DAVID BUSCH'S
CANON® EOS® 5D MARK IV

GUIDE TO DIGITAL SLR PHOTOGRAPHY

David D. Busch

rockynook

David Busch's Canon® EOS® 5D Mark IV
Guide to Digital SLR Photography
David D. Busch

Project Manager: Jenny Davidson
Series Technical Editor: Michael D. Sullivan
Layout: Bill Hartman
Cover Design: Mike Tanamachi
Indexer: Valerie Haynes Perry
Proofreader: Mike Beady

ISBN: 978-1-68198-238-0
1st Edition (5th printing)

© 2017 David D. Busch

All images © David D. Busch unless otherwise noted

Rocky Nook, Inc.
1010 B Street, Suite 350
San Rafael, CA 94901
USA
www.rockynook.com
info@rockynook.com
(415) 747-8756

Distributed in the UK and Europe by Publishers Group UK
Distributed in the U.S. and all other territories by Publishers Group West

Library of Congress Control Number: 2016957326

This book is printed on acid-free paper.
Printed in Korea

rockynook

For Cathy

Acknowledgments

Thanks to everyone at Rocky Nook, including Scott Cowlin, managing director and publisher, for the freedom to let me explore the amazing capabilities of the Canon EOS 5D Mark IV in depth. I couldn't do it without my veteran production team, including project manager, Jenny Davidson, and series technical editor, Mike Sullivan. Also thanks to Bill Hartman, layout; Valerie Hayes Perry, indexing; Mike Beady, proofreading; Mike Tanamachi, cover design; and my agent, Carole Jelen, who has the amazing ability to keep both publishers and authors happy.

About the Author

With more than two million books in print, **David D. Busch** is the world's #1 best-selling camera guide author, and the originator of popular series like *David Busch's Compact Field Guides* and *David Busch's Quick Snap Guides*. He has written more than 100 hugely successful guidebooks for Canon and other digital camera models, including the all-time #1 bestsellers for several different cameras, as well as many popular books devoted to photography, including *Digital SLR Cameras and Photography for Dummies*. As a roving photojournalist for more than 20 years, he illustrated his books, magazine articles, and newspaper reports with award-winning images. He's operated his own commercial studio, suffocated in formal dress while shooting weddings, and shot sports for a daily newspaper and an upstate New York college. His photos and articles have appeared in *Popular Photography, Rangefinder, Professional Photographer*, and hundreds of other publications. He's also reviewed dozens of digital cameras for CNet and other CBS publications.

When About.com first named its top five books on Beginning Digital Photography, debuting at the #1 and #2 slots were Busch's *Digital Photography All-In-One Desk Reference for Dummies* and *Mastering Digital Photography*. He has had as many as 18 books listed in the Top 100 of Amazon.com's Digital Photography Bestseller list—simultaneously! Busch's 250-plus other books published since 1983 include bestsellers like *Mastering Digital SLR Photography*.

Busch is a member of the Cleveland Photographic Society (www.clevelandphoto.org), which has operated continuously since 1887. Visit his website at http://www.canonguides.com.

Contents

Chapter 5
Mastering the Mysteries of Autofocus   107

Chapter 6
Advanced Techniques, Wi-Fi, and GPS 139

Chapter 7
Choosing Your Lens Arsenal 171

Chapter 8
Making Light Work for You 185

Chapter 9
Electronic Flash Basics   201

Chapter 10
Working with Wireless Flash   231

Chapter 11
Customizing with the Shooting Menu   251

Chapter 12
Customizing with the Autofocus Menus   307

Chapter 13
Customizing with the Playback and Set-up Menus   327

Chapter 14
The Custom Functions and My Menus   373

Chapter 15
Using Live View
389

Chapter 16
Capturing Video
403

Chapter 17
Troubleshooting and Prevention

437

Index

457

Preface

If you've invested in a camera as sophisticated as the Canon EOS 5D Mark IV, you're looking for more than good pictures—you demand *outstanding* photos. As the camera of choice for many professional and advanced photo enthusiasts, it boasts 30.2 megapixels of resolution, blazing-fast automatic focus, and cool features like 4K and full HD movie shooting. But your gateway to pixel proficiency is dragged down by the confusing and oddly organized book included in the box as a manual. You know everything you need to know is in there, somewhere, but you probably don't know where to start. In addition, the camera manual doesn't offer much information on photography or digital photography. Nor are you interested in spending hours or days studying a comprehensive book on digital SLR still photography that doesn't necessarily apply directly to your 5D Mark IV.

If you're new to the 5D series, what you need is a guide that explains the purpose and function of the 5D Mark IV's basic controls, how you should use them, and *why*. If you're a veteran who is upgrading from the Mark II or Mark III, you're looking for a refresher on those topics, plus an update on the camera's exciting new features. You're looking for information about autofocus, tips on using the touch screen, and advice on customizing your camera, but you'd prefer to read about those topics only after you've had the chance to go out and take a few hundred great pictures with your new tool. Why isn't there a book that summarizes the most important information in its first two or three chapters, with lots of illustrations showing what your results will look like when you use this setting or that?

Now there is such a book. If you want a quick introduction to the 5D Mark IV's focus controls, wireless flash synchronization options, how to choose lenses, or which exposure modes are best, this book is for you. If you can't decide on what basic settings to use with your camera because you can't figure out how changing ISO or white balance or focus defaults will affect your pictures, you need this guide.

Introduction

Canon makes haste slowly, especially in the case of its most popular advanced camera, which, in its latest iteration is dubbed the Canon EOS 5D Mark IV. The previous Mark III was introduced in March 2012 and remained as the Canon workhorse for nearly four and a half years. It's safe to say that the new Mark IV is one of the most eagerly anticipated upgrades Canon has ever introduced, and this camera does not disappoint. Resolution has been boosted from 22 megapixels to a whopping 30 megapixels, while retaining the excellent high ISO performance (now expandable to the equivalent of ISO 102,400) that Canon is known for. A useful touch screen has been added, making it easy to "type" in comments, while accelerating many menu functions and allowing the photographer to select a focus point (or take a picture) in live view with a quick tap. Thanks to a Dual Pixel CMOS sensor, the 5D Mark IV is the first Canon camera that can continuously autofocus using accurate phase detection in live view. The sensor's innovative split pixels also allow making micro-adjustments to focus, fine-tuning bokeh, and enhancing the camera's anti-flare features.

Also within its rugged body are built-in GPS and Wi-Fi, and a 153,600-pixel exposure sensor that's adept at performing facial recognition that can be passed along to the autofocus system. The 5D Mark IV is an amazing package, indeed. You won't easily outgrow this camera. It's got enough resolution for the most demanding applications, world-class autofocus, and lots of customization options. Canon must love serious photographers, because it seems to work extra hard to give them incredible value for their money.

But once you've confirmed that you made a wise purchase, the question comes up, *how do I use this thing?* All those cool features can be mind numbing to learn, if all you have as a guide is the manual furnished with the camera. Help is on the way. I sincerely believe that this book is your best bet for learning how to use your new camera for still photography, and for learning how to use it well.

If you're a Canon EOS 5D Mark IV owner who's looking to learn more about how to use this great camera, you've probably already explored your options. Some like YouTube videos and online tutorials—but who can learn how to use a camera by sitting in front of a television or computer screen? Do you want to watch a movie or click on HTML links, or do you want to go out and take photos with your camera? Videos are fun, but not the best answer.

Others observe that every feature of the camera is covered in the manual that Canon supplies. The official manual is compact and filled with information, but there's really very little about *why* you should use particular settings or features, and its organization may make it difficult to find what you need. Multiple cross-references may send you flipping back and forth between two or three sections of the book to find what you want to know. The basic manual is also hobbled by black-and-white line drawings and tiny monochrome pictures that aren't very good examples of what you can do.

I've tried to make *David Busch's Canon EOS 5D Mark IV Guide to Digital SLR Photography* different from your other 5D Mark IV learn-up options. The roadmap sections use larger, color pictures to show you where all the buttons and dials are, and the explanations of what they do are longer and more comprehensive. I've tried to avoid overly general advice, including the two-page checklists on how to take a "sports picture" or a "portrait picture" or a "travel picture." Instead, you'll find tips and techniques for using all the features of your Canon EOS 5D Mark IV to take *any kind of picture* you want. If you want to know where you should stand to take a picture of a quarterback dropping back to unleash a pass, there are plenty of books that will tell you that. This one concentrates on teaching you how to select the best autofocus mode, shutter speed, f/stop, or flash capability to take, say, a great sports picture under any conditions.

However, as you explore the pages of this book, you'll see that, in addition to serving as a supplement to the operator's manual furnished with the camera, I attempt to relate every feature, control, and option to actual picture-taking situations, and, still photography in general, at every opportunity. Some readers who visit my blog have told me that the 5D Mark IV is such an advanced camera that few people really need the kind of basics that so many camera guides concentrate on. "Leave out all the basic photography information!" On the other hand, I've had many pleas from those who are trying to master digital photography as they learn to use their 5D Mark IV, and they've asked me to help them climb the steep learning curve.

Rather than write a book for just one of those two audiences, I've tried to meet the needs of both. You veterans will find plenty of information on getting the most from the camera's features, and may even learn something from an old hand's photo secrets. I'll bet there was a time when you needed a helping hand with some confusing photographic topic. And those who are looking to learn about photography and their camera will find just what you need in this book, too. Because most of my readers are still photographers, the emphasis in this book will be on stills rather than video. However, you'll find plenty of information on movie-making here, including an explanation of some advanced topics, such as time codes, optimum frame rates, and ALL-I versus IPB compression schemes. I'll ease budding videographers into some of the sophisticated features of the 5D Mark IV (which is, after all, being used to capture full-length feature films!).

Who Am I?

After spending years as the world's most successful unknown author, I've become slightly less obscure in the past few years, thanks to a horde of camera guidebooks and other photographically oriented tomes. You may have seen my photography articles in *Popular Photography* magazine. I've also written about 2,000 articles for magazines like *Petersen's PhotoGraphic* (which is now defunct through no fault of my own), plus *Rangefinder, Professional Photographer*, and dozens of other photographic publications. But, first, and foremost, I'm a photojournalist and commercial photographer and made my living in the field until I began devoting most of my time to writing books.

Although I love writing, I'm happiest when I'm out taking pictures, which is why I invariably spend several days each week photographing landscapes, people, close-up subjects, and other things. I spend a month or two each year traveling to events, such as Native American "powwows," Civil War re-enactments, county fairs, ballet, and sports (baseball, basketball, football, and soccer are favorites). In recent years, I've spent a lot of time in Europe, strictly to shoot photographs of the people, landscapes, and monuments that I've grown to love. I can offer you my personal advice on how to take photos under a variety of conditions because I've had to meet those challenges myself on an ongoing basis.

Like all my digital photography books, this one was written by someone with an incurable photography bug. My first Canon SLR was a Pellix back in the 1960s, and I've used a variety of newer models since then. I've worked as a sports photographer for an Ohio newspaper and for an upstate New York college. I've operated my own commercial studio and photo lab, cranking out product shots on demand and then printing a few hundred glossy 8 × 10s on a tight deadline for a press kit. I've served as a photo-posing instructor for a modeling agency. People have actually paid me to shoot their weddings and immortalize them with portraits. I even prepared press kits and articles on photography as a PR consultant for a large Rochester, NY, company, which shall remain nameless. My trials and travails with imaging and computer technology have made their way into print in book form an alarming number of times.

In closing, I'd like to ask a special favor: let me know what you think of this book. If you have any recommendations about how I can make it better, visit my website at www.canonguides.com, click on the E-Mail Me tab, and send your comments, suggestions on topics that should be explained in more detail, or, especially, any typos. (The latter will be compiled on the Errata page you'll also find on my website.) I really value your ideas, and appreciate it when you take the time to tell me what you think! Some of the content of the book you hold in your hands came from suggestions I received from readers like yourself. If you found this book especially useful, tell others about it. Visit http://www.amazon.com/dp/1681982382 and leave a positive review. Your feedback is what spurs me to make each one of these books better than the last. Thanks!

1

Canon EOS 5D Mark IV Quick Start

Whether you've already taken a dozen or twelve hundred photos with your new camera, you'll want to take a more considered approach to operating your Canon EOS 5D Mark IV. If you need a quick start, this chapter is designed to get your camera fired up and ready for shooting as quickly as possible. Because I realize that some of you may already have experience with Canon pro cameras, including the previous Mark III, each of the major sections in this chapter will begin with a brief description of what is covered in that section, so you can easily jump ahead to the next if you are in a hurry to get started.

First Things First

This section helps get you oriented with all the things that come in the box with your Canon EOS 5D Mark IV, including what they do. I'll also describe some optional equipment you might want to have. If you want to get started immediately, skim through this section and jump ahead to "Initial Setup" later in this chapter.

The Canon EOS 5D Mark IV comes in an impressive gray-and-red box filled with stuff, including connecting cords, books, CDs, and lots of paperwork. The first thing to do is carefully unpack the camera and double-check the contents with the checklist on one end of the box. It's better to know *now* that something is missing so you can seek redress immediately, rather than discover two months from now that the video cable you didn't need right away (but now *must* have) was never in the box.

At a minimum, the box should have the following:

- **Canon EOS 5D Mark IV digital camera.** It almost goes without saying that you should check out the camera immediately, making sure the color LCD on the back isn't scratched or cracked, the memory card and battery doors open properly, and, when a charged battery is inserted and lens mounted, the camera powers up and reports for duty. Out-of-the-box defects like these are rare, but they can happen. It's probably more common that your dealer played with the camera or, perhaps, it was a customer return. That's why it's best to buy your 5D Mark IV from a retailer you trust to supply a factory-fresh camera.

- **Battery Pack LP-E6N.** You'll need to charge this 7.2V, 1865mAh (milliampere hour) battery before using it. I'll offer instructions later in this chapter. It should be furnished with a protective cover, which should always be mounted on the battery when it is not inside the camera, to avoid shorting out the contacts.

- **Battery Charger LC-E6/LC-E6E.** One of these chargers, described in this section, is required to vitalize the LP-E6N battery.

- **Eyecup Eg.** This will already be attached to the camera viewfinder, but it can be removed and replaced with other eyepiece accessories, such as a magnifier.

- **Interface Cable IFC-150U II.** You can use this 1.5 meter/4.9 foot USB 3.0 cable to transfer photos from the camera to your computer (not recommended), to upload and download settings between the camera and your computer (highly recommended), and to operate your camera remotely using the software included on CD-ROM.

  My recommendation: I don't recommend using the cable to transfer images. Direct transfer uses a lot of battery power, and is potentially slower.

- **Wide strap.** Canon provides you with a "steal me" neck strap emblazoned with your camera model. It's not very adjustable, and, while useful for showing off to your friends exactly which nifty new camera you bought, it's probably not your best option.

  My recommendation: I never attach the Canon strap to my cameras, and instead opt for a more serviceable strap from companies like UPstrap (www.upstrap-pro.com), which has a non-slip pad that offers reassuring traction and eliminates the contortions we sometimes go through to keep the camera from slipping off our shoulder. I prefer that type to holsters and sliding straps that attach to the tripod socket.

- **RF-3 body cap.** The body cap keeps dust from infiltrating your camera when a lens is not mounted. Always carry a body cap (and rear lens cap). When not in use, the body cap/rear lens cap nest together for compact storage.

- **User's manuals.** Canon still provides a printed manual with the 5D Mark IV, a tiny (but thick) little tome that combines 612 pages on the camera itself, and an additional 48 pages on wireless communication. Even if you have this book, you'll probably want to check the printed guide from time to time, if only to check the actual nomenclature for some obscure accessory, or to double-check an error code. You can download a PDF version of the reference book, as well as individual guides for Canon lenses and accessories from the Canon website in your country.

- **CD-ROMs.** You'll find the Canon Digital Solution Disc with software applications and a Software Instruction manual (in PDF form) on the pair of CD-ROMs packaged with the camera.

- **Warranty and registration card.** Don't lose these! You can register your Canon 5D Mark IV by mail, although you don't really need to in order to keep your warranty in force, but you may need the information in this paperwork (plus the purchase receipt/invoice from your retailer) should you require Canon service support.

There are a few things Canon classifies as optional accessories, even though you (and I) might consider some of them essential. Here's a list of what you *don't* get in the box, but might want to think about as an impending purchase. I'll list them roughly in the order of importance:

- **Memory card.** To best use the capabilities of the 5D Mark IV's dual slots, you'll need both a Compact Flash and SD memory card.

  My recommendation: For a 30.1-megapixel camera, you really need a Compact Flash or SD memory card that's a *minimum* of 16GB in size, and a 32GB, 64GB, or larger card would be much better.

- **Extra LP-E6N/LP-E6 battery.** Even though you might get 500 to nearly 1,000 shots from a single battery, it's easy to exceed that figure in a few hours of shooting sports at 7 fps. Batteries can unexpectedly fail, too, or simply lose their charge from sitting around unused for a week or two.

  My recommendation: Buy an extra (I own four, in total), keep it charged, and free your mind from worry. While the latest LP-E6N version is best, if you're upgrading from a previous model that uses the original LP-E6 batteries and have a spare or two, you can use them as well.

- **Add-on Speedlite.** Like most pro cameras, the Canon 5D Mark IV does not include a built-in electronic flash, so you'll need an off-camera Speedlite such as the Canon 600EX II-RT, which was designed especially for cameras in this class.

  My recommendation: Your add-on flash can function as the main illumination for your photo, or softened and used to fill in shadows. If you do much flash photography at all, consider a Speedlite as an important accessory. For the most flexibility when lighting your subject, you'll need *two* flash units: one on the camera to be used as a master, and one off-camera flash triggered wirelessly as a slave. Canon also offers the ST-E2 and ST-E3-RT transmitter/triggers, which can serve as masters.

- **AC Adapter Kit ACK-E6N.** This device is used with a *DC coupler*, the DR-E6, that replaces the LP-E6N battery and powers the Canon 5D Mark IV from AC current.

  My recommendation: There are several typical situations where this capability can come in handy: when you're cleaning the sensor manually and want to totally eliminate the possibility that a lack of juice will cause the fragile shutter and mirror to spring to life during the process; when indoors shooting tabletop photos, portraits, class pictures, and so forth for hours on end; when using your 5D Mark IV for remote shooting as well as time-lapse photography; for extensive review of images on your television; or for file transfer to your computer. These all use prodigious amounts of power, which can be provided by this AC adapter.

- **Angle Finder C right-angle viewer.** This handy accessory fastens in place of the standard rubber eyecup and provides a 90-degree view for framing and composing your image at right angles to the original viewfinder, useful for low-level (or high-level) shooting. (Or, maybe, shooting around corners!)
- **HDMI cable HTC-100.** You'll need this optional cable if you want to connect your camera directly to an HDTV for viewing your images. Because standard-definition television sets are on the way out, Canon no longer supports the Stereo AV Cable AVC-DC400ST that could be used with the previous Mark III camera to connect to an analog television through the set's yellow RCA video jack and red/white RCA audio jacks.

Initial Setup

Most 5D Mark IV owners can skip this section, which describes basic setup steps. I'm including it at the request of ambitious photo buffs who have upgraded to this advanced camera after switching from another brand or an entry-level model.

The initial setup of your Canon EOS 5D Mark IV is fast and easy. Basically, you just need to charge the battery, attach a lens, insert a memory card, and make a few settings.

Power Options

Your Canon EOS 5D Mark IV is a sophisticated hunk of machinery and electronics, but it needs a charged battery to function, so rejuvenating the LP-E6N lithium-ion battery pack furnished with the camera should be your first step. A fully charged power source should be good for approximately 900 shots, based on standard tests defined by the Camera & Imaging Products Association (CIPA) document DC-002. The figure was arrived at based on a fully charged battery and no use of live view or movie settings.

All rechargeable batteries undergo some degree of self-discharge just sitting idle in the camera or in the original packaging. Lithium-ion power packs of this type typically lose a small amount of their charge every day, even when the camera isn't turned on. The small amount of juice used to provide the "skeleton" outline on the top-panel monochrome LCD when the 5D Mark IV is turned off isn't the culprit; Li-ion cells lose their power through a chemical reaction that continues when the camera is switched off. So, it's very likely that the battery purchased with your camera is at least partially pooped out, so you'll want to revive it before going out for some serious shooting.

Several battery chargers are available for the Canon EOS 5D Mark IV. The compact LC-E6 is the charger that most 5D Mark IV owners end up using. Purchasing one of the optional charging devices offers more than some additional features: You gain a spare that can keep your camera running until you can replace your primary power rejuvenator. I like to have an extra charger in case my original charger breaks, or when I want to charge more than one battery at a time. (That's often the case if your using the BG-E20 grip.) Here's a list of your power options:

- **LC-E6.** The standard charger for the 5D Mark IV (and also compatible with earlier cameras that use the LC-E6 or LC-E6N batteries), this one is the most convenient, because of its compact size and built-in wall plug prongs that connect directly into your power strip or wall socket and require no cord. (See Figure 1.1, left.)

- **LC-E6E.** This is similar to the LC-E6, and also charges a single battery, but requires a cord. That can be advantageous in certain situations. For example, if your power outlet is behind a desk or in some other semi-inaccessible location, the cord can be plugged in and routed so the charger itself sits on your desk or another more convenient spot. The cord is standard and works with many different chargers and devices (including the power supply for my laptop), so I purchased several of them and leave them plugged into the wall in various locations. I can connect my 5D Mark IV's charger, my laptop computer's charger, and several other electronic components to one of these cords without needing to crawl around behind the furniture. The cord draws no power when it's *not plugged into a charger.* Unhook the charger from the cord when you're not actively rejuvenating your batteries.

- **Car Battery Charger CBC-E6.** It includes the Car Battery Cable CB-570 (plug into your vehicle's lighter or accessory socket). The vehicle battery option allows you to keep shooting when in remote locations that lack AC power.

- **Battery Grip BG-E20.** This accessory holds one or two LC-E6N batteries. You can potentially double your shooting capacity, while adding an additional shutter release, Main Dial, AE lock/ FE lock, and AF point selection controls for vertically oriented shooting.

- **AC Adapter Kit ACK-E6N.** As I mentioned earlier, this device allows you to operate your EOS 5D Mark IV directly from AC power, with no battery required. Studio photographers need this capability because they often snap off hundreds of pictures for hours on end and want constant, reliable power. The camera is probably plugged into a flash sync cord (or radio device), and the studio flash are plugged into power packs or AC power, so the extra tether to this adapter is no big deal in that environment. You also might want to use the AC adapter when viewing images on a TV connected to your 5D Mark IV, shooting video, or when shooting remote or time-lapse photos.

Charging the Battery

When the battery is inserted into the LC-E6 charger properly (it's impossible to insert it incorrectly), a Charge light begins flashing. It flashes on and off until the battery reaches a 50 percent charge, then blinks in two-flash cycles between 50 and 75 percent charged, and in a three-flash sequence until the battery is 90 percent charged, usually within about 90 minutes. You should allow the charger to continue for about 60 minutes more, until the status lamp glows green steadily, to ensure a full charge. When the battery is charged, flip the lever on the bottom of the camera and slide in the battery (see Figure 1.1, right). To remove the battery from the camera, press the white retaining button.

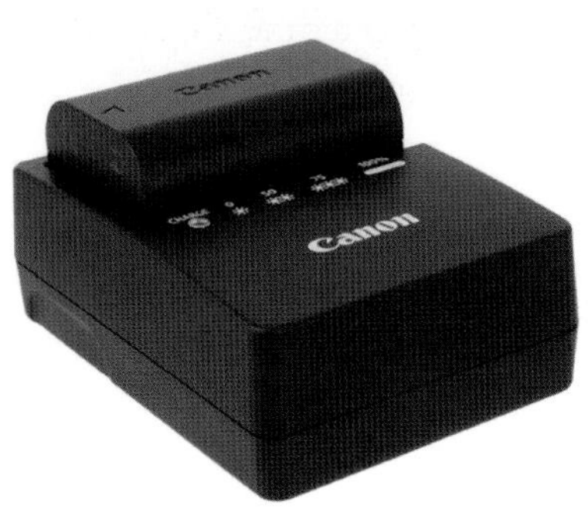
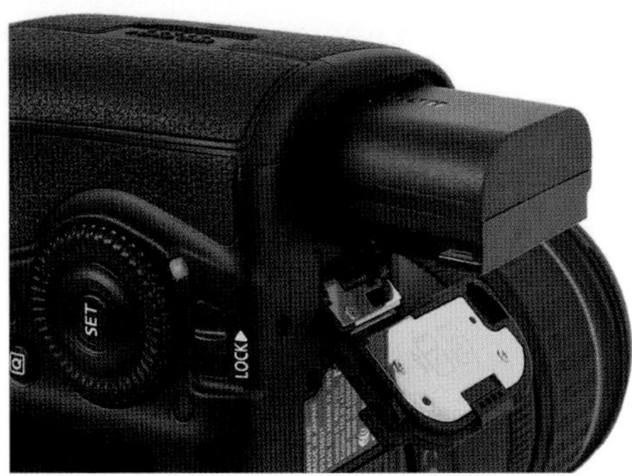

Figure 1.1
The flashing status light indicates that the battery is being charged (left). Insert the battery in the camera; it only fits one way (right).

Final Steps

Your Canon EOS 5D Mark IV is almost ready to fire up and shoot. You'll need to select and mount a lens, adjust the viewfinder for your vision, and insert memory card(s). Each of these steps is easy, and if you've used a previous EOS model, you already know exactly what to do. I'm going to provide a little extra detail for those of you who are new to the Canon or digital SLR worlds.

Mounting the Lens

As you'll see, my recommended lens mounting procedure emphasizes protecting your equipment from accidental damage, and minimizing the intrusion of dust. If your 5D Mark IV has no lens attached, select the lens you want to use and loosen (but do not remove) the rear lens cap. I generally place the lens I am planning to mount vertically in a slot in my camera bag, where it's protected from mishaps, but ready to pick up quickly. By loosening the rear lens cap, you'll be able to lift it off the back of the lens at the last instant, so the rear element of the lens is covered until then.

After that, remove the body cap by rotating the cap toward the shutter release button. You should always mount the body cap when there is no lens on the camera, because it helps keep dust out of the interior of the camera, where it can settle on the mirror, focusing screen, interior mirror box, and potentially find its way past the shutter onto the sensor. (While the 5D Mark IV's sensor cleaning mechanism works fine, the less dust it has to contend with, the better.) The body cap also protects the vulnerable mirror from damage caused by intruding objects (including your fingers, if you're not cautious).

Once the body cap has been removed, remove the rear lens cap from the lens, set it aside, and then mount the lens on the camera by matching the raised red alignment indicator on the lens barrel with the red dot on the camera's lens mount. Rotate the lens away from the shutter release until it seats securely. Set the focus mode switch on the lens to AF (autofocus). If the lens hood is bayoneted on the lens in the reversed position (which makes the lens/hood combination more compact for transport), twist it off and remount with the edge facing outward. A lens hood protects the front of the lens from accidental bumps, stray fingerprints, and reduces flare caused by extraneous light arriving at the front element of the lens from outside the picture area.

EF-S LENSES NOT WELCOME

If you've used any of Canon's non-full-frame cameras with the 1.6X crop factor (more on that in Chapter 7), you may have worked with the EF-S lenses that can be mounted on those models. They feature a square white alignment indicator on the barrel, which mates with a similar indicator on the camera lens mount. These EF-S lenses *cannot* be used with the 5D Mark IV; the rear lens elements extend back into the camera body too far, and would strike the mirror. You can't use EF-S lenses on any of Canon's full-frame cameras, nor on earlier 1.3X crop models, nor 1.6X crop models prior to the EOS 20D, such as the EOS 10D.

Adjusting Diopter Correction

Those of us with less than perfect eyesight can often benefit from a little optical correction in the viewfinder. Your contact lenses or glasses may provide all the correction you need, but if you are a glasses wearer and want to use the EOS 5D Mark IV without your glasses, you can take advantage of the camera's built-in diopter adjustment, which can be varied from –3 to +1 correction. Press the shutter release halfway to illuminate the indicators in the viewfinder, then rotate the diopter adjustment control next to the viewfinder (see Figure 1.2) while looking through the viewfinder until the indicators appear sharp. Technically, you should make the dioptric adjustment using the image frame itself, but the virtual position of the indicators is close enough, and usually easier to focus on.

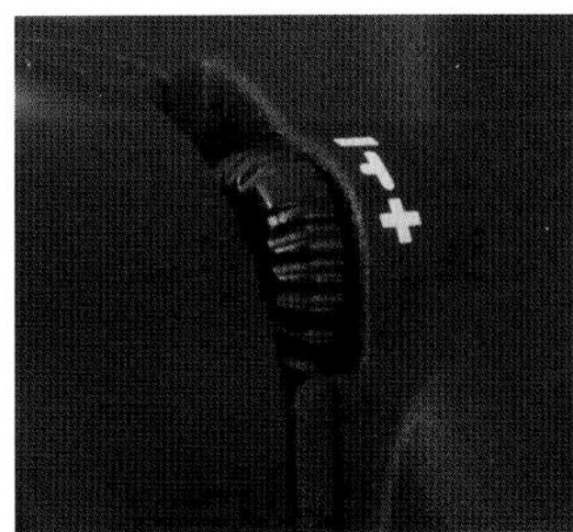

Figure 1.2 Viewfinder diopter correction from –3 to +1 can be dialed in.

If the available correction is insufficient, Canon offers 10 different Dioptric Adjustment Lens Series E correction lenses for the viewfinder window. If more than one person uses your 5D Mark IV, and each requires a different diopter setting, you can save a little time by noting the number of clicks and direction (clockwise to increase the diopter power; counterclockwise to decrease the diopter value) required to change from one user to the other.

Inserting a Memory Card

You can't take photos without a memory card inserted in your EOS 5D Mark IV (although there is a Release Shutter Without Card entry in the Shooting 1 menu that enables/disables shutter release functions when a memory card is absent—covered in Chapter 11). So, your final step will be to insert a memory card. Slide the door on the right side of the body toward the back of the camera to release the cover, and then open it. (You should only remove the memory card when the camera is switched off, but the 5D Mark IV will remind you if the door is opened while the camera is still writing photos to the memory card.)

Insert the memory card into Slot 1 (for Compact Flash) or Slot 2 (for SD cards) with the label facing the back of the camera, as shown in Figure 1.3, oriented so the edge with the double row of tiny holes (on the CF card) or gold contacts (on the SD card) go into the slot first. Close the door, and your preflight checklist is done! (I'm going to assume you remember to remove the lens cap when you're ready to take a picture!) When you want to remove the memory card later, press down on an SD card or the gray button next to a Compact Flash card to make the memory card pop out.

Formatting a Memory Card

There are three ways to create a blank memory card for your 5D Mark IV, and two of them are at least partially wrong. Here are your options, both correct and incorrect:

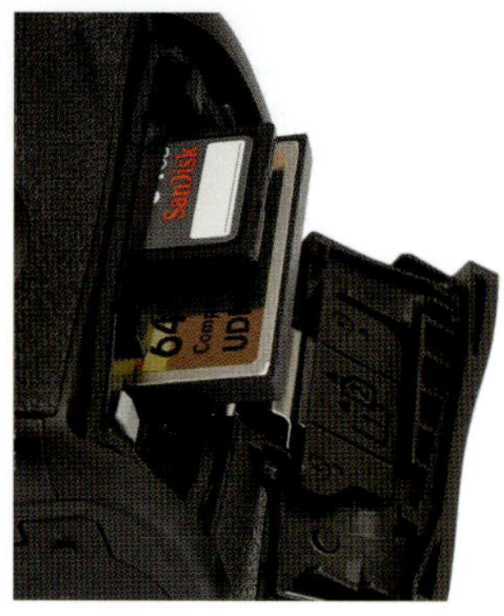

Figure 1.3 Insert the memory card in the slot with the label facing the back of the camera.

- **Transfer (move) files to your computer.** When you transfer (rather than copy) all the image files to your computer from the memory card (either using a direct cable transfer or with a card reader, as described later in this chapter), the old image files are erased from the card, leaving the card blank. Theoretically. This method does *not* remove files that you've labeled as Protected (choosing the Protect images function in the Playback menu) nor does it identify and lock out parts of your memory card that have become corrupted or unusable since the last time you formatted the card. Therefore, I recommend always formatting the card, rather than simply moving the image files, each time you want to make a blank card. The only exception is when you *want* to leave the protected/unerased images on the card for awhile longer, say, to share with friends, family, and colleagues.

- **(Don't) Format in your computer.** With the memory card inserted in a card reader or card slot in your computer, you can use Windows or Mac OS to reformat the memory card. Don't! The operating system won't necessarily arrange the structure of the card the way the 5D Mark IV likes to see it (in computer terms, an incorrect *file system* may be installed). The only way to ensure that the card has been properly formatted for your camera is to perform the format in the camera itself. The only exception to this rule is when you have a seriously corrupted memory card that your camera refuses to format. Sometimes it is possible to revive such a corrupted card by allowing the operating system to reformat it first, then trying again in the camera.

- **Setup menu format.** To use the recommended method to format a memory card, press the MENU button, rotate the Main Dial (located on top of the camera, just behind the shutter release button), choose the Set-up 1 menu (which is represented by a wrench icon), use the Quick Control Dial (that round wheel to the right of the LCD) to navigate to the last entry, Format, and press the SET button in the center of the dial to access the Format screen. Rotate the Quick Control Dial again to select the CF slot or SD slot (the icons resemble the card type, so it's easy to tell the difference). Press the SET button and the screen shown in Figure 1.4 appears. Select OK and press SET one final time to begin the format process.

Figure 1.4
Formatting a
memory card.

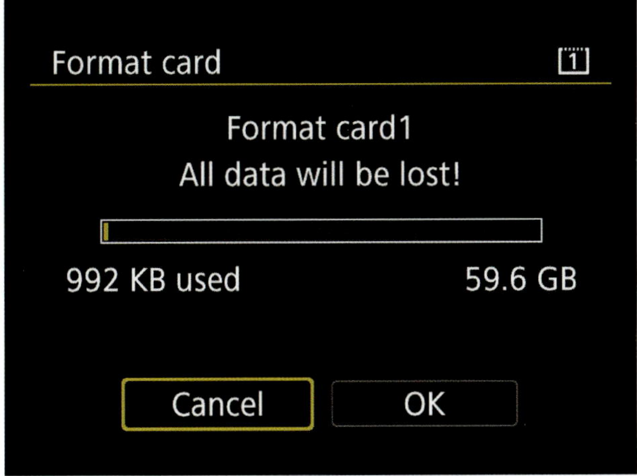

HOW MANY SHOTS REMAINING? GUESS NO MORE!

If the previous model EOS 5D Mark III had a serious flaw, my nomination would be the earlier camera's apparent inability to tell you how many shots you have left. Of course, you know you have a great camera when the counter that keeps track of the number of shots remaining is its most annoying defect. What's the deal? The counter on the monochrome LCD panel on the top of the camera showed only 1999 shots remaining, maximum, even though your memory card had much more capacity remaining. It was easy to exceed that number with today's high-capacity memory cards. Fortunately, Canon has—mostly—remedied the situation. The 5D Mark IV can indicate up to 9999 images remaining on both the top LCD panel and rear LCD monitor, so even if you're using a huge card and shooting in the smallest JPEG size (S3), your shots remaining count will overflow the display only rarely.

Setting the Time and Date

The first time you use the Canon EOS 5D Mark IV, it may ask you to enter the time and date. (This information may have been set by someone checking out your camera on your behalf prior to sale.) Just follow these steps:

1. Press the MENU button, located in the upper-left corner of the back of the 5D Mark IV.

2. Rotate the Main Dial (near the shutter release button on top of the camera) until the Set-up 2 menu is highlighted. It's marked by a wrench and the message SET UP2, as shown at left in Figure 1.5.

3. Rotate the Quick Control Dial (QCD) to move the highlighting down to the Date/Time entry.

4. Press the SET button in the center of the QCD to access the Date/Time setting screen, shown at right in Figure 1.5.

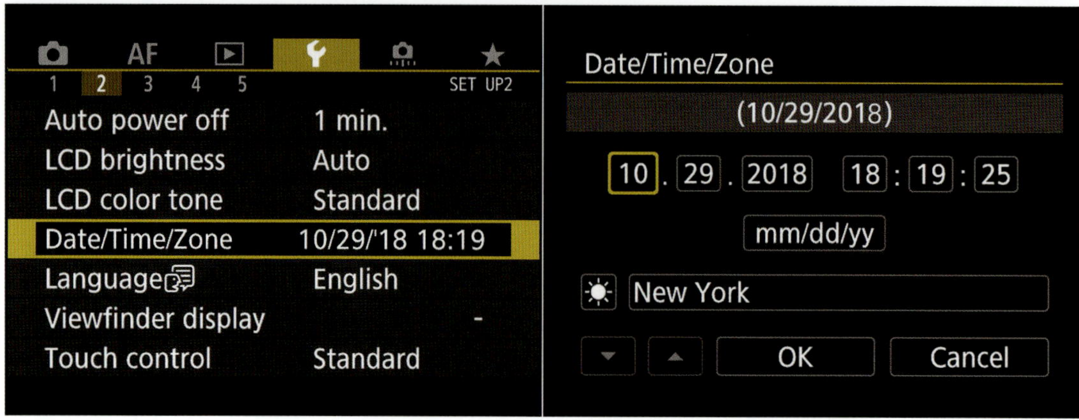

Figure 1.5 Choose the Date/Time entry from the Set-up 2 menu and set the parameters.

5. Rotate the QCD to select the value you want to change. When the gold box highlights the month, day, year, hour, minute, or second format you want to adjust, press the SET button to activate that value. A pair of up/down pointing triangles appears above the value.

6. Rotate the Quick Control Dial to adjust the value up or down. Press the SET button to confirm the value you've entered.

7. Repeat steps 5 and 6 for each of the other values you want to change. The date format can be switched from the default mm/dd/yy to yy/mm/dd or dd/mm/yy. You can activate/deactivate Daylight Saving Time, and select a Time Zone.

8. When finished, rotate the QCD to select either OK (if you're satisfied with your changes) or Cancel (if you'd like to return to the Set-up 2 menu screen without making any changes). Press SET to confirm your choice.

9. When finished setting the date and time, press the MENU button to exit.

REACH OUT AND TOUCH SOMETHING

Your Canon EOS 5D Mark IV has a touch-sensitive screen that is useful for navigating menus, selecting focus points, and other functions. In many cases, you can use the buttons and dials and the touch screen almost interchangeably, but for this Quick Start chapter I'm going to stick to using the physical controls instead of the touch controls. There are two reasons for that. First, it's important you become comfortable using the buttons and dials, because for many functions they are faster, sometimes easier, and work reliably even when your fingers are "encumbered" (say, while you're wearing gloves). In addition, this introductory chapter is intended primarily for those new to the Canon pro world, and I think it's a good idea to give equal weight to the "quick" and "start" of the chapter title. I'll explain how to use the touch screen in Chapter 2.

Selecting a Shooting Mode

The following sections show you how to choose semi-automatic, automatic shooting, or exposure modes; select a metering mode (which tells the camera what portions of the frame to evaluate for exposure); and set the basic autofocus functions. If you understand how to do these things, you can skip ahead to "Other Settings."

Now it's time to fire up your EOS 5D Mark IV and take some photos. The easy part is turning on the power—that OFF-ON switch on the top-left shoulder of the camera, nestled next to the Mode Dial (see Figure 1.6). Turn on the camera, and, if you mounted a lens and inserted a fresh battery and memory card, you're ready to begin. You'll need to select a shooting mode, metering mode, and focus mode.

You can choose a shooting method from the Mode Dial located on the top-left edge of the 5D Mark IV. To rotate the dial, you must press the button in the center to release the dial lock. The camera has one fully automatic mode called Scene Intelligent Auto, which makes virtually all the decisions for you (except when to press the shutter). There are also five *semi-automatic/manual* modes (what Canon calls Creative Zone on its entry- and mid-level models), including Program, Shutter-priority, Aperture-priority, Manual, and Bulb, which allow you to provide input over the exposure and settings the camera uses. There are also three camera user settings (Custom shooting modes) that can be used to store specific groups of camera settings, which you can then recall quickly by spinning the Mode Dial to C1, C2, or C3. You'll find a complete description of fully automatic and semi-automatic/manual modes in Chapter 4, as well as Custom shooting modes in Chapter 14.

Turn your camera on by flipping the power switch to ON. Next, you need to select which shooting mode to use. If you're very new to digital photography, you might want to set the camera to Auto (the green frame on the Mode Dial) or P (Program mode) and start snapping away. These modes will make all the appropriate settings for you for many shooting situations.

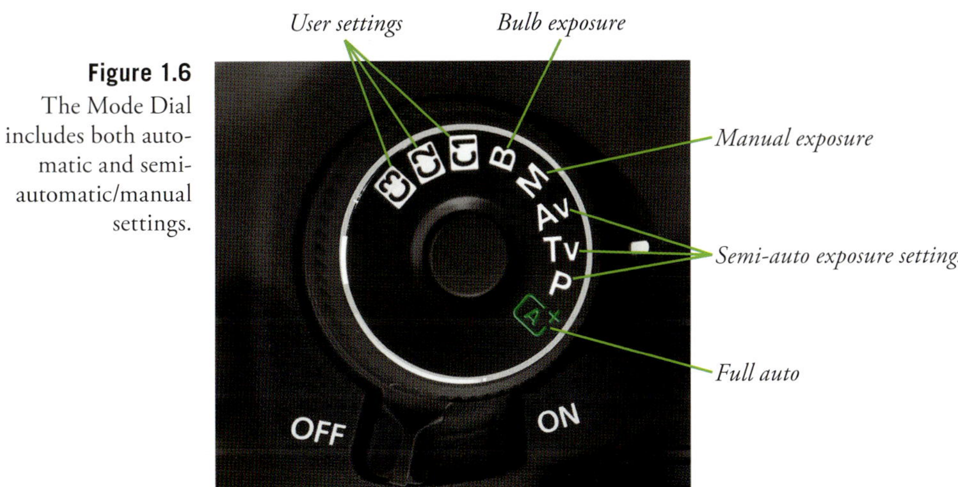

Figure 1.6
The Mode Dial includes both automatic and semi-automatic/manual settings.

Your choices are as follows:

- **Scene Intelligent Auto.** In this mode, the EOS 5D Mark IV makes all the exposure decisions for you.

- **P (Program).** This semi-automatic mode allows the 5D Mark IV to select the basic exposure settings, but you can still override the camera's choices to fine-tune your image.

- **Tv (Shutter-priority).** This mode (Tv stands for *time value*) is useful when you want to use a particular shutter speed to stop action or produce creative blur effects. The 5D Mark IV will select the appropriate f/stop for you.

- **Av (Aperture-priority).** Choose when you want to use a particular lens opening, especially to control sharpness or how much of your image is in focus. The 5D Mark IV will select the appropriate shutter speed for you. Av stands for *aperture value.*

- **M (Manual).** Select when you want full control over the shutter speed and lens opening, either for creative effects or because you are using a studio flash or other flash unit not compatible with the 5D Mark IV's automatic flash metering.

- **B (Bulb).** Choose this mode and the shutter will remain open as long as you hold down the release button. It is useful for making exposures of indeterminate length (say, you want to capture some fireworks, and leave the shutter open until a burst appears, then release the shutter after a few seconds when the light trails have been captured). The B setting can also be used to produce exposures longer than the 30 seconds (maximum) the 5D Mark IV can take automatically.

Choosing a Metering Mode

Metering mode is the next setting you'll want to make. Note that for this and the settings that follow, the 5D Mark IV must be set to one of the semi-automatic and manual modes and *not* to Scene Intelligent Auto. Among the three metering modes I'll describe next, the default Evaluative metering is probably the best choice as you get to know your camera. To change metering modes, press the Metering/WB button (Figure 1.7, which also shows the Main Dial and other controls). The screen shown in Figure 1.8 appears for about six seconds, waiting for your input.

GETTING INFO

If the expected screen does not appear on the LCD monitor, press the INFO. button several times until it is shown. One of the most frequent queries I get from new users asks why, when they follow the directions in my book, the illustrated screen isn't shown. In virtually all cases, it's because the photographer has turned off the LCD display using the INFO. button on the back of the camera to the left of the viewfinder.

BUTTON, BUTTON

Each top-panel button has two functions. To set the right function of each pair (that is Metering mode with the Metering mode/WB button), hold the button and rotate the Main Dial. To set the right function of each pair, rotate the Quick Control Dial located on the right side of the back panel. Each pair of choices appears in a single pop-up screen with Main Dial and QCD icons to remind you which dial sets which function, as you can see in Figure 1.8.

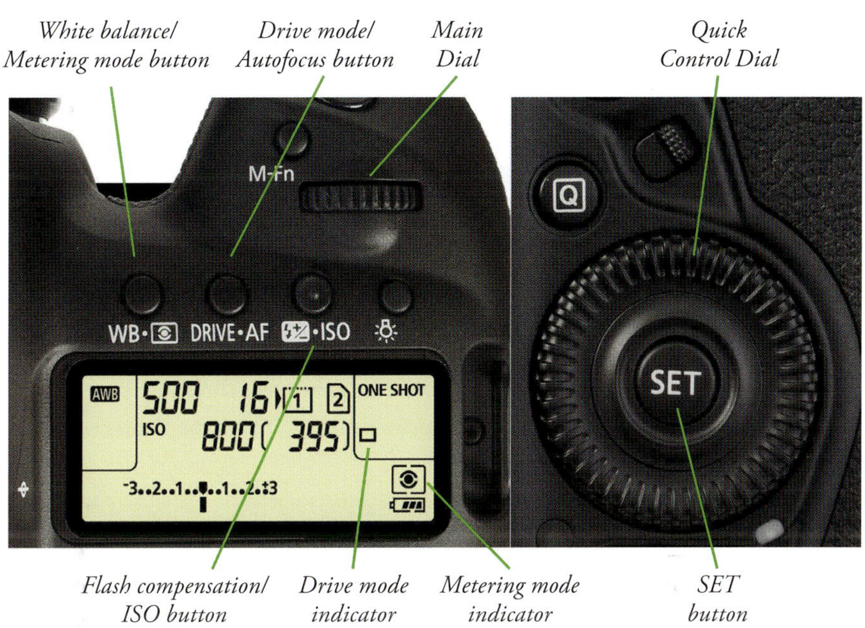

Figure 1.7
The controls you'll use to adjust your settings.

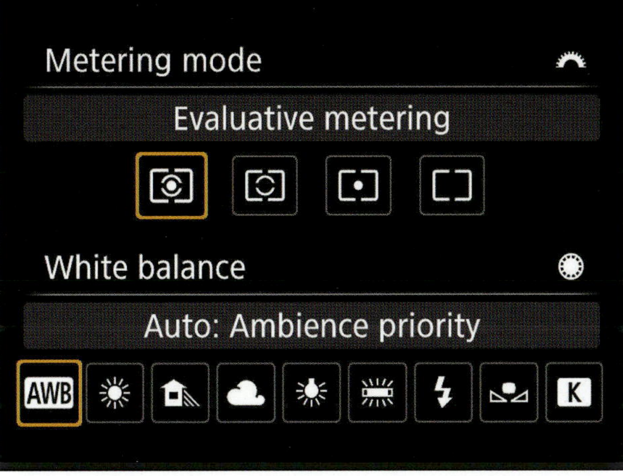

Figure 1.8
Metering modes (left to right, top third of the screen): Evaluative, Partial, Spot, Center-weighted.

Spin the Main Dial to cycle among the following choices:

- **Evaluative metering.** The standard metering mode; the 5D Mark IV attempts to intelligently classify your image and choose the best exposure based on readings from a 150,000-pixel exposure sensor in the viewfinder that detects RGB (red/green/blue) and infrared illumination levels within a 252-zone metering area.
- **Partial metering.** Exposure is based on a central spot, roughly 6.1 percent of the image area.
- **Spot metering.** Exposure is calculated from a smaller central spot, about 1.3 percent of the image area, located in the center of the frame.
- **Center-weighted averaging metering.** The 5D Mark IV meters the entire scene, but gives the most emphasis to the central area of the frame.

You'll find a detailed description of each of these modes in Chapter 4.

Choosing a Focus Mode

You can easily switch between automatic and manual focus by moving the AF/MF switch on the lens mounted on your camera. However, if you're using a semi-automatic shooting mode, you'll still need to choose an appropriate focus mode. (You can read more on selecting focus parameters in Chapter 5.)

To set the focus mode, press the AF-DRIVE button on the top panel of the camera and spin the Main Dial until the mode you want appears in the LCD. (See Figure 1.9.)

The three choices are as follows:

- **One-Shot.** This mode, sometimes called *single autofocus*, locks in a focus point when the shutter button is pressed down halfway, and the focus confirmation light glows in the viewfinder. The focus will remain locked until you release the button or take the picture. If the camera is unable to achieve sharp focus, the focus confirmation light will blink. This mode is best when your subject is relatively motionless.

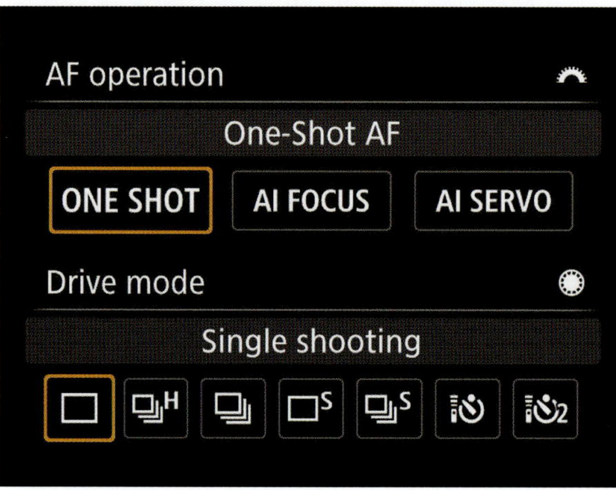

Figure 1.9
Set autofocus mode.

- **AI Servo.** This mode, sometimes called *continuous autofocus*, sets focus when you partially depress the shutter button, but continues to monitor the frame and refocuses if the camera or subject is moved. This is a useful mode for photographing sports and moving subjects.

- **AI Focus.** In this mode, the 5D Mark IV switches between One-Shot and AI Servo as appropriate. That is, it locks in a focus point when you partially depress the shutter button (One-Shot mode), but switches automatically to AI Servo if the subject begins to move. This mode is handy when photographing a subject, such as a child at quiet play, which might move unexpectedly.

Selecting a Focus Point

The Canon EOS 5D Mark IV uses up to 61 different focus points to calculate correct focus. In Full Auto mode, the focus point is selected automatically by the camera. In the other semi-automatic modes, you can allow the camera to select the focus point automatically, or you can specify which focus point should be used.

Your camera has seven different ways of specifying which of the 61 focus points is selected by the camera automatically, or by the user manually. The choices can vary, depending on the lens mounted on the camera (I'll cover these in detail in Chapters 5 and 12.) Your options are as follows:

- **Single-point Spot AF (Manual Selection).** Allows you to manually select a single, reduced-size AF point.

- **Single-point AF (Manual Selection).** For manual selection of a single, slightly larger AF point.

- **AF point expansion (Manual Selection).** You can manually select a single AF point, as well as the four points above, below, and to the left/right of it.

- **AF point expansion (Manual Selection, Surrounding Points).** You can manually select a single AF point, as well as *up to* eight points surrounding it (above, below, left, right, and diagonally from the selected point).

- **Zone AF (Manual Selection of Zone).** AF points are segregated into nine zones, and you can select which zone to use.

- **Large Zone AF (Manual Selection of Zone).** AF points are segregated into three zones (the left, center, and right clusters of AF points), and you can select which zone to use.

- **Automatic Selection AF.** The camera selects one or more focus points automatically within the entire AF area, and highlights them in red in the viewfinder.

The 5D Mark IV offers several ways of choosing the AF area selection mode, including one new method that was not available with the earlier model Mark III, because it employs a brand-new button. Canon, in its wisdom, gave the new control a confusing name.

Here's a quick how-to on choosing the AF area mode:

1. **Press the AF point selection button.** It's located at the far right of the back of the camera. Figure 1.10 shows views from the top (left) and right (center) perspectives. You must press this button each time you want to change the AF area selection *mode* or when you want to select a specific AF *point* after the mode is specified.

2. **Change modes.** Within about six seconds of pressing the AF point selection button, press the M-Fn button (located on top of the camera next to the shutter release button) repeatedly to cycle among the seven available modes. You can *also* opt to press the poorly named AF area selection button (not to be confused with the AF point selection button) on the back of the camera, and shown in Figure 1.10, center. Use which ever control is more convenient for you.

3. **Select AF area mode.** As you press the M-Fn or AF area selection buttons, the screen shown at right in Figure 1.10 appears. The highlighting will change to indicate which mode is selected. Note that the nomenclature that appears on the screen for the modes differs slightly from that used in the Canon manual (and which I've used in the bullet points above). A similar indicator, without the text labels, appears in the viewfinder frame. You might want to use that to change modes while the 5D Mark IV is up to your eye, after you've learned what each mode does. The AF area mode is also shown on the top-surface LCD panel.

SIX-SECOND RULE

Many informational and settings screens will be "live" for about 6 to 16 seconds after you've pressed the relevant button. I won't repeat that information for every setting in this book; if a screen vanishes, just press the appropriate button once more.

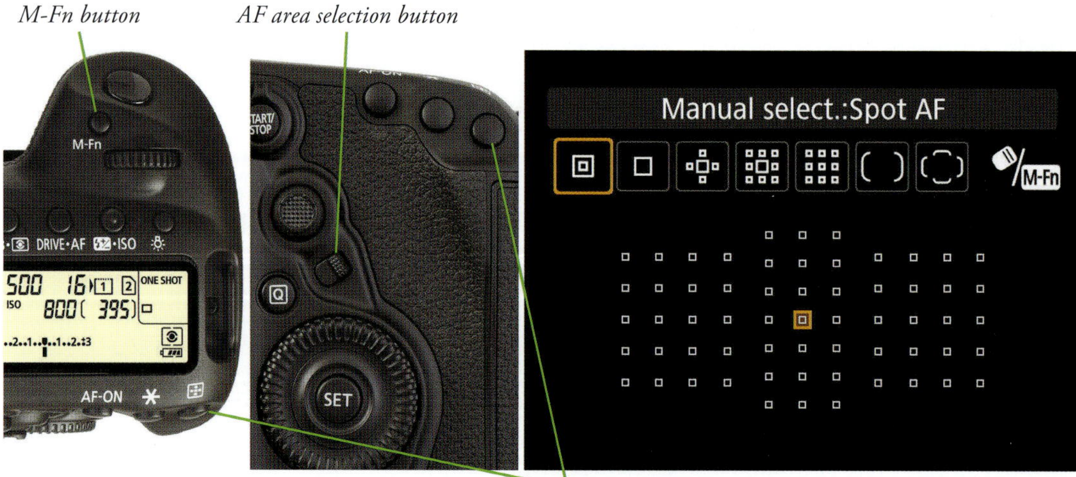

Figure 1.10 Choose AF area mode.

Once you've chosen your AF area mode, there are several ways to set the focus point in any of the manual selection modes:

- **Press the AF point selection button.** The screen shown at right earlier in Figure 1.10 appears. Use the Main Dial to move the selected point, group of points, or zone left or right in the array, and the Quick Control Dial to move the point, group, or zone up or down.

- **Press the multi-controller button.** Use the multi-controller joystick (seen just above and to the left of the AF area selection button in the figure) to move the point, group of points, or zone to any location within the AF frame. Press the multi-controller button inward, and the center AF point or zone will be selected.

- **Rotate either the Main Dial or QCD in Zone AF or Large Zone AF modes.** You can rotate either the Main Dial or QCD to cycle among the available zones for that mode.

BLINKIN' AND NOD

When the AF points are highlighted in red in the viewfinder, the blinking points are those that are sensitive only to horizontal or vertical lines; the solid red points are the 41 *cross-type* sensors. I'll explain the difference between the two types in Chapter 5.

Other Settings

There are a few other options, such as white balance, using the self-timer, or working with flash. You use these right away if you're feeling ambitious, but don't feel ashamed if you postpone using these features until you've racked up a little more experience with your EOS 5D Mark IV.

Adjusting White Balance and ISO

If you like, you can custom-tailor your white balance (color balance) and ISO sensitivity settings. To start out, it's best to set white balance (WB) to Auto, and ISO to ISO 100 or ISO 200 for daylight photos, and ISO 400 for pictures in dimmer light. You'll find complete recommendations for both these settings in Chapter 4. You can adjust either one now by pressing the Metering-WB button (for white balance) and rotating the Quick Control Dial, or by pressing the ISO-Flash exposure compensation button (for ISO sensitivity) and rotating the Main Dial until the setting you want appears on the status LCD. Both buttons were shown earlier in Figure 1.7.

Using the Self-Timer

If you want to set a short delay before your picture is taken, you can use the self-timer. Press the AF-DRIVE button (the screen shown earlier in Figure 1.9 will appear) and rotate the Quick Control Dial until the self-timer icon (for a 10-second delay) or the self-timer icon accompanied by the numeral 2 (for a 2-second delay) appear on the status LCD. Canon supplies a rubber eyepiece cover, which attaches to your camera strap and can be slid over the eyepiece in place of the rubber eyecup. This prevents light from entering through the eyepiece, which can confuse the exposure meter. I've found that extraneous light is seldom a problem unless a bright light source is coming from directly behind the camera, in which case I use my hand or a jacket to shield the viewfinder.

Press the shutter release to lock focus and start the timer. The self-timer lamp will blink and the beeper will sound (unless you've silenced it in the menus) until the final two seconds, when the lamp remains on and the beeper beeps more rapidly.

Taking a Picture

This final section of the chapter guides you through taking your first pictures, reviewing them on the LCD monitor, and transferring your shots to your computer.

Just press the shutter release button halfway to lock in focus at the selected autofocus point for a few seconds. When the shutter button is in the half-depressed position, the exposure, calculated using the shooting mode you've selected, is also locked.

Press the button the rest of the way down to take a picture. At that instant, the mirror flips up out of the light path to the optical viewfinder (assuming you're not using Live View mode, discussed in Chapter 15), the shutter opens, the electronic flash (if attached and enabled) fires, and your 5D Mark IV's sensor absorbs a burst of light to capture an exposure. In fractions of a moment, the shutter closes, the mirror flips back down restoring your view, and the image you've taken is escorted off the CMOS sensor chip very quickly into an in-camera store of memory called a buffer, and the EOS 5D Mark IV is ready to take another photo. The buffer continues dumping your image onto the memory card as you keep snapping pictures without pause (at least until the buffer fills and you must wait for it to get ahead of your continuous shooting, or your memory card fills completely).

Reviewing the Images You've Taken

The Canon EOS 5D Mark IV has a broad range of playback and image review options. Here are the basics, as shown in Figure 1.11. I'll explain more choices, such as rotating the image on review, in Chapter 2:

- **Display image.** Press the Playback button (marked with a blue right-pointing triangle at the lower-left edge of the back of the 5D Mark IV just above the Trash button) to display the most recent image on the LCD monitor in full-screen single image mode. If you last viewed your images using the thumbnail mode (described later in this list), the Index display appears instead.

- **View additional images.** Rotate the Quick Control Dial to review additional images, one at a time. Turn it counterclockwise to review images from most recent to oldest, or clockwise to start with the first image on the memory card and cycle forward to the newest. (You can also move among images using the touch screen, as I'll explain in Chapter 2.)

Figure 1.11
Review your images.

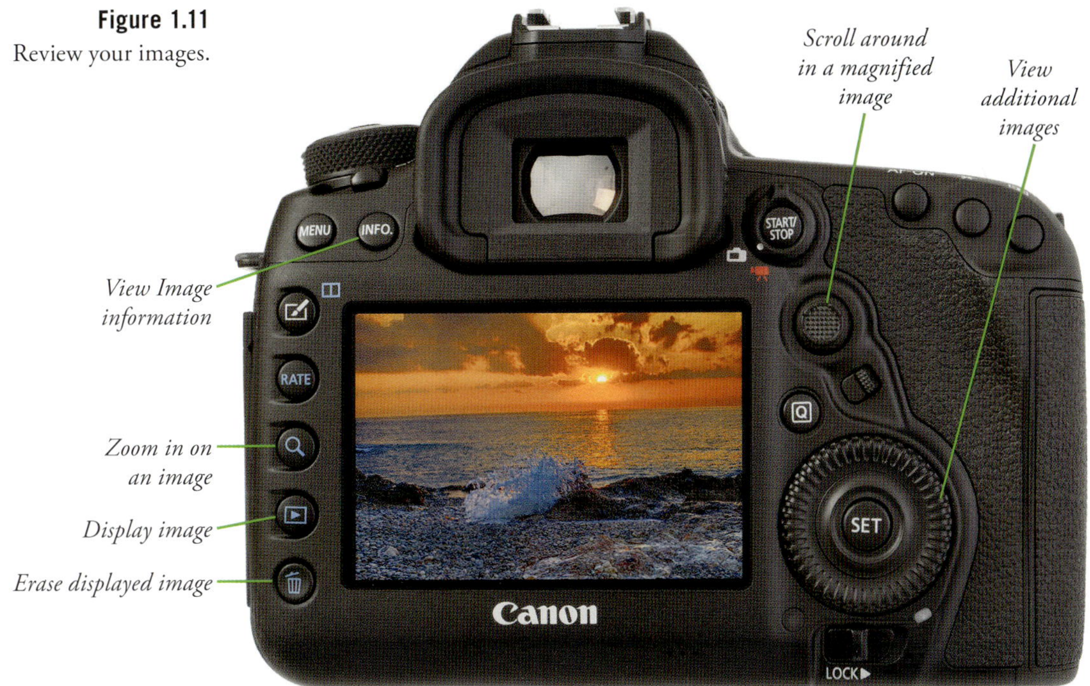

■ **Jump ahead or back.** When you're using the single image display (not zoomed or viewing reduced-size thumbnail images), you can zip through your shots more quickly to find a specific image. Just rotate the Main Dial to leap ahead or back 1, 10, or 100 images, depending on the increment you've set using the last entry in the Playback 2 menu. I find the 5D Mark IV's use of the Main Dial is faster. You can also jump ahead by screens of images, by date, or by folder, and jump among movies, stills, or image "rating." (You can mark favorite images with one to four stars, as I'll explain when I show you how to select all these Playback options in Chapter 14.)

■ **View image information.** Press the INFO. button repeatedly to cycle among overlays of basic image information, detailed shooting information, or no information at all.

■ **Zoom in on an image.** When an image is displayed full-screen on your LCD, press the Magnify/Reduce button (located on the back left of the camera) and rotate the Main Dial to zoom in or out. Press the Playback button to exit magnified display. I'll show you how to specify how much magnification is applied (from 1.5X up to 10X is available) using the Playback 3 menu, in Chapter 13. Pinching and spreading two fingers on the touch screen can also be used to zoom in and out.

- **Scroll around in a magnified image.** Press the Magnify/Enlarge button, then use the multi-controller (that joystick-like knob I mentioned earlier) to scroll around within a magnified image.

- **View thumbnail images.** You can also rapidly move among a large number of images using the Index mode described in the section that follows this list.

- **Compare images.** While reviewing images, you can press the Comparative Photo (Two-Image Display)/Direct Print/Creative Photo button, located fifth from the bottom to the left of the back-panel LCD monitor to split the LCD between two images. The current image is highlighted with a frame. Press SET to swap highlighting to the other image, and then rotate the Quick Control Dial to change to another image. The Q button (to the upper left of the QCD) sets both images to the same magnification. Hold down the Playback button to fill the LCD with the highlighted image. Press the Two-Image button to return to single-image view.

- **Access Functions.** While reviewing pictures in full-image view, you can press the Q button to produce a Quick Control screen that gives you access to many simple functions. You can protect or rate images, resize them, change the jumping method, rotate them, perform RAW image processing, enable or disable highlight alerts, and activate/deactivate AF point display. When the Quick Control screen is visible, use the multi-controller joystick to select the function to perform.

Cruising through Index Views

You can navigate quickly among thumbnails representing a series of images using the 5D Mark IV's Index mode. Here are your basic options.

- **Display thumbnails.** Press the Playback button to display an image on the color LCD monitor. If you last viewed your images using Index mode, an array of images appears automatically (see Figure 1.12). If an image pops up full-screen in single-image mode, press the Magnify/Reduce button once. Then, you can switch between 4, 9, 36, 100, and back to single image view by rotating the Main Dial counterclockwise. A few clicks will take you from magnified view to the four-image index view, (and continuing to rotate counterclockwise will produce fewer/larger index images), while clockwise switches to fewer index images and back to single image mode.

- **Navigate within a screen of index images.** In Index mode, use the QCD or multi-controller joystick to move the highlight box around within the current Index display screen.

- **Check image.** When an image you want to examine more closely is highlighted, press the SET button until the single-image version appears full-screen on your LCD.

- **Compare images.** Two-image review, described earlier, also works in Index mode.

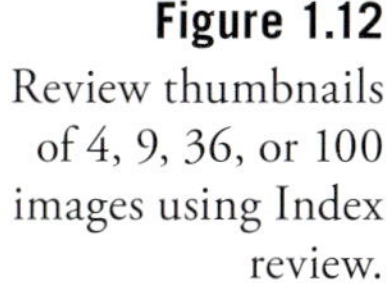

Figure 1.12
Review thumbnails of 4, 9, 36, or 100 images using Index review.

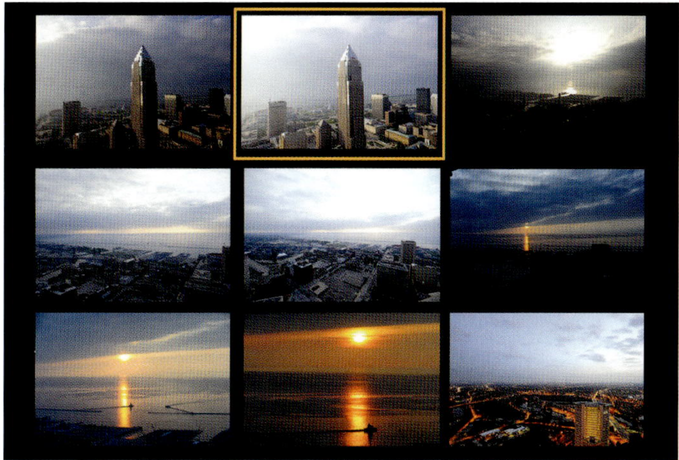

Transferring Photos to Your Computer

The final step in your picture-taking session will be to transfer the photos you've taken to your computer for printing, further review, or image editing. Your 5D Mark IV allows you to print directly to PictBridge-compatible printers and to create print orders right in the camera.

For now, you'll probably want to transfer your images either by using a cable transfer from the camera to the computer or by removing the memory card from the 5D Mark IV and transferring the images with a card reader. The latter option is generally the best, because it's usually much faster and doesn't deplete the battery of your camera. However, you can use a cable transfer when you have the cable and a computer, but no card reader (perhaps you're using the computer of a friend or colleague, or at an Internet café).

To transfer images from the camera to a Mac or PC computer using the USB cable:

1. Turn off the camera.

2. Pry back the rubber cover that protects the EOS 5D Mark IV's USB port, and plug the USB cable furnished with the camera into the USB port. (See Figure 1.13.)

3. Connect the other end of the USB cable to a USB port on your computer.

4. Turn on the camera. Your installed software usually detects the camera and offers to transfer the pictures, or the camera appears on your desktop as a mass storage device, enabling you to drag and drop the files to your computer.

Figure 1.13 Images can be transferred to your computer using a USB cable.

To transfer images from a memory card to the computer using a card reader:

1. Turn off the camera.
2. Slide open the memory card door, and press the gray button, which ejects the Compact Flash card, or press down on the SD card to pop it up for removal.
3. Insert the memory card into your memory card reader. Your installed software detects the files on the card and offers to transfer them. The card can also appear as a mass storage device on your desktop, which you can open and then drag and drop the files to your computer.

2

Canon EOS 5D Mark IV Roadmap

Most of the Canon EOS 5D Mark IV's key functions and settings that are changed frequently can be accessed directly using the array of dials and buttons and knobs that populate the camera's surface. With so many dedicated controls available, you'll find that the bulk of your shooting won't be slowed down by a visit to the vast thicket of text options called Menu-land. That's a distinct paradigm shift from early point-and-shoot cameras, which had only four or five buttons, and relied on menus to control virtually every setting you might want to make. With the 5D Mark IV, you can press specific buttons dedicated to image quality, white balance, ISO sensitivity, shooting mode, exposure compensation, and playback options, and then spin a dial or make adjustments using the multi-controller.

While it might take some time to learn the position and function of each of these controls, once you've mastered them the 5D Mark IV camera is remarkably easy to use. That's because dedicated buttons with only one or two functions each are much faster to access than the alternative—a maze of menus that must be navigated every time you want to use a feature. The advantage of menu systems—dating back to early computer user interfaces of the 1980s—is that they are easy to *learn*. The ironic disadvantage of menus is that they are clumsy to *use*.

Imagine that you are familiar with digital SLRs in general, but know virtually nothing about the Canon EOS 5D Mark IV. You've decided that you want to format the memory card. A-ha! There's a big 'ol MENU button on the left side of the camera. Press it, and you'll see a series of different menu icons, which, when you scroll through them, have entries for shooting options, playback, camera set-up, and customized functions. In the case of the 5D Mark IV, none of the menu screens you see scroll; all the choices available for that screen are shown each time the menu tab appears.

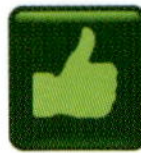

NOTE

When I ask you to *press* or *tap* in this book, I mean you should press and release a button or tap the touch screen (described later). The 5D Mark IV will then give you some time (6 to 16 seconds, depending on the function) to make an adjustment. When I am asking you to keep a button depressed while using another control, I'll say *hold*. For many functions, the camera's exposure meters must be active; just tap the shutter release button lightly to wake them up.

So, with a couple clicks of the Main Dial, you spy a Set-up menu with the Format command as its fifth entry. Scroll down to Format using the other dial (the Quick Control Dial), press the SET ("enter") button, and there you are, looking at the Format screen. A couple more button presses, and you've successfully formatted your memory card.

You didn't really need instructions—the menu system itself led you to the right command. If you don't format another card for weeks and weeks, you can come back to the menus and discover how to perform the task all over again. The main cost to you was the time required to negotiate through all the menus to carry out the function; while menus are easy to learn, the multiple steps they call for (10 or more dial twirls or button presses may be required) can be cumbersome to use.

Direct-access command buttons are the exact opposite: you have to teach yourself how to use them, and then remember what you've learned over time, but, once learned, buttons are much faster to use. For example, to change the autofocus mode with the 5D Mark IV, all you need to do is press the DRIVE-AF button on top of the camera and rotate the Main Dial until the autofocus mode you want to use is indicated on the top-panel LCD. To switch from single exposure to continuous shooting, self-timer, or other "drive" modes, press the same button and rotate the Quick Command Dial. No menus required—but you have to learn the location of the particular button you need to use.

Or, if you need to change the ISO setting on your 5D Mark IV, would you rather press the ISO button and spin the Main Dial until the desired value appears on the LCD—or would you prefer tapping a menu button, using cursor keys to locate the ISO setting submenu, pressing a button to select the ISO menu, navigating to the ISO value you want, and then pressing an OK button to confirm your choice? Yet, that's the procedure mandated by countless point-and-shoot digital cameras and more than a few digital SLRs. The Canon dedicated-button approach (also used by other digital SLR vendors) is a much better design.

So, if you want to operate your 5D Mark IV efficiently, you'll need to learn the location, function, and application of all these controls. What you really need is a street-level roadmap that shows where everything is, and how it's used. But what Canon gives you in the user's manual is akin to a world globe with an overall view and many cross-references to the pages that will tell you what you really need to know. Check out the Nomenclature pages of the Canon 5D Mark IV manual (pages 28 to 30), which offer tiny black-and-white line drawings of the camera body that show front, back, two sides, and the top and bottom of the 5D Mark IV, plus lenses, screens, and other features. There are more than 10 *dozen* callouts pointing to various buttons, dials, controls, components, and icons. If you can find the control you want in this cramped layout, you'll still need to flip back and forth among multiple pages (individual buttons can have several different cross-references!) to locate the information.

Most other third-party books follow this format, featuring black-and-white photos or line drawings of front, back, and top views, and many labels. I originated the up-close-and-personal full-color, street-level roadmap (rather than a satellite view) that I use in this book and my previous camera guidebooks. I provide you with many different views and lots of explanation accompanying each zone of the camera, so that by the time you finish this chapter, you'll have a basic understanding of every control and what it does. I'm not going to delve into menu functions here—you'll find a discussion of your Set-up, Shooting, and Playback menu options in Chapters 11 and 13. Everything here is devoted to the button pusher and dial twirler in you.

You'll also find this "roadmap" chapter a good guide to the rest of the book, as well. I'll try to provide as much detail here about the use of the main controls as I can, but some topics (such as auto-focus and exposure) are too complex to address in depth right away. So, I'll point you to the relevant chapters that discuss things like set-up options, exposure, use of electronic flash, and working with lenses with the occasional cross-reference.

Front View

The front of the 5D Mark IV is the face seen by your victims as you snap away. For the photographer, though, the front is the surface your fingers curl around as you hold the camera, and there are really only three buttons to press, all within easy reach of the fingers of your left hand, plus the shutter button and Main Dial, which are on the top/front of the hand grip. There are additional controls on the lens itself. Figure 2.1 is a view of the front of the EOS 5D Mark IV with the lens detached. The other main components you need to know about are as follows:

- **Shutter release button.** Angled on top of the hand grip is the shutter release button. Press this button down halfway to lock exposure and focus (in One-Shot mode and AI Focus with non-moving subjects).

- **Main Dial.** This dial is used to change shooting settings. When settings are available in pairs (such as shutter speed/aperture), this dial will be used to make one type of setting, such as shutter speed, while the Quick Control Dial (on the back of the camera) will be used to make the other, such as aperture setting.

- **Remote control sensor.** This infrared sensor detects the invisible flash of a Canon remote control, like the RC-6.

- **Self-timer lamp.** When using the self-timer, this lamp also flashes to mark the countdown until the photo is taken. (You can turn off the lamp if you don't want it.)

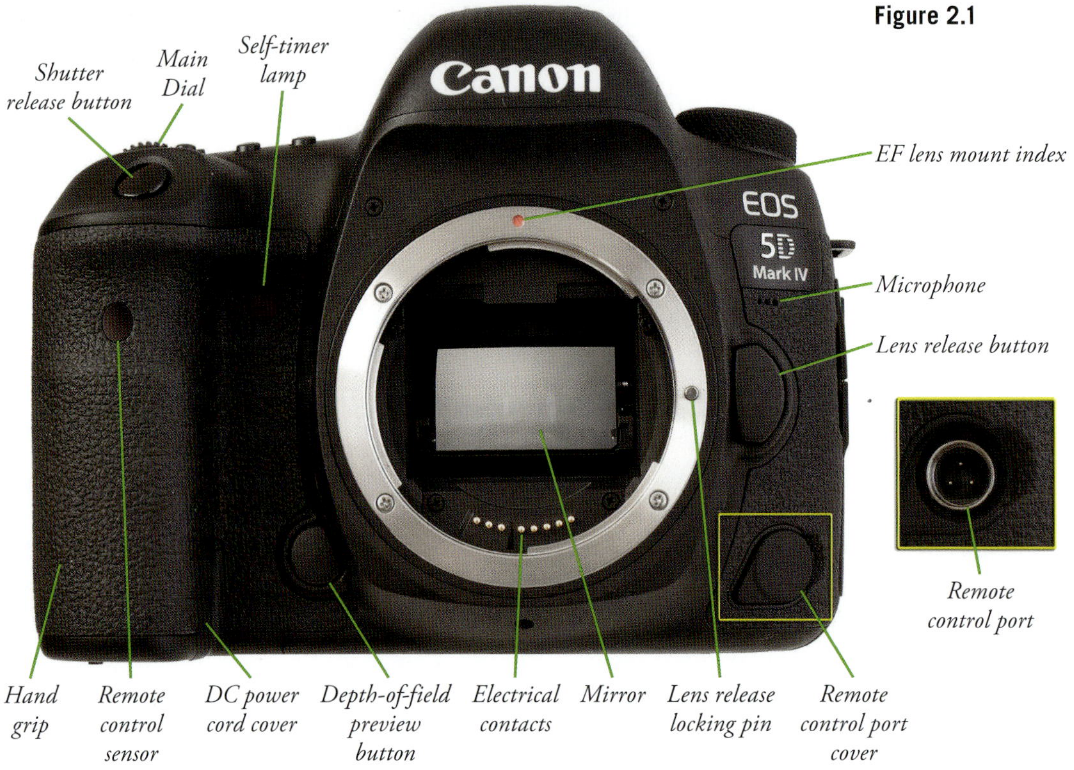

- **DC power cord cover.** This cover, on the inside edge of the hand grip, opens to allow the DC power cable to connect to the 5D Mark IV through the battery compartment.

- **Hand grip.** This provides a comfortable hand-hold, and also contains the 5D Mark IV's battery.

- **Lens release button.** Press and hold this button to unlock the lens so you can rotate the lens to remove it from the camera.

- **Lens release locking pin.** This pin on the lens flange retracts when the release button is held down to unlock the lens.

- **Depth-of-field preview button.** This button, adjacent to the lens mount, stops down the lens to the taking aperture so you can see in the viewfinder how much of the image is in focus. The view grows dimmer as the aperture is reduced.

- **EF lens mount index.** Line up this dot with the raised red dot on the barrel of your EF lens to align the lens as you mount it on the camera. If your lens has a raised white square instead, it's an EF-S lens and cannot be mounted on the 5D Mark IV!

- **Mirror.** The partially silvered mirror reflects light up to the optical viewfinder, and allows some light to pass downward to the autofocus sensor.

- **Electrical contacts.** These contacts connect to matching points on the lens to allow the camera and lens to communicate electronically.

- **Microphone.** The 5D Mark IV has only a monophonic microphone. To record stereo sound, you'll need to plug in an external mic, as described later.

- **Remote control port/cover.** The remote control port cover protects the remote control port (shown in the inset). You can connect a variety of devices to this three-pin port, including the RS-80N3 remote switch, TC80N3 timer/remote controller, or LC-5 wireless controller.

You'll find more controls on the side of the 5D Mark IV, shown in Figure 2.2. In the illustration, you can see the Mode Dial on top, and the rubber cover on the side that protects the camera's USB, TV, HDMI, external flash, and remote control ports. The main buttons shown include:

- **Lens mounting index mark.** Line up this raised dot on an EF lens with the red dot on the lens flange to align the lens as you mount it on the camera. As I noted, non-compatible EF-S lenses have a raised white square indicator instead.

- **Port covers.** The 5D Mark IV's ports are behind these two rubber covers.

- **Neck strap mount.** Attach your neck strap here, and to the matching mount on the opposite edge of the camera.

- **Autofocus/Manual focus lens and Image stabilizer switches.** Canon autofocus lenses have a switch to allow changing between automatic focus and manual focus, and, in the case of IS lenses, another switch to turn image stabilization on and off.

Figure 2.2

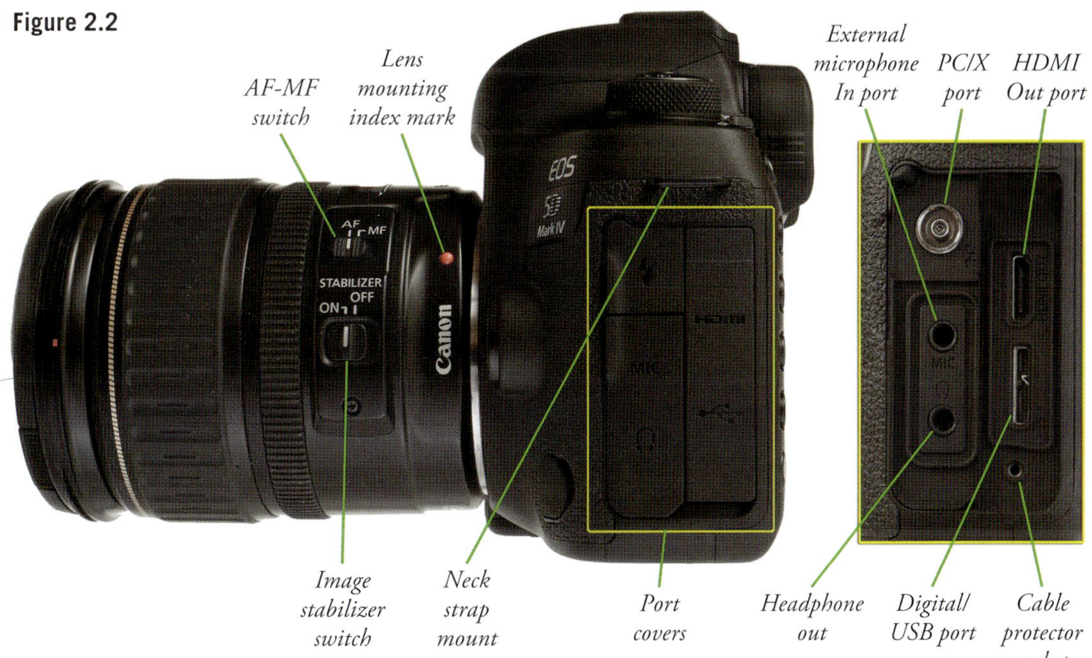

The main feature on the side of the EOS 5D Mark IV are two rubber covers (see Figure 2.2, inset) that protect the five connector ports underneath from dust and moisture.

- **Digital/USB port.** Plug the IFC-150U II interface USB cable furnished with your EOS 5D Mark IV into this digital port and connect the other end to a USB port in your computer to transfer photos, or to your PictBridge-compatible printer to output hard copies. The optional 15.4 foot IFC-500U II interface cable can be purchased if you need a longer link-up. The port can be used with the Wireless File Transmitter WFT-E7 II and GPS Receiver GP-E2.
- **Headphone out.** Connect headphones or other audio playback gear here. It accepts a 3.5mm stereo mini-plug.
- **PC/X port.** This connector is for a non-dedicated electronic flash unit, including studio flash.
- **HDMI Out port.** You need to buy an accessory cable to connect your 5D Mark IV to an HDMI-compatible television, video recorder, or other device, as one to fit this port is not provided with the camera. If you have a high-definition television, it's worth the expenditure to be able to view your camera's output in all its glory. Canon's HDMI cable HTC-100, and other Type C HDMI cables are compatible.
- **External microphone In port.** Connect an external stereo microphone with a 3.5mm stereo mini-plug here to bypass the internal microphone when recording sound.
- **Cable protector socket.** The included cable protector, which prevents cables from accidentally pulling out of their terminals, connects here.

The Canon EOS 5D Mark IV's Business End

The back panel of the EOS 5D Mark IV (see Figure 2.3) bristles with more than a dozen different controls, buttons, and knobs. That might seem like a lot of controls to learn, but you'll find, as I noted earlier, that it's a lot easier to press a dedicated button and spin a dial than to jump to a menu every time you want to change a setting.

Figure 2.3

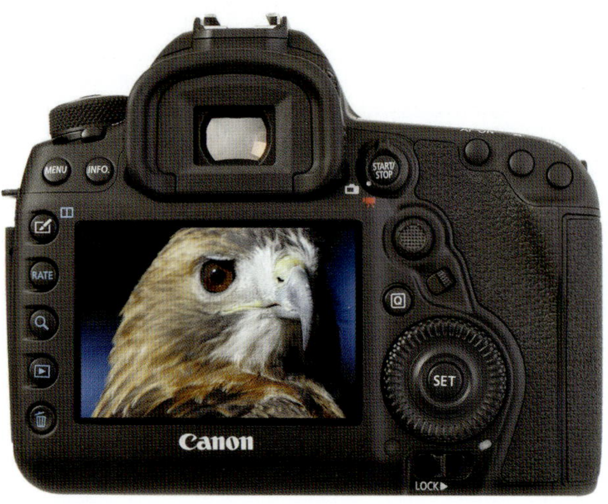

You can see the controls clustered on the left side of the 5D Mark IV in Figure 2.4. The key buttons and components and their functions are as follows:

- **Viewfinder eyepiece.** You can frame your composition by peering into the viewfinder. It's surrounded by a soft rubber eyecup/frame that seals out extraneous light when pressing your eye tightly up to the viewfinder, and it also protects your eyeglass lenses (if worn) from scratching. It can be removed and replaced by the cap attached to your neck strap when you use the camera on a tripod, to ensure that light coming from the back of the camera doesn't venture inside and possibly affect the exposure reading.

- **LCD monitor.** This upgraded 3.2-inch, 1,620,000-dot full-color liquid crystal display presents your menus, review images, and live previews as you make adjustments, shoot, and evaluate your images. Although often referred to as just the *LCD*, the official name is *LCD monitor*, because the monochrome panel on top of the 5D Mark IV is called the *LCD panel.* In Chapter 13, I'll show you how to adjust the LCD monitor's brightness and color balance.

  One major change Canon made for the Mark IV was the introduction of a touch screen. I'll explain how to use the touch screen at the end of this chapter.

- **MENU button.** Summons/exits the menu displayed on the rear LCD monitor of the 5D Mark IV. When you're working with submenus, this button also serves to exit a submenu and return to the main menu.

Figure 2.4

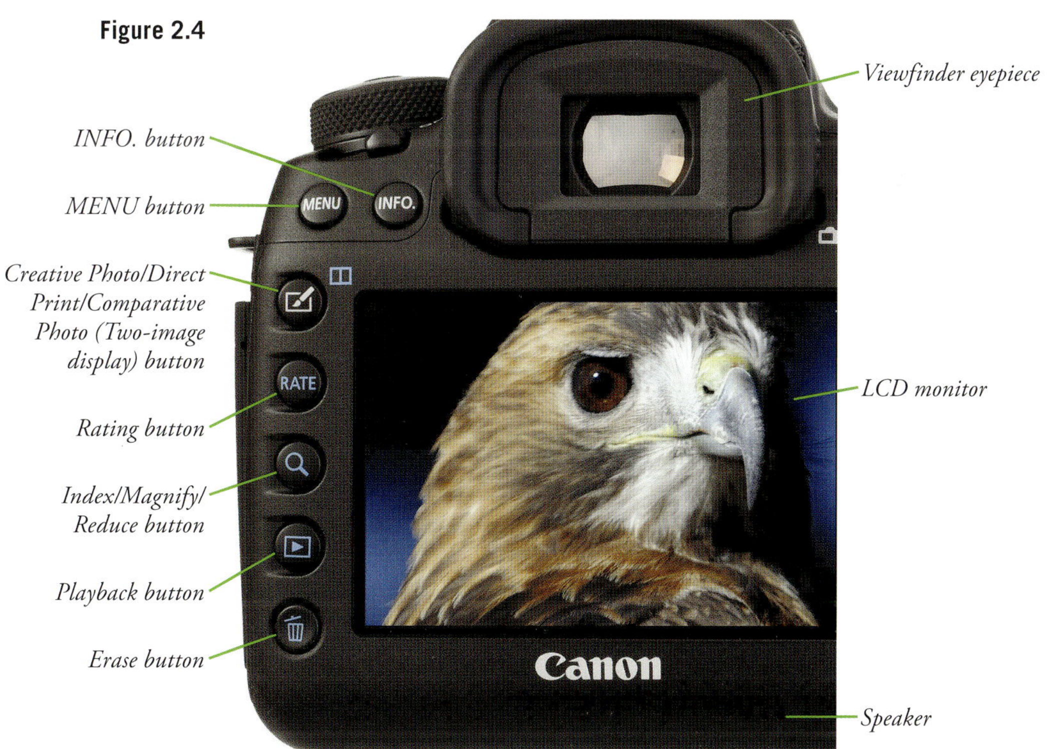

- **Creative Photo/Direct Print/Comparative Photo (Two-image display) button.** In Shooting mode (including Live View still mode), this useful button gives you quick access to Picture Style, Multiple Exposure, and HDR (high dynamic range) features. When you press the button, the screen shown in Figure 2.5 pops up on the LCD monitor so you can select one of these creative effects. In Live View/Movie mode, only Picture Styles are available.

  In Playback mode, this button activates the Direct Printing function, as described in Chapter 13, when you're connected to a PictBridge-compatible device. Otherwise, in Playback mode, the button produces the Comparative Photo/Two-image display described in Chapter 1.

- **Rating button.** This button can be used to assign a star rating to an image during picture review, or to protect an image from accidental erasure. In Shooting mode, it has no function. Although image "ratings" has long been a feature on amateur cameras, Canon has been especially clever in implementing it for advanced models like the 5D Mark IV. See the "Rating Images" section that follows for some ideas for using this feature that you might not have thought of.

- **INFO. button.** When pressed, cycles among Electronic Level, Camera Settings and Shooting Functions screens, and Off (no information displayed). You can disable any of these (except Off) using the INFO. Button Display Options entry in the Set-up 3 menu, as described in Chapter 13. Electronic Level allows you to orient the camera; use the Camera Settings screen to review the current settings. When the Shooting Functions screen is visible, you can adjust the values of the settings. Choose Off when you want a blank screen and no distractions or to save power.

  - **Camera settings.** Shows a list of basic settings for the camera, including color space, white balance information, and the actual number of free shots remaining on your memory card. (Up to 9999.) (See Figure 2.6.)

  - **Electronic level.** This readout includes indicators that show the amount of front/back tilt of the camera and horizontal rotation (along the axis passing through the center of the lens). The 5D Mark IV has three different modes for this feature. The INFO. button produces the electronic level on the LCD monitor in both still shooting (see Figure 2.7) and Live View/ Movie shooting modes. You can also view a slightly different leveling display in the optical viewfinder, using the AF points to show orientation. That display is not activated using the INFO. button; you must assign the viewfinder electronic level to a custom control, as described in Chapter 13.

  - **Shooting functions.** Displays the current shooting settings of the camera, including shutter speed, aperture, ISO sensitivity, battery status, and image quality settings. (See Figure 2.8.) Press the Q button on the back of the camera, and the Quick Control screen appears, as described in the sidebar that follows. (See Figure 2.9.)

  - **Custom Quick Control.** This screen, shown in Figure 2.10, functions similarly to the Quick Control screen, but it can be customized to show only the shooting functions you most frequently adjust, using a layout you select. I'll show you how to create this custom QC screen within the Set-up 3 menu in Chapter 13.

Figure 2.5
Choose from Picture
Style, Multiple
Exposure, or HDR
features.

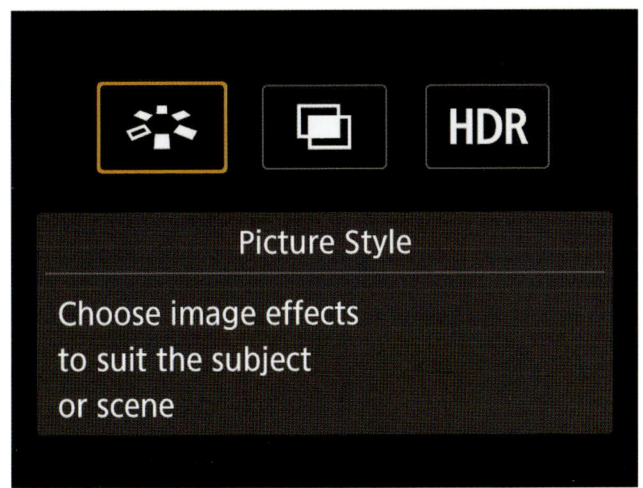

Shooting mode for C1, C2, and C3 user settings

Figure 2.6
This is the Camera
Settings screen.

Color temperature

*Possible shots
remaining on
CF card*

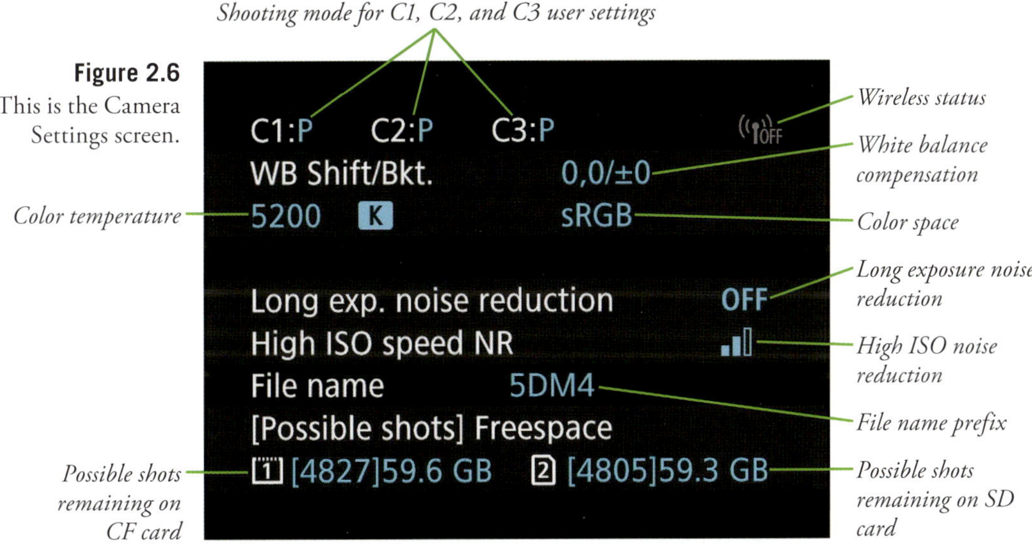

Wireless status

*White balance
compensation*

Color space

*Long exposure noise
reduction*

*High ISO noise
reduction*

File name prefix

*Possible shots
remaining on SD
card*

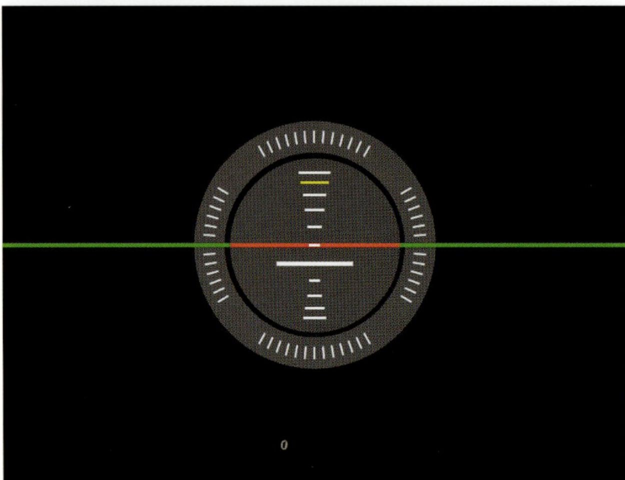

Figure 2.7
The outer ring shows the amount of horizontal rotation; the inner circle shows front/back tilt. When the bar turns from red to green, the camera is level.

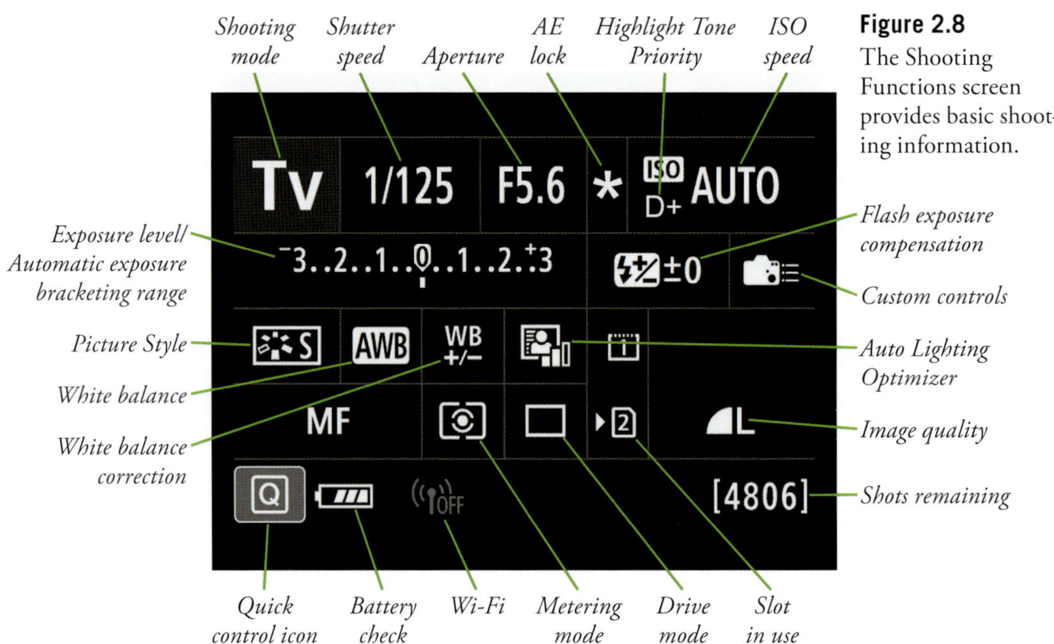

Figure 2.8
The Shooting Functions screen provides basic shooting information.

Figure 2.9
Quick Control
screen.

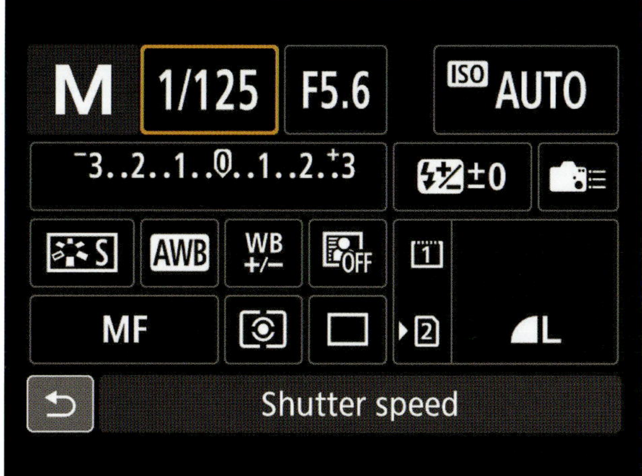

Figure 2.10
Custom Quick
Control screen

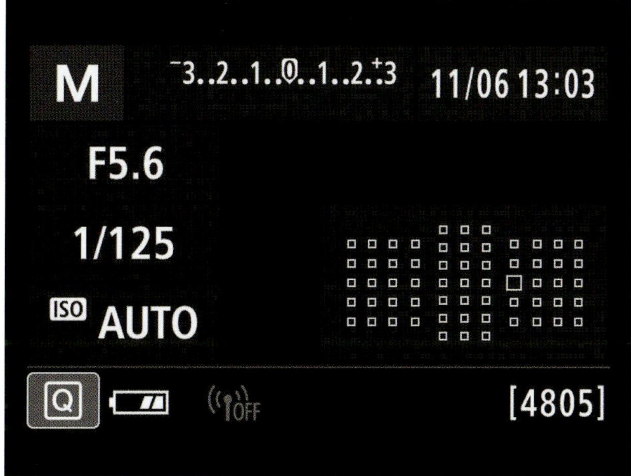

USING THE QUICK CONTROL SCREEN

You can activate the Quick Control screen (shown earlier in Figure 2.9) by pressing the Q button located just below the multi-controller, to the right of the color LCD monitor. Then, use the multi-controller joystick to highlight one of the settings in the screen.

You can't change the exposure mode; instead rotate the Mode Dial to Bulb, Manual, Av (Aperture-priority), Tv (Shutter-priority), or P (Program). The choices you can select change, depending on the position of the Mode Dial.

Once you've highlighted a setting, you can change it by rotating either the Main Dial or Quick Control Dial. You can then move the highlighting to a different setting using the multi-controller, if you want to make multiple changes. Press the Q button a second time to lock in the settings and exit the Quick Control screen.

■ **INFO. button (Live View/Movie shooting modes).** When pressed repeatedly while using Live View or Movie mode, the INFO. button cycles among a slightly different set of informational screens. I'll show you those screens, and how to use them, in Chapter 15, which shows you how to use Live View mode and shoot video clips with your EOS 5D Mark IV.

■ **INFO. button (Playback mode).** In Playback mode, while reviewing images, pressing the INFO. button cycles among three displays of the image: a single-frame version of the image, a similar view with basic information about the shot arrayed at the top and bottom of the frame (see Figure 2.11), and a detailed display with a thumbnail of the image with basic shooting information plus a brightness histogram (upper left in Figure 2.12).

You can scroll down this screen using the multi-controller joystick to add additional details:

- RGB histogram, plus lens information (Figure 2.12, upper right).
- White balance data (Figure 2.12, second row, left).
- Picture Style sharpness information (Figure 2.12, second row right).
- Picture Style contrast information (Figure 2.12, third row left).
- Color space and noise reduction data (Figure 2.12, third row right).
- Peripheral illumination and distortion correction data (Figure 2.12, bottom left).
- Digital lens optimizer, chromatic aberration, and diffraction correction data (Figure 2.12, bottom right).
- GPS/IPTC information (optional; not shown in the figures). If you've used the 5D Mark IV's built-in GPS to record location data, or have added IPTC (International Press Information Council) information to your shots, you can scroll down to it here. I'll explain the use of these two types of data in Chapter 13.

■ **INFO. button (other modes).** When setting Picture Styles, the INFO. button is used to select a highlighted Picture Style for modification. When trimming an image, the INFO. button selects the orientation.

■ **Index/Magnify/Reduce button.** During Playback zooms in to magnify image, and zooms out to full screen and index views.

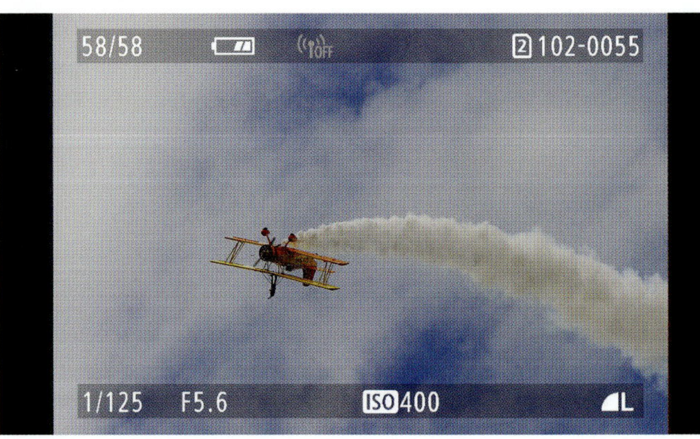

Figure 2.11
Single image playback.

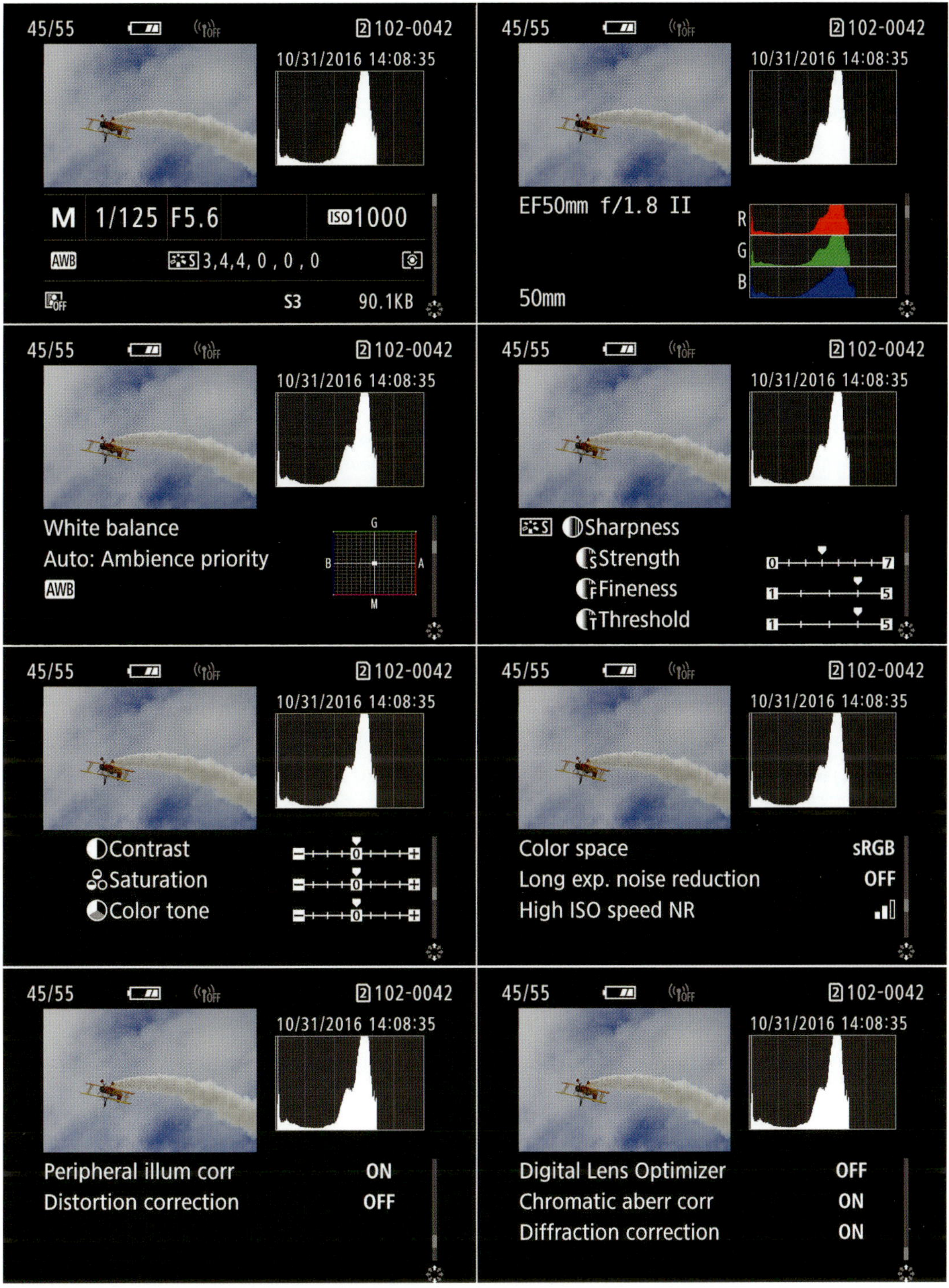

Figure 2.12 Scrolling through the detail screens.

- **Playback button.** Displays the last picture taken. Thereafter, you can move back and forth among the available images by rotating the Quick Control Dial, to advance or reverse one image at a time, or the Main Dial, to jump forward or back using the jump method described in the discussion of the Playback menu in Chapter 13. To quit playback, press this button again. The 5D Mark IV also exits Playback mode automatically when you press the shutter button (so you'll never be prevented from taking a picture on the spur of the moment because you happened to be viewing an image).

- **Erase button.** Press to erase the image shown on the LCD. A menu will pop up displaying Cancel and Erase choices. Rotate the Quick Control Dial to select one of these actions; then press the SET button to activate your choice.

- **Speaker.** Sounds emitting from your camera emanate from here.

Rating Images

Why did Canon assign a button located on prime back-panel real estate to the Rating function alone? Isn't this the equivalent of pasting a shiny Gold Star sticker on your images, like amateur snapshooters are wont to do? Think again, because Canon has put a powerful tool at your disposal. There's a lot more you can do with this button than specify, "This shot's nice, but this other one is better!"

- **Think categories.** Instead of equating the one to five stars you can apply to quality, consider them to represent other types of image categories. These categories can be very broad, or very specific. The assignments are up to you. Once you instigate a particular system, you'll find it easy to memorize and recall when you're actually applying ratings.

- **Specify types of images.** You might want to use one star for landscapes; two stars for portraits; three stars for action; four stars for close-ups; and five stars for concerts and performances. Then, you can use the 5D Mark IV's Main Dial Jump by Rating capability to quickly move through all your images of a particular type. Canon software that can "read" ratings can be used to group these picture types together.

- **Group by venue.** You can access images by date created, but using the Rating system you can also "mark" them by logical locations. If you're on a long trip to Spain, assign one star to pictures taken in Madrid; two stars to photos captured in Toledo; three stars to Granada and Seville; four stars to Barcelona and Valencia; and five stars for everywhere else.

- **Categorize by style or type or subject.** Say you're at a track meet. You can assign different star ratings to running, jumping, or throwing events. Or, you can use ratings for individual and relay events. Differentiate between trials and finals if you like. That gives you the freedom to wander around among simultaneous events, and mark all your shots (or just your best ones) for easy retrieval.

- **Assemble slide shows.** You can select images for display in a slide show based on ratings. You can choose specific star ratings to display in your show, as described in Chapter 13. For example, your presentation can include All, only images marked with five stars (your best ones, if you use a quality rating system), or those marked with either two or four stars (if you used some sort of category system).

- **"Protect" images.** The Rating button can be reassigned to mark images as Protected, instead. And the protection attribute does a lot more than just keep you from accidentally erasing photos. For example, the Eye-Fi wireless card can be set so that it will upload only images you've marked as Protected, rather than every single shot you take.

To rate images during picture review, just follow these steps (you can also rate/protect images in the Playback 1 menu):

1. **Display the image or movie to be rated.** Use the Quick Control Dial (QCD) to advance/rewind among your images (or use one of the other image review tools, such as Jumping or Index thumbnails) to find an image to mark.

2. **Press the RATE button.** Each time the RATE button is pressed, the rating will change, cycling from one star to five stars and then to None. *However,* you can disable a particular star rating, so that you can apply, say, one, three, and five stars (only), or, if you've mentally assigned categories to star ranks, you could use only two, four, and five stars. I'll show you how to do this using the Rate Button Function setting in the Set-up 3 menu in Chapter 13.

3. **Protect instead.** If you've reassigned the RATE button to the Protect function, you can mark the displayed image as Protected instead.

4. **Continue marking.** Press the Playback button when you're finished to exit the ranking function.

Right Side Controls

More buttons reside on the right side of the back panel, as shown in Figure 2.13. The key controls and their functions are as follows:

- **Diopter adjustment knob.** Rotate this knob to adjust the diopter correction for your eyesight.

- **Live View/Movie switch.** Flip to switch between Live View and Movie modes.

- **Start/Stop button.** Press once to begin live view or movie capture, and again to exit.

- **Multi-controller.** This joystick-like button can be shifted up, down, side to side, and diagonally for a total of eight directions, or pressed. It can be used for several functions, including AF point selection, scrolling around a magnified image, trimming a photo, or setting white balance correction.

- **AF-ON button.** Press this button to activate the autofocus system without needing to partially depress the shutter release. This control, used with other buttons, allows you to lock exposure and focus separately. Lock exposure by pressing the shutter release halfway, or by pressing the AE Lock button; autofocus by pressing the shutter release halfway, or by pressing the AF-ON button. Functions of this button will be explained in more detail in Chapter 5.

- **AE/FE (autoexposure/flash exposure) lock.** In Shooting mode, it locks the exposure or external flash exposure that the camera sets when you partially depress the shutter button. The exposure lock indication (*) appears in the viewfinder. If you want to recalculate exposure with the shutter button still partially depressed, press the * button again. The exposure will be unlocked when you release the shutter button or take the picture. To retain the exposure lock for subsequent photos, keep the * button pressed while shooting.

  When using external flash, pressing the * button fires an extra pre-flash when you partially depress the shutter button that allows the unit to calculate and lock exposure prior to taking the picture.

- **AF point selection button.** In Shooting mode, this button activates autofocus point selection. (See Chapter 5 for information on setting autofocus/exposure point selection.)

- **AF area selection button.** In Shooting mode, this button duplicates the default behavior of the M-Fn button (located on top of the camera and shown later). Press the AF point selection button first, and then this button to cycle through the available AF area modes. You can assign a different behavior for this button using the Custom Controls entry of the Custom Functions menu. Your choices include direct AF area selection, AE lock, AE lock (hold), toggle between selected AF point and center/registered AF point, set ISO speed, exposure compensation, and off (to disable the button).

- **Memory card access lamp.** When lit or blinking, this lamp indicates that the Compact Flash card is being accessed.

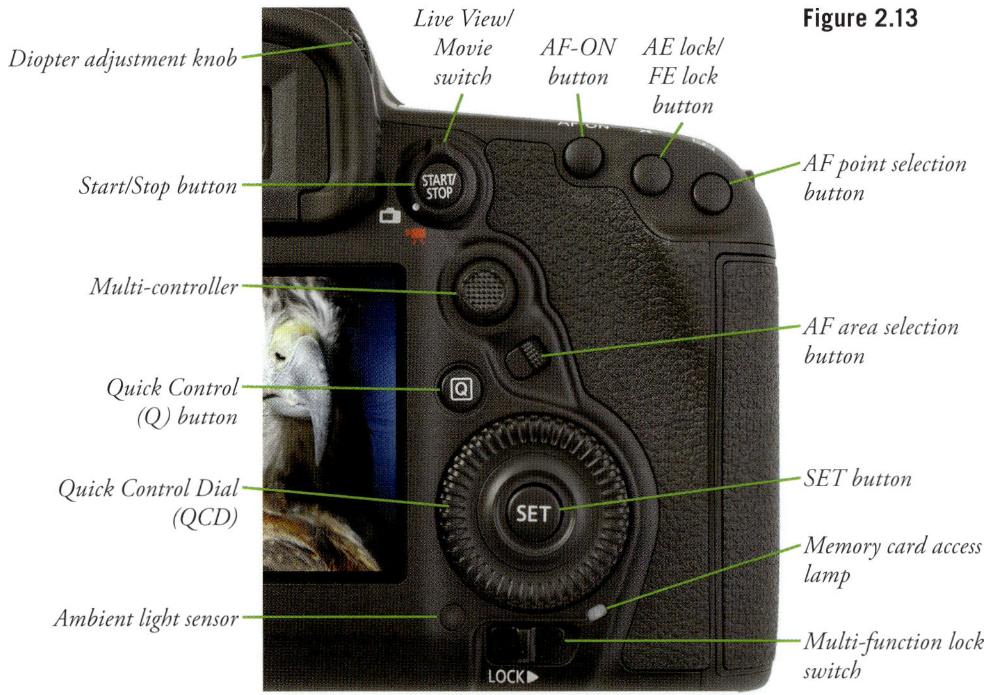

- **Quick Control (Q) button.** Press this button to produce the Quick Control screen, which gives you access to many features when in Shooting mode. When you're reviewing images in Playback, a different Quick Control screen pops up that allows you to protect or rate images, change jump method, resize, or perform other functions.

- **Quick Control Dial (QCD).** Used to select shooting options, such as f/stop or exposure compensation value, or to navigate through menus. It also serves as an alternate controller for some functions set with other controls, such as AF point.

- **SET button.** Selects a highlighted setting or menu option.

- **Multi-function lock switch.** Set to the right, it prevents the Main Dial, QCD, and multi-controller from changing a setting. If you try to use one of these locked controls, an L warning will be displayed in the optical viewfinder and the LCD panel; in the Shooting Settings display, Lock will be shown. You can select which of the three are locked out using the Multi Function Lock entry in the Custom Functions 2 menu. Choose any combination of one, two, or all three controls to freeze with this lock switch.

- **Ambient light sensor.** The 5D Mark IV is smart enough to automatically adjust the brightness of the LCD monitor for ambient light levels. The sensor that measures the amount of light is located here. You can fine-tune the brightness levels in the Set-up 2 menu, as described in Chapter 13.

Going Topside

The top surface of the Canon EOS 5D Mark IV has its own set of frequently accessed controls. The three of them, just forward of the status LCD panel, have dual functions and are marked with hyphenated labels. Press the relevant button (you don't need to hold it down) and then rotate the Main Dial to choose the left function of the pair, such as metering mode, autofocus, or ISO, and the Quick Control Dial to select the right function, such as white balance, drive mode, or flash exposure compensation. The settings you make will be indicated in the LCD status panel, which is described in the section that follows this one. The key controls, shown in Figure 2.14, are as follows:

- **Shutter release button.** Partially depress this button to lock in exposure and focus. Press all the way to take the picture. Tapping the shutter release when the camera has turned off the autoexposure and autofocus mechanisms reactivates both. When a review image is displayed on the back-panel color LCD, tapping this button removes the image from the display and reactivates the autoexposure and autofocus mechanisms.

- **M-Fn button.** This multi-function button can be used to change the autofocus area selection mode (as described in Chapter 5). You can assign an additional function to this control using the Custom Controls feature, as described in Chapter 14. Your choices include Flash Exposure Lock, Autoexposure Lock (both toggle and hold versions), One-touch image quality setting (both toggle and hold versions), and activate viewfinder electronic level.

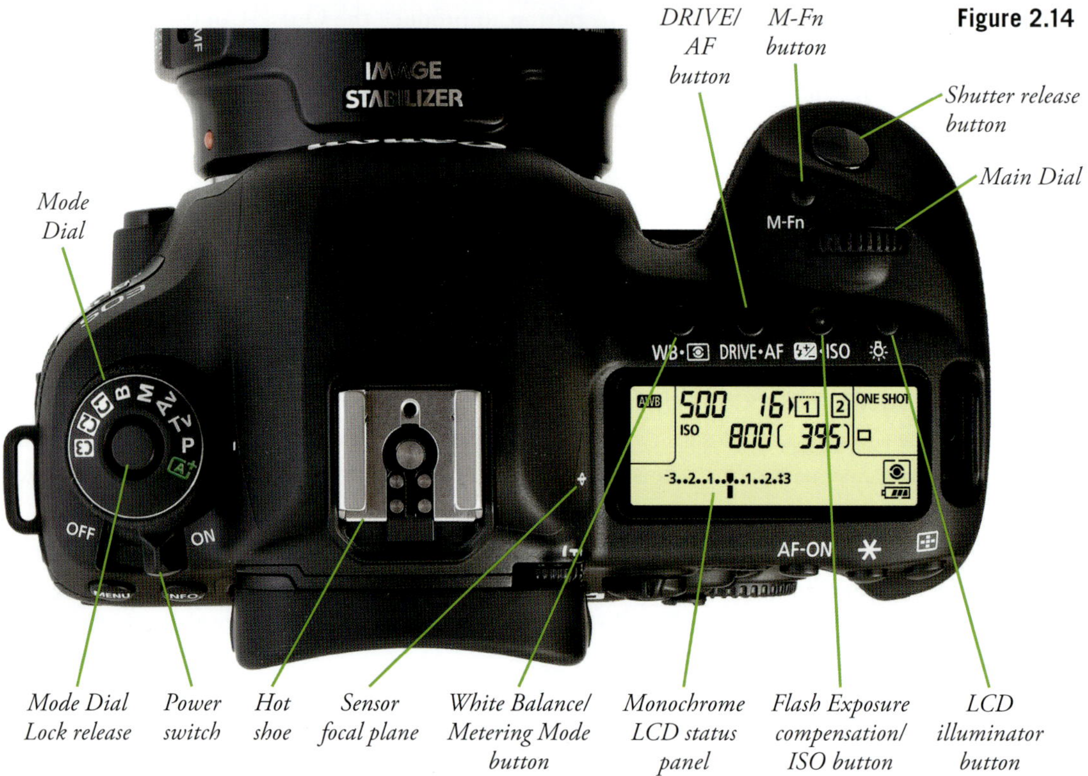

- **Mode Dial.** Hold down the Mode Dial Lock release and rotate this dial to switch among exposure modes, and to choose one of the camera user settings (C1, C2, or C3). You'll find these modes and options described in more detail in Chapter 13 (where I show you how to register your settings in the C1/C2/C3 "slots").

- **Sensor focal plane.** Precision macro and scientific photography sometimes requires knowing exactly where the focal plane of the sensor is. The symbol on the side of the pentaprism marks that plane.

- **Hot shoe.** Slide an electronic flash into this multi-purpose accessory shoe when you need an external Speedlite. A dedicated flash unit, like those from Canon, can use the multiple contact points shown to communicate exposure, zoom setting, white balance information, and other data between the flash and the camera. There's more on using electronic flash in Chapters 9 and 10.

- **LCD illuminator button.** Press this button to turn on the amber LCD panel lamp that back-lights the LCD status panel for about six seconds, or to turn it off if illuminated. The lamp will remain lit beyond the six-second period if you are using the Mode Dial or other shooting control.

■ **White Balance/Metering Mode button.** This button has two functions. Rotate the Main Dial after pressing this button to change between Evaluative, Partial, Spot, or Center-weighted metering. Rotate the Quick Control Dial to cycle among AWB (Automatic White Balance), Daylight, Shade, Cloudy/Twilight/Sunset, Tungsten, White Fluorescent, Flash, Custom, and Color Temperature. You'll find more information about customizing white balance in Chapter 11.

■ **DRIVE/AF button.** Press once and then rotate the Main Dial to change between One-Shot, AI Focus, and AI Servo autofocus modes (you'll find more about those modes in Chapter 5). Drive mode settings include single shooting, continuous (up to 7 fps), and 10- or 2-second self-timer/remote control, selected by holding down the button and rotating the Quick Control Dial.

■ **Flash Exposure compensation/ISO button.** Press and rotate the Main Dial to choose an ISO setting; use the Quick Control Dial to change electronic flash exposure compensation. You'll find more about ISO options in Chapter 4, and flash EV settings in Chapter 9. The functions for all three buttons are shown in Table 2.1

■ **Monochrome LCD status panel.** The LCD panel provides information about the status of your camera and its settings, including exposure mode, number of pictures remaining, battery status, and many other settings. I'll illustrate all these in the next section.

■ **Main Dial.** This dial is used to make many shooting settings. When settings come in pairs (such as shutter speed/aperture in Manual shooting mode), the Main Dial is used for one (for example, shutter speed), while the Quick Control Dial is used for the other (aperture). When an image is on the screen during playback, this dial also specifies the leaps that skip a particular number of images during playback of the shots you've already taken. Jumps can be 1 image, 10 images, 100 images, jump by date, or jump by screen (that is, by screens of thumbnails when using Index mode), date, or folder. (Jump method is selected in the Playback 2 menu, as described in Chapter 13.) This dial is also used to move among tabs when the MENU button has been pressed, and is used within some menus (in conjunction with the Quick Control Dial) to change pairs of settings.

Table 2.1 Control Button Functions

Button	Quick Control Dial	Main Dial
WB/Metering	Auto/Daylight/Shade/Cloudy/Tungsten/White Fluorescent/Flash/Custom/Kelvin color temperatures	Evaluative/Partial/Spot/Center-weighted average metering modes
DRIVE/AF	Single shooting/Continuous/Self-timer 2 seconds/Self-timer 10 seconds/Remote	One-Shot/AI Focus/AI Servo autofocus modes
Flash EV/ISO	Flash compensation (+ or − up to 2 stops)	ISO Auto/ISO 100-6400/ H1 (12800)–H2(102800)

LCD Panel Readouts

The top panel of the EOS 5D Mark IV (see Figure 2.15) contains an amber-colored (when backlit) monochrome LCD readout that displays status information about most of the shooting settings. All of the information segments available are shown in Figure 2.16. I've color-coded the display to make it easier to differentiate them; the information does *not* appear in color on the actual 5D Mark IV.

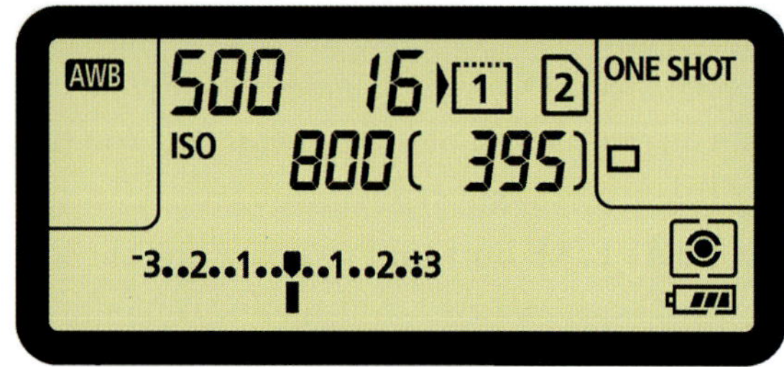

Figure 2.15

Many of the information items are mutually exclusive (that is, in the white balance area at upper left, only one of the possible settings illustrated will appear).

Some of the items on the status LCD also appear in the viewfinder, such as the shutter speed and aperture (pictured at top in blue in the figure), and the exposure level (in yellow at the bottom).

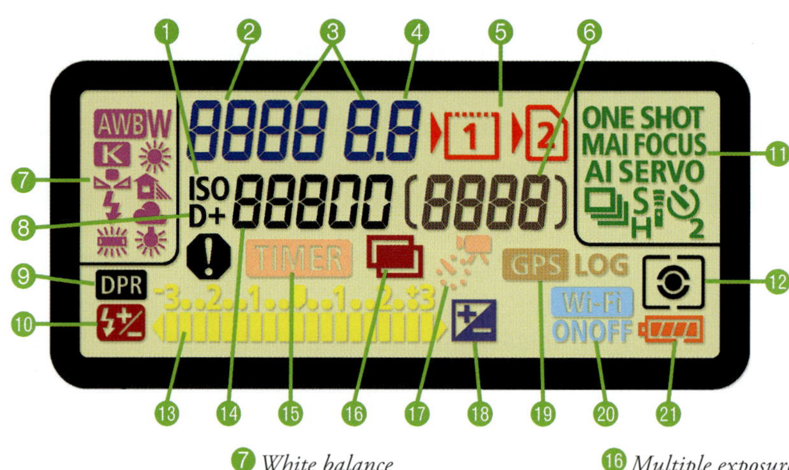

1 *ISO*

2 *Shutter speed/FE lock/Remaining time-lapse exposures/busy/Multi-function lock/Cleaning sensor/No card/Error*

3 *AF point selection/Card warning*

4 *Aperture/Dust Data Delete*

5 *Card selected*

6 *Possible shots/Self-timer countdown/Bulb exposure time/ Card error/Error number/ Remaining images*

7 *White balance*

8 *Highlight tone priority*

9 *Dual pixel RAW*

10 *Flash exposure compensation*

11 *Drive mode*

12 *Metering mode*

13 *Exposure level/Exposure/Flash exposure compensation amount/ Autoexposure bracket range*

14 *ISO speed*

15 *Bulb/Interval timer*

16 *Multiple exposure*

17 *Time-lapse movie*

18 *Exposure compensation*

19 *GPS*

20 *Wi-Fi*

21 *Battery*

Figure 2.16

Lens Components

The typical lens, like the one shown in Figures 2.17 and 2.18, has seven or eight common features:

- **Filter thread.** Lenses have a thread on the front for attaching filters and other add-ons. Some also use this thread for attaching a lens hood (you screw on the filter first, and then attach the hood to the screw thread on the front of the filter).
- **Lens hood bayonet mount.** This is used to mount the lens hood for lenses that don't use screw-mount hoods (the majority).
- **Zoom ring.** Turn this ring to change the zoom setting.
- **Zoom scale.** These markings on the lens show the current focal length selected.
- **Focus ring.** This is the ring you turn when you manually focus the lens.
- **Focus scale.** This is a readout that rotates in unison with the lens's focus mechanism to show the distance at which the lens has been focused. It's a useful indicator for double-checking autofocus, roughly evaluating depth-of-field, and for setting manual focus guesstimates.

Figure 2.17

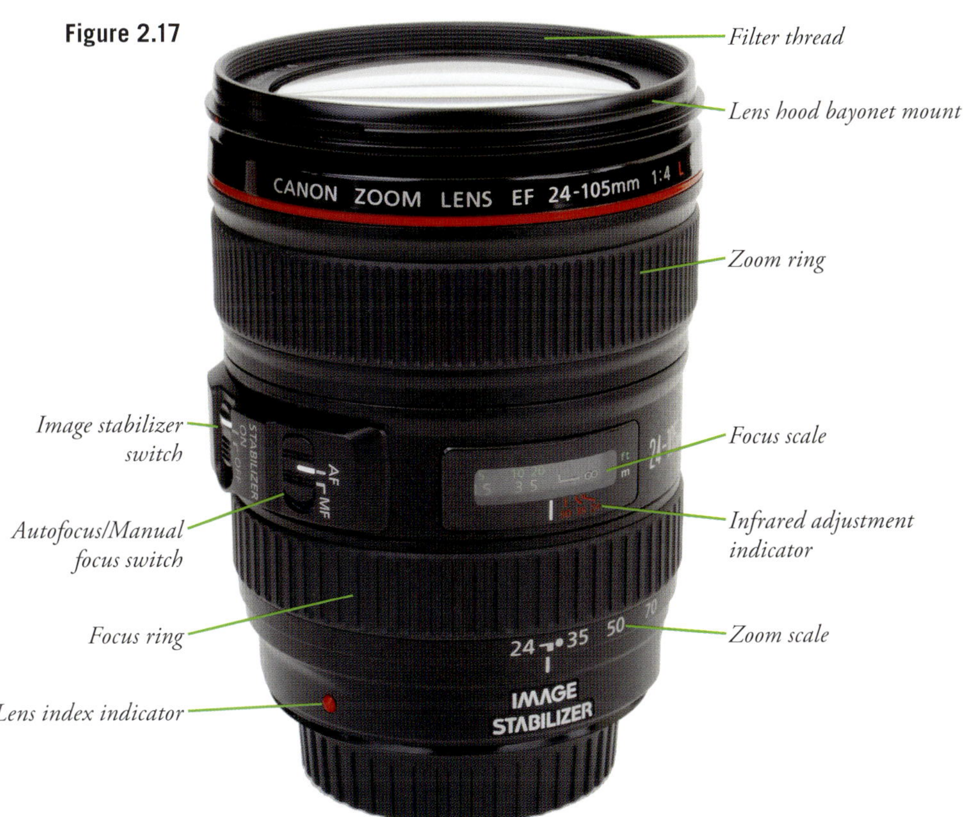

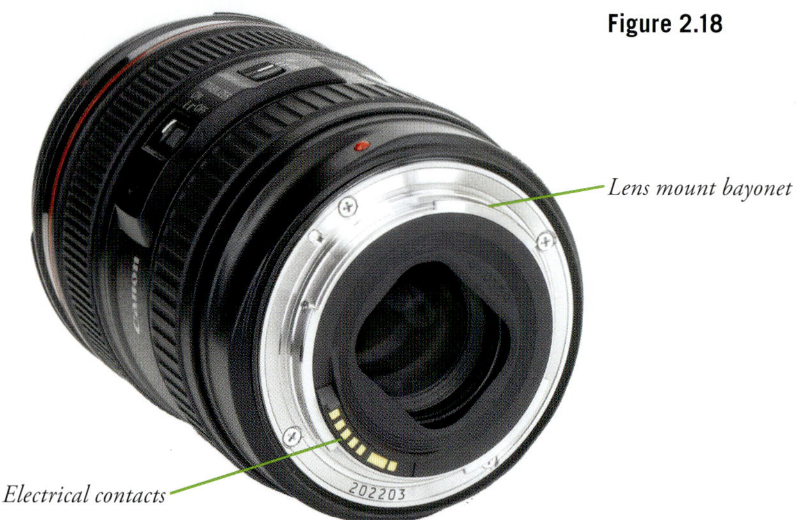

- **Autofocus/Manual focus switch.** Allows you to change from automatic focus to manual focus.

- **Image stabilizer switch.** Lenses with IS include a separate switch for adjusting the stabilization feature.

- **Infrared adjustment indicator.** If you're shooting infrared photos (with a suitable visible light cut-off filter), you should know that IR illumination focuses at a different point from ordinary light. If you want the most accurate focus and you're using a lens with IR indicators, the focus point should be adjusted from the white line on the lens barrel to the red line representing your current zoom setting. With the 24-105mm lens shown, indicators are provided for 24mm, 35mm, and 50mm focal lengths. The focus difference diminishes as focal length increases; from 50 to 105mm you can "guestimate" the correct adjustment, or ignore it altogether. In many cases, depth-of-field (when using f/stops of f/8 or smaller) may take care of the disparity.

- **Electrical contacts.** The gold contacts on the rear of the lens mate with the contacts on the camera body, allowing the lens and camera to communicate electronically (shown in Figure 2.18).

- **Lens mount bayonet.** This is the component used to mount the lens on the camera (shown in Figure 2.18).

Looking Inside the Viewfinder

Much of the important shooting status information is shown inside the viewfinder of the EOS 5D Mark IV. As with the status LCD up on top, not all of this information will be shown at any one time. Figure 2.19 shows what you can expect to see.

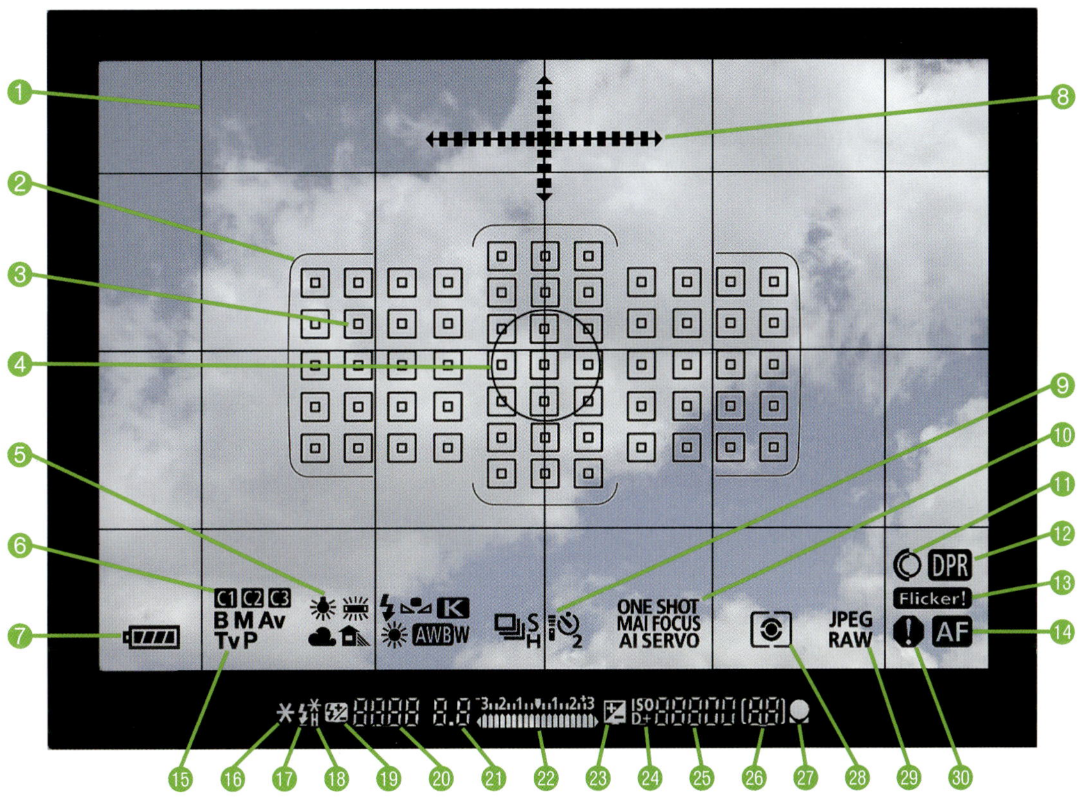

Figure 2.19

1. Grid
2. AF area frame
3. AF points
4. Spot metering circle
5. White balance
6. User settings
7. Battery check
8. Electronic level
9. Drive mode
10. Focus mode
11. Digital lens optimizer
12. Dual pixel RAW
13. Flicker detection
14. Autofocus status
15. Shooting mode
16. AE lock/Autoexposure bracketing in progress
17. Flash ready/Improper FE lock warning
18. High-speed sync
19. Flash exposure compensation
20. Shutter speed/FE lock/Busy
21. Aperture/AF point selection
22. Exposure level indicator/Exposure compensation amount/Flash exposure compensation amount/Autoexposure bracketing range
23. Exposure compensation
24. Highlight Tone Priority
25. ISO speed
26. Maximum burst
27. Focus confirmation light
28. Metering mode
29. JPEG/RAW
30. Warning

Underneath Your EOS 5D Mark IV

There's not a lot going on with the bottom panel of your EOS 5D Mark IV. You'll find a tripod socket, which secures the camera to a tripod, and is also used to lock on the optional BG-E20 battery grip, which provides more juice to run your camera to take more exposures with a single charge. It also adds a vertically oriented shutter release, Main Dial, AE lock/FE lock, and AF point selection controls for easier vertical shooting. To mount the grip, slide the battery door latch to open the door, then push down on the small pin that projects from the hinge. That will let you remove the battery door. Then slide the grip into the battery cavity, aligning the pin on the grip with the small hole on the other side of the tripod socket. Tighten the grip's tripod socket screw to lock the grip onto the bottom of your 5D Mark IV. Figure 2.20 shows the underside view of the camera

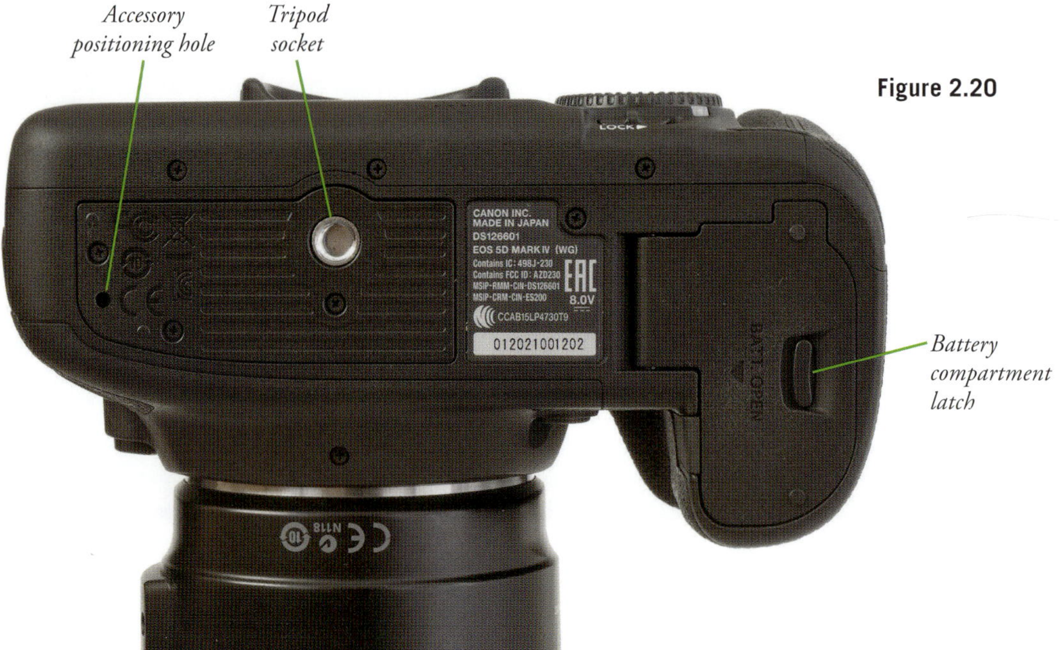

Mastering the Touch Screen

Touch screens are finally making the migration from consumer cameras and smartphones to high-end cameras like the 5D Mark IV. This section will show you how to activate/deactivate it in the Set-up 2 menu, and how to use its functions. Using the touch screen, you can perform many routine operations, including menu navigation/selection functions by tapping the screen. For many veteran shooters, touch-friendly tasks are no quicker than the button/dial procedures we are used to, and can even be more awkward for those with large fingers or who need/want to wear gloves.

However, there are several uses for the touch screen that border on outstanding:

- **Touch focus.** In live view and, more importantly, when shooting movies, you can tap the screen to focus on the subject at that point on the screen. There are two reasons why this is a stellar capability. First, it eliminates the need to press a button that's been assigned the AF-ON feature. Any vibration of the camera from depressing a button will be visible during video. A light tap on the screen is much less likely to generate vibrations. That's especially useful if the camera is mounted on a tripod or secured in a Steadicam-style video stabilizer rig. Advanced videographers can also use touch focus to create pull focus/rack focus effects, a creative tool that involves adjusting focus from one subject to another during a shot.

- **Selecting a focus point.** When not using live view, you can still use the touch screen to specify a focus point. In any manual focus point selection mode, press the point selection button, and then swipe your finger around the touch screen to move the focus point, as represented by the green arrows in Figure 2.21.

Figure 2.21
Use the touch screen to select a focus point manually.

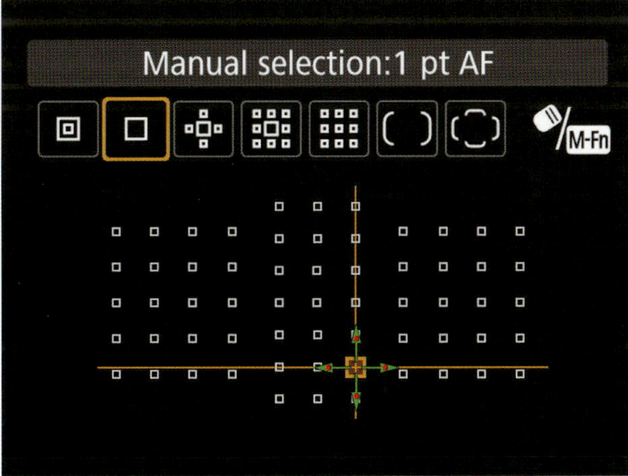

- **Text entry.** If you've ever had to type in copyright information, tried to rename the My Menu tab, or performed any other text entry operation using the 5D Mark IV's buttons and dials, you'll appreciate the ability to just tap on the virtual keyboard to input your data. It's a shame that the EOS Utility must still be used to enter ITPC (International Press Telecommunications Council) metadata into image files. Photojournalists (a primary user base for the 5D Mark IV) would *love* this capability for entering data on the fly at a news scene as an alternative to their laptop.

- **Playback.** As you'll see, you can scroll through images rapidly during review, zoom in and out, and perform other functions that are much clumsier with buttons and dials—even if you've had years of experience and are adept with the old-school methods.

Although some menu entries work better with the touch screen (which can be activated/deactivated in the Set-up 2 menu) than others (you'll have to try them to see which are convenient for you), the Quick Control menu has some settings that are ideal. You can adjust sliders with a fingertip to set ISO, make exposure or flash exposure compensation adjustments, and just slide your finger around the White Balance Shift/Amber-Blue/Green-Magenta grid to set color bias to your heart's content. It's also very fast to press one of the top-panel direct access buttons (WB/Meter Mode, DRIVE-AF, Flash Comp./ISO) and then immediately tap the option you want on the screen. Most will love the touch screen, but will pick and choose exactly how they prefer to use it.

TIP: YOUR CHOICE

Throughout this book, I may not explicitly say "tap the screen, or use the button, or visit the menu" for every single operation. Given the large number of how-to entries in this book, that would require unnecessarily long descriptions and extra verbiage. I'm going to assume that once you master the touch screen using the information in this section, you'll make your own choice and use whichever method you prefer. I'll generally stick to using the physical controls that we're all accustomed to. But, unless I specifically say to use the touch screen or physical controls, assume I mean you can use either one.

When a main menu, adjustment screen, or the Quick Control menu is displayed, you will often elect to use the touch screen to make your changes. Optionally, you can resort to the physical controls that provide the equivalent functions, including the available buttons and navigational buttons. However, I think that once you become familiar with the speed with which the touch screen allows you to make these adjustments, you'll be reluctant to go back to the "old" way of doing things.

The 5D Mark IV's touch screen is *capacitive* rather than *resistive*, making it more like the current generation of smartphones than earlier computer touch-sensitive screens. The difference is that your camera's LCD responds to the electrical changes that result from *contact* rather than the force of *pressure* on the screen itself. That means that the screen can interpret your touches and taps in more complex ways. It "knows" when you're using two fingers instead of one, and can react to multi-touch actions and gestures, such as swiping (to scroll in any direction), and pinching/spreading of fingers to zoom in and out. Since you probably have been using a smartphone for a while, these actions have become ingrained enough to be considered intuitive. Virtually every main and secondary function or menu operation can be accessed from the touch screen. However, if you want to continue using the buttons and dials, the 5D Mark IV retains that method of operation.

Here's what you need to know to get started:

- **Tap to select.** Tap (touch the LCD screen briefly) to select an item, including a menu heading or icon. Any item you can tap will have a frame or box around it. Figure 2.22 shows the taps needed to select a menu tab and specific entry within that menu and then make your adjustments on the screen that appears. On settings screens, tappable items will have a box around them.

- **Drag/swipe to select.** Many functions can be selected by touching the screen and then sliding your finger to the right or left until the item you want is highlighted. For example, instead of tapping, you can slide horizontally along the main menu's tabs to choose any Shooting, Playback, Custom, or My Menu tab. However, you can't slide vertically to choose an individual menu entry; tap the desired entry instead. The swiping motion is represented by the arrows in Figure 2.22.

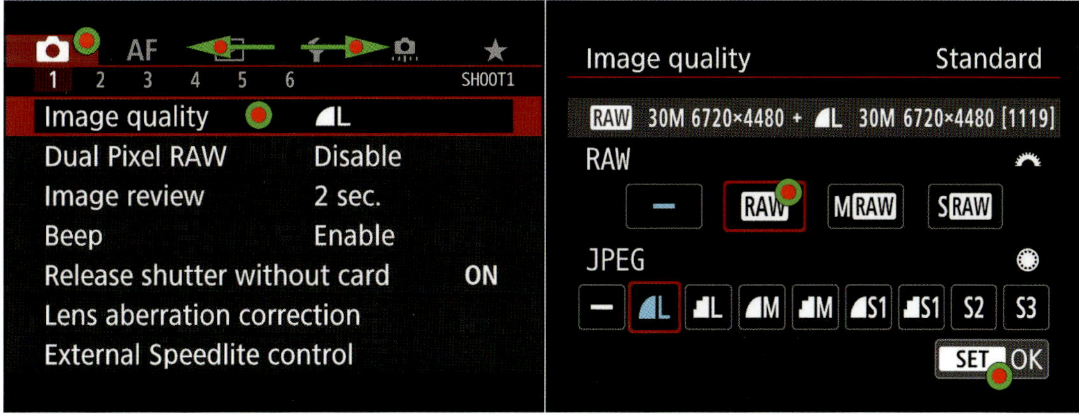

Figure 2.22 Select a menu tab and entry (left) and change settings (right).

■ **Drag/swipe to adjust scales.** Screens that contain a sliding scale can be adjusted by dragging. In Figure 2.23, left, the arrows show how you can drag along the exposure compensation scale to make adjustments. You can also tap the minus/plus buttons, and exit by tapping the return arrow at lower right. Even when you are using the touch screen, you can still opt for the Main Dial or QCD to make your changes. Note that some scales, such as the LCD brightness scale in Figure 2.23, right, don't respond to dragging. Instead, tap on the scale's fixed-size intervals.

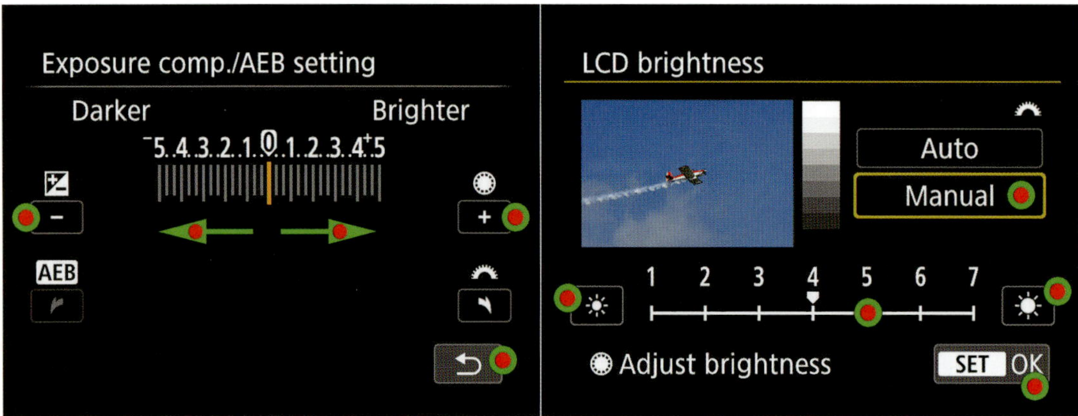

Figure 2.23 Use sliding scales or tap icons to make adjustments.

■ **Drag/swipe to scroll among single images.** In Playback single-image mode, as you review your images, you can drag your finger left and right to advance from one image to another, much as you might do with a smartphone or tablet computer. Use one finger to scroll one image at a time, and two to jump using the image jump method you've chosen in the Playback 2 menu, as described in Chapter 13. The arrows at the bottom of Figure 2.24, left, represent this function.

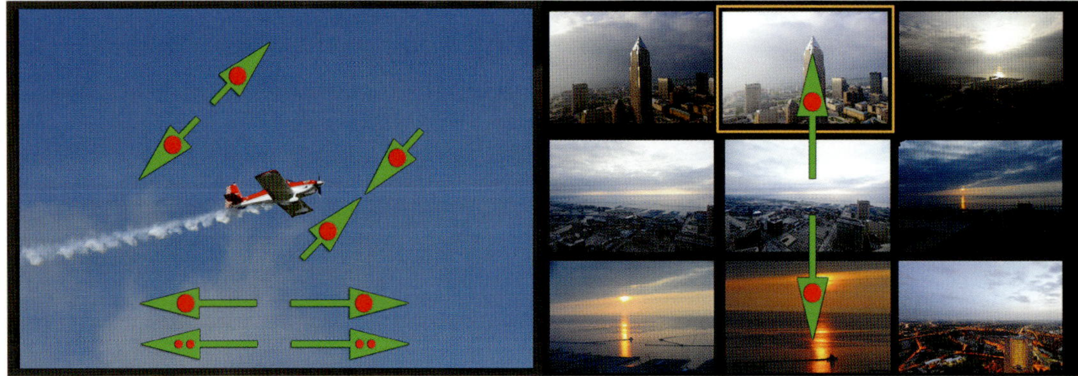

Figure 2.24 In Playback, pinch or spread fingers to magnify or reduce images, and swipe/drag to move/jump among them.

- **Drag to scroll among thumbnails.** When viewing thumbnails, you can drag through the thumbnail screen to quickly move among sets of index images, as represented in Figure 2.24, right.

- **Pinch/spread to reduce/enlarge.** During playback, you can use two fingers to "pinch" the screen to reduce/shrink the image, from, say, single image to index view. Tap on a thumbnail to view it full size. Spread those two fingers apart to enlarge an image, to zoom in from, say, a nine-image index array to the four-image display, then to single image. If you continue spreading, you can magnify the image up to about 10X. Tap the return icon to resume single-image display. (See the arrows in the top half of Figure 2.24, left.)

- **Fine-tune touch features.** As I'll explain in Chapter 9, you can enable or disable touch operation and change sensitivity from Standard to Sensitive in the Set-up 2 menu under the Touch Control entry. The click sound the touch feature makes can be turned on or off using the Beep setting in the Shooting 1 menu.

- **Avoid "protective" sheets, moisture, and sharp implements.** The LCD uses capacitive technology to sense your touch, rather than pressure sensitivity. LCD protectors or moisture can interfere with the touch functions, and styluses or sharp objects (such as pens) won't produce the desired results. I have, in fact, used "skins" on my 5D Mark IV's LCD with good results (even though the screen is quite rugged and really doesn't need protection from scratches), but there is no guarantee that all such protectors will work for you.

As I noted, the choice of whether to use the traditional buttons or touch screen is up to you. I've found that with some screens, the controls are too close together to be easily manipulated with my wide fingers. The touch screen can be especially dangerous when working with some functions, such as card formatting. In screens where the icons are large and few in number, such as the screen used to adjust LCD brightness, touch control works just fine. Easiest of all is touch operation during Playback. It's a no-brainer to swipe your finger from side to side to scroll among images and pinch/spread to zoom out and in.

3

Recommended Settings

This chapter is purely optional, especially for those who are new to an advanced Canon at the 5D Mark IV's level, who should skip it entirely for now, and return when they've gained some experience with this full-featured camera. This section is for the benefit of those who want to know *now* some of the most common changes I recommend to the default settings of your 5D Mark IV. Canon has excellent reasons for using these settings as a default; I have better reasons for changing them.

Changing Default Settings

Even if this is your first experience with a Canon digital SLR, you can easily make a few changes to the default settings that I'm going to recommend, and then take your time learning *why* I suggest these changes when they're explained in the more detailed chapters of this book. I'm not going to provide step-by-step instructions for changing settings here; I'll give you an overview of how to make any setting adjustment, and leave you to navigate through the fairly intuitive 5D Mark IV menu system to make the changes yourself. Or, you can jump ahead to Chapters 11 to 14 for more detailed instructions on a particular setting.

Resetting the Canon 5D Mark IV

If you want to change from the factory default values, you might think that it would be a good idea to make sure that the Canon 5D Mark IV is set to the factory defaults in the first place. After all, even a brand-new camera might have had its settings changed at the retailer, or during a demo. Most of the time, however, you'll prefer to use the Clear All Camera Settings option in the Set-up 5 menu, which returns most settings (other than Custom Functions) to their default values. The tables that follow show the settings defaults after using the Clear All Camera Settings menu option.

Table 3.1 Shooting Settings Defaults

AF operation	One-Shot AF
AF area selection mode	Single-point AF (Manual selection)
AF point selection	Center
Registered AF point	Canceled
Metering mode	Evaluative
ISO	
ISO speed	Auto
Range for stills	Minimum: 100 Maximum 32,000
Auto	Minimum: 100 Maximum 12,800
Minimum shutter speed for Auto	Auto
Drive mode	Single Shooting
Exposure comp./AEB	Canceled
Flash exposure comp.	Canceled
Multiple exposure	Disable
HDR mode	Disable
Interval timer	Disable
Bulb timer	Disable
Anti-flicker	Disable
Mirror lockup	Disable
Viewfinder information	
Electronic level	Hide
Grid display	Hide
Show in viewfinder	Only flicker detection
Custom Functions	Unchanged
External Speedlite control	
Flash firing	Enable
E-TTL II flash metering	Evaluative flash metering
Flash sync speed in Av mode	Auto

Table 3.2 AF Settings Defaults

Case 1–6	Cleared
AI Servo 1st image priority	Equal
AI Servo 2nd image priority	Equal
Lens electronic manual focus	Enable after One-Shot
AF-assist beam firing	Enable
One-Shot AF release priority	Focus
Lens drive when AF impossible	Continue focus search
Selectable AF point	61 points
Select AF area selection mode	All modes
AF area selection method	M-Fn button
Orientation-linked AF point	Same for both
Initial AF point AI Servo	Auto
Auto AF point selection: EOS iTR AF	Auto
AF point selection movement	Stops at AF area edges
AF point display during focus	Selected (constant)
VF display illumination	Auto
AF point during AI Servo AF	Disable
AF operation display in viewfinder	Enabled
AF microadjustment	Disable/Amount retained

Table 3.3 Image Recording Settings Defaults

Image quality	Large	White balance shift	Canceled
Dual Pixel RAW	Disable	White balance bracketing	Canceled
Picture Style	Standard		
Lens aberration correction		Color space	sRGB
Peripheral illumination correction	Enable	Long exposure noise reduction	Disable
Distortion correction	Disable	High ISO speed NR	Standard
Digital lens optimizer	Disable	Highlight tone priority	Disable
Chromatic aberration correction	Enable	Record Function+card/folder selection	
Diffraction	Enable	*Record function*	Standard
White balance	Auto (Ambience priority)	*Record and playback*	Unchanged
		File numbering	Continuous
		File name	Preset code
Custom White balance	Canceled	Dust Delete Data	Erased

Table 3.4 Camera Settings Defaults

Image review time	2 sec.	Touch control	Standard
Beep	Enable	Video system	Unchanged
Release shutter without card	Enable	Auto cleaning	Enable
Image jump with dial	Enable	INFO. button display options	All items
Highlight alert	Disable	Custom Quick Control	Unchanged
AF point display	Disable	INFO button live view display options	All items
Playback grid	Off		
Histogram display	Brightness	RATE button function	Rating
Movie playback count	Unchanged	GPS	Disable
Magnification (Approximate)	2x (from center)	Built-in wireless setting — Wi-Fi/NFC	Disable
Control over HDMI	Disable	FTP transfer setting — Automatic transfer	Disable
Auto rotate vertical images	Camera/Computer		
		Multi function lock	QCD only
Auto power off	1 min.	Custom shooting modes	Unchanged
LCD brightness	Auto	Copyright information	Unchanged
LCD color tone	2: Standard	Configure: My Menu	Unchanged
Date/Time/Zone	Unchanged	*Menu display*	Normal
Language	Unchanged		

Table 3.5 Live View Shooting Settings Defaults

Live View Shooting	Enable	Aspect ratio	3:2
AF Method	Face+Tracking	Exposure simulation	Enable
Touch shutter	Disable	Silent LV shooting	Mode 1
Grid display	Off	Metering timer	8 sec.

Table 3.6 Movie Settings Defaults

ISO speed	Auto	Metering timer	8 sec.
Range for movies	Minimum: 100 Maximum 25,600	Time code	
Range for 4K	Minimum 100 Maximum 12,800	*Count up*	Unchanged
		Start time	Unchanged
Movie Servo AF	Enable	*Movie recording count*	Unchanged
AF method	Face+Tracking	*Movie playback count*	Unchanged
Grid display	Off	*HDMI*	Computer monitor only
Movie recording quality		*Drop frame*	Unchanged
MOV/MP4	MOV	Shutter button function	Half press: Metering+AF
Movie recording size	NTSC: 1920 × 1080 29.97 fps		
	PAL: 1920 × 1080 25.00 fps	Fully press: No function	
24.00P	Disable	Time-lapse movie	Disable
High frame rate	Disable	HDMI display	Computer monitor only
Sound recording	Auto	HDMI frame rate	Auto
Wind filter	Disable	Remote control shooting	Disable
Attenuator	Disable		
Movie Servo AF speed			
When active	Always on		
AF speed	0 (Standard)		

Recommended Default Changes

Although I won't be explaining how to use the Canon 5D Mark IV's menu system in detail until Chapters 11 to 14, you can make some simple changes now. These general instructions will serve you to make any of the setting changes I recommend next. It's likely that experienced photographers won't need the settings charts that follow, but I'm including some basic recommendations for those who want some guidance in shooting particular types of subjects. You'll find specific types for functions like autofocus and other features later in this book.

The 5D Mark IV divides its menu entries into "tabbed" sections—Shooting, Autofocus, Playback, Set-up, Custom Functions, and My Menu—which, except for My Menu, each have separate pages. The available pages can vary, depending on your shooting mode, as I'll explain in Chapter 11.

To access menus, tap the MENU button. Use the Main Dial to move from menu to menu, and the Quick Control Dial to highlight a particular menu entry. Press the SET button to select a menu item. You can also navigate with the joystick-like multi-controller or use the touch screen. When you've highlighted the menu item you want to work with, press the SET button to select it. The current settings for the other menu items in the list will be hidden, and a list of options for the selected menu item (or a submenu screen) will appear. Or, you may be shown a separate settings screen for that entry. Within the menu choices, you can scroll up or down with the Quick Control Dial; press SET to select the choice you've made; and press the MENU button again to exit.

Once you've made changes for a specific type of shooting, you should store each set of parameters in one of the Custom Shooting mode user slots C1, C2, or C3 in the Set-up 4 menu, as explained in Chapter 13. Here are some recommended settings to consider. Note that these tables don't correspond to entire menus; I'm listing only the settings that need attention. If a particular parameter is not listed, you can use a setting of your choice.

Table 3.7 Default, All Purpose, Sports: Outdoors, Sports: Indoors

	Default	All Purpose	Sports: Outdoors	Sports: Indoors
SETTINGS				
Exposure Mode	Your choice	Your choice	Tv	Tv
Autofocus Mode	One-Shot	AI Focus	AI Servo	AI Servo
Drive Mode	Single Shooting	Single Shooting	Continuous Shooting	Continuous Shooting
SHOOTING MENUS				
Beep	Enable	Enable	Enable	Enable
Image Review	2 sec.	2 sec.	Off	Off
Metering Mode	Evaluative	Evaluative	Evaluative	Evaluative
Color Space	sRGB	sRGB	sRGB	sRGB
Picture Style	Auto	Auto	Standard	Standard
ISO Speed	Auto	Auto	800–3200	800–3200
ISO Speed Range	100–32000	100–12800	200–3200	200–12800
Auto ISO Range	100–12800	100–6400	200–6400	400–12800
ISO Auto Minimum Shutter Speed	Auto	Auto	1/250	1/250
Long Exposure NR	Disable	Disable	Disable	Disable
High ISO speed NR	Standard	Standard	Standard	Standard
Highlight Tone Priority	Disable	Disable	Disable	Disable
AF MENUS				
Case	Case 1	Case 1	Case 4	Case 2/Case 4
AF Assist Beam	Enable	Enable	Disable	Disable
Selectable AF Point	61 points	61 points	9 points	15 points
Select AF Area Selection Mode	61-point automatic selection AF	61-point automatic selection AF	AF-point expansion	AF-point expansion
SET-UP MENUS				
Auto Power Off	1 minute	30 sec.	Off	Off
LCD Brightness	Auto	Medium	Medium	Medium

Table 3.8 Stage Performances, Long Exposure, HDR, Portrait

	Stage Performances	Long Exposure	HDR	Portrait
SETTINGS				
Exposure Mode	Your choice	Manual/Your choice	One-Shot	One-Shot
Autofocus Mode	One-Shot	AI Focus	AI Servo	AI Servo
Drive Mode	Continuous Shooting	Single Shooting	Continuous Shooting	Continuous Shooting
SHOOTING MENUS				
Beep	Disable	Enable	Enable	Enable
Image Review	Off	Off	Off	2 sec.
Metering Mode	Spot	Center-weighted	Evaluative	Center-weighted
Color Space	Adobe RGB	Adobe RGB	Adobe RGB	Adobe RGB
Picture Style	User—Reduce contrast, add sharpening	Neutral	Standard	Portrait
ISO Speed	800–3200	800–3200	Auto	Auto
ISO Speed Range	100–32000	100–12800	200–3200	200–1600
Auto ISO Range	100–12800	100–6400	200–6400	100–3200
ISO Auto Minimum Shutter Speed	Auto	Auto	1/250	1/250
Long Exposure NR	Disable	Disable	Disable	Disable
High ISO Speed NR	Standard	Standard	Standard	Standard
Highlight Tone Priority	Disable	Disable	Disable	Disable
AF MENUS				
Case	Case 1	Case 1	Case 1	Case 1
AF Assist Beam	Disable	Disable	Disable	Disable
Selectable AF Point	61 points	61 points	61 points	15 points
Select AF Area Selection Mode	61-point automatic selection AF	61-point automatic selection AF	61-point automatic selection AF	61-point automatic selection AF
SET-UP MENUS				
Auto Power Off	1 minute	Disable	Disable	Disable
LCD Brightness	Dimmer	Dimmer	Medium	Medium

Table 3.9 Studio Flash, Landscape, Macro, Travel, E-Mail

	Studio Flash	Landscape	Macro	Travel	Email
SETTINGS					
Exposure Mode	Manual	Av	Tv	Tv	Av
Autofocus Mode	One-Shot	One-Shot	Manual	One-Shot	One Shot
Drive Mode	Single Shooting	Single Shooting	Single Shooting	Single Shooting	Single Shooting
SHOOTING MENUS					
Beep	Disable	Enable	Enable	Enable	Enable
Image Review	2 sec.	2 sec.	2 sec.	2 sec.	2 sec.
Metering Mode	Evaluative	Evaluative	Spot	Evaluative	Evaluative
Color Space	Adobe RGB	Adobe RGB	Adobe RGB	Adobe RGB	Adobe RGB
Picture Style	User—Reduce contrast, add sharpening	Landscape	Auto	Landscape	Auto
ISO Speed	100–400	100–1600	100–1600	Auto	Auto
ISO Speed Range	100–32000	100–12800	200–3200	200–1600	100–3200
Auto ISO Range	100–12800	100–6400	200–6400	100–3200	100–6400
ISO Auto Minimum Shutter Speed	Auto	Auto	1/250	1/250	Auto
Long Exposure NR	Disable	Disable	Disable	Disable	Disable
High ISO Speed NR	Standard	Standard	Standard	Standard	Standard
Highlight Tone Priority	Disable	Enable	Disable	Enable	Enable
AF MENUS					
Case	Case 1	Case 1	Case 1	Case 1	Case 1
AF Assist Beam	Disable	Disable	Disable	Disable	Disable
Selectable AF Point	61 points	61 points	61 points	15 points	15 points
Select AF Area Selection Mode	61-point automatic selection AF	61-point automatic selection AF	61-point automatic selection AF	61-point automatic selection AF	61-point automatic selection AF
SET-UP MENUS					
Auto Power Off	1 minute	Disable	Disable	Disable	Disable
LCD Brightness	Dimmer	Dimmer	Medium	Medium	Medium

4

Nailing the Right Exposure

As you learn to use your 5D Mark IV creatively, you're going to find that the right settings—as determined by the camera's exposure meter and intelligence—need to be *adjusted* to account for your creative decisions or to fine-tune the image for special situations.

For example, when you shoot with the main light source behind the subject, you end up with *back-lighting*, which results in an overexposed background and/or an underexposed subject. The 5D Mark IV recognizes backlit situations nicely, and can properly base exposure on the main subject, producing a decent photo. Features like Highlight Tone Priority and the Auto Lighting Optimizer can fine-tune exposure to preserve detail in the highlights and shadows.

But what if you *want* to underexpose the subject, to produce a silhouette effect? Or, perhaps, you might want to use an external electronic flash to fill in the shadows on your subject. The more you know about how to use your 5D Mark IV, the more you'll run into situations where you want to creatively tweak the exposure to provide a different look than you'd get with a straight shot.

This chapter shows you the fundamentals of exposure, so you'll be better equipped to override the 5D Mark IV's default settings when you want to, or need to. After all, correct exposure is one of the foundations of good photography, along with accurate focus and sharpness, appropriate color balance, freedom from unwanted noise and excessive contrast, as well as pleasing composition.

The 5D Mark IV gives you a great deal of control over all of these, although composition is entirely up to you. You must still frame the photograph to create an interesting arrangement of subject matter, but all the other parameters are basic functions of the camera. You can let your 5D Mark IV set them for you automatically, you can fine-tune how the camera applies its automatic settings, or you can make them yourself, manually. The amount of control you have over exposure, sensitivity (ISO settings), color balance, focus, and image parameters like sharpness and contrast make the 5D Mark IV a versatile tool for creating images.

In the next few pages, I'm going to give you a grounding in one of those foundations, and explain the basics of exposure, either as an introduction or as a refresher course, depending on your current level of expertise. When you finish this chapter, you'll understand most of what you need to know to take well-exposed photographs creatively in a broad range of situations with the EOS 5D Mark IV.

Getting a Handle on Exposure

This section explains the fundamental concepts that go into creating an exposure. If you already know about the role of f/stops, shutter speeds, and sensor sensitivity in determining an exposure, you might want to skip to the next section, which explains how the 5D Mark IV calculates exposure.

In the most basic sense, exposure is all about light. Exposure can make or break your photo. Correct exposure brings out the detail in the areas you want to picture, providing the range of tones and colors you need to create the desired image. Poor exposure can cloak important details in shadow, or wash them out in glare-filled featureless expanses of white. However, getting the perfect exposure requires some intelligence—either that built into the camera or the smarts in your head—because digital sensors can't capture all the tones we can see. If the range of tones in an image is extensive, embracing both inky black shadows and bright highlights, we often must settle for an exposure that renders most of those tones—but not all—in a way that best suits the photo we want to produce.

As the owner of a 5D Mark IV, you're probably aware of the traditional "exposure triangle" of aperture (quantity of light and light passed by the lens), shutter speed (the amount of time the shutter is open), and the ISO sensitivity of the sensor—all working proportionately and reciprocally to produce an exposure. The trio is itself affected by the amount of illumination that is available to work with. So, if you double the amount of light, increase the aperture by one stop, make the shutter speed twice as long, or boost the ISO setting 2X, you'll get twice as much exposure. Similarly, you can increase any of these factors while decreasing one of the others by a similar amount to keep the same exposure.

Working with any of the three controls involves trade-offs. Larger f/stops provide less depth-of-field, while smaller f/stops increase depth-of-field (and potentially at the same time can *decrease* sharpness through a phenomenon called *diffraction*). Shorter shutter speeds do a better job of reducing the effects of camera/subject motion, while longer shutter speeds make that motion blur more likely. Higher ISO settings increase the amount of visual noise and artifacts in your image, while lower ISO settings reduce the effects of noise. (See Figure 4.1.)

Exposure determines the look, feel, and tone of an image, in more ways than one. Incorrect exposure can impair even the best-composed image by cloaking important tones in darkness, or by washing them out so they become featureless to the eye. On the other hand, correct exposure brings out the detail in the areas you want to picture, and provides the range of tones and colors you need to create the desired image. However, getting the perfect exposure can be tricky, because digital sensors can't capture all the tones we can see. If the range of tones in an image is extensive,

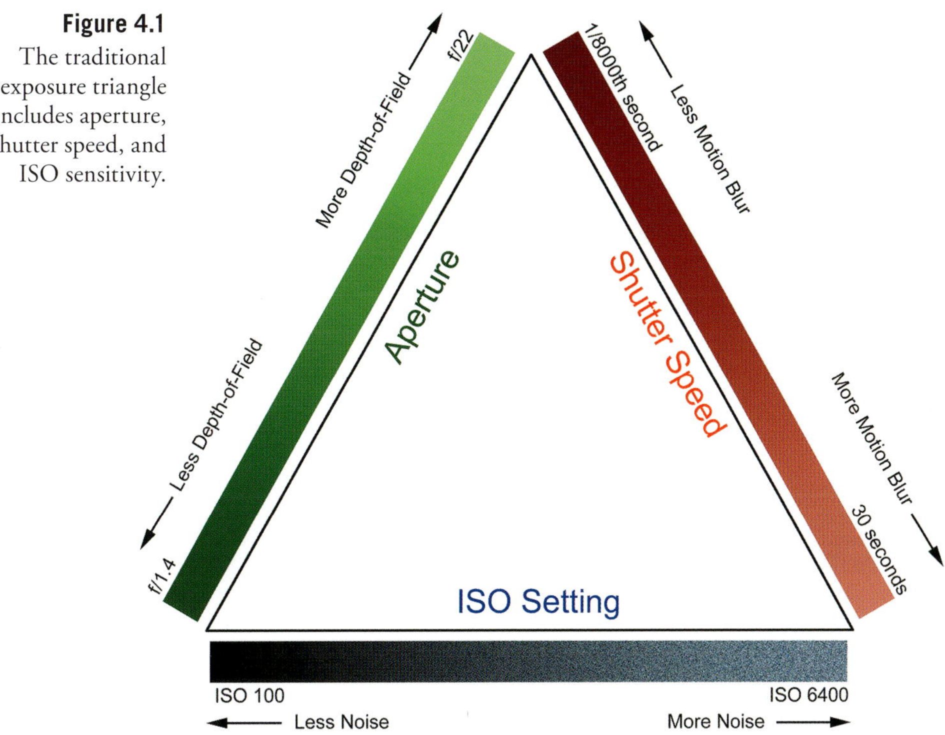

Figure 4.1
The traditional exposure triangle includes aperture, shutter speed, and ISO sensitivity.

embracing both inky black shadows and bright highlights, the sensor may not be able to capture them all. Sometimes, we must settle for an exposure that renders most of those tones—but not all—in a way that best suits the photo we want to produce. You'll often need to make choices about which details are important, and which are not, so that you can grab the tones that truly matter in your image. That's part of the creativity you bring to bear in realizing your photographic vision.

For example, look at two bracketed exposures presented at top in Figure 4.2. For the image at upper left, the highlights (chiefly the clouds at upper left and the top-left edge of the skyscraper) are well exposed, but everything else in the shot is seriously underexposed. The version on the upper right, taken an instant later with the tripod-mounted camera, shows detail in the shadow areas of the buildings, but the highlights are completely washed out. The camera's sensor simply can't capture detail in both dark areas and bright areas in a single shot.

With digital camera sensors, it's tricky to capture detail in both highlights and shadows in a single image, because the number of tones, the *dynamic range* of the sensor, is limited. The solution, in this case, was to resort to a technique called High Dynamic Range (HDR) photography, in which the two exposures from Figure 4.2 were combined in an image editor such as Photoshop, or a specialized HDR tool like Photomatix (about $100 from www.hdrsoft.com). The resulting shot is shown at bottom in Figure 4.2. I'll explain more about HDR photography later in this chapter. For now, though, I'm going to concentrate on showing you how to get the best exposures possible without resorting to such tools, using only the features of your 5D Mark IV.

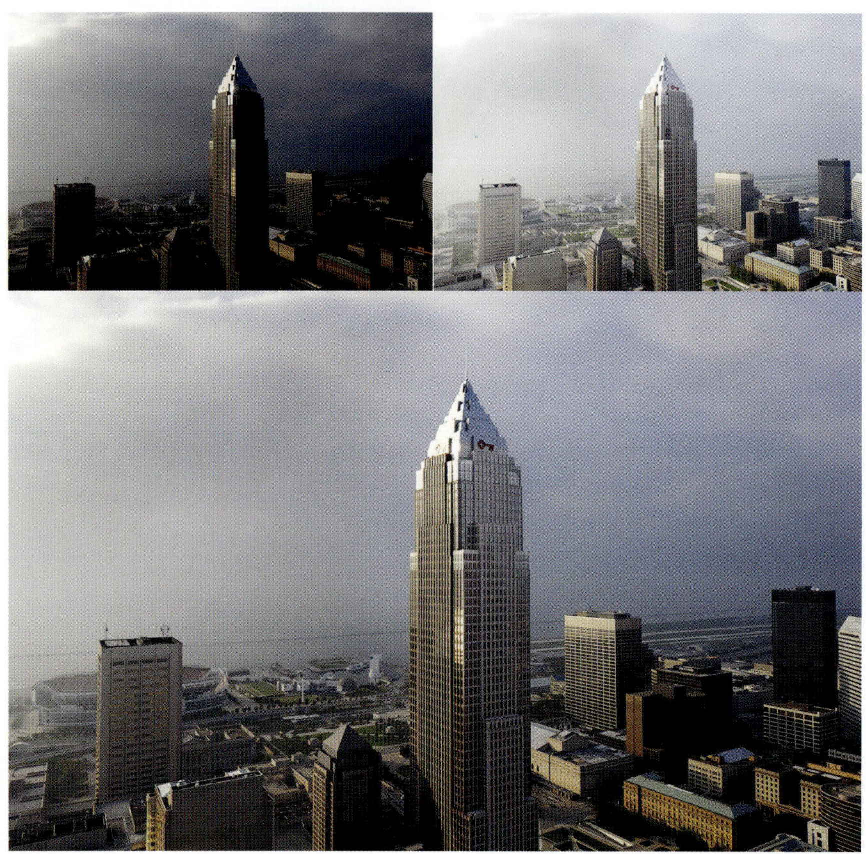

Figure 4.2
The image is exposed for the highlights, losing shadow detail (upper left). At upper right, the exposure captures detail in the shadows, but the background highlights are washed out. Combining the two exposures produces the best compromise image (bottom).

To understand exposure, you need to understand the six aspects of light that combine to produce an image. Start with a light source—the sun, an interior lamp, or the glow from a campfire—and trace its path to your camera, through the lens, and finally to the sensor that captures the illumination. Here's a brief review of the things within our control that affect exposure.

- **Light at its source.** Our eyes and our cameras—film or digital—are most sensitive to that portion of the electromagnetic spectrum we call *visible light.* That light has several important aspects that are relevant to photography, such as color and harshness (which is determined primarily by the apparent size of the light source as it illuminates a subject). But, in terms of exposure, the important attribute of a light source is its *intensity.* We may have direct control over intensity, which might be the case with an interior light that can be brightened or dimmed. Or, we might have only indirect control over intensity, as with sunlight, which can be made to appear dimmer by introducing translucent light-absorbing or reflective materials in its path.

- **Light's duration.** We tend to think of most light sources as continuous. But, as you'll learn in Chapter 9, the duration of light can change quickly enough to modify the exposure, as when the main illumination in a photograph comes from an intermittent source, such as an electronic flash.

- **Light reflected, transmitted, or emitted.** Once light is produced by its source, either continuously or in a brief burst, we can see and photograph objects by the light that is reflected from our subjects toward the camera lens; transmitted (say, from translucent objects that are lit from behind); or emitted (by a candle or television screen). When more or less light reaches the lens from the subject, we need to adjust the exposure. This part of the equation is under our control to the extent we can increase the amount of light falling on or passing through the subject (by adding extra light sources or using reflectors), or by pumping up the light that's emitted (by increasing the brightness of the glowing object).

- **Light passed by the lens.** Not all the illumination that reaches the front of the lens makes it all the way through. Filters can remove some of the light before it enters the lens. Inside the lens barrel is a variable-sized diaphragm that dilates and contracts to vary the size of the aperture and control the amount of light that enters the lens. You, or the 5D Mark IV's autoexposure system, can control exposure by varying the size of the aperture. The relative size of the aperture is called the *f/stop*.

- **Light passing through the shutter.** Once light passes through the lens, the amount of time the sensor receives it is determined by the 5D Mark IV's shutter, which can remain open for as long as 30 seconds (or even longer if you use the Bulb setting) or as briefly as 1/8,000th second.

- **Light captured by the sensor.** Not all the light falling onto the sensor is captured. If the number of photons reaching a particular photosite doesn't pass a set threshold, no information is recorded. Similarly, if too much light illuminates a pixel in the sensor, then the excess isn't recorded or, worse, spills over to contaminate adjacent pixels. We can modify the minimum and maximum number of pixels that contribute to image detail by adjusting the ISO setting. At higher ISOs, the incoming light is amplified to boost the effective sensitivity of the sensor.

F/STOPS AND SHUTTER SPEEDS

If you're *really* new to more advanced cameras (and I realize that many soon-to-be-ambitious photographers do purchase the 5D Mark IV as their first digital SLR), you might need to know that the lens aperture, or f/stop, is a ratio, much like a fraction, which is why f/2 is larger than f/4, just as 1/2 is larger than 1/4. However, f/2 is actually *four times* as large as f/4. (If you remember your high school geometry, you'll know that to double the area of a circle, you multiply its diameter by the square root of two: 1.4.)

Lenses are usually marked with intermediate f/stops that represent a size that's twice as much/half as much as the previous aperture. So, a lens might be marked f/2, f/2.8, f/4, f/5.6, f/8, f/11, f/16, f/22, with each larger number representing an aperture that admits half as much light as the one before.

Shutter speeds are actual fractions (of a second), but the numerator is omitted, so that 60, 125, 250, 500, 1,000, and so forth represent 1/60th, 1/125th, 1/250th, 1/500th, and 1/1,000th second. To avoid confusion, Canon uses quotation marks to signify longer exposures: 2", 2"5, 4", and so forth representing 2.0-, 2.5-, and 4.0-second exposures, respectively.

These factors—the quantity of light produced by the light source, the amount reflected or transmitted toward the camera, the light passed by the lens, the amount of time the shutter is open, and the sensitivity of the sensor—all work proportionately and reciprocally to produce an exposure. That is, if you double the amount of light that's available, increase the aperture by one stop, make the shutter speed twice as long, or boost the ISO setting 2X, you'll get twice as much exposure. Similarly, you can increase any of these factors while decreasing one of the others by a similar amount to keep the same exposure.

Most commonly, exposure settings are made using the aperture and shutter speed, followed by adjusting the ISO sensitivity if it's not possible to get the preferred exposure; that is, the one that uses the "best" f/stop or shutter speed for the depth-of-field (range of sharp focus) or action stopping we want (produced by short shutter speeds, as I'll explain later). Table 4.1 shows equivalent exposure settings using various shutter speeds and f/stops.

When the 5D Mark IV is set for P (Program) mode, the metering system selects the correct exposure for you automatically, but you can change quickly to an equivalent exposure by locking the current exposure, and then spinning the Main Dial until the desired *equivalent* exposure combination is displayed. You can use this standard Program Shift feature more easily if you remember that you need to rotate the dial toward the *left* when you want to increase the amount of depth-of-field or use a slower shutter speed; rotate to the *right* when you want to reduce the depth-of-field or use a faster shutter speed. The need for more/less DOF and slower/faster shutter speed are the primary reasons you'd want to use Program Shift. I'll explain Program mode exposure shifting options in more detail later in this chapter.

In Aperture-priority (Av) and Shutter-priority (Tv) modes, you can change to an equivalent exposure using a different combination of shutter speed and aperture, but only by either adjusting the aperture in Aperture-priority mode (the camera then chooses the shutter speed) or shutter speed in Shutter-priority mode (the camera then selects the aperture). I'll cover all these exposure modes and their differences later in the chapter.

Table 4.1 Equivalent Exposures

Shutter Speed	f/stop	Shutter Speed	f/stop
1/30th second	f/22	1/1,000th second	f/4
1/60th second	f/16	1/2,000th second	f/2.8
1/125th second	f/11	1/4,000th second	f/2
1/250th second	f/8	1/8,000th second	f/1.4
1/500th second	f/5.6		

How the 5D Mark IV Calculates Exposure

When using the optical viewfinder, your 5D Mark IV calculates exposure by measuring the light that passes through the lens and is bounced up by the mirror toward a 153,600-pixel exposure sensor that's laid out in a 480 × 320–pixel RGB array that's also sensitive to infrared illumination. This RGB-IR metering sensor is located near the focusing surface. (**Note:** In live view, the sensor image is used instead to calculate exposure, as I'll explain later.) Light is evaluated using a pattern you can select (more on that later) and based on the assumption that each area being measured reflects about the same amount of light as a neutral gray card that reflects a "middle" gray of about 12- to 18-percent reflectance. (The photographic "gray cards" you buy at a camera store have an 18-percent gray tone, which does represent middle gray; however, your camera is calibrated to interpret a somewhat darker 12-percent gray; I'll explain more about this later.) That "average" 12- to 18-percent gray assumption is necessary, because different subjects reflect different amounts of light. In a photo containing, say, a white cat and a dark gray cat, the white cat might reflect five times as much light as the gray cat. An exposure based on the white cat will cause the gray cat to appear to be black, while an exposure based only on the gray cat will make the white cat appear washed out.

This is more easily understood if you look at some photos of subjects that are dark (they reflect little light), those that have predominantly middle tones, and subjects that are highly reflective. The next few figures show a simplified scale with a middle-gray 18-percent tone, plus black and white patches, along with a human figure (not a cat) to illustrate how different exposure measurements actually do affect an exposure.

Correctly Exposed

The image shown in Figure 4.3 represents how a photograph might appear if you inserted the patches shown at bottom left into the scene, and then calculated exposure by measuring the light reflecting from the middle-gray patch, which, for the sake of illustration, we'll assume reflects approximately 12 to 18 percent of the light that strikes it. The exposure meter in the 5D Mark IV sees an object that it thinks is a middle gray, calculates an exposure based on that, and the patch in the center of the strip is rendered at its proper tonal value. Best of all, because the resulting exposure is correct, the black patch at left and white patch at right are rendered properly as well.

When you're shooting pictures with your 5D Mark IV, and the meter happens to base its exposure on a subject that averages that "ideal" middle gray, then you'll end up with similar (accurate) results. The camera's exposure algorithms are concocted to ensure this kind of result as often as possible, barring any unusual subjects (that is, those that are backlit, or have uneven illumination). The 5D Mark IV has four different metering modes (described next), each of which is equipped to handle certain types of unusual subjects, as I'll outline.

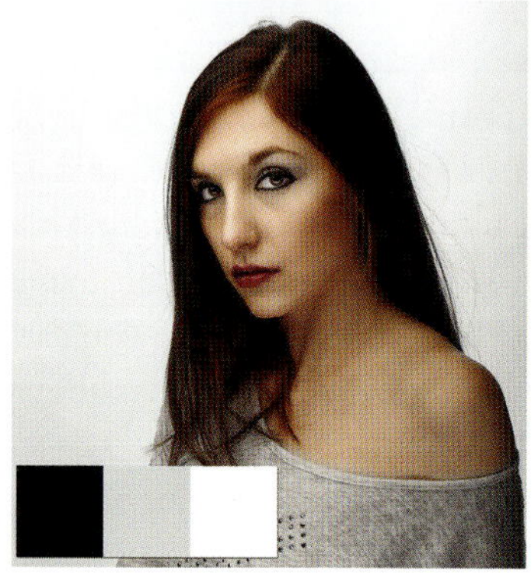

Figure 4.3 When exposure is calculated based on the middle-gray tone in the center of the card, the black and white patches are rendered accurately, too, and our model is properly exposed.

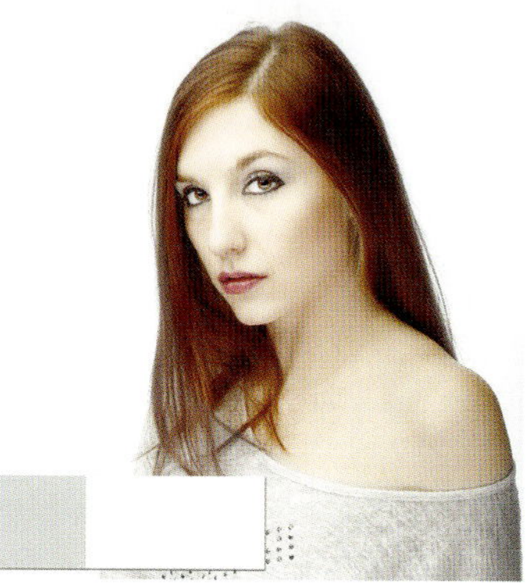

Figure 4.4 When exposure is calculated based on the black square at lower left, the black patch looks gray, the gray patch appears to be a light gray, and the white square is seriously overexposed.

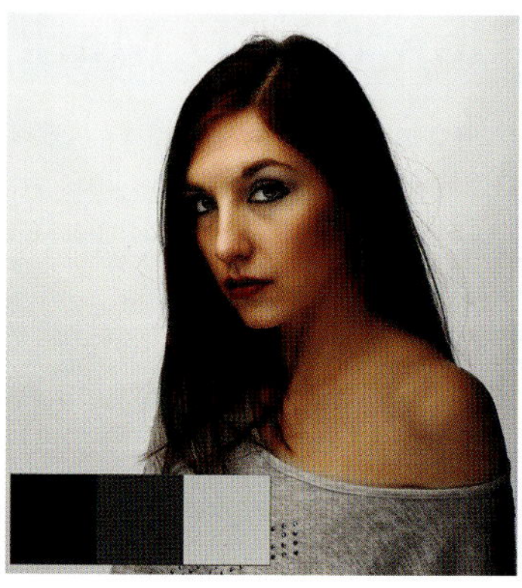

Figure 4.5 When exposure is calculated based on the white patch on the right, the other two patches, and the photo, are underexposed.

Overexposed

Figure 4.4 shows what would happen if the exposure were calculated based on metering the left-most, black patch, which is roughly the same tonal value of the darkest areas of the subject's hair. The light meter sees less light reflecting from the black square than it would see from a gray middle-tone subject, and so figures, "Aha! I need to add exposure to brighten this subject up to a middle gray!" That lightens the "black" patch, so it now appears to be gray.

But now the patch in the middle that was *originally* middle gray is overexposed and becomes light gray. And the white square at right is now seriously overexposed and loses detail in the highlights, which have become a featureless white. Our human subject is similarly overexposed. (Ignore the fact that this high-key image may appear to be a more effective photograph than the properly exposed version; we're concerned only with exposure here.)

Underexposed

The third possibility in this simplified scenario is that the light meter might measure the illumination bouncing off the white patch, and try to render *that* tone as a middle gray. A lot of light is reflected by the white square, so the exposure is *reduced*, bringing that patch closer to a middle-gray tone. The patches that were originally gray and black are now rendered too dark. Clearly, measuring the gray card—or a substitute that reflects about the same amount of light—is the only way to ensure that the exposure is precisely correct in this example. (See Figure 4.5.)

In some very bright scenes (like a snowy landscape or a lava field), you won't have a mid-tone to meter. Another substitute for a gray card is the palm of a human hand (the backside of the hand is too variable). But a human palm, regardless of ethnic group, is even brighter than a standard gray card, so instead of one-half stop more exposure, you need to add one additional stop. That is, if your meter reading is 1/500th of a second at f/11, use 1/500th second at f/8 or 1/200th second at f/11 instead. (Both exposures are equivalent.)

Or, you might want to resort to using an evenly illuminated gray card mentioned earlier. Small versions are available that can be tucked in a camera bag. Place it in your frame near your main subject, facing the camera, and with the exact same even illumination falling on it that is falling on your subject. Then, use the Spot metering function (described in the next section) to calculate exposure.

But, the standard Kodak gray card reflects 18 percent of the light while, as I noted, your camera is calibrated for a somewhat darker 12-percent tone. If you insisted on getting a perfect exposure, you would need to add about one-half stop more exposure than the value provided by taking the light meter reading from the card. Of course, in most situations, it's not necessary to do this. Your camera's light meter will do a good job of calculating the right exposure, especially if you use the exposure tips in the next section. But, I felt that explaining exactly what is going on during exposure calculation would help you understand how your 5D Mark IV's metering system works.

ORIGIN OF THE 18-PERCENT MYTH

Why are so many photographers under the impression that camera light meters are calibrated to the 18-percent "standard," rather than the true value, which may be 12 to 14 percent, depending on the vendor? You'll find this misinformation in an alarming number of places. I've seen the 18-percent myth taught in camera classes; I've found it in books, and even been given this wrong information from the technical staff of camera vendors. (They should know better—the same vendors' engineers who design and calibrate the cameras have the right figure.)

The most common explanation is that during a revision of Kodak's instructions for its gray cards in the 1970s, the advice to open up an extra half stop was omitted, and a whole generation of shooters grew up thinking that a measurement off a gray card could be used as-is. The proviso returned to the instructions by 1987, it's said, but by then it was too late. Next to me is a (c)2006 version of the instructions for KODAK Gray Cards, Publication R-27Q (still available in authorized versions from non-Kodak sources). The current directions read (with a bit of paraphrasing from me in italics):

■ For subjects of normal reflectance increase the indicated exposure by 1/2 stop.

■ For light subjects use the indicated exposure; for very light subjects, decrease the exposure by 1/2 stop. *(That is, you're measuring a subject that's lighter than middle gray.)*

■ If the subject is dark to very dark, increase the indicated exposure by 1 to 1-1/2 stops. *(You're shooting a dark subject.)*

EXTERNAL METERS CAN BE CALIBRATED

The light meters built into your 5D Mark IV are calibrated at the factory. But if you use a handheld incident or reflective light meter, you *can* calibrate it, using the instructions supplied with your meter. Because a handheld meter, of both the reflective and incident type, *can* be calibrated to the 18-percent gray standard (or any other value you choose), my rant about the myth of the 18-percent gray card doesn't apply.

Choosing a Metering Method

To calculate exposure automatically, you need to tell the 5D Mark IV *where* in the frame to measure the light (this is called the *metering method*) and *what controls* should be used (aperture, shutter speed, or both) to set the exposure. That's called *exposure mode,* and includes Program (P), Shutter-priority (Tv), Aperture-priority (Av), or Manual (M) options, plus Scene Intelligent Auto. I'll explain all these next.

But first, I'm going to introduce you to the four metering methods. You can select any of the four if you're working with P, Tv, Av, or M exposure modes; if you're using Scene Intelligent Auto, Evaluative metering is selected automatically and cannot be changed. In Live View mode, only Evaluative and Center-weighted averaging modes can be selected.

Choose a metering mode by pressing the Metering mode/White balance selection button on the top panel, and using the Main Dial until the icon for the mode you want appears in the status LCD. You can also select the metering mode by pressing the Q button and navigating to the metering mode icon in the bottom row of the Quick Control screen. Then, choose your mode:

- **Evaluative.** The 5D Mark IV slices up the frame into 252 different zones, shown as cyan rectangles at left in Figure 4.6. (Don't confuse these zones with the 61 *autofocus* zones; they are different. Both the 61 AF points and 252 exposure zones are shown in the figure.) Within those exposure zones are the 153,600 RGB-IR exposure sensors in a 480 × 320–pixel array, represented by tiny red rectangles in the figure.

  The exposure zones used are linked to the autofocus system such that as the camera evaluates the measurements, it gives extra emphasis to the metering zones that indicate sharp focus. From this data, it makes an educated guess about what kind of picture you're taking, based on examination of thousands of different real-world photos in the camera's database. For example, if the top sections of a picture are much lighter than the bottom portions, the algorithm can assume that the scene is a landscape photo with lots of sky. This mode is the best all-purpose metering method for most pictures. I'll explain how to choose an autofocus/exposure zone in the section on autofocus operation later in this chapter. See Figure 4.6, right for an example of a scene that can be easily interpreted by the Evaluative metering mode.

- **Partial.** This is a *faux* spot mode, using roughly 6.1 percent of the image area to calculate exposure, which, as you can see at left in Figure 4.7, is a rather large spot, represented by the larger cyan circle. The status LCD icon is shown in the upper-left corner. Use this mode if the background is much brighter or darker than the subject, as in Figure 4.7, right.

- **Spot.** This mode confines the reading to a limited area in the center of the viewfinder, as shown at left in Figure 4.8, making up only 1.3 percent of the image. This mode is useful when you want to base exposure on a small area in the frame, such as the gray portions of the structure in Figure 4.8, right. If that area is in the center of the frame, so much the better. If not, you'll have to make your meter reading and then lock exposure by pressing the shutter release halfway, or by pressing the AE lock (*) button. Note that spot metering is *not* linked to the focus point.

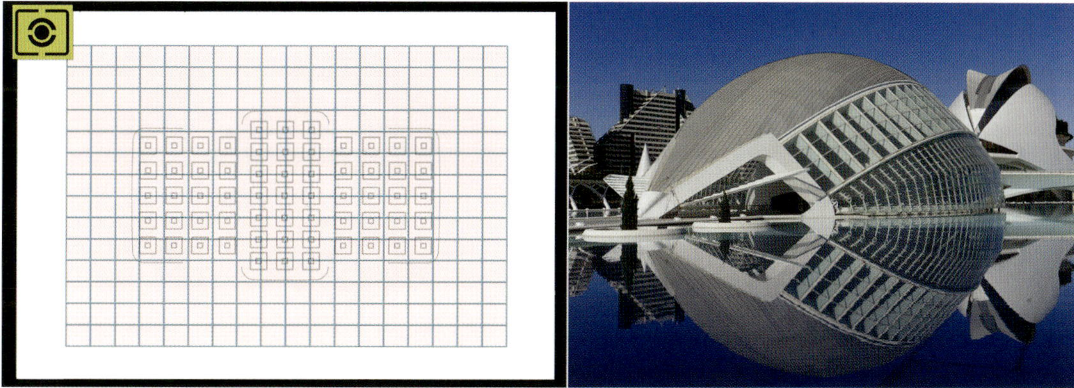

Figure 4.6 Evaluative metering uses 252 zones and 153,600 exposure sensors (left) and is effective for evenly lit scenes (right).

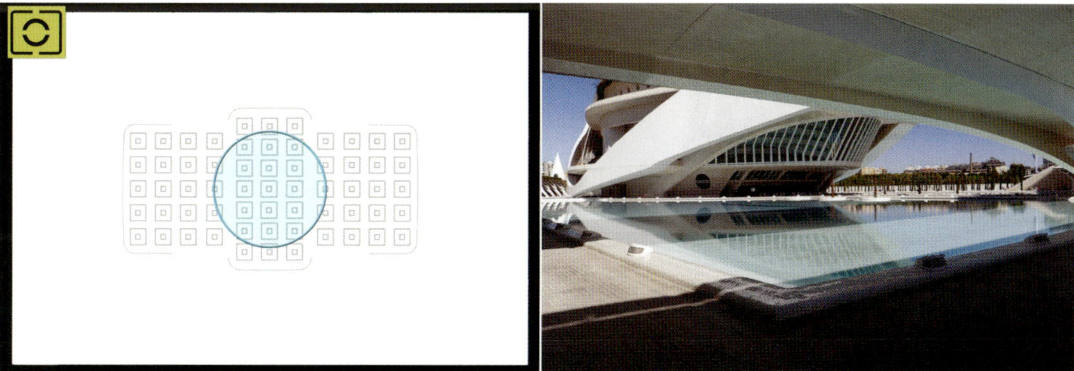

Figure 4.7 Partial metering uses a center spot that's roughly 6.1 percent of the frame area (left), and is excellent for images with the most important areas in the center (right).

- **Center-weighted averaging.** In this mode, the exposure meter emphasizes a zone in the center of the frame to calculate exposure, as shown at left in Figure 4.8, on the theory that, for most pictures, the main subject will be located in the center. Center-weighting works best for portraits, architectural photos, and other pictures in which the most important subject is located in the middle of the frame, as in Figure 4.9, right. As the name suggests, the light reading is *weighted* toward the central portion, but information is also used from the rest of the frame. If your main subject is surrounded by very bright or very dark areas, the exposure might not be exactly right. However, this scheme works well in many situations if you don't want to use one of the other modes.

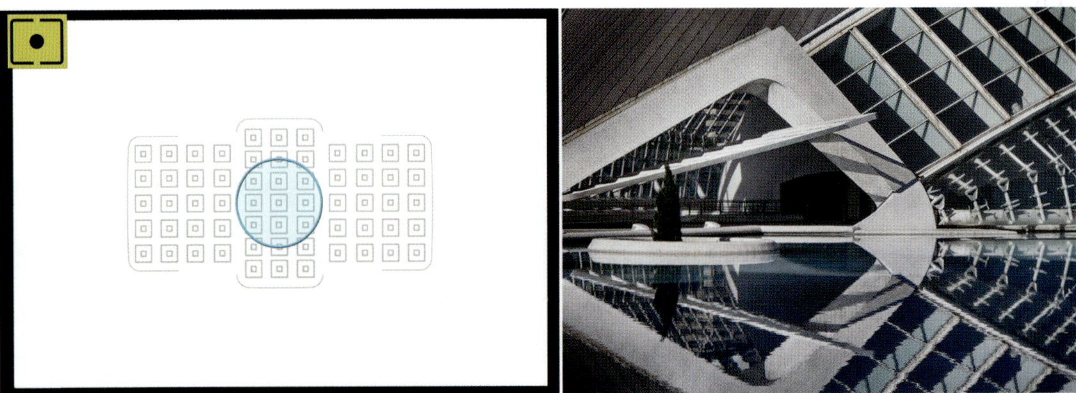

Figure 4.8 Spot metering calculates exposure based on a center spot that's only 1.3 percent of the image area (left), and allows measuring specific areas, such as the gray portions of the structure (right).

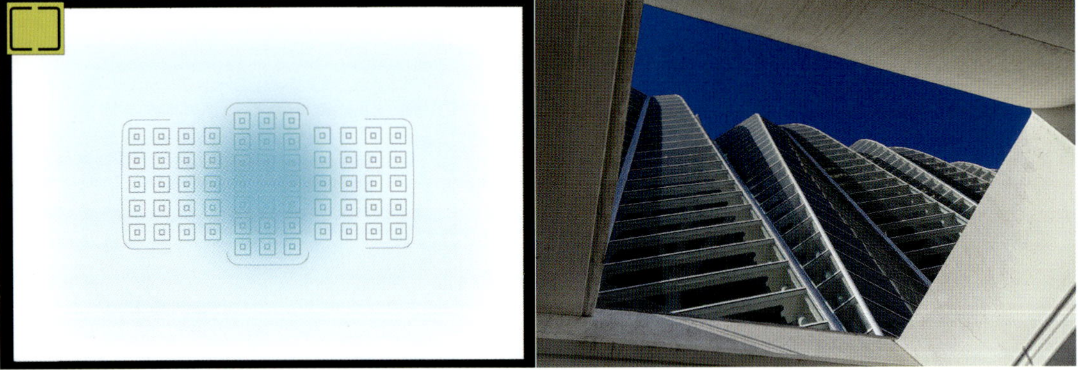

Figure 4.9 Center-weighted metering calculates exposure based on the full frame, but emphasizes the center area (left). Exposure for the image on right was calculated from the large area in the center of the frame, with less emphasis on the darker surroundings.

Choosing an Exposure Method

You'll find four methods for choosing the appropriate shutter speed and aperture: Program (P), Shutter-priority (Tv), Aperture-priority (Av), and Manual (M). To select one of these modes, just spin the Mode Dial (located at the top-left side of the camera) to choose the method you want to use.

Your choice of which exposure method is best for a given shooting situation will depend on things like your need for lots of (or less) depth-of-field, a desire to freeze action or allow motion blur, or how much noise you find acceptable in an image. (Remember that exposure triangle at the beginning of the chapter.) Each of the 5D Mark IV's exposure methods emphasizes one of those aspects of image capture or another. This section introduces you to all of them.

In Scene Intelligent Auto mode, the 5D Mark IV selects an appropriate ISO sensitivity setting, color (white) balance, Picture Style, color space, noise reduction features, and use of the Auto Lighting Optimizer. Use the Scene Intelligent Auto exposure mode when you hand your camera to a friend to take a picture (say, of you standing in front of the Eiffel Tower), and want to be sure they won't accidentally change any settings.

Aperture-Priority

In Av mode, you specify the lens opening used, and the 5D Mark IV selects the shutter speed. Aperture-priority is especially good when you want to use a particular lens opening to achieve a desired effect. Perhaps you'd like to use the smallest f/stop possible to maximize depth-of-field in a close-up picture. Or, you might want to use a large f/stop to throw everything except your main subject out of focus, as in Figure 4.10. Maybe you'd just like to "lock in" a particular f/stop smaller than the maximum aperture because it's the sharpest available aperture with that lens. Or, you might prefer to use, say, f/2.8 on a lens with a maximum aperture of f/1.4, because you want the best compromise between speed and sharpness.

Aperture-priority can even be used to specify a *range* of shutter speeds you want to use under varying lighting conditions, which seems almost contradictory. But think about it. You're shooting a soccer game outdoors with a telephoto lens and want a relatively high shutter speed, but you don't care if the speed changes a little should the sun duck behind a cloud. Set your 5D Mark IV to Av, and adjust the aperture until a shutter speed of, say, 1/1,000th second is selected at your current ISO setting. (In bright sunlight at ISO 400, that aperture is likely to be around f/11.) Then, go ahead and shoot, knowing that your 5D Mark IV will maintain that f/11 aperture (for sufficient DOF as the soccer players move about the field), but will drop down to 1/750th or 1/500th second if necessary should the lighting change a little.

If the shutter speed in the viewfinder or on the Shooting Settings screen is blinking, that indicates that the 5D Mark IV is unable to select an appropriate shutter speed at the selected aperture and that overexposure (the 8000 is blinking) or underexposure (the 30 shutter speed is blinking) will occur at the current ISO setting. To correct overexposure, select a smaller aperture (if available) or choose a lower ISO sensitivity. Fix underexposure conditions by choosing a larger aperture (if possible) or a higher ISO setting.

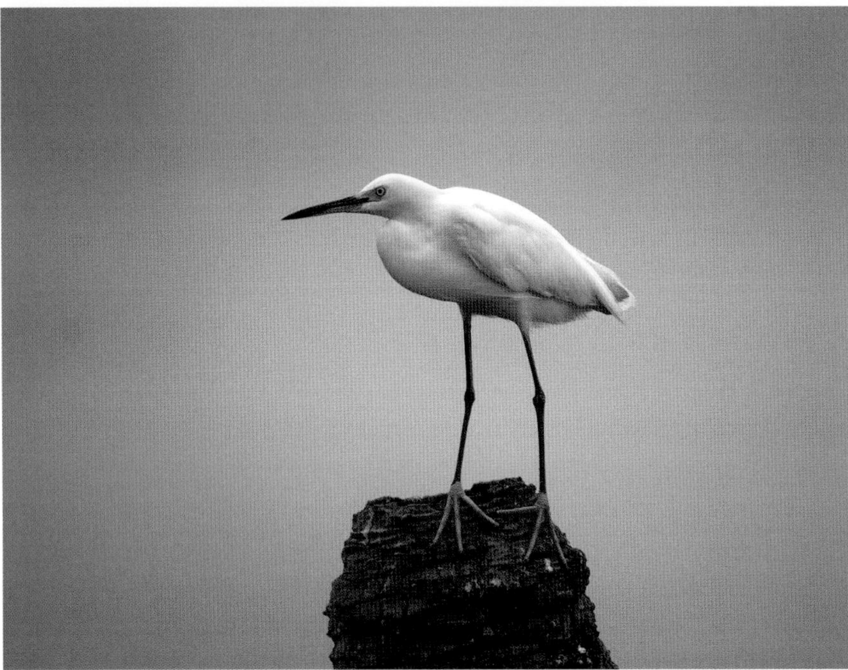

Figure 4.10
Use Aperture-priority to "lock in" a large f/stop when you want to blur the background.

That's the major pitfall of using Av: you might select an f/stop that is too small or too large to allow an optimal exposure with the available shutter speeds. For example, if you choose f/2.8 as your aperture and the illumination is quite bright (say, at the beach or in snow), even your camera's fastest shutter speed might not be able to cut down the amount of light reaching the sensor to provide the right exposure. Or, if you select f/8 in a dimly lit room, you might find yourself shooting with a very slow shutter speed that can cause blurring from subject movement or camera shake. Aperture-priority is best used by those with a bit of experience in choosing settings. Many seasoned photographers leave their 5D Mark IV set on Av all the time.

When to use Aperture-priority:

- **General landscape photography.** The 5D Mark IV is a great camera for landscape photography, of course, because its 30MP of resolution allows making huge, gorgeous prints, as well as smaller prints that are filled with eye-popping detail. Aperture-priority is a good tool for ensuring that your landscape is sharp from foreground to infinity, if you select an f/stop that provides maximum depth-of-field.

  If you use Av mode and select an aperture like f/11 or f/16, it's your responsibility to make sure the shutter speed selected is fast enough to avoid losing detail to camera shake, or that the 5D Mark IV is mounted on a tripod. One thing that new landscape photographers fail to account for is the movement of distant leaves and tree branches. When seeking the ultimate in sharpness, go ahead and use Aperture-priority, but boost ISO sensitivity a bit, if necessary, to provide a sufficiently fast shutter speed, whether shooting hand-held or with a tripod.

- **Specific landscape situations.** Aperture-priority is also useful when you have no objection to using a long shutter speed, or, particularly, *want* the 5D Mark IV to select one. Waterfalls are a perfect example. You can use Av mode, set your camera to ISO 100, use a small f/stop, and let the camera select a longer shutter speed that will allow the water to blur as it flows. Indeed, you might need to use a neutral-density filter to get a sufficiently long shutter speed. But Aperture-priority mode is a good start.

- **Portrait photography.** Portraits are the most common applications of selective focus. A medium-large aperture (say, f/5.6 or f/8) with a longer lens/zoom setting (in the 85mm-135mm range) will allow the background behind your portrait subject to blur. A *very* large aperture (I frequently shoot wide open with my 85mm f/1.2 lens) lets you apply selective focus to your subject's *face.* With a three-quarters view of your subject, as long as their eyes are sharp, it's okay if the far ear or their hair is out of focus.

- **When you want to ensure optimal sharpness.** All lenses have an aperture or two at which they perform best, providing the level of sharpness you expect from a camera with the resolution of the 5D Mark IV. That's usually about two stops down from wide open, and thus will vary depending on the maximum aperture of the lens. My 85mm f/1.2 is good wide open, but it's even sharper at f/2.8 or f/4; I shoot my 70-200mm f/2.8 wide open at concerts, but, if I can use f/4 instead, I'll get better results. Aperture-priority allows me to use each lens at its very best f/stop.

- **Close-up/Macro photography.** Depth-of-field is typically very shallow when shooting macro photos, and you'll want to choose your f/stop carefully. Perhaps you need the smallest aperture you can get away with to maximize DOF. Or, you might want to use a wider stop to emphasize your subject, as I did with the photo of the bird in Figure 4.10. Av mode comes in very useful when shooting close-up pictures. Because macro work is frequently done with the 5D Mark IV mounted on a tripod, and your close-up subjects, if not living creatures, may not be moving much, a longer shutter speed isn't a problem. Aperture-priority (Av mode) can be your preferred choice.

Shutter-Priority

Shutter-priority (Tv) is the inverse of Aperture-priority: you choose the shutter speed you'd like to use, and the camera's metering system selects the appropriate f/stop. Perhaps you're shooting action photos and you want to use the absolute fastest shutter speed available with your camera; in other cases, you might want to use a slow shutter speed to add some blur to a sports image that would be mundane if the action were completely frozen. Motor sports and track-and-field events particularly lend themselves to create use of slower speeds, as you can see in Figure 4.11. Shutter-priority mode gives you some control over how much action-freezing capability your digital camera brings to bear in a particular situation.

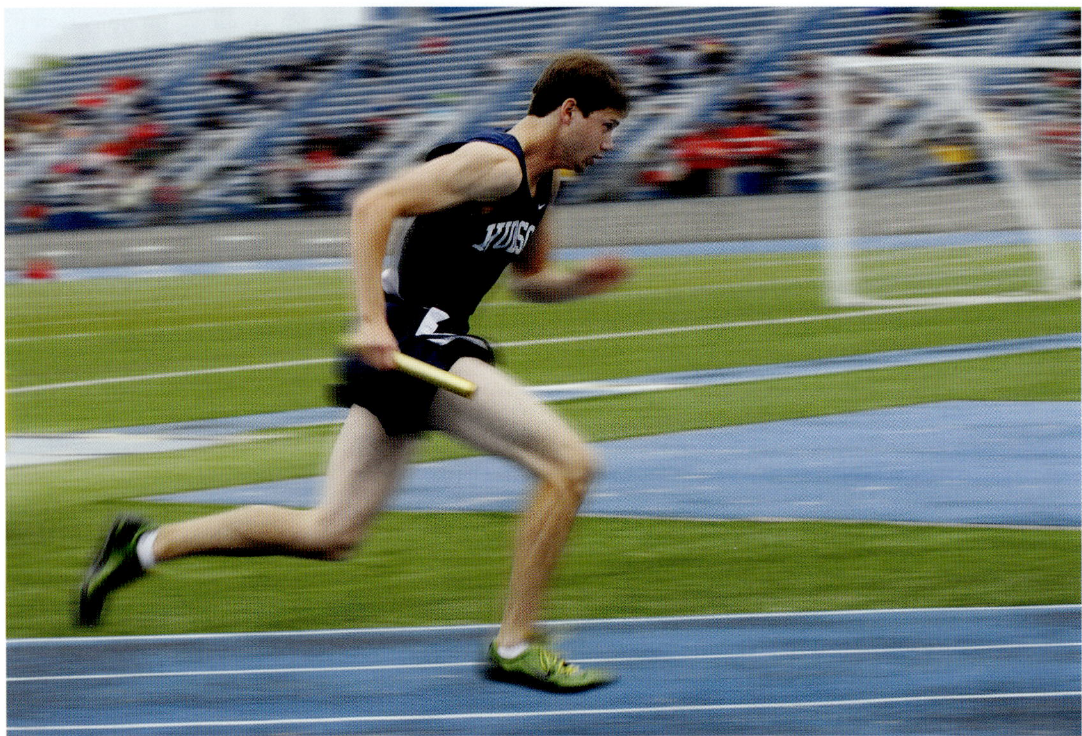

Figure 4.11 Lock the shutter at a slow speed to introduce a little blur into an action shot, seen here in this panned image of a relay runner.

You'll also encounter the same problem as with Aperture-priority when you select a shutter speed that's too long or too short for correct exposure under some conditions. I've shot outdoor soccer games on sunny fall evenings and used Shutter-priority mode to lock in a 1/1,000th second shutter speed, which triggered the blinking warning, even with the lens wide open.

Like Av mode, it's possible to choose an inappropriate shutter speed. If that's the case, the maximum aperture of your lens (to indicate underexposure) or the minimum aperture (to indicate overexposure) will blink. To fix, select a longer shutter speed or higher ISO setting (for underexposure), or a faster shutter speed/lower ISO setting (for overexposure).

When to use Shutter-priority:

- **To reduce blur from subject motion.** Set the shutter speed of the 5D Mark IV to a higher value to reduce the amount of blur from subjects that are moving. The exact speed will vary depending on how fast your subject is moving and how much blur is acceptable. You might want to freeze a basketball player in mid-dunk with a 1/1,000th second shutter speed, or use 1/250th second to allow the spinning wheels of a motocross racer to blur a tiny bit to add the feeling of motion.

- **To add blur from subject motion.** There are times when you want a subject to blur, say, when shooting waterfalls with the camera set for a one- or two-second exposure in Shutter-priority mode.

- **To add blur from camera motion when *you* are moving.** Say you're panning to follow a pair of relay runners. You might want to use Shutter-priority mode and set the 5D Mark IV for 1/60th second, so that the background will blur as you pan with the runners. The shutter speed will be fast enough to provide a sharp image of the athletes.

- **To reduce blur from camera motion when *you* are moving.** In other situations, the camera may be in motion, say, because you're shooting from a moving train or auto, and you want to minimize the amount of blur caused by the motion of the camera. Shutter-priority is a good choice here, too.

- **Landscape photography hand-held.** If you can't use a tripod for your landscape shots, you'll still probably want the sharpest image possible. Shutter-priority can allow you to specify a shutter speed that's fast enough to reduce or eliminate the effects of camera shake. Just make sure that your ISO setting is high enough that the 5D Mark IV will select an aperture with sufficient depth-of-field, too.

- **Concerts, stage performances.** I shoot a lot of concerts with my 70-200mm f/2.8 lens, and have discovered that, when image stabilization is taken into account, a shutter speed of 1/180th second is fast enough to eliminate blur from hand-holding the 5D Mark IV with this lens, and also to avoid blur from the movement of all but the most energetic performers. I use Shutter-priority and set the ISO so the camera will select an aperture in the f/4–5.6 range.

Program AE Mode

Program mode (P) uses the 5D Mark IV's built-in smarts to select the correct f/stop and shutter speed using a database of picture information that tells it which combination of shutter speed and aperture will work best for a particular photo. If the correct exposure cannot be achieved at the current ISO setting, the shutter speed or aperture indicator in the viewfinder will blink, indicating under- or overexposure. You can then boost or reduce the ISO to increase or decrease sensitivity.

The 5D Mark IV's recommended exposure can be overridden if you want. Use the EV setting feature (described later, because it also applies to Tv and Av modes) to add or subtract exposure from the metered value. And, as I mentioned earlier in this chapter, you can change from the recommended setting to an equivalent setting (as shown in Table 4.1) that produces the same exposure, but using a different combination of f/stop and shutter speed. To accomplish this:

1. Press the shutter release halfway to lock in the current base exposure, or press the AE Lock button (*) on the back of the camera (in which case the * indicator will illuminate in the viewfinder to show that the exposure has been locked).

2. If the camera cannot select an appropriate exposure, the shutter speed and aperture display will blink:

   - **Underexposure.** The 30 shutter speed indicator will flash, along with the maximum (largest) aperture of the lens. (The exact number will vary, depending on which lens you are using.) To compensate, you must either use a higher ISO setting or provide additional illumination, such as electronic flash.

   - **Overexposure.** The 8000 shutter speed indicator will flash, along with the minimum (smallest available) f/stop, such as f/16, f/22, or f/32, depending on the lens you are using. You can usually compensate for this by reducing the ISO speed to a lower setting. Your scene must be *very* bright indeed to trigger overexposure at a shutter speed of 1/8,000th second and the lowest L (ISO 50 equivalent) sensitivity setting. But if you're photographing, say, a blast furnace, and still have an overexposure situation, you can resort to a neutral density filter or find some way to reduce the amount of illumination.

3. Once an exposure is set, you can spin the Main Dial to change to a different combination of settings. Rotate left to select a longer shutter speed/smaller aperture, or to the right to choose a faster shutter speed/larger aperture.

Your adjustment remains in force for a single exposure; if you want to change from the recommended settings for the next exposure, you'll need to repeat those steps.

When to use Program mode priority:

- **When you're in a hurry to get a grab shot.** The 5D Mark IV will do a pretty good job of calculating an appropriate exposure for you, without any input from you.

- **When you hand your camera to a novice.** Set the 5D Mark IV to P, hand the camera to your friend, relative, or trustworthy stranger you meet in front of the Eiffel Tower, point to the shutter release button and viewfinder, and say, "Look through here, and press this button."

- **When no special shutter speed or aperture settings are needed.** If your subject doesn't require special anti- or pro-blur techniques, and depth-of-field or selective focus aren't important, use P as a general-purpose setting. You can still make adjustments to increase/decrease depth-of-field or add/reduce motion blur with a minimum of fuss.

Scene Intelligent Auto

On first consideration, including an exposure mode with no user options might seem counterintuitive on a camera as advanced as the 5D Mark IV, because it essentially transforms a sophisticated pro/enthusiast camera into a point-and-click snapshooter. Delve deeper, and you'll discover that there is method in Canon's madness, and that Scene Intelligent Auto is a lot more than a less versatile version of Program mode. The key is the *Intelligent* part of the mode's nomenclature.

With P mode, only the shutter speed and aperture are determined by the camera. You can change the metering mode, autofocus mode, white balance, and virtually all other settings. In Scene Intelligent Auto mode, the 5D Mark IV will analyze your scene, even to the extent of evaluating whether or not your subject is static or moving, and then intelligently choose optimum settings without any input from you. Its choices include:

- **ISO speed.** The camera will choose an ISO sensitivity automatically.
- **Picture Style.** The A (automatic) Picture Style is active, and the camera will choose appropriate settings. Note that if you have made changes to the Auto Picture Style (I'll show you how to do that in Chapter 11), they will be ignored in Scene Intelligent Auto.
- **White balance.** White balance is set automatically and cannot be changed.
- **Auto Lighting Optimizer.** Always active in Scene Intelligent Auto mode.
- **Color space.** Forced to sRGB.
- **Autofocus.** AI Focus AF is always used, and AF area selection modes cannot be specified. AF point selection is always automatic, and the AF-assist beam activated.
- **Metering mode.** Evaluative metering is always used.

Things that you *can* choose in Scene Intelligent Auto mode include:

- **Manual focus.** Manual focus can be chosen by toggling the AF/MF switch on the lens to Manual.
- **Drive mode.** You use the Quick Control screen or Drive mode button to choose from single shooting, high-/low-speed continuous shooting, silent single shooting, silent continuous shooting, and 10 sec./2 sec. self-timer modes.
- **Memory card options.** The Q button will also give you access to the options for your Card 1 or Card 2 storage.
- **Image quality/size.** Press the Q button to select among your RAW, JPEG, and other image size options.

Some shooting options are available from the truncated three-tab menu system offered in Scene Intelligent Auto mode. I'll explain all menu entries for all exposure modes in Chapters 11 to 14. While some Playback and Set-up menu choices are accessible, those you most commonly might need to access while shooting include:

- Image Quality
- Dual Pixel RAW
- Image Review Duration
- Beep Enable/Disable
- Release Shutter without Card
- Interval Timer
- Lens Aberration Correction
- Live View Enable/Disable
- AF Mode in Live View
- Live View Touch Shutter
- Live View Grid Display

Manual Exposure

Part of being an experienced photographer comes from knowing when to rely on your 5D Mark IV's automation (including Scene Intelligent Auto or P mode), when to go semi-automatic (with Tv or Av), and when to set exposure manually (using M). Some photographers actually prefer to set their exposure manually most of the time, as the 5D Mark IV will be happy to provide an indication of when its metering system judges your settings provide the proper exposure, using the analog exposure scale at the bottom of the viewfinder and on the status LCD.

Manual exposure can come in handy in some situations. You might be taking a silhouette photo and find that none of the exposure modes or EV correction features give you exactly the effect you want. For example, when I shot the ballet dancer in Figure 4.12 in front of a mostly dark background highlighted by an illuminated curtain off to the right, there was no way any of my 5D Mark IV's exposure modes would be able to interpret the scene the way I wanted to shoot it, even with Spot metering, which didn't have a narrow enough field-of-view from my position. So, I took a couple test exposures, and set the exposure manually using the exact shutter speed and f/stop I needed. You might be working in a studio environment using multiple flash units. The additional flash are triggered by slave devices (gadgets that set off the flash when they sense the light from another flash, or, perhaps from a radio or infrared remote control). Your camera's exposure meter doesn't compensate for the extra illumination, and can't interpret the flash exposure at all, so you need to set the aperture manually.

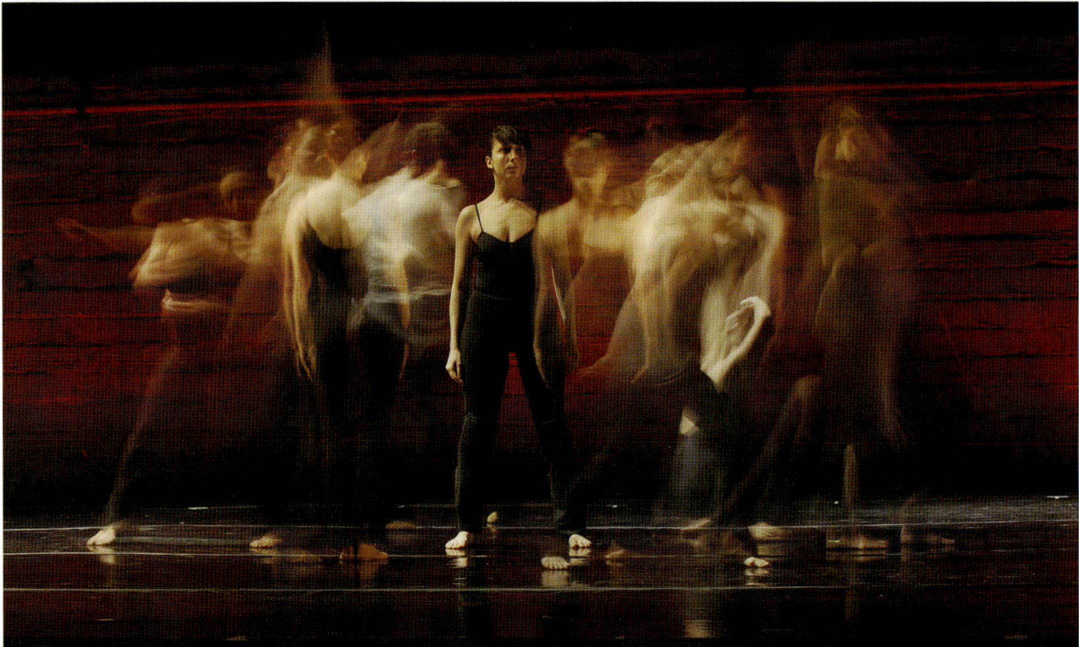

Figure 4.12 Manual exposure allows selecting both f/stop and shutter speed, especially useful when you're experimenting, as with this shot of ballet dancers.

Because, depending on your proclivities, you might not need to set exposure manually very often, you should still make sure you understand how it works. Fortunately, the 5D Mark IV makes setting exposure manually very easy. Just set the Mode Dial to M, turn the Main Dial to set the shutter speed, and hold down the Av button while rotating the Main Dial to adjust the aperture. Press the shutter release halfway or press the AE Lock button, and the exposure scale in the viewfinder shows you how far your chosen setting diverges from the metered exposure.

When to use Manual exposure:

- **When working in the studio.** If you're working in a studio environment, you generally have total control over the lighting and can set exposure exactly as you want. The last thing you need is for the 5D Mark IV to interpret the scene and make adjustments of its own. Use M and the shutter speed, aperture, and (as long as you don't use ISO-Auto) ISO setting are totally up to you.

- **When using non-dedicated flash.** External Canon-dedicated flash units are cool, but if you're working with a non-compatible flash unit, particularly studio flash plugged into the side-mounted PC/X socket, or into a PC/X sync adapter mounted on the hot shoe, the camera has no clue about the intensity of the flash, so you'll have to dial in the appropriate aperture manually.

- **If you're using a hand-held light meter.** The appropriate aperture, both for flash exposures and shots taken under continuous lighting, can be determined by a hand-held light meter, flash meter, or combo meter that measures both kinds of illumination. With an external meter, you can measure highlights, shadows, backgrounds, or additional subjects separately, and use Manual exposure to make your settings.

- **When you want to outsmart the metering system.** Your 5D Mark IV's metering system is "trained" to react to unusual lighting situations, such as backlighting, extra-bright illumination, or low-key images with murky shadows. In many cases, it can counter these "problems" and produce a well-exposed image. But what if you don't *want* a well-exposed image? Manual exposure allows you to produce silhouettes in backlit situations, wash out all the middle tones to produce a luminous look, or underexpose to create a moody or ominous dark-toned photograph.

Adjusting Exposure with ISO Settings

Another way of adjusting exposures is by changing the ISO sensitivity setting. Sometimes photographers forget about this option, because the common practice is to set the ISO once for a particular shooting session (say, at ISO 100 or 200 for bright sunlight outdoors, or ISO 800 when shooting indoors) and then forget about it. ISOs higher than ISO 100 or 200 are seen as "bad" or "necessary evils." However, changing the ISO is a valid way of adjusting exposure settings, particularly with the Canon EOS 5D Mark IV, which produces good results at ISO settings that create grainy, unusable pictures with some other camera models.

Indeed, I find myself using ISO adjustment as a convenient alternate way of adding or subtracting EV when shooting in Manual mode, and as a quick way of choosing equivalent exposures when in Auto or semi-automatic modes. For example, I've selected a Manual exposure with both f/stop and shutter speed suitable for my image using, say, ISO 200. I can change the exposure in one-third-stop increments by pressing the ISO button on top of the camera, and spinning the Main Dial one click at a time. The difference in image quality/noise at the base setting of ISO 200 is negligible if I dial in ISO 100 to reduce exposure a little, or change to ISO 400 to increase exposure. I keep my preferred f/stop and shutter speed, but still adjust the exposure.

Or, perhaps, I am using Tv mode and the metered exposure at ISO 200 is 1/500th second at f/11. If I decide on the spur of the moment I'd rather use 1/500th second at f/8, I can press the ISO button and spin the Main Dial to switch to ISO 100. Of course, it's a good idea to monitor your ISO changes, so you don't end up at ISO 1600 accidentally. ISO settings can, of course, also be used to boost or reduce sensitivity in particular shooting situations.

When not using Scene Intelligent Auto (which sets ISO automatically), the 5D Mark IV can set ISO speeds manually for stills. (In video mode, Auto ISO must be used in all modes except Manual exposure.) The ISO Speed Settings entry in the Shooting 2 menu allows you to specify what speeds are available and how they are used:

- **ISO Speed.** This scale allows you to choose from the enabled ISO speeds, plus Auto, using a sliding scale that can be adjusted using the QCD, multi-controller, or the touch screen. Pressing INFO. when the scale is visible activates Auto.

- **Range for Stills.** You can specify the minimum and maximum ISO sensitivity available, including "expanded" settings such as Low (ISO 50 equivalent) and H1 or H2 (ISO 51200 and 102400 equivalent, respectively). I find myself using this feature frequently to keep me from accidentally switching to a setting I'd rather not use (or need to avoid). For example, at concerts I may switch from ISO 1600 to 6400 as the lighting changes, and I set those two values as my minimum or maximum. Outdoors in daylight, I might prefer to lock out ISO values lower than ISO 100 or higher than ISO 800.

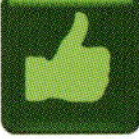

> **Tip**
>
> The Lo, H1, and H2 settings enables *ISO expansion,* which may produce excessive noise, irregular colors, banding, and lower resolution. Use them with caution.

■ **Auto Range.** This is the equivalent "safety net" for Auto ISO operation. You can set the minimum no lower than ISO 100 and the maximum to ISO 32000, and no further. Use this to apply your own "smarts" to the Auto ISO setting.

■ **Minimum Shutter Speed.** You can choose whether to allow the 5D Mark IV to select the slowest shutter speed used before Auto ISO kicks in. The idea here is that you'll probably want to boost ISO sooner if you're using a long lens with P and Av modes (in which the camera selects the shutter speed). If you specify, for example, a minimum shutter speed of 1/250th second, if P or Av mode needs a slower shutter speed for the proper exposure, it will boost ISO instead, within the range you've specified with Auto Range.

This setting has two modes. In Auto mode, the camera decides when the shutter speed is too low. You can fine-tune this by choosing Slower or Faster on the scale (–3 to +3) that appears. Or, you can manually select the "trigger" shutter speed, from 1 second to 1/8000th second.

By default, both the exposure level increments (size of shutter speed or f/stop changes) are in 1/3-stop jumps. In the Custom Functions 1 menu, you can set exposure level increments to 1/3 or 1/2 stops, and ISO changes to 1/3- or 1-stop increments. The larger 1-stop step for ISO allows rapid switching through ISO 100, 200, 400, 800, and so forth.

Table 4.2 show the available ISO settings for each shooting mode, both with and without flash. The ISO speed range depends, of course, on the minimum and maximum values you enable.

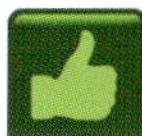

Tip

Find yourself locked out of ISO settings lower than 200 or higher than 32000? You've probably set Highlight Tone Priority to Enable in the Shooting 3 menu, as described in Chapter 11.

Table 4.2 Available ISO Settings

Shooting Mode	ISO—No Flash	ISO—Flash
Scene Intelligent Auto	ISO 100–ISO 12800	ISO 100–ISO 1600
Tv/Av	ISO 100–ISO 32000	ISO 400
P	ISO 100–ISO 32000	ISO 400 (ISO 400–1600 available when using bounce flash)
M	ISO 100–ISO 32000	ISO 400 (Lower settings may be used with fill flash to avoid overexposure)
Bulb	ISO 400	ISO 400 (Lower settings may be used with fill flash to avoid overexposure)

Dealing with Visual Noise

Visual image noise is that random grainy effect that some like to use as a special effect, but which, most of the time, is objectionable because it robs your image of detail even as it adds that "interesting" texture. Noise is caused by two different phenomena: high ISO settings and long exposures.

High ISO noise commonly first appears when you raise your camera's sensitivity setting above ISO 3200. With Canon cameras, which are renown for their good ISO noise characteristics, noise is usually fairly noticeable at ISO 6400 and above. At the H1 and H2 settings (ISO 51200 and 102400 equivalents), noise is usually quite bothersome, which is why those lofty sensitivity ratings are disabled by default and must be activated with ISO expansion. This kind of noise appears as a result of the amplification needed to increase the sensitivity of the sensor. Because your sensor has twice as many green pixels as red and blue pixels, such noise is typically worse in areas that have red, blue, and magenta tones, because the green signals don't have to be amplified as much to produce detail. While higher ISOs do pull details out of dark areas, they also amplify non-signal information randomly, creating noise.

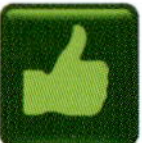

NOTE

The structure of your sensor is a bit off-topic here, but you'll learn a little more about why it has twice as many green photosites in Chapter 5, under the discussion of the 5D Mark IV's Dual Pixel RAW feature. While your camera's "split" (dual) pixels have applications for image microadjustment, bokeh shift, and ghost reduction (all explained in Chapter 5), they have no effect on the sensor's ISO behavior.

A similar noisy phenomenon occurs during long time exposures, which allow more photons to reach the sensor, increasing your ability to capture a picture under low-light conditions. However, the longer exposures also increase the likelihood that some pixels will register random phantom photons, often because the longer an imager is "hot," the warmer it gets, and that heat can be mistaken for photons. There's also a special kind of noise that CMOS sensors like the one used in the 5D Mark IV are potentially susceptible to. With a CCD, the entire signal is conveyed off the chip and funneled through a single amplifier and analog-to-digital conversion circuit. Any noise introduced there is, at least, consistent. CMOS imagers, on the other hand, contain millions of individual amplifiers and A/D converters, all working in unison. Because all these circuits don't necessarily process in precisely the same way all the time, they can introduce something called fixed-pattern noise into the image data.

Fortunately, Canon's electronics geniuses have done an exceptional job minimizing noise from all causes in the 5D Mark IV. Even so, you might still want to apply the optional long exposure noise reduction that can be activated in the Shooting 3 menu. This type of noise reduction involves the 5D Mark IV taking a second, blank exposure, and comparing the random pixels in that image with the photograph you just took. Pixels that coincide in the two represent noise and can safely be suppressed. This noise reduction system, called *dark frame subtraction,* effectively doubles the amount of time required to take a picture, and is used only for exposures longer than one second. Noise reduction can reduce the amount of detail in your picture, as some image information may be removed along with the noise. So, you might want to use this feature with moderation. Some types of images don't require noise reduction, because the grainy pattern tends to blend into the overall scene.

To activate your 5D Mark IV's long exposure noise reduction features, go to the Shooting 3 menu, as explained further in Chapter 11.

You can also apply noise reduction to a lesser extent using Photoshop or Canon Digital Photo Professional (or, DPP, which is necessary for working with Dual Pixel RAW images in any case), and when converting RAW files to some other format, using your favorite RAW converter, or an industrial-strength product like Noise Ninja (www.picturecode.com) to wipe out noise after you've already taken the picture.

Making EV Changes

Sometimes you'll want more or less exposure than indicated by the 5D Mark IV's metering system. Perhaps you want to underexpose to create a silhouette effect, or overexpose to produce a high-key look. It's easy to use the 5D Mark IV's exposure compensation system to override the exposure recommendations, available in any non-automatic mode except Manual. There are three ways to make exposure value (EV) changes with the 5D Mark IV.

- **Viewfinder/Quick Control Dial.** When looking through the optical viewfinder, you can add/subtract exposure compensation +/–3 stops by tapping the shutter release halfway (you don't have to hold it down) and then rotating the Quick Control Dial. Turn clockwise to add exposure, or counter-clockwise to reduce exposure. The exposure scale at the bottom of the screen and in the top-panel monochrome LCD will indicate the amount of exposure compensation you've dialed in. (See Figure 4.13, top.)

- **Quick Control screen.** Press the Q button and use the multi-controller to select the exposure scale. Then rotate the QCD. Rotate clockwise to add exposure, or counter-clockwise to reduce exposure. (As always, you can use the touch screen to access these controls.) The exposure scale on the screen will indicate the amount of exposure compensation. (See Figure 4.13, bottom.)

- **Shooting 2 menu.** Press the MENU button and rotate the Main Dial to select the Shooting 2 menu. Then rotate the QCD or use the multi-controller joystick to highlight the Expo. Comp/AEB entry. Press SET or the multi-controller to access the screen shown in Figure 4.14. Then rotate the QCD or slide a finger across the scale to select the amount of exposure compensation. The screen has helpful labels (Darker on the left and Brighter on the right) to make sure you're adding/subtracting when you really want to.

  Note that this method has two advantages: you can choose up to five stops of exposure compensation (rather than just three with the first two methods), and you can specify automatic exposure bracketing from this screen just by rotating the Main Dial. I'll explain bracketing in more detail next.

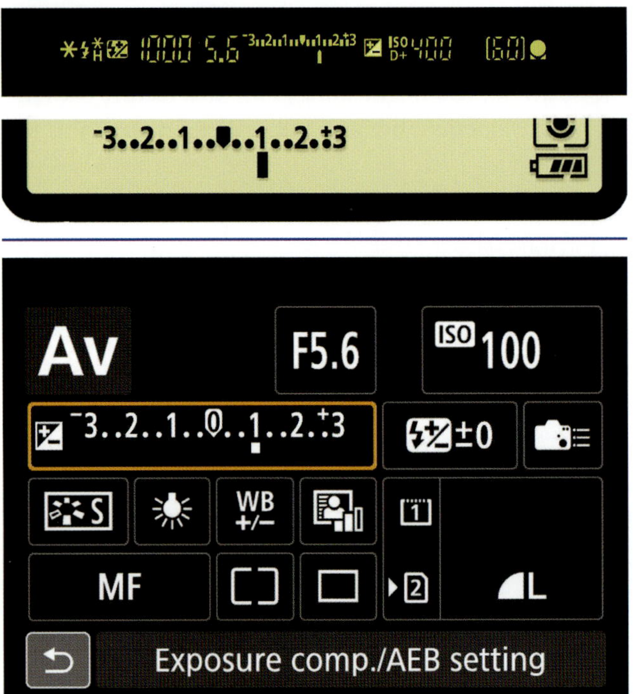

Figure 4.13
When you set exposure compensation with the Quick Control Dial, the amount of adjustment is shown in the viewfinder and top-panel monochrome LCD (top). You can also use the Quick Control screen (bottom).

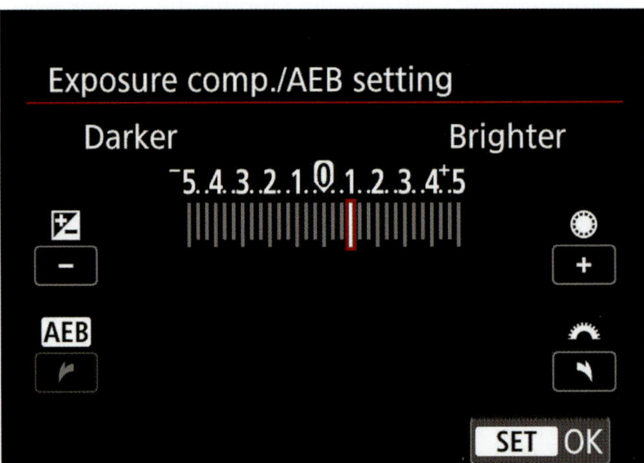

Figure 4.14
A wider range of exposure compensation adjustments (up to five stops) can be made using the Expo. Comp/AEB entry in the Shooting 2 menu.

Bracketing Parameters

Bracketing is a method for shooting several consecutive exposures using different settings, as a way of improving the odds that one will be exactly right. Before digital cameras took over the universe, it was common to bracket exposures, shooting, say, a series of three photos at 1/125th second, but varying the f/stop from f/8 to f/11 to f/16. In practice, smaller than whole-stop increments were used for greater precision. Plus, it was just as common to keep the same aperture and vary the shutter speed, although in the days before electronic shutters, film cameras often had only whole-increment shutter speeds available. Figure 4.15 shows a typical bracketed series.

Today, cameras like the 5D Mark IV can bracket exposures much more precisely, and bracket white balance as well (using the WB Shift/Bkt entry found in the Shooting 2 menu and described in Chapter 11). While WB bracketing is sometimes used when getting color absolutely correct in the camera is important, autoexposure bracketing (AEB) is used much more often. When this feature is activated, the 5D Mark IV takes a series of shots, all at a different exposure value—one at the standard exposure, and the others with more or less exposure. (See Figure 4.16.) In Av mode, the shutter speed will change, whereas in Tv mode, the aperture speed will change. The next sections will explain the parameters you can select.

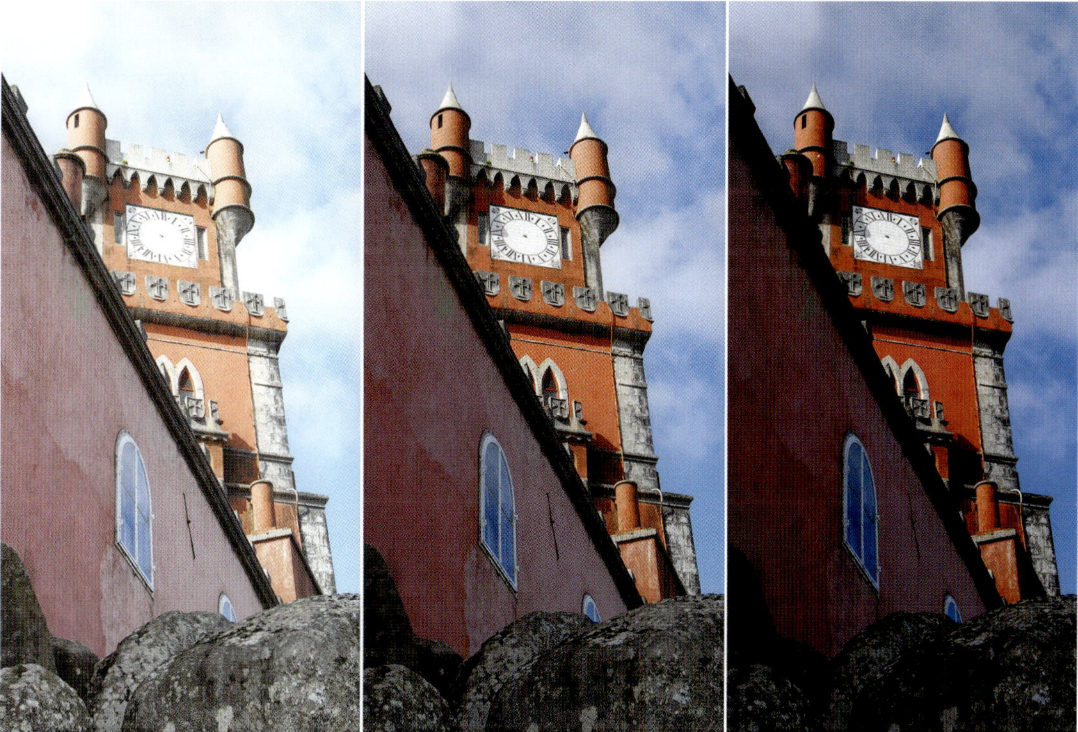

Figure 4.15 In this bracketed series, you can see overexposure (left), metered exposure (center), and underexposure (right).

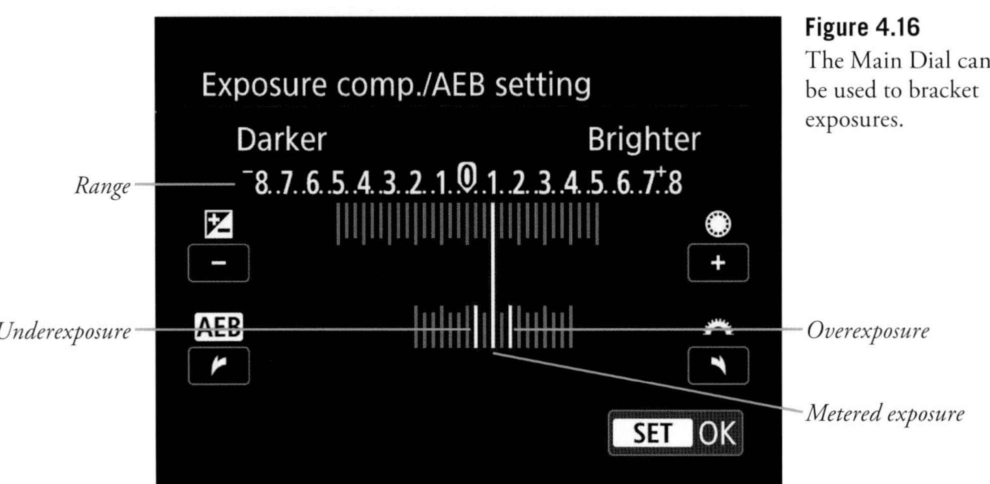

Figure 4.16
The Main Dial can be used to bracket exposures.

Number of Exposures

In the Custom Function 1 menu, under the Number of Bracketed Shots entry, you can elect to bracket 2, 3, 5, or 7 shots:

- **2 shots.** The 5D Mark IV will capture one image at the *base* or standard exposure (which can be the metered exposure, or one that's more or less than the metered exposure, as I'll explain shortly). It then takes one additional shot that provides either *more* or *less* exposure relative to that "base" image. Rotate the QCD to the right to specify more exposure for the second shot, or to the left to specify less exposure. The *amount* of additional/less exposure is determined by the increment you select. (Read on! I'll tie all the parameters together in an upcoming section.)

- **3, 5, 7 shots.** The camera captures one image at the base exposure, and then two, four, or six shots bracketed around that exposure, respectively. That translates to one over/one under at the 3-shot setting, two over/two under at the 5-shot setting, and three over/three under when using the 7-shot option.

Bracketing Sequence

Also in the Custom Function 1 menu, you'll find a Bracketing Sequence entry, which allows you to specify the order in which the autoexposure bracketing series are exposed. Your choice will depend both on personal preference, and what you intend to do with the bracketed shots.

The options include:

- **0 – +:** The exposure sequence is standard exposure, decreased exposure, increased exposure. With this default value, your base exposure will be captured and saved first on your memory card, followed by the progressively reduced exposure images, then the shots with increased exposure. You might prefer this order if you expect your standard exposure will be the preferred image and arranged first in the queue of each bracket set, and want the alternate exposures to follow.

- **– 0 +:** The sequence is decreased exposure, standard exposure, increased exposure. This order is the most logical to use if you're shooting with the intention to combine images using HDR (high dynamic range) techniques in your image editor or HDR utility. The final bracketed array is stored on your memory card starting with the most underexposed shot, and progressing to the best exposed, and then on to the overexposures. That makes it easy to use all of your bracketed shots in the HDR sequence, or to select only some of them to combine.

- **+ 0 –:** This sequence is the inverse of the last one, progressing from increased exposure to standard exposure and decreased exposure. You might prefer this order if you expect to see your best exposures on the plus side of the exposure sequence, and want them to be displayed first.

Bracketing Auto Cancel

The final relevant entry in the Custom Function 1 menu is Bracketing Auto Cancel. When you activate bracketing (in the Shooting 2 menu, described shortly), the 5D Mark IV continues to shoot bracketed exposures until you manually turn the bracket feature off, assuming you have this setting disabled. That's a good thing. If you're out shooting a series of bracketed exposures (especially for HDR), it's convenient to have your bracket setting be "sticky" and still be active even if you turn your camera off. Some shooters like to bracket virtually *everything* and leave bracketing on routinely.

However, much of the time you'll want to turn bracketing off, and you may not want to visit the Shooting 2 menu to deactivate it manually. Set Bracketing Auto Cancel to Enable, and bracketing is cancelled when you turn the 5D Mark IV off, change lenses, use the flash, or change memory cards. When this setting is set to Disable, bracketing remains in effect until you manually turn it off *or use the flash*. The flash still cancels bracketing, but your settings are retained.

Increment Between Exposures

You can choose the size of the jump between each of the bracketed exposures. To do that, you'll need to visit the Expo. Comp/AEB entry in the Shooting 2 menu. There, you can select from plus/minus 1/3 to 3 full stops in 1/3-stop increments, by rotating the Main Dial. The next section provides instructions for producing a bracketed set.

Creating a Bracketed Set

Using autoexposure bracketing is trickier than it needs to be, but has been made more flexible than with some earlier models. With the 5D Mark IV you are not limited to only three exposures (up to seven shots can be taken), and you can choose to bracket only overexposures or underexposures—a very useful improvement! Just follow these steps:

1. **Specify number of exposures and sequence.** Choose the number of bracketed exposures you want and the sequence in which they will be shot in the Custom Function 1 menu, as described earlier.

2. **Activate the Expo. Comp./AEB screen.** Press the MENU button and navigate to the Shooting 2 menu, where you'll find the Expo. Comp./AEB option. Press SET to select this entry.

3. **Set the bracket range/increment.** Rotate the Main Dial to spread out or contract the three bars to include the desired range and exposure increment you want to use. The wider the spread, the larger the increment and the larger the range of bracketed shots you'll end up with. The Main Dial will allow you to set the bracket range to up to three stops on either side of the standard (middle) exposure.

   For example, in Figure 4.17 (top), the red highlighted bars are separated from the center bar by a full f/stop, so the bracketing will produce one image at one stop *less* than the zero point (the large center bar), one at the zero point, and one at one stop more than that. Figure 4.17 (bottom) shows the bars more widely separated, for a bracketed set three stops under and three stops over the midpoint, or standard/base exposure.

4. **Adjust zero point/standard exposure.** By default, the bracketing is zeroed around the center of the scale, which represents the correct exposure as metered by the 5D Mark IV. But you might want to have your three bracketed shots *all* biased toward overexposure or underexposure. Perhaps you feel that the metered exposure will be too dark or too light, and you want the bracketed shots to lean in the other direction. Use the Quick Control Dial to move the bracket spread toward one end of the scale or the other. Figure 4.17 (top) shows the bracketing biased toward overexposure, while in 4.17 (bottom), the zero point is clustered around underexposure. (Actually, the exposure bar at left will be four stops under the metered exposure, the center bar two stops under, and the right bar ends up at the metered value.)

NON-BRACKETING IS EXPOSURE COMPENSATION

When the three bracket indicators aren't separated, using the QCD simply, in effect, adds or subtracts exposure compensation. You'll be shooting a "bracketed" set of one picture, with the zero point placed at the portion of the scale you indicated. Until you rotate the Main Dial to separate the three bracket indicators by at least one indicator, this screen just supplies EV adjustment. Also, keep in mind that the increments shown will be either 1/3 stop or 1/2 stop, depending on how you've set Exposure Level Increments in the Custom Function 1 menu.

Figure 4.17
Use the Quick Control Dial to bias the bracketing toward more or less exposure, and the Main Dial to set the bracket range.

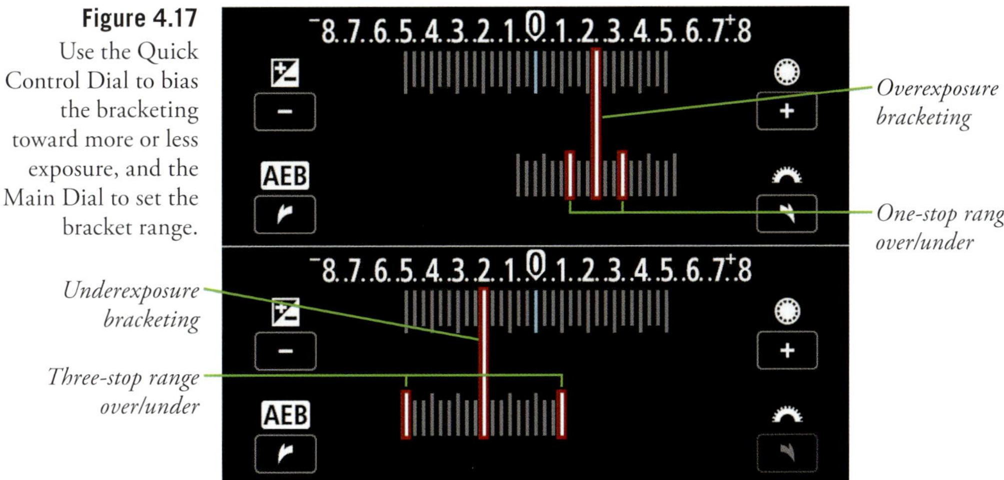

5. **Confirm your choice.** Press the SET button to enter the settings.

6. **Take your photo sequence.** Press the shutter release to start capturing the bracketed sequence. The drive mode you select will determine when they are taken:

   - **Single shooting/Silent single shooting.** Press the shutter release one time for each exposure in the sequence.

   - **High-speed continuous/Low-speed continuous/Silent continuous.** You can hold down the shutter release and all the shots in the sequence will be exposed. The 5D Mark IV stops shooting when the series is complete.

   - **10 sec./2 sec. self-timer modes.** After the appropriate delay, all the shots in the sequence will be taken.

7. **Monitor your shots.** As the images are captured, three indicators will appear on the exposure scale in the viewfinder, with one of them flashing for each bracketed photo, showing when the base exposure, underexposure, and overexposure are taken.

8. **Turn bracketing off when done.** Bracketing remains in effect when the set is taken so you can continue shooting bracketed exposures until you use the electronic flash, turn off the camera, or return to the menu to cancel bracketing.

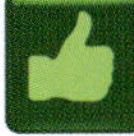

NOTE

AEB is disabled when you're using flash, Multi Shot Noise Reduction, taking long time exposures with the Bulb setting, or have enabled the Auto Lighting Optimizer in the Shooting 2 menu (in which case the optimizer will probably override and nullify bracketing).

Working with HDR

High dynamic range (HDR) photography is quite the rage these days, and entire books have been written on the subject. It's not really a new technique—film photographers have been combining multiple exposures for ages to produce a single image of, say, an interior room while maintaining detail in the scene visible through the windows.

Suppose you wanted to photograph a dimly lit room that had a bright window showing an outdoors scene. Proper exposure for the room might be on the order of 1/60th second at f/2.8 at ISO 200, while the outdoors scene probably would require f/11 at 1/400th second. That's almost a 7 EV step difference (approximately 7 f/stops) and effectively beyond the dynamic range of any digital camera, including the 5D Mark IV.

Until camera sensors gain much higher dynamic ranges (which may not be as far into the distant future as we think), special tricks like Active D-Lighting and HDR photography will remain basic tools. With the 5D Mark IV, you can create in-camera HDR exposures, or shoot HDR the old-fashioned way—with separate bracketed exposures that are later combined in a tool like Photomatix or Adobe's Merge to HDR Pro image-editing feature. I'm going to show you how to use both.

The 5D Mark IV's in-camera HDR feature is simple, flexible, and surprisingly effective in creating high dynamic range images. It's also remarkably easy to use. Although it combines only three images to create a single HDR photograph, and while it's not always as good as the manual HDR method I'll describe in the section after this one, it's a *lot* faster.

Figure 4.18 shows you a typical situation in which you might want to use this setting. When the exposure is set for the interior of the cathedral, the beautiful backlit stained glass windows are washed out and have no detail (top left). When the exposure is adjusted to produce detail in the glass panes (bottom left), the rest of the cathedral goes dark. HDR allows combining the detail

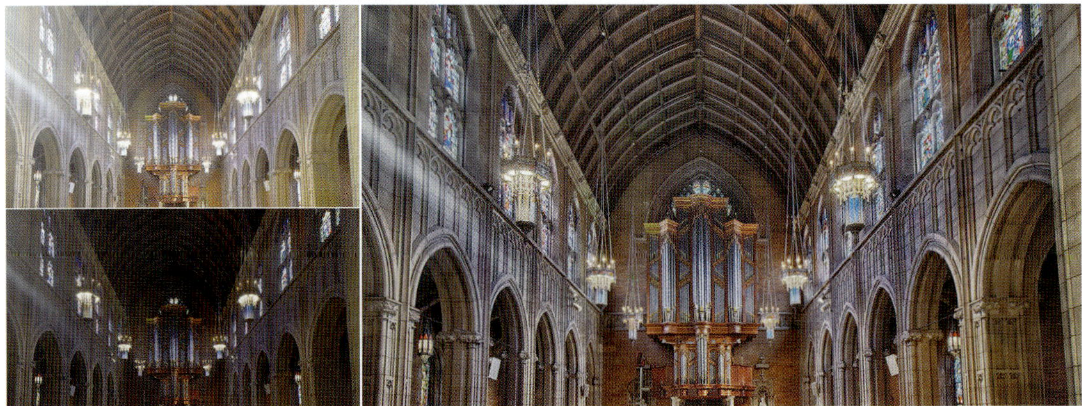

Figure 4.18 Exposing for the cathedral interior produces overexposed backlit stained glass windows, while exposing for the windows captures a murky cathedral interior (left). HDR allows combining tones to produce an image similar to the one at right.

from multiple images—not just the two shown at left, but as many as you want, if you combine them manually (as I'll show you later).

However, a quickie solution is to use the 5D Mark IV's HDR mode, described next. It captures three consecutive images and then merges them as a JPEG image that preserves both highlight and shadow detail.

Using HDR Mode

Here are some tips for using this feature:

- **Use a tripod if possible.** Because there may be some camera movement between the continuous shots, you'll get better results if you mount the 5D Mark IV on a tripod.

- **Moving objects may produce ghosts.** In this case, there may be some *subject* motion between shots, producing "ghost" effects.

- **Misalignment.** If you *don't* use a tripod, when Auto Image Align is activated, this mode does a good job of realigning your multiple images when they are merged. However, it can't do a perfect job, particularly with repetitive patterns that are difficult for the camera's "brains" to sort out. Some misalignment is possible.

- **Shutter speeds vary.** The camera brackets by adjusting the shutter speed within the increment range selected, *even if you're using Tv or M modes and have specified a shutter speed.*

- **Unwanted cropping.** Because the processor needs to be able to shift each individual image slightly in any (or all) of four directions in Auto Align mode (described next), it needs to crop the image slightly to trim out any non-image areas that result. Your final image will be slightly smaller than one shot in other modes.

- **Weird colors.** Some types of lighting, including fluorescent and LED illumination, "cycle" many times a second, and colors can vary between shots. You may not even notice this when single shooting, but it becomes more obvious when using any continuous shooting mode, including HDR mode. The combined images may have strange color effects.

- **Can't use any RAW mode, or ISOs higher than 32000.** Your image will be recorded as a Large JPEG only, and HDR is disabled when you're using ISO expansion to enable sensitivity settings higher than 32000. While you can use HDR mode if Auto Lighting Optimizer has been enabled, the camera will disable it while shooting your HDR images, then re-enable it when you turn HDR mode off.

- **The process takes time.** Forget about firing off a large number of HDR shots in a row. After the 5D Mark IV captures its three images, it takes a few seconds to process them and save your final image. Be patient.

Although you can locate HDR Mode in the Shooting 3 menu, it's faster to press the Creative Photo button, located to the upper left of the LCD monitor on the back panel of the 5D Mark IV, just above the RATE button. Rotate the QCD to choose HDR Mode from the screen that pops up (see Figure 4.19, left), press the SET button, and you'll be taken to the menu shown in Figure 4.19, right.

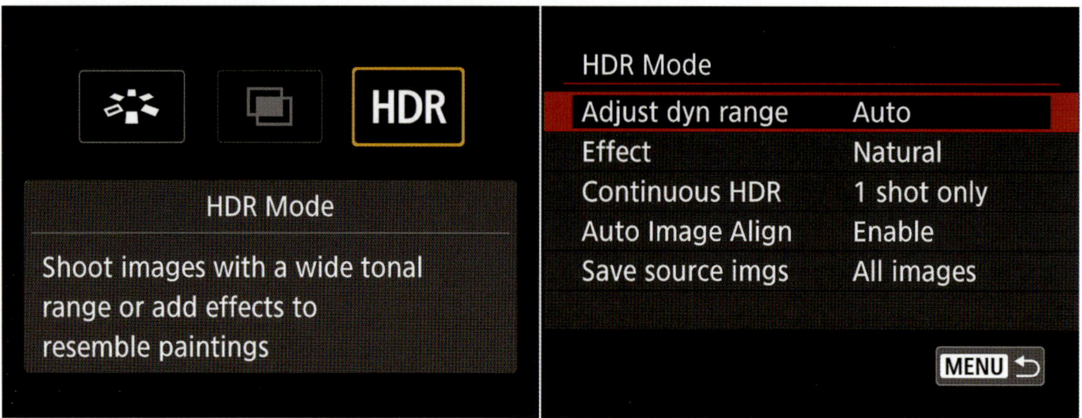

Figure 4.19 Press the Creative Photo button and choose HDR mode (left). The HDR Mode menu has five entries (right).

This menu has five separate entries:

- **Adjust Dynamic Range.** There are five choices in this entry. Select Disable HDR to turn HDR completely off. The others select the number of stops of dynamic range improvement the HDR feature will provide. Choose Auto to allow the 5D Mark IV to examine your scene and select an appropriate EV range. As you gain experience you might want to select the range yourself, in order to achieve a particular look. You can choose plus/minus 1, 2, or 3 EV.

- **Effect.** If you've worked with HDR utilities (such as Photomatix) in the past, you know that various parameters can be adjusted while combining HDR images to produce various effects. These include the amount of color saturation (the "richness" of the hues); the boldness of the edge transitions between portions of the image (producing mild to distinct outlines); brightness of the resulting image; and contrast/tone. Various combinations of these settings produce what can only be called special effects. Select from what Canon terms Natural, Art Standard, Art Vivid, Art Bold, or Art Embossed. Note that these effects are *added* to the settings of any Picture Style currently in use.

- **Continuous HDR.** Choose 1 Shot Only if you plan to take just a single HDR exposure and want the feature disabled automatically thereafter, or Every Shot to continue using HDR mode for all subsequent exposures until you turn it off.

- **Auto Image Align.** HDR images are ideally produced with the camera on a tripod, in order to reduce the ghosting effects from a series of pictures that each aren't perfectly aligned with the other. You can choose Enable to have the camera attempt to align all three HDR exposures, or select Disable when using a tripod. The success of the automatic alignment will vary, depending on the shutter speed used (higher is better), and the amount of camera movement (less is better!).

■ **Save Source Images.** When the 5D Mark IV has finished creating its HDR image from your three shots, you can choose to save all the images on your memory card (so you can manually combine them later or perform other manipulations using your image editor). Or, you can elect to save your final HDR image only. You might prefer that choice to save card space, reduce the number of images you won't be using anyway, or if shooting a lot of HDR and are confident that the camera's results will suit your needs.

SPECIAL HDR EFFECTS

The Effect parameters generate five different special effects (see Figure 4.20):

■ **Natural.** Provides the most useful range of highlight and shadow details.

■ **Art Standard.** Offers a great deal of highlight and shadow detail, but with lower overall contrast and outlines accentuated, making the image look more like a painting. Saturation, bold outline, and brightness are adjusted to the default levels, and tonal range is lower in contrast.

■ **Art Vivid.** Similar to Art Standard, but saturation is boosted to produce richer colors, and the bold outlines are not as strong, producing a poster-like effect.

■ **Art Bold.** Even higher saturation than Art Vivid, with emphasized edge transitions, producing what Canon calls an "oil painting" effect.

■ **Art Embossed.** Reduces saturation, darker tones, and lower contrast, and gives the image a faded, aged look. The edge transitions are brighter or darker to emphasize them.

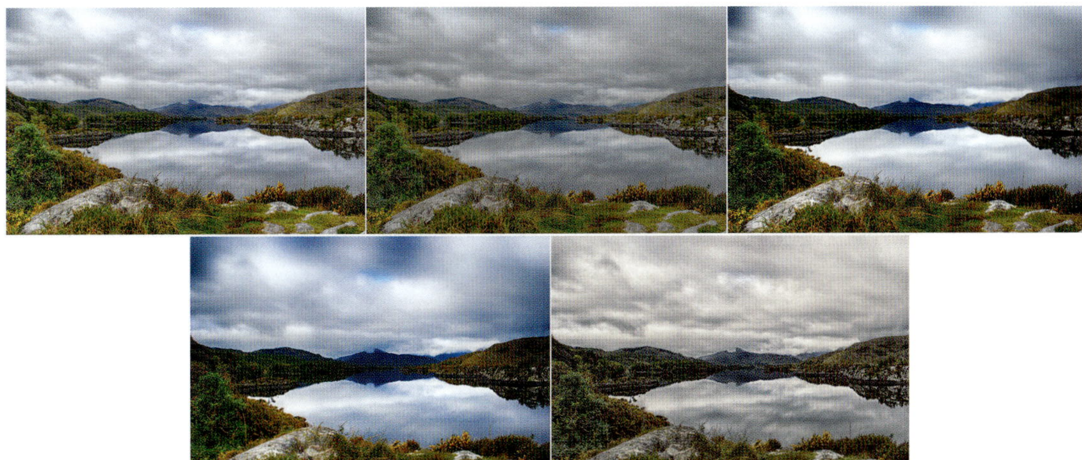

Figure 4.20 Top row (left to right): Natural, Art Standard, Art Vivid; bottom row: Art Bold, Art Embossed.

Bracketing and Merge to HDR

HDR (high dynamic range) photography was, for awhile, an incredibly popular fad. There are even entire books that do nothing but tell you how to shoot HDR images. Everywhere you looked there were overprocessed, garish HDR images that had little relationship to reality. I've been able to resist the temptation to overdo my landscape and travel photography (unlike the deliberately awful example I created for Figure 4.21). The phony-looking skies, the unnatural halos that appear at the edges of some objects, and the weird textures are usually a giveaway. My rule of thumb is that, if you can tell it's HDR, it's been done wrong—unless your intent was to show off what HDR can do.

The technique does have its uses, especially if done subtly, or as a special effect. That's what I was looking for when I shot Alastair Greene, guitarist for the Alan Parsons Project for Figure 4.22. I wanted an edgy, posterlike quality, and so applied HDR liberally, but with the hope that the effect might not be evident on first glance.

Although the 5D Mark IV does have its built-in HDR feature, you can usually get much better, more tasteful results if you create your high dynamic range images manually. You can use a tool such as Photoshop's Merge to HDR Pro feature, a stand-alone HDR utility, or a third-party Photoshop plug-in.

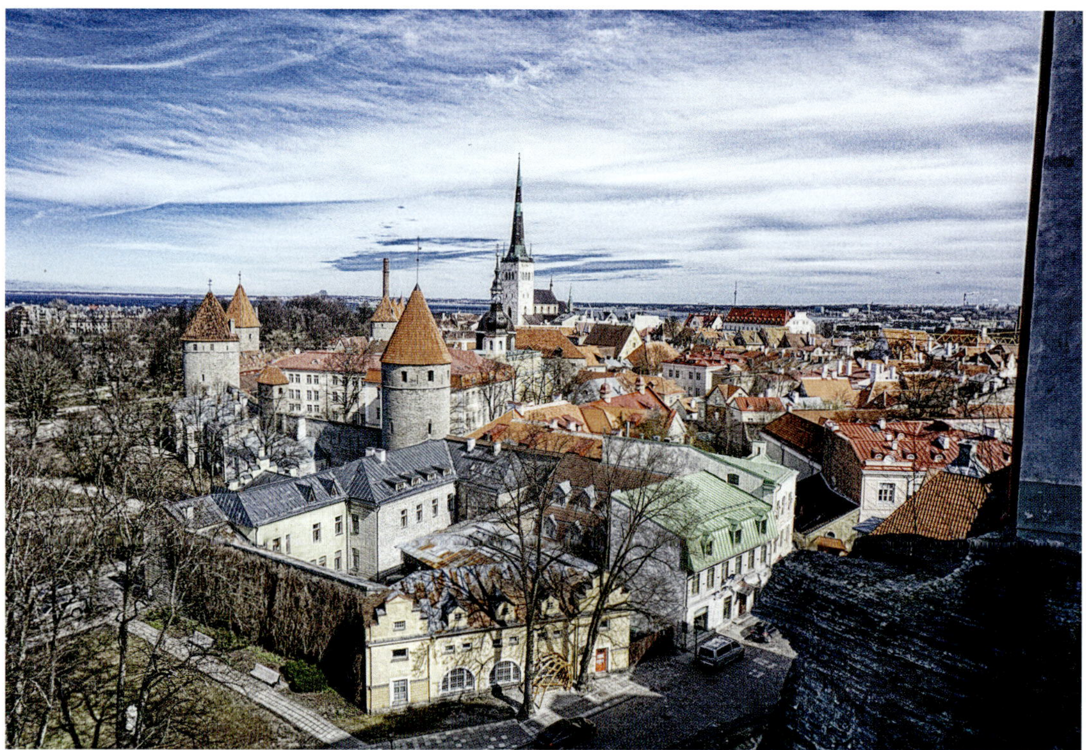

Figure 4.21 A deliberately overcooked HDR photo.

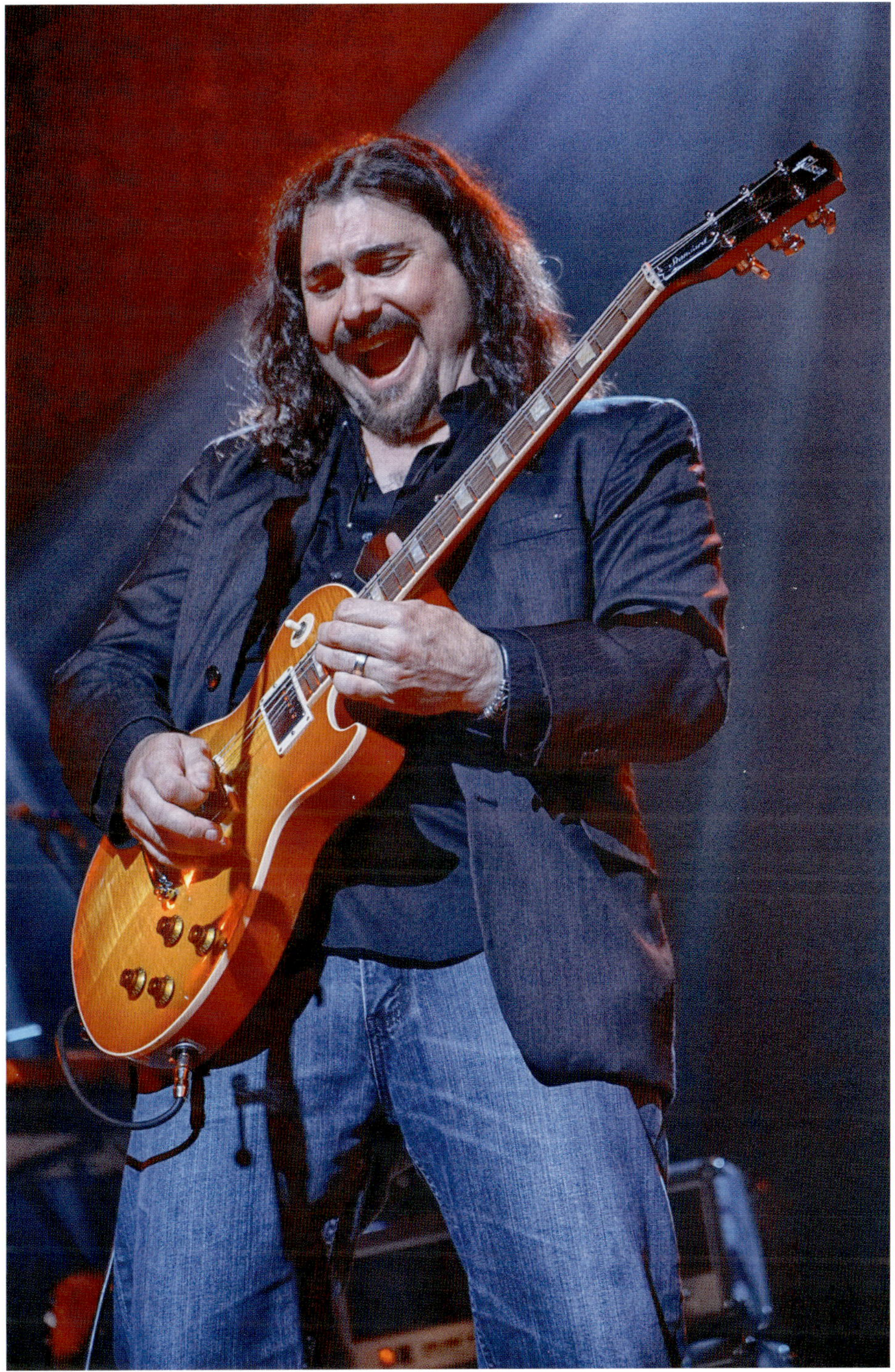

Figure 4.22 In this case, HDR added a desired posterlike effect.

When you're using Merge to HDR Pro in Adobe Photoshop (similar functions are available in other programs, including the Mac/PC utility Photomatix [www.hdrsoft.com; free to try, $39–$99 to buy, depending on the version you select]), you'd take and combine several pictures. As I mentioned earlier, one would be exposed for the shadows, one for the highlights, and perhaps one for the midtones. Then, you'd use the Merge to HDR command (or the equivalent in other software) to combine all of the images into one HDR image that integrates the well-exposed sections of each version. You can use the camera's bracketing feature to produce those images.

The next steps show you how to combine the separate exposures into one merged high dynamic range image. The sample images in Figure 4.23 show the results you can get from a three-shot (manually) bracketed sequence. The images should be as identical as possible, except for exposure.

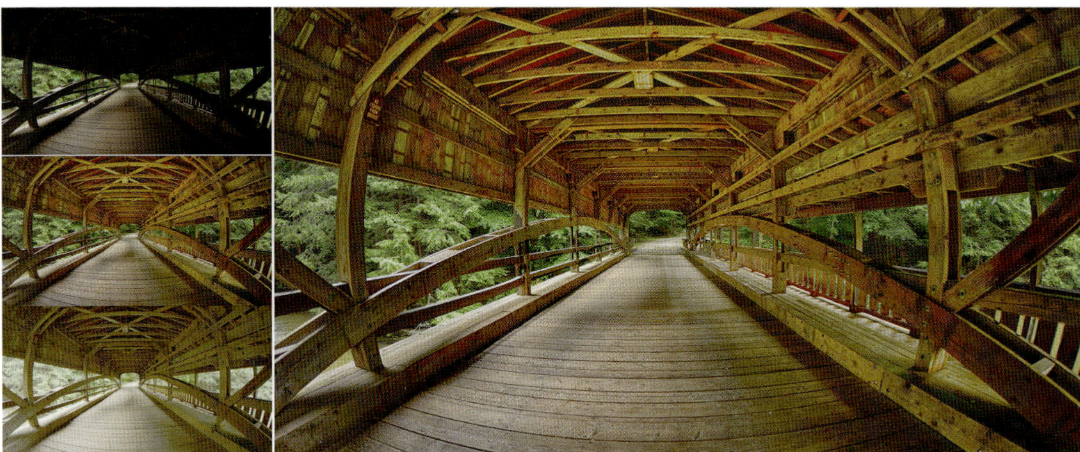

Figure 4.23 Three bracketed photos should look like this (left). The finished image is shown at right.

So, as with HDR mode, it's a good idea to mount the 5D Mark IV on a tripod, use a remote release, and take all the exposures at once. Just follow these steps:

1. **Set up the camera.** Mount the 5D Mark IV on a tripod.

2. **Choose an f/stop and Av mode.** Select an aperture that will provide a correct exposure at your initial settings for the series of bracketed shots. *And then leave this adjustment alone!* You don't want the aperture to change for your series, as that would change the depth-of-field, and, subtly, the size of some elements of the image as they move more or less out of focus. You want the 5D Mark IV to adjust exposure *only* using the shutter speed.

3. **Choose manual focus.** You don't want the focus to change between shots, so set the 5D Mark IV to manual focus, and carefully focus your shot.

4. **Choose RAW exposures.** Set the camera to take RAW files, which will give you the widest range of tones in your images.

5. **Set up your bracketed set.** Use the instructions earlier in this chapter to set the number of bracketed images you take, and the increment between them. After you've created your first few manual HDR photos, you'll learn to judge what increment is best (larger isn't always better). However, the more shots you have to work with, the better your results can be.

6. **Take your photos.** With the camera in continuous shooting mode, press the button on the remote (or carefully press the shutter release or use the self-timer) and take the set of bracketed exposures.

7. **Continue with the Merge to HDR Pro steps listed next.** You can also use a different program, such as Photomatix, if you know how to use it.

The next steps show you how to combine the separate exposures into one merged high dynamic range image.

1. **Copy your images to your computer.** If you use an application to transfer the files to your computer, make sure it does not make any adjustments to brightness, contrast, or exposure. You want the real raw information for Merge to HDR Pro to work with.

2. **Activate Merge to HDR Pro.** Choose File > Automate > Merge to HDR Pro.

3. **Select the photos to be merged.** Use the Browse feature to locate and select your photos to be merged. You'll note a checkbox that can be used to automatically align the images if they were not taken with the camera mounted on a rock-steady support. This will adjust for any slight movement of the camera that might have occurred when you changed exposure settings.

4. **Choose parameters (optional).** The first time you use Merge to HDR Pro, you can let the program work with its default parameters. Once you've played with the feature a few times, you can read the Adobe help files and learn more about the options than I can present in this non-software-oriented camera guide.

5. **Click OK.** The merger begins.

6. **Save.** Once HDR merge has done its thing, save the file to your computer.

What if you don't have the opportunity, inclination, or skills to create several images at different exposures, as described? If you shoot in RAW format, you can still use Merge to HDR, working with a *single* original image file. What you do is import the image into Photoshop several times, using Adobe Camera Raw to create multiple copies of the file at different exposure levels.

For example, you'd create one copy that's too dark, so the shadows lose detail, but the highlights are preserved. Create another copy with the shadows intact and allow the highlights to wash out. Then, you can use Merge to HDR to combine the two and end up with a finished image that has the extended dynamic range you're looking for. (This concludes the image-editing portion of the chapter. We now return you to our alternate sponsor: photography.)

Fixing Exposures with Histograms

Your 5D Mark IV's histograms are a simplified display of the numbers of pixels at each of 256 brightness levels, producing an interesting mountain range effect. Although separate charts may be provided for brightness and the red, green, and blue channels, when you first start using histograms, you'll want to concentrate on the brightness histogram.

Each vertical line in the graph represents the number of pixels in the image for each brightness value, from 0 (black) on the left to 255 (white) on the right, although the resolution of the LCD monitor isn't sufficient to actually show each of the 256 lines. The vertical axis measures that number of pixels at each level. The 5D Mark IV provides a "live" histogram on the screen when using Live View mode, and offers two different histogram views in playback mode when using the default shooting information display with a brightness histogram at upper right (Figure 4.24, left). You can scroll down to view a screen with an RGB histogram added (Figure 4.24, right). The former shows a simple brightness/luminance histogram, while the Histogram display allows you to see brightness as well as separate red, green, and blue channel histograms.

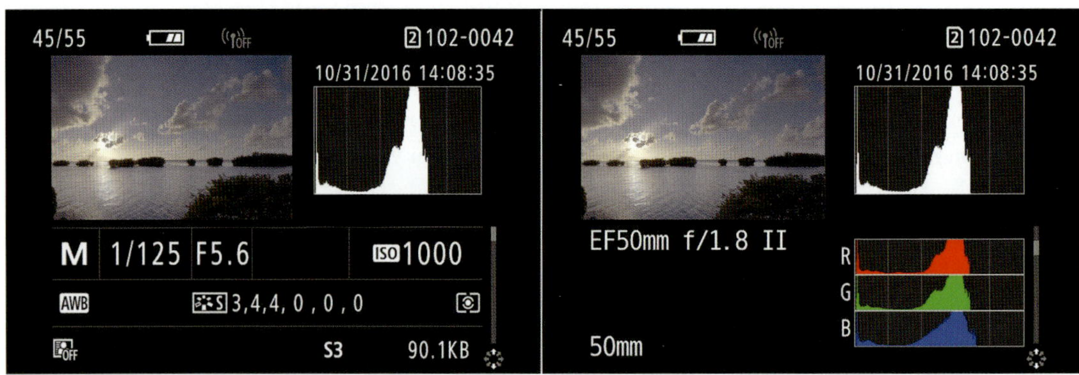

Figure 4.24 Shooting information display, with luminance histogram (left); Histogram display with luminance, red, green, and blue histograms (right).

Histograms and Contrast

Although histograms are most often used to fine-tune exposure, you can glean other information from them, such as the relative contrast of the image. Figure 4.25 shows a histogram representing an image having normal contrast. In such an image, most of the pixels are spread across the image, with a healthy distribution of tones throughout the midtone section of the graph. That large peak at the right side of the graph represents all those light tones in the sky. A normal-contrast image you shoot may have less sky area, and less of a peak at the right side, but notice that very few pixels hug the right edge of the histogram, indicating that the lightest tones are not being clipped because they are off the chart.

With a lower-contrast image, like the one shown in Figure 4.26, the basic shape of the previous histogram will remain recognizable, but gradually will be compressed together to cover a smaller area of the gray spectrum. The squished shape of the histogram is caused by all the grays in the original image being represented by a limited number of gray tones in a smaller range of the scale.

Instead of the darkest tones of the image reaching into the black end of the spectrum and the whitest tones extending to the lightest end, there is a small gap at either end. Consequently, the blackest areas of the scene are now represented by a light gray, and the whites by a somewhat lighter gray. The overall contrast of the image is reduced. Because all the darker tones are actually a middle gray or lighter, the scene in this version of the photo appears lighter as well.

Figure 4.25
This image has fairly normal contrast, even though there is a peak of light tones at the right side representing the sky.

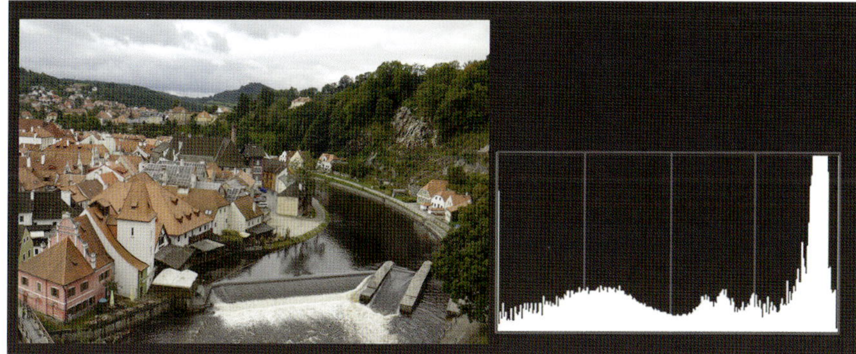

Figure 4.26
This low-contrast image has all the tones squished into one section of the grayscale.

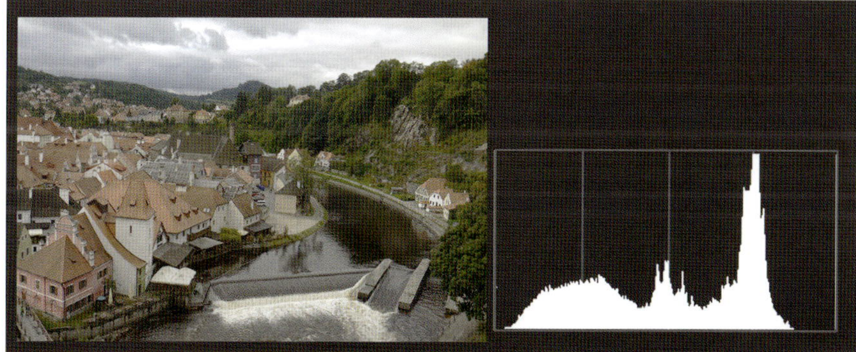

Figure 4.27
A high-contrast image produces a histogram in which the tones are spread out.

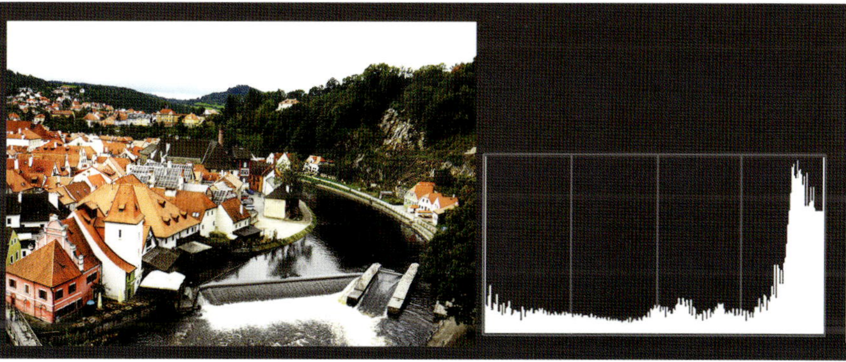

Going in the other direction, increasing the contrast of an image produces a histogram like the one shown in Figure 4.27. In this case, the tonal range is now spread over the entire width of the chart, but, except for the bright sky (which you can see peaks at right), there is not much variation in the middle tones; the mountain "peaks" are not very high. When you stretch the grayscale in both directions like this, the darkest tones become darker (that may not be possible) and the lightest tones become lighter (ditto). In fact, shades that might have been gray before can change to black or white as they are moved toward either end of the scale.

The effect of increasing contrast may be to move some tones off either end of the scale altogether, while spreading the remaining grays over a smaller number of locations on the spectrum. That's exactly the case in the example shown. The number of possible tones is smaller and the image appears harsher.

Understanding Histograms

The important thing to remember when working with the histogram display in your 5D Mark IV is that changing the exposure does *not* change the contrast of an image. The curves illustrated in the previous three examples remain exactly the same shape when you increase or decrease exposure. I repeat: The proportional distribution of grays shown in the histogram doesn't change when exposure changes; it is neither stretched nor compressed. However, the tones as a whole are moved toward one end of the scale or the other, depending on whether you're increasing or decreasing exposure. You'll be able to see that in some illustrations that follow.

So, as you reduce exposure, tones gradually move to the black end (and off the scale), while the reverse is true when you increase exposure. The contrast within the image is changed only to the extent that some of the tones can no longer be represented when they are moved off the scale.

To change the *contrast* of an image, you must do one of the following things:

- **Change the 5D Mark IV's contrast setting** using the menu system. You'll find these adjustments in your camera's Picture Styles, as explained in Chapter 11.
- **Use your camera's tone "booster."** The Highlight Tone Priority and Auto Lighting Optimizer features, described in Chapter 11, can also adjust contrast.
- **Alter the contrast of the scene itself,** for example, by using a fill light or reflectors to add illumination to shadows that are too dark.
- **Attempt to adjust contrast in post-processing** using your image editor or RAW file converter. You may use features such as Levels or Curves (in Photoshop, Photoshop Elements, and many other image editors), or work with HDR software to cherry-pick the best values in shadows and highlights from multiple images.

Of the four of these, the third—changing the contrast of the scene—is the most desirable, because attempting to fix contrast by fiddling with the tonal values is unlikely to be a perfect remedy. However, adding a little contrast can be successful because you can discard some tones to make the image more contrasty. However, the opposite is much more difficult. An overly contrasty image rarely can be fixed, because you can't add information that isn't there in the first place.

What you *can* do is adjust the exposure so that the tones *that are already present in the scene* are captured correctly. Figure 4.28 shows the histogram for an image that is badly underexposed. You can guess from the shape of the histogram that many of the dark tones to the left of the graph have been clipped off. There's plenty of room on the right side for additional pixels to reside without having them become overexposed. So, you can increase the exposure (either by changing the f/stop or shutter speed, or by adding an EV value) to produce the corrected histogram shown in Figure 4.29.

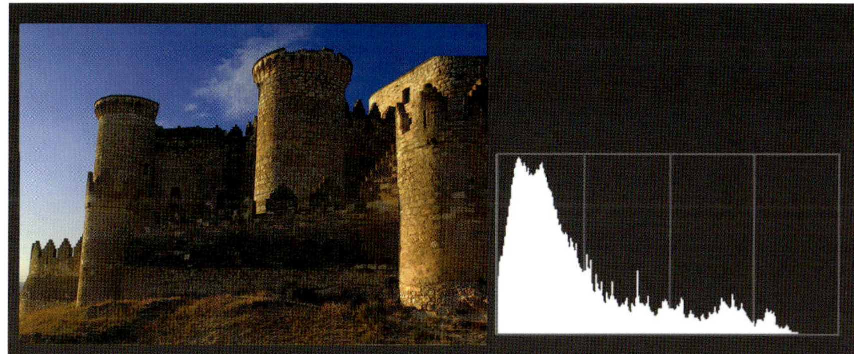

Figure 4.28

A histogram of an underexposed image may look like this.

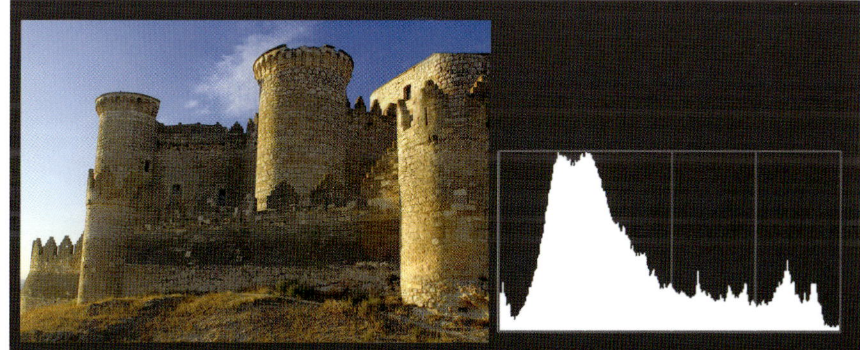

Figure 4.29

Adding exposure will produce a histogram like this one.

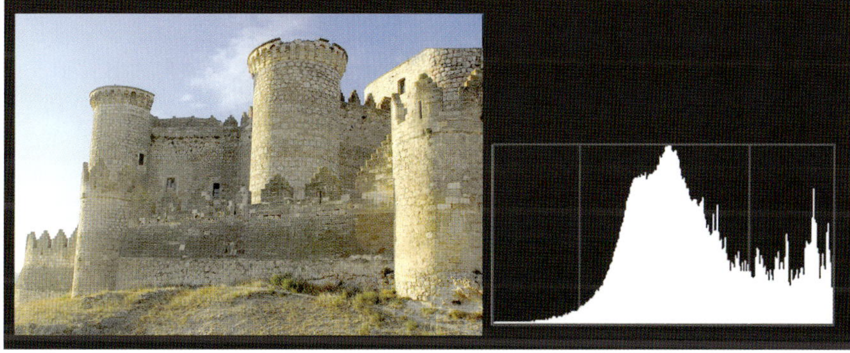

Figure 4.30

A histogram of an overexposed image will show clipping at the right side.

Conversely, if your histogram looks like the one shown in Figure 4.30, with bright tones pushed off the right edge of the chart, you have an overexposed image, and you can correct it by reducing exposure. In addition to the histogram, the 5D Mark IV has its Highlight Alert option (found in the Playback 3 menu), which, when activated, shows areas that are overexposed with flashing tones (often called "blinkies") in the review screen. Depending on the importance of this "clipped" detail, you can adjust exposure or leave it alone. For example, if all the dark-coded areas in the review are in a background that you care little about, you can forget about them and not change the exposure, but if such areas appear in facial details of your subject, you may want to make some adjustments.

A traditional technique for optimizing exposure is called "expose to the right," (ETTR) which involves adding exposure to push the histogram's curve toward the right side *but not far enough to clip off highlights.* The rationale for this method is that extra shadow detail will be produced with a minimum increase in noise, especially in the shadow areas. It's said that half of a digital sensor's response lies in the brightest areas of an image, and so require the least amount of amplification (which is one way to increase digital noise). ETTR can work, as long as you're able to capture a satisfactory amount of information in the shadows.

Exposing to the Right

It's easier to understand exposing to the right if you divide the histogram into fifths, as you see on the display used by the 5D Mark IV. And, for the sake of simplicity and smaller numbers, with a 14-bit file like that produced with your camera's ordinary RAW file, the maximum number of tones that can be captured is 16,383. However, each fifth of the histogram does *not* encompass 3,277 tones (one-fifth of 16,384, rounded up).

Instead, the right-most fifth, the highlights, accounts for 8,192 different captured tones. Moving toward the left, the next fifth represents 4,096, followed by 2,048 levels, 1,024 levels, and, in the left-most section where the deepest shadows reside, only 512 different tones are captured. When processing your RAW file, there are only 512 tones to recover in the shadows (compared to the whopping 8,192 in the highlights), which is why boosting/amplifying them as you raise the ISO increases noise. (As I mentioned earlier, the effect is most noticeable in the red and blue channels; your sensor's Bayer array has twice as many green-sensitive pixels as red or blue.)

Instead, you want to add exposure—as long as you don't push highlights off the right edge of the histogram—to brighten the shadows. Because there are 8,192 tones available in the highlights, even if the RAW image *looks* overexposed, it's possible to use your RAW converter's Exposure slider (such as the one found in Adobe Camera Raw) to bring back detail captured in that surplus of tones in the highlights. This procedure is the exact opposite of what was recommended for film of the transparency variety—it was fairly easy to retrieve detail from shadows by pumping more light through them when processing the image, while even small amounts of extra exposure blew out highlights. You'll often find that the range of tones in your image is so great that there is no way to keep your histogram from spilling over into the left and right edges, costing you both highlight and shadow detail. Exposing to the right may not work in such situations. A second school of thought recommends *reducing* exposure to bring back the highlights, or "exposing to the left." You would then attempt to recover shadow detail in an image editor, using tools like Adobe Camera Raw's Exposure slider. But remember, above all, that this procedure will also boost noise in the shadows, and so the technique should be used with caution. In most cases, exposing to the right is your best bet.

The more you work with histograms, the more useful they become. One of the first things that histogram veterans notice is that it's possible to overexpose one channel even if the overall exposure appears to be correct. For example, flower photographers soon discover that it's really, really difficult to get a good picture of a red rose. The exposure and luminance histogram may look okay—but there's no detail in the rose's petals. Looking at the RGB histograms can show why: the red channel is probably blown out. If you look at the red histogram, you'll probably see a peak at the right edge that indicates that highlight information has been lost. In fact, the green channel may be blown, too, and so the green parts of the flower also lack detail. Only the blue channel's histogram would typically be entirely contained within the boundaries of the chart, and, on first glance, the white luminance histogram at top of the column of graphs seems fairly normal.

Any of the primary channels, red, green, or blue, can blow out all by themselves, although bright reds seem to be the most common problem area. More difficult to diagnose are overexposed tones in one of the "in-between" hues on the color wheel. Overexposed yellows (which are very common) will be shown by blowouts in *both* the red and green channels. Too-bright cyans will manifest as excessive blue and green highlights, while overexposure in the red and blue channels reduces detail in magenta colors. As you gain experience, you'll be able to see exactly how anomalies in the RGB channels translate into poor highlights and murky shadows.

The only way to correct for color channel blowouts is to reduce exposure. As I mentioned earlier, you might want to consider filling in the shadows with additional light to keep them from becoming too dark when you decrease exposure. In practice, you'll want to monitor the red channel most closely, followed by the blue channel, and slightly decrease exposure to see if that helps. Because of the way our eyes perceive color, we are more sensitive to variations in green, so green channel blowouts are less of a problem, unless your main subject is heavily colored in that hue. If you plan on photographing a frog hopping around on your front lawn, you'll want to be extra careful to preserve detail in the green channel, using bracketing or other exposure techniques outlined in this chapter.

While you can often recover poorly exposed photos in your image editor, your best bet is to arrive at the correct exposure in the camera, minimizing the tweaks that you have to make in post-processing.

5

Mastering the
Mysteries of Autofocus

Capturing a compelling photograph involves a lot more than just correct exposure. The right tonal range, proper white balance, good color, and other factors all can help elevate your image from good to exceptional. But one of the most important and, sometimes, the most frustrating aspects of shooting with a highly automated—yet fully adjustable—camera like the EOS 5D Mark IV is achieving sharp focus. Your camera has lots of AF controls and options, and new users and veterans alike can quickly become confused. In this chapter, I'm going to clear up the mysteries of autofocus and show you exactly how to use your 5D Mark IV's AF features to their fullest. I'll even tell you when to abandon the autofocus system and turn to the ancient art of manual focus, too.

How Focus Works

This section describes the differences between contrast detection and phase detection autofocus, and details how linear and cross-type AF sensors work in the 5D Mark IV's advanced focusing system. Even those who are familiar with these concepts should still read this section carefully, because Canon has made some revolutionary changes in AF with the introduction of its Dual Pixel CMOS AF sensor design in which every single pixel used for autofocus is split into two photodiodes that can be used to provide advanced autofocus features in Live View and Movie modes.

Although Canon added autofocus capabilities in the 1980s, back in the day of film cameras, prior to that focusing was always done manually. Honest. Even though viewfinders were bigger and brighter than they are today, special focusing screens, magnifiers, and other gadgets were often used to help the photographer achieve correct focus. Imagine what it must have been like to focus manually under demanding, fast-moving conditions such as sports photography.

Manual focusing was problematic because our eyes and brains have poor memory for correct focus, which is why your eye doctor must shift back and forth between sets of lenses and ask "Does that look sharper—or was it sharper before?" in determining your correct prescription. Similarly, manual focusing involves jogging the focus ring back and forth as you go from almost in focus, to sharp focus, to almost focused again. The little clockwise and counterclockwise arcs decrease in size until you've zeroed in on the point of correct focus. What you're looking for is the image with the most contrast between the edges of elements in the image.

The camera also looks for these contrast differences among pixels to determine relative sharpness. There are two ways that sharp focus is determined: phase detection and contrast detection. The camera also looks for these contrast differences among pixels to determine relative sharpness. To get the most from your camera, you really need to understand both. We'll start with the easier of the two: contrast detection.

Contrast Detection

Contrast detection is a slower mode and was used exclusively by Canon dSLRs in Live View and Movie modes until relatively recently, when Canon added a small number of special pixels to the sensor of its most recent cameras. That small number allowed a limited type of phase detection autofocus. The Dual Pixel CMOS AF used by the Canon 5D Mark IV goes much further, as I'll explain later in this chapter. To appreciate the innovation, you need to understand traditional contrast detection first.

The relatively slow contrast detection method was necessary because, to allow live viewing of the sensor image, the camera's mirror has to be flipped up out of the way so that the illumination from the lens can continue through the open shutter to the sensor. Your view through the viewfinder is obstructed, of course, and there is no partially silvered mirror to reflect some light down to the autofocus sensors. So, an alternate means of autofocus must be used in Live View, and that method has traditionally been *contrast detection.* Contrast detection is a bit easier to understand and is illustrated by Figure 5.1, which uses an extreme enlargement of a shot of some wood siding (actually a

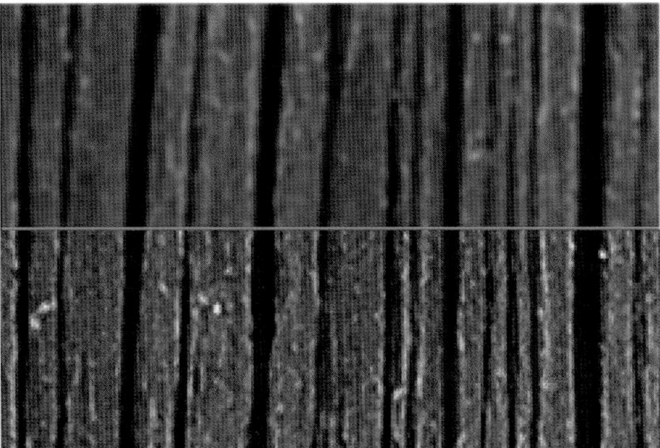

Figure 5.1 Focus in contrast detection mode evaluates the increase in contrast in the edges of subjects, starting with a blurry image (top) and producing a sharp, contrasty image (bottom).

19th century outhouse). At top in the figure, the transitions between pixels are soft and blurred. When the image is brought into focus (bottom), the transitions are sharp and clear. Although this example is a bit exaggerated so you can see the results on the printed page, it's easy to understand that when maximum contrast in a subject is achieved, it can be deemed to be in sharp focus.

As I noted, contrast detection is used in Live View and Movie mode, even when Dual Pixel CMOS AF is also active. (In effect, you get two AF systems from one sensor.) Contrast detection works best and is very accurate with static subjects, but it is inherently slower and not well suited for tracking moving objects. Contrast detection works less well than phase detection in dim light, because its accuracy is determined by its ability to detect variations in brightness and contrast. You'll find that contrast detection works better with faster lenses, too, because larger lens openings admit more light that can be used by the sensor to measure contrast.

Phase Detection

Like all digital SLRs that use an optical viewfinder and mirror system to preview an image (that is, when not in Live View mode), the Canon EOS 5D Mark IV calculates focus using what is called a *passive phase detection* system. It's passive in the sense that the ambient illumination in a scene (or that illumination augmented with a focus-assist beam) is used to determine correct focus. (An *active* phase detection system might employ a laser, sonar, or other special signal, and is not currently used by any digital SLR camera.) The system used in the Mark IV is called a *high-density reticular* auto-focus system. It's high density because there are now 61 different AF sensors, and reticular just means that the AF pattern forms a network.

Parts of the image from two opposite sides of the lens are directed down to the floor of the camera's mirror box, where an autofocus sensor array resides; the rest of the illumination from the lens bounces upward toward the optical viewfinder system and the autoexposure sensors. Figure 5.2 is a wildly over-simplified illustration that may help you visualize what is happening.

As light emerges from the rear element of the lens, most of it is reflected upward toward the focusing screen, where the relative sharp focus (or lack of it) is displayed (and which can be used to evaluate manual focus). It then bounces off two more reflective surfaces in the pentaprism (in the 5D Mark IV; other cameras may use a less expensive and less bright *pentamirror* system instead), emerging at the optical viewfinder correctly oriented left/right and up/down. (The image emerges from the lens reversed.) Some of the illumination is directed to the autoexposure sensor at the top of the penta-prism housing.

SIMPLIFICATION MADE OVERLY SIMPLE

To reduce the complexity of the diagram, it doesn't show the actual path of the light passing through the lens, as it converges to the point of focus. That point is either the viewfinder screen when the mirror is down or the sensor plane when the mirror is flipped up and the shutter has opened. Nor does it show the path of the light directed to the autoexposure sensor. Only two of the pairs of autofocus microlenses are shown, and greatly enlarged so you can see their approximate position. All we're concerned about here is how light reaches the autofocus sensor.

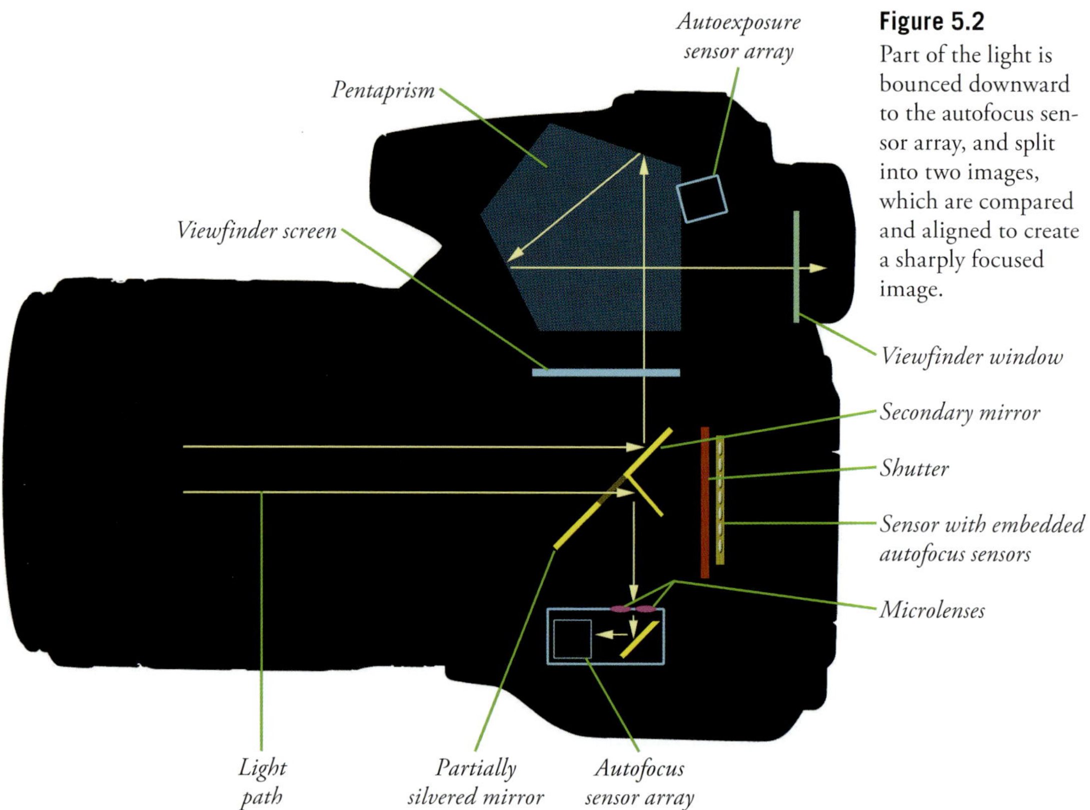

Figure 5.2
Part of the light is bounced downward to the autofocus sensor array, and split into two images, which are compared and aligned to create a sharply focused image.

A small portion of the illumination passes through the partially silvered center of the main mirror, and is directed downward to the autofocus sensor array, which includes 61 separate autofocus "detectors." Conceptually, these function as shown in Figure 5.3, another simplified illustration. The illumination arrives from opposite sides of the lens surface and is directed through separate microlenses, producing two half-images. These images are compared with each other, much like (actually, *exactly* like) a two-window rangefinder used in surveying, weaponry, and non-SLR cameras like the venerable Leica M film models.

When the image is out of focus—or out of phase—as in Figure 5.4 (top), the two halves, each representing a slightly different view from opposite sides of the lens, don't line up. Sharp focus is achieved when the images are "in phase," and aligned, as in Figure 5.4 (bottom).

As with any rangefinder-like function, accuracy is better when the "base length" between the two images is larger. (Think back to your high school trigonometry; you could calculate a distance more accurately when the separation between the two points where the angles were measured was greater.) For that reason, phase detection autofocus is more accurate with larger (wider) lens openings than with smaller lens openings, and may not work at all when the f/stop is smaller than f/5.6 or f/8. Obviously, the "opposite" edges of the lens opening are farther apart with a lens having an f/2.8 maximum aperture than with one that has a smaller, f/5.6 maximum f/stop, and the base line is

Figure 5.3

In phase detection, parts of an image are split in two and compared.

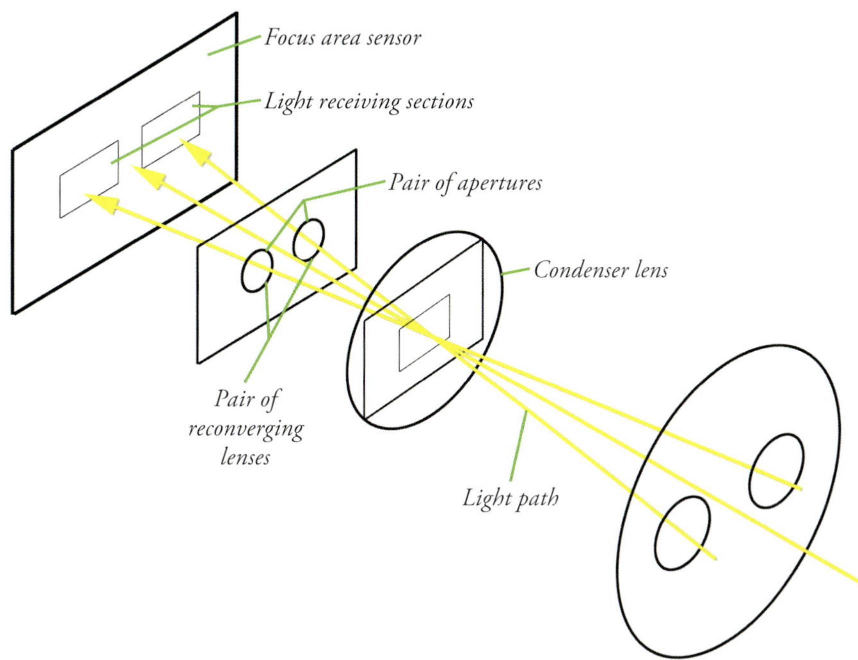

Figure 5.4

When the image is in focus, the two halves of the image align, as with a rangefinder.

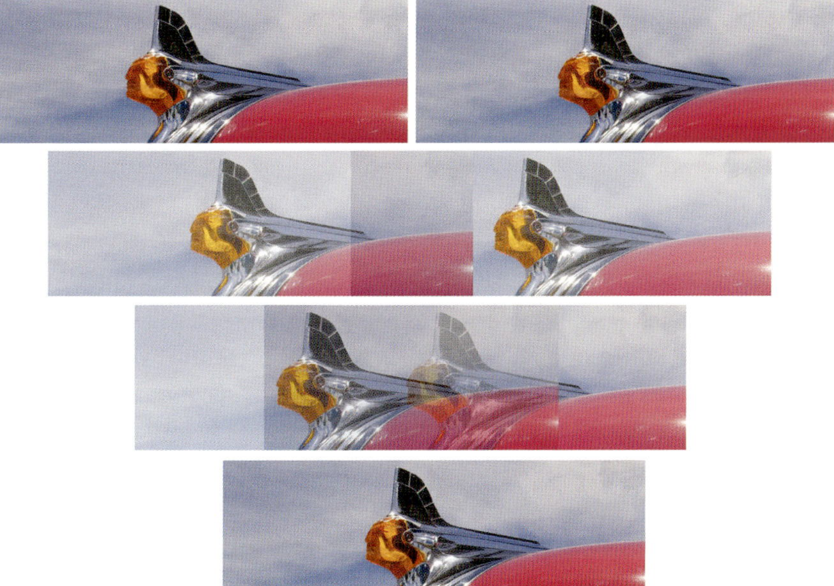

much longer. The 5D Mark IV is able to perform these comparisons and then move the lens elements directly to the point of correct focus very quickly, in milliseconds.

Unfortunately, while the 5D Mark IV's focus system finds it easy to measure degrees of apparent focus at each of the focus points in the viewfinder, it doesn't really know with any certainty *which* object should be in sharpest focus. Is it the closest object? The subject in the center? Something lurking *behind* the closest subject? A person standing over at the side of the picture? Many of the techniques for using autofocus effectively involve telling the EOS 5D Mark IV exactly what it should be focusing on, by choosing a focus zone or by allowing the camera to choose a focus zone for you. I'll address that topic shortly.

Dual Pixel CMOS AF

So far, we've explored how the 5D Mark IV autofocuses when using the optical viewfinder. A completely different AF system comes into play when you're capturing stills or movies in live view. Understanding contrast and phase detection helps you appreciate the marvel that is Canon's Dual Pixel CMOS AF system. Used in Live View mode while shooting stills and movies, it works much more quickly than the camera's more traditional contrast detection system alone.

An array of special pixels, which cover 80 percent of the frame horizontally and vertically, provide the same type of split-image rangefinder phase detection AF that is available when using the optical viewfinder. The most important aspect of the system is that it doesn't rob the camera of any imaging resolution. It would have been possible to place AF sensors *between* the pixels used to capture the image, but that would leave the sensor with less area with which to capture light. Keep in mind that CMOS sensors, unlike earlier CCD sensors, have more on-board circuitry which already consumes some of the light-gathering area. Microlenses are placed above each photosensitive site to focus incoming illumination on the sensor and to correct for the oblique angles from which some photons may approach the imager. (Older lenses, designed for film, are the worst offenders in terms of emitting light at severely oblique angles; newer "digital" lenses do a better job of directing photons onto the sensor plane with a less "slanted" approach.)

With the Dual Pixel CMOS AF system, the same photosites capture both image and autofocus information. Each pixel is divided into two photodiodes, facing left and right when the camera is held in horizontal orientation (or above and below each other in vertical orientation; either works fine for autofocus purposes). Each pair functions as a separate AF sensor, allowing a special integrated circuit to process the raw autofocus information before sending it on to the 5D Mark IV's digital image processor, which handles both AF and image capture. For the latter, the information grabbed by *both* photodiodes is combined, so that the full photosensitive area of the sensor pixel is used to capture the image.

While traditional contrast detection frequently involves frustrating "hunting" as the camera continually readjusts the focus plane trying to find the position of maximum contrast, adding Dual Pixel CMOS AF phase detection allows the 5D Mark IV to focus smoothly, which is important for speed, and essential when shooting movies (where all that hunting is unfortunately captured for posterity). Movie Servo AF tracking is improved, allowing shooting movies of subjects in motion. The system works with (at this writing) 103 different lenses, both current and previously available optics, and works especially well with lenses that have speedy USM or STM motors. I'll explain the 5D Mark IV's AF operation in live view and movie shooting in more detail in Chapter 15.

An interesting adjunct to the dual pixel autofocus approach is the 5D Mark IV's ability to save Dual Pixel RAW image files, which allow including the rangefinder-like focus information in RAW files that can later be manipulated in Digital Photo Professional to provide focus microadjustment during post-processing, adjustment of bokeh (the out-of-focus regions of a photograph in both foreground and background), and to reduce flare and ghosting effects. The important thing to keep in mind is that while Dual Pixel CMOS AF is active *only* in Live View and Movie modes, only the files captured in Dual Pixel RAW mode can be manipulated, whether you used the optical viewfinder *or* live view.

Cross-Type Focus Point

Returning to the optical viewfinder's AF system, we're going to explore one special aspect next. So far, we've only looked at focus sensors that calculate focus in a single direction. Figure 5.5 (top left and right) illustrates a horizontally oriented linear focus sensor evaluating a subject that is made up, predominantly, of vertical lines. But what does such a sensor do when it encounters a subject that isn't conveniently aligned at right angles to the sensor array? You can see the problem in Figure 5.5 (bottom left), which pictures the same weathered wood siding rotated 90 degrees. The horizontal grain of the wood isn't divided as neatly by the split image, so focusing using phase detection is more difficult. The lines in the grain don't cross the AF sensor at right angles any more.

You can see the "solution" at bottom right in Figure 5.5, in the form of a vertical linear sensor, which does a better job of interpreting horizontal lines. By mixing both types in a focusing system, the vertical sensors could detect differences in horizontal lines, while the horizontal sensors took care of the vertical lines. Both varieties are equally adept at handling *diagonal* lines, which crossed each type of line sensor at a 45-degree angle.

However, a better solution is the use of a *cross-type* sensor, which is a merger of vertical and horizontal linear sensors, thus including sensitivity to horizontal, vertical, and lines at any diagonal angle. In lower light levels, with subjects that are moving, or with subjects that have no pattern and less contrast to begin with, the cross-type sensor not only works faster but can focus subjects that a horizontal- or vertical-only sensor can't handle at all.

In practice, these sensors consist of an *array* of lines and, in the 5D Mark IV, none of them are strictly horizontal or vertical in orientation. Instead, the AF points are arranged as shown at left in Figure 5.6, using what are called *cross-type* sensors that form a plus-sign shape. Of the 5D Mark IV's 61 AF points, 41 of them are potentially cross sensors. The number available will depend on the aspect ratio you select and the lens mounted on your camera (some AF points cannot function in cross mode with certain lenses, as I'll explain shortly). In cross sensor mode, such sensors are a merger of vertical and horizontal linear sensors, thus including sensitivity to horizontal, vertical,

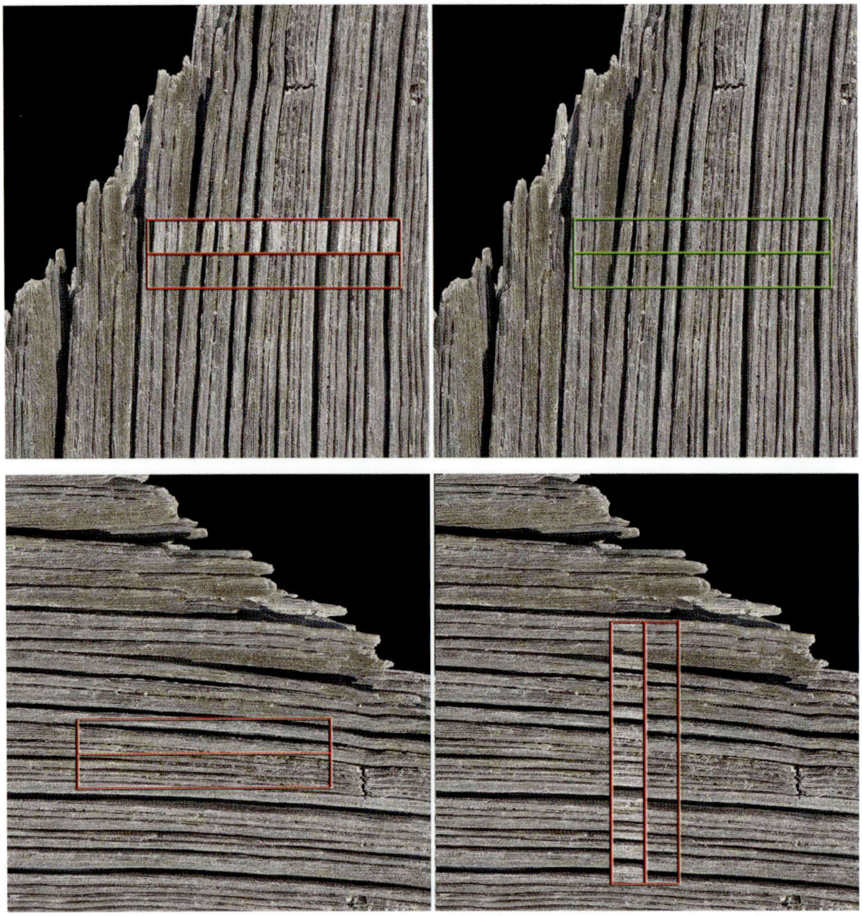

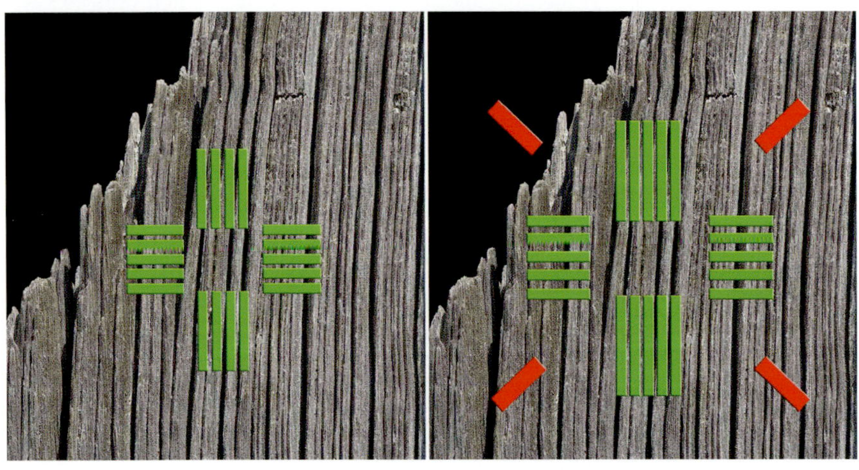

Figure 5.5

A horizontally oriented sensor handles vertical lines easily (top). A horizontal sensor has problems with subjects that have parallel horizontal lines (bottom left). A vertically oriented sensor is really needed for that type of subject (bottom right).

Figure 5.6

Cross-type sensors can achieve sharp focus with horizontal, vertical, and diagonal lines (left). The center focus point (right) has additional diagonal sensors (in red) that function with lenses with an f/2.8 or larger maximum aperture.

and lines at any diagonal angle. In lower light levels, with subjects that are moving, or with subjects that have no pattern and less contrast to begin with, the cross-type sensor not only works faster but can focus subjects that a horizontal- or vertical-only sensor can't handle at all.

All of the 41 AF cross-type sensors function with lenses that have a maximum aperture of f/5.6 or larger (remember that smaller numbers equal larger apertures; f/4 is larger than f/5.6, for example). So, if you're using a lens with an f/stop from, say, f/1.2 through f/5.6, all 41 AF cross-type points will function as cross-type sensors. (Some may function in cross mode with a few f/8 lenses.) If your maximum aperture is even larger—f/2.8 or greater—a column of five *center* AF points will also use a pair of diagonal sensors, represented in red at right in Figure 5.6. Note that the baseline of these diagonal AF points is much larger than that of the green vertically/horizontally oriented sensors. Coupled with the larger baseline of lenses with, say, f/1.2 to f/2.8 maximum apertures, the center AF sensors are significantly more accurate than those at the other 60 locations in the frame. Figure 5.7 shows the layout of each type of sensor.

- **Vertical linear sensors (green).** The system has 20 vertically oriented sensors that are optimized for lenses having a maximum aperture of f/5.6 or larger (that is, f/1.2 to f/5.6). Keep in mind that you may own a lens that offers an f/3.5 maximum aperture at its widest focal length, but only f/5.6 (or smaller) when you crank them out to the telephoto position. In addition, teleconverters rob you of an f/stop or more (which is why an f/4 tele won't autofocus with a 2X converter with certain cameras; its effective maximum f/stop is just f/8). Extension tubes and bellows also decrease the effective maximum aperture.

Luckily, the 5D Mark IV includes some more robust AF sensors that can perform even with lower light levels.

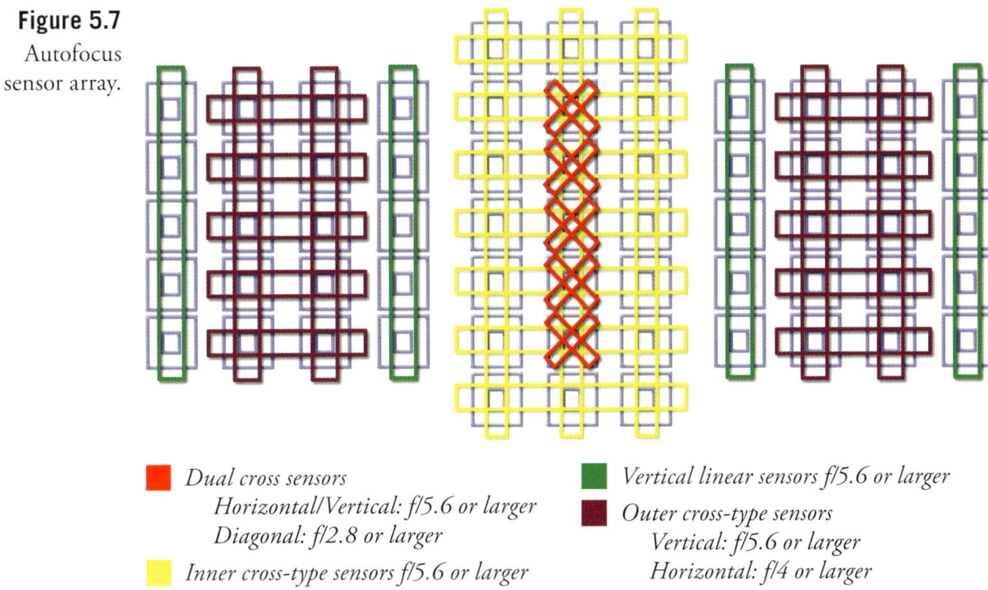

Figure 5.7
Autofocus sensor array.

- **Outer cross-type sensors (purple).** These 20 sensors are located just outside the central focusing area, as shown in Figure 5.7, and are truly a combination of vertical and horizontal sensors, and they operate as if you had separate horizontal and vertical sensors at each position. The vertical component performs like a vertical linear sensor and operates with lenses having a maximum aperture of f/5.6 or larger. The horizontal component requires a maximum aperture of f/4 or greater. So, if you're using a lens with an effective maximum aperture of f/5.6, these perform as if they were vertical linear sensors.

- **Inner cross-type sensors (yellow).** These 16 sensors form a "ring" around the central dual cross sensors, and require lenses with f/5.6 or larger apertures. They perform as if you had both vertical and horizontal sensors, but as both types are active with f/5.6 and faster lenses, you generally won't notice the difference.

- **Dual cross sensors (red).** The remaining five sensors are arrayed in a vertical line in the center of the frame. They consist of sensors of the "inner cross" type (horizontal and vertical arrays used with lenses with f/5.6 or larger apertures), plus each has a second X-shaped diagonal cross sensor component. That component kicks in to add precision when your lens has a maximum aperture of f/2.8 or larger. In other words, these five dual cross sensors are actually inner cross-types with enhanced sensitivity with fast lenses, thanks to the additional diagonal sensor.

    If you don't have or use f/1.2–f/2.8 lenses, you are, in effect, working with 41 cross sensors of two types, and 20 vertical sensors.

Usable AF Points and Lens Groups

While your camera has a mixture of linear, cross, and dual cross sensors, you can elect to use *only* the sensors of the cross variety. Some photographers have found that when shooting subjects with lots of vertical lines in horizontal orientation exclusively, the non-cross (vertical linear) sensors, which are optimized to interpret *horizontal* lines, "interfere" with the focus process. It's a rather esoteric situation, but shows how extensively Canon allows you to fine-tune your 5D Mark IV. Visit the AF 4 menu, choose Selectable AF Point, and choose Only Cross-Type AF Points to disable the vertical sensors. As I'll explain in Chapter 12, you can also choose whether the camera uses all 61 points, 15 points, or just 9 points. Keep in mind that in any autofocus mode, the exact number of sensors and sensor types at work will vary depending on the lens and its maximum aperture.

To help you determine which AF points are active and how they operate, Canon has helpfully divided all of its current lenses into eight different groups, labeled Group A to Group H. If you want to know which group your own lenses belong to, check out the six pages of dense tables on pages 115–125 of the manual furnished with your camera. As much as I favor one-stop shopping, I won't duplicate those tables here; you're likely to need them just once to look up your particular lenses.

- **Groups A–E.** Autofocusing with all 61 points is possible, so you can choose any of the AF area selection modes (described later in this chapter). However, the center row of high-precision dual cross sensors function as ordinary cross sensors with Groups C and E lenses. The tables in the Canon manual provide charts showing the functions of each usable focus point within a particular group.

- **Group F.** With these lenses, autofocusing is available with 47 points, with the 21 points in the three center columns functioning as ordinary cross sensors (dual cross sensor mode is disabled). The remaining 14 points, positioned at the edges of the point array, are disabled and not displayed in the viewfinder when you have one of those lenses mounted.

- **Group G.** Lenses in this group can use just 33 focus points, including 15 cross-type sensors in the center of the viewfinder, and 9 horizontal sensors (18 total) flanking them on either side.

- **Group H.** The two lenses in this group (the EF35-105 f/4.5-5.6 and EF35-105 f/4.5-5.6 USM optics) allow using only the center cross-type AF point for focusing (you can't move the focus point to another point), and the only AF selection modes available are Single-point AF (Manual Selection) and Single-point Spot AF (Manual Selection).

Adding Circles of Confusion

You know that increased depth-of-field brings more of your subject into focus. But more depth-of-field also makes autofocusing (or manual focusing) more difficult because the contrast is lower between objects at different distances. This is an added factor *beyond* the rangefinder aspects of lens opening size in phase detection. An image that's dimmer is more difficult to focus with any type of focus system, phase detection, contrast detection, or manual focus.

So, focus with a 200mm lens (or zoom setting) may be easier in some respects than at a 28mm focal length (or zoom setting) because the longer lens has less apparent depth-of-field. By the same token, a lens with a maximum aperture of f/1.8 will be easier to autofocus (or manually focus) than one of the same focal length with an f/4 maximum aperture, because the f/4 lens has more depth-of-field *and* a dimmer view. That's yet another reason why lenses with a maximum aperture smaller than f/5.6 can give your 5D Mark IV's autofocus system fits—increased depth-of-field joins forces with a dimmer image that's more difficult to focus using phase detection.

To make things even more complicated, many subjects aren't polite enough to remain still. They move around in the frame, so that even if the 5D Mark IV is sharply focused on your main subject, it may change position and require refocusing. An intervening subject may pop into the frame and pass between you and the subject you meant to photograph. You (or the 5D Mark IV) have to decide whether to lock focus on this new subject, or remain focused on the original subject. Finally, there are some kinds of subjects that are difficult to bring into sharp focus because they lack enough contrast to allow the 5D Mark IV's AF system (or our eyes) to lock in. Blank walls, a clear blue sky, or other subject matter may make focusing difficult.

If you find all these focus factors confusing, you're on the right track. Focus is, in fact, measured using something called a *circle of confusion*. An ideal image consists of zillions of tiny little points, which, like all points, theoretically have no height or width. There is perfect contrast between the point and its surroundings. You can think of each point as a pinpoint of light in a darkened room. When a given point is out of focus, its edges decrease in contrast and it changes from a perfect point to a tiny disc with blurry edges (remember, blur is the lack of contrast between boundaries in an image). (See Figure 5.8.)

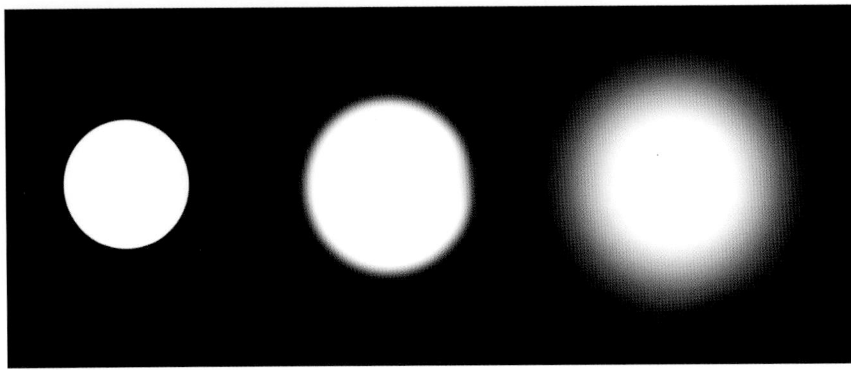

Figure 5.8
When a pinpoint of light (left) goes out of focus, its blurry edges form a circle of confusion (center and right).

If this blurry disc—the circle of confusion—is small enough, our eye still perceives it as a point. It's only when the disc grows large enough that we can see it as a blur rather than a sharp point that a given point is viewed as out of focus. You can see, then, that enlarging an image, either by displaying it larger on your computer monitor or by making a large print, also enlarges the size of each circle of confusion. Moving closer to the image does the same thing. So, parts of an image that may look perfectly sharp in a 5 × 7–inch print viewed at arm's length, might appear blurry when blown up to 11 × 14 and examined at the same distance. Take a few steps back, however, and it may look sharp again.

To a lesser extent, the viewer also affects the apparent size of these circles of confusion. Some people see details better at a given distance and may perceive smaller circles of confusion than someone standing next to them. For the most part, however, such differences are small. Truly blurry images will look blurry to just about everyone under the same conditions.

Technically, there is just one plane within your picture area, parallel to the back of the camera (or sensor, in the case of a digital camera), that is in sharp focus. That's the plane in which the points of the image are rendered as precise points. At every other plane in front of or behind the focus plane, the points show up as discs that range from slightly blurry to extremely blurry until the out-of-focus areas become one large blur that de-emphasizes an unattractive textured white background.

In practice, the discs in many of these planes will still be so small that we see them as points, and that's where we get depth-of-field. Depth-of-field is just the range of planes that include discs that we perceive as points rather than blurred splotches. The size of this range increases as the aperture is reduced in size and is allocated roughly one-third in front of the plane of sharpest focus, and two-thirds behind it. The range of sharp focus is always greater behind your subject than in front of it.

Working with the AF System

> This section begins the practical explanations that show you how to choose the most important settings for autofocus with the Canon EOS 5D Mark IV. If you want entry-by-entry listings of the functions in the AF menu, check out Chapter 12.

Now that you understand the basics of how the 5D Mark IV's autofocus system works, it's time to jump into the actual settings and options you have at your disposal. To achieve tack-sharp focus every time, you'll need to master focus modes (*when* to evaluate a scene and lock in focus) and focus area selection (you or the camera decides *what* to focus on). The following sections concentrate on achieving focus when *not* using live view or movie-making modes; in other words, when you're framing a picture using the optical viewfinder.

Focus Modes

Focus modes tell the camera *when* to evaluate and lock in focus. They don't determine *where* focus should be checked; that's the function of other autofocus features. Focus modes tell the camera whether to lock in focus once, say, when you press the shutter release halfway (or use some other control, such as the AF-ON button), or whether, once activated, the camera should continue tracking your subject and, if it's moving, adjust focus to follow it.

The 5D Mark IV has manual focus through the optical viewfinder, plus magnified (up to 10X manual focus using live view), and three AF modes: One-Shot AF (also known as single autofocus), AI Servo (continuous autofocus), and AI Focus AF (which switches between the two as appropriate). I'll explain all of these in more detail later in this section.

Choosing the right autofocus mode and the way in which focus points are selected is your key to success. Using the wrong mode for a particular type of photography can lead to a series of pictures that are all sharply focused—on the wrong subject. When I first started shooting sports with an autofocus SLR (back in the film camera days), I covered one game alternating between shots of base runners and outfielders with pictures of a promising young pitcher, all from a position next to the third base dugout. The base runner and outfielder photos were great, because their backgrounds didn't distract the autofocus mechanism. But all my photos of the pitcher had the focus tightly zeroed in on the fans in the stands behind him. Because I was shooting film instead of a digital camera, I didn't know about my gaffe until the film was developed. A simple change, such as locking in focus or focus zone manually, or even manually focusing, would have done the trick.

To save battery power, your 5D Mark IV doesn't start to focus the lens until you partially depress the shutter release. But, autofocus isn't some mindless beast out there snapping your pictures in and out of focus with no feedback from you after you press that button. There are several settings you can modify that return at least a modicum of control to you. Your first decision should be whether

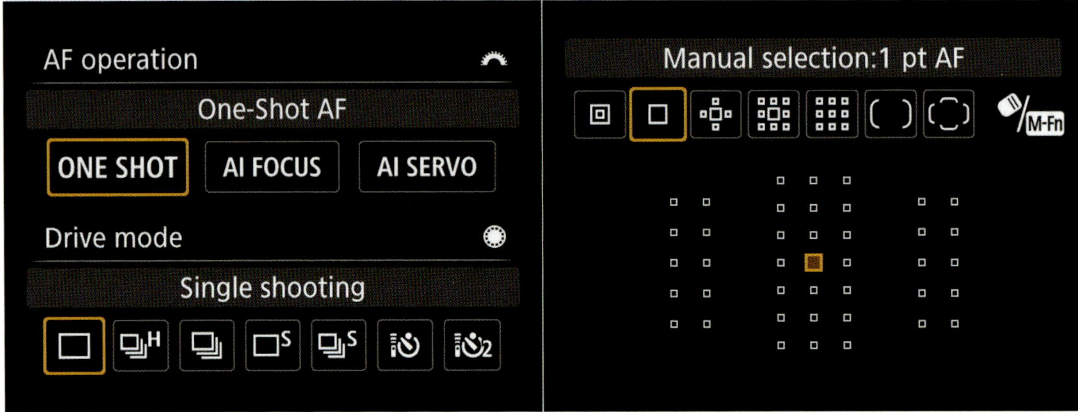

Figure 5.9 Choose an autofocus mode (left), or AF area selection mode (right).

you set the 5D Mark IV to One-Shot, AI Servo AF, or AI Focus AF. With the camera set for one of the non-auto modes, press the DRIVE-AF button and spin the Main Dial until the choice you want is displayed on the rear color LCD monitor (if you've set the screen to display Shooting Functions) and LCD status panel (see Figure 5.9, left). (The AF/M switch on the lens must be set to AF before you can change autofocus mode.)

Manual Focus

With manual focus activated by sliding the AF/MF switch on the lens, your 5D Mark IV lets you set the focus yourself. There are some advantages and disadvantages to this approach. While your batteries will last longer in manual focus mode, it will take you longer to focus the camera for each photo, a process that can be difficult. Modern digital cameras, even dSLRs, depend so much on autofocus that the viewfinders of models that have less than full-frame-sized sensors are no longer designed for optimum manual focus. Pick up any film camera and you'll see a bigger, brighter viewfinder with a focusing screen that's a joy to focus on manually. You really needed to use a full-frame digital camera, like the Canon EOS 5D Mark IV, to get such a bright view and easy manual focus.

One-Shot AF

In this mode, also called *single autofocus*, focus is set once and remains at that setting until the button is fully depressed, taking the picture, or until you release the shutter button without taking a shot. This mode is best for subjects that are not moving around a great deal. So, for non-action photography, this setting is usually your best choice, as it minimizes out-of-focus pictures (at the expense of spontaneity). The drawback here is that you might not be able to take a picture at all while the camera is seeking focus; you're locked out until the autofocus mechanism is happy with the current setting. One-Shot AF/single autofocus is sometimes referred to as *focus-priority* for that reason, although you can change the priority using the One-Shot AF Release Prior. option in the

AF 3 menu. Because of the small delay while the camera zeroes in on correct focus during focus-priority operation, you might experience slightly more shutter lag. This mode uses less battery power than the other autofocus modes.

When sharp focus is achieved, the selected focus point will flash red in the viewfinder (you can adjust the behavior of the focus point using the AF 4 menu, as described in Chapter 12), and the focus confirmation light at the lower right will flash green. If you're using Evaluative metering, the exposure will be locked at the same time. By keeping the shutter button depressed halfway, you'll find you can reframe the image while retaining the focus (and exposure) that's been set. You can also use the AE Lock/FE Lock button to retain the exposure calculated from the center AF point while reframing.

AI Servo AF

This mode, also known as *continuous autofocus*, is the mode to use for sports and other fast-moving subjects, and is often used with continuous shooting modes. With AI Servo AF, once the shutter release is partially depressed, the camera sets the focus on the point that's selected (by the camera or by you manually), but continues to monitor the subject, so that if it moves or you move, the lens will be refocused to suit. Focus and exposure aren't really locked until you press the shutter release down all the way to take the picture. You'll find that AI Servo AF produces the least amount of shutter lag of any autofocus mode: press the button and the camera fires. It also uses the most battery power, because the autofocus system operates as long as the shutter release button is partially depressed.

You'll often see continuous autofocus referred to as *release-priority,* because that's the way it has been traditionally used. In that mode, if you press the shutter release down all the way while the system is refining focus, the camera will go ahead and take a picture, even if the image is slightly out of focus. However, you can specify the priority for the first image in a series, and, if you're shooting in continuous mode, for the second shot in a series. Select release-priority, focus-priority, or give equal weight to each. Use the AF 2 menu, described in Chapter 12.

AI Servo AF uses a technology called *predictive AF,* which allows the 5D Mark IV to calculate the correct focus if the subject is moving toward or away from the camera at a constant rate. It uses either the automatically selected AF point or the point you select manually to set focus. AI Servo AF's characteristics can be fine-tuned for particular types of subjects and scenes, called *cases,* as I'll explain later.

AI Focus AF

This setting is actually a combination of the first two. When selected, the camera focuses using One-Shot AF and locks in the focus setting. But, if the subject begins moving, it will switch automatically to AI Servo AF and change the focus to keep the subject sharp. AI Focus AF is a good choice when you're shooting a mixture of action pictures and less dynamic shots and want to use One-Shot AF when possible. The camera will default to that mode, yet switch automatically to AI Servo AF when it would be useful for subjects that might begin moving unexpectedly.

Setting the AF Area Selection Mode

You or the 5D Mark IV can select the AF point(s) to be used. There are six modes in which you select the initial point or zone of points (with variations on what additional points will also be used). A seventh mode allows the camera to use all the useable points (up to 61 total) to select the initial focus point automatically.

You can quickly switch among any of the AF area selection modes by pressing the AF selection button on the upper-right corner of the camera's back panel, and then pressing the M-Fn button repeatedly while the available modes cycle on the screen shown at right in Figure 5.9, and on the LCD monitor. If you generally use only a few of the seven total modes, Canon gives you the ability to "hide" the others using the Select AF Area Selec. Mode entry in the AF4 menu. You'll find a description of all the options in the four AF menus in Chapter 12.

Once you've selected one of the modes below, you can change which of the (up to) 61 focus points the Canon EOS 5D Mark IV uses to calculate correct focus. There are several methods to set the focus point/zone in any of the manual modes. You can press the AF point selection button on the back of the camera, look through the viewfinder, and use the multi-controller (to the right and below the viewfinder window) to move the focus point to the zone you want to use.

For example, press the AF point selection button, and then shift the multi-controller straight up or down, and the top or bottom focus points are selected; to the left or right, and the side points are selected. Movements to the two o'clock, four o'clock, seven o'clock, or ten o'clock positions choose the in-between focus sensors. Press the multi-controller in, and the center focus point becomes active. You can also use the QCD and Main Dial to move the active focus point around among the available choices.

Manual Selection: Spot AF

In this mode, you can zero in and focus on the tiny area covered by a single spot in the 61-point focus array. Use the controls described above to move the highlighted spot to a different point within the entire available focus zone. This precision can be too much of a good thing, however; camera movement (as when shooting hand-held, especially with a front-heavy long lens), and subject movement can easily move the focus spot away from your primary subject. Figure 5.10, left, shows the focus area in the center of the frame for simplicity; you can actually move it to any other focus point.

This mode may be your best choice when you want to focus precisely on a subject that is surrounded by fine detail, as shown at right in Figure 5.10. The heron was not moving and my camera and 400mm lens were mounted on a sturdy tripod, so it was easy to place the focus spot exactly where I wanted it. Keep in mind that the portion of the sensor used to autofocus is not precisely represented by the rectangle shown in the viewfinder, so if you're focusing on, say, the near eye of a portrait subject turned at a 45-degree angle with a wide aperture, you might end up focusing on the bridge of their noise instead. Single-Point AF (Manual Selection) is not a good choice for moving subjects.

Manual Selection: 1 Point AF

This mode uses the larger focus area shown at left in Figure 5.11, and is more practical for scenes where you want to focus on a certain point, but your subject may be moving slowly, like the gondola seen at right in Figure 5.11. Position the active focus point with the controls, as described earlier. You can use Manual Selection: 1 Point AF for everyday shooting where precision is needed, and the subject contains sufficient detail within the area covered by the sensor. If such a small area of your subject is a bit amorphous, you'll want to use one of the selection modes described next, which allow the AF system to take into account surrounding focus points as well as the manually selected point.

Expand AF Area

In this mode, the focus point you select is used, along with the points immediately above, below, and to either side of it (until the manually selected point reaches the edge of the array and one or more of the additional points scroll off). (See Figure 5.12, left.) This mode is better for moving objects, like the pelican shown at right in Figure 5.12, because the larger effective zone makes it

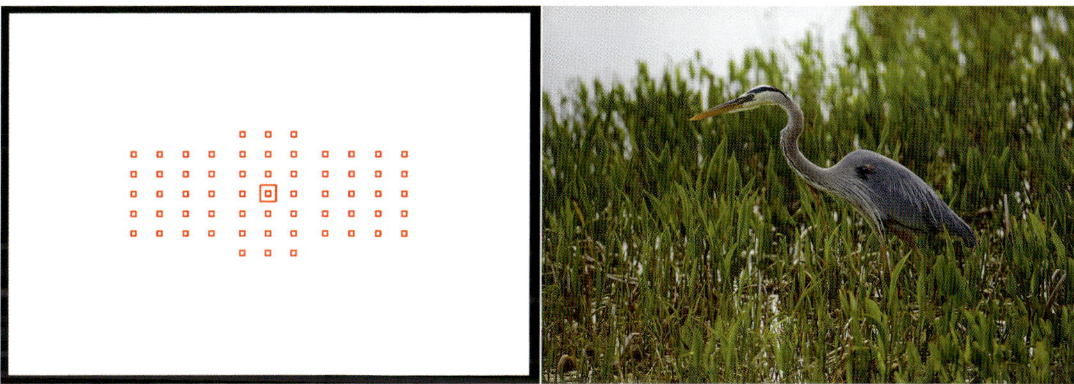

Figure 5.10 Manual Selection: Spot AF mode allowed focusing precisely on the heron, despite the surrounding detail.

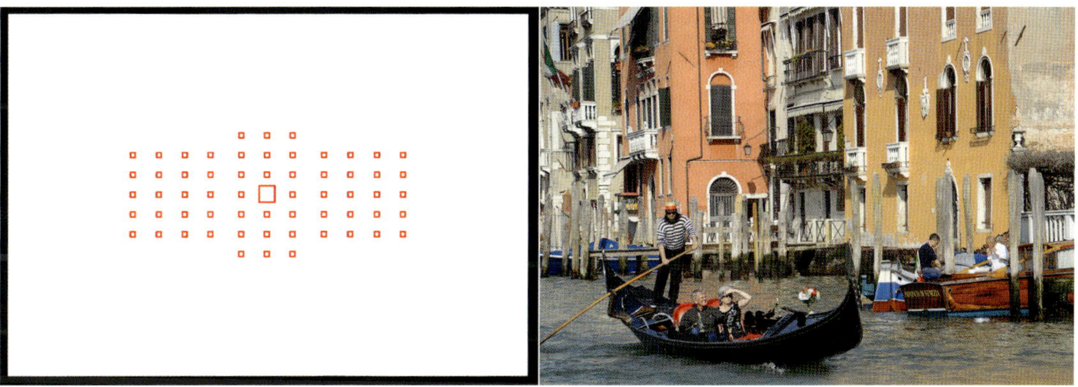

Figure 5.11 Slow-moving subjects are suitable for Single-Point AF.

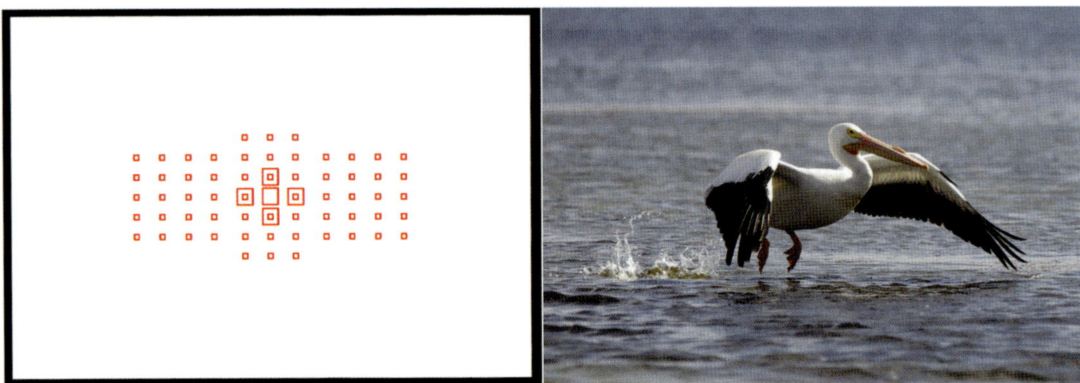

Figure 5.12 A larger AF area when using Expand AF Area allows autofocus of moving subjects.

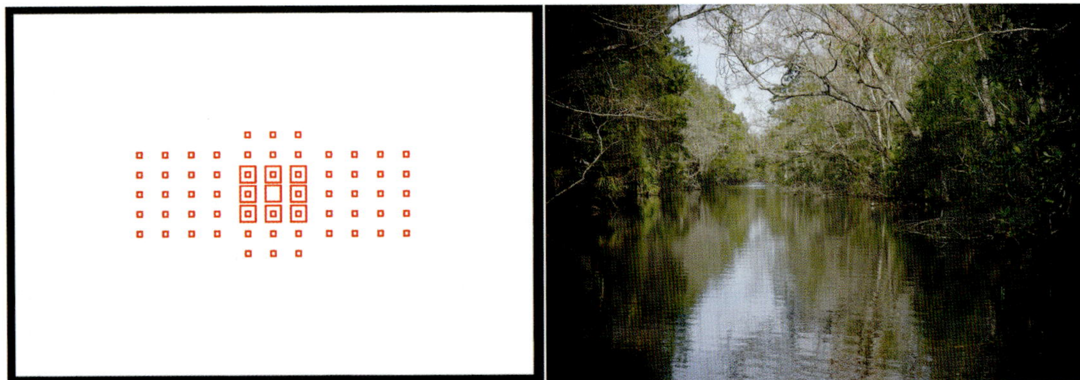

Figure 5.13 Expand AF Area: Surround is excellent for subjects without a great deal of detail in large areas of the frame.

easier to track subjects that are moving within the frame. As the subject moves outside the area defined by the selected focus point, three to four of the surrounding focus points can pick up and track the movement. In One-Shot AF mode, the manually selected focus point and expanded point used will be displayed in the viewfinder.

Expand AF Area: Surround

This mode is similar to the one above, except that the four points located diagonally in relation to the manually selected point are included in the focusing array. It is slightly better for subjects that don't contain a lot of detail at the manually selected focus point, and the 3 to 8 additional points surrounding the initial focus point improve your results. This mode is better for larger moving objects, even though it offers a bit less precision. As always, while the active points are shown in the center of the frame (at left in Figure 5.13), you can move the active area around while looking through the viewfinder. At right in the figure, you can see a subject that can benefit from this AF area mode.

Manual Selection: Zone AF

This is a zone-oriented point selection method, in which the 61 AF points are divided into nine possible zones, shown color-coded in Figure 5.14 for clarity. (They don't appear in color in your viewfinder.) When you move the focus "point" using the controls, you are actually simply switching from one entire zone to the next; all the points in a given zone are used to achieve focus. This mode works well when you know the approximate area where your subject will reside, and want to cover a particular zone. For Figure 5.15, I knew all the rodeo action was going to be roughly in the center of the frame, and often in the bottom half of the focus area sensor array, so I alternated between the two orange zones shown at top and in the middle of Figure 5.14.

Figure 5.14

Nine zones are available.

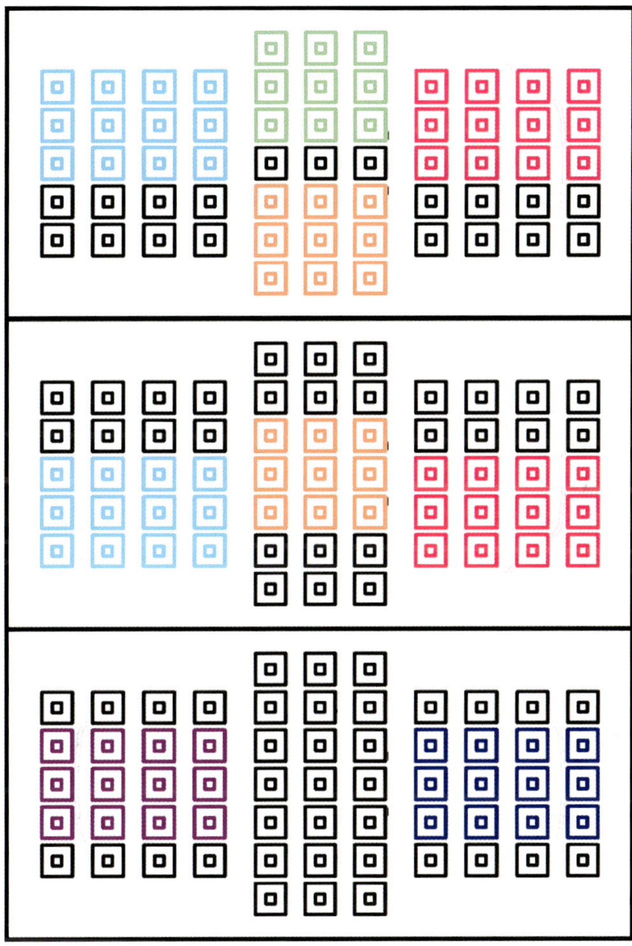

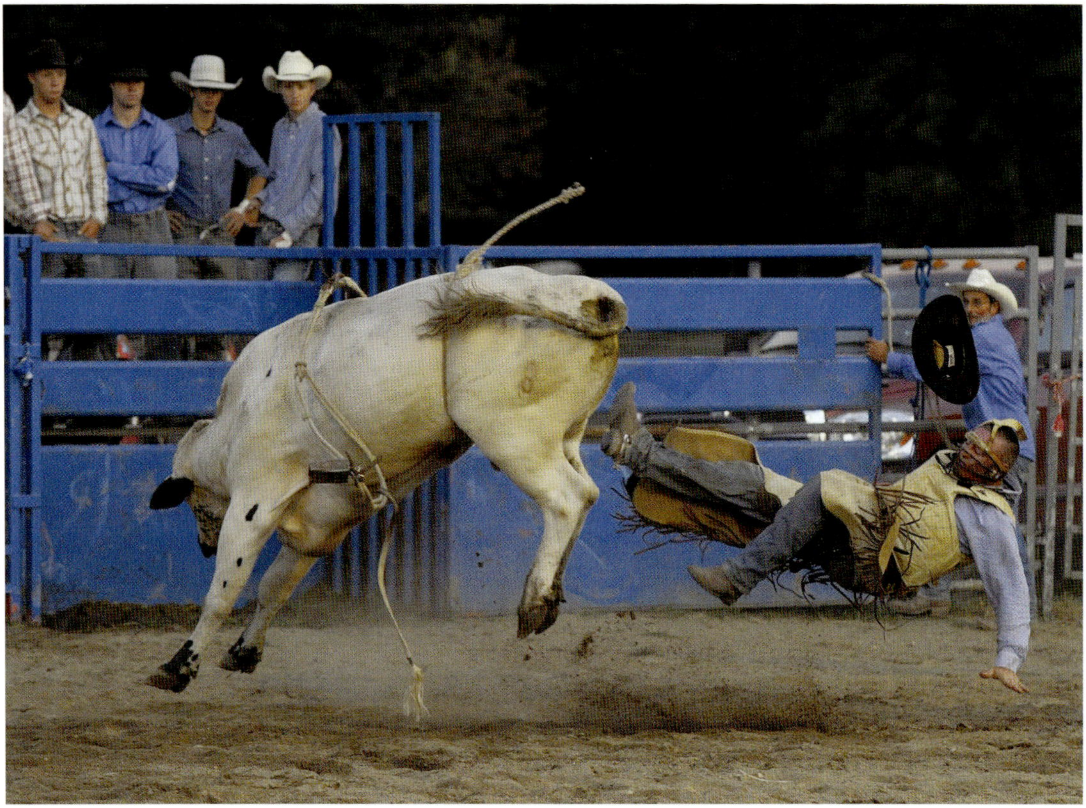

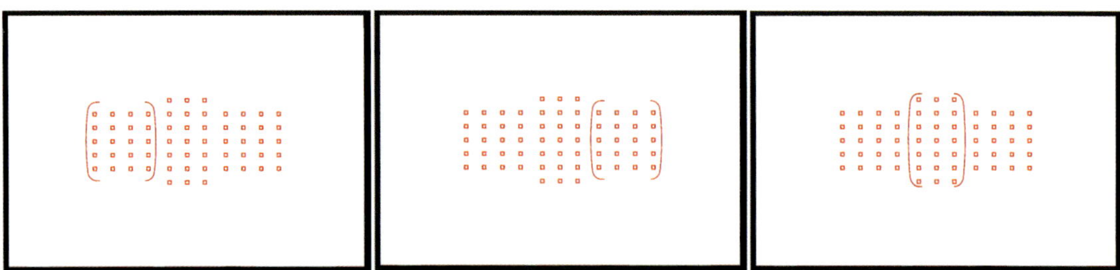

Figure 5.15 The zone near the bottom of the focus area was used for this shot.

Manual Selection: Large Zone AF

This is another zone-oriented point selection method, in which the 61 AF points are divided into only three possible zones: left, right, and center, as shown in Figure 5.16. When you move the focus "point" using the controls, you are actually simply switching from one entire zone to the next; all the points in a given zone are used to achieve focus. This mode also is excellent when you know the approximate area where your subject will be, and the zone is rather large.

Figure 5.16 Three zones are available.

Auto Selection AF

If you choose this mode, the camera will be able to use as many as all 61 points to achieve focus. Use this method when your subject will reside in the center of the frame, and you thus don't need to rely on selecting the initial focus point manually every single time. This method is automatically activated when using Scene Intelligent Auto exposure. It's a good choice for general-purpose shooting and action in the center of the scene.

In One-Shot AF focus mode, the focus area will look like Figure 5.17, left, until you press the shutter button halfway. In most cases, focus will lock on the subject closest to the camera. Then, the AF points used to achieve focus—from one to all 61—will be illuminated. In AI Servo AF mode, you can select the initial focus point manually, but the camera will use any of the others automatically as needed (see Figure 5.17, right). The point(s) used will be highlighted.

Figure 5.17
In One-Shot AF mode (left); in AI Servo AF mode (right).

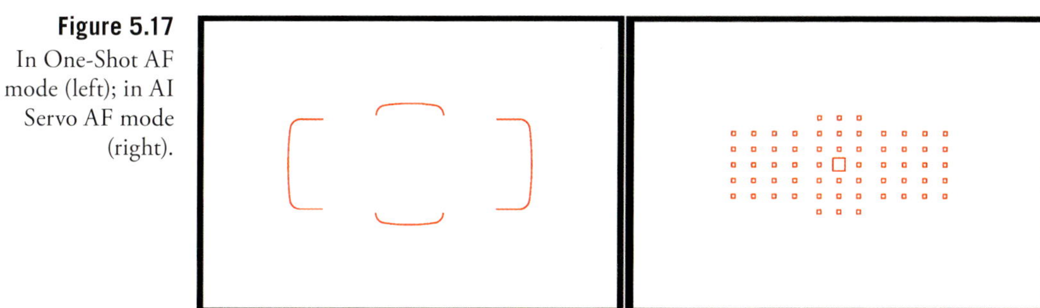

Fine-Tuning Your Autofocus

The options available for the Canon EOS 5D's autofocus can be overwhelming at times, which is why I'm devoting two full chapters to explaining them, this one, and Chapter 12, which deals exclusively with autofocus menu options. If the modes and parameters described so far aren't enough, Canon allows you do some additional fine-tuning, as I'll describe in this section. You can select from six different configuration setups (which Canon calls "Cases"), each tailored for a specific type of shooting when using AI Servo AF. You are able to further tweak how each Case performs if the factory defaults don't suit you. One additional modification, AF Microadjustment (one or more of your lenses consistently focuses in front of or behind your actual subject) is performed very rarely (or never), and will be discussed in Chapter 12. The section that follows is devoted to the AF adjustments available in the AF 1 menu.

AF Configuration Tool

In the AF 1 menu tab, you'll find six factory-defined Cases (actually, typical autofocus situations) that have been set up to provide good results with a half-dozen different types of scenes when using AI Servo AF (continuous autofocus).

Each of the Cases uses different combinations of settings for three different parameters:

- **Tracking sensitivity.** This determines how quickly the AF system switches to a new subject entering the focus area. Your choices are –2 (Locked On) to +2 (Responsive). Negative numbers allow you to retain focus on the original subject even if it briefly leaves the area covered by the focus points, making tracking easier. The drawback is that if the camera selects the wrong subject, there is a longer delay before the correct subject is captured. Positive numbers cause the AF system to more quickly switch to a new subject. However, such a quick response can cause the camera to focus on the wrong subject.

- **Acceleration/deceleration tracking.** This parameter determines how the AF system responds to sudden acceleration, deceleration, or stopping. Your choices are 0 (for subjects that move at a constant speed) to 2 (for faster reactions to subjects that suddenly change speed). Lower values can cause the camera to be "fooled" if a subject that was moving consistently suddenly stops; focus may change to the position where the subject *would* have been if it'd kept moving. A higher value may cause inconsistent focus with subjects that move at a constant speed.

- **AF point auto switching.** This setting determines how quickly the AF system changes from the current AF point to an adjacent one when the subject moves away from the current point, or an intervening object moves across the frame into the area interpreted by the current point. Your choices are 0 (switch more slowly so focus is stable, with slower tracking response) to 2 (switch to an adjacent point quickly). This parameter operates in 61 Point Auto Selection, Zone AF, and AF Point Expansion area selection modes.

You can adjust any of these three parameters for any Case (with the option of returning the Case to its default values later) by rotating the QCD and pressing SET to select it. I'll show you how to do that later in this section. You should use each Case extensively to get a feeling for how it operates before making any changes. First, check out the default behavior of each of the six Cases (see Figure 5.18):

- **Case 1: Versatile multi-purpose setting.** Use this as your default setting, as it works well with many moving subjects (and moving subject matter is why you selected AI Servo AF, isn't it?). Use with any type of action that isn't one of the special cases described next. It's good for some motor sports, many track meet events, and action that's moving toward or away from the camera.

Figure 5.18
The AF 1 menu is used to select and adjust autofocus Cases.

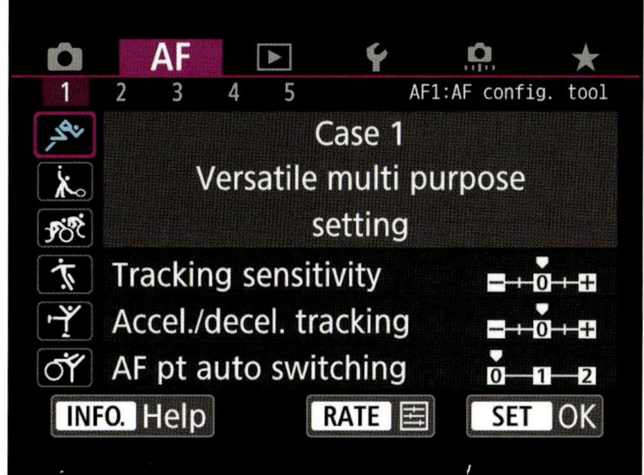

- **Case 2: Continue to track subject, ignoring possible obstacles.** This Case could be your mainstay for football games, because you can track a running back, receiver, or another player of interest without having focus disrupted when a referee, coach, or another player passes between you. The camera will delay refocusing on the new object long enough to resume following the original subject.

- **Case 3: Instantly focus on subjects suddenly entering AF points.** This Case is ideal when you're photographing a relatively static scene in anticipation of a moving subject, such as a runner, skier, or bicyclist entering the frame. You could, for example, frame the finish line of a horse race, and the Mark IV would instantly lock focus on the winning steed as it crosses the line (or perhaps several horses if one wins "by a nose").

- **Case 4: For subjects that accelerate or decelerate quickly.** Canon earmarks this one for motor sports, but I find that race cars often move predictably at relatively constant speeds. This Case is better for basketball and soccer, because you can have players racing toward you one instant, and crossing your field of view the next.

- **Case 5: For erratic subjects moving quickly in any direction.** This is my choice for hockey games and anything that involves skates—as well as small children and pets. It's also excellent for that most difficult of subjects: birds in flight (often abbreviated to just BIF because photographers talk about the challenges of photographing pesky avians so frequently). (See Figure 5.19.)

- **Case 6: For subjects that change speed and move erratically.** This works with 61 Point Auto Selection, Zone AF, and AF Point Expansion area selection modes. (In other words, it doesn't operate with Single-Point Spot AF or Single-Point AF manual selection modes.) I use this one for basketball, too, and you might try it with children and small pets to see if it works better for you than Case 5.

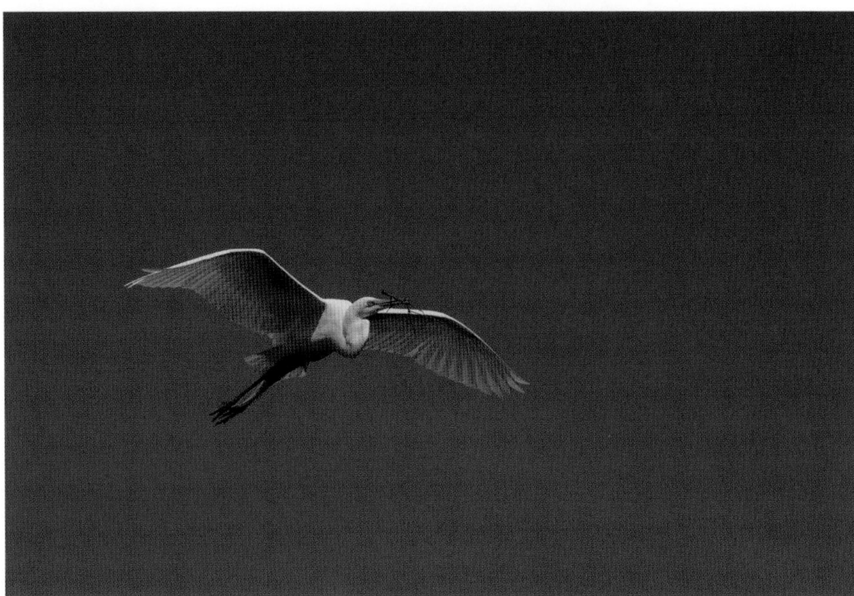

Figure 5.19
Birds in flight are one of the most difficult subjects for any autofocus system to handle.

Modifying Cases

To change the values of any of the six AF Cases, just follow these steps:

1. **Access menu.** Navigate to the AF 1 menu and rotate the QCD to highlight the Case you want to modify.

2. **Choose Detail Set.** Press the Rate button located to the left of the LCD. The Tracking Sensitivity parameter will be highlighted.

3. **Select parameter to change.** Use the QCD or multi-controller joystick to select the parameter you want to modify, and press SET.

4. **Make adjustment.** Use the QCD or multi-controller joystick to move the indicator along the scale to the value you want.

5. **Confirm.** Press SET to confirm. Note that the default value for the Case you've modified will be noted with an additional gray indicator so you can tell at a glance that you've changed the factory settings.

6. **Exit.** Press MENU to exit, or press the Trash button to restore that Case's settings to their defaults.

7. **Store in C1–C3 (Optional).** It's probably smart to store your modified settings in one of the three User slots. You can, in effect, use the factory default Cases, plus additional sets of Cases you've created for specific shooting situations. You can register settings in the Set-up 4 menu, as described in Chapter 13.

AF with Color Tracking

The 153,000-pixel RGB+infrared exposure sensor mentioned in Chapter 4 can also be used to facilitate autofocus. The color information can recognize colors equivalent to skin tones, and thus enhance AF sensitivity when shooting still photos of human subjects. As I'll explain in Chapter 12, you can activate this feature using the AF 4 menu. The default is EOS iTR AF (Face-priority), which tells the 5D Mark IV to automatically select AF points using color information, which can include human skin. It works well in One-Shot mode to lock in focus; in AI Servo AF mode, focusing on humans is enhanced (if no skin tones are detected, the camera will focus on the nearest object). As AI Servo AF continues to refocus as required until the shutter release is pressed down all the way, the 5D Mark IV continues to select focus points representing the colors of the subject first focused on. Under lighting conditions dim enough to trigger an attached electronic flash's AF-assist beam, color information is not used. This mode gives *focus-priority* to faces, so if there are humans in your frame and you don't want the AF system to zero in on them (say, you're photographing objects in the foreground, with the people located behind) use a different mode.

That mode could be plain old EOS iTR AF 1. In that case, human face and color tones are considered, but in AI Servo AF mode, the point where focus was first achieved will be used. In other words, face/color information is used, but it isn't given the top priority. If you really need to ignore people in your frame, use Disable to tell the camera to select AF points without regard to color information. Disabling the color tracking feature may result in faster autofocus, which can be useful for birds-in-flight (no human faces involved) and sports photography.

Other AF Options

In addition to the Case adjustments in the AF 1 menu, you'll find additional adjustments available in AF 2, AF 3, AF 4, and AF 5. Most of these aren't used in day-to-day shooting, which is the case with the options explained in this chapter. Instead, the AF 2 to AF 5 settings are those that you'll change once, or perhaps modify only occasionally.

- **AF 2:** AI Servo-priority Release/Focus-priority.

- **AF 3:** Use of electronic focus ring with certain USM lenses; AF-Assist Beam Enable/Disable; One-Shot AF Release-priority.

- **AF 4:** You can tell the Mark IV how to behave when AF is impossible; which AF points can be selected; choose an AF area selection mode; whether the M-Fn or Main Dial is used to choose AF area selection method; and whether AF points are linked to the camera's vertical or horizontal orientation.

- **AF 5:** Whether AF point selection wraps around at boundaries; how AF points are displayed during focus; viewfinder focus point display; and Autofocus micro adjustment.

Dual Pixel RAW Focus Adjustments

My guides emphasize getting great pictures *in the camera,* rather than through post-processing, so I generally don't cover software tools like the EOS Utility or Digital Photo Professional in any detail. However, most of you will be curious about the focus enhancements that the new Dual Pixel RAW format makes possible, so I'll provide a brief overview here. A more complete discussion of what you can do with this format can be found in the Digital Photo Profession PDF on the Software CD included in the box with your 5D Mark IV.

Dual Pixel RAW is a special double-size RAW format that can be manipulated in an image editor (as I write this, only Digital Photo Pro has that capability) to make microadjustments to the focus plane, slightly improve bokeh effects (the smoothness of the out-of-focus areas of the image), and make corrections to ghosting and flare. Dual Pixel RAW files also offer the opportunity for advanced users to recover up to one additional stop in the highlights. When activated, Dual Pixel RAW saves, in effect, two different RAW files (and takes twice as long to do so), combined into a single file on your memory card. One half contains information from both sets of pixels (call them Sets A+B) while the other half includes information only from the pixels in Set B.

As I will remind you in Chapter 11, to use Dual Pixel RAW, you must select RAW (but not M RAW or S RAW) or RAW+JPEG as your Image Quality, and then enable the dual pixel feature in the Shooting 1 menu. A DPR alert will then be displayed on the monochrome LCD panel on top of the camera. You cannot use DPR if you want to shoot multiple exposures, use automatic HDR, One-Touch image quality, or the Digital Lens Optimizer. It is also unavailable if you're trying to save RAW files to one memory card and M RAW or S RAW to the other using the Record Separately in the Record Function+Card/Folder Selection entry in the Set-up 1 menu.

While you can save Dual Pixel RAW files whether using the optical viewfinder or live view/movies, continuous shooting will be slower when working with the optical viewfinder. And in live view, continuous shooting is not available, and if set will switch back to single-shot mode.

We're primarily concerned with the focus plane microadjustment feature here. DPR doesn't improve the resolution of your image: those 30-megapixel split pairs don't give you 60 megapixels of resolution. What the DPR file does do is make use of the sensor's phase-detection information, even though, when you're using the optical viewfinder, that data played no part in determining the focus plane of your finished image.

What you *can* do is make very small adjustments in the plane of focus, amounting to just a few millimeters in front of or behind the original plane. This is similar to what Lytro's *light field photography* does (Google it for more information), although on a reduced scale. These are *micro* adjustments. As a practical matter, it might mean that a portrait photographer who discovers that an image captured wide open with a portrait-friendly lens or focal length (Canon's 85mm f/1.2 optic comes to mind) is focused on the subject's eyelashes, the plane of focus can be moved back to the eyes instead.

You'll locate Start Dual Pixel RAW Optimizer in the Tools menu of Digital Photo Pro, with an image area and tool palette like the one shown in Figure 5.20. There are four palettes, and you can activate *only one of them* (plus sharpness) at a time for a particular image by putting a check mark in the box at upper left of the palette you want to work with. Your options include:

- **Image Microadjustment.** You can zoom in and out from 100% to 400% to view the focus plane changes you're making in real time. You'll generally use some level of zoom because, as I noted, the adjustments are very small. A vertical slider lets you move the focus plane toward the front or back of your subject, in increments of five. You can also specify the strength of the adjustment from 1 to 10. Figure 5.21 shows a zoomed-in view of a Dual Pixel RAW image that has had its focal plane moved to the maximum forward and backward positions.

- **Bokeh Shift.** You can shift background or foreground "bokeh" left or right, again in values of 1–5 in either direction. Click the Select Area button and you can drag an area the adjustment is applied to. I've found the effect to be very subtle.

- **Ghosting Reduction.** Reduces ghosting superimposed on your subject and flare from bright light sources in the frame. You can select the area affected, but not the amount of correction. Because flare may differ from the light gathered from one side of the lens or the other, the Dual Pixel RAW feature can be an effective way of detecting it and making corrections.

- **Sharpness.** This feature allows you to adjust overall sharpness or apply an unsharp mask to the image, either alone or in conjunction with the other effects of this tool. Strength, fineness, and threshold can be applied in a manner similar to most other image processing sharpeners, including Canon's in-camera Picture Controls.

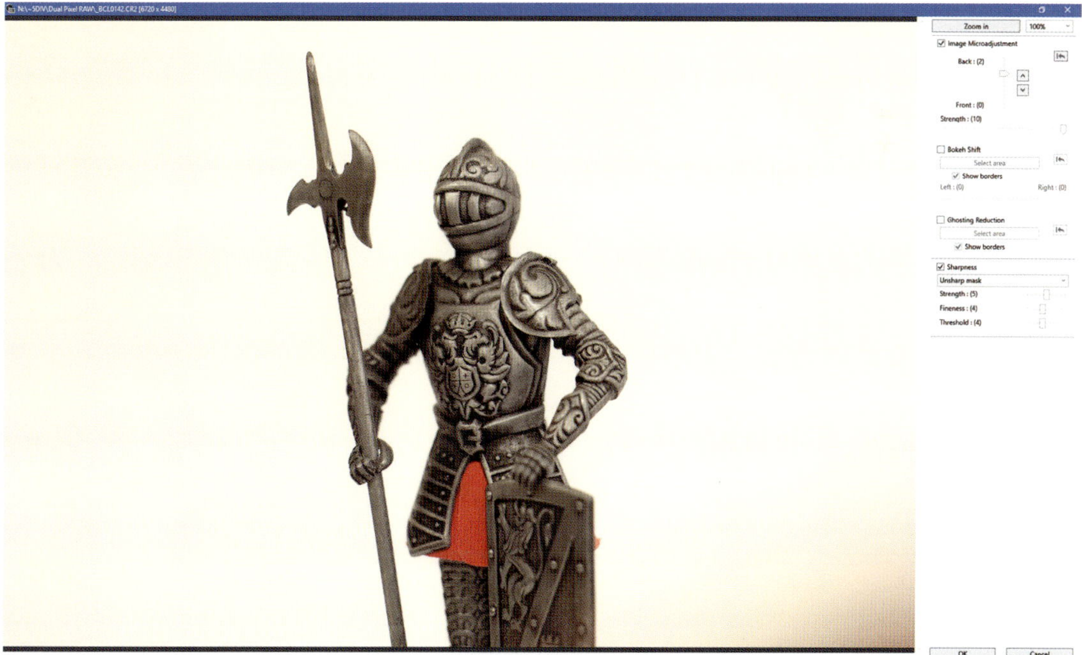

Figure 5.20 Four palettes are available in the Dual Pixel RAW pane.

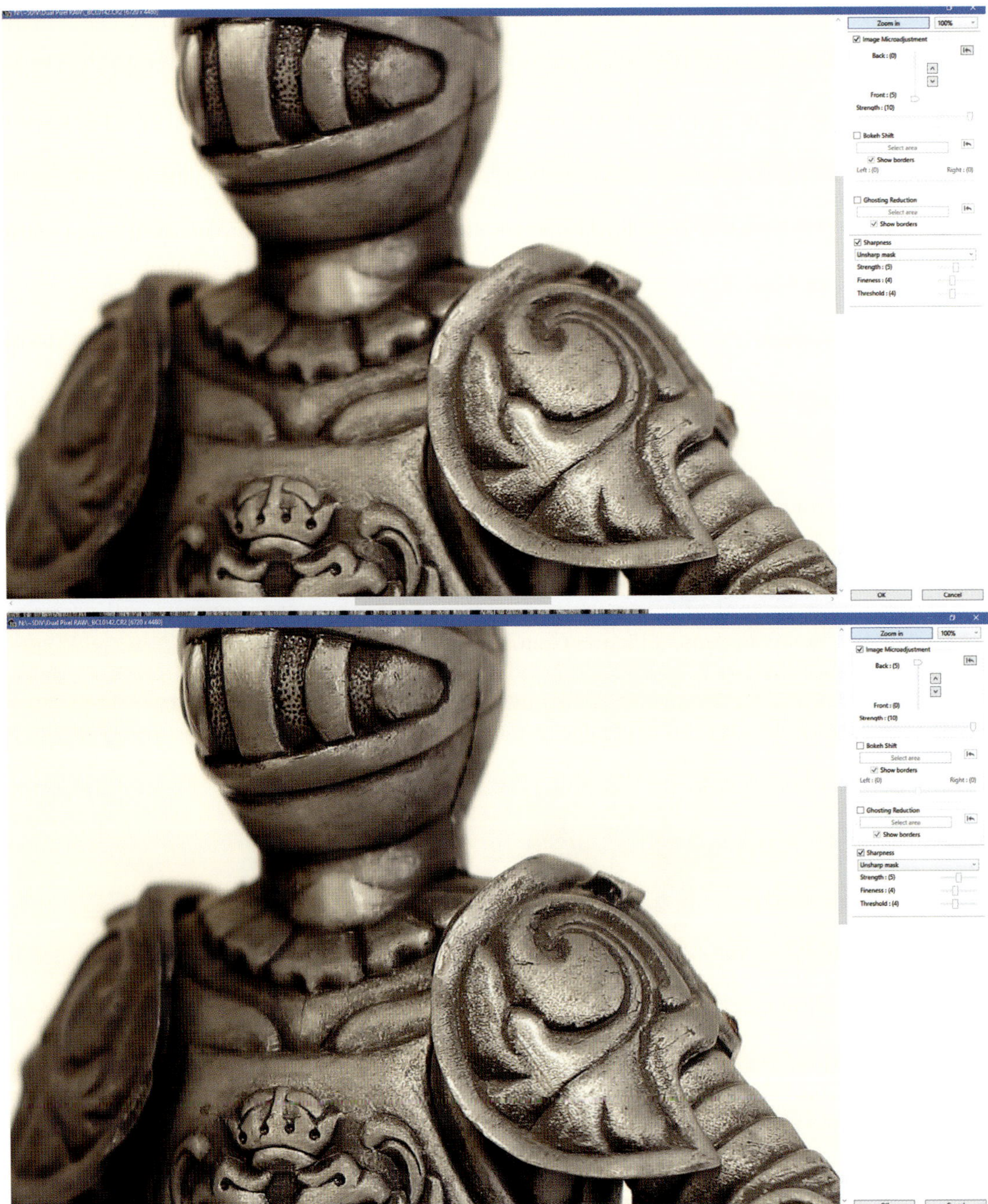

Figure 5.21 Focus plane the maximum amount forward (top) and back (bottom).

As you might expect, any adjustments you make to a Dual Pixel RAW file are implemented *only* in the JPEG or other file you save from DPP; the original RAW file remains untouched, so you're free to play around with this feature as much as you like.

As I write this, the Dual Pixel RAW features are too new for much solid documentation to have been produced by Canon or others. Canon notes that the effects produced can vary depending on the particular lens in use, shooting conditions, and whether the camera is held in vertical or horizontal orientations. For example, the tool is most effective if the lens is used at its maximum aperture. That makes sense, because depth-of-field is less when the lens is wide open, so adjustments in focus plane, bokeh, sharpness, and perhaps ghosting/flare will be more obvious.

Back-Button Focus

Once you've been using your camera for a while, you'll invariably encounter the terms *back focus* and *back-button focus*, and wonder if they are good things or bad things. Actually, they are *two different things,* and are often confused with each other. *Back focus* is a bad thing, and occurs when a particular lens consistently autofocuses on a plane that's *behind* your desired subject. This malady may be found in some of your lenses, or all your optics may be free of the defect. The good news is that if the problem lies in a particular lens (rather than a camera misadjustment that applies to *all* your lenses), it can be fixed. I'll show you how to do that at the end of this chapter.

Back-button focus, on the other hand, is a tool you can use to separate two functions that are commonly locked together—exposure and autofocus—so that you can lock in exposure while allowing focus to be attained at a later point, or vice versa. It's a *good* thing, although using back-button focus effectively may require you to unlearn some habits and acquire new ways of coordinating the action of your fingers.

As you have learned, the default behavior of your 5D Mark IV is to set both exposure and focus (when AF is active) when you press the shutter release down halfway. When using One Shot mode, that's that: both exposure and focus are locked and will not change until you release the shutter button, or press it all the way down to take a picture and then release it for the next shot. In AI Servo mode, exposure is locked and focus set when you press the shutter release halfway, but the 5D Mark IV will continue to refocus if your subject moves for as long as you hold down the shutter button halfway. Focus isn't locked until you press the button down all the way to take the picture. In AI Focus mode, the camera will start out in One Shot mode, but switch to AI Servo if your subject begins moving.

What back-button focus does is *decouple* or separate the two actions. You can retain the exposure lock feature when the shutter is pressed halfway, but assign autofocus *start* and/or autofocus *lock* to a different button. So, in practice, you can press the shutter button halfway, locking exposure, and reframe the image if you like (perhaps you're photographing a backlit subject and want to lock in exposure on the foreground, and then reframe to include a very bright background as well).

But, in this same scenario, you *don't* want autofocus locked at the same time. Indeed, you may not want to start AF until you're good and ready, say, at a sports venue as you wait for a ballplayer to streak into view in your viewfinder. With back-button focus, you can lock exposure on the spot where you expect the athlete to be, and activate AF at the moment your subject appears. The 5D Mark IV gives you a great deal of flexibility, both in the choice of which button to use for AF, and the behavior of that button. You can *start* autofocus, *lock* autofocus at a button press, or *lock it while holding the button.* That's where the learning of new habits and mind-finger coordination comes in. You need to learn which back-button focus techniques work for you, and when to use them.

Back-button focus lets you avoid the need to switch from One Shot to AI Servo when your subject begins moving unexpectedly. You retain complete control. It's great for sports photography when you want to activate autofocus precisely based on the action in front of you. It also works for static shots. You can press and release your designated focus button, and then take a series of shots using the same focus point. Focus will not change until you once again press your defined back button. (See Figure 5.22.)

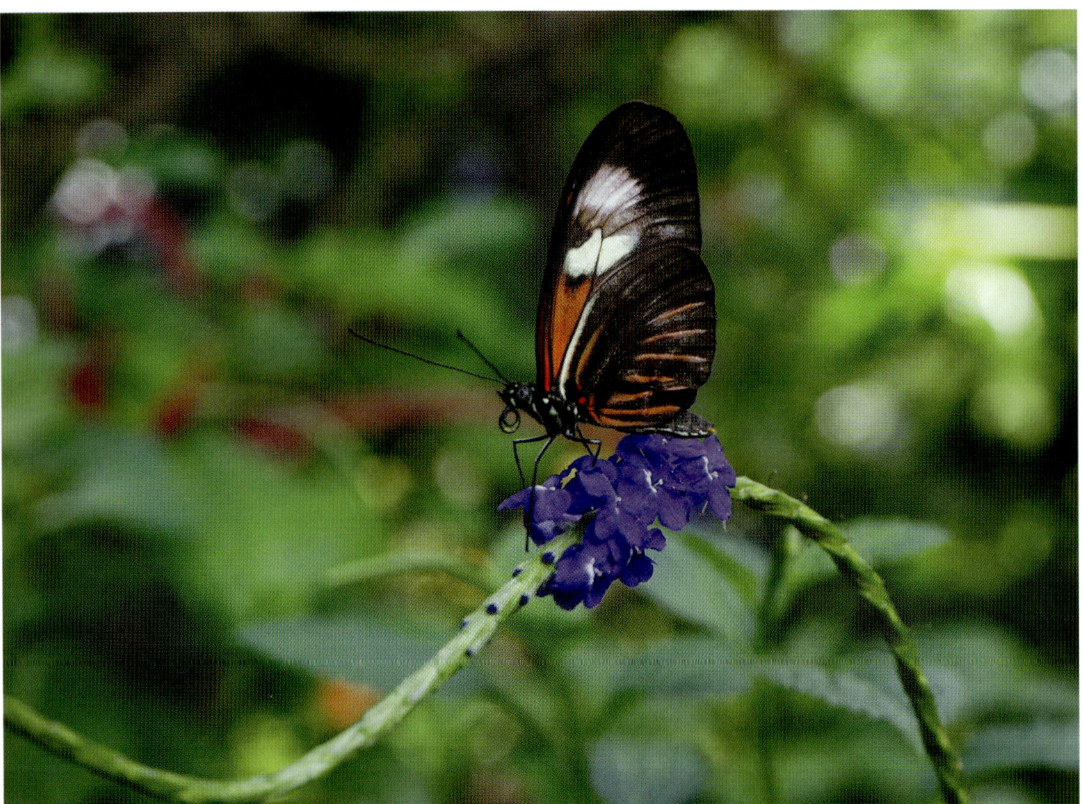

Figure 5.22 Lock your exposure for the garden by pressing the shutter release halfway, then activate autofocus when the butterfly decides where to land.

Want to reframe after focus is achieved? Use back-button focus to zero in focus on that location, then reframe. Focus will not change. Don't want to miss an important shot at a wedding on a photojournalism assignment? If you're set to *focus-priority* your camera may delay taking a picture until the focus is optimum; in *release-priority* there may still be a slight delay. With back-button focus you can focus first, and wait until the decisive moment to press the shutter release and take your picture. The 5D Mark IV will respond immediately and not bother with focusing at all.

Back-button focus can also save battery power. Ordinarily, your image stabilized (IS) lens will begin adjusting for camera shake as soon as you begin focusing. Constantly refocusing can consume a lot of power. With back-button focus, the IS isn't switched on until you actually decide to autofocus on your subject. To summarize, the advantages of back-button focus are these:

- **Great for unwanted subjects in action photography.** Earlier in this chapter I talked about using the tracking sensitivity settings in the AF 1 menu to minimize the camera locking onto an intervening object (in football, that might be a yardline marker, another player, or a ref) during an action shot. With back-button focus, you can not only initiate focus whenever you want, you can *pause* focus temporarily by releasing the back button and then pressing it again when the intervening subject is no longer in the frame.

- **Exact timing of focus.** Sports photographers also like the ability of back-button focus to allow them to focus at a decisive moment. You may be following the action through the viewfinder, seeking a subject to capture, and decide to capture an image of a wide receiver reaching out for the ball. Frame the receiver in the viewfinder and press the back button to lock in focus, and then press the shutter release all the way to actually take the picture.

- **Reframing.** As I mentioned earlier, you can lock focus with the back button, then release the button and reframe before taking the picture with the shutter release button. The camera will not refocus when the shutter button is pressed.

- **Fine-tuning focus.** Many Canon lenses allow you to fine-tune focus even when the lens is set for autofocus. With those lenses, you can go ahead and initiate autofocus using the back button; then, if you want to fine-tune focus manually, release the button and rotate the focusing ring. The camera will not refocus when you press the shutter release button, and you won't have to switch the lens' AF/MF switch to Manual. This technique works particularly well for macro photography, which often benefits from precise manual focusing on the exact plane that you want to be sharpest. Go ahead and pre-focus using the autofocus feature, then release the back button and manually set your focus. It's faster than focusing entirely in manual focus mode.

Activating Back-Button Focus

To use back-button focus, you need to define one of your rear buttons for that function. While the AF-ON button is the most logical choice, the exposure lock button (marked with an asterisk and located to its immediate right) can also be used. Either can be reached with your right thumb while your index finger remains poised over the shutter release button.

The easiest way to activate back-button focus is to make a quick trip to the Custom Controls entry in the Custom Functions 3 menu, as described in Chapter 14. Once you've activated this feature, you press one of two buttons: either the rear AE Lock button (marked with an asterisk or star icon) or the rear AF-ON button. Either is relatively easy to reach with your right thumb on the back of the camera as you shoot.

Here's what you need to do:

1. **Redefine the shutter release button.** In Custom Controls, highlight the Shutter Button entry, as shown at left in Figure 5.23. Press SET.

2. **Choose Metering Start.** When selected, pressing the shutter release activates metering, but *not* autofocus. press SET to confirm.

3. **Select Back Button.** The default value for the AF-ON button works fine (see Figure 5.23, right). When you press the AF-ON button, autofocus will initiate *and* metering will be performed, continuously updating both until you release the button. When the shutter release button is pressed, metering will take place and the exposure will be locked. If you want to lock exposure before the picture is taken, press the AE Lock (*) button.

   Alternatively, you can define the AE Lock (*) button with the Metering and AF Start function and use that for back-button focus instead. In that case, you'll want to redefine the AF-ON button to the AE lock function (the asterisk icon in Figure 5.23, right). If you do this, you have effectively swapped the buttons' functions.

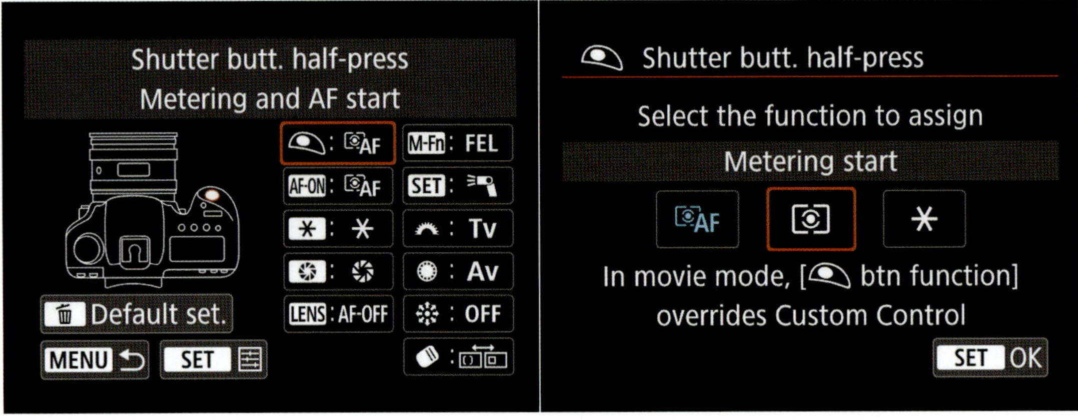

Figure 5.23 Activating back-button focus.

6

Advanced Techniques, Wi-Fi, and GPS

You can happily spend your entire shooting career using the techniques and features already explained in this book. Great exposures, sharp pictures, and creative compositions are all you really need to produce great shot after great shot. But, those with enough interest in getting the most out of their Canon EOS 5D Mark IV who buy this book probably will be interested in going beyond those basics to explore some of the more advanced techniques and capabilities of the camera. Capturing the briefest instant of time, transforming common scenes into the unusual with lengthy time exposures, and working with new tools like GPS and Wi-Fi are all tempting avenues for exploration. So, in this chapter, I'm going to offer longer discussions of some of the more advanced techniques and capabilities that I like to put to work.

Continuous Shooting

The Canon EOS 5D Mark IV's continuous shooting mode reminds me how far digital photography has brought us. The first accessory I purchased when I worked as a sports photographer some years ago was a motor drive for my film SLR. It enabled me to snap off a series of shots in rapid succession, which came in very handy when a fullback broke through the line and headed for the end zone. Even a seasoned action photographer can miss the decisive instant when a crucial block is made, or a baseball superstar's bat shatters and pieces of cork fly out. Continuous shooting simplifies taking a series of pictures, either to ensure that one has more or less the exact moment you want to capture or to capture a sequence that is interesting as a collection of successive images.

The 5D Mark IV's "motor drive" capabilities are, in many ways, much superior to what you get with a film camera. For one thing, a motor-driven film camera can eat up film at an incredible pace, which is why many of them are used with cassettes that hold hundreds of feet of film stock. At three frames per second (typical of film cameras), a short burst of a few seconds can burn up as much as half of an ordinary 36 exposure roll of film. Digital cameras, in contrast, have reusable "film," so if you waste a few dozen shots on non-decisive moments, you can erase them and shoot more. Save only the best shots, like the series shown in Figure 6.1.

To use the 5D Mark IV's continuous shooting mode, press the DRIVE-AF button and rotate the Quick Control Dial to select High-speed continuous (up to 7 frames per second), Low-speed continuous (3 fps), or Silent continuous shooting (3 fps). Alternatively, you can press the Q button to pop up the Quick Control screen and select the drive mode icon, which is located in the middle of the bottom row of icons.

When you partially depress the shutter button, the viewfinder will display a number representing the maximum number of shots you can take at the current quality settings. (If your battery is low, this figure will be lower.) The display shows a maximum of 99 shots remaining; it's possible that the camera can take more than that, so the 99 will remain lit until the actual number remaining drops below that value. When the internal buffer is full, a "buSY" indicator will be shown. Generally speaking, there is no actual limit on the number of JPEG shots you can take continuously (other than your card's capacity), as write speeds with standard and high-speed memory cards outpace the camera's capture rate when shooting Large, Medium, and all Small image sizes and compression ratios. The lone exception is with a Large JPEG Fine image and standard speed CF or SD card; you may be limited to about 110–130 frames before the buffer fills. (Canon does not specify the exact speed of its "benchmark" Compact Flash/Secure Digital standard/high-speed cards.)

Continuous shooting can be affected by the speed with which your 5D Mark IV is able to focus. So, in AI Servo AF mode, the frames-per-second rate may be lower. Lenses that inherently focus more slowly (see Chapter 7 for information on the various types of autofocus motors built into Canon lenses), and scenes that are poorly lit can also affect the frame rate.

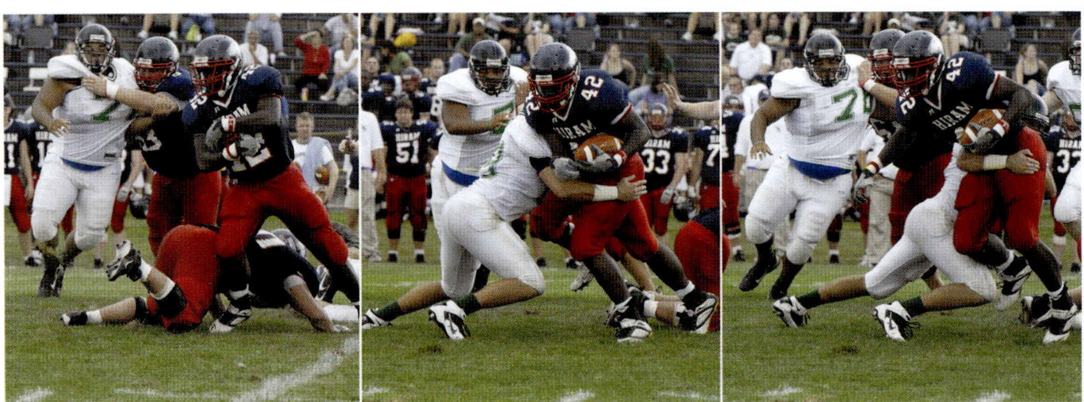

Figure 6.1 Continuous shooting allows you to capture an entire sequence of exciting moments as they unfold.

When the 5D Mark IV's internal buffer fills, the camera will stop capturing images until enough pictures have been written to the memory card to allow shooting to resume. As you might expect, the number of continuous shots you can fire off before that happens varies with the format you choose and the write speed of your card.

The reason the size of your bursts is limited by the buffer is that continuous images are first shuttled into the 5D Mark IV's internal memory, then doled out to the memory card as quickly as they can be written to the card. Technically, the 5D Mark IV takes the RAW data received from the digital image processor and converts it to the output format you've selected—either JPG or CR2 (RAW) or both—and deposits it in the buffer ready to store on the card.

This internal "smart" buffer can suck up photos much more quickly than the memory card and, indeed, some memory cards are significantly faster or slower than others. You'll get the best results when using a shutter speed of 1/500th second, the widest opening of the lens, One-Shot autofocus, and when image stabilization is turned off. However, when One-Shot AF is active, the 5D Mark IV will focus only once at the beginning of the sequence, and then use that focus setting for the rest of the shots in the burst. If your subject is moving, you can use AI Servo AF instead, at a slightly slower continuous frame rate.

Setting High ISO Speed Noise Reduction to High also limits the length of your continuous burst. You'll also see a decrease if lens aberration correction is active, or you have the camera set to do white balance bracketing. (In such cases, the 5D Mark IV stores multiple copies of each image snapped, slowing down the burst rate.) Anti-flicker shooting, and Dual Pixel RAW also reduce the continuous shooting speed. While you can use flash in continuous mode, the camera will wait for the flash to recycle between shots, slowing down the continuous shooting rate. In Live View mode, if you use Servo AF, the maximum shooting speed is likely to be no more than 4.3 frames per second.

BURSTS NOT JUST FOR ACTION

I often use continuous shooting mode even when I'm not busy shooting action. As I've mentioned before, bursts make sense when you're shooting HDR or bracketing. But here's a technique you might not have thought of—continuous shooting can give you sharper images!

When I'm photographing concerts, I most frequently use my 70-200mm f/2.8 IS zoom, hand-held, with image stabilization turned on, and using the highest continuous frame rate at my disposal. I enjoy greater mobility by not using a monopod (and a tripod would be even more of a ball-and-chain, even if not forbidden by the venue). I'm generally shooting at around 1/180th second, which is usually fast enough to eliminate blur from the performers' motion. IS has no effect on stopping *their* movement, of course, and it does a fairly good job of eliminating camera/photographer shake. However, I invariably find that if I shoot in continuous, one of the middle frames in a sequence will be sharpest. Even the most seasoned photographer will add a little bump to the camera when they squeeze (not stab) the shutter release.

More Exposure Options

In Chapter 4, you learned techniques for getting the *right* exposure, but I haven't explained all your exposure options just yet. You'll want to know about the *kind* of exposure settings that are available to you with the Canon EOS 5D Mark IV. There are options that let you control when the exposure is made, or even how to make an exposure that's out of the ordinary in terms of length (time or bulb exposures). The sections that follow explain your camera's special exposure features, and even discuss a few it does not have (and why it doesn't).

A Tiny Slice of Time

Exposures that seem impossibly brief can reveal a world we didn't know existed. In the 1930s, Dr. Harold Edgerton, a professor of electrical engineering at MIT, pioneered high-speed photography using a repeating electronic flash unit he patented called the *stroboscope*. As the inventor of the electronic flash, he popularized its use to freeze objects in motion, and you've probably seen his photographs of bullets piercing balloons and drops of milk forming a coronet-shaped splash.

Electronic flash freezes action by virtue of its extremely short duration—as brief as 1/50,000th second or less. You can read more about using electronic flash to stop action in Chapter 9.

Of course, the 5D Mark IV is fully capable of immobilizing all but the fastest movement using only its shutter speeds, which range all the way up to 1/8,000th second. Indeed, you'll rarely have need for such a brief shutter speed in ordinary shooting. If you wanted to use an aperture of f/2.8 at ISO 100 outdoors in bright sunlight, for some reason, a shutter speed of 1/8,000th second would more than do the job. You'd need a faster shutter speed only if you moved the ISO setting to a higher sensitivity (but why would you do that?). Under less than full sunlight, 1/8,000th second is more than fast enough for any conditions you're likely to encounter.

Most sports action can be frozen at 1/2,000th second or slower, and for many sports a slower shutter speed is actually preferable—for example, to allow the wheels of a racing automobile or motorcycle, or the propeller on a classic aircraft to blur realistically.

But if you want to do some exotic action-freezing photography without resorting to electronic flash, the 5D Mark IV's top shutter speed is at your disposal. Here are some things to think about when exploring this type of high-speed photography:

- **You'll need a lot of light.** High shutter speeds cut very fine slices of time and sharply reduce the amount of illumination that reaches your sensor. To use 1/4,000th second at an aperture of f/6.3, you'd need an ISO setting of 800—even in full daylight. To use an f/stop smaller than f/6.3 or an ISO setting lower than 800, you'd need *more* light than full daylight provides. (That's why electronic flash units work so well for high-speed photography when used as the sole illumination; they provide both the effect of a brief shutter speed and the high levels of illumination needed.)

- **Don't combine high shutter speeds with electronic flash.** You might be tempted to use an electronic flash with a high shutter speed. Perhaps you want to stop some action in daylight with a brief shutter speed and use electronic flash only as supplemental illumination to fill in the shadows. Unfortunately, under most conditions you can't use flash in subdued illumination with your 5D Mark IV at any shutter speed faster than 1/200th second. That's the fastest speed at which the camera's focal plane shutter is fully open: at shorter speeds, the "slit" (described in more detail in Chapter 9) comes into play. (Check out "Avoiding Sync Speed Problems" in Chapter 9 if you want to see how you *can* use shutter speeds shorter than 1/200th second with certain Canon Speedlites, albeit at much-reduced effective power levels.)

Working with Short Exposures

You can have a lot of fun exploring the kinds of pictures you can take using very brief exposure times, whether you decide to take advantage of the action-stopping capabilities of your built-in or external electronic flash or work with the Canon EOS 5D Mark IV's faster shutter speeds. Here are a few ideas to get you started:

- **Take revealing images.** Fast shutter speeds can help you reveal the real subject behind the façade, by freezing constant motion to capture an enlightening moment in time. Legendary fashion/portrait photographer Philippe Halsman used leaping photos of famous people, such as the Duke and Duchess of Windsor, Richard Nixon, and Salvador Dali to illuminate their real selves. Halsman said, "*When you ask a person to jump, his attention is mostly directed toward the act of jumping and the mask falls so that the real person appears.*" Try some high-speed portraits of people you know in motion to see how they appear when concentrating on something other than the portrait. (See Figure 6.2.)

- **Create unreal images.** High-speed photography can also produce photographs that show your subjects in ways that are quite unreal. A helicopter in mid-air with its rotors frozen makes for an unusual picture. Figure 6.3 shows a pair of pictures. At top, a shutter speed of 1/1,000th

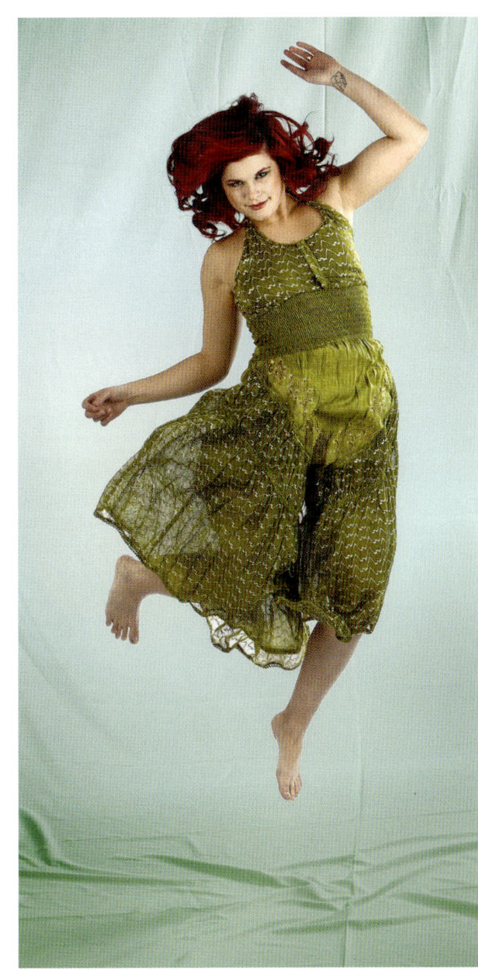

Figure 6.2 When your subjects leap, the real person inside emerges.

second virtually stopped the rotation of the chopper's rotors, while the bottom image, shot at 1/200th second, provides a more realistic view of the blurry blades as they appeared to the eye.

- **Capture unseen perspectives.** Some things are *never* seen in real life, except when viewed in a stop-action photograph. Edgerton's balloon bursts were only a starting point. Freeze a hummingbird in flight for a view of wings that never seem to stop. Or, capture the splashes as liquid falls into a bowl, as shown in Figure 6.4. No electronic flash was required for this image (and wouldn't have illuminated the water in the bowl as evenly). Instead, a clutch of high-intensity lamps and an ISO setting of 1600 allowed the EOS 5D Mark IV to capture this image at 1/2,000th second.

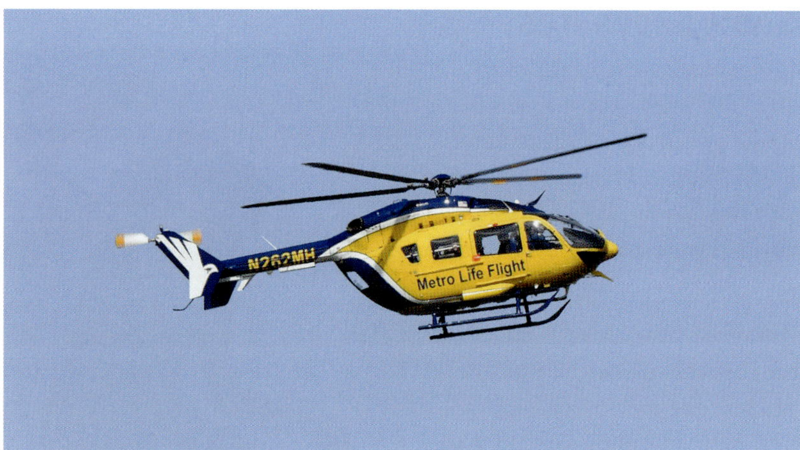

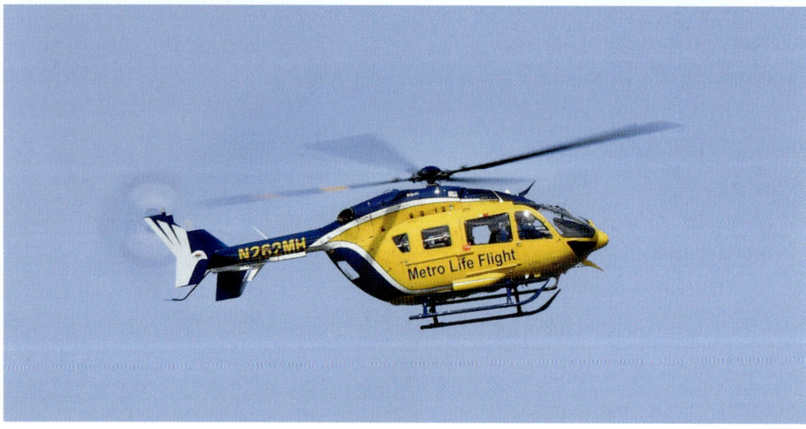

Figure 6.3
Top: the chopper's blades are frozen at 1/1,000th second; bottom: a more realistic blurry rendition at 1/200th second shutter speed.

Figure 6.4
A large amount of artificial illumination and an ISO 1600 sensitivity setting allowed capturing this shot at 1/2,000th second without use of an electronic flash.

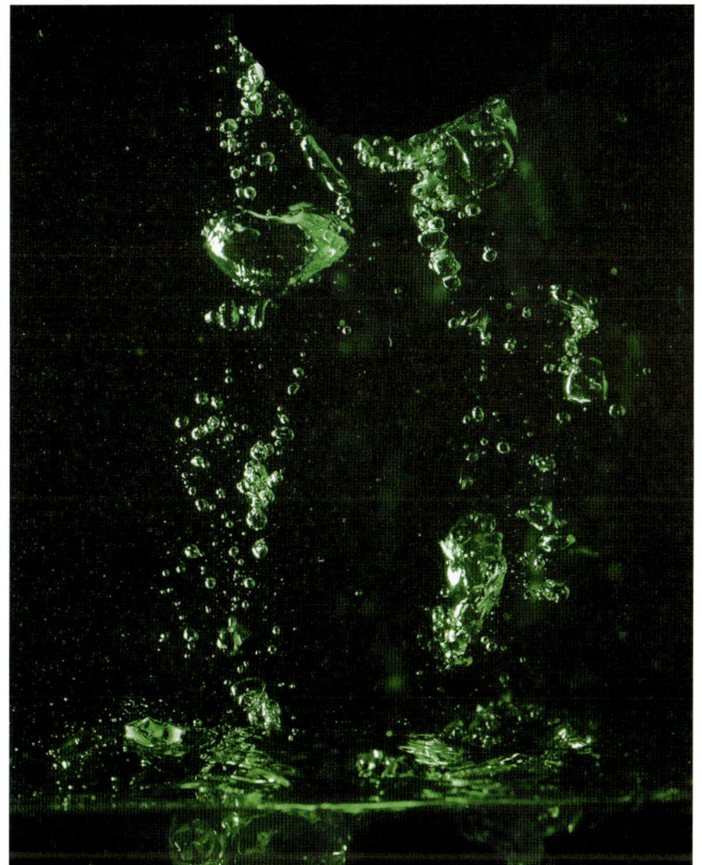

■ **Vanquish camera shake and gain new angles.** Here's an idea I mentioned earlier in this chapter that's so obvious it isn't always explored to its fullest extent. A high enough shutter speed can free you from the tyranny of a tripod, making it easier to capture new angles, or to shoot quickly while moving around, especially with longer lenses. I tend to use a monopod or tripod for almost everything when I'm not using an image-stabilized lens, and I end up missing some shots because of a reluctance to adjust my camera support to get a higher, lower, or different angle. If you have enough light and can use an f/stop wide enough to permit a high shutter speed, you'll find a new freedom to choose your shots. I have a favored 170mm-500mm lens that I use for sports and wildlife photography, almost invariably with a tripod, as I don't find the "reciprocal of the focal length" rule particularly helpful in most cases. (I would *not* hand-hold this hefty lens at its 500mm setting with a 1/500th second shutter speed under most circumstances.) However, at 1/2,000th second or faster, and with a sufficiently high ISO setting (I recommend ISO 800–1600) to allow such a speed, it's entirely possible for a steady hand to use this lens without a tripod or monopod's extra support, and I've found that my whole approach to shooting animals and other elusive subjects changes in high-speed mode. Selective focus allows dramatically isolating my prey wide open at f/6.3, too.

Long Exposures

Longer exposures are a doorway into another world, showing us how even familiar scenes can look much different when photographed over periods measured in seconds. At night, long exposures produce streaks of light from moving, illuminated subjects like automobiles or amusement park rides. Extra-long exposures of seemingly pitch-dark subjects can reveal interesting views using light levels barely bright enough to see by. At any time of day, including daytime (in which case you'll often need the help of neutral-density filters, which reduce the amount of light passing through the lens, to make the long exposure practical), long exposures can cause moving objects to vanish entirely, because they don't remain stationary long enough to register in a photograph.

WATCH OUT FOR AMP NOISE

When exposures extend past 30 seconds into the realm of several minutes—or more—all digital cameras are theoretically susceptible to a phenomenon called *amp noise*, which manifests itself as a purplish glow, often around the edges of an image, creating an aurora borealis–style ghost effect. Amp noise happens when the sensor heats up during a long exposure, and some cameras fall victim more readily than others. The EOS 5D Mark IV resists this phenomenon better than most dSLRs, but you should be aware it exists, even if you'd need to use an uncommon exposure (on the order of 30 minutes or so) to create the effect with your camera.

Three Ways to Take Long Exposures

There are actually three common types of lengthy exposures: *timed exposures*, *bulb exposures*, and *time exposures*. The EOS 5D Mark IV offers all three. Because of the length of the exposure, all of the following techniques should be used with a tripod to hold the camera steady.

- **Timed exposures.** These are long exposures from 1 second to 30 seconds, measured by the camera itself. To take a picture in this range, simply use Manual or Tv modes and use the Main Dial to set the shutter speed to the length of time you want, choosing from preset speeds of 1.0, 1.5, 2.0, 3.0, 4.0, 6.0, 8.0, 10.0, 15.0, 20.0, or 30.0 seconds (if you've specified ½-stop increments for exposure adjustments), or 1.0, 1.3, 1.6, 2.0, 2.5, 3.2, 4.0, 5.0, 6.0, 8.0, 10.0, 13.0, 15.0, 20.0, 25.0, and 30.0 seconds (if you're using 1/3-stop increments). The advantage of timed exposures is that the camera does all the calculating for you. There's no need for a stopwatch. If you review your image on the LCD and decide to try again with the exposure doubled or halved, you can dial in the correct exposure with precision. The disadvantage of timed exposures is that you can't take a photo for longer than 30 seconds.

- **Bulb exposures.** This type of exposure is so-called because in the olden days the photographer squeezed and held an air bulb attached to a tube that provided the force necessary to keep the shutter open. Traditionally, a bulb exposure is one that lasts as long as the shutter release button is pressed; when you release the button, the exposure ends. To make a bulb exposure with the 5D Mark IV, set the camera on B using the Mode Dial. Then, press the shutter to start the exposure, and press it again to close the shutter.

■ **Timed exposures.** This is a setting found on some cameras to produce longer exposures. With the 5D Mark IV, it's actually an enhancement of the Bulb exposure feature. With the camera's Mode Dial set to Bulb, locate the Bulb Timer setting in the Shooting 4 menu. Press SET, and in the screen that pops up, highlight Enable. Press SET again, and a screen appears that will allow you to set an exposure time of up to 99 hours, 59 minutes, and 59 seconds. You'll rarely need extra-long exposures (unless you're shooting continuous star trails), but many exposures longer than 30 seconds are quite useful. For example, if many star photographers shoot multiple one-minute exposures (any longer than that, and the star pinpoints become blurs) and then merge them together to get a different kind of sky photograph.

When using this type of Bulb exposure, you can press the shutter release button, go off for a few minutes, and come back to take your next shot (assuming your camera is still there). The disadvantages of this mode are exposures must be timed manually, and with shorter exposures, it's possible for the vibration of manually opening and closing the shutter to register in the photo. For longer exposures, the period of vibration is relatively brief and not usually a problem—and there is always the release cable option to eliminate photographer-caused camera shake entirely.

Working with Long Exposures

Because the EOS 5D Mark IV produces such good images at longer exposures, and there are so many creative things you can do with long-exposure techniques, you'll want to do some experimenting. Get yourself a tripod or another firm support and take some test shots with long exposure noise reduction both enabled and disabled using the entry in the Shooting 3 menu, as explained in Chapter 11 (to see whether you prefer low noise or high detail), and get started. Here are some things to try:

■ **Make people invisible.** One very cool thing about long exposures is that objects that move rapidly enough won't register at all in a photograph, while the subjects that remain stationary are portrayed in the normal way. That makes it easy to produce people-free landscape photos and architectural photos at night or, even, in full daylight if you use a neutral-density filter (or two or three) to allow an exposure of at least a few seconds. At ISO 100, f/22, and a pair of 8X (three-stop) neutral-density filters, you can use exposures of nearly two seconds; overcast days and/or more neutral-density filtration would work even better if daylight people-vanishing is your goal. They'll have to be walking *very* briskly and across the field of view (rather than directly toward the camera) for this to work. At night, it's much easier to achieve this effect with the 20- to 30-second exposures that are possible, as you can see in Figure 6.5.

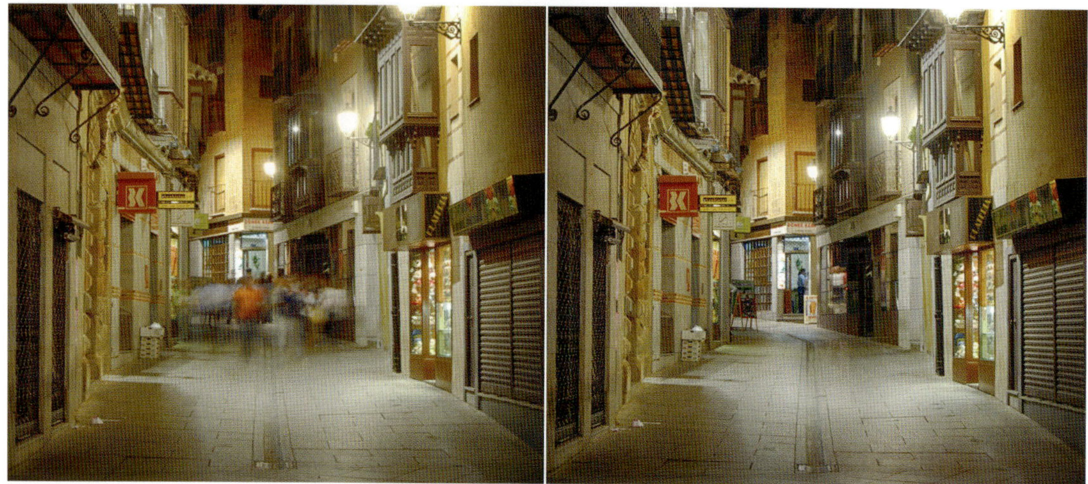

Figure 6.5 This alleyway is thronged with people, as you can see in this two-second exposure using only the available illumination (left). With the camera still on a tripod, a 30-second exposure rendered the passersby almost invisible (right).

- **Create streaks.** If you aren't shooting for total invisibility, long exposures with the camera on a tripod or monopod can produce some interesting streaky effects, as you can see in Figure 6.6. You don't need to limit yourself to indoor photography, however. Even a single 8X ND filter will let you shoot at f/22 and 1/6th second in full daylight at ISO 100.

- **Produce light trails.** At night, car headlights and taillights and other moving sources of illumination can generate interesting light trails. Your camera doesn't even need to be mounted on a tripod; hand-holding the 5D Mark IV for longer exposures adds movement and patterns to your trails. If you're shooting fireworks (preferably with a tripod), a longer exposure of several seconds may allow you to combine several bursts into one picture. Or, you can record the movement of a Ferris wheel, as shown in Figure 6.7.

- **Blur waterfalls, etc.** You'll find that waterfalls and other sources of moving liquid produce a special type of long exposure blur, because the water merges into a fantasy-like veil that looks different at different exposure times, and with different waterfalls. Cascades with turbulent flow produce a rougher look at a given longer exposure than falls that flow smoothly. Although blurred waterfalls have become almost a cliché, there are still plenty of variations for a creative photographer to explore, as you can see in Figure 6.8.

- **Show total darkness in new ways.** Even on the darkest nights, there is enough starlight or glow from distant illumination sources to see by, and, if you use a long exposure, there is enough light to take a picture, too. Figure 6.9 shows San Juan, Puerto Rico late at night.

Figure 6.6
These dancers produced a swirl of movement during the 1/8th second exposure.

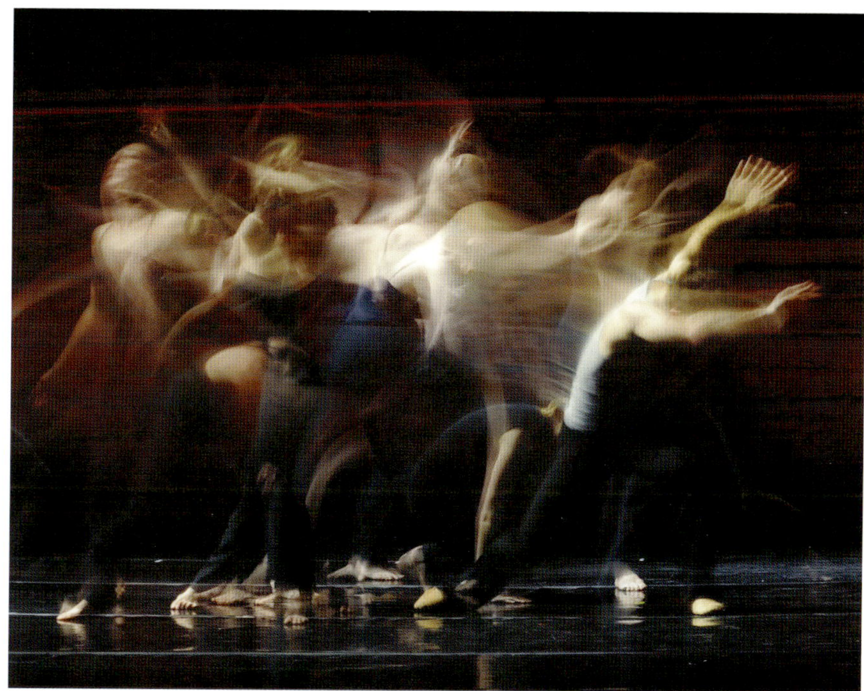

Figure 6.7
A long exposure allows capturing the movement of this Ferris wheel.

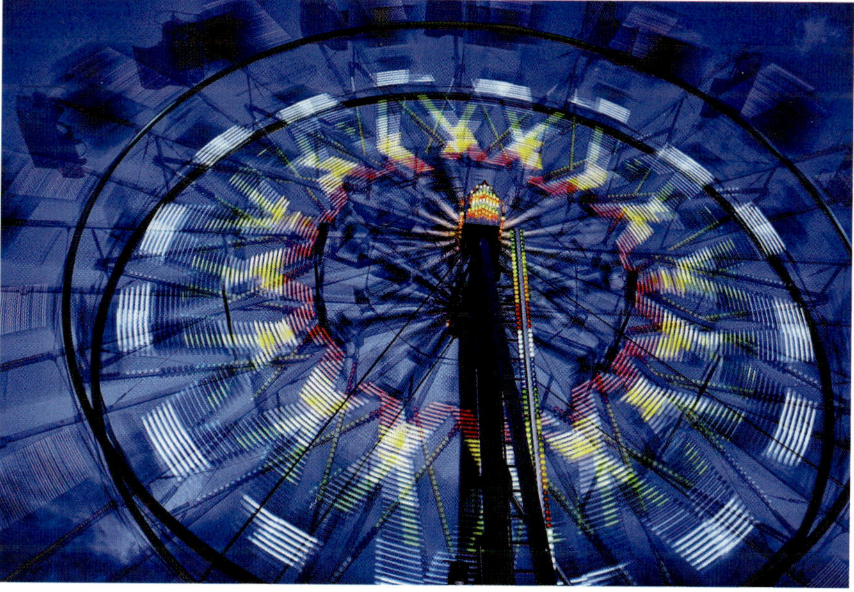

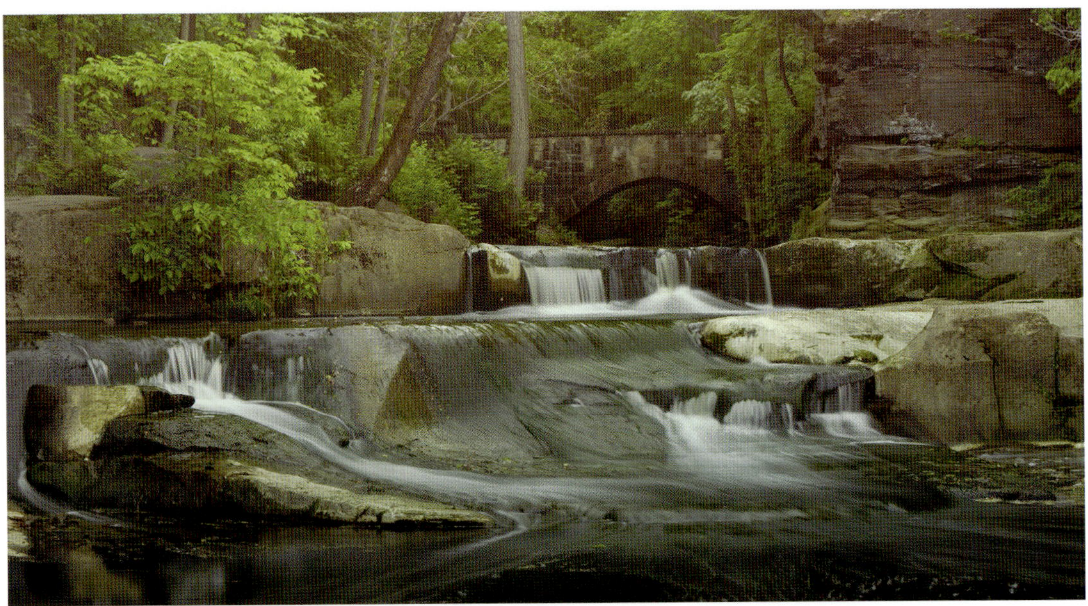

Figure 6.8 A 1/4-second exposure blurred the falling water.

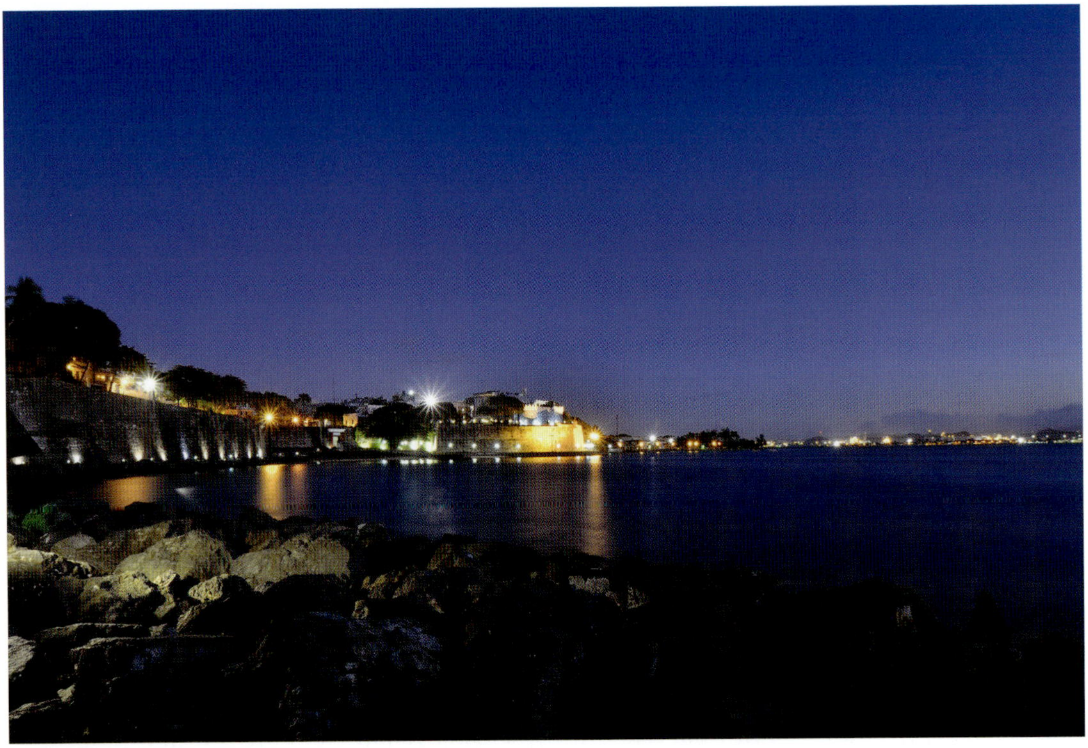

Figure 6.9 A 20-second exposure revealed this view of San Juan, Puerto Rico.

Delayed Exposures

Sometimes it's desirable to have a delay of some sort before a picture is actually taken. Perhaps you'd like to get in the picture yourself, and would appreciate it if the camera waited 10 seconds after you press the shutter release to actually take the picture. Maybe you want to give a tripod-mounted camera time to settle down and damp any residual vibration after the release is pressed to improve sharpness for an exposure with a relatively slow shutter speed. It's possible you want to explore the world of time-lapse photography. The next sections present your delayed exposure options.

Self-Timer

The EOS 5D Mark IV has a built-in self-timer with 10-second and 2-second delays. Activate the timer by pressing the DRIVE-AF button and rotating the QCD to select the drive modes. Press the shutter release button halfway to lock in focus on your subjects (if you're taking a self-portrait, focus on an object at a similar distance and use focus lock). When you're ready to take the photo, continue pressing the shutter release the rest of the way. The lamp on the front of the camera will blink slowly for eight seconds (when using the 10-second timer) and the beeper will chirp (if you haven't disabled it in the Shooting menu, as described in Chapter 11). During the final two seconds, the beeper sounds more rapidly and the lamp remains on until the picture is taken. The top-panel LCD displays a countdown while all this is going on.

Another way to use the self-timer is with the mirror lockup feature (which can be enabled using the Shooting 4 menu entry, as explained in Chapter 11). This is something you might want to do if you're shooting close-ups, landscapes, or other types of pictures using the self-timer, to trip the shutter in the most vibration-free way possible. Forget to bring along your tripod, but still want to take a close-up picture with a precise focus setting? Set your digital camera to the self-timer function, then put the camera on any reasonably steady support, such as a fence post or a rock. When you're ready to take the picture, press the shutter release. The camera might teeter back and forth for a second or two, but it will settle back to its original position before the self-timer activates the shutter. The self-timer remains active until you turn it off—even if you power down the 5D Mark IV, so remember to turn it off when finished.

Interval/Time Lapse Photography

Who hasn't marveled at interval stills, shot moments or minutes apart to document an event, or wasn't enrapt by a time-lapse movie of a flower opening, a series of shots of the moon marching across the sky, or one of those extreme interval or time-lapse photography productions showing something that takes a very, very long time, such as a building under construction.

You probably won't be shooting such construction shots, unless you have a spare 5D Mark IV you don't need for a few months (or are willing to go through the rigmarole of figuring out how to set up your camera in precisely the same position using the same lens settings to shoot a series of pictures at intervals). However, other kinds of time-lapse photography are entirely within reach.

The 5D Mark IV has built-in features that allow you to create a set of still photographs taken at intervals you specify, or shoot time-lapse movies easily. Before I explain how to use these features, here are a few things to keep in mind:

- **Use AC power.** If you're shooting a long sequence, consider connecting your camera to an AC adapter, as leaving the 5D Mark IV on for long periods of time will rapidly deplete the battery. The optional Canon DC Coupler DR-E6 and AC Adapter AC-6N are perfect for this application. While shooting time-lapse movies, auto power off will not take place.

- **Disabled functions.** While capturing time-lapse movies, ISO must be ISO 6400 or slower; shooting and menu functions and playback are disabled, along with Movie Servo AF. You can't shoot time-lapse movies if digital zoom is enabled, and sound is not recorded.

- **Make sure you have enough storage space.** Unless your memory card has enough capacity to hold all the images you'll be taking, you might want to change to a higher compression rate or reduced resolution to maximize the image count.

- **Protect your camera.** If your camera will be set up for an extended period of time (longer than an hour or two), make sure it's protected from weather, earthquakes, animals, young children, innocent bystanders, and theft.

- **Vary intervals.** Experiment with different time intervals. You don't want to take pictures or frames too often or less often than necessary to capture the changes you hope to image in your movies or still series.

Interval Timer

The 5D Mark IV allows you to shoot a series of still shots at intervals you specify. The function is similar to time-lapse movie shooting (described next) in many respects, but must be done in still photography mode (with the Live View/Movie switch set to the Live View position, although you cannot be in Live View mode to use this feature). Nor can you shoot movies or use Bulb exposures while Interval Timer is enabled. Here are some other things to consider:

- **Interval timing can be combined with other functions.** You can use auto exposure and white balance bracketing, shoot multiple exposures, or access HDR mode. I particularly like to shoot multiple exposures combined with interval shots when doing manual HDR work. For example, I've set my 5D Mark IV on a tripod and configured it to shoot bracketed shots of a sunset at intervals, so I ended up with groups of pictures taken over a span of time that I could combine in Photoshop.

- **The 5D Mark IV is smart enough to override auto power off settings.** After powering down, it will turn itself on roughly one minute before the next shot is taken.

- **You don't have to use the menu to disable interval shooting.** Just turn the 5D Mark IV off.

- **Use manual focus if you can.** If the camera is unable to autofocus, the shot will not be captured.

- **Flash is okay.** But make sure the interval between shots is longer than the flash's normal recycling time.

Just follow these steps:

1. **Access Interval Timer.** Visit the Shooting 4 menu and choose Interval Timer, the first entry on the screen.

2. **Enable.** Highlight Enable and the settings display shown in Figure 6.10, left, appears.

3. **Access settings.** Press the INFO. button to produce the Adjust Interval/Shots screen seen in Figure 6.10, right.

4. **Choose an interval between exposures,** in hours, minutes, and seconds, from 00:00:01 to 99:59:59.

5. **Specify number of shots.** Choose from 01 to 99, or you can select Unlimited (00) and the camera will continue to capture stills until you stop the timer, the memory card fills, or the battery runs out of juice.

6. **Confirm.** Highlight OK and press SET.

7. **Make other settings.** In the screen that appears next, you can Enable/Disable Anti-Flicker correction. When active, anti-flicker (enabled in the Shooting 4 menu, discussed in Chapter 8) may slow down capture. You can also Enable/Disable a Bulb exposure timer, turn mirror lockup on or off, and specify an aspect ratio for the image's capture.

8. **Exit.** When finished setting up press the MENU button to exit.

9. **Press the shutter release to begin.** The Timer indicator on the top-panel LCD status panel will blink. Once the series is complete, the 5D Mark IV will cancel interval timer shooting automatically.

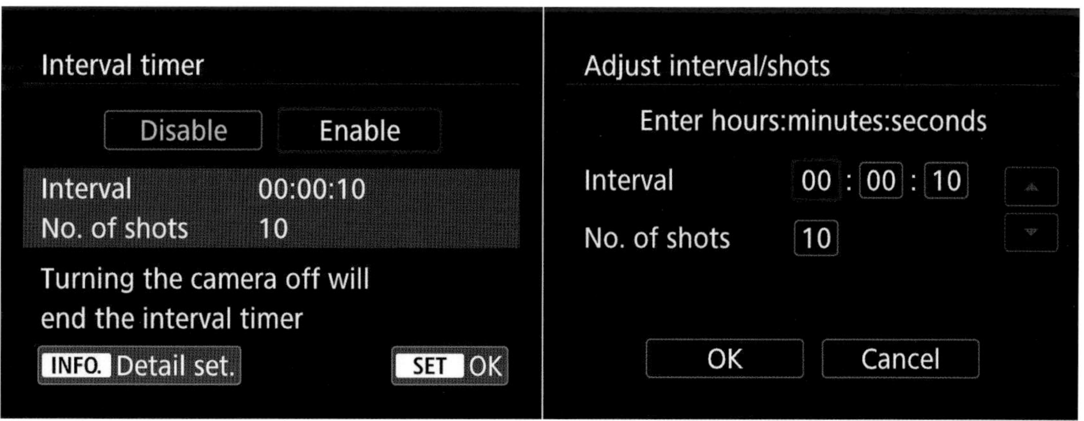

Figure 6.10 Enable the interval timer (left) and adjust the interval and number of shots (right).

Time-lapse Movies

The 5D Mark IV's time-lapse movie facility is actually a still photography mode that shoots images at intervals you specify, and then stitches them together automatically to create a MOV-format movie in Full HD (1920 × 1080) at a playback rate of 30/25 fps. To create a time-lapse movie, just follow these steps:

1. **Set the Live View/Movie switch to the Movie position.** Even though time-lapse clips are a series of stills, you must be in Movie mode to access the feature. Even though individual images are still photographs, no stills are stored; the 5D Mark IV converts them to a movie file even if you take only one shot in time-lapse mode.

2. **Navigate to the Shooting 5 (Movie) menu.** (Use the Shooting 3 menu if the Mode Dial is set to Scene Intelligent Auto.) Select Time-Lapse Movie and press SET.

3. **Choose Enable.** The current settings will be shown, as in Figure 6.11, left.

4. **Press the INFO. button.** (*Not* the SET button). The options shown in Figure 6.11, right, appear. Highlight each one and press SET, and use the up/down buttons to select values. You can choose the interval between shots, up to 99 hours, 59 minutes, and 59 seconds, and the total number of shots to take in the sequence. The expected elapsed time for the entire sequence is shown near the bottom of the screen.

5. **Confirm.** When finished setting parameters, highlight OK and press SET to confirm.

6. **Exit menu and test settings.** Press MENU to exit the menu system. A message appears on the LCD monitor advising you to make your exposure settings and press the shutter release to take a test shot. Note that you can use a full range of shutter speeds from 1/8,000th to 1/30th second and if you've selected a speed slower than 1/60th second, when capture ends the camera will change to a shutter speed allowable for movie shooting.

7. **Exit setup.** When satisfied with your exposure settings, press OK to exit the set-up screen.

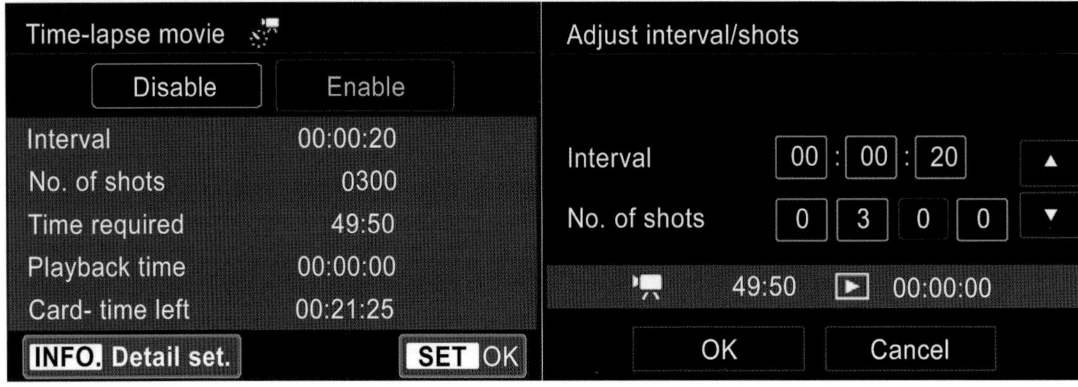

Figure 6.11 Enable/disable and check settings on this screen (left). Choose interval and number of shots here (right).

8. **Check settings (optional).** You can check your settings by accessing the Shooting 5 (Movie) menu and selecting Time-Lapse Movie again. The current settings appear in the screen as shown earlier at left in Figure 6.11.

9. **Start time-lapse.** When ready to begin, press the Start/Stop button to commence your time-lapse movie.

10. **Stop capture.** While the time-lapse movie is recording, you can press the shutter release to start or stop capture, or the Start/Stop button to return to the exposure set-up screen. When time-lapse shooting ends, the settings are cleared and the 5D Mark IV resumes normal Movie shooting mode.

Introducing Wi-Fi

Your 5D Mark IV has built-in wireless communications capabilities that allow you to link the camera to multiple devices. The various permutations and features are complex, to the extent that Canon includes a 48-page basic Wi-Fi manual as part of its basic 5D Mark IV product guide, and a separate exhaustive (and exhausting) 180-page Wireless Communication Function Instruction Manual. This book concentrates on still photography rather than information technology and, obviously, I can't devote 48 pages or 180 pages just to Wi-Fi topics. However, I think you'll find enough information in the following sections to get you started.

First, here is a list of the connections you can make with the 5D Mark IV's built-in Wi-Fi:

- **Phones and tablets.** You can connect to a smartphone or tablet and use an app on the device to operate the camera remotely or review images on your memory card. Both Android and iOS are supported. Quick connection with Android devices using NFC (Near Field Communications) is available, but, to date Apple's iOS supports NFC only for Apple Pay. That may change while this book is in print, given the expected long product life of the 5D Mark IV.

- **Connect Station.** Canon offers the Connect Station, a 1TB storage device that can download images from the 5D Mark IV over a wireless connection, or transfer them directly using its two memory card slots. The transferred images can be viewed using a web browser, or directed to an HDMI-compatible monitor/HDTV over a cable connection. An included remote control allows you to display the images in slide-show fashion.

- **Remote control.** The 5D Mark IV can be operated remotely using a computer with EOS Utility software installed.

- **Direct printing.** If you have a Wi-Fi-compatible printer that supports PictBridge, you can make hard copies of your images with a wireless connection.

- **FTP transfer.** You can send your images to an FTP server for immediate availability by anyone with permissions to access that server.

- **Web upload.** The free Canon iMage Gateway can be used to share your images with colleagues, family, or friends over the Internet.

I'll explain all of these in the next sections, but first you need to consider some general guidelines for the 5D Mark IV's built-in wireless functions.

General Wi-Fi Guidelines

Here are some general tips for using the EOS 5D Mark IV's built-in Wi-Fi functions:

- **Conserve processing power.** Wi-Fi uses some of your camera's internal CPU's processing muscle, so when the 5D Mark IV is busy communicating with another device, give Wi-Fi top priority. Don't press the shutter release, rotate the Mode Dial, or review images with the Playback button. If you do, Wi-Fi functions may be interrupted.

- **Some functions are disabled.** When Wi-Fi is enabled the 5D Mark IV cannot communicate with a computer, printer, external monitor, GPS, or other device with a direct (cable) connection, USB, or HDMI cable link. For example, if you're viewing your camera's output on a monitor using an HDMI connection, the monitor will go dark during Wi-Fi communication. In addition, you can't use an Eye-Fi card (an SD card with its own built-in Wi-Fi functions) and the internal Wi-Fi functions simultaneously; if you've set the 5D Mark IV's Wi-Fi functions to Enable, any Eye-Fi card is automatically disabled. The camera cannot be connected to other NFC devices, including printers, when you're using the NFC function.

- **No auto shutoff.** When using Wi-Fi, the camera's power-saving shutdown feature is disabled.

- **Monitor connection status.** Wi-Fi status can be seen within the information displays on both the camera's LCD monitor and LCD panel. When Wi-Fi is disabled, or enabled but no connection is available, an OFF indicator is shown in both places. When a connection is available, the indicators are animated when data is being transmitted, and blink if the camera is waiting for a reconnection or there is a connection error.

Using Wi-Fi and NFC

Your 5D Mark IV can communicate using standard Wi-Fi communications or, with Android devices, NFC (Near Field Communications). The latter is a radio protocol similar to Bluetooth that makes automatic connections simply by touching the NFC indicator on the side of the camera with the memory card door to the NFC indicator on the Android phone or tablet. To activate and begin using the 5D Mark IV's Wi-Fi capabilities, just follow these steps:

1. **Download App.** If you plan to link your 5D Mark IV to an Android or iOS smart device, visit your device's store and download the Canon Camera Connect app to your smartphone or tablet.

2. **Enable Wi-Fi.** Navigate to the Set-up 4 menu and select Communication Settings. (See Figure 6.12, upper left.) Choose Built-In Wireless Settings (Figure 6.12, upper right), press SET, and choose Enable from the next screen (Figure 6.12, lower left).

3. **Activate NFC (Android only).** If you plan to link an Android device to your camera, press the INFO. button to allow NFC connections. (NFC does not currently work with iOS devices.) Press/tap SET to confirm and exit back to the previous menu. Because wireless communications use power, you'll want to Disable the feature when it is not needed, or when in areas where such electronic features are prohibited (chiefly onboard airplanes or in hospitals).

4. **Set Camera Nickname.** The first time you use Wi-Fi, the camera will ask you to choose a nickname. You can also name or rename your camera at any time by scrolling down to the Nickname entry (fourth from the top in Figure 6.12, lower left). The sidebar that follows explains how to enter the nickname.

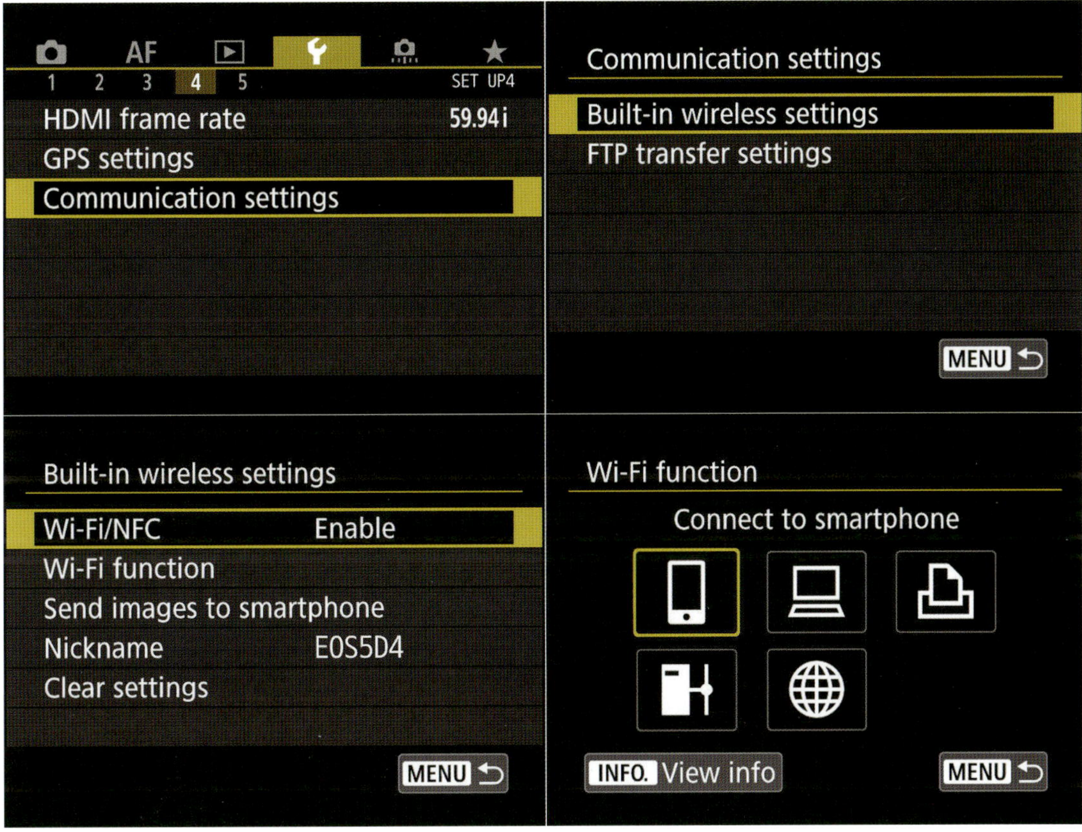

Figure 6.12 Set-up 4 menu (upper left); Communications Settings (upper right); Built-in Wireless settings (lower left); Wi-Fi functions (lower right).

5. **Select function.** When your camera has acquired a nickname, or you choose Wi-Fi Function in the Built-In Wireless Settings screen, the display shown in Figure 6.12, lower right, appears. Use the left/right directional buttons, the Quick Control Dial, or touch screen to navigate to the Wi-Fi function you want to activate and press/tap SET. Choose from:

   - Transfer images between cameras.

   - Connect to a smartphone.

   - Remote control (EOS Utility).

   - Print from a Wi-Fi printer.

   - Transfer images to an FTP server.

   - Upload to web service on the Internet.

   - Press INFO. to view error details, or your camera's MAC (Media Access Control) address. That's the "label" the network uses to identify individual wireless devices that are connected. You probably won't need it unless you need to block a particular MAC address from access to a network for some reason, or simply want to use your router's screens to see what devices are connected.

6. **Enter parameters.** Each of the modes has its own set of parameters, described in the sections that follow.

ENTERING TEXT

The entry screen has two sections, the entered text area, and an alphabetical character selection area. (See Figure 6.13.) You'll find the touch screen the easiest way to enter this information. Press/tap the Q button to toggle between the two. In the selection area, navigate to the character you want to add and press/tap SET. You can enter up to 10 characters in your nickname, such as "Busch5D4" or "EOS5D4" and you cannot have a nickname with no characters at all. If Touch Control is enabled, you'll find all the available characters on multiple screens; when disabled, all are available on a single screen. Press the Trash button to erase a character, the INFO. button to cancel text entry, and MENU to finish and confirm your nickname by selecting OK on the screen that pops up. If you later want to change the nickname, return to this menu entry in the Wireless Communications screen.

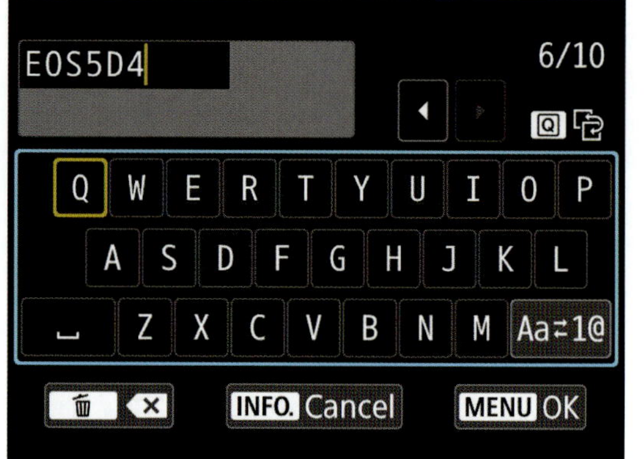

Figure 6.13 Enter a nickname.

Making an NFC Connection

While the sections that follow this one describe making Wi-Fi connections between devices, if you have an Android phone or tablet with NFC, you can link easily just by touching the NFC icon on your 5D Mark IV to the matching icon on your device. (Note that with the 5D Mark IV, NFC can be used only between the camera and phones and tablets or the Canon Connection Station, and not between printers or other NFC-enabled devices.)

You must first visit the Communications Settings screen in the Set-Up 4 menu, and choose Wi-Fi/NFC. Select Enable, and press the INFO. button to permit NFC connections. Then, all you need to do is touch the smartphone/tablet's icon to the camera's. The Camera Connect app on your device (which you have previously downloaded from the Google Play app store) makes the connection automatically. You can then carry out the functions described in the next few sections.

Connecting to a Smartphone

Your 5D Mark IV can use its Wi-Fi connection to interface when using stills mode (but not movie mode) with a smartphone using an app that's available for both iOS and Android operating systems. Navigate to your phone's App store or Google Play and download the free Canon Camera Connect application.

The camera and phone connect through a wireless LAN, either an external network (such as your home network, or one at a hotel or other site) or using the camera itself as an access point (so that no separate network is required). The latter mode is especially convenient, because you can use it anywhere if the camera and phone are located within range of the 5D Mark IV's network capabilities. Using an external LAN might be your choice if you wanted to communicate between your camera and the phone over a greater distance.

To link up through your camera's internal access point, just follow these steps the first time. Once you've connected successfully, you won't need to repeat them, and can instead use the "Send Images to Smartphone" entry in the Wireless Communications Settings screen when you just want to transmit photos.

1. Enable Wi-Fi in the Set-up 4 menu, then navigate to Wi-Fi Function in the Wireless Connections entry, as described earlier.

2. Choose the Connect to Smartphone option, the leftmost icon in the top row of the Wi-Fi Function screen shown earlier in Figure 6.12.

3. Select Easy Connection from the Connection Method screen that appears next (see Figure 6.14, left), and press SET. OK will be highlighted, and you can press SET again to continue.

4. A message appears "Waiting to connect." The screen displays the name of the 5D Mark IV's internal access point (the SSID, or *service set identifier* and an encryption key). This will be the nickname you chose for the camera earlier. The *encryption key* shown on this screen is the password you'll need to log into your camera's access point. (See Figure 6.14, right.)

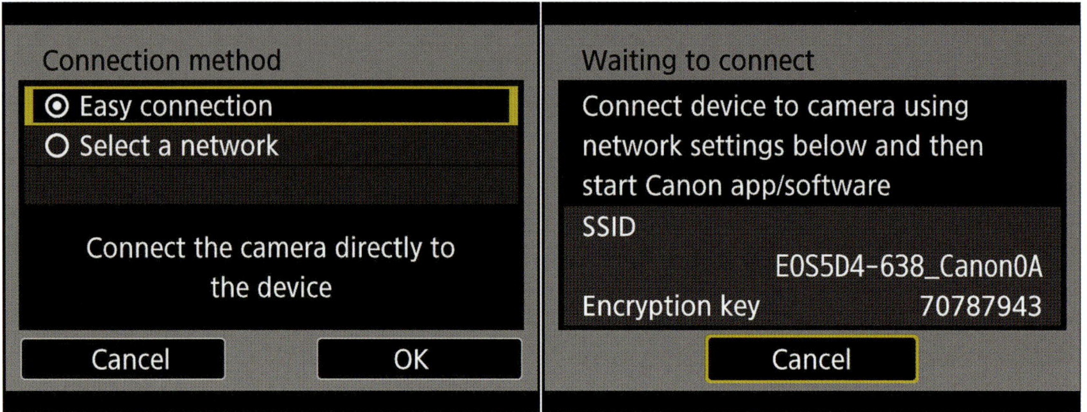

Figure 6.14 Choose Easy Connection (left). The SSID and encryption key of the camera appears (right).

5. Switch to your smartphone and use its Settings utility to connect to the camera's access point SSID displayed on the 5D Mark IV. You'll be asked for a password—the encryption key displayed on the camera. (Figure 6.15 shows the screens I see on my iPhone 6s Plus.)

6. Once you're connected, a screen will appear on the camera's LCD with the message "Start the EOS app on the smartphone." The 5D Mark IV's SSID (nickname), the encryption key (password), IP address, and Mac address will also be displayed. For most of us, that data is just informational, and needed only by networking gurus with special applications for it.

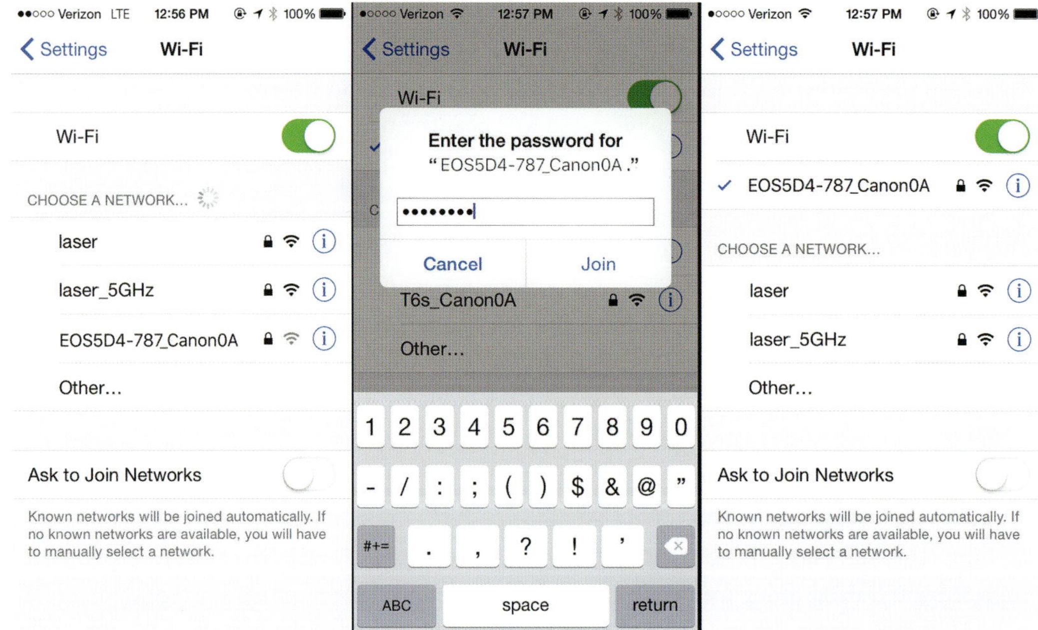

Figure 6.15 Select the camera's built-in network on your smart device.

7. Launch the Canon Camera Connect app. It will automatically search for camera access points and display the name of your detected camera. Tap the name of the camera on the screen of the smartphone. (See Figure 6.16.)

8. When pairing is complete, a message appears on the 5D Mark IV's LCD monitor offering to connect to the smartphone. Choose OK and press SET.

9. The current settings needed to link the 5D Mark IV and your smartphone are stored in the camera, and given the name SET1. You can change this name to something else, such as "David's iPhone" by highlighting the current settings label and pressing SET. The 5D Mark IV's text entry screen, described earlier, appears. Once settings are stored, reconnecting the camera to that smartphone is as simple as choosing the settings name from the camera, and activating the camera's access point on the phone.

10. Once the camera and smartphone are linked, you can access available functions (see Figure 6.17, left). You can use the phone to view images, control the camera remotely (see Figure 6.17 center), or change camera settings (see Figure 6.17, right).

11. Terminate the connection by highlighting Disconnect/Exit on the screen displayed on the camera and pressing SET, then confirming by choosing OK and pressing SET once again.

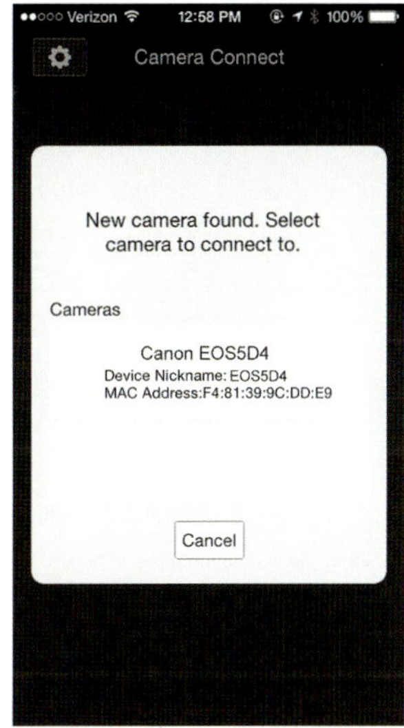

Figure 6.16 Once connected, the Camera Connect software will invite you to link up.

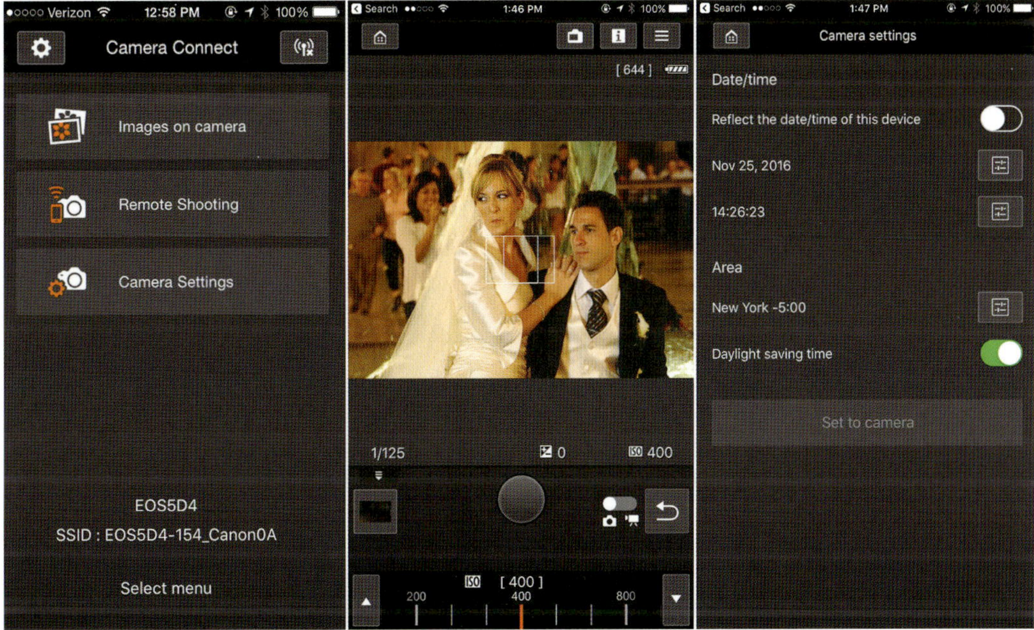

Figure 6.17 Available functions (left); remote control (center); camera settings (right).

OTHER CONNECTIONS

If you prefer to link your EOS 5D Mark IV to another device (including smartphones, printers, or computers) using a Wi-Fi connection other than the camera's built-in access point, you can set up a standard link, either semi-automatically using Easy Connection or Find Network functions or manually by entering the information about the external network. It would be impossible to cover all the options for connecting to a network/access point, and choosing among WPS (Wi-Fi Protected Setup) variations for the various Windows and Mac operating systems in this book. I recommend using the 5D Mark IV's internal access point to everyone who isn't intimately familiar with wireless networking. Canon does provide a 180-page Wireless Communication Function Instruction Manual with all the parameters a LAN-savvy photographer needs to connect to a favorite network. As I noted earlier, this is a photography book rather than computer manual. I'm not going to go into depth on any advanced options.

Remote Control with EOS Utility

While you can control your 5D Mark IV using the Camera Connect app on your smartphone as described above, you can also use a laptop or desktop computer to wirelessly operate your camera using the free EOS Utility that can be downloaded from the Canon website.

Connection is done in a similar way:

1. Choose Remote Control (EOS Utility) from the Wi-Fi Function screen shown earlier in Figure 6.12. (It's the desktop computer icon.)

2. Select Easy Connection on the camera as described earlier to display the SSID and encryption key (password) on the 5D Mark IV's LCD monitor.

3. Access your particular computer/operating system's wireless settings. Keep in mind that while virtually all laptops have wireless built-in, not all desktop computers do. The screen shown for my Windows 10 OS appears in Figure 6.18.

4. Select the camera's SSID from the list and enter the password/encryption/network security key.

5. Start the EOS Utility 3 on your computer, and select Pairing Over Wi-Fi/LAN.

6. Choose OK when the Start Pairing Device notice shows up on the 5D Mark IV.

7. When pairing is accomplished, you will be able to access the camera wirelessly using the EOS Utility.

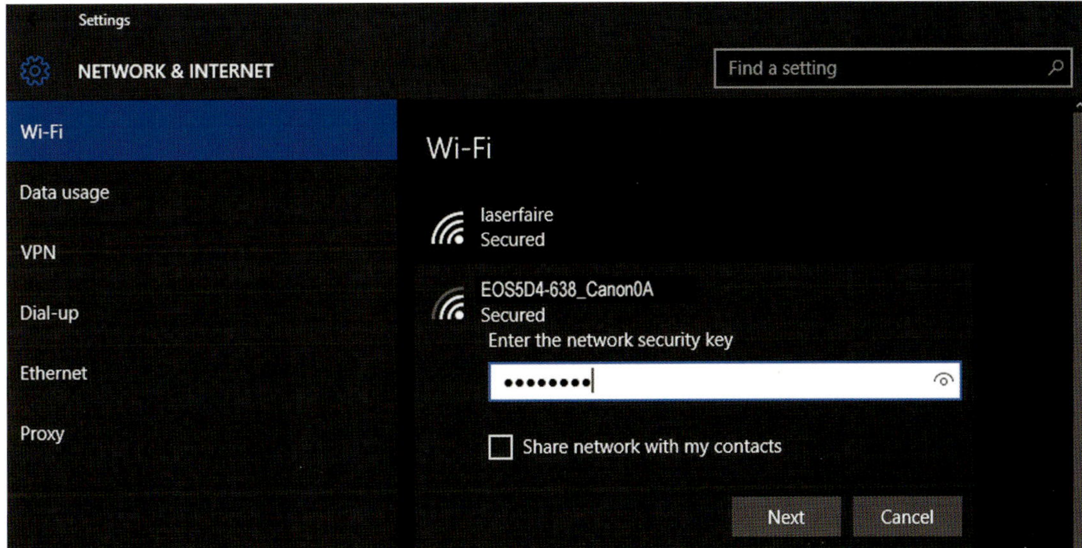

Figure 6.18 Choose the camera's SSID from your operating system's network connections screen.

Printing from a Wi-Fi Printer

Many (perhaps most) printers today have built-in wireless capabilities, allowing you to print out directly from your computer without a physical link between the computer and printer. The EOS 5D Mark IV adds the same function to your camera/printer setup, so you can make hard copies of your images from files in your camera without the bother of transferring them to a computer first. All you need is your 5D Mark IV and a PictBridge-compatible printer that conforms to the DPS over IP standard. (More alphabet soup: *Digital Photo Solutions* and *Internet Protocol*.) To use this feature, you must:

- **Configure your printer for wireless printing.** The instructions vary from printer to printer, so you should consult your printer manual for the procedures. Once you've done this, you'll be able to print photos from your camera, plus files from your computer and other compatible devices, such as smartphones. Wireless printing is *not* limited to camera-to-printer communications.

- **Link your camera to the printer.** The procedures are the same as those mentioned earlier. You can use your camera's built-in access point or connect to your local area network (*infrastructure network*). A list of detected printers is displayed, and, as before, you can save the camera-printer connection to a setting for re-use later. Multiple printer connections can be registered.

    If your printer *does not* connect wirelessly, you can still connect to the camera using your LAN, as described previously.

- **Printing images.** Once linked, you can print by pressing the Playback button and scrolling to the image you want to output. Select printing parameters, number of prints, and other settings just as you would for printing over a wired connection to a PictBridge printer.

Transfer to an FTP Server

One nifty feature, especially for professional photographers, is the ability to automatically transfer your still images (but *not* movies) from the 5D Mark IV to an FTP server immediately after the image is captured. You can, however, also opt to transfer to the FTP server after all the images are taken using a batch transfer process. In that case, both movies and stills can be uploaded. Here's an overview of the process:

- **Access Communications Settings.** Use the entry in the Set-up 4 menu, as described earlier, but instead of Built-in Wireless Settings, select FTP Transfer Settings, shown as the second entry in Figure 6.12, upper right.

- **Enable automatic transfer.** If you want the still photos to upload as you shoot, enable Automatic transfer. (See Figure 6.19, left.)

- **Select image size.** You can choose the size of the JPEG and RAW sizes to transfer, and choose whether to transfer JPEG only, RAW only, or both during an upload. (See Figure 6.19, right.)

- **Transfer with SET.** You can enable/disable transfer initiation with the SET button, as you prefer.

- **Enter/Update FTP server settings.** As described earlier, select the Transfer to FTP Server icon in the Wi-Fi Function menu. It's the icon at far left in the bottom row, as seen in Figure 6.12, lower right. You can then choose a connection set you've already defined, review settings, or delete settings.

- **First time setup of an FTP connection.** Screens appear allowing you to choose your connection, select an FTP mode, enter the ftp address of the site, enable/disable passive mode, use a proxy server, and enter your username/password (or log in anonymously). If you've used FTP sites with your computer or other device, the screens shown in Figure 6.20 will hold few mysteries for you. Advanced photographers who need/want FTP services will probably understand these settings anyway. If you need additional help, the Canon Wi-Fi manuals will lead you through the process.

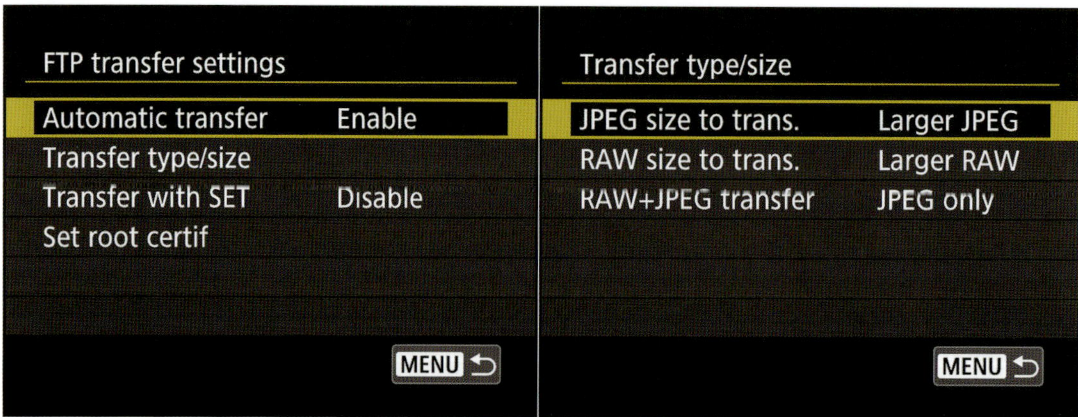

Figure 6.19 Enable transfer (left); select image size (right).

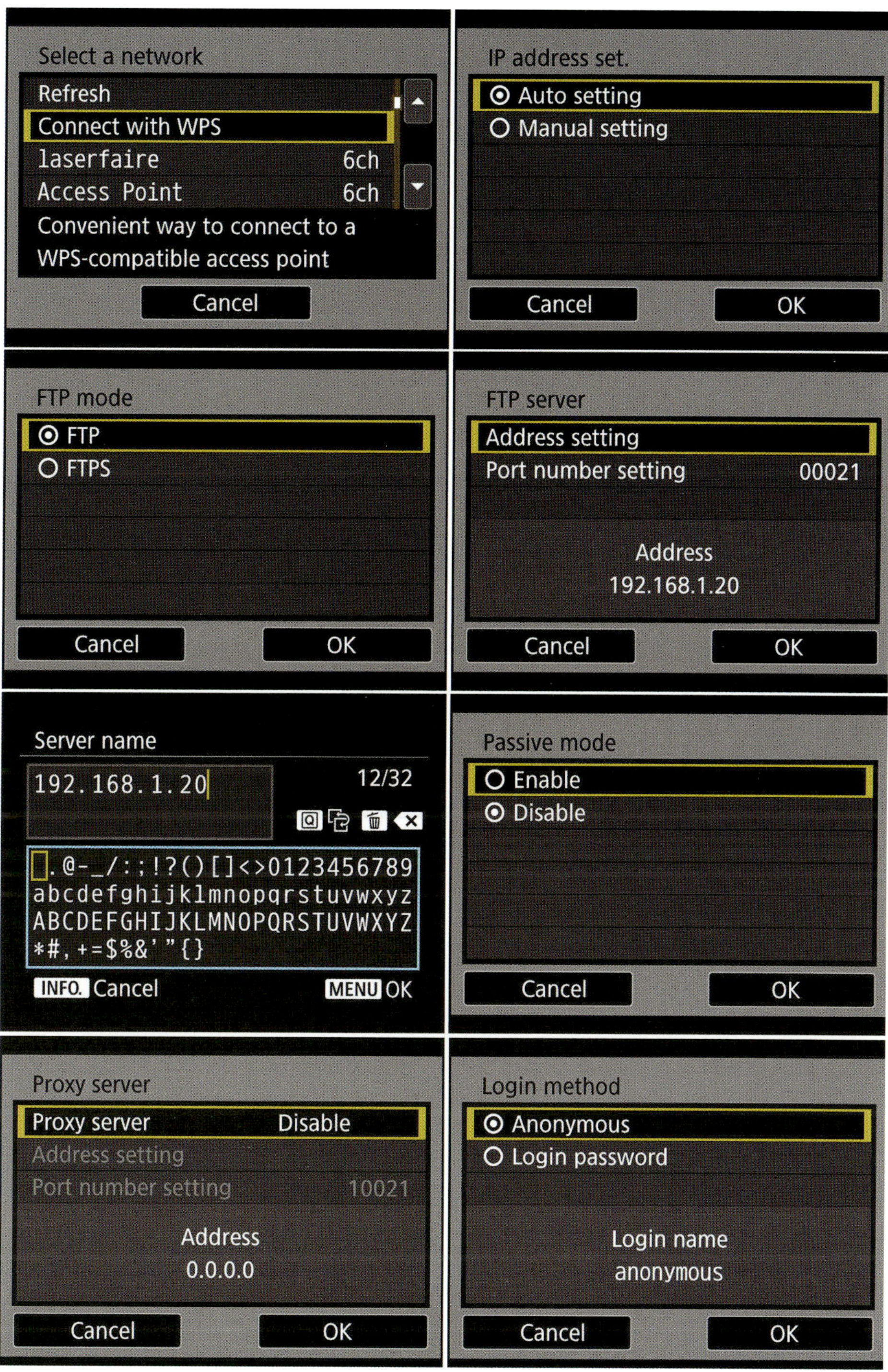

Figure 6.20 FTP connection screens.

Uploading to a Web Service

This wireless option allows you to select images and upload them to the Canon iMage Gateway, which is a free-of-charge service. You can register online through your computer and through this entry. Once you've become a member, you can upload photos, create photo albums, and use other Canon Image Gateway services. The site also can interface with other web services you have an account with, including e-mail, Twitter, YouTube, and Facebook.

All you need is your EOS 5D Mark IV and a computer with the EOS Utility installed. Before you can interface with the Canon gateway wirelessly, you must connect your camera and computer using the conventional digital/USB connection, log onto the Gateway through the "globe" icon, and configure the camera's settings to allow access to the web services. (Remember that Wireless capabilities must be set to Disable any time you want to use a wired connection between your camera and computer.)

Then, you can remove the direct link, turn wireless features back on, and connect to your computer through the wireless access methods described earlier in this chapter. Still images can be uploaded to the Gateway, and movies to YouTube. Images can be uploaded directly to Facebook, or shared with Facebook and Twitter users by posting a link back to the Canon Image Gateway location of the files. As with the image transfer features described earlier, you can resize images before uploading, and send photos one by one or in batches.

Geotagging

Geotagging is most important as a way to associate the geographical location where the photographer was when a picture was taken, with the actual photograph itself. Geotagging can also be done by attaching geographic information to the photo after it's already been taken. This is often done with online services that allow you to associate your uploaded photographs with a map, city, street address, or postal code. When properly geotagged and uploaded to compatible sites, users can browse through your photos using a map, finding pictures you've taken in a given area, or even searching through photos taken at the same location by other users.

You EOS 5D Mark IV includes a built-in GPS receiver. It records locational data such as latitude, longitude, and altitude, and saves it to the EXIF metadata in your image files, where it can be retrieved by compatible software to plot to maps or insert into your uploads to Flickr or other sites. You can even track your trajectory of movement with the receiver's logging function.

The 5D Mark IV is the very first professional Canon dSLR with GPS features integrated right into the body, at the top of the camera body, near the accessory shoe. In most cases, its features are all you need for geotagging your photographs. The big advantages of the internal receiver are that you don't need to carry an extra piece of equipment, or remember to attach it when geotagging is wanted, or give up use of your camera's hot shoe for other accessories, including a flash. (While geotagging is generally performed outdoors, you still might want to use flash, if only for fill outside, when working with GPS.)

If your familiarity with GPS is limited to that gadget that sits atop your dashboard, you'll be pleasantly surprised at the things that a GPS-equipped camera can do with locational information. When active, the GPS system records the latitude and longitude of each location where a picture is snapped, the elevation, Coordinated Universal Time Code (UTC), and the satellite reception status. This information is embedded in the EXIF metadata included in each photo, where it can be read and manipulated by compatible software. That includes Canon utilities, such as the Map Utility, Digital Photo Professional, and ImageBrowser EX programs; third-party image-editing software, including iPhoto for the Mac and the Map Module in Lightroom; and many photo-sharing sites that can display the location where each image was taken when you upload your pictures to an online album. Google Earth can also use your EXIF data.

You can view GPS data on the 5D Mark IV's LCD monitor as you review images. Press the INFO. button until the view with a histogram appears, then scroll down using the multi-controller until you reach the screen shown at left in Figure 6.21. When the GPS is active, you can also view the information for your current location in the GPS menu, as I'll describe shortly. I often use this feature when I am traveling around and want to record a specific site that I want to return to at a later time. I can view the latitude and longitude and enter them into my portable Garmin Etrex GPS, or the GPS in my car, and then return by accessing the data I've saved. While GPS data is most often used to pinpoint the shooting location of individual images, the receiver's logging function allows you to re-create the route you took in capturing those photos, thanks to the Canon Map Utility.

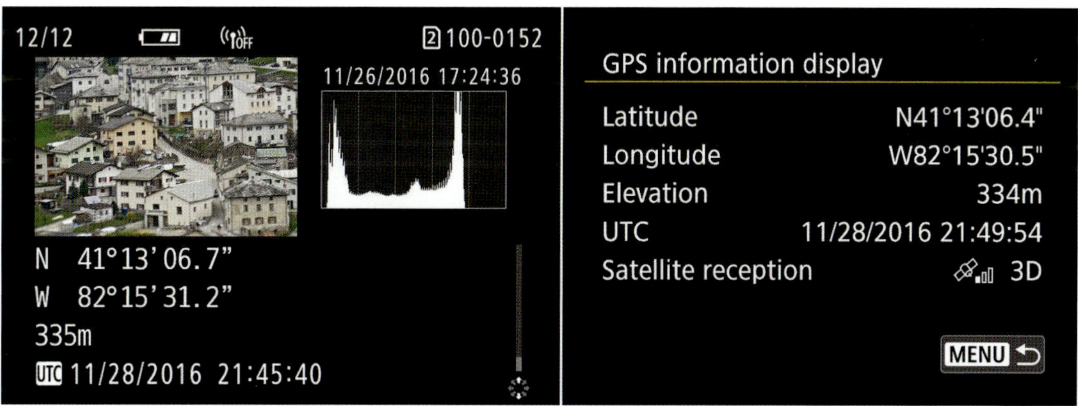

Figure 6.21 Display GPS information about an image (left) or your camera's current location (right).

Using the Internal GPS Receiver

To activate your 5D Mark IV's internal GPS receiver, just follow these steps:

1. **Navigate to the Set-up 4 menu and choose GPS Settings.** The screen shown in Figure 6.22 appears.

2. **Set GPS mode.** You can disable GPS here (to save power), or choose one of two modes:

   - **Mode 1.** When the camera is powered down, the GPS receiver still functions at intervals, keeping track of your location. That's useful if you'll be using GPS a lot during a shooting session and don't want to wait for the receiver to re-acquire GPS satellites (it can take valuable seconds or even minutes). The penalty is that the 5D Mark IV draws power continually and your battery life is shortened. Carry plenty of extra batteries if you use this mode.

   - **Mode 2.** When you turn the camera off, GPS is turned off too and no longer drains power. However, if the camera goes to "sleep" due to your auto power off setting, the GPS will receive signals at intervals and draw some power. This mode uses less power than Mode 1, but gives you the option of shutting off the GPS when you know you won't be using it for a while, but not disabling it when your auto power off setting kicks in.

3. **Choose time update.** With the Auto time setting option, the 5D Mark IV can use time data embedded in the GPS signal to set the camera's internal clock accurately. You can choose Auto Update to set the time automatically whenever the camera is powered up and GPS data is available; disable this function, or Set Now to update immediately. The receiver must be able to link with at least five GPS satellites for the time function to operate; when activated, the time setting in your camera will maintain plus/minus one-second accuracy. (This feature is great for synchronizing several GPS-equipped cameras, especially when shooting and editing videos and still shots contemporaneously.)

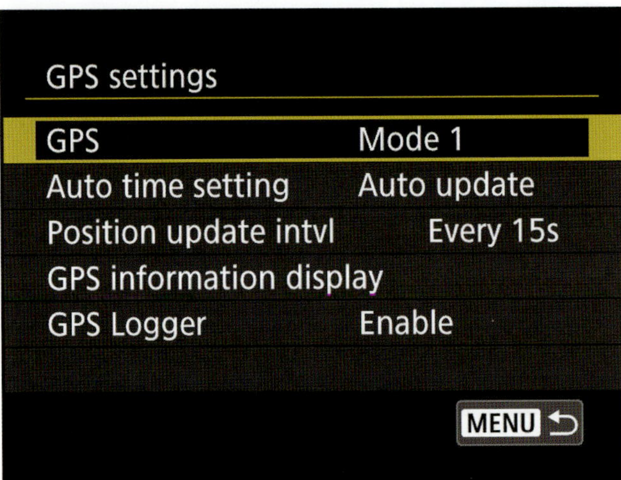

Figure 6.22
GPS settings.

4. **Position update timing.** Use this to specify the interval the GPS device uses to update position information. Choose from every 1, 5, 10, 15, or 30 seconds, or every 1, 2, or 5 minutes. Select a shorter interval when you are moving and/or accuracy is critical, or a longer interval to save power, when GPS reception is not optimal, or you are shooting from one position for a longer period.

5. **GPS information display.** This entry simply displays a screen of current GPS information, including latitude, longitude, elevation, UTC time (essentially Greenwich Mean Time), and Satellite reception strength/status, as shown earlier in Figure 6.21, right.

6. **GPS logger.** Allows you to enable or disable tracking of GPS position data, transfer log data to your memory card for later manipulation by an appropriate software program, or to delete the camera's current GPS log. (See Figure 6.23.) Nature and wildlife photographers (now, *where* did I photograph those rare flowers?), law enforcement personnel, business users, and anyone wandering through a strange city during a vacation will love the ability to track not only individual locations but the routes taken to get from one shooting spot to another.

Your Canon Map Utility, when connected to the Internet through your computer, can easily trace a path for you on a standard road map or satellite view (see Figure 6.24). The logger's NMEA-0813 format log file, which includes all the information for a single day's shooting, can be converted by the utility to a .KMZ file and uploaded to Google Earth, where it can be shared and viewed. A new log is created each day, or each time you change time zones. Depending on how often the position update timing is recorded (from every second to every five minutes), the 5D Mark IV can store from less than a week to as much as 100 days' worth of data. However, you'll probably use the Transfer Log Data to Card option more often than that.

Figure 6.23
Enable, disable logger; transfer log data to a memory card; delete log data.

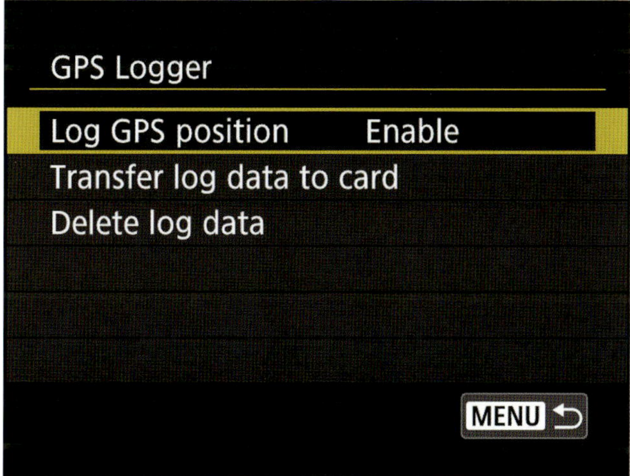

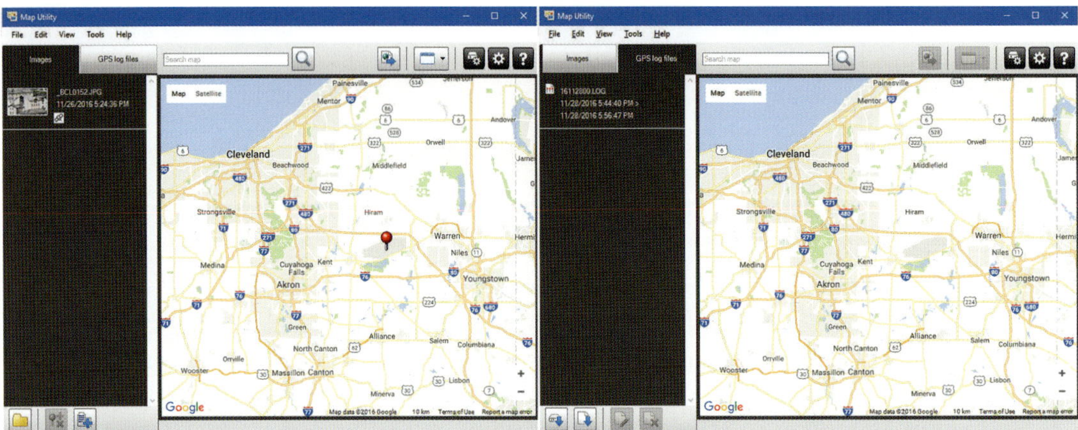

Figure 6.24 Canon's Map Utility can display the GPS data for an image (left), or show you the log data for a shooting session (right).

7. **Begin using GPS.** After a delay of about 30 to 60 seconds while the receiver connects to the optimum number of satellites, GPS functions will be activated, and remain so until you return to the menu to disable GPS features. If you turn the camera off, it will automatically re-acquire the satellites within a few seconds when it's powered up again, assuming that GPS reception is available at that location.

7

Choosing Your Lens Arsenal

In September 2016, Canon announced that it had produced its 120 millionth EF-series lens, roughly 25 years after the company's current autofocus mount was introduced (back in the film era). Considering that it took 11 years for Canon to sell its first 10 million copies of its EF lens line, but only *nine months* to peddle its most recent 10 million lenses, it's easy to see that the digital photography revolution can take credit for the most recent explosion.

With nearly five dozen full-frame compatible lenses in its current lineup, Canon is catering to the wide-ranging needs of a broad user base, from novice photo enthusiasts to advanced amateur and professional photographers. It's this mind-bending assortment of high-quality lenses available to enhance the capabilities of cameras like the Canon EOS 5D Mark IV that make the product line so appealing. Thousands of current and older lenses introduced by Canon and third-party vendors since 1987 can be used to give you a wider view, bring distant subjects closer, let you focus closer, shoot under lower-light conditions, or provide a more detailed, sharper image for critical work. Other than the sensor itself, the lens you choose for your dSLR is the most important component in determining image quality and perspective of your images. This chapter explains how to select the best lenses for the kinds of photography you want to do.

Your First Lenses

Back in ancient times (the pre-zoom, pre-autofocus era before the mid-1980s), choosing the first lens for your camera was a no-brainer: you had few or no options. Canon cameras (which used a different lens mount in those days) were sold with a 50mm f/1.4, a 50mm f/1.8, or, if you had deeper pockets, a super-fast 50mm f/1.2 lens. It was also possible to buy a camera as a body alone, which didn't save much money back when a film SLR like the Canon A-1 sold for $435—*with lens*.

Today, your choices are more complicated, and Canon lenses, which now include zoom, autofocus, and, more often than not, built-in image stabilization (IS) features, tend to cost a lot more compared to the price of a camera. (Adjusted for inflation, that $435 A-1 costs around $900 in today's dollars.)

The Canon EOS 5D Mark IV is frequently purchased with a lens, even now, often the upgraded Canon EF 24-105mm f/4L IS II USM lens introduced in August 2016. It has improved image stabilization, less vignetting in the corners, a 10-blade circular aperture with incredible bokeh (creamy background blur), and a coating that does a better job of reducing flare and ghost images.

However, the 5D Mark IV can also be purchased in a body-only configuration, because advanced shooters and professionals are very likely buying the new model to replace an older camera, or adding an additional body to their kit. Because I was in replacement mode, I opted to get the body, and use it with the older version of the lens, shown in Figure 7.1. As you might expect, even the older "L" (luxury) optic is a remarkable performer. At this writing, both the old and new lens remain in the Canon line. The Mark II lens is priced $100 higher at $1,099, and I expect the original version will be phased out as quantities are depleted. Unless there are close-out discounts, most will choose the newer lens for such a slight price difference.

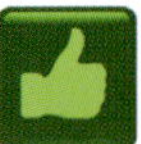

Tip

Throughout this chapter, I'm going to use the current Canon manufacturer suggested list price (MSRP) when it's available. (I'll use the Canon store price if it's not.) You should know that many lenses are available for less at the Canon store for your country or at retailers, and that prices can (and will) change throughout the life of this book.

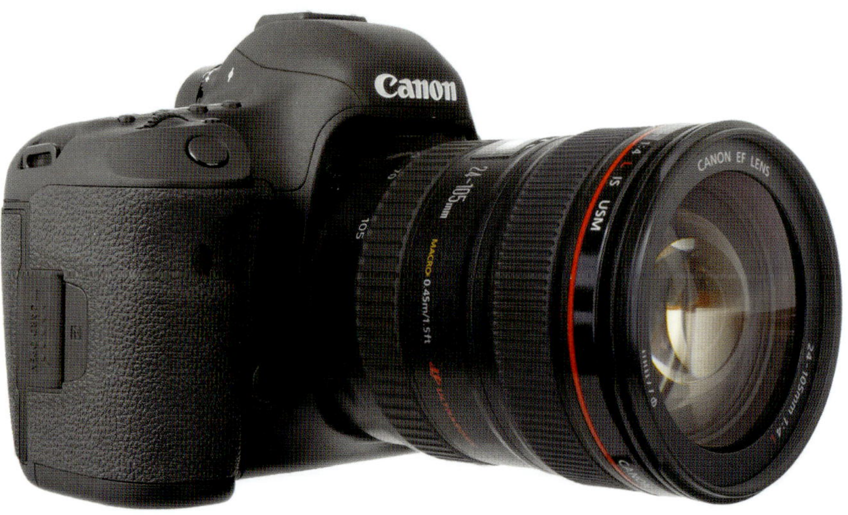

Figure 7.1
The Canon EF 24-105mm f/4 IS L autofocus lens is often packaged with the 5D Mark IV in a kit.

If you are switching to full frame and don't already own a lens compatible with your 5D Mark IV, you can't go wrong with the 24-105mm optic. Many photographers, especially old-school film shooters, prefer working with zoom lenses as much as they can, and may prefer a "normal" lens, like the EF 50mm f/1.4 USM ($399 MSRP) or the sublime EF 50mm f/1.2L ($1,349).

So, depending on which category you fall into, you'll need to make a decision about what lens to buy, or decide what other kind of lenses you need to fill out your complement of Canon optics. This section will cover "first lens" concerns, while later in the chapter we'll look at "add-on lens" considerations. When deciding on your initial lens purchases, there are several factors you'll want to consider:

- **Cost.** You might have stretched your budget a bit to purchase your 5D Mark IV, so you might want to keep the cost of your add-on lenses fairly low. Fortunately, there are excellent lenses available that will add from $100 to $500 to the price of your camera if purchased at the same time.

- **Zoom range.** If you have only one lens, you'll want a fairly long zoom range to provide as much flexibility as possible. Fortunately, several of the most popular basic lenses for the 5D Mark IV have 3X to 5X zoom ranges, extending from moderate wide-angle/normal out to medium telephoto. These are fine for everyday shooting, portraits, and some types of sports.

- **Adequate maximum aperture.** You'll want an f/stop of at least f/3.5 to f/4 for shooting under fairly low-light conditions. The thing to watch for is the maximum aperture when the lens is zoomed to its telephoto end. You may end up with no better than an f/5.6 maximum aperture. That's not great, but you can often live with it.

- **Image quality.** Your starter lens should have good image quality, befitting a camera with 30MP of resolution, because that's one of the primary factors that will be used to judge your photos.

- **Size matters.** A good walking-around lens is compact in size and light in weight. My favorite, the 24-105mm f/4 isn't tiny, but having it mounted on the camera most of the time isn't a burden, either. Considering its image quality and zoom range, I think it's worth every ounce.

- **Fast/close focusing.** Your first lens should have a speedy autofocus system (which is where the ultrasonic motor/USM or STM found in nearly all moderately priced lenses is an advantage). Close focusing (to 12 inches or closer) will let you use your basic lens for some types of macro photography.

You can find comparisons of the lenses discussed in the next section, as well as third-party lenses from Sigma, Tokina, Tamron, and other vendors, in online groups and websites. There are many excellent third-party optics, especially since Sigma introduced its top-notch Art and Sport lineup. Because of the sheer number of options, I'm going to concentrate on Canon lenses only, even though I own and use quite a few non-Canon lenses (with the Sigma company's aging, but capable 15mm f/2.8 EX DG fisheye among my favorites). I'll provide my recommendations, but more information available from online sources is always helpful.

Buy Now, Expand Later

The 5D Mark IV is commonly available with several good, basic lenses that can serve you well as a "walk-around" lens (one you keep on the camera most of the time, especially when you're out and about without your camera bag). The number of options available to you is actually quite amazing, even if your budget is limited.

One important thing to keep in mind is that Canon has been producing EF lenses for a very long time, and some excellent lenses have been replaced with newer models, or dropped from the Canon lineup entirely. If you want to choose from the broadest variety of lenses at reduced prices, you definitely should consider buying gently used optics.

I highly recommend KEH Camera in Smyrna, Georgia, as a source for affordable used gear. I've purchased many lenses from their website (www.keh.com). Their prices may not be the lowest available, but you'll save significantly from the new price for the same lens, and the company is notorious for exceeding their own lens grading standards: the lenses I've purchased from them listed as Excellent were difficult to tell from new, and their "Bargain" optics often show only minor wear and near-perfect glass. For each lens you're considering, you can usually select from three or more different grades, plus choose lenses with or without hoods and/or front and rear caps. Because of the ready availability of used and discontinued lenses for Canon full-frame models, I'm going to cast a broad net when making my recommendations for lenses you should consider. Canon's best-bet first lenses are as follows:

- **Canon EF 17-40mm f/4L USM lens.** Not everyone needs a wide angle to medium telephoto lens, and this $799 optic is perfect for those who tend to see the world from a wide-angle perspective. It provides a broader 104-degree field of view than your typical walk-around lens (which usually start at around 24mm), and zooms only to a near-normal 40mm. Its f/4 *constant maximum aperture* (it delivers f/4 at every zoom position) is large enough for much low-light shooting, particularly since it is sharp wide open. It focuses down to about 11 inches.

- **Canon Zoom Wide-Angle-Telephoto EF 24-70mm f/2.8L II USM lens.** I couldn't leave the latest version of this premium lens out of the mix, even though it costs $1,899. As part of Canon's L-series line, it offers better sharpness over its focal range than many of the other lenses in this list. Best of all, it's fast (for a zoom), with an f/2.8 maximum aperture that *doesn't change* as you zoom out. Unlike some other lenses, which may offer only an f/5.6 maximum f/stop at their longest zoom setting, this is another constant aperture lens, which retains its maximum f/stop. The added sharpness, constant aperture, and ultra-smooth USM motor are what you're paying for with this lens.

- **Canon EF 24-85mm f/3.5-4.5 USM Autofocus Wide-Angle Telephoto Zoom lens.** If you can get by with wide angle to short telephoto range, this older ("classic") consumer-grade lens might suit you. It can often be found used in the $300 price range and offers a useful range of focal lengths.

- **Canon EF 24-105mm f/4L IS USM Autofocus Wide-Angle Telephoto Zoom lens.** This is the previous version, now replaced by the Mark II. It is still the first choice of many 5D Mark IV owners at its new MSRP of $999 (or even cheaper if bought in a kit), and is the closest you can come to a true do-everything zoom. Like the new lens, it focuses no closer than about 18 inches however, but at 3.3 × 4.2 inches and less than 24 ounces, it's compact and lightweight.

- **Canon EF 28-105mm f/3.5-4.5 II USM Autofocus Wide-Angle Telephoto Zoom lens.** Discontinued only a few years ago, this lens is a little slower than its 28-105mm L-class counterpart, but it's priced roughly in the range of the 24-85mm lens mentioned earlier and offers more reach.

- **Canon EF 28-135mm f/3.5-5.6 IS USM Image-Stabilized Autofocus Wide-Angle Telephoto Zoom lens.** Image stabilization is especially useful at longer focal lengths, which makes this lens worth its $479 price tag. Several retailers are packing this lens with the 5D Mark IV as a kit. (See Figure 7.2.)

- **Canon EF 28-200mm f/3.5-5.6 USM Autofocus Wide-Angle Telephoto Zoom lens.** If you want one affordable lens to do everything except ultra-wide-angle photography, this discontinued 7X zoom lens can be found used for around $250.

- **Canon EF 55-200mm f/4.5-5.6 II USM Telephoto Zoom lens.** This one goes from normal to medium-long focal lengths. It features a desirable ultrasonic motor. Best of all, it's very affordable at an MSRP of $349.

- **Canon EF 40mm f/2.8 STM lens.** This fairly fast prime lens (less than $200) has the quiet STM motor, making it perfect as a wide/normal lens for video. It's cheap enough to keep around as a "pancake" walk-around lens for street photography. (See Figure 7.3.)

- **Canon EF 50mm f/1.8 STM lens.** If a "normal" lens is not your cup of tea for everyday use, you can skip Canon's f/1.4 and f/1.2 options, and add this $125 lens to your kit for less than you might pay for a high-quality 77mm polarizing filter.

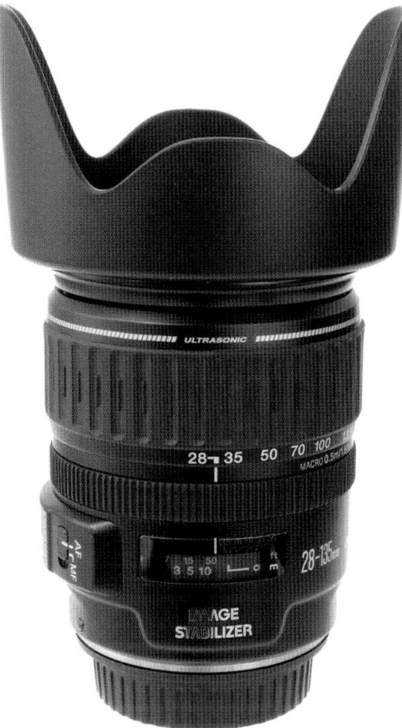

Figure 7.2 The Canon EF 28-135mm f/3.5-5.6 lens is compact, sharp, and inexpensive.

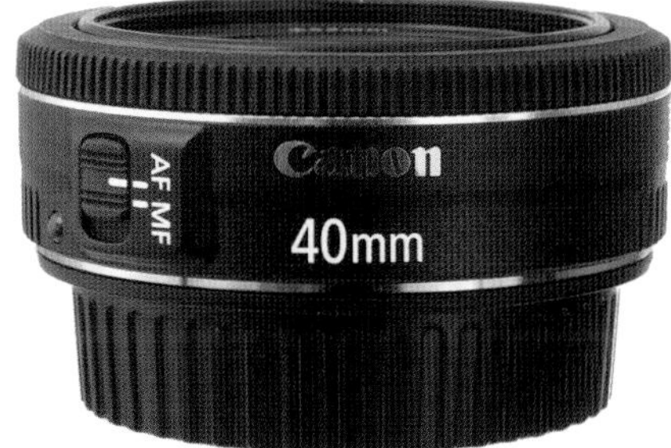

Figure 7.3 Another budget option is the 40mm f/2.8 STM lens.

What Lenses Can You Use?

The previous section helped you sort out what lens you might want to buy with your 5D Mark IV (assuming you already didn't own any Canon lenses). Now, you're probably wondering what lenses can be added to your growing collection (trust me, it will grow). You need to know which lenses are suitable and, most importantly, which lenses are fully compatible with your 5D Mark IV.

With the Canon 5D Mark IV, the compatibility issue is a simple one: It accepts any lens with the EF designation, with full availability of all autofocus, auto aperture, autoexposure, and image-stabilization features (if present). It's comforting to know that any EF lens will work as designed with your camera. As I noted at the beginning of the chapter, that's *millions* of lenses! You *cannot* use Canon EF-S lenses, or lenses from other vendors offered in EF-S or APS-C mounts. They won't fit on your camera at all.

But wait, there's more. You can also attach Canon F mount, Leica R, Olympus OM, and M42 ("Pentax screw mount") lenses with a simple adapter, if you don't mind losing automatic focus and aperture control. If you use one of these lenses, you'll need to focus manually (even if the lens operates in Autofocus mode on the camera it was designed for), and adjust the f/stop to the aperture you want to use to take the picture. That means that lenses that don't have an aperture ring must be used only at their maximum aperture if you use them with a simple adapter. However, Novoflex makes expensive adapter rings (the Canon-Lens-on-Canon-Camera version is called EOS/NIK NT) with an integral aperture control that allows adjusting the aperture of lenses that do not have an old-style aperture ring. Expect to pay as much as $300 for an adapter of this type.

Because of these limitations, you probably won't want to make extensive use of "foreign" lenses on your 5D Mark IV, but an adapter can help you when you really, really need to use a particular focal length but don't have a suitable Canon-compatible lens. For example, I occasionally use an older 400mm lens that was originally designed for the Nikon line on my 5D Mark IV. The lens needs to be mounted on a tripod for steadiness, anyway, so its slower operation isn't a major pain. Another good match is the 105mm Micro-Nikkor I sometimes use with my Canon 5D Mark IV. Macro photos, too, are most often taken with the camera mounted on a tripod, and manual focus makes a lot of sense for fine-tuning focus and depth-of-field. Because of the contemplative nature of close-up photography, it's not much of an inconvenience to stop down to the taking aperture just before exposure.

The limitations on use of lenses within Canon's own product line (as well as lenses produced for earlier Canon SLRs by third-party vendors) are fairly clear cut. The 5D Mark IV cannot be used with any of Canon's earlier lens mounting schemes for its film cameras, including the immediate predecessor to the EF mount, the FD mount (introduced with the Canon F1 in 1964 and used until the Canon T60 in 1990), FL (1964–1971), or the original Canon R mount (1959–1964). While you'll find FD-to-EF adapters for about $40, you'll lose so many functions that it's rarely worth the bother. Nor, as I noted, can you use EF-S lenses. (Don't even try.) That's really all you need to know.

WHY SO MANY LENS MOUNTS?

Four different lens mounts in 40-plus years might seem like a lot of different mounting systems, especially when compared to the Canon F mount of 1959, which retained quite a bit of compatibility with that company's film and digital camera bodies during that same span. However, in digital photography terms, the EF mount itself is positively ancient, having remained reasonably stable for almost two decades. Lenses designed for the EF system work reliably with every EOS film and digital camera ever produced.

However, at the time, yet another lens mount switch, especially a change from the traditional breech system to a more conventional bayonet-type mount, was indeed a daring move by Canon. One of the reasons for staying with a particular lens type is to "lock" current users into a specific camera system. By introducing the EF mount, Canon in effect cut loose every photographer in its existing user base. If they chose to upgrade, they were free to choose another vendor's products and lenses. Only satisfaction with the previous Canon product line and the promise of the new system would keep them in the fold.

In retrospect, the switch to the EF mount seems like a very good idea, as the initial EOS film cameras can now be seen as the beginning of Canon's rise to eventually become the leader in film and (later) digital SLR cameras. By completely revamping its lens mounting system, the company was able to take advantage of the latest advances in technology without compromise.

For example, when the original EF bayonet mount was introduced in 1987, the system incorporated new autofocus technology (EF actually stands for "electro focus") in a more rugged and less complicated form. A tiny motor was built into the lens itself, eliminating the need for mechanical linkages with the camera. Instead, electrical contacts are used to send power and the required focusing information to the motor. That's a much more robust and resilient system that made it easier for Canon to design faster and more accurate autofocus mechanisms just by redesigning the lenses.

EF vs. EF-S

Lenses with the EF-S designation cannot be used with your 5D Mark IV. The EF-S (the S stands for "short back focus") mount has one important chief difference (as you might expect), with lens components that extend farther back into the camera body of some of Canon's latest non-full-frame digital cameras, such as the 7D series, and digital Rebel models. As I'll explain next, this refinement allows designing more compact, less-expensive lenses especially for those cameras, but *not* for models like the EOS 5D Mark IV and other full-frame cameras.

Canon's EF-S lens mount variation was born in 2003, when the company virtually invented the consumer-oriented digital SLR category by introducing the original EOS 300D/Digital Rebel, a dSLR that cost less than $1,000 *with lens* at a time when all other interchangeable-lens digital cameras (including the latest 7D's "grandparent," the original EOS 10D) were priced closer to $2,000 with a basic lens. Like the EOS 10D, the 7D and similar cameras feature a smaller than full-frame sensor with a 1.6X crop factor (Canon calls this format APS-C). But the EOS Digital Rebel, unlike the 10D, accepted lenses that took advantage of the shorter mirror found in APS-C cameras, with elements of shorter focal length lenses (wide angles) that extended *into* the camera, space that was off limits in other models because the mirror passed through that territory as it flipped up to expose the shutter and sensor. (Canon even calls its flip-up reflector a "half mirror.")

In short (so to speak), the EF-S mount made it easier to design less-expensive wide-angle lenses that could be used *only* with 1.6X-crop cameras, and featured a simpler design and reduced coverage area suitable for those non-full-frame models. The new mount made it possible to produce lenses like the ultra-wide EF-S 10-22mm f/3.5-4.5 USM lens, which has the equivalent field of view as a 16-35mm zoom on a full-frame camera.

Suitable cameras for EF-S lenses include all the entry-level models from the original Digital Rebel to the latest Rebels and the Canon EOS xxD line, such as the 80D. The EF-S lenses cannot be used on the APS-C-sensor EOS 10D, any Canon 1D series APS-H models (which have a 28.7mm × 19.1mm sensor with a 1.3X crop factor), or any of the full-frame digital or film EOS models. It's easy to tell an EF lens from an EF-S lens: The latter incorporates EF-S into their name! Plus, EF lenses have a raised red dot on the barrel that is used to align the lens with a matching dot on the camera when attaching the lens. EF-S lenses and compatible bodies use a white square instead. Some EF-S lenses also have a rubber ring at the attachment end that provides a bit of weather/dust sealing and protects the back components of the lens if a user attempts to mount it on a camera that is not EF-S compatible.

Ingredients of Canon's Alphanumeric Soup

The actual product names of individual Canon lenses are fairly easy to decipher; they'll include either the EF or EF-S designation, the focal length or focal length range of the lens, its maximum aperture, and some other information. Additional data may be engraved or painted on the barrel or ring surrounding the front element of the lens, as shown in Figure 7.4. Here's a decoding of what the individual designations mean:

- **EF/EF-S.** If the lens is marked EF, it can safely be used on any Canon EOS camera, film or digital. If it is an EF-S lens, it should be used only on an EF-S-compatible camera.

- **Focal length.** Given in millimeters or a millimeter range, such as 60mm in the case of a popular Canon macro lens, or 24-105mm, used to describe a medium-wide to short-telephoto zoom.

- **Maximum aperture.** The largest f/stop available with a particular lens is given in a string of numbers that might seem confusing at first glance. For example, you might see 1:1.8 for a fixed-focal length (prime) lens, and 1:4.5-5.6 for a zoom. The initial 1: signifies that the f/stop given is actually a ratio or fraction (in regular notation, f/ replaces the 1:), which is why a 1:2 (or f/2) aperture is larger than a 1:4 (or f/4) aperture—just as 1/2 is larger than 1/4. With most zoom lenses, the maximum aperture changes as the lens is zoomed to the telephoto position, so a range is given instead: 1:4.5–5.6. (Some zooms, called constant aperture lenses, keep the same maximum aperture throughout their range.)

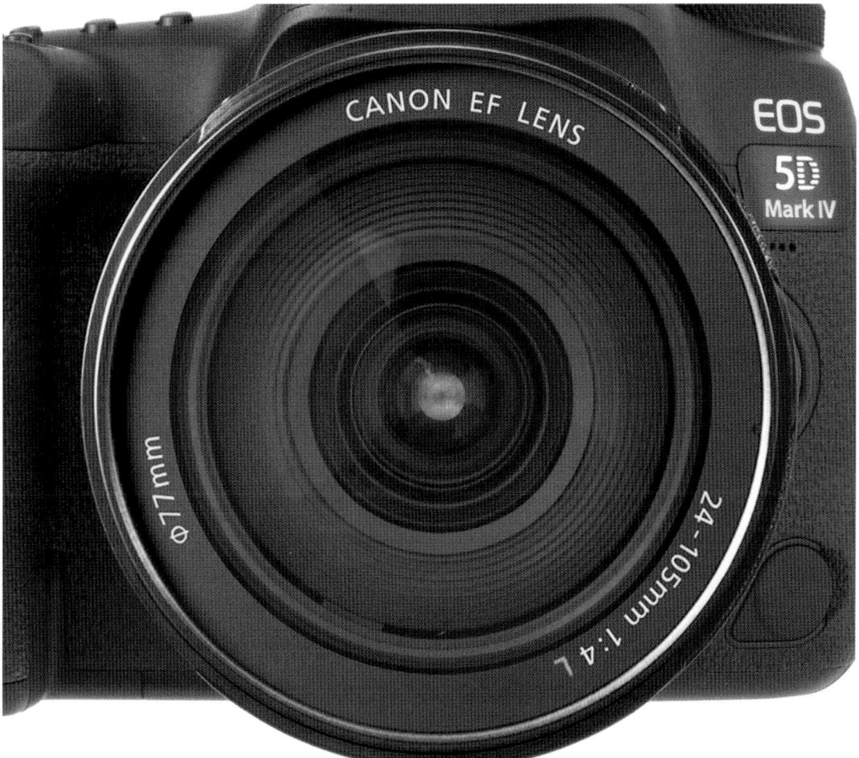

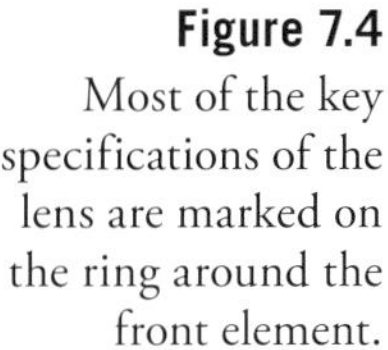

Figure 7.4
Most of the key specifications of the lens are marked on the ring around the front element.

- **Autofocus type.** Most newer Canon lenses that aren't of the bargain-basement type use Canon's *ultrasonic motor* autofocus system (more on that later) and are given the USM designation. If USM does not appear on the lens or its model name, the lens may use the less sophisticated AFD (arc-form drive) autofocus system or the micromotor (MM) drive mechanism. The newer STM designation indicates a stepper-motor drive, which is quieter and especially useful for video.

- **Series.** Canon adds a Roman numeral to many of its products to represent an updated model with the same focal length or focal length range, so some lenses will have a II or III added to their name. The revamped EF 24-70mm f/2.8L II USM lens is an example of a series update.

- **Pro quality.** Canon's more expensive lenses with more rugged construction and higher optical quality, intended for professional use, include the letter L (for "luxury") in their product name. You can further differentiate these lenses visually by a red ring around the lens barrel and the off-white color of the metal barrel itself in virtually all telephoto L-series lenses. (Some L-series lenses have shiny or textured black plastic exterior barrels.) Internally, every L lens includes at least one lens element that is built of ultra-low dispersion glass, is constructed of expensive fluorite crystal, or uses an expensive ground (not molded) aspheric (non-spherical) lens component.

- **Filter size.** You'll find the front lens filter thread diameter in millimeters included on the lens, preceded by a Ø symbol, as in Ø67 or Ø77. One advantage of Canon's L lenses is that many of them use 77mm filters, so you don't have to purchase a new set (or step-up/step-down adapter rings) each time you buy a lens.

- **Special-purpose lenses.** Some Canon lenses are designed for specific types of work, and they include appropriate designations in their names. For example, lenses with perspective control features preface the lens name with T-S (for tilt-shift). Lenses with built-in image-stabilization features include *IS* in their product names.

SORTING THE MOTOR DRIVES

Incorporating the AF motor inside the lens was an innovative move by Canon, and this allowed the company to produce more sophisticated lenses as technology became available to upgrade the focusing system. You'll find four types of motors in Canon-designed lenses.

- **AFD (Arc-form drive)** and **Micromotor (MM)** drives are built around tiny versions of electromagnetic motors, which generally use gear trains to produce the motion needed to adjust the focus of the lens. Both are slow, noisy, and not particularly effective with larger lenses. Manual focus adjustments are possible only when the motor drive is disengaged.

- **Micromotor ultrasonic motor (USM)** drives use high-frequency vibration to produce the motion used to drive the gear train, resulting in a quieter operating system at a cost that's not much more than that of electromagnetic motor drives. With the exception of a couple lenses that have a slipping clutch mechanism, manual focus with this kind of system is possible only when the motor drive is switched off and the lens is set in Manual mode. This is the kind of USM system you'll find in lower-cost lenses.

- **Ring ultrasonic motor (USM)** drives, available in two different types (*electronic focus ring USM* and *ring USM*), also use high-frequency movement, but generate motion using a pair of vibrating metal rings to adjust focus. Both variations allow a feature called Full Time Manual (FTM) focus, which lets you make manual adjustments to the lens's focus even when the autofocus mechanism is engaged. With electronic focus ring USM, manual focus is possible only when the lens is mounted on the camera and the camera is turned on; the focus ring of lenses with ring USM can be turned at any time.

- **Stepper motor (STM) drives.** In autofocus mode, the precision motor of STM lenses, along with a new aperture mechanism, allows lenses equipped with this technology to focus quickly, accurately, silently, and with smooth continuous increments. If you think about video capture, you can see how these advantages pay off. Silent operation is a plus, especially when noise from autofocusing can easily be transferred to the camera's built-in microphones through the air or transmitted through the body itself. In addition, because autofocus is often done *during* capture, it's important that the focus increments are continuous. USM motors are not as smooth, but are better at jumping quickly to the exact focus point. You can adjust focus manually, using a focus-by-wire process. As you rotate the focus ring, that action doesn't move the lens elements; instead, your rotation of the ring sends a signal to the motor to change the focus.

More Interesting Optics

There are lots of interesting lenses that belong in your camera bag, and this chapter wouldn't be complete without me mentioning some of them. The next sections will give you a quick summary of some potential objects of your Lens Lust.

The Magic Three

If you cruise the forums, you'll find the same three lenses mentioned over and over, often referred to as "The Trinity," "The Magic Three," or some other affectionate nickname. They are the three lenses you'll find in the kit of just about every serious Canon photographer (including me). They're fast, expensive, heavier than you might expect, and provide such exquisite image quality that once you equip yourself with the Trinity, you'll never be happy with anything else.

There are actually dual versions of each focal length, and I've arbitrarily divided them into two groups, the (relatively) affordable versions, and the deluxe, top-of-the-line trio.

The Affordable Magic Three

Neither lens trio is cheap, but these three lenses carry relatively reasonable price tags for anyone with the means to spring for a camera like the 5D Mark IV. All of them share a number of attributes. All are full frame L-series lenses; all have f/4 maximum apertures; and they each cost up to half the price of their top-of-the-line stablemates.

- **EF 17-40mm f/4L USM lens.** I recommended this lens earlier as a "kit" lens for wide-angle shooters because of its moderate $799 price tag, but it can be an integral part of anyone's three-lens kit. When I am shooting landscapes, doing street photography, or some types of indoor sports, this lens can go on my 5D Mark IV and never come off. The lens is slower than its top-line equivalent, but provides a useful focal length range, and accepts 77mm filters (use thin filters to avoid vignetting at the 17mm setting).

- **EF 24-70mm f/4L IS USM lens.** The f/4 maximum aperture of this $899 lens isn't truly a handicap, because it includes image stabilization, and Canon's f/2.8 version does not. That makes them roughly equivalent for hand-held photography of subjects that aren't moving (and when you don't need the reduced depth-of-field of an f/2.8 aperture). This lens is wonderfully sharp, and well-suited for anything from sports to portraiture that falls within its focal length range. I know many photographers who aren't heavily into landscapes who use this lens as their main lens. It focuses down to 1.25 feet, so you can get decent magnification by moving close to your subjects at 70mm.

- **EF 70-200mm f/4L IS USM lens.** Canon offers no fewer than *four* 70-200mm zooms, and this $1,099 version is your best bet among the affordable alternatives. While you can also choose one of two others with an f/4 and f/2.8 maximum apertures (for $599 and $1,249, respectively), neither have image stabilization. Unless you absolutely *must* have the largest possible maximum aperture (or need to save some bucks), this one is the best overall choice. It is perfect for some indoor and many outdoor sports, on a monopod, or hand-held, and can be used for portraiture, street photography, wildlife (especially with the 1.4X teleconverter), and even distant scenics. I use it for concerts, too, alternating between this lens and my 85mm f/1.2. It takes me in close to the performer, and can be used wide-open or at f/5.6 with good image quality. Its chief drawbacks are that it focuses only down to about 4 feet, and uses 67mm filters.

The Reigning Magic Three

If you have around $6,500 burning a hole in your pocket, you can purchase the top tier of the Canon line. If their 6.6-pound heft seems like a lot (the 5D Mark IV itself weighs less than a third as much), remember that this trio of lenses embraces every focal length from 16mm to 200mm, with maximum apertures of f/2.8 over the full range. The deluxe lineup looks like this:

- **EF 16-35mm f/2.8L III USM lens.** The image quality of this $2,199 lens is incredible, with very low barrel distortion (outward bowing at the edges) and very little of the chromatic aberrations common to lenses this wide. It focuses down to about 11 inches, allowing for some interesting close-up/wide-angle effects. The downside? The outward curving front element requires the use of large, expensive, 82mm filters—of course, as the use of polarizers, in particular, would be problematic at wider focal lengths. The polarizing effect would be highly variable because of this lens's extremely wide field of view.

- **EF 24-70mm f/2.8 II USM lens.** This lens, at $1,899 MSRP, provides outstanding image quality thanks to its single Super UD lens element paired with two UD elements to minimize chromatic aberrations. But if you have the cash and opportunity to purchase this newer lens, you won't be making a mistake. Some were surprised when it was introduced without the IS feature, but Canon has kept the size of this useful lens down, while maintaining a reasonable price for a "pro" level lens. It's another lens that uses 82mm filters, so if you own the 16-35mm optic, too, your filters can do double duty.

- **EF 70-200mm f/2.8L IS USM lens.** This is my all-time favorite Canon lens. I'm a telephoto/selective focus kind of shooter, and if I could afford only one Magic Three lens, this $2,099 lens would be the one I would get. There's an older version, also with IS, for less, and, as I mentioned earlier, an f/2.8 version with no stabilization at all. But of Canon's three 70-200mm f/2.8 lenses (which all take 77mm filters), this one is the sharpest, focuses the fastest and closest, and is more ruggedly built. You might end up making this your workhorse, as I have.

More Winners

Although all the five or six dozen readily available Canon lenses are beyond the scope of this book, the company makes a variety of other interesting lenses. Here are some of my favorites.

- **EF 8-15mm f/4L Fisheye USM lens.** Yup, a fisheye *zoom*. I was enamored of a Tokina (*nee* Pentax) 10-17mm fisheye zoom for APS-C cameras for a long time, but it wasn't particularly sharp and had chromatic aberrations that wouldn't quit. For a mere $1,249 you can buy the coolest lens you own, and start capturing some mind-bending images, or just add some interest to a simple landscape shot, like the one in Figure 7.5.

- **EF 100-400mm f/4.5-5.6L II USM lens.** A 400mm lens really comes in handy when shooting field sports, wildlife, and other distant subjects. This $2,199 lens is long enough and fast enough to prove useful in a variety of demanding situations. And, it's a lot more affordable than Canon's "exotic" lenses in this range, such as the EF 400mm f/2.8L II USM lens ($9,999). Although, at three pounds, this lens isn't really the boat anchor you might think it is; you'll want to mount it on a sturdy tripod (for wildlife) or monopod (for sports) to get the sharpest images.

- **EF 85mm f/1.2L II USM lens.** This exquisite lens is the perfect optic for head-and-shoulders portraits, with its remarkable bokeh, excellent sharpness, and shallow depth-of-field for selective focus effects. The $1,999 MSRP lens's huge maximum aperture means you can hand-hold it for sports, portraits, or other types of shooting. As I write this, there are rumors that Canon is about to introduce an updated 85mm f/1.4L lens. Price and other specs are unknown, but the new lens is sharper wide open and has comparable bokeh; many photographers will be willing to give up the f/1.2 versions slight maximum aperture advantage for an all-new design.

Figure 7.5
Because lines at the center of the frame aren't bent, some fisheye shots don't look like fisheye images on first glance.

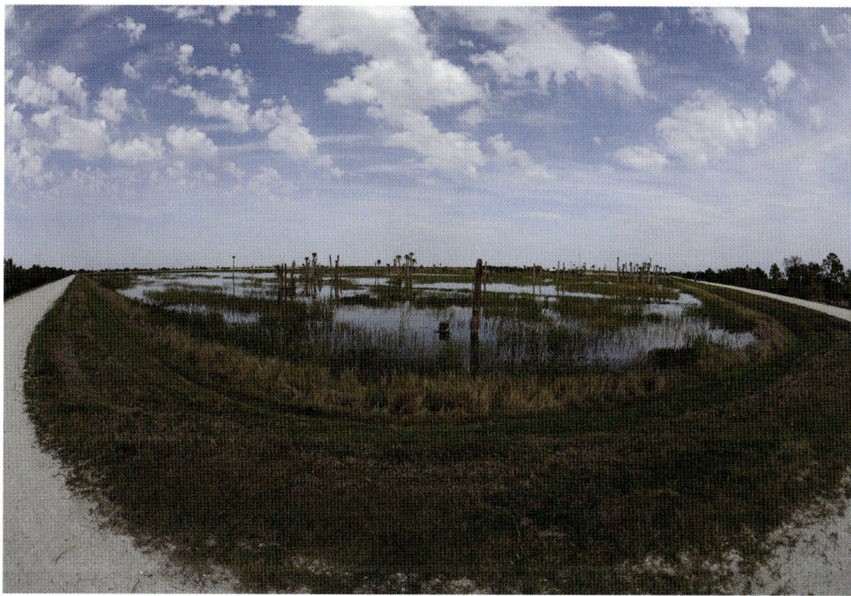

- **Extender EF 1.4X III lens.** This focal-length multiplier is almost a must for anyone owning one of Canon's 70-200mm f/2.8 lenses. It transforms your workhorse into a 98-280mm f/4 lens with virtually no loss in sharpness, for about $429. It performs the same magic with any other compatible lens, too. Canon also offers a 2X extender for the same price, but this one is the most "transparent" in use, so to speak.

- **TS-E 90mm f/2.8 lens (or any other tilt-shift lens).** Manual focus won't bother you with this lens, because the most exciting capability of any tilt-shift lens is to let you manipulate the plane of focus in useful and/or interesting ways. Whether you want to correct the focal plane for architectural images, create "miniature" special effects, or produce unusual selective focus in portraits, these lenses offer interesting capabilities. The 90mm f/2.8 optic at $1,399 is relatively affordable, but Canon also offers 17mm, 24mm, and 45mm TS-E lenses for around $1,399 to $2,149.

- **A macro.** Canon offers an assortment of full-frame macro lenses, priced at less than $400 to less than $1,399, including the unique MP-E 65mm f/2.8 1-5X macro for close-up use only (it doesn't focus to infinity). All are non-zooms and they range in focal length from 50mm to 180mm, and one (the EF 100mm f/2.8L Macro IS USM) includes image stabilization for hand-held work. Choose your lens based on how close you want to work from your subject, and their closest focusing distance. Everybody needs a macro, especially for a rainy day when you want to photograph your collection of salt-shakers rather than venture out into the elements.

- **Super-bargain telephoto.** Canon makes a number of inexpensive telephoto zooms, but for my money, the super-bargain of the line is the EF 75-300mm f/4-5.6 III, shown in Figure 7.6. Its strongest feature is its price: $199, which makes it irresistible to those who feel they have little need for a tele zoom (because they use prime lenses or wide angles for most of their work), but would like to have one in their kit for occasional sports or casual wildlife photography. You don't get image stabilization, but the lens weighs just over one pound and focuses down to 4.9 feet. The f/5.6 maximum aperture at 300mm is only about a stop slower than many more expensive lenses with a similar range. The main quirk is that the lens gets longer—by quite a bit—as you zoom and focus, as you can see at right in the figure. It uses that low-end Micromotor focus mechanism I mentioned earlier, so don't expect lightning-fast focus. Still, it's reasonably sharp and on a dollars-per-millimeter of focal length basis, it's inexpensive.

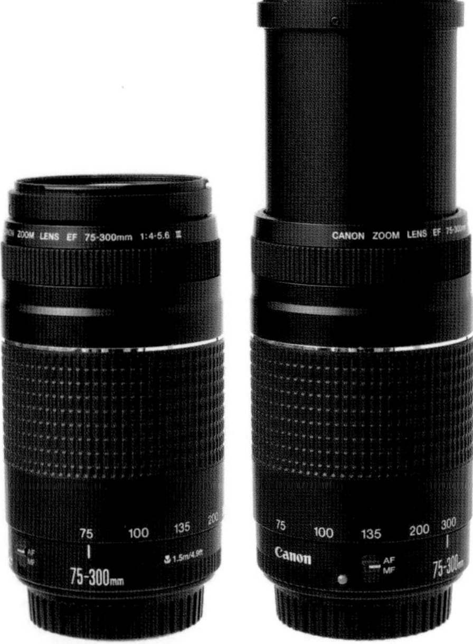

Figure 7.6 An inexpensive telephoto zoom alternative (left) that gets longer as you zoom out (right).

8

Making Light Work for You

Successful photographers and artists have an intimate understanding of the importance of light in shaping an image. Rembrandt was a master of using light to create moods and reveal the character of his subjects. Late artist Thomas Kinkade's official tagline was "Painter of Light." Dean Collins, co-founder of Finelight Studios, revolutionized how a whole generation of photographers learned and used lighting. Photo guru Ed Pierce conducted seminars called "Captivated by the Light," that reveal his secrets for portrait lighting. It's impossible to underestimate how the use of light adds to—and how misuse can detract from—your photographs.

All forms of visual art use light to shape the finished product. Sculptors don't have control over the light used to illuminate their finished work, so they must create shapes using planes and curved surfaces so that the form envisioned by the artist comes to life from a variety of viewing and lighting angles. Painters, in contrast, have absolute control over both shape and light in their work, as well as the viewing angle, so they can use both the contours of their two-dimensional subjects and the qualities of the "light" they use to illuminate those subjects to evoke the image they want to produce.

Photography is a third form of art. The photographer may have little or no control over the subject (other than posing human subjects) but can often adjust both viewing angle *and* the nature of the light source to create a compelling image. The direction and intensity of the light sources create the shapes and textures that we see. The distribution and proportions determine the contrast and tonal values: whether the image is stark or high key, or muted and low in contrast. The colors of the light (because even "white" light has a color balance that the sensor can detect), and how much of those colors the subject reflects or absorbs, paint the hues visible in the image.

This chapter introduces using *continuous* lighting (such as daylight, incandescent, or fluorescent sources) for those who have rarely used auxiliary lights. More advanced photographers can skim through this chapter quickly, and move ahead to the discussion of electronic flash in the two chapters that follow this one.

Continuous Illumination versus Electronic Flash

Continuous lighting is exactly what you might think: uninterrupted illumination that is available all the time during a shooting session. Daylight, moonlight, and the artificial lighting encountered both indoors and outdoors count as continuous light sources (although all of them can be "interrupted" by passing clouds, solar eclipses, a blown fuse, or simply by switching a lamp off). Indoor continuous illumination includes both the lights that are there already (such as incandescent lamps or overhead fluorescent lights indoors) and fixtures you supply yourself, including photoflood lamps or reflectors used to bounce existing light onto your subject.

Electronic flash is notable because it can be much more intense than continuous lighting, lasts only a moment, and can be much more portable than supplementary incandescent sources. It's a light source you can carry with you and use anywhere. There are advantages and disadvantages to each type of illumination. Here's a quick checklist of pros and cons:

- **Lighting preview—Pro: continuous lighting.** With continuous lighting, you always know exactly what kind of lighting effect you're going to get and, if multiple lights are used, how they will interact with each other. Figure 8.1 shows a portrait taken in the simplest of environments, an industrial-type loft converted to a studio, with a large frosted glass window located to the left and slightly behind the subject providing all the illumination. A white piece of foamcore to the right of the camera filled in the shadows, and an aperture of f/4 assured that the rough white wall in the background would be featureless and out of focus.

- **Lighting preview—Con: electronic flash.** With electronic flash, the general effect you're going to see may be a mystery until you've built some experience, and you may need to review a shot on the LCD monitor, make some adjustments, and then reshoot to get the look you want. (In this sense, a digital camera's review capabilities replace the Polaroid test shots pro photographers relied on in decades past.) An image like the one in Figure 8.1 would have been difficult to achieve with an off-camera battery-powered flash unit, because it would be tricky to preview exactly how the shadows would fall without a true continuous modeling light.

- **Exposure calculation—Pro: continuous lighting.** Your 5D Mark IV has no problem calculating exposure for continuous lighting, because it remains constant and can be measured through the exposure sensor that interprets the light reaching the viewfinder (or, when using live view, the sensor). The amount of light available just before the exposure will, in almost all cases, be the same amount of light present when the shutter is released. The 5D Mark IV's Spot metering mode can be used to measure and compare the proportions of light in the highlights and shadows, so you can make an adjustment (such as using more or less fill light) if necessary. You can even use a hand-held light meter to measure the light yourself.

- **Exposure calculation—Con: electronic flash.** Electronic flash illumination doesn't exist until the flash fires, and so can't be measured by the 5D Mark IV's sensors at the moment of exposure. Instead, the light must be measured by metering the intensity of a *pre-flash* triggered an instant before the main flash, as it is reflected back to the camera and through the lens.

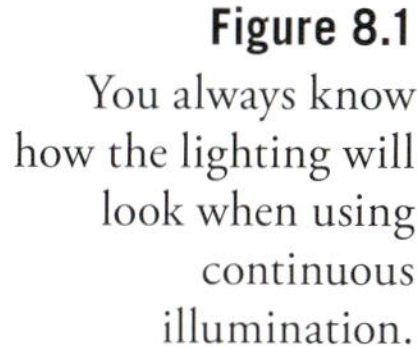

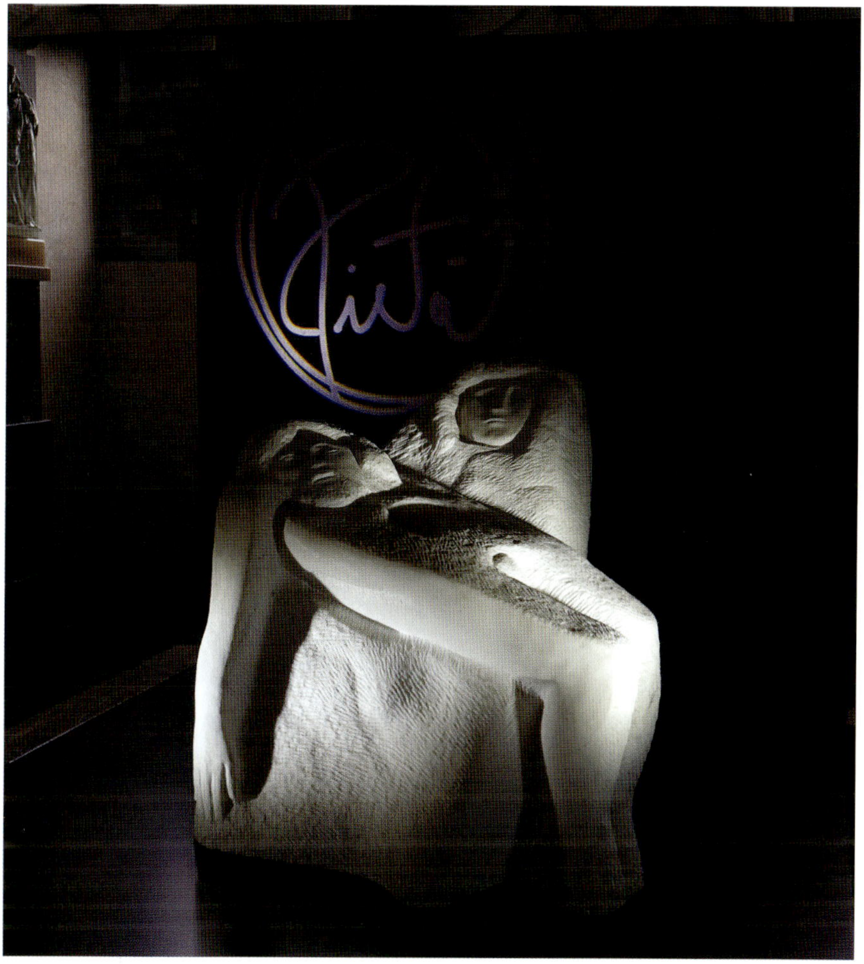

Figure 8.1
You always know how the lighting will look when using continuous illumination.

A less attractive alternative, available with higher-end Canon flash units like the Speedlite 600EX II-RT, is to use a sensor built into the external flash itself and measure reflected light that bounces back, but which has not traveled through the lens. If you have a do-it-yourself bent, there are hand-held flash meters, too, including models that measure both flash and continuous light, so you need only one meter for both types of illumination.

■ **Evenness of illumination—Pro/con: continuous lighting.** Of the continuous light sources, daylight, in particular, provides illumination that tends to fill an image completely, lighting up the foreground, background, and your subject almost equally. Shadows do come into play, of course, so you might need to use reflectors like the one used for Figure 8.1, or fill-in additional light sources to even out the illumination further. But, barring objects that block large sections of your image from daylight, the light is spread fairly evenly. Indoors, however, continuous lighting is commonly less evenly distributed. The average living room, for example, has hot spots near the lamps and overhead lights, and dark corners located farther from those light sources. But on the plus side, you can easily *see* this uneven illumination and compensate with additional lamps.

- **Evenness of illumination—Con: electronic flash.** Electronic flash units, like continuous light sources such as lamps that don't have the advantage of being located 93 million miles from the subject, suffer from the effects of their proximity. The *inverse square law*, first applied to both gravity and light by Sir Isaac Newton, dictates that as a light source's distance increases from the subject, the amount of light reaching the subject falls off proportionately to the square of the distance. In plain English, that means that a flash or lamp that's 12 feet away from a subject provides only one-quarter as much illumination as a source that's 6 feet away (rather than half as much). (See Figure 8.2.) This translates into relatively shallow "depth-of-light."

- **Action stopping—Pro: electronic flash.** When it comes to the ability to freeze moving objects in their tracks, the advantage goes to electronic flash. The brief duration of electronic flash serves as a very high "shutter speed" when the flash is the main or only source of illumination for the photo. Your 5D Mark IV's shutter speed may be set for 1/200th second during a flash exposure, but if the flash illumination predominates, the *effective* exposure time will be the 1/1,000th to 1/50,000th second or less duration of the flash, as you can see in Figure 8.3, because the flash unit reduces the amount of light released by cutting short the duration of the flash. The only fly in the ointment is that, if the ambient light is strong enough, it may produce a secondary, "ghost" exposure, as I'll explain later in this chapter.

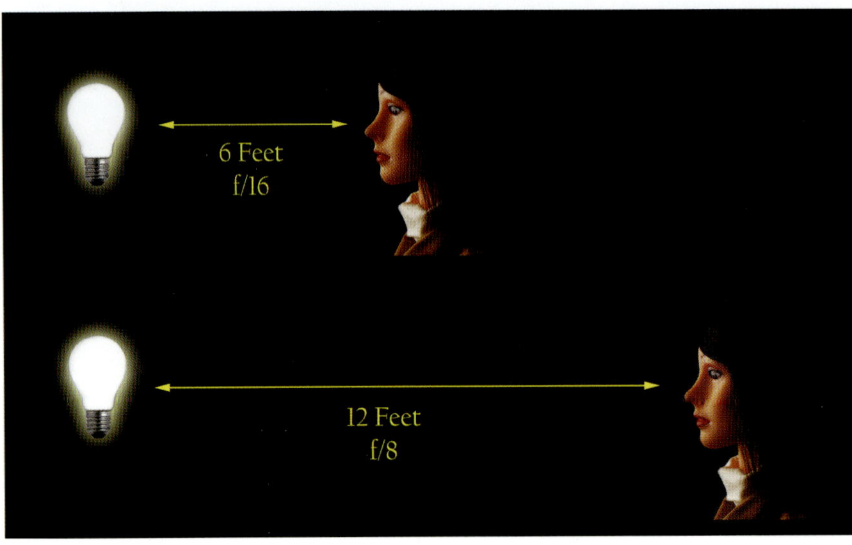

Figure 8.2
A light source that is twice as far away provides only one-quarter as much illumination.

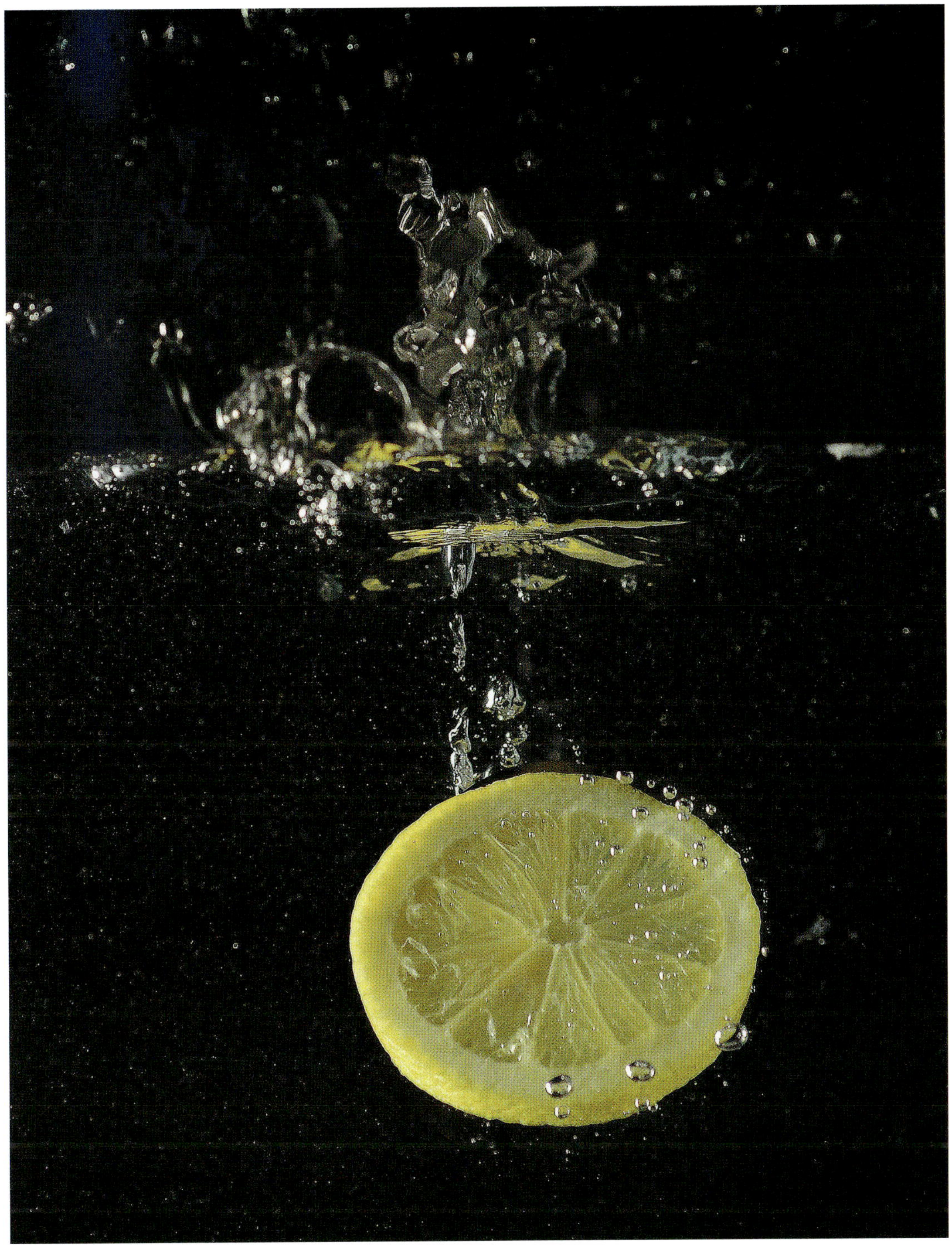

Figure 8.3 Electronic flash can freeze almost any action.

- **Action stopping—Con: continuous lighting.** Action stopping with continuous light sources is completely dependent on the shutter speed you've dialed in on the camera. And the speeds available are dependent on the amount of light available and your ISO sensitivity setting. Outdoors in daylight, there will probably be enough sunlight to let you shoot at 1/2,000th second and f/6.3 with a non-grainy sensitivity setting for your 5D Mark IV of ISO 400. That's a useful combination of settings if you're not using a super-telephoto with a small maximum aperture. But inside, the reduced illumination quickly has you pushing your 5D Mark IV to its limits. For example, if you're shooting indoor sports, there probably won't be enough available light to allow you to use a 1/2,000th second shutter speed (although I routinely shoot non-flash indoor basketball with my 5D Mark IV at ISO 1600 and 1/500th second at f/4). But in many indoor sports situations, the lack of available light, and the 5D Mark IV's increased visual noise at settings of ISO 6400 and above, you may find yourself limited to 1/500th second or slower.

- **Cost—Pro: continuous lighting.** Incandescent or fluorescent lamps are generally much less expensive than electronic flash units, which can easily cost several hundred dollars. I've used everything from desktop high-intensity lamps to reflector flood lights for continuous illumination at very little cost. There are lamps made especially for photographic purposes, too. Maintenance is economical, too: many incandescent or fluorescents use bulbs that cost only a few dollars.

- **Cost—Con: electronic flash.** Electronic flash units aren't particularly cheap. The lowest-cost dedicated flash designed specifically for the Canon dSLRs is about $150, and is probably not one that will be favored by many 5D Mark IV owners. Such units are limited in features, however, and intended for those with entry-level cameras. Plan on spending some money to get the features that a sophisticated electronic flash offers. I paid more than $600 for my 600EX II-RT, and only a little less for its "mate," a 580EX II that I purchased a couple years ago. I've got nearly $1,000 sunk into just two battery-operated strobes, and also invested that much—and more—in studio flash units.

- **Flexibility—Pro: electronic flash.** Electronic flash's action-freezing power allows you to work without a tripod in the studio (and elsewhere), adding flexibility and speed when choosing angles and positions. Flash units can be easily filtered, and, because the filtration is placed over the light source rather than the lens, you don't need to use high-quality filter material. For example, Roscoe or Lee lighting gels, which may be too flimsy to use in front of the lens, can be mounted or taped in front of your flash with ease.

- **Flexibility—Con: continuous lighting.** Because incandescent and fluorescent lamps are not as bright as electronic flash, the slower shutter speeds required (see "Action stopping," above) mean that you may have to use a tripod more often, especially when shooting portraits. The incandescent variety of continuous lighting gets hot, especially in the studio, and the side effects range from discomfort (for your human models) to disintegration (if you happen to be shooting perishable foods like ice cream). The heat also makes it more difficult to add filtration to incandescent sources.

Continuous Lighting Basics

While continuous lighting and its effects are generally much easier to visualize and use than electronic flash, there are some factors you need to take into account, particularly the color temperature of the light, how accurately a given form of illumination reproduces colors (we've all seen the ghastly looks human faces assume under mercury-vapor lamps outdoors), and other considerations.

One important aspect is color temperature. Of course, color temperature concerns aren't exclusive to continuous light sources, but the variations tend to be more extreme and less predictable than those of electronic flash, which output relatively consistent daylight-like illumination.

Living with Color Temperature

In practical terms, color temperature is how "bluish" or how "reddish" the light appears to be to the digital camera's sensor. Indoor illumination is quite warm, comparatively, and appears reddish to the sensor. Daylight, in contrast, seems much bluer to the sensor. Our eyes (our brains, actually) are quite adaptable to these variations, so white objects don't appear to have an orange tinge when viewed indoors, nor do they seem excessively blue outdoors in full daylight. Yet, these color temperature variations are real and the sensor is not fooled. To capture the most accurate colors, we need to take the color temperature into account in setting the color balance (or *white balance*) of the 5D Mark IV—either automatically using the camera's intelligence or manually using our own knowledge and experience.

While Canon has been valiant in its efforts to smarten up the 5D Mark IV's ability to adjust for color balance automatically, an entire cottage industry has developed to provide us additional help, including gadgets like the ExpoDisc filter/caps (see Figure 8.4) and their ilk (www.expoimaging.com), which allow the camera's add-on external custom white balance measuring feature to evaluate the illumination that passes through the disc/cap/filter/Pringle's can lid, or whatever neutral-color substitute you employ. (A white or gray card also works.) Unfortunately, to help us tangle with the many different types of non-incandescent/non-daylight sources, Canon has provided the 5D Mark IV with only a single White Fluorescent setting (some competing models offer more than a half-dozen differ-

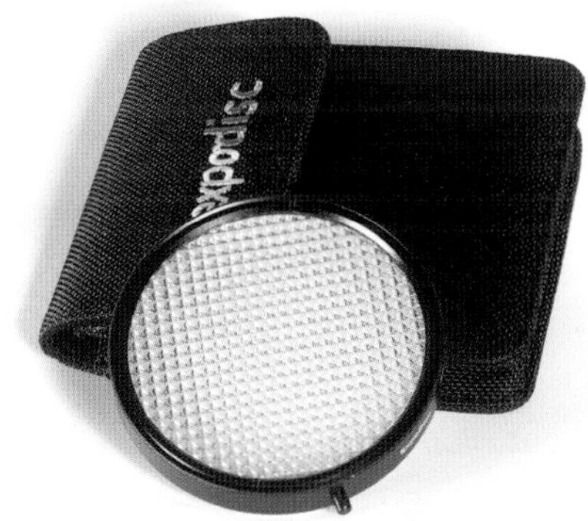

Figure 8.4 The ExpoDisc is placed on a lens and used as a neutral subject for measuring white balance.

ent presets for fluorescents, sodium-vapor, and mercury vapor illumination.) When it comes to zeroing in on the exact color temperature for a scene, your main tools will be custom white balances set using neutral targets like the ExpoDisc, and adjustment of RAW files when you import photos into your image editor.

The only time you need to think in terms of actual color temperature is when you're making adjustments using the Color Temp. setting in the White Balance entry, as I'll describe in Chapter 11. It allows you to dial in exact color temperatures, if known. You can also shift and bias color balance along the blue/amber and magenta/green axes, and bracket white balance.

In most cases, however, the Auto setting in the Shooting menu's White Balance entry will do a good job of calculating white balance for you. Auto can be used as your choice most of the time. Use the preset values or set a custom white balance that matches the current shooting conditions when you need to.

Remember that if you shoot RAW, you can specify the white balance of your image when you import it into Photoshop, Photoshop Elements, or another image editor using Adobe Camera Raw, or your preferred RAW converter. While color-balancing filters that fit on the front of the lens exist, they are primarily useful for film cameras, because film's color balance can't be tweaked as extensively as that of a sensor.

White Balance Bracketing

When using WB bracketing, the 5D Mark IV takes a single shot, and then saves multiple JPEG copies, each with a different color balance. It's not necessary to capture multiple shots, as the camera uses the raw information retrieved from the sensor for the single exposure and then processes it to generate the multiple different versions. The bracketing adjustments are made only on the amber/blue axis (no bracketing in the magenta/green bias is possible), but you can select whether the bracketed shots are spread in the blue *or* amber directions (that is, each one bluer/less blue or yellower/less yellow) or balanced to provide both blue- and amber-oriented brackets.

Making these adjustments are the only times you're likely to be confused by a seeming contradiction in how color temperatures are named: warmer (more reddish) color temperatures (measured in degrees Kelvin) are the *lower* numbers, while cooler (bluer) color temperatures are *higher* numbers. It might not make sense to say that 3,400K is warmer than 6,000K, but that's the way it is. If it helps, think of a glowing red ember contrasted with a white-hot welder's torch, rather than fire and ice.

The confusion comes from physics. Scientists calculate color temperature from the light emitted by a mythical object called a black body radiator, which absorbs all the radiant energy that strikes it, and reflects none at all. Such a black body not only *absorbs* light perfectly, but it *emits* it perfectly when heated (and since nothing in the universe is perfect, that makes it mythical).

At a particular physical temperature, this imaginary object always emits light of the same wavelength or color. That makes it possible to define color temperature in terms of actual temperature in degrees on the Kelvin scale that scientists use. Incandescent light, for example, typically has a color temperature of 3,200K to 3,400K. Daylight might range from 5,500K to 6,000K. Each type of illumination we use for photography has its own color temperature range—with some cautions.

Daylight

Daylight is produced by the sun, and so is moonlight (which is just reflected sunlight). Daylight is present, of course, even when you can't see the sun. When sunlight is direct, it can be bright and harsh. If daylight is diffused by clouds, softened by bouncing off objects such as walls or your photo reflectors, or filtered by shade, it can be much dimmer and less contrasty.

Daylight's color temperature can vary quite widely. It is highest in temperature (most blue) at noon when the sun is directly overhead, because the light is traveling through a minimum amount of the filtering layer we call the atmosphere. The color temperature at high noon may be 6,000K. At other times of day, the sun is lower in the sky and the particles in the air provide a filtering effect that warms the illumination to about 5,500K for most of the day. Starting an hour before dusk and for an hour after sunrise, the warm appearance of the sunlight is even visible to our eyes when the color temperature may dip to 5,000K–4,500K, as shown in Figure 8.5.

Because you'll be taking so many photos in daylight, you'll want to learn how to use or compensate for the brightness and contrast of sunlight, as well as how to deal with its color temperature. I'll provide some hints later in this chapter.

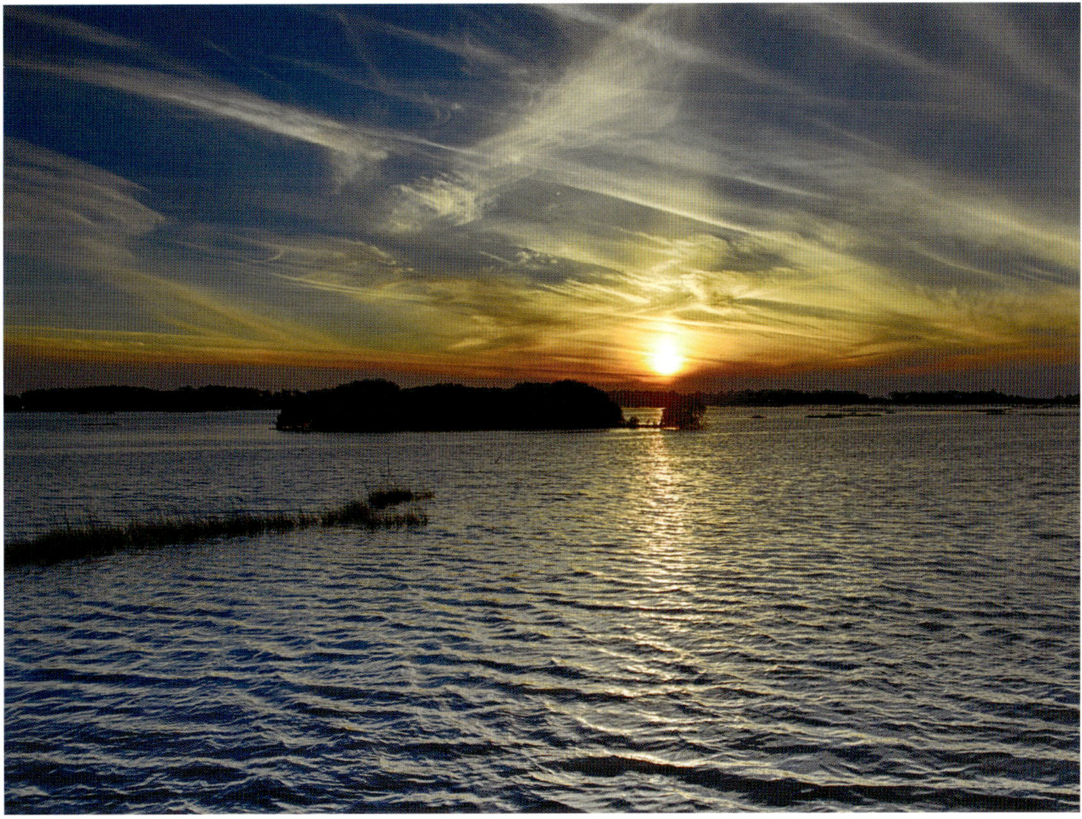

Figure 8.5 At dawn and dusk, the color temperature of daylight may dip as low as 4,500K.

Incandescent/Tungsten Light

The term incandescent or tungsten illumination is usually applied to the direct descendents of Thomas Edison's original electric lamp. Such lights consist of a glass bulb that contains a vacuum, or is filled with a halogen gas, and contains a tungsten filament that is heated by an electrical current, producing photons and heat. Tungsten-halogen lamps are a variation on the basic light-bulb, using a more rugged (and longer-lasting) filament that can be heated to a higher temperature, housed in a thicker glass or quartz envelope, and filled with iodine or bromine ("halogen") gases. The higher temperature allows tungsten-halogen (or quartz-halogen/quartz-iodine, depending on their construction) lamps to burn "hotter" and whiter. Although popular for automobile headlamps today, they've also been used for photographic illumination.

Although incandescent illumination isn't a perfect black body radiator, it's close enough that the color temperature of such lamps can be precisely calculated and used for photography without concerns about color variation (at least, until the very end of the lamp's life). Of course, old-style tungsten lamps are (mostly) long gone by now, replaced, at first, by compact fluorescent lights (CFL) more energy efficient tungsten halogen bulbs, or, most recently by affordable LED lamps. The other qualities of this type of lighting, such as contrast, are dependent on the distance of the lamp from the subject, type of reflectors used, and other factors that I'll explain later in this chapter.

Fluorescent Light/Other Light Sources

Fluorescent light has some advantages in terms of illumination, but some disadvantages from a photographic standpoint. This type of lamp generates light through an electro-chemical reaction that emits most of its energy as visible light, rather than heat, which is why the bulbs don't get as hot. The type of light produced varies depending on the phosphor coatings and type of gas in the tube. So, the illumination fluorescent bulbs produce can vary widely in its characteristics.

That's not great news for photographers. Different types of lamps have different "color temperatures" that can't be precisely measured in degrees Kelvin, because the light isn't produced by heating. Worse, fluorescent lamps have a discontinuous spectrum of light that can have some colors missing entirely. A particular type of tube can lack certain shades of red or other colors (see Figure 8.6), which is why fluorescent lamps and other alternative technologies such as sodium-vapor illumination can produce ghastly looking human skin tones. Their spectra can lack the reddish tones we associate with healthy skin and emphasize the blues and greens popular in horror movies.

Vendors, such as GE and Sylvania, may actually provide a figure known as the *color rendering index* (or CRI), which is a measure of how accurately a particular light source represents standard colors, using a scale of 0 (some sodium-vapor lamps) to 100 (daylight and most incandescent lamps). Daylight fluorescents and deluxe cool white fluorescents might have a CRI of about 79 to 95, which is perfectly acceptable for most photographic applications. Warm white fluorescents might have a CRI of 55. White deluxe mercury vapor lights are less suitable with a CRI of 45, while low-pressure sodium lamps can vary from CRI 0 to 18.

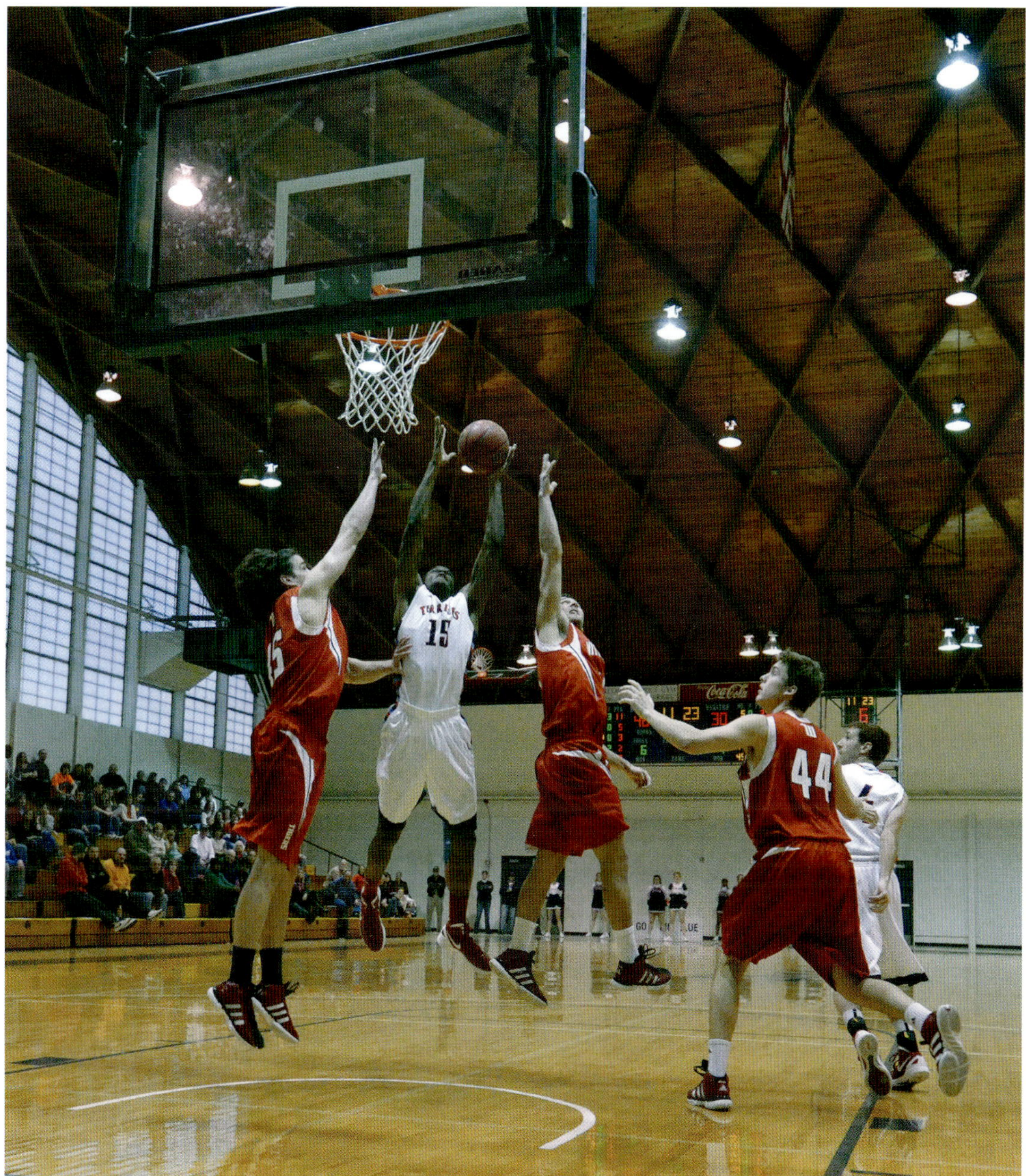

Figure 8.6 The uncorrected lighting in the gym added a distinct greenish cast to this image when exposed with a daylight white balance setting.

Other Lighting Accessories

Once you start working with light, you'll find there are plenty of useful accessories that can help you. Here are some of the most popular that you might want to consider. These all work well with both continuous lighting, discussed in this chapter, as well as with electronic flash, which will be our focus in the chapter that follows.

Do-It-Yourself Lighting

The cool thing about continuous lighting is that anything that lights up can be used as a lighting tool for your 5D Mark IV. Even simple lighting can produce exquisite effects, as you can see in Figure 8.7 in a photograph taken by Cleveland jewelry designer David Wilkinson of one of his creations. Flashlights (for "painting with light" techniques), shop work lights, or even desktop high-intensity lamps can be pressed into service, too, at little or no cost (if you already happen to own something that will work). I used a desk lamp to shoot the two images seen in Figure 8.8, simply because the lamp was bright enough to let me use a small f/stop to maximize depth-of-field, and it was really easy to see the lighting effect and move the lamp an inch or two to get different effects.

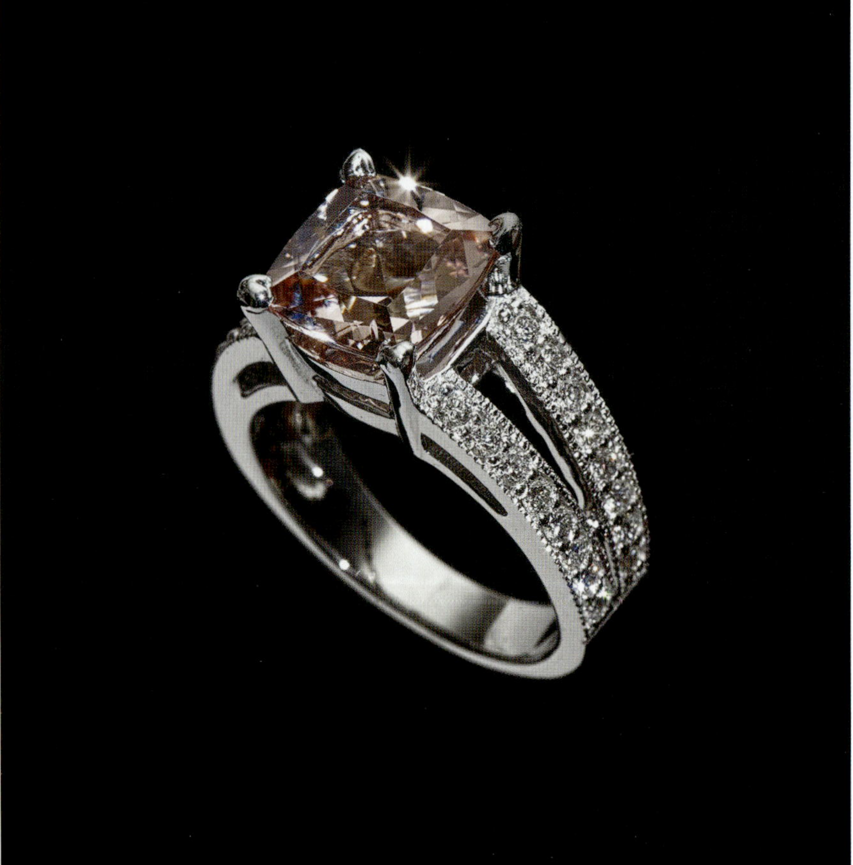

Figure 8.7
Even simple lighting can produce exquisite results.

Photo by David Wilkinson Designs (www.wilkinsonjewelry.com.)

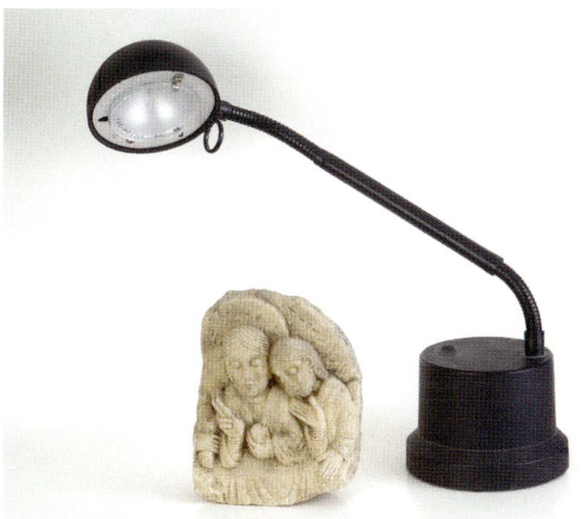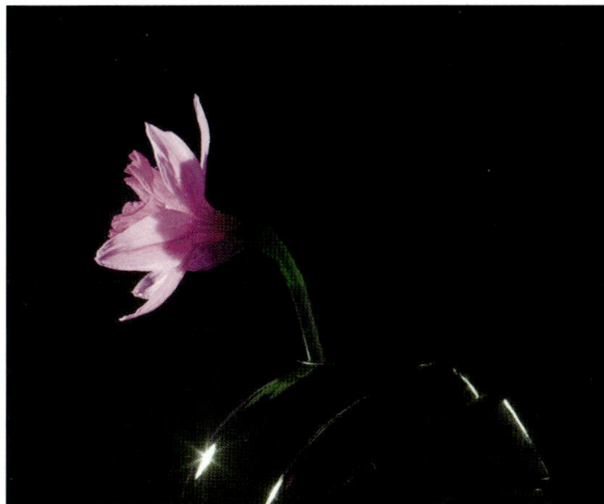

Figure 8.8 A desk lamp was used for both these photographs.

Umbrellas

Umbrellas are just what you might think, a variation on those trusty shields-on-a-stick that protect us from the ravages of sun, rain, snow, or other elements of nature. Whether we know them as parasols (for the sun) or paraguas (for the water) on the Costa del Sol, as parapluies/ombrelles on the Riviera, or Sonnenschirme/Regenschirme (gotta love those Germans!), these inexpensive accessories are just as versatile for reflecting light as blocking it.

Indeed, you can use umbrellas in multiple roles:

- **Light reflector.** A silver umbrella can provide a softer, but not *too* soft light source, or a much softer source of illumination when a non-shiny white umbrella is used. The quality and quantity of the light that your 5D Mark IV sees can be further adjusted simply by moving the umbrella closer to your subject (for a softer illumination) or farther away (for more contrast).

- **Light diffuser.** A white umbrella diffuses and softens light, but a translucent white umbrella (of the "shoot-through" variety) can be reversed so that the illumination passes through the fabric and becomes even more soft and diffuse.

- **Light blocker.** Some umbrellas have a white or silver interior surface, and a black cover that prevents any light from leaking through the umbrella. Those models can be used to *block* light from other sources of illumination—even outdoors in daylight—to allow you to create subtle lighting effects.

- **Light colorizer.** Umbrellas may have a shiny golden, silver, or blue interior surface (as do many flat reflectors), and so can be used to add a rich warm tone, neutral sheen, or cold bluish cast to an image or shadows. You can use umbrella "colorizing" to create an effect or balance multiple light sources.

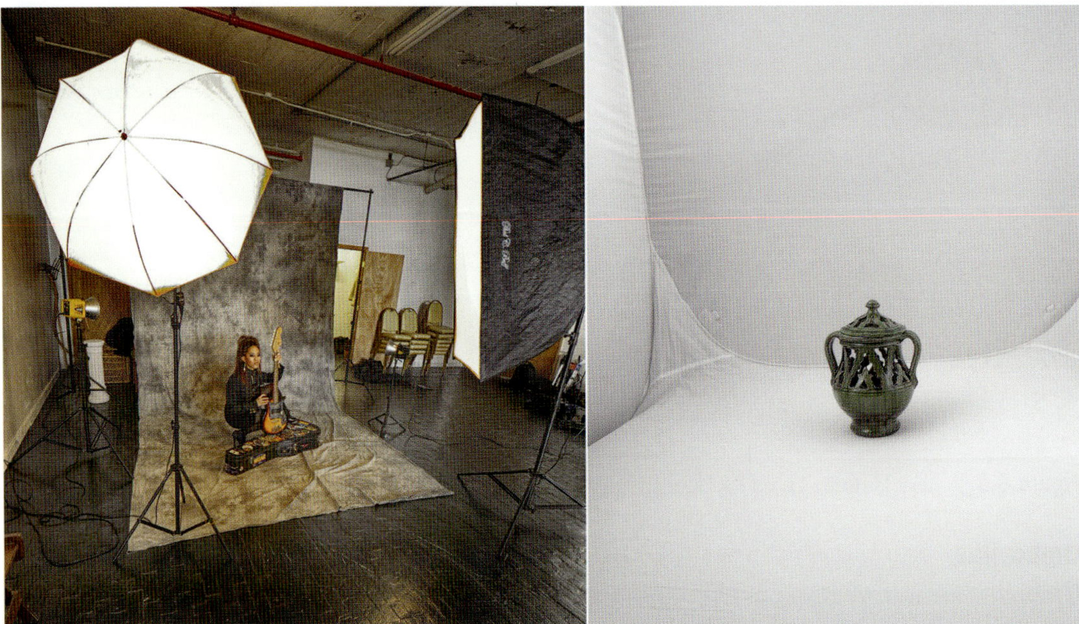

Figure 8.9 Umbrellas and soft boxes, seen at opposite sides of the frame, provide a soft, diffuse light source (left). Tents provide shadowless lighting for shiny objects (right).

- **Soft box in an instant.** Many umbrellas can be fitted with a cover over their front that transforms them into a soft box. This conversion is more practical for use with electronic flash (covered in the next chapter) than for some kinds of continuous lighting, because of heat build-up. "Colder" forms of continuous lighting, such as fluorescent lights designed specially for photographic applications, can be used in soft box mode, however. Figure 8.9 shows both an umbrella and a soft box.

Tents

Tents, like the one seen in at right Figure 8.9, are useful for photographing shiny objects or any subject where you want to reduce the shadows and reflections to a minimum. The fabric of the tent is translucent, so you place the light sources around the sides or above, and a soft glow filters through to illuminate the image. You can still maintain subtle lighting effects by choosing to light up—or not light up—individual sides of the cube.

The lens of the 5D Mark IV protrudes through a hole or slit in the tent, so you can photograph the shiniest subject without having you or your camera show up in the final picture.

Soft Boxes

Soft boxes are also handy for photographing shiny objects. They not only provide a soft light, but if the box itself happens to reflect in the subject (say you're photographing a chromium toaster), the box will provide an interesting highlight that's indistinct and not distracting.

You can buy soft boxes or make your own. Some lengths of friction-fit plastic pipe and a lot of muslin cut and sewed just so may be all that you need. Soft boxes are large square, rectangular, or round or octagonal devices that may resemble an umbrella with a front cover, and produce a similar lighting effect. They can extend from a few feet square to massive boxes that stand five or six feet tall—virtually a wall of light. With a light source or two inside a soft box, you have a very large, semi-directional light source that's very diffuse and very flattering for portraiture and other people photography.

Light Stands

Both electronic flash and incandescent lamps can benefit from light stands. These are lightweight, tripod-like devices (but without a swiveling or tilting head) that can be set on the floor, tabletops, or other elevated surfaces and positioned as needed. Light stands should be strong enough to support an external lighting unit, up to and including a relatively heavy flash with soft box or umbrella reflectors. You want the supports to be capable of raising the lights high enough to be effective. Look for light stands capable of extending six to seven feet high. The nine-foot units usually have larger, steadier bases, and extend high enough that you can use them as background supports. You'll be using these stands for a lifetime, so invest in good ones. I bought my light stands when I was in college, and I have been using them for decades (see Figure 8.10).

Figure 8.10
A good-quality light stand can last a lifetime.

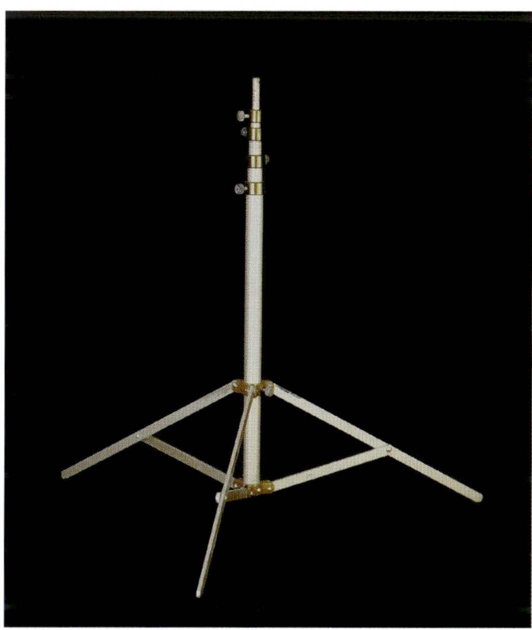

Backgrounds

Backgrounds can be backdrops of cloth, sheets of muslin you've painted yourself using a sponge dipped in paint, rolls of seamless paper, or any other suitable surface your mind can dream up. Backgrounds provide a complementary and non-distracting area behind subjects (especially portraits) and can be lit separately to provide contrast and separation that outlines the subject, or which helps set a mood.

I like to use plain-colored backgrounds for portraits, and white or gray seamless paper backgrounds for product photography. You can usually construct these yourself from cheap materials and tape them up on the wall behind your subject, or mount them on a pole stretched between a pair of light stands.

Snoots and Barn Doors

These fit over the flash unit and direct the light at your subject. Snoots are excellent for converting a light source into a hair light, while barn doors (shown in Figure 8.11) give you enough control over the illumination by opening and closing their flaps that you can use another flash as a background light, with the capability of feathering the light exactly where you want it on the background.

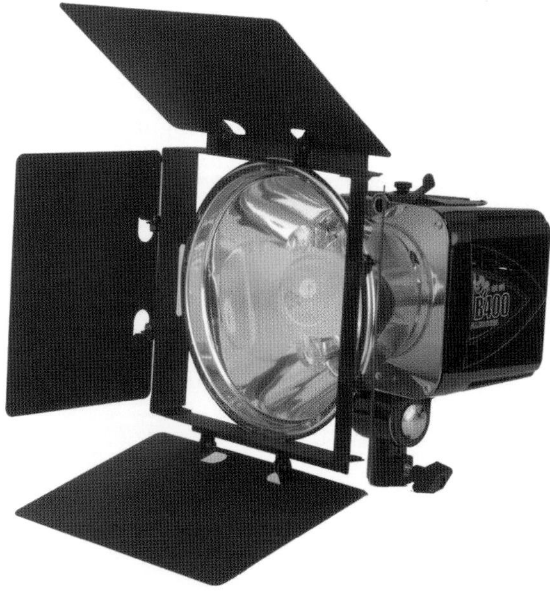

Figure 8.11
Barn doors allow you to control and feather the light.

Electronic Flash Basics

9

Until you delve into the situation deeply enough, it might appear that serious photographers have a love/hate relationship with electronic flash. You'll often hear that flash photography is less natural looking, and that the built-in flash in most cameras should never be used as the primary source of illumination because it provides a harsh, garish look. Indeed, most "pro" cameras like the Canon EOS 1D X and 5D Mark IV don't have a built-in flash at all. Available ("continuous") lighting is praised, and built-in flash photography seems to be roundly denounced.

In truth, however, the bias is against *bad* flash photography, the kind produced when you clamp a flash on top of the camera (as shown in Figure 9.1) and point it directly at your subject. In that mode, you'll often end up with well-exposed (thanks to Canon's e-TTL II metering system), but *harshly lit* images. Yet, in other configurations, flash has become the studio light source of choice for pro photographers, because it's more intense (and its intensity can be varied to order by the photographer), freezes action, frees you from using a tripod (unless you want to use one to lock down a composition), and has a snappy, consistent light quality that matches daylight. (While color balance changes as the flash duration shortens, some Canon flash units can communicate to the camera the exact white balance provided for that shot.) And even pros will cede that an external flash has some important uses as an adjunct to existing light, particularly to illuminate dark shadows using a technique called *fill flash*. Moreover, creative photographers can use an external Speedlite with their 5D Mark IV in remarkably creative ways, especially in wireless and multiple flash modes (which I'll explain in Chapter 10).

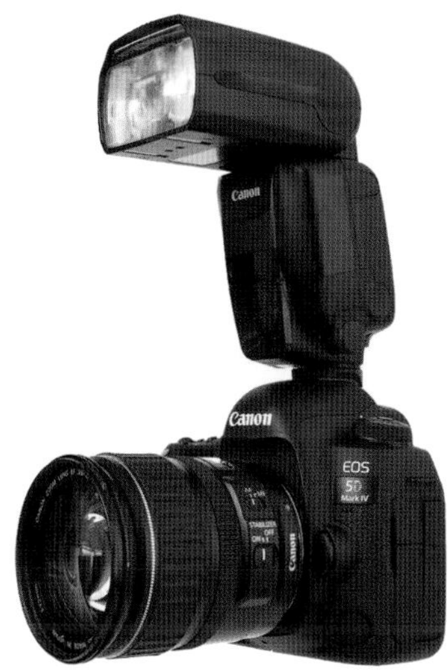

Figure 9.1 An add-on flash is a versatile accessory.

But electronic flash isn't as inherently easy to use as continuous lighting. As I noted in Chapter 8, electronic flash units are more expensive, don't show you exactly what the lighting effect will be (unless you use a second, relatively continuous source called a *modeling light* for a preview), and the exposure of electronic flash units is more difficult to calculate accurately.

How Electronic Flash Works

The bursts of light we call electronic flash are produced by a flash of photons generated by an electrical charge that is accumulated in a component called a *capacitor* and then directed through a glass tube containing xenon gas, which absorbs the energy and emits the brief flash. For a typical external flash attached to the EOS 5D Mark IV, such as the top-of-the-line Speedlite 600EX II-RT, the full burst of light lasts about 1/1,000th of a second and provides enough illumination to shoot a subject 12 feet away at f/16 using the ISO 100 setting.

Because the duration of the burst is so brief, if the external flash is the main source of illumination, the effective exposure time is short, typically 1/1,000th to 1/50,000th second, freezing a moving subject dramatically, as shown in Figure 9.2. These short bursts can also be repeated, producing multiple-exposure/stroboscopic effects, as described later in this chapter.

An electronic flash is triggered at the instant of exposure, during a period when the sensor is fully exposed by the shutter. The 5D Mark IV has a vertically traveling shutter that consists of two curtains. The first curtain opens and moves to the opposite side of the frame, at which point the shutter is completely open. The flash can be triggered at this point (so-called *first-curtain sync*), making the flash exposure. Then, after a delay that can vary from 30 seconds to 1/200th second (with the EOS 5D Mark IV; other cameras may sync at a faster or slower speed), a second curtain begins moving across the sensor plane, covering up the sensor again. If the flash is triggered just before the second curtain starts to close, then *second-curtain sync* is used. In both cases, though, a shutter speed of 1/200th second is the maximum that can be used to take a photo (unless you're using high-speed sync, discussed later in this chapter).

Figure 9.3 illustrates how this works. At upper left, you can see a fanciful illustration of a generic shutter (your EOS 5D Mark IV's shutter does *not* look like this), with both curtains tightly closed. At upper right, the first curtain begins to move downward, starting to expose a narrow slit that reveals the sensor behind the shutter. At lower left, the first curtain moves downward farther until, as you can see at lower right in the figure, the sensor is fully exposed.

When first-curtain sync is used, the flash is triggered at the instant that the sensor is completely exposed. The shutter then remains open for an additional length of time (from 30 seconds to 1/200th second), and the second curtain begins to move downward, covering the sensor once more. When second-curtain sync is activated, the flash is triggered *after* the main exposure is over, just before the second curtain begins to move downward.

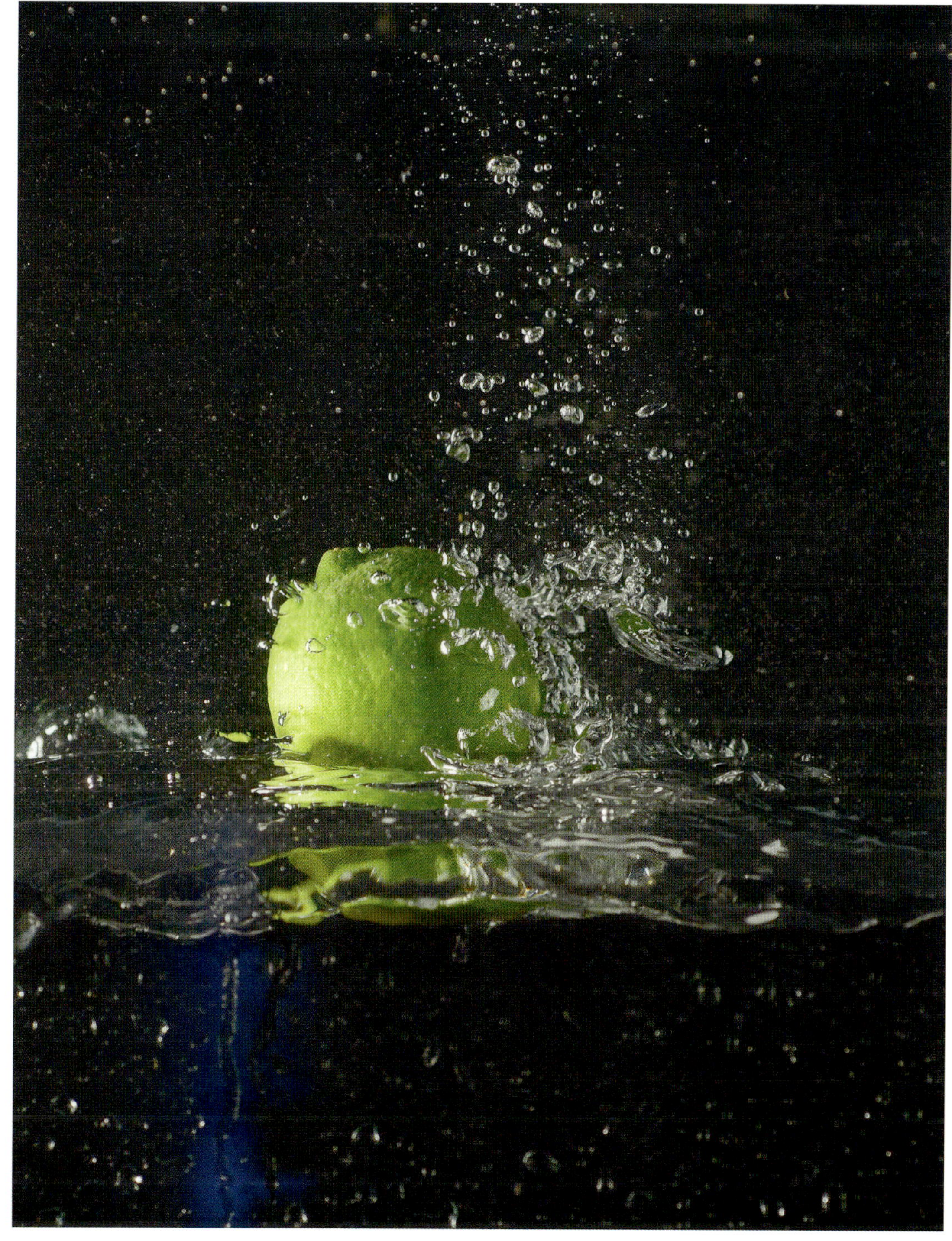

Figure 9.2 An external flash placed to the left produced a brief burst that froze this lime in mid-fall.

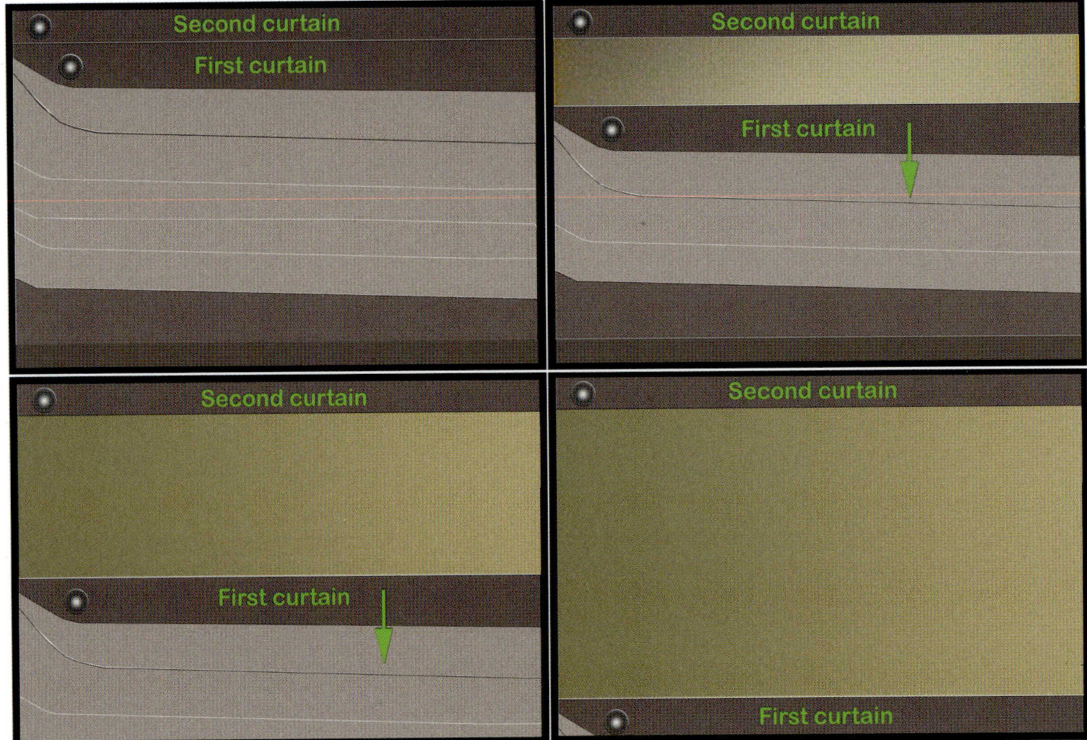

Figure 9.3 A focal plane shutter has two curtains, the upper, or front curtain, and a lower, second curtain.

Ghost Images

The difference between triggering the flash when the shutter just opens, or just when it begins to close might not seem like much. But whether you use first-curtain sync (the default setting) or second-curtain sync (an optional setting) can make a significant difference to your photograph *if the ambient light in your scene also contributes to the image.* You can set either of these sync modes in the Shooting 1 menu, under External Speedlite control where you'll find the Flash Function setting option.

At faster shutter speeds, particularly 1/200th second, there isn't much time for the ambient light to register, unless it is very bright. It's likely that the electronic flash will provide almost all the illumination, so first-curtain sync or second-curtain sync isn't very important. However, at slower shutter speeds, or with very bright ambient light levels, there is a significant difference, particularly if your subject is moving, or the camera isn't steady.

In any of those situations, the ambient light will register as a second image accompanying the flash exposure, and if there is movement (camera or subject), that additional image will not be in the same place as the flash exposure. It will show as a ghost image and, if the movement is significant enough, as a blurred ghost image trailing in front of or behind your subject in the direction of the movement.

As I noted, when you're using first-curtain sync, the flash's main burst goes off the instant the shutter opens fully (a pre-flash used to measure exposure in auto flash modes fires *before* the shutter opens). This produces an image of the subject on the sensor. Then, the shutter remains open for an additional period (30 seconds to 1/200th second, as I said). If your subject is moving, say, toward the right side of the frame, the ghost image produced by the ambient light will produce a blur on the right side of the original subject image, making it look as if your sharp (flash-produced) image is chasing the ghost. For those of us who grew up with lightning-fast superheroes who always left a ghost trail *behind them*, that looks unnatural (see Figure 9.4).

So, Canon uses second-curtain sync to remedy the situation. In that mode, the shutter opens, as before. The shutter remains open for its designated duration, and the ghost image forms. If your subject moves from the left side of the frame to the right side, the ghost will move from left to right, too. *Then*, about 1.5 milliseconds before the second shutter curtain closes, the flash is triggered, producing a nice, sharp flash image *ahead* of the ghost image. Voilà! We have monsieur *Speed Racer* outdriving his own trailing image.

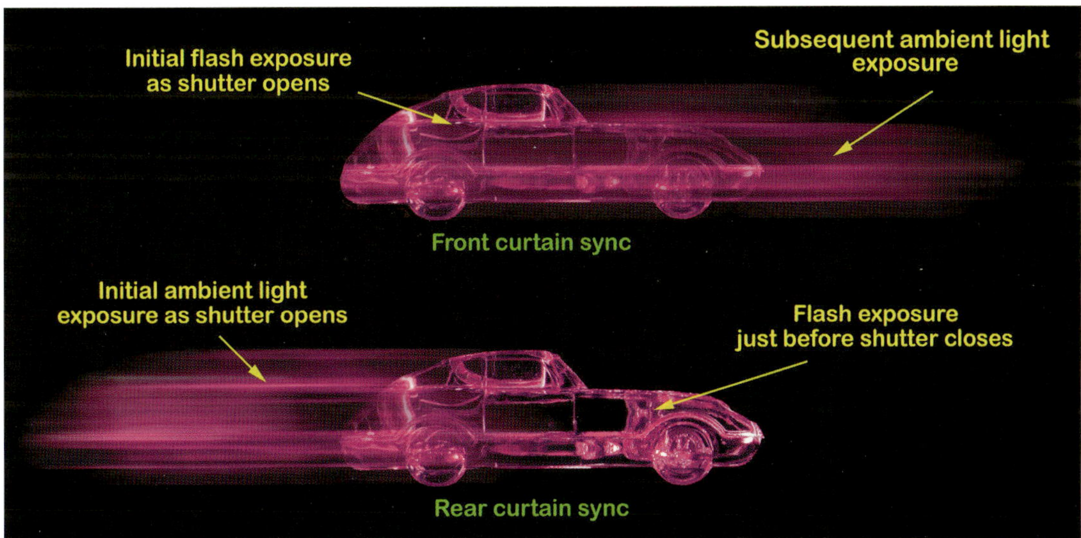

Figure 9.4 First-curtain sync produces an image that trails in front of the flash exposure (top), whereas second-curtain sync creates a more "natural-looking" trail behind the flash image.

Avoiding Sync Speed Problems

Using a shutter speed faster than 1/200th second can cause problems. Triggering the electronic flash only when the shutter is completely open makes a lot of sense if you think about what's going on. To obtain shutter speeds faster than 1/200th second, the 5D Mark IV exposes only part of the sensor at one time, by starting the second curtain on its journey before the first curtain has completely opened, as shown in Figure 9.5. That effectively provides a briefer exposure as a slit, narrower than the full height of the sensor, passes above its surface. If the flash were to fire during the time when the first and second curtains partially obscured the sensor, only the slit that was actually open would be exposed.

You'd end up with only a narrow band, representing the portion of the sensor that was exposed when the picture is taken. For shutter speeds *faster* than 1/200th second, the second curtain begins moving *before* the first curtain reaches the bottom of the frame. As a result, a moving slit, the distance between the first and second curtains, exposes one portion of the sensor at a time as it moves from the top to the bottom. Figure 9.5 shows three views of our typical (but imaginary) focal plane shutter. At left is pictured the closed shutter; in the middle version you can see the first curtain has moved down about 1/4 of the distance from the top; and in the right-hand version, the second curtain has started to "chase" the first curtain across the frame toward the bottom.

If the flash is triggered while this slit is moving, only the exposed portion of the sensor will receive any illumination. You end up with a photo like the one shown in Figure 9.6. Note that a band across the bottom of the image is black. That's a shadow of the second shutter curtain, which had started to move when the flash was triggered. Sharp-eyed readers will wonder why the black band is at the *bottom* of the frame rather than at the top, where the second curtain begins its journey. The answer is simple: your lens flips the image upside down and forms it on the sensor in a reversed position. You never notice that, because the camera is smart enough to show you the pixels that make up your photo in their proper orientation. But this image flip is why, if your sensor gets dirty and you detect a spot of dust in the upper half of a test photo, if cleaning manually, you need to look for the speck in the *bottom* half of the sensor.

I generally end up with sync speed problems only when shooting in the studio, using studio flash units rather than my 5D Mark IV's Canon-dedicated Speedlite. That's because if you're using a

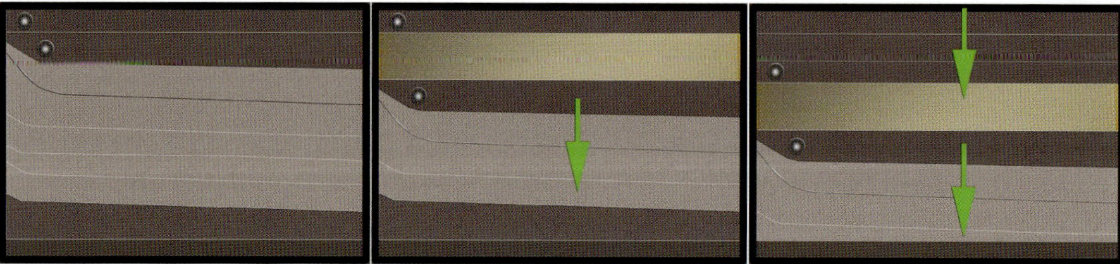

Figure 9.5 A closed shutter (left); partially open shutter as the first curtain begins to move downward (middle); only part of the sensor is exposed as the slit moves (right).

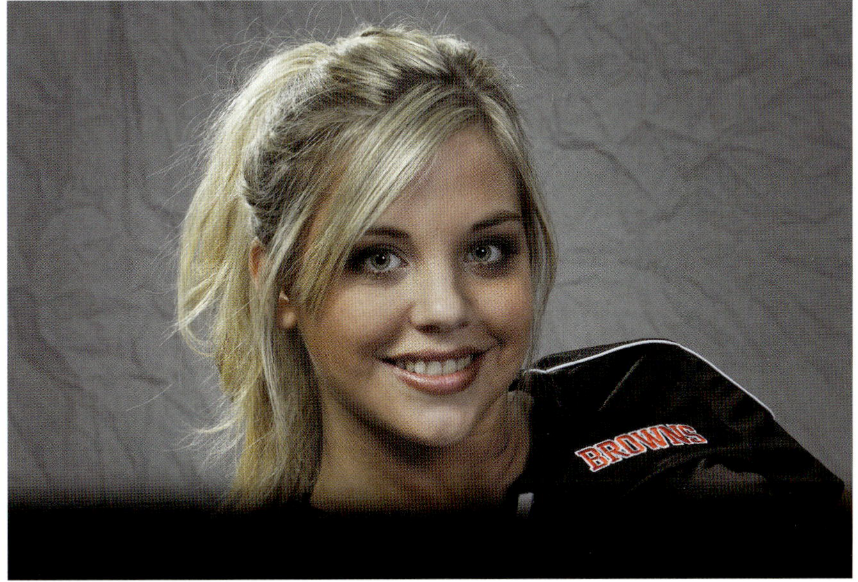

Figure 9.6
If a shutter speed faster than 1/200th second is used, you can end up photographing only a portion of the image.

"smart" (dedicated) flash, the camera knows that a strobe is attached, and remedies any unintentional goof in shutter speed settings. If you happen to set the 5D Mark IV's shutter to a faster speed in Tv or M mode, the camera will automatically adjust the shutter speed down to 1/200th second. In Av, P, or any of the automatic modes, where the 5D Mark IV selects the shutter speed, it will never choose a shutter speed higher than 1/200th second when using flash. In P mode, shutter speed is automatically set between 1/60th to 1/200th second when using flash.

But when using a non-dedicated flash, such as a studio unit plugged into the 5D Mark IV's PC/X connector, the camera has no way of knowing that a flash is connected, so shutter speeds faster than 1/200th second can be set inadvertently. Note that the 5D Mark IV can use a feature called *high-speed sync* that allows shutter speeds faster than 1/200th second with certain external dedicated Canon flash units. When using high-speed sync (HSS), the flash fires a continuous series of bursts at *reduced power* for the entire exposure, so that the duration of the illumination is sufficient to expose the sensor as the slit moves. High-speed sync is set using the controls on the attached and powered-up compatible external flash. I'll explain HSS later.

Determining Exposure

Calculating the proper exposure for an electronic flash photograph is a bit more complicated than determining the settings by continuous light. The right exposure isn't simply a function of how far away your subject is (which the 5D Mark IV can figure out based on the autofocus distance that's locked in just prior to taking the picture). Various objects reflect more or less light at the same distance so, obviously, the camera needs to measure the amount of light reflected back and through the lens. Yet, as the flash itself isn't available for measuring until it's triggered, the 5D Mark IV has nothing to measure.

The solution is to fire the flash multiple times. The initial shot is a pre-flash that can be analyzed, then followed by a main flash that's given exactly the calculated intensity needed to provide a correct exposure. If the main flash is serving as a master to trigger off-camera flash units, additional coded pulses can convey settings information to the slave flashes and trigger their firing. Of course, if *radio* signals rather than optical signals are in play, the sequences may be different. I'll cover various radio and optical wireless flash modes in Chapter 10; this chapter just explains the basics.

Because of the need to abbreviate or quench a flash burst in order to provide the optimum exposure, the primary flash may be longer for distant objects and shorter for closer subjects, depending on the required intensity. This through-the-lens evaluative flash exposure system is called E-TTL II, and it operates whenever you have attached a Canon dedicated flash unit to the 5D Mark IV.

Guide Numbers

Guide numbers, usually abbreviated GN, are a way of specifying the power of an electronic flash in a way that can be used to determine the right f/stop to use at a particular shooting distance and ISO setting. In fact, before automatic flash units became prevalent, the GN was actually used to do just that. A GN is usually given as a pair of numbers for both feet and meters that represent the range at ISO 100. For example, consider the Canon Speedlite 270EX II, the least powerful of Canon's current external flash units (aside from the mini 90EX, primarily intended for use on Canon's non-dSLR models). The 270EX II has a GN of 89 at ISO 100. That Guide Number applies when the flash is set to the 50mm zoom setting (so that the unit's coverage is optimized to fill up the frame when using a 50mm focal length on a *full-frame* camera body like the 5D Mark IV). (The effective Guide Number is just 72 when the flash is mounted on a "cropped" sensor camera like the EOS 7D II.) If you're using the 270EX II set to the 28mm zoom position, the light spreads out more to cover the wider area captured at that focal length, and the Guide Number of the unit drops to 79.

Of course, the question remains, what can you *do* with a Guide Number, other than to evaluate relative light output when comparing different flash units? In theory, you could use the GN to calculate the approximate exposure that would be needed to take a photo at a given distance. To calculate the right exposure at ISO 100, you'd divide the guide number by the distance to arrive at the appropriate f/stop. (Remember that the shutter speed has no bearing on the *flash* exposure; the flash burst will occur while the shutter is wide open, and will have a duration of *less* than the time the shutter is open.)

Again, using the 270EX II as an example, at ISO 100 with its GN of 89, if you wanted to shoot a subject at a distance of 11 feet, you'd use f/8 (89 divided by 11). At approximately 16 feet, an f/stop of f/5.6 would be used. Some quick mental calculations with the GN will give you any particular electronic flash's range. You can easily see that the 270EX II would begin to peter out at about 32 feet, where you'd need an aperture of roughly f/2.8 at ISO 100. Of course, in the real world you'd probably bump the sensitivity up to a setting of ISO 400 so you could use a more practical f/5.6 at that distance.

You should use Guide Numbers as an *estimate* only. Other factors can affect the relative "power" of a flash unit. For example, if you're shooting in a small room. Some light will bounce off ceilings and walls—even with the flash pointed straight ahead—and give your flash a slight boost, especially if you're not shooting extra close to your subject. Use the same flash outdoors at night, say, on a football field, and the flash will have less relative power, because helpful reflections from surrounding objects are not likely.

So, today, guide numbers are most useful for comparing the power of various flash units. You don't need to be a math genius to see that an electronic flash with a GN of, say, 197 (like the 600EX II-RT) would be *a lot* more powerful than that of the 270EX II. You could use f/12 instead of f/5.6 at 16 feet. That's slightly more than two full f/stops' difference. As a Canon 5D Mark IV owner, we can safely assume you'll be using one of the more powerful flash units in the Canon line (or perhaps a similar unit from a third-party vendor).

Getting Started with Electronic Flash

The Canon EOS 5D Mark IV's accessory flash is one of the most useful add-ons you can have. I'll include detailed explanations of your flash settings options later in the chapter. This section will get you started quickly.

When you're using Scene Intelligent Auto, P, Av, Tv, B, or Manual exposure modes, attach the flash and turn it on. The behavior of the external flash varies, depending on which exposure mode you're using:

- **Scene Intelligent Auto.** When the 5D Mark IV is set to this mode, the flash will fire automatically, if it is attached and powered up.
- **P.** In Program mode, the 5D Mark IV fully automates the exposure process, giving you subtle fill flash effects in daylight, and fully illuminating your subject under dimmer lighting conditions. The camera selects a shutter speed from 1/60th to 1/200th second and sets an appropriate aperture.
- **Av.** In Aperture-priority mode, you set the aperture as always, and the 5D Mark IV chooses a shutter speed from 30 seconds to 1/200th second. Use this mode with care, because if the camera detects a dark background, it will use the flash to expose the main subject in the foreground, and then leave the shutter open long enough to allow the background to be exposed correctly, too. If you're not using an image-stabilized lens, you can end up with blurry ghost images even of non-moving subjects at exposures longer than 1/30th second, and if your camera is not mounted on a tripod, you'll see these blurs at exposures longer than about 1/8th second even if you are using IS.

  To disable use of a slow shutter speed with flash, access Flash Sync. Speed in Av mode from the External Speedlite Control entry in the Shooting 1 menu, and change from the default setting (Auto) to either 1/200-1/60sec. auto or 1/200sec. (fixed).

- **Tv.** When using flash in Tv mode, you set the shutter speed from 30 seconds to 1/200th second, and the 5D Mark IV will choose the correct aperture for the correct flash exposure. If you accidentally set the shutter speed higher than 1/200th second, the camera will reduce it to 1/200th second when you're using the flash.

- **M/B.** In Manual or Bulb exposure modes, you select both shutter speed (30 seconds to 1/200th second) and aperture. The camera will adjust the shutter speed to 1/200th second if you try to use a faster speed with a flash. The E-TTL II system will provide the correct amount of exposure for your main subject at the aperture you've chosen (if the subject is within the flash's range, of course). In Bulb mode, the shutter will remain open for as long as the release button on top of the camera is held down, or the release of your remote control is activated. If you use the Bulb timer, you can specify long exposures.

Flash Exposure Compensation and FE Lock

If you want to lock flash exposure for a subject that is not centered in the frame, you can use the FE Lock (the * button) to lock in a specific flash exposure. Just depress and hold the shutter button halfway to lock in focus, then center the viewfinder on the subject you want to correctly expose and press the * button. The pre-flash fires and calculates exposure, displaying the FEL (flash exposure lock) message in the viewfinder. The 5D Mark IV remembers the correct exposure until you take a picture, and the FEL indicator in the viewfinder is your reminder. If you want to recalculate your flash exposure, just press the * button again. When you're ready to shoot, recompose your photo and press the shutter down the rest of the way to take the picture.

You can also manually add or subtract exposure to the flash exposure calculated by the 5D Mark IV on the camera itself, without needing to touch the flash. When using any of the exposure modes *except* Scene Intelligent Auto (that is, Program AE, Aperture-priority, Shutter-priority or Manual), you can access flash exposure compensation (FEC) in five different ways, with three of them illustrated in Figure 9.7, and arranged from fastest to slower (the two slowest aren't illustrated).

- **Press the Flash Compensation/ISO button.** Located on top of the camera, this button produces the screen shown at top in Figure 9.7. When it's visible, just rotate the Quick Control Dial clockwise to add exposure, and counterclockwise to reduce exposure.

- **Press the Fn button.** Use the multi-controller to navigate to the Flash Exposure compensation area on the Quick Control screen (if necessary), and when it's highlighted, rotate the QCD *or* the Main Dial to add or subtract flash exposure. If you subsequently want to make another adjustment and haven't used the Quick Control screen for any other function, the next time you press the Q button, Flash Exposure compensation will automatically be highlighted. (See Figure 9.7, center.)

- **Press SET on the Quick Control screen** when Flash Exposure compensation is highlighted. It produces the screen seen at bottom of Figure 9.7. You might want to do this if you preferred to use the touch screen to make your adjustments, or needed the extra legibility the larger screen provides.

Figure 9.7

Flash exposure compensation can be set from the Quick Control screen.

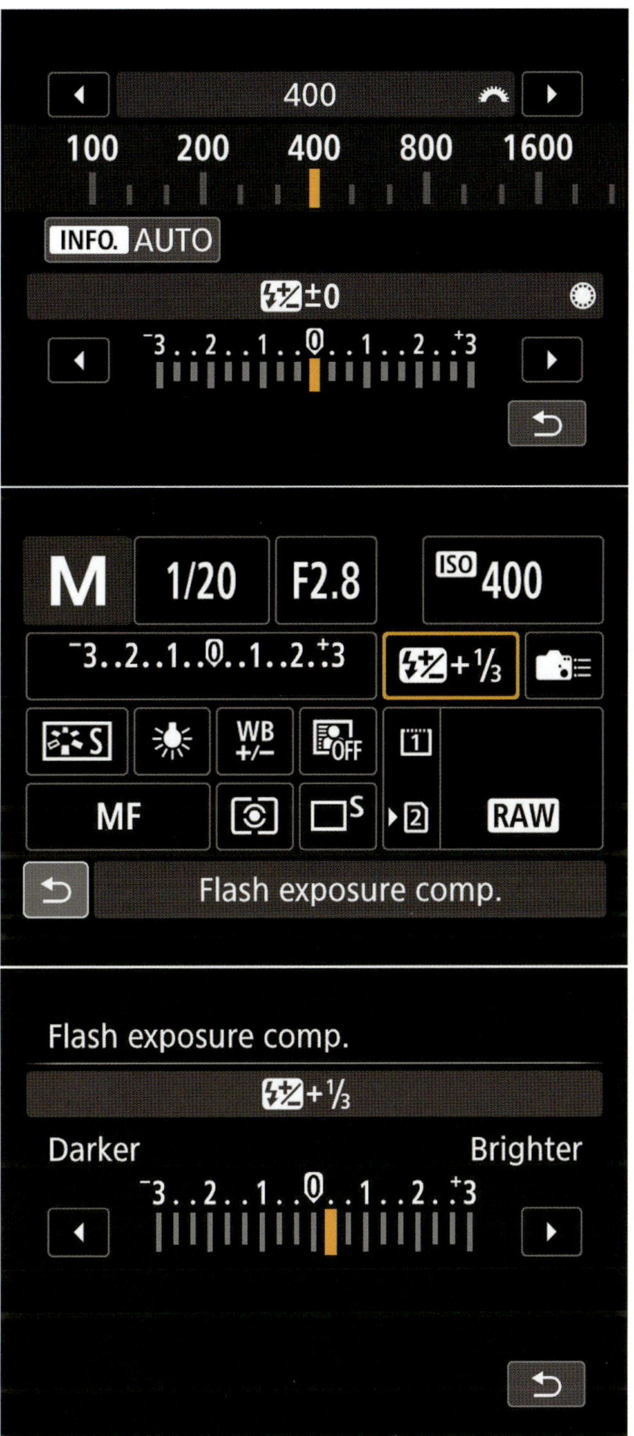

- **Press the INFO. button.** If you've enabled the Quick Control or Custom Quick Control screens for display by the INFO. button, you can press it and use those screens to adjust flash exposure compensation.

- **Access External Speedlite Control.** Find it in the Shooting 1 menu, press SET, and, if your flash is attached and powered up, select Flash Function settings. Then navigate to the Flash Exposure Compensation icon in the second row of the screen. You might go this route if you were making multiple settings, including FEC, from that screen.

SETTING FEC ON THE FLASH

While setting flash exposure compensation within the camera is usually most convenient, with some Canon Speedlites (such as the 600EX II-RT), you can set exposure compensation on the external flash instead. With either unit, in ETTL, M, or MULTI modes, press the #2 button to highlight the +/- FEC indicator, then rotate the flash's Select dial to set the specific amount. Press the Select/SET button to confirm your choice.

If you want to avoid accidentally changing the FEC value on the flash, say, while making other adjustments, use either flash unit's C.Fn-13 (not to be confused with the 5D Mark IV's own Custom Functions). When set to the default, 0, rotating the Select dial specifies the amount; change to 1, instead, and you must *first* press the Select/SET button before rotating the dial.

Flash exposure compensation can work in tandem with non-flash exposure compensation, so you can adjust the amount of light registered from the scene by ambient light even while you're tweaking the amount of illumination absorbed from your flash unit. As with non-flash exposure compensation, the compensation you make remains in effect for the pictures that follow, and even when you've turned the camera off, remember to cancel the flash exposure compensation adjustment by reversing the steps used to set it when you're done using it.

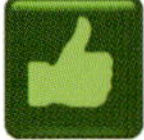

Tip

If you've enabled the Auto Lighting Optimizer in the Shooting 2 menu, it may cancel out any EV you've subtracted using flash exposure compensation. Disable the Auto Lighting Optimizer if you find your images are still too bright when using flash exposure compensation.

Flash Range

The illumination of the EOS 5D Mark IV's external flash varies with distance, focal length, and ISO sensitivity setting.

- **Distance.** The farther away your subject is from the camera, the greater the light fall-off, thanks to the inverse square law discussed earlier. Keep in mind that a subject that's twice as far away receives only one-quarter as much light, which is two f/stops' worth.

- **Focal length.** A non-zooming flash "covers" only a limited angle of view, which doesn't change. So, when you're using a lens that is wider than the default focal length, the frame may not be covered fully, and you'll experience dark areas, especially in the corners. As you zoom in using longer focal lengths, some of the illumination is outside the area of view and is "wasted." (This phenomenon is why some external flash units, such as the 600EX II-RT or 580EX II, automatically "zoom" to match the zoom setting of your lens to concentrate the available flash burst onto the actual subject area.)

- **ISO setting.** The higher the ISO sensitivity, the more photons captured by the sensor. So, doubling the sensitivity from ISO 100 to 200 produces the same effect as, say, opening up your lens from f/8 to f/5.6.

External Speedlite Control

The Shooting 1 menu's External Speedlite control menu offers six options (see Figure 9.8). The next sections will explain your choices.

Figure 9.8
The External Speedlite control menu has six options.

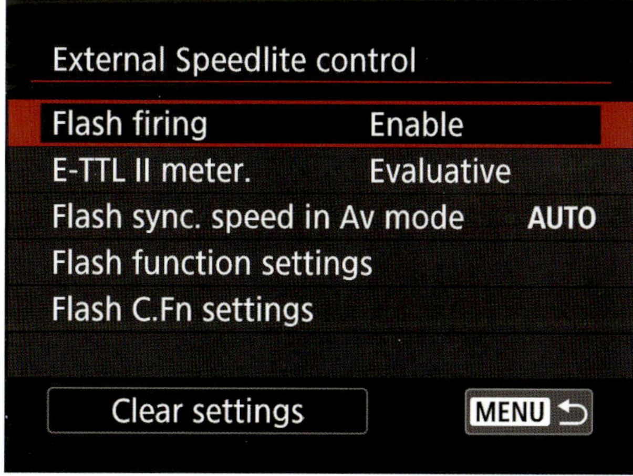

Flash Firing

This menu entry has two options: Enable and Disable. It can be used to activate or deactivate any attached external electronic dedicated flash unit. When disabled, the flash cannot fire even if you have an accessory flash attached and turned on. However, you should keep in mind that the AF-assist beam can still be used. If you want to disable that, too, you'll need to turn it off using the AF-Assist Beam Firing entry in the AF 3 menu.

E-TTL II Meter.

When you're using E-TTL II mode, you can specify whether the 5D Mark IV uses Evaluative (Matrix) or Average metering modes for the electronic flash exposure meter. Evaluative metering intelligently looks at selected areas in the scene and compares its measurements to a database of typical scene "layouts" to calculate exposure, while Average calculates flash exposure by reading the entire scene. Your choice becomes active when you select E-TTL II as your flash mode, using the entry listed first on this menu screen, and described in more detail in the next section.

Flash Sync Speed in Av Mode

You can select the flash synchronization speed that will be used when working in Aperture-priority mode. In Aperture-priority mode when using flash, you specify the f/stop to be locked in. The exposure is then adjusted by varying the output of the electronic flash (rather than by adjusting the shutter speed, which is norm with non-flash images). Because the primary exposure comes from the flash, the main effect of the shutter speed selected is on the *secondary* exposure from the ambient light within the scene.

Auto is your best choice under most conditions. The 5D Mark IV will choose a shutter speed that balances the flash exposure and available, ambient light. The 1/200th–1/60th second setting locks out slower shutter speeds, preventing blur from camera/subject movement in the secondary ("ghost") exposure. However, the background may be rendered dark, if the flash is not strong enough to illuminate it. The 1/200th second (fixed) setting further reduces the chance of getting those blurry ghosts, but there is more of a chance the background will be dark.

- ***Auto.** The camera selects the shutter speed from 30 seconds to 1/200th second; however, high-speed sync (HSS) can also be activated at the flash.

- ***1/200-1/60 auto.** Only shutter speeds from 1/200th to 1/60th second will be used. This locks out shutter speeds slower than 1/60th second, and is useful when you want to avoid blur in the secondary, ambient light exposure due to subject movement and/or camera shake. The 5D Mark IV will always expose the main subject correctly using the flash, but, as noted earlier, the unavailability of slower shutter speeds may mean that the camera is unable to balance the flash with ambient illumination, making the background too dark. HSS is not possible in Av mode with this setting.

- ***1/200 sec. (fixed).** A shutter speed of 1/200th second will be used with flash at all times. Use this setting when you want to make sure that the highest flash sync speed is used, minimizing the possibility of blur in the secondary, ambient light exposure. As with the previous setting, using a fixed 1/200th second shutter speed may cause the background to appear darker because less of the ambient light can be used to balance the exposure. HSS is not possible in Av mode with this setting.

Flash Function Settings

This entry (see Figure 9.9) provides access to functions that may differ between different flash units. Because the available features may vary, you can't access this screen unless the Speedlite you'll be using is attached and powered up; the 5D Mark IV needs to know what flash it is working with to properly display this submenu. It has six sections that can be used to adjust flash mode, wireless functions, zoom head coverage, shutter sync, flash exposure compensation, and flash exposure bracketing.

- **Flash mode.** This entry offers five choices:
  - **E-TTL.** This E-TTL II is the standard mode for EX-series Speedlites.
  - **M.** This Manual flash can be used to set a fixed flash output, from full power (1/1) to 1/128th power.
  - **MULTI.** This MULTI flash is used to produce stroboscopic effects.
  - **Ext. A/Ext. M.** These two, Auto External Flash and Manual External flash, don't measure light through the lens at all, but, instead, meter the illumination falling on an external sensor (with an unvarying 20-degree angle of view) that's built into the flash. The former method performs automatic exposure calculation using this information, while the latter provides data you can use for manual flash exposure. I don't recommend either of those two, but you can find more information about them in your flash's manual.

Figure 9.9
The entries in the Flash Function Settings screen.

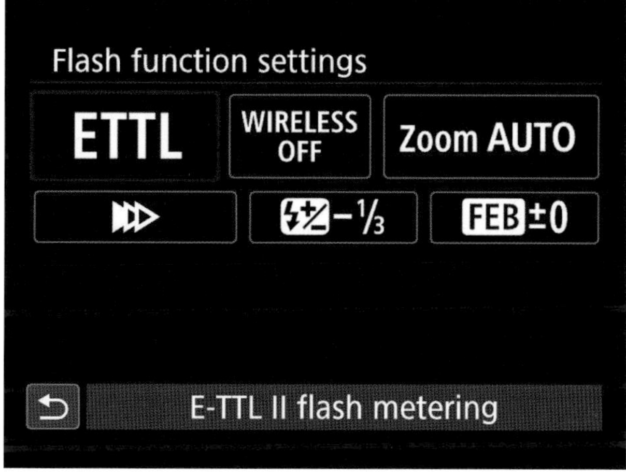

- **Wireless functions.** Functions vary, depending on the attached Speedlite. If you're not working with wireless flash, your only choice is Wireless: OFF. If you do want to use an attached flash (or a flash trigger unit) as a master flash, you may be able to select Wireless: Optical Transmission; Wireless: Radio Transmission; and, with either of those two, additional functions, such as mode, channel, firing group, and other options become available. These options are explained in Chapter 10.

- **Zoom.** Select this entry and press the SET button. Then, you can rotate the Quick Control Dial to choose Auto (the flash zooms to the correct setting based on information about focal length supplied to the flash by the camera), or 24, 28, 35, 50, 70, 80, or 105mm (available with the older 580EX II) plus 135 and 200mm (with the 600EX II-RT).

- **Shutter sync.** You can choose First-curtain sync (which fires the main flash as soon as the shutter is completely open) or Second-curtain sync (which waits until just before the shutter starts to close to fire the main flash). If you have a compatible Canon Speedlite attached, you can also select High-speed sync (HSS), which allows using shutter speeds faster than 1/200th second.

- **Flash exposure compensation.** If you'd rather adjust flash exposure using a menu than with the Quick Control screen or by using the ISO-Exposure compensation button, you can do that here. Select this option with the SET button, then dial in the amount of flash EV compensation you want using the multi-controller or Quick Control Dial. The EV that was in place before you started to make your adjustment is shown as a blue indicator, so you can return to that value quickly. Press SET again to confirm your change, then press the MENU button twice to exit. Keep in mind that using this entry overrides any flash exposure compensation you might set using the ISO-Exposure compensation button on top of the camera, or with any flash function settings.

- **Flash exposure bracketing (FEB).** This operates similarly to regular exposure bracketing, discussed in Chapter 4. Highlight this entry, press SET, and you can rotate the Quick Control Dial to specify up to three stops of compensation over/under the metered exposure for a set of three flash pictures.

If you enable wireless flash, additional options appear in this menu. I'll cover these in more detail in Chapter 10:

- **Channel.** All flashes used wirelessly can communicate on one of four channels. This setting allows you to choose which channel is used. Channels are especially helpful when you're working around other Canon photographers; each can select a different channel so one photographer's flash units don't trigger those of another photographer.

- **Master flash.** You can enable or disable use of the external flash as the master controller for the other wireless flashes. When set to enable, the attached external flash is used as the master.

- **Flash Firing Group.** Multiple flash units can be assigned to a group. This choice allows specifying which groups are triggered, A/B, A/B plus C, or All. The 600EX-RT/600EX II-RT offer additional groups when using radio control mode, Groups D and E.

- **A:B fire ratio.** If you select A/B or A/B plus C, this option appears, and allows you to set the proportionate outputs of Groups A and B, in ratios from 8:1 to 1:8 as explained in Chapter 12.

- **Group C exposure compensation.** If you select A/B plus C, this option appears, too, allowing you to set flash exposure compensation separately for Group C flashes.

Flash C.Fn Settings

This menu entry produces a screen that allows you to set any available Custom Functions in your flash, *from the camera.* The functions available will depend on the C.Fn's included in the flash unit. (See Figure 9.10.) To set flash Custom Functions, rotate the QCD to choose the C.Fn number to be adjusted, then press SET. Rotate the Quick Control Dial again to choose from that function's options, then press SET again to confirm.

Clear Settings

Select this menu entry, located at the bottom of the screen, and you'll be asked if you want to change all the flash settings to their factory default values. You have two choices: Clear Flash Settings (the settings internal to the 5D Mark IV) and Clear All Speedlite C.Fn's, which returns all the *attached* Speedlite's Custom Function settings to their factory defaults. The only exception is C. Fn-0: Distance Indicator Display, which will remain at its set value.

Figure 9.10
Custom Functions for your Speedlite can be set from the camera's Flash C.Fn menu.

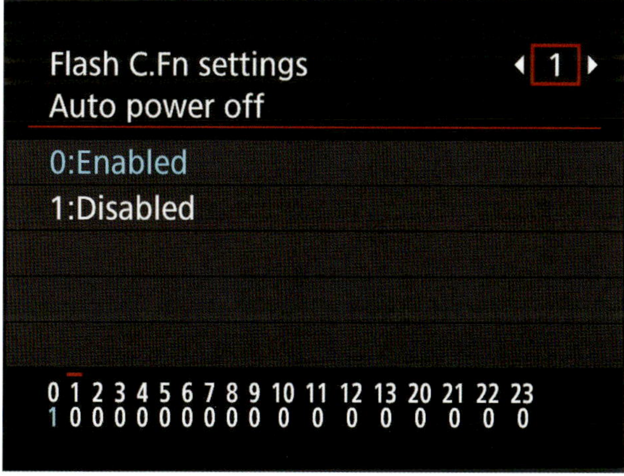

Using Flash Settings

This section includes some tips for using the available Flash settings.

When to Disable Flash Firing

There are a few applications where I always disable my flash and AF-assist beam, even though my 5D Mark IV won't fire an attached flash without my intervention anyway. Some situations are too important to take chances.

- **Venues where flash is forbidden.** I've discovered that many No Photography signs actually mean "No Flash Photography," either because those who make the decisions feel that flash is distracting or they fear it may potentially damage works of art. Tourists may not understand the difference between flash and available-light photography, or may be unable to set their camera to turn off the flash. One of the first phrases I learn in any foreign language is "Is it permitted to take photos if I do not use flash?" A polite request, while brandishing an advanced camera like the 5D Mark IV (which may indicate you know what you are doing), can often result in permission to shoot away.

- **Venues where flash is ineffective anyway.** We've all seen the concert goers who stand up in the last row to shoot flash pictures from 100 yards away. I tend to not tell friends that their pictures are not going to come out, because they usually come back to me with a dismal, grainy shot (actually exposed by the dim available light) that they find satisfactory, just to prove I was wrong.

- **Venues where flash is annoying.** If I'm taking pictures in a situation where flash is permitted, but mostly supplies little more than visual pollution, I'll disable or avoid using it. Concerts or religious ceremonies may *allow* flash photography, but who needs to add to the blinding bursts when you have a camera that will take perfectly good pictures at ISO 3200? Of course, I invariably see one or two people flashing away at events where flash is not allowed, but that doesn't mean I am eager to join in the festivities.

More on Flash Modes

In choosing Flash mode, you have three choices. The available modes are E-TTL II, the standard mode for EX-series Speedlites; Manual flash, which you can use to set a fixed flash output, from full power (1/1) to 1/128th power; and MULTI flash, used to produce stroboscopic effects.

E-TTL II

You'll leave Flash mode at this setting most of the time. In this mode, the camera fires a pre-flash prior to the exposure, and measures the amount of light reflected to calculate the proper settings. As noted earlier, when you've selected the E-TTL II flash mode, you can also choose either Evaluative or Average metering methods. If you select Manual flash or MULTI flash, that option is removed from the menu.

Manual Flash

Use this setting when you want to specify exactly how much light is emitted by the flash, and don't want the 5D Mark IV's E-TTL II exposure system to calculate the f/stop for you. When you activate this option, a new entry appears in the Flash Func. Setting menu, with a sliding scale from 1/1 (full power) to 1/128th power. Highlight the scale and press the SET button. You can then rotate the Quick Control Dial and choose any of the settings. (Only 1/4, 1/2, 1/1, and the intermediate settings between them appear when 1/1 is chosen; view the other power settings by rotating the QCD counterclockwise.) A blue dot appears under the 1/1 setting, and a white dot under your new setting, a reminder that you've chosen something other than full power.

Here are some situations where you might want to use manual flash settings:

- **Close-ups.** You're shooting macro photos and the E-TTL II exposure is not precisely what you'd like. You can dial in exposure compensation, or set the output manually. Close-up photos are problematic, because the power of the flash may be too much (choose 1/128th power to minimize the output), or the reflected light may not be interpreted accurately by the through-the-lens metering system. Manual flash gives you greater control.

- **Fill flash.** Although E-TTL II can be used in full daylight to provide fill flash to brighten shadows, using manual flash allows you to tweak the amount of light being emitted in precise steps. Perhaps you want just a little more illumination in the shadows to retain a dramatic lighting effect without the dark portions losing all detail. Again, you can try using exposure compensation to make this adjustment, but I prefer to use manual flash settings. (See Figure 9.11.)

- **Action stopping.** The lower the power of the flash, the shorter the effective exposure. Use 1/128th power in a darkened room (so that there is no ambient light to contribute to the exposure and cause a "ghost" image) and you can end up with a "shutter speed" that's the equivalent of 1/50,000th second!

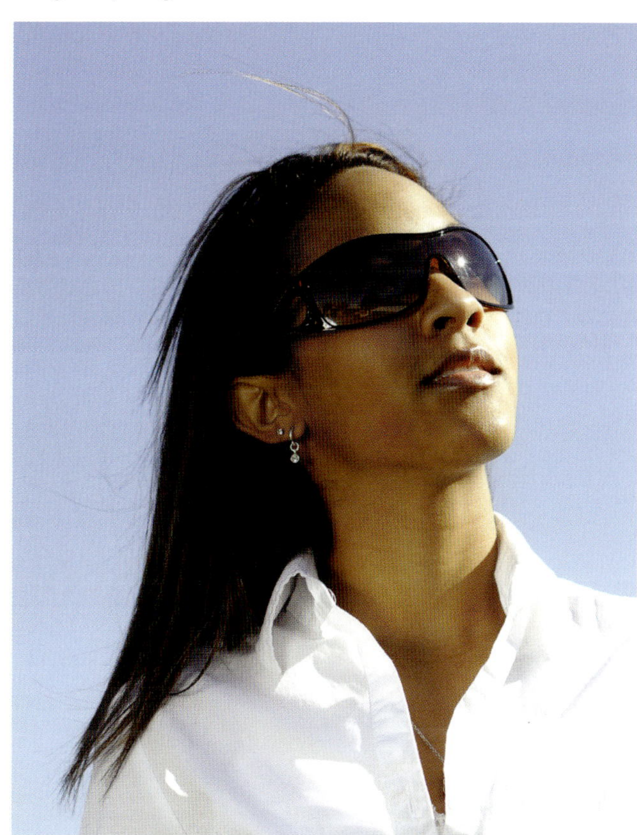

Figure 9.11 You can fine-tune fill illumination by adjusting the output of your camera's flash manually.

MULTI Flash

The MULTI flash setting makes it possible to shoot cool stroboscopic effects, with the flash firing several times in quick succession. You can use the capability to produce multiple images of moving objects, to trace movement (say, your golf swing). When you've activated MULTI flash, three parameters appear on the Flash Function Setting menu, as shown in Figure 9.12. They include:

- **Flash Output (Power level).** Similar to the Flash Output option in Manual mode, you can choose the intensity of each individual flash in your multiple flash sequence, from 1/4 to 1/128th power (the 1/1 and 1/2 power settings are not available).

- **Frequency (Times per second).** This figure specifies the number of bursts per second. With the external flash, you can choose (theoretically) 1 to 199 bursts per second. The actual number of flashes produced will be determined by your flash count (which turns off the flash after the specified number of flashes), flash output (higher output levels will deplete the available energy in your flash unit), and shutter speed.

- **Flash Count (Number of shots).** This setting determines the number of flashes in a given burst, and can be set from 1 to 30 flashes.

These factors work together to determine the maximum number of flashes you can string together in a single shot. The exact number will vary, depending on your settings and your Speedlite model.

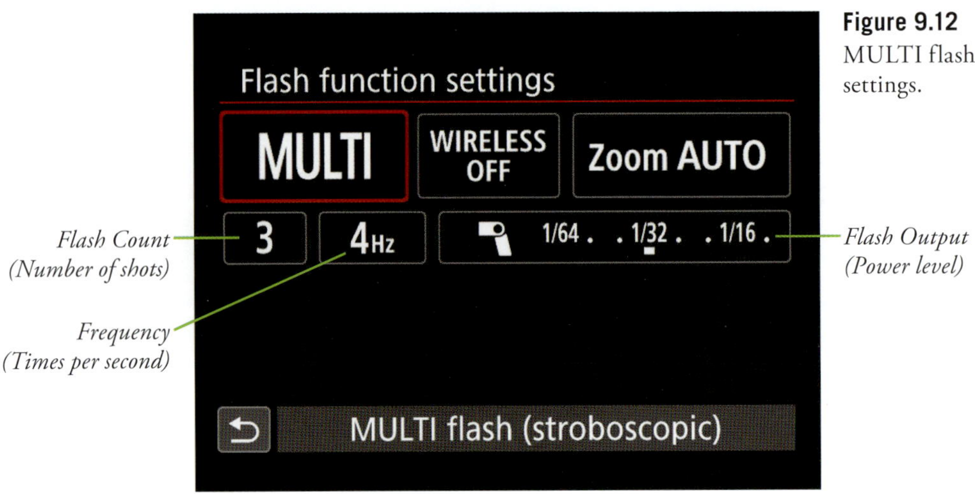

Figure 9.12
MULTI flash settings.

Here are some guidelines you can use:

- **Output.** As you cut the power from 1/4 to 1/128th, the output of the flash drops dramatically, and so does the maximum distance you can shoot at any particular f/stop. The 1/4 power setting, the most powerful setting available with MULTI flash, will give you the greatest flash range in this mode. With your 5D Mark IV's sensitivity set to ISO 1600, your flash will allow you to photograph a subject at 10 feet using f/8 and one-quarter power. (If you remember the discussion of guide numbers from earlier in this chapter, the flash would have an effective GN of 80 at ISO 1600.)

  If you wanted to use the 1/16th power setting instead, you'd need to use f/4 to account for the reduced output of the flash. By the time you dial down to 1/128th power, your flash has a feeble guide number of about 14 (at ISO 1600!), so to shoot at f/4 you'd be able to locate your subject *no farther* than 3.5 feet from the camera.

  The output level also determines the maximum number of flashes that are possible before the charge stored in your flash's capacitor is depleted. The capacitor partially recharges itself as you shoot, so the number of flashes also varies by the flashes-per-second rate. At the 1Hz (one flash per second) rate and 1/4 power, you can expect about 6 to 7 flashes before the Speedlite's power poops out. By the time you reach 10Hz (10 flashes per second) and higher, the unit can crank out no more than two flashes per second at 1/4 power.

  Logically, as output levels decrease, more flashes can be pumped out in a given time period. At 1/128th power, you can expect as many as 100 flashes at the 1Hz rate, and up to 40 consecutive flashes at the 20Hz to 199Hz frequency.

- **Flashes per second.** Cycles per second are, by convention, measured using an increment called *Hertz*. The more flashes you want during the time the shutter is open, the higher the rate you must select. You can select rates of 1Hz to 199Hz, or 1 to 199 flashes per second, plus "- -" (more on that later). To maximize the number of flashes in a second, you'll also need to choose the lowest power output level that you find acceptable. The flash unit can emit a lot more fractional 1/128th power bursts in a given period of time than it can more robust (relatively) 1/4 power bursts.

  When you choose "- -" for your frequency, the flash will continue firing until the shutter closes, or its internal storage is depleted. (In any case, you should not use the MULTI flash feature for more than 10 consecutive pictures. At that point, you should allow the flash to "rest" for at least 15 minutes. But don't worry, the unit will shut down automatically to avoid overheating.)

- **Flash count.** Chose the number of flashes, from 1 to 30, that you want in your multiple exposure, given the output and flash frequency constraints described above.

High-Speed Sync

High-speed sync is a special mode that allows you to synchronize a compatible external flash at all shutter speeds, rather than just 1/200th second and slower. The entire frame is illuminated by a series of continuous bursts as the shutter opening moves across the sensor plane, so you do *not* end up with a horizontal black band, as shown earlier in Figure 9.6.

HSS is especially useful in three situations, all related to problems associated with high ambient light levels:

- **Eliminate "ghosts" with moving images.** When shooting with flash, the primary source of illumination may be the flash itself. However, if there is enough available light, a secondary image may be recorded by that light (as described under "Ghost Images" earlier in this chapter). If your main subject is not moving, the secondary image may be acceptable or even desirable. But if your subject is moving, the secondary image creates a ghost image.

  High-speed sync gives you the ability to use a higher shutter speed. If ambient light produces a ghost image at 1/200th second, upping the shutter speed to 1/500th or 1/1,000th second may eliminate it.

  Of course, HSS *reduces* the amount of light the flash produces. If your subject is not close to the camera, the waning illumination of the flash may force you to use a larger f/stop to capture the flash exposure. So, while shifting from 1/200th second at f/8 to 1/500th second at f/8 *will* reduce ghost images, if you switch to 1/500th second at f/5.6 (because the flash is effectively less intense), you'll end up with the same ambient light exposure. Still, it's worth a try.

- **Improved fill flash in daylight.** The 5D Mark IV can use an attached flash unit to fill in inky shadows—both automatically and using manually specified power ratios, as described earlier in this chapter. However, both methods force you to use a 1/200th second (or slower) shutter speed. That limitation can cause three complications.

  First, in very bright surroundings, such as beach or snow scenes, it may be difficult to get the correct exposure at 1/200th second. You might have to use f/16 or a smaller f/stop to expose a given image, even at ISO 100. If you want to use a larger f/stop for selective focus, then you encounter the second problem—1/200th second won't allow apertures wider than f/8 or f/5.6 under many daylight conditions at ISO 100. (See the discussion of fill flash with Aperture-priority in the next bullet.)

  Finally, if you're shooting action, you'll probably want a shutter speed faster than 1/200th second, if at all possible, under the current lighting. That's because, in fill flash situations, the ambient light (often daylight) provides the primary source of illumination. For many sports and fast-moving subjects, 1/500th second, or faster, is desirable. HSS allows you to increase your shutter speed and still avail yourself of fill flash. This assumes that your subject is close enough to your camera that the fill flash has some effect; forget about using fill and HSS with subjects a dozen feet away or farther. The flash won't be powerful enough to have much effect on the shadows.

■ **When using fill flash with Aperture-priority.** The difficulties of using selective focus with fill flash, mentioned earlier, become particularly acute when you switch to Av exposure mode. Selecting f/5.6, f/4, or a wider aperture when using flash is guaranteed to create problems when photographing close-in subjects, particularly at ISO settings higher than ISO 100. If you own a compatible external flash unit, HSS may be the solution you are looking for.

To use High-speed sync, just follow these steps:

1. **Attach the flash.** Mount/connect the external flash on the 5D Mark IV, using the hot shoe or a dedicated flash cable. (HSS cannot be used in wireless radio mode with the 600EX II-RT, nor with a flash linked through the PC terminal.)

2. **Power up.** Turn the flash and camera on.

3. **Select HSS in the camera.** Set the External Flash Function setting *in the camera* to HSS as the 5D Mark IV's sync mode.

4. **Choose HSS on the flash.** Activate HSS (FP flash) on your attached external flash. With the older (but still common) Speedlite 580EX II, press the High-speed sync/Sync button on the back of the flash unit (it's the second from the right under the LCD). If you're using the 600EX II-RT, press the #4 function button (of the array under the LCD) until the HSS icon appears on the LCD.

5. **Confirm HSS is active.** The HSS icon will be displayed on the flash unit's LCD (at the upper-left side with the 580EX II and 600EX II-RT), and at bottom left in the 5D Mark IV's viewfinder. If you choose a shutter speed of 1/200th second or slower, the indicator will not appear in the viewfinder, as HSS will not be used at slower speeds.

6. **View minimum/maximum shooting distance.** Choose a distance based on the maximum shown in the line at the bottom of the flash's LCD display (from 0.5 to 18 meters).

7. **Shoot.** Take the picture. To turn off HSS, press the button on the flash again. Remember that you can't use MULTI flash or Wireless flash when working with high-speed sync.

Using External Electronic Flash

Once the capacitor is charged, the burst of light that produces the main exposure can be initiated by a signal from the 5D Mark IV that commands the internal or connected flash units to fire. External strobes can be linked to the camera in several different ways:

■ **Camera-mounted/hardwired external dedicated flash.** Units offered by Canon or other vendors that are compatible with Canon's lighting system can be clipped onto the accessory "hot" shoe on top of the camera or linked through a wired system such as the Canon Off Shoe Camera Cord OC-E3.

- **Wireless dedicated flash.** A compatible unit can be triggered by signals produced by a pre-flash (before the main flash burst begins), which offers two-way communication between the camera and flash unit. The triggering flash can be an external flash unit in Master mode, or a wireless non-flashing accessory, such as the Canon Speedlite Transmitter ST-E2 and new radio-controlled wireless trigger, the Speedlite Transmitter ST-E3-RT, which each do nothing but "talk" to the external flashes. You'll find more on this mode in Chapter 10.

- **Wired, non-intelligent mode.** If you connect a flash to the 5D Mark IV's PC/X connector, you can use non-dedicated flash units, including studio strobes, through a non-intelligent camera/flash link that sends just one piece of information, one way: it tells a connected flash to fire. There is no other exchange of information between the camera and flash. The PC/X connector can be used to link the 5D Mark IV to studio flash units, manual flash, flash units from other vendors that can use a PC cable, or even Canon-brand Speedlites that you elect to connect to the 5D Mark IV in "unintelligent" mode.

- **Infrared/radio transmitter/receivers.** Another way to link flash units to the 5D Mark IV is through third-party wireless infrared or radio *transmitters*, like a Pocket Wizard, Radio Popper, or the Paul C. Buff CyberSync trigger. These are generally mounted on the accessory shoe of the camera, and emit a signal when the 5D Mark IV sends a command to fire through the hot shoe. The simplest of these function as a wireless PC/X connector, with no other communication between the camera and flash (other than the instruction to fire). However, sophisticated units have their own built-in controls and can send additional commands to the receivers when connected to compatible flash units. I use one to adjust the power output of my Alien Bees studio flash from the camera, without the need to walk over to the flash itself.

- **Simple slave connection.** In the days before intelligent wireless communication, the most common way to trigger off-camera, non-wired flash units was through a *slave* unit. These can be small external triggers connected to the remote flash (or built into the flash itself), and set off when the slave's optical sensor detects a burst initiated by the camera itself. When it "sees" the main flash (from the 5D Mark IV's attached external flash, or another flash), the slave flash units are triggered quickly enough to contribute to the same exposure. The main problem with this type of connection—other than the lack of any intelligent communication between the camera and flash—is that the slave may be fooled by any pre-flashes that are emitted by the other strobes, and fire too soon. Modern slave triggers have a special "digital" mode that ignores the pre-flash and fires only from the main flash burst.

Canon offers a broad range of accessory electronic flash units for the 5D Mark IV. They can be mounted to the flash accessory shoe, or used off-camera with a dedicated cord that plugs into the flash shoe to maintain full communications with the camera for all special features. (Non-dedicated flash units, such as studio flash, can be connected using the camera's PC/X terminal.) They range from the Speedlite 600EX II-RT and Speedlite 580EX II, which can correctly expose subjects up to 24 feet away at f/11 and ISO 200, to the 270EX II, which is good out to 9 feet at f/11 and ISO 200. (You'll get greater ranges at even higher ISO settings, of course.) There are also two electronic flash units specifically for specialized close-up flash photography.

I power my Speedlites with Panasonic Eneloop AA nickel metal hydride batteries, seen in Figure 9.13. These are a special type of rechargeable battery with a feature that's ideal for electronic flash use. The Eneloop cells, unlike conventional batteries, don't self-discharge over relative short periods of time. Once charged, they can hold onto most of their juice for a year or more. That means you can stuff some of these into your Speedlite, along with a few spares in your camera bag, and not worry about whether the batteries have retained their power between uses. There's nothing worse than firing up your strobe after not using it for a month, and discovering that the batteries are dead.

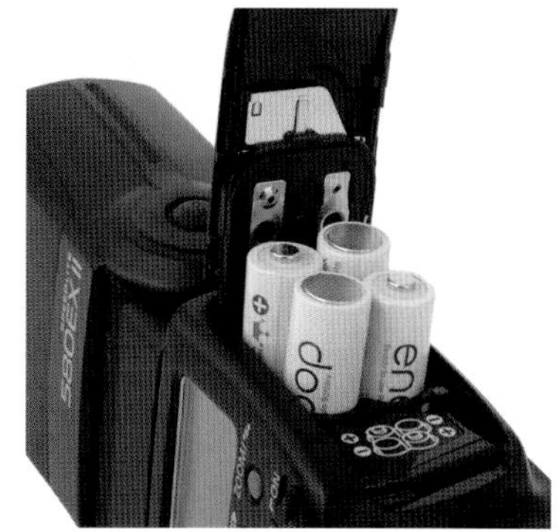

Figure 9.13 Panasonic's Eneloop AA batteries are a perfect power source for Canon Speedlites.

Speedlite 600EX-RT/600EX II-RT

This flagship of the Canon accessory flash line (and most expensive at about $550) is the most powerful unit the company offers, with a GN of 197 and a manual/automatic zoom flash head that covers the full frame of lenses from 24mm wide angle to 200mm telephoto. (There's a flip-down, wide-angle diffuser that spreads the flash to cover a 14mm lens's field of view, too.) All angle specifications given by Canon refer to full-frame sensors, but this flash unit automatically converts its field of view coverage to accommodate the crop factor of the 5D Mark IV and the other 1.6X crop Canon dSLRs. The latest 600EX II-RT version was not available while this book was being written, but Canon states it will have improved continuous flash firing rates (up to 2X faster with an optional CP-E4N battery pack).

The 600EX-RT shares its basic features with the discontinued (but still widely used) 580EX II, described next, so I won't repeat them here, because the typical veteran Canon owner is more likely to own multiple Speedlites.

The killer feature of this unit is the new wireless two-way radio communication between the camera and this flash (or ST-E3-RT wireless controller and the flash) at distances of up to 98 feet. You can link up to 15 different flash units with radio control, using *five* groups (A, B, C, D, and E), and no line-of-sight connection is needed. (You can hide the flash under a desk or in a potted plant.) With the latest Canon cameras having a revised "intelligent" hot shoe (which includes the 5D Mark IV), a second 600EX-RT/600EX II-RT can be used to trigger a *camera* that also has a 600EX-RT/600EX II-RT mounted, from a remote location. That means you can set up multiple cameras equipped with multiple flash units to all fire simultaneously! For example, if you were shooting a wedding, you could photograph the bridal couple from two different angles, with the second camera set up on a tripod, say, behind the altar. A pro shooter might find the 5D Mark IV to be an excellent, affordable second (or third) camera to use in such situations.

600EX (NON-RADIO)

If you see references to a 600EX model (non-RT), you'll find that a version with the radio control crippled is sold only outside the USA in countries where obtaining permission to use the relevant radio spectrum is problematic.

The 600EX II-RT maintains backward compatibility with optical transmission used by earlier cameras. However, it's a bit pricey for the average EOS 5D Mark IV owner, who is unlikely to be able to take advantage of all its features. If you're looking for a high-end flash unit and don't need radio control, I still recommend the Speedlite 580EX II (described next), which is still widely available and is the most-used high-end flash Canon has ever offered.

Remember that with the 600EX II-RT, you can't use radio control and some other features unless you own at least *two* radio-controlled Speedlites, such as a 600EX II-RT or 430EX III-RT (described later) or one 600EX II-RT plus the ST-E3-RT, which costs about $300. Radio control is possible only between a camera that has a radio-capable flash or ST-E3-RT in the hot shoe, and an additional radio-capable flash or ST-E3-RT.

Some Custom Functions of the 600EX II-RT can be set using the 5D Mark IV's External Flash C.Fn Setting menu. Additional Personal Functions can be specified on the flash itself. The 5D Mark IV–friendly functions include:

C.Fn-00 Distance indicator display (Meters/Feet)

C.Fn-01 Auto power off (Enabled/Disabled)

C.Fn-02 Modeling flash (Enabled-DOF preview button/Enabled-test firing button/ Enabled-both buttons/Disabled)

C.Fn-03 FEB Flash exposure bracketing auto cancel (Enabled/Disabled)

C.Fn-04 FEB Flash exposure bracketing sequence (Metered > Decreased > Increased Exposure/Decreased > Metered > Increased Exposure)

C.Fn-05 Flash metering mode (E-TTL II/E-TTL/TTL/External metering: Auto/ External metering: Manual)

C.Fn-06 Quickflash with continuous shot (Disabled/Enabled)

C.Fn-07 Test firing with autoflash (1/32/Full power)

C.Fn-08 AF-assist beam firing (Enabled/Disabled)

C.Fn-09 Auto zoom adjusted for image/sensor size (Enabled/Disabled)

C.Fn-10 Slave auto power off timer (60 minutes/10 minutes)

C.Fn-11 Cancellation of slave unit auto power off by master unit (within 8 hours/within 1 hour)

C.Fn-12 Flash recycling on external power (Use internal and external power/Use only external power)

C.Fn-13   Flash exposure metering setting button (Speedlite button and dial/Speedlite dial only)

C.Fn-20   Beep (Enable/Disable)

C.Fn-21   Light distribution (Standard, Guide number priority, Even coverage)

C.Fn-22   LCD panel illumination (On for 12 seconds, Disable, Always on)

C.Fn-23   Slave flash battery check (AF-assist beam/Flash lamp, Flash lamp only)

The Personal Functions available include the following. Note that you can set the LCD panel color to differentiate at a glance whether a given flash is functioning in Master or Slave mode.

P.Fn-01   LCD panel display contrast (Five levels of contrast)

P.Fn-02   LCD panel illumination color: Normal (Green, Orange)

P.Fn-03   LCD panel illumination color: Master (Green, Orange)

P.Fn-04   LCD panel illumination color: Slave (Green, Orange)

P.Fn-05   Color filter auto detection (Auto, Disable)

P.Fn-06   Wireless button toggle sequence (Normal > Radio > Optical, Normal < > Radio, Normal < > Optical)

P.Fn-07   Flash firing during linked shooting (Disabled, Enabled)

Speedlite 580EX II

If you were using Canon cameras prior to purchasing your 5D Mark IV, you might already own this deposed flagship of the Canon accessory flash line. Despite the introduction of the 600EX-RT/600EX II-RT, this unit is still the most widely used Canon Speedlite, popular because of its relatively lower price and wide availability new (from some retailers) or used. The 580EX II is the second-most powerful unit the company offered, with a GN of 190, and a manual/automatic zoom flash head that covers the full frame of lenses from 24mm wide angle to 105mm telephoto, as well as 14mm optics with a flip-down diffuser.

Like the 600EX II-RT, this unit offers full-swivel, 180-degrees in either direction, and has its own built-in AF-assist beam and an exposure system that's compatible with the nine focus points of the 5D Mark IV. Powered by economical AA-size batteries, the unit recycles in 0.1 to 6 seconds, and can squeeze 100 to 700 flashes from a set of alkaline batteries.

The 580EX II automatically communicates white balance information to your camera, allowing it to adjust WB to match the flash output. You can even simulate a modeling light effect: When you press the depth-of-field preview button on the 5D Mark IV, the 580EX II emits a one-second burst of light that allows you to judge the flash effect. If you're using multiple flash units with Canon's wireless E-TTL system, this model can serve as a master flash that controls the slave units you've set up (more about this later) or function as a slave itself.

It's easy to access all the features of this unit, because it has a large backlit LCD panel on the back that provides information about all flash settings. There are 14 Custom Functions that can be controlled from the flash, numbered from 00 to 13. These functions are (the first setting is the default value):

C.Fn-00 Distance indicator display (Meters/Feet)

C.Fn-01 Auto power off (Enabled/Disabled)

C.Fn-02 Modeling flash (Enabled-DOF preview button/Enabled-test firing button/ Enabled-both buttons/Disabled)

C.Fn-03 FEB Flash exposure bracketing auto cancel (Enabled/Disabled)

C.Fn-04 FEB Flash exposure bracketing sequence (Metered > Decreased > Increased Exposure/Decreased > Metered > Increased Exposure)

C.Fn-05 Flash metering mode (E-TTL II-E-TTL/TTL/External metering: Auto/ External metering: Manual)

C.Fn-06 Quickflash with continuous shot (Disabled/Enabled)

C.Fn-07 Test firing with autoflash (1/32/Full power)

C.Fn-08 AF-assist beam firing (Enabled/Disabled)

C.Fn-09 Auto zoom adjusted for image/sensor size (Enabled/Disabled)

C.Fn-10 Slave auto power off timer (60 minutes/10 minutes)

C.Fn-11 Cancellation of slave unit auto power off by master unit (within 8 hours/within 1 hour)

C.Fn-12 Flash recycling on external power (Use internal and external power/Use only external power)

C.Fn-13 Flash exposure metering setting button (Speedlite button and dial/Speedlite dial only)

Speedlite 430EX III-RT

This less pricey electronic flash (available for less than $300) is an affordable replacement for the 580EX II for those who don't need the beefy power of the older Speedlite. It also makes radio control wireless triggering available to those who can't afford the 600EX-RT's price tag. The 430EX III-RT has automatic and manual zoom coverage from 24mm to 105mm, and the same wide-angle pullout panel found on the 600EX-RT/600EX II-RT that covers the area of a 14mm lens on a full-frame camera, and automatic conversion to the cropped frame area of the 5D Mark IV and other 1.6X crop Canon dSLRs. The 430EX III-RT also communicates white balance information with the camera, and has its own AF-assist beam. Compatible with Canon's wireless E-TTL system, it makes a good slave unit, but cannot serve as a master flash. It, too, uses AA batteries, and offers recycle times of 0.1 to 3.7 seconds for 200 to 1,400 flashes, depending on subject distance.

This long-overdue replacement for the 430EX II has as its biggest selling point the ability to communicate either optically (as a slave) with any compatible master flash, or by radio transmission (as either master or slave) with other RT flashes, including the 600EX RT. Previously, you needed either two of the expensive 600EX RT/600EX II-RT units or one 600EX RT/600EX II-RT and an ST-E3-RT trigger to use radio communications.

The Canon Speedlite 430EX III-RT offers a sophisticated set of features, including an LCD panel that allows you to navigate the unit's menu and view its status. These features, along with powerful output and automatic zoom means this unit has more in common with Canon's high-end Speedlites than it does with the 320EX or the 270EX II. The Speedlite 430EX III-RT is compatible with E-TTL II and earlier flash technologies. It can serve as a slave unit in an optical wireless configuration. The Speedlite 430EX III-RT has a Guide Number of 43/141 (meters/feet) at ISO 100, at 105mm focal length.

Speedlite 320EX

This $249 flash has a GN of 105. Lightweight and more pocket-sized than the 430EX III-RT and 600EX-RT, this bounceable (both horizontally and vertically) flash has some interesting features, including a built-in LED video light that can be used for shooting movies with the 5D Mark IV, or as a modeling light or even AF-assist beam when shooting with live view. Canon says that this efficient LED light can provide up to four hours of illumination with a set of AA batteries. (See Figure 9.14.) It can be used as a wireless slave unit, and has a new flash release function that allows the shutter to be triggered remotely with a two-second delay.

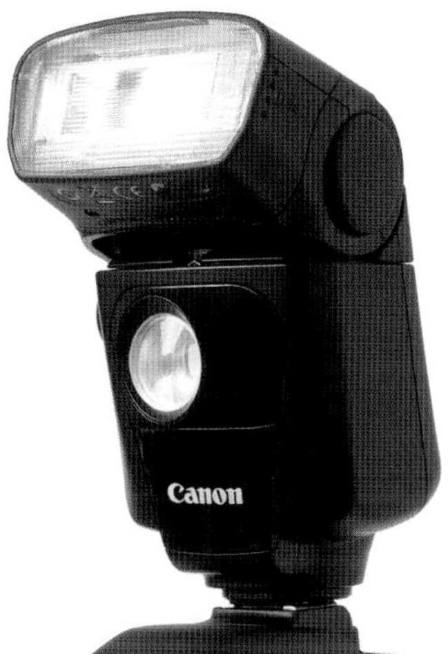

Figure 9.14 The Speedlite 320EX has a built-in video lamp.

Speedlite 270EX II

The Canon Speedlite 270EX II is designed to work with compatible EOS cameras utilizing E-TTL II and E-TTL automatic flash technologies. This flash unit is entirely controlled from the camera, making it as simple to use as a built-in flash. Its options can be selected and set via the camera's menu system. The 270EX II can also be used as an off-camera slave unit when controlled by a master Speedlite, transmitter unit, or a camera with an integrated Speedlite transmitter. One interesting feature of this unit is that it is also a remote control transmitter, allowing you to wirelessly release the shutter on cameras compatible with certain remote controller units. The Speedlite 270EX II has a Guide Number of 27/89 (meters/feet) at ISO 100, with the flash head pulled forward.

This $170 ultra-compact unit is Canon's entry-level Speedlite, and suitable for 5D Mark IV owners who want a simple strobe for occasional use, without sacrificing the ability to operate it as a wireless slave unit. With its modest guide number, it provides a little extra pop for fill flash applications. It has vertical bounce capabilities of up to 90 degrees, and can be switched between Tele modes to Normal (28mm full-frame coverage) at a reduced guide number of 72.

The 270EX II functions as a wireless slave unit triggered by any Canon EOS unit or flash (such as the 430EX III-RT) with a Master function. It also has the new flash release function with a two-second delay that lets you reposition the flash. There's a built-in AF-assist beam, and this 5.5-ounce, 2.6 × 2.6 × 3–inch unit is powered by just two AA-size batteries.

Close-Up Lites

Canon has offered two lites, especially suitable for close-up photography: the Macro Ring Lite MR-14EX II and Macro Twin Lite flash MD-24EX. As you might guess from their names, these lites are especially suitable for close-up, or macro photography, because they provide a relatively shadowless illumination. It's always tricky photographing small subjects up close, because there often isn't room enough between the camera lens and the subject to position lights effectively. Ring lites, in particular, especially those with their own modeling lamps to help you visualize the illumination you're going to get, mount around the lens at the camera position, and help solve many close-up lighting problems.

But, in recent years, the ring lite has gone far beyond the macro realm and is now probably even more popular as a light source for fashion and glamour photography. The right ring lite, properly used, can provide killer illumination for glamour shots, while eliminating the need to move and reset lights for those shots that lend themselves to ring lite illumination. As you, the photographer, move around your subject, the ring lite moves with you.

One of the key drawbacks to ring lites (whether used for macro or glamour photography) is that they are somewhat bulky and clumsy to use (they must be fastened around the camera lens itself, or the photographer must position the ring lite, and then shoot "through" the opening or ring). That means that you might not be moving around your subject as much as you thought and will, instead, mount the ring lite and camera on a tripod, studio stand, or other support.

Another drawback is the cost. The MR-14EX and MR-24EX close-up lites are priced in the $550 and $830 range, respectively. You have to be planning a *lot* of macro or fashion work to pay for one of those. Specialists take note. I tend to favor a third-party substitute for close-up photography, the Alien Bees ABR800 Ringflash. It's priced at about $400, and, besides, it integrates very well with my other Alien Bees studio flash units.

10

Working with Wireless Flash

As I mentioned in the last chapter, one of the chief objections to the use of electronic flash is the stark, flat look of direct/on-camera flash. But as flash wizard Joe McNally, author of *The Hotshoe Diaries*, has proven, small flash units can produce amazingly creative images when used properly.

The key to effective flash photography is to get the flash off the camera, so its illumination can be used to paint your subject in interesting and subtle ways from a variety of angles. But, sometimes, using a cable to liberate your flash from the accessory shoe isn't enough. Nor is the use of just a single electronic flash always the best solution. What we really have needed is a way to trigger one—or more—flash units wirelessly, giving us the freedom to place the electronic flash anywhere in the scene and, if our budgets and time allow, to work in this mode with multiple flashes.

Wireless Evolution

For *all* Canon cameras prior to the introduction of the original Canon EOS 7D back in 2009, wireless operation was strictly an add-on option. The on-camera flash of those earlier cameras was not capable of triggering any off-camera Canon Speedlite with full E-TTL exposure automation. (And, of course, cameras like EOS 5D Mark IV, which do not have any on-camera flash at all, were in the same boat.)

Because wireless triggering was not built into the camera itself, to control other flash units it was necessary to use either a Canon Speedlite Transmitter ST-E2 (a $250 accessory that uses hard-to-find and expensive 2CR5 batteries) or mount a "master" flash on the camera. Dedicating a flash meant sinking another $300 or more into a unit like the Speedlite 430EX III-RT, the now-discontinued, but popular Speedlite 580EX II, or, more recently, a 600EX-RT/600EX II-RT (at a cost south of $600) just to trigger your wireless strobes. It was especially frustrating when you did not want to use the on-camera flash to contribute to the exposure. Your "triggering" device was invariably an expensive accessory. This, of course, led to the popularity of third-party triggers, like the Pocket Wizard and Radio Popper product lines.

The situation has changed dramatically since then. Most Canon cameras with a built-in flash include internal wireless triggering capabilities using the on-camera flash. Of course, the ability of an on-camera flash to serve as a wireless master provides little comfort to 5D Mark IV owners—we're still stuck with using other flash units or add-ons to trigger our wireless units. However, most users of this camera are advanced photographers and can generally abide the equipment requirements that accompany useful wireless capabilities.

It's not possible to cover every aspect of wireless flash in one chapter. There are too many permutations involved. For example, you can use the 5D Mark IV's external flash, or the ST-E2 optical transmitter (or ST-E3-RT radio transmitter) as the master. You may have one external "slave" flash, or use several. It's possible to control all your wireless flash units as if they were one multi-headed flash, or you can allocate them into "groups" that can be managed individually. You may select one of several "channels" to communicate with your strobes (or any of multiple wireless IDs when using radio controlled units like the 600EX-RT). These are all aspects that you'll want to explore as you become used to working with the 5D Mark IV's amazing wireless capabilities.

What I hope to do in this chapter is provide the introduction to the basics that you won't find in the other guidebooks, so you can learn how to operate the 5D Mark IV's wireless capabilities quickly, and then embark on your own exploration of the possibilities. You'll find more complete information in *David Busch's Guide to Canon Flash Photography* or similar publications from Rocky Nook.

YOUR STEPS MAY VARY

This chapter is intended to teach you the basics of wireless flash: why to use it, how a dedicated flash or add-on controller can be used to trigger and manipulate additional units, and what lighting ratios, channels, and groups are. I'm going to provide instructions on getting set up with wireless flash, but, depending on what flash unit you're working with (and how many you have), your specific steps may vary. The final authority on working with wireless flash has to be the manual furnished with your flash unit.

Elements of Wireless Flash

Here are some of the key concepts to electronic flash and wireless flash that I'll be describing in this chapter. Learn what these are, and you'll have gone a long way toward understanding how to use wireless flash. You need to understand the various combinations of flashes that can be used, how they can be controlled individually and together, and why you might want to use multiple and off-camera flash units. I'm going to address all these points in this section.

Flash Combinations

Your 5D Mark IV's attached on-camera external flash can be used alone, or, if it has the capability to serve as a *master flash* (not all Canon Speedlites do), in combination with other, external flash units. Here's a quick summary of the permutations available to you.

- **On-camera flash used alone.** Your on-camera flash can function as the only flash illumination used to take a picture. In that mode, the flash can provide the primary illumination source (the traditional "flash photo") with the ambient light in the scene contributing little to the overall exposure. (See Figure 10.1, left.) Or, the on-camera flash can be used in conjunction with the scene's natural illumination to provide a balanced lighting effect. (Figure 10.1, center.) In this mode, the flash doesn't overpower the ambient light, but, instead, serves to supplement it. Finally, the on-camera flash can be used as a "fill" light in scenes that are illuminated predominantly by a natural main light source, such as daylight. In this mode, the flash serves to brighten dark shadows created by the primary illumination, such as the glaring daylight in Figure 10.1, right.

- **On-camera flash used simultaneously with off-camera flash.** You can use the off-camera flash as a *main light* and supply *fill light* from the on-camera flash to produce interesting effects and pleasing portraits.

- **On-camera flash used as a trigger only for off-camera flash.** Use the 5D Mark IV's on-camera wireless flash controller to command single or multiple Speedlites for studio-like lighting effects, without having the flash contribute to the exposure itself.

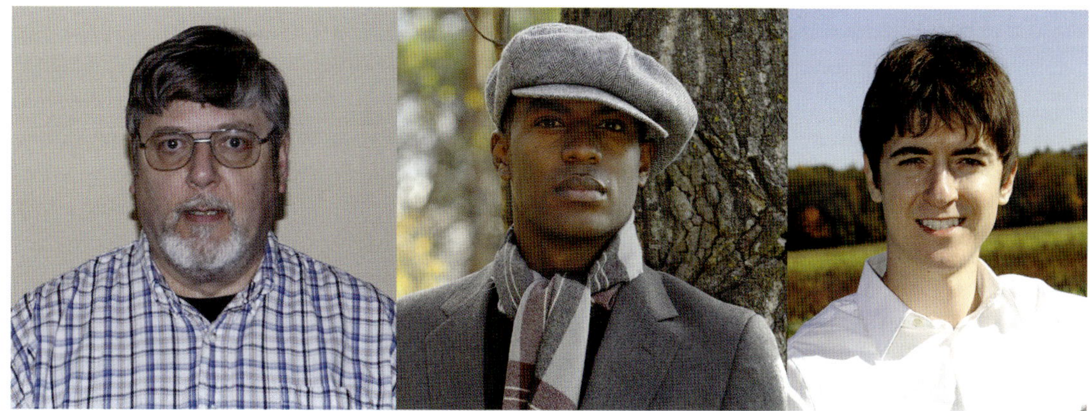

Figure 10.1 On-camera flash alone (left), as a supplement (center), and for fill flash (right).

Controlling Flash Units

There are multiple ways of controlling flash units, both through direct or wired connections and wirelessly. Here are the primary methods used:

- **Direct connection.** The on-camera flash, of course, is directly connected to the 5D Mark IV, and triggered electronically when a picture is taken. External flash units can also be controlled directly by linking them to a camera with a dedicated flash cord that in turn attaches to the accessory hot shoe, such as the Canon OC-E3 EOS Dedicated TTL off-camera shoe cord.

  When used in these modes, the camera has full communication with the flash, which can receive information about zoom lens position, correct exposure required, and the signals required to fire the flash. You can also plug a non-dedicated strobe, such as studio flash units, into the Mark IV's PC/X connector, located on the left side of the camera. The PC/X connection is "dumb" and conveys no information other than the signal to fire.

- **Dedicated wireless optical signals.** In this mode, external flash units communicate with the camera through a pre-flash, which is used to measure exposure prior to the "real" flash burst an instant later. The pre-flashes can also wirelessly send information from the camera to the flash unit, to determine the duration of the burst to achieve the desired exposure. The pulses also can be used to adjust zoom head position (if the flash has that feature). In the case of Canon flash units, the pre-flash information is sent and received as visible light, sent so quickly just before the main burst that you may not be able to distinguish them from the "real" flash.

- **Dedicated wireless infrared signals.** Some devices, such as the Canon ST-E2 Speedlite Transmitter, can communicate with dedicated flash units through infrared signals—much like the remote control of your television. (And, also like your TV remote, the IR signal can bounce around the room somewhat, but you more or less need a line-of-sight connection for the communication to work properly.) The transmitter attaches to the accessory shoe or is connected to the accessory shoe through a dedicated cable. It was an option for wireless flash for Canon cameras prior to the EOS 7D (and later models with an in-camera wireless controller), as well as for Canon cameras that have no flash unit at all (such as the EOS 1D and 5D series). Although the ST-E2 costs about $250, it's still less expensive than using a unit like the 580EX II or 600EX II as a master controller, particularly when on-camera flash is not desired.

- **Canon and third-party IR and radio transmitters.** The 600EX-RT/600EX II-RT, 430EX III-RT, and ST-E3-RT from Canon can communicate as master flash units using radio signals. The 600EX-RT/600EX II-RT can also serve as a master optical flash, and as a radio or optical slave, while the 430 EX III-RT functions as a slave only in optical mode.

  In addition, some excellent wireless flash controllers that use IR or radio signals to operate external flash units are available from sources like PocketWizard and RadioPopper. One advantage some of these third-party units has is the ability to dial in exposure/output adjustments from the transmitter mounted on the accessory shoe of the camera.

■ **Optical slave units.** A relatively low-tech/low-versatility option is to use optical slave units that trigger the off-camera flash units when they detect the firing of the main flash. Slave triggers are inexpensive, but dumb: they don't allow making any adjustments to the external flash units, and are not compatible with the 5D Mark IV's E-TTL II exposure system. Moreover, you should make sure that the slave trigger responds to the *main* flash burst only, rather than a pre-flash, using a so-called *digital* mode. Otherwise, your slave units will fire before the main flash, and not contribute to the exposure.

Why Use Wireless Flash?

Canon's wireless flash system gives you a number of advantages that include the ability to use directional lighting, which can help bring out detail or emphasize certain aspects of the picture area. It also lets you operate multiple strobes; with models like the old favorite 580EX II that's as many as four flash units in each of three groups, or twelve in all (although most of us won't own 12 Canon Speedlites). With the 600EX-RT/600EX II-RT and 430EX III-RT, which also have radio control in addition to optical transmission, you can control many more flash units optically, but only 15 radio-controlled Speedlites, in five different groups.

You can set up complicated portrait or location lighting configurations. Since the two top Canon Speedlites pump out a lot of light for a shoe-mount flash, a set of these units can give you near studio-quality lighting. Of course, the cost of these high-end Speedlites approaches or exceeds that of some studio monolights—but the Canon battery-powered units are more portable and don't require an external AC or DC power source.

Key Wireless Concepts

There are three key concepts you must understand before jumping into wireless flash photography: channels, groups, and flash ratios. Here is an explanation of each:

■ **Channel controls.** Canon's wireless flash system offers users the ability to determine on which of four possible channels the flash units can communicate. (The pilots, ham radio operators, or scanner listeners among you can think of the channels as individual communications frequencies.) When using optical transmission, the channels are numbered 1, 2, 3, and 4, and each flash must be assigned to one of them. Moreover, in general, each of the flash units you are working with should be assigned to the *same* channel, because the slave Speedlites will respond *only* to a master flash that is on the same channel.

When using the 600EX-RT or 430EX III-RT in radio control mode, there are 15 different channels, plus an Auto setting that allows the flash to select a channel. In addition, you can assign a four-digit Wireless Radio ID that further differentiates the communications channel your flashes use.

The channel ability is important when you're working around other photographers who are also using the same system. Photojournalists, including sports photographers, encounter this situation frequently. At any event populated by a sea of "white" lenses, you'll often find photographers who are using Canon flash units triggered by Canon's own optical or (now) radio control. Third-party triggers from PocketWizard or RadioPopper are also popular, but Canon's technology remains a mainstay for many shooters.

Each photographer sets flash units to a different channel so as to not accidentally trigger other users' strobes. (At big events with more than four photographers using Canon flash and optical transmission, you may need to negotiate.) I use this capability at workshops I conduct where we have two different setups. Photographers working with one setup use a different channel than those using the other setup, and can work independently even though we're at opposite ends of the same large room.

There is less chance of a channel conflict when working with radio control and all radio-compatible Canon flash units. With 15 channels to select from, and almost 10,000 wireless radio IDs to choose from, any overlap is unlikely. (It's smart not to use a radio ID like 0000, 1111, 2222, etc., to avoid increasing the chances of conflicts. I use the last four digits of my mother-in-law's Social Security Number.) Remember that you must use either all optical or all radio transmission for all your flash units; you can't mix and match.

- **Groups.** Canon's wireless flash system lets you designate multiple flash units in separate groups. There can be as many as three groups with earlier Speedlites like the 580EX II, labeled A, B, and C.

With the 600EX-RT, 430EX III-RT, and ST-E3-RT, up to five groups (A, B, C, D, and E) can be used with as many as 15 different flash units. All the flashes in all the groups use the exact same *channel* and all respond to the same master controller, but you can set the output levels of each group separately. So, Speedlites in Group A might serve as the main light, while Speedlites in Group B might be adjusted to produce less illumination and serve as a fill light. It's convenient to be able to adjust the output of all the units within a given group simultaneously. This lets you create different styles of lighting for portraits and other shots.

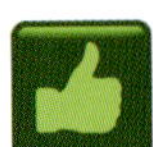

TIP

It's often smart to assign flash units that will reside to the left of the camera to the A group, and flashes that will be placed to the right of the camera to the B group. It's easier to adjust the comparative power ratios because you won't have to stop and think where your groups are located. That's because the adjustment controls in the *menus* are always arranged in the same A-B-C left-to-right alignment.

For example, if your A group is used as a main light on the left, and the B group as fill on the right, you intuitively know to specify more power to the A group, and less output to the B group. Reserve the C group (if used) to some other purpose, such as background or hair lights.

■ **Flash ratios.** This ability to control the output of one flash (or set of flashes) compared to another flash or set allows you to produce lighting *ratios*. You can control the power of multiple off-camera Speedlites to adjust each unit's relative contribution to the image, for more dramatic portraits and other effects.

Which Flashes Can Be Operated Wirelessly?

A particular Speedlite can have one of two functions. It can serve as a *master* flash that's capable of triggering other compatible Canon units that are on the same channel. Or, a Speedlite can be triggered wirelessly as a *slave unit* that's activated by a *master*, with full control over exposure through the camera's eTTL flash system. The second function is easy: all current and many recent Canon shoe-mount flash, including the 600EX-RT, 580EX II, 430EX II, 430EX III, 430EX III-RT, 320EX, and 270EX II can be triggered wirelessly. In addition, some Speedlites have the ability to serve as a master flash.

I'm not going to discuss older flash units in this chapter; if you own one, particularly a non-Canon unit, it may or may not function as a slave. For example, the early Speedlite 380EX lacked the wireless capabilities added with later models, such as the 420EX, 430EX, 430EX II, 430EX III, and 430EX III-RT.

Here's a quick rundown of current flash capabilities:

■ **Canon Speedlite 600EX-RT/600EX II-RT.** These top-of-the-line flashes can function as a master flash when physically attached to any Canon EOS model, using either optical or radio transmission, and can be triggered wirelessly by another master flash, such as a compatible EOS model, another 600EX-RT/600EX II-RT or 580EX II, or the ST-E2/ST-E3-RT transmitters.

■ **Canon Speedlite 580EX II.** This discontinued flash can function as a master flash when physically attached to any Canon EOS model, and can be triggered wirelessly by an optical (not radio) transmission from another master flash from a compatible EOS camera, another 580EX II, a 600EX-RT, 600EX II-RT, 430EX III-RT, or the ST-E2 transmitter. (The ST-E3-RT transmitter operates in radio mode only.)

■ **Canon Speedlite 430EX III.** This sibling of the radio-compatible version described next cannot function as a master, but can be used as a slave when working with optical triggering technology.

■ **Canon Speedlite 430EX III-RT.** This newer flash can function as a master (in radio mode only) and as a slave when using both optical and radio technology.

■ **Canon Speedlite 430EX II.** This discontinued flash cannot function as a master, but can be triggered wirelessly by a master flash, including a compatible EOS camera, a Speedlite 600EX-RT/580EX II, or the ST-E-2 transmitters.

- **Canon Speedlite 320EX.** This flash can be triggered wirelessly by a master flash, including a compatible EOS camera, a 600EX-RT/600EX II-RT, 580EX II, or the ST-E-2 transmitter.

- **Canon Speedlite 270EX II.** This flash can be triggered wirelessly by a compatible camera's master flash, a 600EX-RT/600EX II-RT, 580EX II, or the ST-E-2 and ST-E3-RT transmitters in optical mode.

You can use any combination of compatible flash units in your wireless setup. You can use an attached 600EX-RT/600EX II-RT, 580EX II, 430EX III-RT, or ST-E2/ST-E3-RT as a master, with any number of 600EX-RT, 580EX II, 430EX III, 430EX III-RT, 430EX II, 320EX, or 270EX II units (or older compatible Speedlites not discussed in this chapter) as wireless slaves. I'll get you started assigning these flash to groups and channels later on.

Setting Up a Master Flash or Controller

The first step in working with wireless flash is to set up one unit (either a flash or controller) as the *master*. You can mount a Speedlite 580EX, 580EX II, or 600EX-RT/600EX II-RT to your camera, which can serve as the master unit, transmitting E-TTL II optical signals to one or more off-camera Speedlite *slave* units. The master unit can have its flash output set to "off" so that it controls the remote units with the pre-flash, but omitting the main flash so the master unit does not contribute any illumination of its own to the exposure. This is useful for images where you don't want noticeable flash illumination coming in from the camera position. The next sections explain your options for setting up a master unit for fully automatic, E-TTL II exposure. You can also use manual exposure instead of E-TTL II automatic exposure in wireless mode. Setting up your master flash for manual operation is beyond the scope of this introductory wireless chapter.

Using a Speedlite as an Optical Master

Here are the steps to follow to set up and use a compatible Speedlite as a camera-mounted master unit for automatic exposure. For each individual flash unit described below, check your flash's manual if you have any questions about particular button location.

600EX-RT/600EX II-RT

1. Press the Wireless button repeatedly until the LCD panel indicates you are in optical wireless master mode.

2. Press MODE to cycle through the ETTL, M, and Multi modes.

3. Use the menu system to control and make changes to RATIO, output, and other options on the master and slave units.

580EX II

1. Press and hold the ZOOM button to bring up the wireless options. Use the Select dial to cycle through the OFF, MASTER on, and SLAVE on options. Select and confirm MASTER on.

2. Press MODE to cycle through the ETTL, M, and Multi modes.

3. Press the ZOOM button repeatedly to cycle through the following options: Flash zoom, RATIO, CH., flash emitter ON/OFF. Use the Select dial and Select/SET button to make any changes to these options.

4. Use the Select/SET button to select and confirm the output power settings when using Manual and Multi modes, or to use FEC or FEB when in ETTL mode.

580EX

1. Slide the OFF/MASTER/SLAVE wireless switch near the base of the unit to MASTER.

2. Press MODE to cycle through the ETTL, M, and Multi modes.

3. Press the ZOOM button repeatedly to cycle through the following options: Flash zoom, RATIO, CH., flash emitter ON/OFF. Use the Select dial and Select/SET button to make any changes to these options.

4. Use the Select/SET button to select and confirm the output power settings when using Manual and Multi modes, or to use FEC or FEB when in ETTL mode.

Using the ST-E2 Transmitter as Master

Canon's Speedlite Transmitter (ST-E2) is mounted on the camera's hot shoe and provides a way to control one or more Speedlites and/or units assigned to Groups A and B. The ST-E2 does not provide any flash output of its own and will not trigger units assigned to Group C. It has the following features and controls:

- **Transmitter.** Located on the top front of the unit, the transmitter emits E-TTL II pulses through an infrared filter.

- **AF-assist beam emitter.** Just below the transmitter, the AF-assist beam emitter works similarly to the Speedlite 430EX II and higher models.

- **Battery compartment.** The ST-E2 uses a 6.0V 2CR5 lithium battery. The battery compartment is accessed from the top of the unit.

- **Lock slider and mounting foot.** The lock slider is located on the right side of the unit when facing the front. Sliding it to the left lowers the lock pin in the mounting foot (located on the bottom of the unit) to secure it to the camera's hot shoe.

■ **Back panel.** The rear of the unit features several indicators and controls:

- **Ratio indicator.** A series of red LED lights indicating the current A:B ratio setting.

- **Flash ratio control lamp.** A red LED that lights up when flash ratio is in use.

- **Flash ratio setting button.** Next to the flash ratio control lamp. Press this button to activate flash ratio control.

- **Flash ratio adjustment buttons.** Two buttons with raised arrows (same color as buttons) pointing left and right. Use these to change the A:B ratio setting.

- **Channel indicator.** The channel number in use (1–4) glows red.

- **Channel selector button.** Next to the channel indicator. Press this button to select the communication channel.

- **High-speed sync (FP flash) indicator.** A red LED that glows when high-speed sync is in use.

- **High-speed sync button.** Press this button to activate/deactivate high-speed sync.

- **ETTL indicator.** A red LED that glows when E-TTL II is in use.

- **Off/On/HOLD switch.** Slide this switch to turn the unit off, on, or on with adjustments disabled (HOLD). The ST-E2 will power off after approximately 90 seconds of idle time. It will turn back on when the shutter button or test transmission button is pressed.

- **Pilot lamp/Test transmission button.** This lamp works similarly to the Speedlite pilot lamp/test buttons. The lamp glows red when ready to transmit. Press the lamp button to send a test transmission to the slave units.

- **Flash confirmation lamp.** This lamp glows green for about three seconds when the ST-E2 detects a good flash exposure.

Here are the steps to follow to set up and use the ST-E2 transmitter (see Figure 10.2) as a camera-mounted master unit:

1. Mount the ST-E2 unit on your 5D Mark IV.

2. Make sure both the ST-E2 unit and your camera are powered on.

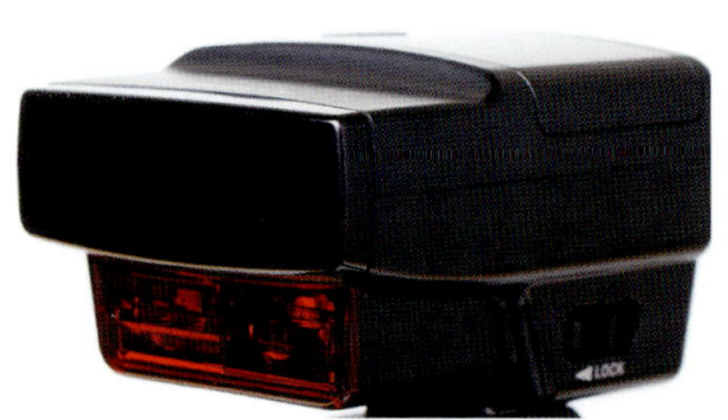

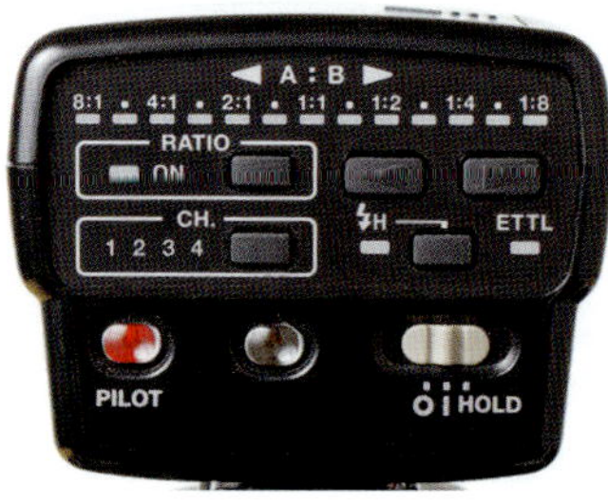

Figure 10.2
ST-E2 transmitter.

3. Make sure the slave units are set to E-TTL II, assigned to the appropriate group(s), and that all units are operating on the same channel.

4. If you'd like to set a flash ratio between Groups A and B, press the flash ratio setting button and flash ratio adjustment buttons to select the desired ratio. Press the high-speed sync button to use high-speed sync (often helpful with outdoor shooting).

Using the Speedlite 600EX-RT/600EX II-RT as Radio Master

The Speedlite 600EX-RT/600EX II-RT can serve as the master unit when mounted to your camera, transmitting radio signals to one or more off-camera Speedlite 600EX-RT/600EX II-RT slave units. The master unit can have its flash output set to "off" so that it controls the remote units without contributing any flash output of its own to the exposure. This is useful for images where you don't want noticeable flash illumination coming in from the camera position.

Here are the steps to follow to set up and use a Speedlite 600EX-RT/600EX II-RT as a camera-mounted master unit for radio wireless E-TTL II operation.

1. Mount the Speedlite 600EX-RT/600EX II-RT to your 5D Mark IV.

2. Make sure the 600EX-RT master units, slave units, and the camera are powered on.

3. Set the camera-mounted unit to radio wireless MASTER mode. Press the Wireless button until the LCD panel indicates you are on radio wireless master mode.

4. Set the slave 600EX-RT/600EX II-RT or 430EX III-RT units to radio wireless SLAVE mode. For each 600EX-RT unit, press the Wireless button until the LCD panel indicates you are on radio wireless slave mode. For each 430EX III-RT slave, press the left directional key and rotate the Select dial until Slave appears on the LCD. Then press the Select button to confirm.

5. Confirm that all units are set to E-TTL II, assigned to the appropriate group(s), and that all units are operating on the same channel and ID number. The LINK lamps on all units should glow green.

Using the Speedlite 430EX III-RT as Radio Master

The Speedlite 430EX III-RT can serve as a radio master unit to trigger another 430EX III-RT or a 600EX-RT flash. Just follow these steps:

1. Press the left directional key on the Select dial. It's marked with a lightning bolt symbol.

2. Rotate the Select dial until MASTER appears on the LCD.

3. Press the Select button in the center of the Select dial.

4. Set any 600EX-RT or 430EX III-RT units that you will be using as slaves to the Slave mode.

   - For the 600EX-RT, press the Wireless button until the LCD panel indicates you are in radio wireless slave mode.

   - For any 430EX III-RT slaves, press the left directional key and rotate the Select dial until Slave appears on the LCD. Then press the Select button to confirm.

5. Repeat Step 4 for any additional Slave units.

6. When master and slaves are communicating, the LINK lamps on all units will glow green.

Using the ST-E3-RT as Radio Master

The ST-E3-RT transmitter can be mounted to the camera's hot shoe and used as a master controller to one or more slave Speedlite 600EX-RT units. The ST-E3-RT and the 600EX-RT share essentially the same radio control capabilities except that the ST-E3-RT does not produce flash, provide AF-assist, or otherwise emit light and is therefore incapable of optical wireless transmission.

The layout of the ST-E3-RT's control panel is virtually identical to the 600EX-RT. So is the menu system and operation, except that, as stated earlier, it will only operate as a radio wireless transmitter. Here are the steps to follow to set up and use the ST-E3-RT transmitter as a camera-mounted master unit for radio wireless E-TTL II operation:

1. Mount the ST-E3-RT unit on your 5D Mark IV.

2. Make sure both the ST-E3-RT unit and your camera are powered on.

3. Set the slave 600EX-RT or 430EX III-RT units to radio wireless SLAVE mode. For each 600EX-RT unit, press the Wireless button until the LCD panel indicates you are on radio wireless slave mode. For each 430EX III-RT slave, press the left directional key and rotate the Select dial until Slave appears on the LCD. Then press the Select button to confirm.

4. Confirm that all units are set to E-TTL II, assigned to the appropriate group(s), and that all units are operating on the same channel and ID number. The LINK lamps on all units should glow green.

The ST-E3-RT controls slave units as described earlier in the section, "Speedlite 600EX-RT/600EX II-RT as Radio Master."

Setting Up a Slave Flash

The whole point of working wirelessly is to have a master flash/controller trigger and adjust one or more slave flash units. So, once you've defined your master flash, the next step is to switch your remaining Speedlites into slave mode. That's done differently with each particular Canon Speedlite.

To enter slave mode:

- **Speedlite 600EX-RT/600EX II-RT.** Press the Wireless button repeatedly until the LCD panel indicates that the unit is in optical wireless slave mode or radio wireless slave mode. In this mode, the 600EX-RT is assigned a flash mode by the master transmitter, either a flash or ST-E2 or ST-E3-RT.

- **Speedlite 580EX II.** Press and hold the ZOOM button until the wireless setting options appear. Use the Select dial and Select/SET button to select and confirm that wireless is on and in slave mode.

- **Speedlite 430EX III/430EX III-RT.** For each 430EX III-RT slave, press the left directional key and rotate the Select dial until Slave appears on the LCD. Then press the Select button to confirm.

- **Speedlite 430EX II.** Press and hold the ZOOM button for two seconds or more until the wireless setting options appear. Use the Select dial and Select/SET button to select and confirm that wireless is on and in slave mode.

- **Speedlite 320EX.** This flash has an On/Off/Slave switch at the lower left of the back panel. In Slave mode, you can use the flash's C.Fn-10 to tell the unit to power down after either 10 or 60 minutes of idle time. That can help preserve the 320EX's batteries. The unit's C.Fn-11 can be set to allow the master transmitter to "wake" a sleeping 320EX after your choice of within 1 hour or within 8 hours. Note that the C.Fn settings of the 320EX and 270EX II (described next) can be set only while the Speedlites are connected to the camera with the hot shoe.

- **Speedlite 270EX II.** This flash has an Off/Slave/On switch. If left on and idle, the 270EX II will power itself off after approximately 90 seconds. C.Fn-1 can be used to disable auto power off. As with the 320EX, in Slave mode, you can use the flash's C.Fn-10 to tell the unit to power down after either 10 or 60 minutes of idle time. The unit's C.Fn-11 can be set to allow the master transmitter to "wake" a sleeping unit after your choice of within 1 hour or within 8 hours.

Choosing a Channel

In optical mode, Canon's wireless flash system can work on any of four channels, so if more than one photographer is using the Canon system, each can set his gear to a different channel so they don't accidentally trigger each other's strobes. You need to be sure all of your gear is set to the same channel. Selecting a channel is done differently with each particular flash model.

The ability to operate flash units on a particular channel isn't really important unless you're shooting in an environment where other photographers are also using the Canon wireless flash system. If the system only offered one channel, then each photographer's wireless flash controller would be firing every Canon flash set for wireless operation. By having four channels available, the photographers can coordinate their use to avoid that problem. Such situations are common at sporting events and other activities that draw a lot of shooters.

It's always a good idea to double-check your flash units before you set them up to make sure they're all set to the same channel, and this should also be one of your first troubleshooting questions if a flash doesn't fire the first time you try to use it wirelessly.

You do this as follows:

1. **Set flash units to the channel you want to use for all your groups.** Before you use the 5D Mark IV's controls to configure your flash exposures, you must first make adjustments on the external Speedlite. Each flash unit may use its own procedure for setting that strobe's channel. Consult your Speedlite's manual for instructions. With the 580EX II, press the Zoom button repeatedly until the CH. Indicator blinks, then rotate the control dial to select Channel 1, 2, 3, or 4. Press the control dial center button to confirm. With the 600EX-RT/600EX II-RT, press Fn Button 4 until Menu 2 appears, then press Fn Button 1 to select a channel.

2. **Activate wireless operation.** From the External Speedlite Control entry in the Shooting 1 menu, navigate to the Flash Function Settings choice, Flash Functions. Highlight the second icon from the left in the top row (as seen in Figure 10.3, left) and press SET. Then choose Wireless: Optical Transmission from the screen that appears (Figure 10.3, right). Press SET to confirm and exit.

3. **Navigate to the 5D Mark IV's channel selection option.** Navigate to the Channel Setting (highlighted in red at left in Figure 10.3) and push the SET button.

4. **Select the channel your flashes are set to.** You can then use the QCD to cycle the channel number from 1 to 4.

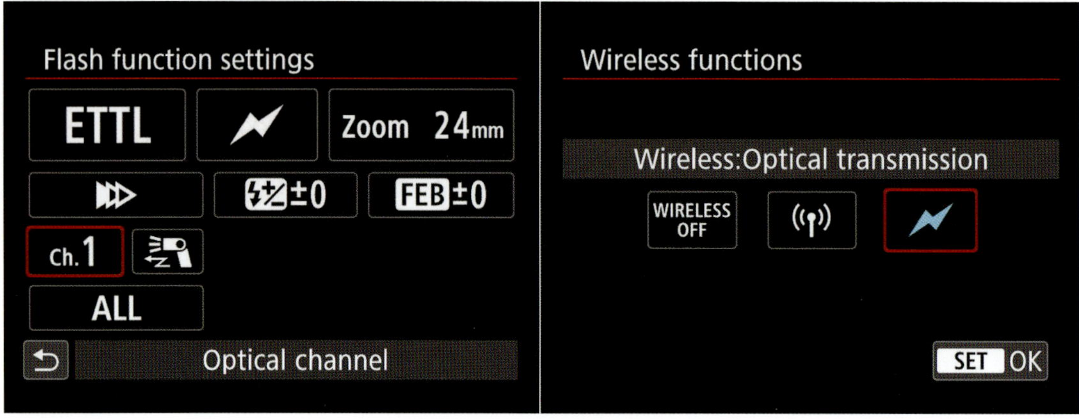

Figure 10.3 You can choose the Channel, Groups, and other parameters from the Flash Functions Settings screen (left); activate wireless functions (right).

5. **Enable/disable master flash firing.** The icon to the immediate right of the Channel Setting icon allows you to enable or disable firing of the master flash. When disabled, the master flash will still control external flashes wirelessly with a preflash burst, but won't contribute to the exposure. This is useful if you want all the illumination to come from your slave flash units, such as when shooting close-up or macro images, or when you're simulating a studio flash setup with Speedlites.

6. **Double-check to make sure your off-camera flash units are set to the appropriate channel.** Your wireless flash units must be set to the same channel as the 5D Mark IV's wireless flash controller; otherwise, the Speedlites won't fire.

Working with Groups

With what you've already learned, you can shoot wirelessly using your camera's on-camera flash and one or more external flash units. All these strobes will work together with the 5D Mark IV for automatic exposure using E-TTL II exposure mode. You can vary the power ratio between your on-camera flash and the external units. As you become more comfortable with wireless flash photography, you can even switch the individual external flash units into manual mode, and adjust their lighting ratios manually.

But there's a lot more you can do if you've splurged and own two or more compatible external flash units (some photographers I know own five or six Speedlite 580EX II or 600EX II-RT units). Canon wireless photography lets you collect individual strobes into *groups*, and control all the Speedlites within a given group together. You can operate as few as two strobes in two groups or three strobes in three groups, while controlling more units if desired. You can also have them fire at equal output settings (A+B+C mode) versus using them at different power ratios (A:B or A:B C modes). Setting each group's strobes to different power ratios gives you more control over lighting for portraiture and other uses.

This is one of the more powerful options of the EOS wireless flash system. I prefer to keep my Speedlites set to different groups normally. I can always set the power ratio to 1:1 if I want to operate the flash units all at the same power. If I change my mind and need to make adjustments, I can just change the wireless flash controller and then manipulate the different groups' output as desired.

Canon's wireless flash system works with a number of Canon flashes and even some third-party units. I routinely mix a 600EX-RT, 600EX II-RT, 580EX II, 550EX, and 420EX. I control these flash units either with the EOS 5D Mark IV's on-camera external flash or using a Canon ST-E2 Speedlite Transmitter.

The ST-E2 is a hot shoe mount device that offers wireless flash control for a wide variety of Canon wireless flash capable strobes and can even control flash units wirelessly for high-speed sync (HSS) photography. (HSS is described in Chapter 9.) The ST-E2 can only control two flash groups though, not three like the 5D Mark IV and also can support flash exposure bracketing. Its range isn't as great as the 5D Mark IV's though.

Here's how you set up groups:

1. **Set flash units to the group you want to assign them to.** Each flash unit may use its own procedure for setting that strobe's group. Consult your Speedlite's manual for instructions.

2. **Navigate to the 5D Mark IV's group selection option.** From the External Speedlite Control entry in the Shooting 1 menu, navigate to the Flash Function Settings choice, Flash Functions. Navigate to the Group setting (located just below the Channel and Master Flash Firing options) and push the SET button.

3. **Select the Group Configuration you want.** You can then use the QCD to cycle to select ALL, A:B, or A:B C. If you're using the 600EX-RT/600EX II-RT in radio control mode, you can also activate Groups D and E.

4. **Double-check to make sure your flash units are set to the appropriate channel.** Your wireless flash units must be set to the same channel as the 5D Mark IV's wireless flash controller; otherwise, the Speedlites won't fire.

Ratio Control

By default, all the flashes in each group will fire at full power. However, for more advanced lighting setups, you can select lighting ratios.

Your on-camera master flash and your wireless slave flash units have their own individual *oomph*— how much illumination they put out. This option lets you choose the relationship between these units, a *power ratio* between your on-camera flash and your wireless flash units—the relative strength of each. That ability can be especially useful if you want to use the on-camera flash for just a little fill light, while letting your off-camera units do the heavy work.

Having the ability to vary the power of each flash unit or group of flash units wirelessly gives you greater flexibility and control. Varying the light output of each flash unit makes it possible to create specific types of lighting (such as traditional portrait lighting, which frequently calls for a 3:1 lighting ratio between main light and fill light) or to use illumination to highlight one part of the photo while reducing contrast in another.

Lighting ratios determine the contrast between the main light (sometimes called a "key" light) and fill light. For portraiture, usually the main light is placed at a 45-degree angle to the subject (although there are some variations), with the fill-in light on the opposite side or closer to the camera position. Choosing the right lighting ratio can do a lot to create a particular look or mood. For instance, a 1:1 ratio produces what's known as "flat" lighting. While this is good for copying or documentation, it's not usually as interesting for portraiture. Instead, making the main light more powerful than the fill light creates interesting shadows for more dramatic images. (See Figure 10.4.)

By selecting the power ratio between the flash units, you can change the relative illumination between them. Figure 10.5 shows a series of four images with a single main flash located at a 45-degree angle off to the right and slightly behind the model. The on-camera flash at the camera provided illumination to fill in the shadows on the side of the face closest to the camera. The ratio between the two Speedlites flash was varied using 2:1 (upper left), 3:1 (upper right), 4:1 (lower left), and 5:1 (lower right) ratios.

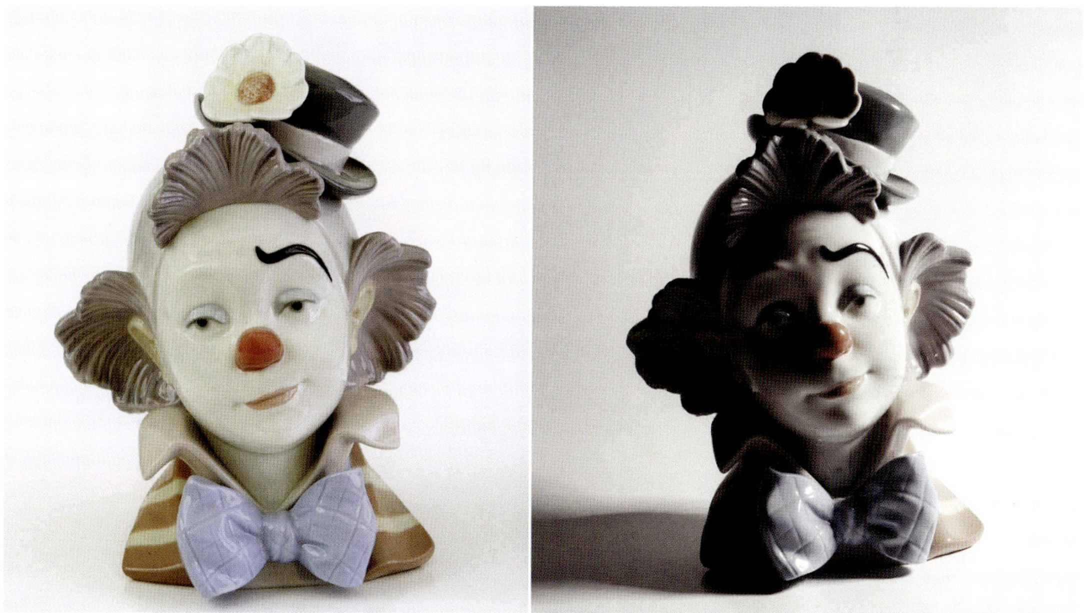

Figure 10.4 More dramatic lighting ratios produce more dramatic-looking illumination.

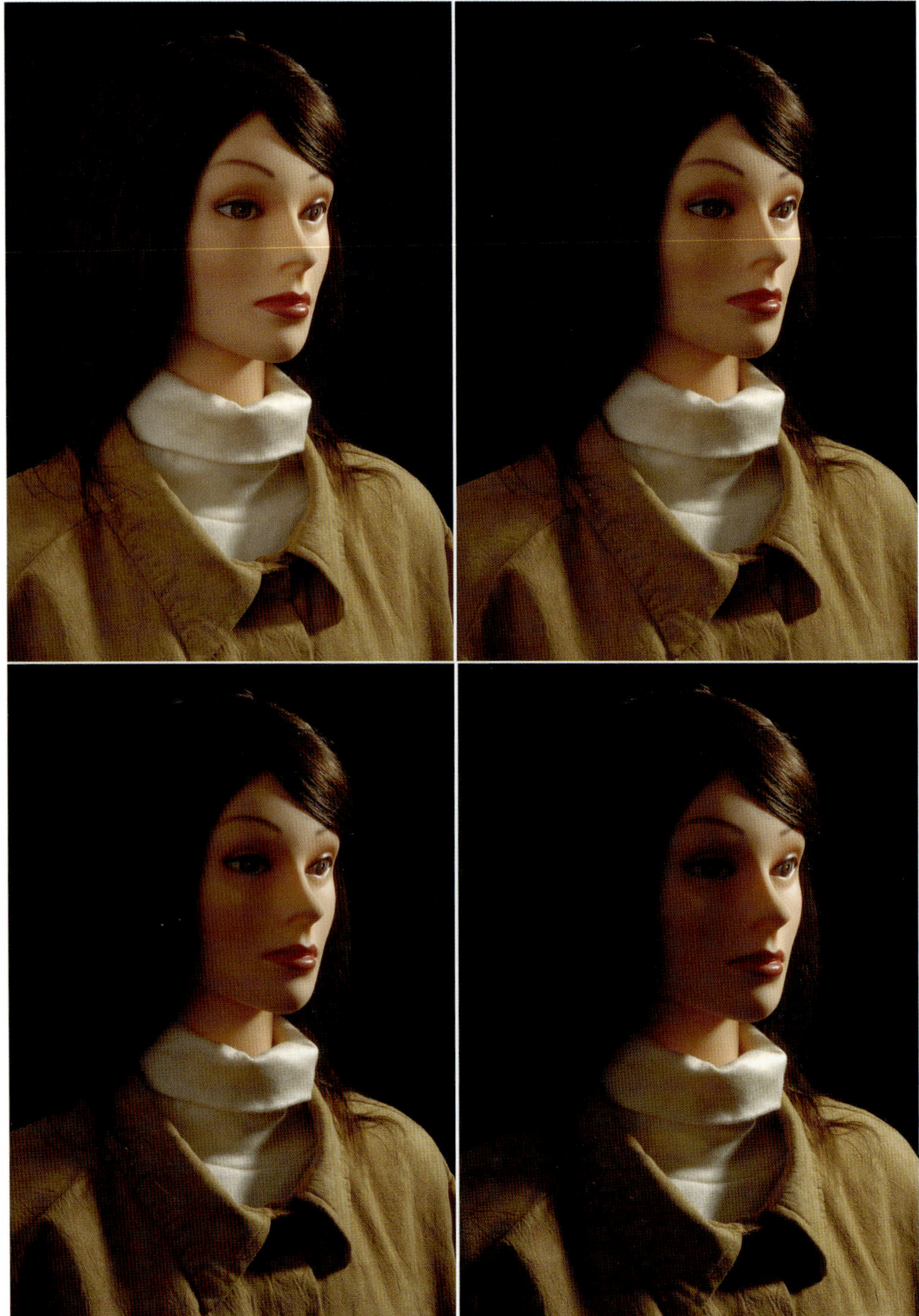

Figure 10.5 The main light (to the right and behind the model) and fill light (at the camera position) were varied using 2:1 and 3:1 (top row, left to right) as well as 4:1 and 5:1 (bottom row, left to right) ratios.

Here's how to set the lighting ratio between the master flash and one additional external wireless flash unit:

1. **Navigate to the 5D Mark IV's Flash Group selection option.** With wireless flash already activated, visit the External Speedlite Control entry in the Shooting 1 menu, navigate to the Flash Function Settings choice, Flash Functions. Navigate to the Flash Group choice at the lower left of the screen, and push the SET button.

2. **Choose Group Configuration.** You can select ALL, A:B, or A:B C. If you're using the 600EX-RT/600EX II-RT in radio transmission mode, you can also select Groups D and E. Press SET to confirm.

3. **Select Ratio.** If you've chosen A:B C, use the QCD to navigate to the A:B Ratio Control option, highlighted in red at left in Figure 10.6, press SET and select a ratio from 8:1 to 1:8 (see Figure 10.6, right). Group A at 1:8 supplies 1/8th the output of Group B. At 8:1, the ratio is reversed.

4. **Confirm.** Press SET to confirm your ratio.

Here's how the various basic Group Configurations work:

■ **ALL.** All groups will fire at the power level set at the flash unit itself. That may be full power, or you may have set individual flashes to fire at some other power level. It's usually simpler to set your flashes at full power and allow the master to control their output.

■ **A:B.** In this configuration, you can specify the ratio of the power levels of Groups A and B, as described in Step 3 above.

■ **A:B C.** In this Group Configuration, you can specify the power ratio between Groups A and B, but *not* the output of Group C flashes. Those can be controlled only using Flash Exposure Compensation, the option immediately above the A:B Power Ratio setting in Figure 10.6.

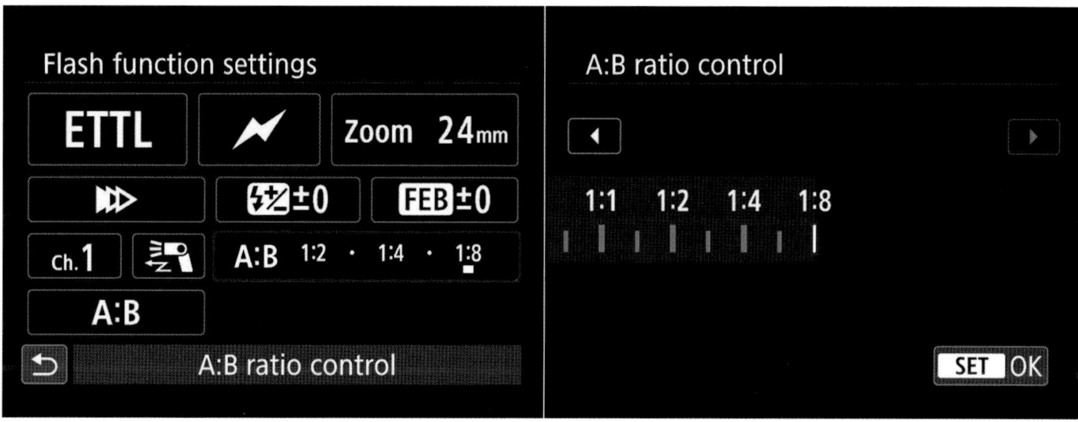

Figure 10.6 Select your Group Configuration.

Flash Release Function

The Canon Speedlite 600EX-RT, 600EX II-RT, 430EX III, 320EX, and Speedlite 270EX II have a nifty feature called the Remote Release Function, which, as I write this, is completely novel in the Canon accessory flash lineup. The feature allows you to detach the Speedlite from certain EOS cameras (right now the 5DS/5DS R, 5D Mark II, Mark III, and Mark IV, 6D, 7D, 7D II, 60D, 70D, 80D, T6s, T6i, T5i, T4i, T3i, T2i, T1i, Xsi, Xti, XT, and 2003-era original Digital Rebel), and then use a button on the flash unit as a remote control to trigger the camera from up to 16 feet away. That's right, your 320EX and 270EX II can function as a wireless remote control, just like the Canon RC-6, RC-5, and RC-1 infrared controls! Your Speedlite Transmitter ST-E3-RT can also be used for this function.

As you can see from the list of cameras, it works with any EOS camera that can be triggered by an IR remote. There's a (mandatory) two-second delay after you press the flash's remote release, and the flash itself does not have to fire and contribute to the exposure. An invisible infrared signal emitted by the flash triggers the camera.

To use the feature with the 5D Mark IV, use the Drive function, described earlier, and select the self-timer/infrared remote option. With the compatible flash turned on and detached from the camera, position the flash so it "sees" the remote control sensor on the front of the camera. Press the remote release button on the side of the flash, and the camera will fire two seconds later. If you're taking a picture of yourself, this delay allows you to stash the flash out of sight and grin. The flash will not fire.

If you prefer to have the flash fire and contribute to the exposure, move the On/Off switch on the back to the middle "slave" position. In this mode, the camera itself must serve as the master, or you must have another master unit physically attached to the camera. Or, you can connect a 580EX II, set to master mode, either by putting it in the accessory shoe or linked with a cable, such as the Off Camera Cord OC-E3. Alternatively, you can connect the Speedlite Transmitter ST-E2 or ST-E3-RT (when using radio triggering).

When you're ready, point the flash at the front of the camera/master flash within 16 feet of the camera, and press the remote control button on the side of the flash. During the two-second delay, you can then point the flash in a different direction (as is likely, because you're probably using this feature to illuminate the scene, not the camera). That's the real reason for the two-second delay, by the way: giving you the ability to reposition the "remote" release flash.

The 600EX-RT/600EX II-RT has its own remote release function, which allows you to use a slave unit to trigger your camera by remote control when using radio transmission mode. EOS cameras released since 2012 can be triggered in this way through the intelligent hot shoe, using a 600EX-RT mounted on the camera as a receiver, and the slave 600EX-RT/600EX II-RT off camera as the remote trigger. Older cameras can still be used in this mode, but you'll need to connect the on-camera 600EX-series flash to the camera's N3 remote control terminal using an optional Release Cable SR-N3. (If your camera uses a different type of remote release, you're out of luck.)

11

Customizing with the Shooting Menu

This chapter and the next three will help you sort out the settings you can make to customize how your Canon EOS 5D Mark IV uses its features, shoots photos, displays images, and processes the pictures after they've been taken. I'm not going to waste a lot of space on some of the more obvious menu choices. For example, you can probably figure out that the Release Shutter without Card option in the Shooting 1 menu deals with whether you can "take" a picture even if no memory card is present. You can certainly decipher the import of the two options available (Enable and Disable). In this chapter, I'll devote no more than a sentence or two to the blatantly obvious settings and concentrate on the more confusing aspects of 5D Mark IV set-up, such as Automatic Exposure Bracketing.

The six Shooting menu tabs discussed in this chapter are those available in still shooting mode. If you rotate the Live View/Movie switch to the Movie position, only the first three Shooting menus are available, and the specialized Movie Shooting 4 and 5 menus are activated. I'll explain the Movie Shooting menus in Chapter 16, where I've collected all the basic video capture information for the 5D Mark IV. For now, let's start off with an overview of the 5D Mark IV's menus themselves.

Anatomy of the 5D Mark IV's Menus

The 5D Mark IV divides the entries into six major sections—Shooting, Autofocus, Playback, Set-up, Custom Functions, and My Menu—each of which (except for the last) is further subdivided into three to six separate pages. Each page's listings are shown as a separate screen with no scrolling.

The menus are easy to use, too. Just press the MENU button, spin the Main Dial to highlight the menu tab and page you want to access, and then scroll up and down within a menu with the Quick Control Dial. What could be easier?

Tapping the MENU button brings up a typical menu like the one shown in Figure 11.1. (If the camera goes to "sleep" while you're reviewing a menu, you may need to wake it up again by tapping the shutter release button.) Different menu tabs are provided, depending on the shooting mode, shown in Table 11.1.

The 5D Mark IV's tabs are color-coded: red for Shooting, magenta for Autofocus, blue for Playback, amber for Set-up, brown for Custom Functions, and Green for My Menu. The currently selected menu tab's icon is white within a background corresponding to its color code. A lineup immediately underneath shows the page numbers available, and, at far right, the name of the page (for example, SHOOT1). The current screen's number is highlighted. All the inactive menus are gray and dimmed.

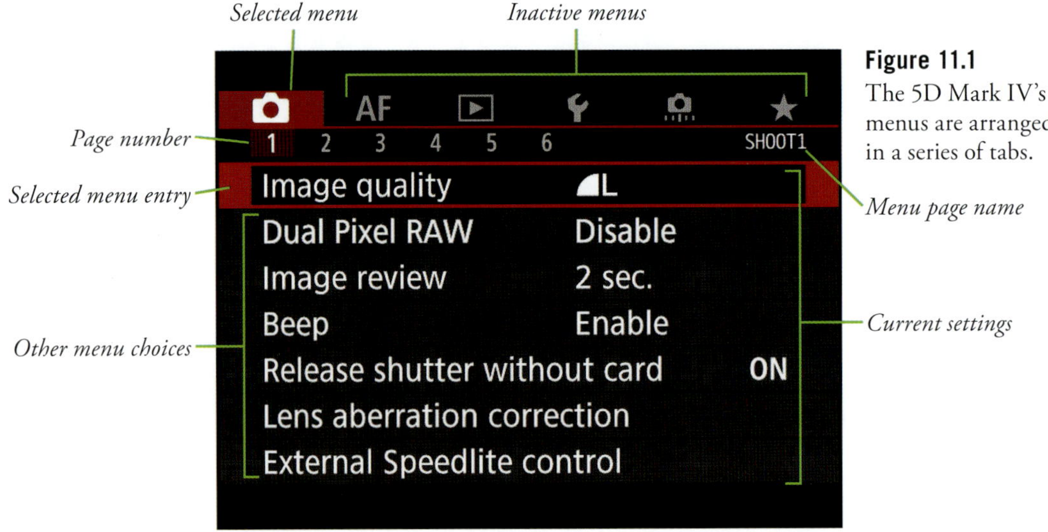

Figure 11.1
The 5D Mark IV's menus are arranged in a series of tabs.

Table 11.1 Available Menus	
Modes	**Available Menu Tabs**
Bulb, M, Tv, Av, P Modes	Shooting 1–4, Shooting 5 (Live View), Shooting 6 (Live View), Playback 1–3, Set-up 1–5, Custom Functions 1–5, My Menu
Scene Intelligent Auto	Shooting 1, Shooting 2, Shooting 3 (Live View), Playback 1–3, Set-up 1–5 (Only selected entries)
Movie mode	Shooting 1, Shooting 2 (Movie), Shooting 3 (Movie), Playback 1–3, Set-up 1–5

HYPER MENU NAVIGATION

As I mentioned, you can use the Main Dial to move from menu to menu, and the Quick Control Dial to highlight a menu entry. Press the SET button to select a menu item. That procedure is probably the best way to start out, because those controls are used to make so many settings with the EOS 5D Mark IV that they quickly become almost intuitive. The 5D Mark IV manual uses the Main Dial/Quick Control Dial method in its Menu Setting description. But, there are two alternate methods.

You can use the touch screen to tap on a specific menu tab, page number, and individual entry, if you like. Or, if you have an agile thumb, you can do all your menu navigation with the joystick-like multi-controller:

- Shift the multi-controller left/right to jump from tab to tab.

- Press the multi-controller up/down to move within the menu choices of a given tab.

- Press the multi-controller in to select a menu item, and press it again to return to the menu choices.

It gets even better. You can jump from tab to tab even if you've highlighted a menu setting on another tab—and the 5D Mark IV will remember which menu entry you've highlighted when you return to that menu. The memorization works even if you leave the menu system or turn off your camera. The 5D Mark IV always remembers the last menu entry you used with a tab. So, if you generally use the Format command each time you access the Set-up 1 menu, that's the entry that will be highlighted when you choose that tab. The camera remembers which tab was last used, too, so, potentially, formatting your memory card might take just a couple presses (the MENU button, the SET button to select the highlighted Format command, then a click of the Quick Control Dial to choose OK, and another press of SET to start the format process).

Here are the things to watch for as you navigate the menus:

- **Menu tabs.** In the top row of the menu screen, the menu that is currently active will be highlighted as described earlier. The numbers within the tab let you know if you are in, say, Set-up 1, Set-up 2, Set-up 3, or Set-up 4. Just remember that the red camera icons stand for still, live view, and movie shooting options; the blue right-pointing triangles represent playback options; the yellow wrench icons stand for set-up options; the brown camera icons represent Custom Functions; and the green star stands for personalized menus defined for the star of the show—you.

- **Selected menu item.** The currently selected menu entry within a given tab will have a black background and will be surrounded by a box the same hue as its color code.

- **Other menu choices.** The other menu items visible on the screen will have a dark gray background.

- **Current setting.** The current settings for visible menu items are shown in the right-hand column, until one menu entry is selected (by pressing the SET key). Current settings aren't appropriate for some menu entries (for example, the Protect Images or Resize options in the Playback 1 and 2 screens), so the right column is left blank.

When you've moved the menu highlighting to the menu item you want to work with, press the SET button to select it. The current settings for the other menu items in the list will be hidden, and a list of options for the selected menu item (or a submenu screen) will appear. Or, you may be shown a separate settings screen for that entry. Within the menu choices, you can scroll up or down with the Quick Control Dial; press SET to select the choice you've made; and press the MENU button again to exit.

Shooting Menu Options

The various direct setting buttons on the top panel of the camera for metering mode/white balance, autofocus/drive mode, and ISO/flash exposure compensation are likely to be the most common settings changes you make, with changes during a session common. You'll find that the Shooting menu options are those that you access second most frequently when you're using your 5D Mark IV. You might make such adjustments as you begin a shooting session, or when you move from one type of subject to another. Canon makes accessing these changes very easy.

This section explains the options of the Shooting menus and how to use them. The options you'll find in these red-coded menus include:

- Image Quality
- Dual Pixel RAW
- Image Review
- Beep
- Release Shutter without Card
- Lens Aberration Correction
- External Speedlite Control
- Exposure Compensation/AEB (Automatic Exposure Bracketing)
- ISO Speed Settings
- Auto Lighting Optimizer
- White Balance
- Custom White Balance
- WB Shift/Bkt
- Color Space
- Picture Style
- Long Exposure Noise Reduction

- High ISO Speed Noise Reduction
- Highlight Tone Priority
- Dust Delete Data
- Multiple Exposure
- HDR Mode
- Interval Timer
- Bulb Timer
- Anti-flicker Shooting
- Mirror Lockup
- Live View Shooting
- AF Method
- Touch Shutter
- Grid Display
- Aspect Ratio
- Exposure Simulation
- Silent Live View Shooting
- Metering Timer

Image Quality

Options: Resolution: Large (default), Medium, Small 1, Small 2, Small 3; JPEG Compression: Fine (default), Standard; JPEG (default), RAW, or RAW+JPEG

My preference: Resolution: Large; JPEG Compression: Fine; RAW+JPEG

You can choose the image quality settings used by the 5D Mark IV to store its files. This is the first entry in the Shooting 1 menu (see Figure 11.1). You have three choices to make when selecting a quality setting:

- **Resolution.** The number of pixels captured determines the absolute resolution of the photos you shoot with your 5D Mark IV. Your choices range from 30 megapixels (Large or L), measuring 6720 × 4480; 13 megapixels (Medium or M), measuring 4464 × 2976; 7.5 megapixels (Small 1 or S1), measuring 3360 × 2240; 2.5 megapixels (Small 2 or S2), measuring 1920 × 1280; and 350,000 pixels (Small 3 or S3), measuring 720 × 480. You can also choose RAW-only sizes of RAW (6720 × 4480; 30MP); M-RAW (5040 × 3360, 17MP); or S-RAW (3360 × 2240, 7.5MP). (A double-size Dual Pixel RAW format can also be selected using the entry discussed after this one.)

- **JPEG compression.** To reduce the size of your image files and allow more photos to be stored on a given memory card, the 5D Mark IV uses JPEG compression to squeeze the images down to a smaller size. This compacting reduces the image quality a little, so you're offered your choice of Fine compression and Normal compression. The symbols help you remember that Fine compression (represented by a quarter-circle) provides the smoothest results, while Normal compression (signified by a stair-step icon) provides "jaggier" images.

- **JPEG, RAW, or both.** You can elect to store only JPEG versions of the images you shoot or you can save your photos as uncompressed, loss-free RAW files, which consume about four times as much space on your memory card. Or, you can store both at once as you shoot. Many photographers elect to save *both* a JPEG and a RAW file, so they'll have a JPEG version that might be usable as-is, as well as the original "digital negative" RAW file in case they want to do some processing of the image later. You'll end up with two different versions of the same file: one with a JPG extension, and one with the CR2 extension that signifies a Canon RAW file.

To choose the combination you want, access the menus, scroll to Image Quality, and press the SET button. A screen similar to the one shown in Figure 11.2 will appear with two rows of choices. Spin the Main Dial to choose from: -- (no RAW), RAW, M RAW, or S RAW. Rotate the QCD to select one of the JPEG choices: -- (no JPEG), Large, Medium, or Small in Fine or Normal compression (represented by smooth and stepped icons, respectively), plus Small 2 or Small 3 JPEG, at the resolutions listed above. A red box appears around the currently selected choice. If you choose "--" for both RAW and JPEG, then JPEG Fine will be used. As always, when you've highlighted your selection, press SET to confirm.

Why so many choices? There are some limited advantages to using the Medium and Small resolution settings, Normal JPEG compression setting, and the two lower resolution RAW formats. They

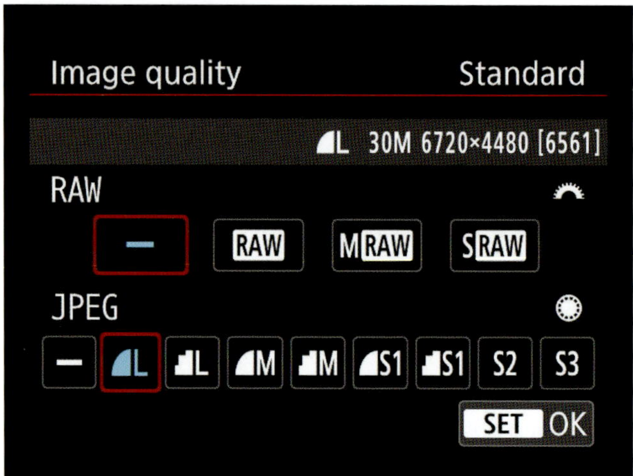

Figure 11.2
Choose your resolution, JPEG compression, and file format from this screen.

all allow stretching the capacity of your memory card so you can shoehorn quite a few more pictures onto a single memory card. That can come in useful when on vacation and you're running out of storage, or when you're shooting non-critical work that doesn't require full resolution. The Small 2 and Small 3 settings can be useful for photos taken for real estate listings, web page display, photo ID cards, or similar non-critical applications.

For most work, using lower resolution and extra compression is often false economy. You never know when you might need that extra bit of picture detail. Your best bet is to have enough memory cards to handle all the shooting you want to do until you have the chance to transfer your photos to your computer or a personal storage device.

However, reduced image quality can sometimes be beneficial if you're shooting sequences of photos rapidly, as the 5D Mark IV is able to hold more of them in its internal memory buffer before transferring to the memory card. Still, for most sports and other applications, you'd probably rather have better, sharper pictures than longer periods of continuous shooting.

Note that the screen shown in the figure may vary slightly, depending on how you've set the Record Function+Card/Folder Selection entry in the Set-up 1 menu (also described in Chapter 13). That entry determines which memory card(s) are used to store the RAW and JPEG file formats you select here. The Record Function feature, which is active when you have more than one memory card inserted in the 5D Mark IV, can be set to:

- **Standard.** All images will be recorded only to the memory card specified by the Record/Play setting of the Record Function+Card/Folder Selection entry in the Set-up 1 menu, using the settings established in the Image Quality screen.
- **Auto Switch Card.** All images will be recorded only to the memory card specified by the Record/Play setting using the Image Quality specifications you apply, but when that card is full, the camera switches automatically to the other card.

- **Rec. separately.** When this option is active, all images will be stored on *both* cards, but you can specify the image recording quality separately for each memory card in the Image Quality screen.
- **Rec. to Multiple.** All images are stored on both cards, using the quality settings you specify in the Image Quality screen.

JPEG vs. RAW

You'll sometimes be told that RAW files are the "unprocessed" image information your camera produces, before it's been modified. That's nonsense. RAW files are no more unprocessed than your camera film is after it's been through the chemicals to produce a negative or transparency. A lot can happen in the developer that can affect the quality of a film image—positively and negatively—and, similarly, your digital image undergoes a significant amount of processing before it is saved as a RAW file. Canon even applies a name (DIGIC 6+) to the digital image processing (DIP) chip used to perform this magic.

A RAW file is more like a film camera's processed negative. It contains all the information, captured in 14-bit channels per color (and stored in a 16-bit space), with no compression, no sharpening, no application of any special filters or other settings you might have specified when you took the picture. Those settings are *stored* with the RAW file so they can be applied when the image is converted to a form compatible with your favorite image editor. However, using RAW conversion software such as Adobe Camera Raw or Canon's Digital Photo Professional, you can override those settings and apply settings of your own. You can select essentially the same changes there that you might have specified in your camera's picture-taking options.

RAW exists because sometimes we want to have access to all the information captured by the camera, before the camera's internal logic has processed it and converted the image to a standard file format. RAW doesn't save as much space as JPEG. What it does do is preserve all the information captured by your camera after it's been converted from analog to digital form. Of course, the 5D Mark IV's RAW format preserves the *settings* information.

So, why don't we always use RAW? Although some photographers do save only in RAW format, it's more common to use either RAW plus one of the JPEG options or just shoot JPEG and avoid RAW altogether. That's because having only RAW files to work with can significantly slow down your workflow. While RAW is overwhelmingly helpful when an image needs to be fine-tuned, in other situations working with a RAW file, when all you really need is a good-quality, un-tweaked JPEG image, consumes time that you may not want to waste. For example, RAW images take longer to store on the memory card, and require more post-processing effort, whether you elect to go with the default settings in force when the picture was taken, or just make minor adjustments.

Thus, those who depend on speedy access to images or who shoot large numbers of photos at once may prefer JPEG over RAW. Wedding photographers, for example, might expose several thousand photos during a bridal affair and offer hundreds to clients as electronic proofs for possible inclusion in an album or transfer to a CD or DVD. These wedding shooters, who want JPEG images as their final product, take the time to make sure that their in-camera settings are correct, minimizing the need to post-process photos after the event. Given that their JPEGs are so good (in most cases thanks, in large part, to the pro photographer's extensive experience), there is little need to get bogged down shooting RAW.

JPEG was invented as a more compact file format that can store most of the information in a digital image, but in a much smaller size. JPEG predates most digital SLRs, and was initially used to squeeze down files for transmission over slow dialup connections. Even if you were using an early dSLR with 1.3 megapixel files for news photography, you didn't want to send them back to the office over a modem (Google it) at 1,200 bps.

But, as I noted, JPEG provides smaller files by compressing the information in a way that loses some image data. JPEG remains a viable alternative because it offers several different quality levels. At the highest-quality Fine level, you might not be able to tell the difference between the original RAW file and the JPEG version. You've squeezed the image significantly without losing much visual information at all. (See Figure 11.3.)

In my case, I shoot virtually everything at RAW+JPEG Fine. Most of the time, I'm not concerned about filling up my memory cards, as I usually have a minimum of five fast 32GB or 64GB memory cards with me. If I think I may fill up all those cards, I have Apple's Camera Connection Kit for my iPad, and can transfer photos to that device. As I mentioned earlier, when shooting sports, I'll

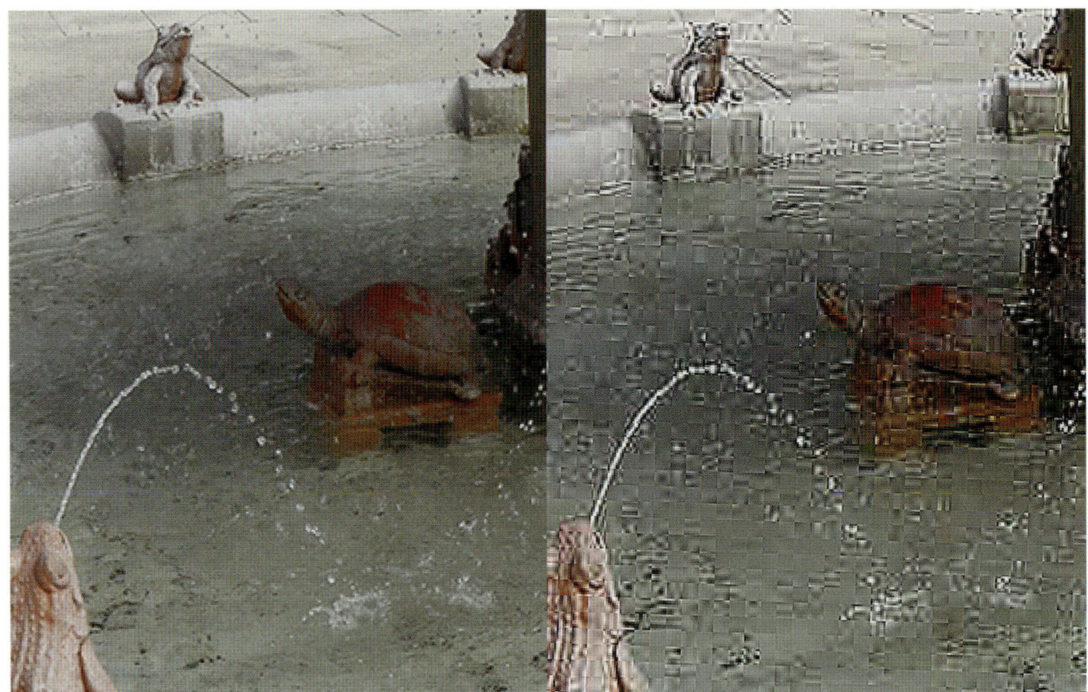

Figure 11.3 Low compression yields the best image (left); at high compression, pixelation and artifacts rear their ugly heads.

shift to JPEG Fine (with no RAW file) to squeeze a little extra speed out of my 5D Mark IV's continuous shooting mode, and to reduce the need to wade through eight-photo bursts taken in RAW format. On the other hand, on my last trip to Europe, I took only RAW (instead of my customary RAW+JPEG) photos to fit more images onto my iPad, as I planned on doing at least some post-processing on many of the images for a travel book I was working on.

Dual Pixel RAW

Options: Enable, Disable (default)

My preference: Disable unless this special format is needed

Dual Pixel RAW is a special RAW format that can be manipulated in an image editor to make microadjustments to the focus plane, slightly improve bokeh effects (the smoothness of the out-of-focus areas of the image), and make corrections to ghosting and flare. Dual Pixel RAW files also offer the opportunity for advanced users to recover up to one additional stop in the highlights. In effect, the camera saves two different RAW files: one containing information from both sets of pixels (call them Sets A+B) while the other contains only the pixels in Set B. The software can then process each subset separately. I explained Dual Pixel Raw more completely in Chapter 5, which deals primarily with autofocus, but offers explanations of the other features of the format.

To use Dual Pixel RAW, you must select RAW (but not M RAW or S RAW) or RAW+JPEG as your Image Quality, and then enable the dual pixel feature here. DPR will then be displayed on the monochrome LCD panel on top of the camera. This feature is not available if you want to shoot multiple exposures, use automatic HDR, One Touch image quality, or the Digital Lens Optimizer. It is also unavailable if you're trying to save RAW files to one memory card and M RAW or S RAW to the other using the Record Separately in the Record Function+Card/Folder Selection entry in the Set-up 1 menu.

While you can save Dual Pixel RAW files whether using the optical viewfinder or live view/movies, continuous shooting will be slower when working with the optical viewfinder. And in live view, continuous shooting is not available, and if set will switch back to single-shot mode.

Image Review

Options: 2 sec. (default), Off, 4 sec., 8 sec., Hold

My preference: 2 sec.

You can adjust the amount of time an image is displayed for review on the LCD after each shot is taken. You can elect to disable this review entirely (Off), or choose display times of 2, 4, or 8 seconds. You can also select Hold, an indefinite display, which will keep your image on the screen until you use one of the other controls, such as the shutter button, Main Dial, or Quick Control Dial. Turning the review display off or choosing a brief duration can help preserve battery power. However, the 5D Mark IV will always override the review display when the shutter button is partially or fully depressed, so you'll never miss a shot because a previous image was on the screen.

Choose Review Time from the Shooting 1 menu, and select Off, 2 sec., 4 sec., 8 sec., or Hold. If you want to retain an image on the screen for a longer period, but don't want to use Hold as your default, press the Erase button under the LCD monitor. The image will display until you choose Cancel or Erase from the menu that pops up at the bottom of the screen. A longer review time gives you an opportunity to delete a non-keeper quickly without a visit to the menu system.

Beep

Options: Enable (default), Disable for touch screen, Disable

My preference: Disable

The 5D Mark IV's internal beeper provides a helpful chirp to signify various functions, such as the countdown of your camera's self-timer. You can switch it off if you want to avoid the beep because it's annoying, impolite, or distracting (at a concert or museum), or undesired for any other reason. It's one of the few ways to make the 5D Mark IV a bit quieter, other than Live View's "silent shoot" mode. (I've had new dSLR owners ask me how to turn off the "shutter sound" the camera makes; such an option was available in the point-and-shoot camera they'd used previously.) Select Beep from the menu, press SET, and use the Quick Control Dial to choose Enable, Disable (for touch screen only) or Disable (for all functions). Press SET again to activate your choice.

Release Shutter without Card

Options: Enable (default), Disable

My preference: Disable

This entry in the Set-up 1 menu gives you the ability to snap off "pictures" without a memory card installed—or to lock the camera shutter release if that is the case. It is sometimes called Play mode, because you can experiment with your camera's features or even hand your 5D Mark IV to a friend to let him/her fool around, without any danger of pictures being taken. Back in our film days, we'd sometimes finish a roll, rewind the film back into its cassette surreptitiously, and then hand the camera to a child to take a few pictures—without wasting any film. It's hard to waste digital film, but Release Shutter without Card mode is still appreciated by some, especially camera vendors who want to be able to demo a camera at a store or trade show, but don't want to have to equip every demonstrator model with a memory card. Choose this menu item, press SET, select Enable or Disable, and press SET again to turn this capability on or off.

Lens Aberration Correction

Options: Peripheral illumination correction: Enable (default)/Disable; Chromatic Aberration correction: Enable (default)/Disable; Distortion correction: Enable/Disable (default); Digital Lens Optimizer: Enable/Disable (default); Diffraction Correction

My preference: Use the default values

The 5D Mark IV can automatically partially correct for lens aberrations in five different ways, if you are using a lens for which correction data is available. Previously, several of these corrections were available only when post-processing the image in Digital Photo Professional or another utility. The five choices (see Figure 11.4), all described in detail in the following sections:

- **Peripheral illumination correction.** Fixes light fall-off at the edges of an image.
- **Distortion correction.** Adjusts for barrel and pincushion distortion.
- **Digital lens optimizer.** Corrects for a variety of characteristics, taking into account the lens, subject distance, focal length, aperture, and low-pass (anti-aliasing) filter over the sensor.
- **Chromatic aberration correction.** Reduces color fringes around the edges of subjects.
- **Diffraction correction.** Corrects for moiré effects produced when shooting at a very small aperture.

I'll explain what each of these components do one at a time, and include some examples of those aspects that can be easily illustrated.

Peripheral Illumination Correction

One defect is caused by a phenomenon called *vignetting*, which is a darkening of the four corners of the frame because of a slight amount of fall-off in illumination at those nether regions. This menu option allows you to activate Peripheral Illumination Correction, a clever feature built in to the 5D Mark IV that partially (or fully) compensates for this effect for any lens included in the camera's internal, updateable (through firmware upgrades) database. Depending on the f/stop you use, the lens mounted on the camera, and the focal length setting, vignetting can be non-existent, slight, or may be so strong that it appears you've used a too-small hood on your camera. (Indeed, the wrong lens hood can produce a vignette effect of its own.) Vignetting can be affected by the use of a telephoto converter (more on those in Chapter 7, too).

Figure 11.4
The Lens Aberration Correction screen.

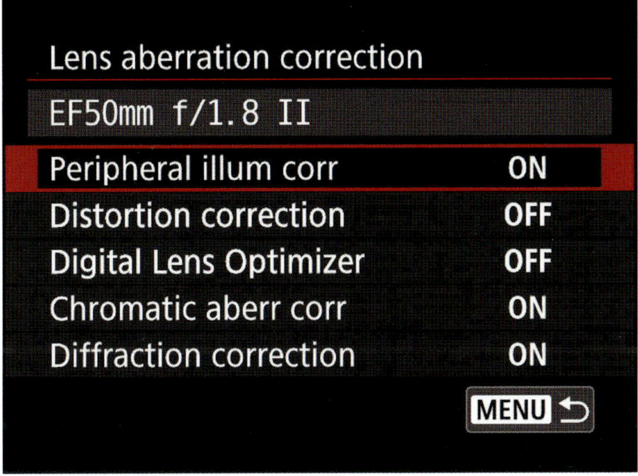

Peripheral illumination drop-off, even if pronounced, may not be much of a problem. I actually *add* vignetting, sometimes, when shooting portraits and some other subjects. Slightly dark corners tend to focus attention on a subject in the middle of the frame. On the other hand, vignetting with subjects that are supposed to be evenly illuminated, such as landscapes, is seldom a benefit.

To minimize the effects of corner light fall-off, you can process RAW files using Digital Photo Professional or, if you want your JPEG files fixed as you shoot them, by using this menu option. Figure 11.5 shows an image at top left without peripheral illumination correction, and a corrected image at bottom left. I've exaggerated the vignetting a little to make it more evident on the printed page. Keep in mind that the amount of correction available with Digital Photo Pro can be a little more intense than that applied in the camera. In addition, the higher the ISO speed, the less correction is applied. If you see severe vignetting with a particular lens, focal length, or ISO setting, you might want to turn off this feature, shoot RAW, and apply correction using DPP instead.

When you select this menu option from the Shooting 1 menu, the screen shown in Figure 11.4 appears. The lens currently attached to the camera is shown, along with a notation whether correction data needed to brighten the corners is already registered in the camera. (Information about 25 of the most popular lenses is included in the 5D Mark IV's firmware.) If so, you can use the Quick Control Dial to choose Enable to activate the feature, or Disable to turn it off. Press the SET button to confirm your choice. Note that in-camera correction must be specified *before* you take the photo, so that the DIGIC 6+ processing engine can lighten the corners of your photo before it is saved to the memory card.

Distortion Correction

This option adjusts to correct barrel and pincushion distortion, based on information in the camera's database.

Barrel distortion is found in some wide-angle lenses, and causes straight lines to bow outward, with the strongest effect at the edges. In fisheye (or *curvilinear*) lenses, this defect is a feature. When distortion is not desired, you'll need to use a lens that has corrected barrel distortion. Manufacturers like Canon do their best to minimize or eliminate it (producing a *rectilinear* lens), often using *aspherical* lens elements (which are not cross-sections of a sphere). You can also minimize less severe barrel distortion simply by framing your photo with some extra space all around, so the edges where the defect is most obvious can be cropped out of the picture. If none of the above work, you can apply this feature, which is disabled by default, to "undistort" your image with some bending of its own.

Pincushion distortion is a trait of many telephoto lenses, producing lines that curve inward toward the center of the frame. You might find after a bit of testing that it is worse at certain focal lengths with your particular zoom lens. Like chromatic aberration, it can be partially corrected using tools like Photoshop's Lens Correction filter and Photoshop Elements' Correct Camera Distortion filter, Digital Photo Professional, or this in-camera feature.

Digital Lens Optimizer

This option is a general-purpose fixer-upper based on the 5D Mark IV's database understanding of its list of lenses and characteristics of the camera and sensor. It applies a whole range of corrections and can apply them separately to the center or edges of the frame, fixing spherical aberration, axial chromatic aberration, curvature of field, astigmatism, chromatic aberration, sagittal halo, and chromatic magnification. Many of these are technical aspects that are beyond the scope of this book. The feature is turned off by default, as I recommend, but can be activated by advanced users, particularly those who had been using Digital Photo Pro to fine tune these aspects during post-processing.

Chromatic Aberration

Another defect involves fringes of color around backlit objects, produced by *chromatic aberration*, which comes in two forms: *longitudinal/axial*, in which all the colors of light don't focus in the same plane; and *lateral/transverse*, in which the colors are shifted in one direction. (See Figure 11.5, top right.) When this feature is enabled, the camera will automatically correct images taken with one of the supported lenses to reduce or eliminate the amount of color fringing seen in the final photograph. (See Figure 11.5, bottom right.)

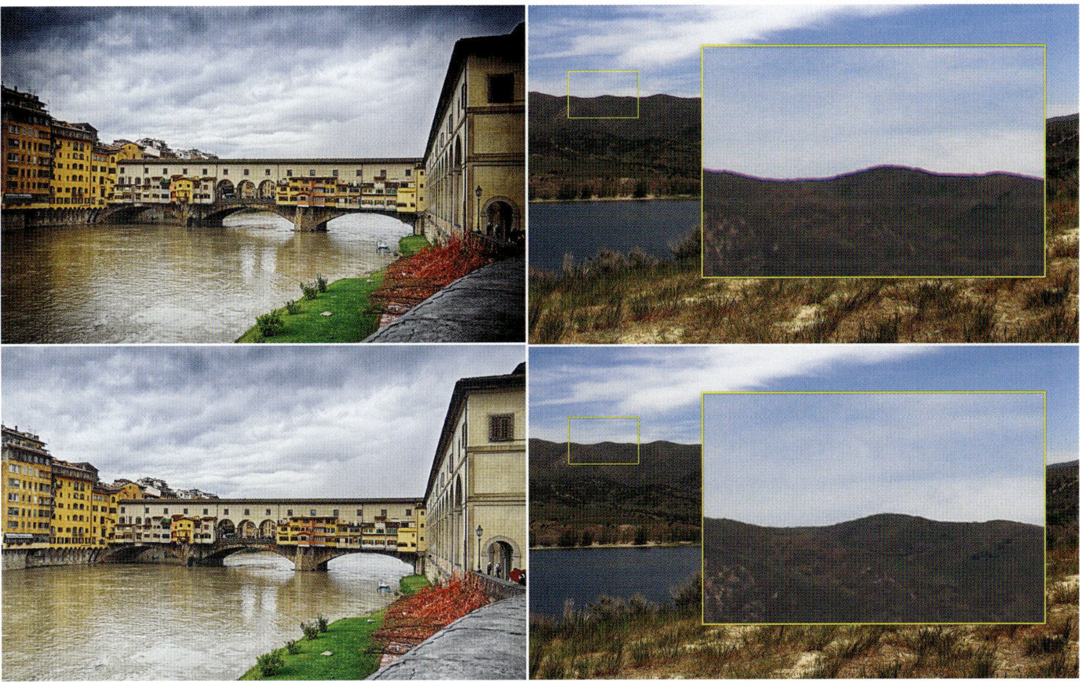

Figure 11.5 Left: Vignetting (top) is undesirable. You can correct this defect in the camera (bottom). Right: Color fringes can be corrected using the lens aberration correction feature (right top and bottom).

Diffraction Correction

Diffraction is a phenomenon that can cause a reduction in the apparent sharpness of your image due to scattering and interference of photons as they pass through smaller lens openings. In effect, the edges of your lens aperture affect proportionately more photons as the f/stop grows smaller. The relative amount of space available to pass freely decreases, and the amount of edge surface that can collide with incoming light increases.

The best analogy I can think of is a pond with two floating docks sticking out into the water, as shown in Figure 11.6. Throw a big rock in the pond, and the ripples pass between the docks relatively smoothly if the structures are relatively far apart (top). Move them closer together (bottom), and some ripples rebound off each dock to interfere with the incoming wavelets. In a lens, smaller apertures produce the same effect.

The 5D Mark IV's sensor includes a so-called "anti-aliasing" filter (technically known as an *optical low-pass filter,* or OLPF), designed to eliminate moiré. You might see it on your television when a guest wears a checked shirt with a pattern that's very close to the interval, or frequency, of the lines that produce the video image. Or, it might show up when photographing a window screen (see

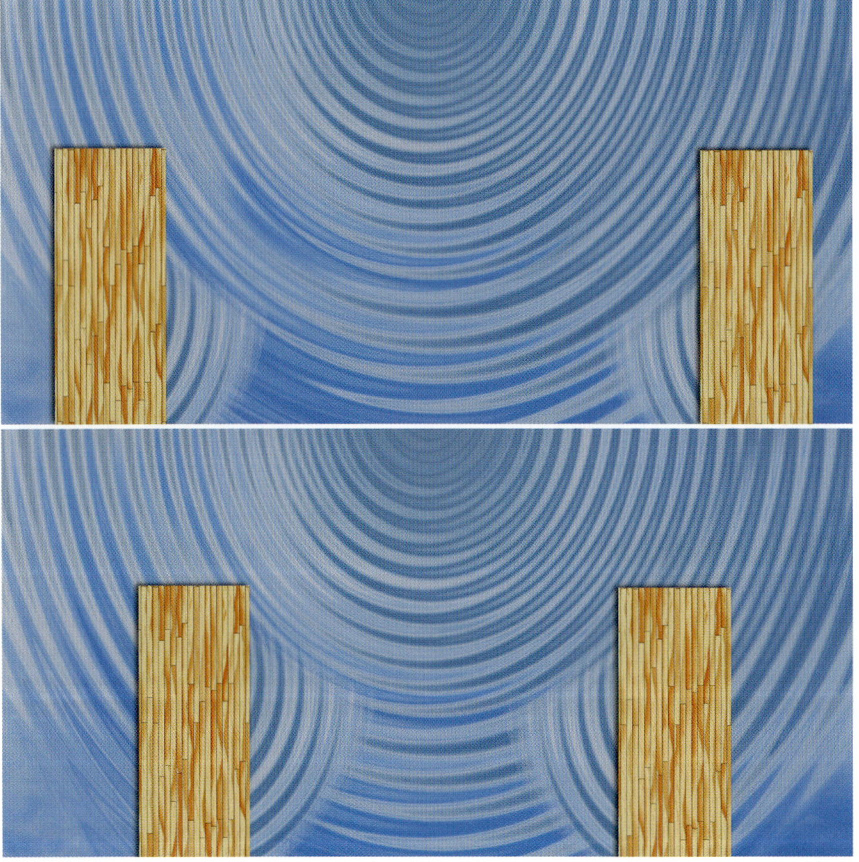

Figure 11.6
Diffraction interference can be visualized as ripples on a lake.

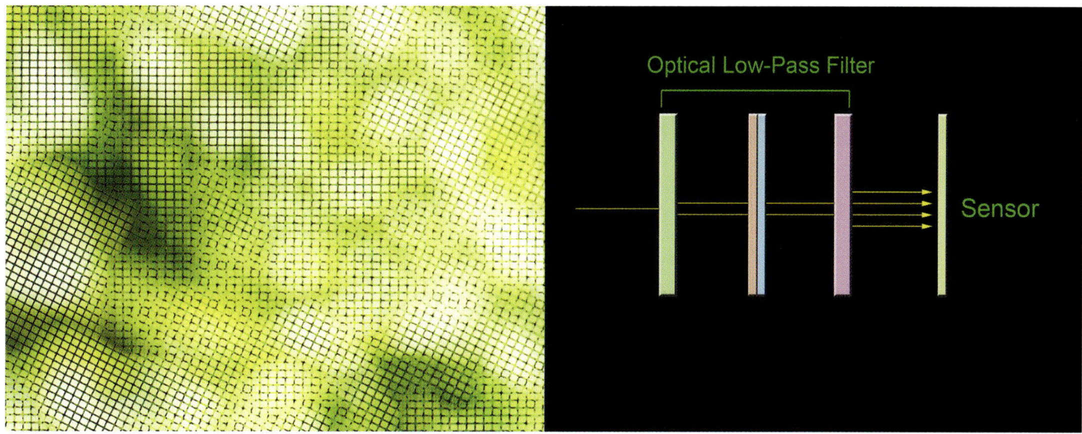

Figure 11.7 Moiré effect (left); The optical low-pass filter (right).

Figure 11.7, left). The optical low-pass filter blocks most of that moiré by blurring the image slightly in a special way. Figure 11.7, right, shows what happens. The components described below are shown from left to right in the figure.

1. **Low-pass Filter #1 (Green).** Light arriving at the filter pack in front of the sensor first moves through low-pass filter #1, at the left side of the illustration. This filter splits the beam of light in the horizontal direction.

2. **Wave plate (Red).** The next component takes the split beam of light and polarizes it circularly, so all the beams of light are pulsating in the same orientation.

3. **IR filter (Blue).** The polarized beams next pass through an IR cut-off filter that removes most (but not all) of the light in the infrared range, which keeps the IR illumination (which focuses at a different plane than visible light) from tainting the image.

4. **Low-pass Filter #2 (Purple).** The split beams next arrive at the second low-pass filter, where they are split once again in the vertical direction.

5. **Sensor.** What was originally a single beam of light arrives at the sensor in four pieces, producing a *slight* blurring effect. The 5D Mark IV's Diffraction Correction feature analyzes the image and counteracts excessive blurring, performing some sharpening internally before saving the image to your memory card with reduced blur.

With the 5D Mark IV, Canon has greatly expanded the list of lens data included within the camera itself. However, if lens aberration correction information for your lens is not registered in the camera, you can often remedy that deficit using the most recent version of the EOS Utility. Just follow these steps:

1. **Link up your camera.** Connect your 5D Mark IV to your computer using the USB cable supplied with the camera.

2. **Launch the EOS utility.** Load the utility and click on Camera Settings/Remote Shooting from the splash screen that appears.

3. **Select the Shooting menu.** It's located on the menu bar located about midway in the control panel that appears on your computer display. The Shooting menu icon is the white camera on a red background.

4. **Click on the Lens Aberration Correction choice.** The selection screen will appear.

5. **Choose your lens.** Select the category containing the lens you want to register from the panels at the top of the new screen; then place a check mark next to all the lenses you'd like to register in the camera.

6. **Confirm your choice.** Click OK to send the data from your computer to the 5D Mark IV and register your lenses.

7. **Activate correction.** When a newly registered lens is mounted on the camera, you will be able to activate the anti-vignetting feature for that lens from the Set-up 1 menu.

External Speedlite Control

This multi-level menu entry includes settings for controlling the Canon 5D Mark IV's accessory flash units attached to the camera (see Figure 11.8). I'll provide in-depth coverage of how you can use these options in Chapters 9 and 10, but will list the main options here for reference.

Flash Firing

Use this option to enable or disable the attached electronic flash. Choose Enable, and the flash fires normally when it's attached to the camera and powered up. Select Disable, and the flash itself will not fire, but the AF-assist beam emitted by the unit will function normally. You might want to use the latter option when you prefer to shoot under low levels of existing light, but still need the auto-focusing boost the flash's AF beam provides.

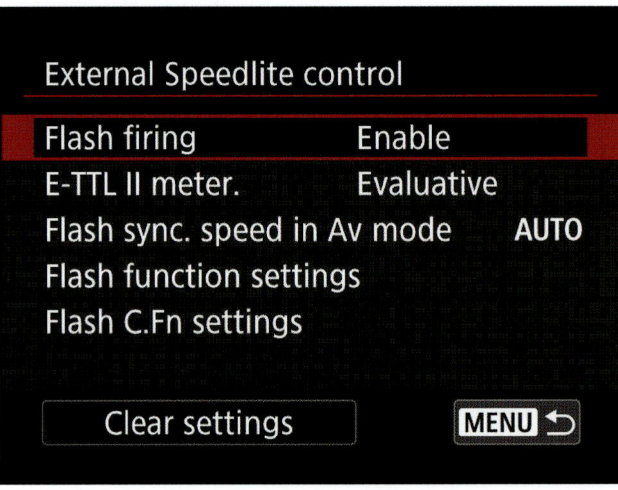

Figure 11.8
The External Speedlite Control menu.

E-TTL II Metering

You can choose Evaluative (Matrix) or Average metering modes for the electronic flash exposure meter. Evaluative looks at selected areas in the scene to calculate exposure, and is the best choice for most images because it attempts to interpret the type of scene being shot; Average calculates flash exposure by reading the entire scene, and it is possibly a good option if you want exposure to be calculated for the overall scene.

Flash Sync. Speed in Av Mode

You can select the flash synchronization speed that will be used when working in Aperture-priority mode; choose from Auto (the 5D Mark IV selects the shutter speed from 30 seconds to 1/200th second), to a range embracing only the speeds from 1/200th to 1/60th second, or fixed at 1/200th second.

Normally, in Aperture-priority mode when using flash, you specify the f/stop to be locked in. The camera then adjusts exposure by varying the output of the electronic flash. Because the primary exposure comes from the flash, the main effect of the shutter speed selected is on the secondary exposure from the ambient light remaining on the scene.

Auto is your best choice under most conditions. The 5D Mark IV will choose a shutter speed that balances the flash exposure and available, ambient light. The 1/200th–1/60th second setting locks out slower shutter speeds, preventing blur from camera/subject movement in the secondary ("ghost") exposure. However, the background may be rendered dark if the flash is not strong enough to illuminate it. The 1/200th second (fixed) setting further reduces the chance of getting those blurry ghosts, but there is more of a chance the background will be dark. You'll find a more detailed explanation of these options in Chapter 9.

Flash Function Settings

There is a total of six possible choices for this menu screen, plus Clear Settings. The additional options are grayed out unless you're working in wireless flash mode. All these are explained in Chapters 9 and 10.

- **Flash mode.** This entry allows you to choose from automatic exposure calculation (E-TTL II) or manual flash exposure.

- **Wireless functions.** These choices include Mode, Channel, Firing Group, and other options used only when you're working in wireless mode to control a wireless-capable external flash. If you've disabled wireless functions, the other options don't appear on the menu. I'm going to leave the explanation of these options for Chapter 10, which is an entire chapter dedicated to using the 5D Mark IV's wireless shooting capabilities.

- **Zoom.** Use this to select a flash zoom head setting to adjust coverage area of compatible Speedlites.

- **Shutter sync.** You can choose First-curtain sync, which fires the pre-flash used to calculate the exposure before the shutter opens, followed by the main flash as soon as the shutter is completely open. This is the default mode, and you'll generally perceive the pre-flash and main flash as a single burst. Alternatively, you can select Second-curtain sync, which fires the pre-flash as soon as the shutter opens, and then triggers the main flash in a second burst at the end of the exposure, just before the shutter starts to close. (If the shutter speed is slow enough, you may clearly see both the pre-flash and main flash as separate bursts of light.) This action allows photographing a blurred trail of light of moving objects with sharp flash exposures at the beginning and the end of the exposure. This type of flash exposure is slightly different from what some other cameras produce using Second-curtain sync. I'll explain how it works in Chapter 9.

  If you have an external compatible Speedlite attached, you can also choose High-speed sync, which allows you to use shutter speeds faster than 1/200th second, using the External Flash Function Setting menu.

- **Flash exposure compensation.** If you'd rather adjust flash exposure using a menu than with the ISO/Flash exposure compensation button, you can do that here. (If you happen to specify a value with both, this menu entry overrides the button-selected value.) Select this option with the SET button, then dial in the amount of flash EV compensation you want using the Quick Control Dial. The EV that was in place before you started to make your adjustment is shown as a blue indicator, so you can return to that value quickly. Press SET again to confirm your change, then press the MENU button twice to exit.

- **Flash exposure bracketing.** Use these settings to specify options for adjusting the output of your unit when using bracketing with your compatible electronic flash.

Flash Custom Function Settings

Many external Speedlites from Canon include their own list of Custom Functions, which can be used to specify things like flash metering mode and flash bracketing sequences, as well as more sophisticated features, such as modeling light/flash (if available), use of external power sources (if attached), and functions of any slave unit attached to the external flash. This menu entry allows you to set an external flash unit's Custom Functions from your 5D Mark IV's menu. The exact functions available will vary by flash unit. For example, with the Speedlite 320EX, only Custom Functions 1 (Auto Power Off), 6 (Quick Flash with Continuous Shot), 10 (Slave Auto Power Off Timer), and 11 (Slave Auto Power Off Cancel) are available. With high-end units, like the Speedlite 600EX-RT, a broader range of choices (described in Chapter 9) are at your disposal.

Clear Settings

This entry allows you to zero-out any changes you've made to your external flash's Custom Functions, and return them to their factory default settings. The exception is C.Fn-00 Distance Indicator Display (if available for your flash). That setting remains as adjusted until you change it yourself. Note that a flash's Personal Functions (P.Fn) cannot be set or reset from the camera; you must use the Speedlite's controls instead.

Exposure Compensation/Automatic Exposure Bracketing

Options: Exposure comp/Auto exposure bracketing
My preference: N/A

The first entry on the Shooting 2 menu is Expo. Comp./AEB, or exposure compensation and automatic exposure bracketing. (See Figure 11.9.) As you learned in Chapter 4, exposure compensation (added/subtracted by pressing the Quick Control Dial while this menu screen is visible) increases or decreases exposure from the metered value.

Exposure bracketing using the 5D Mark IV's AEB feature is a way to shoot several consecutive exposures using different settings, to improve the odds that one will be exactly right. Automatic exposure bracketing is also an excellent way of creating the base exposures you'll need when you want to combine several shots to create a high dynamic range (HDR) image. (You'll find a discussion of HDR photography in Chapter 4, too.)

To activate automatic exposure bracketing, select this menu choice, then rotate the Main Dial to spread or contract the three lines beneath the scale until you've defined the range you want the bracket to cover, which can be up to plus/minus three stops from the base exposure, as shown in Figure 11.10. Then, use the Quick Control Dial to move the bracket set right or left, moving the

Figure 11.9

Exposure compensation/AEB is the first entry in the Shooting 2 menu.

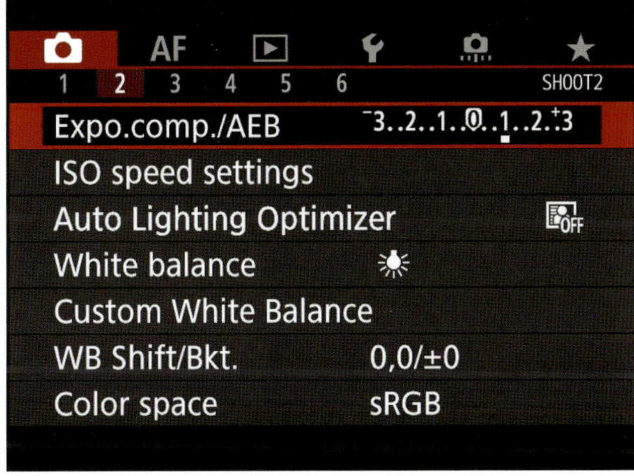

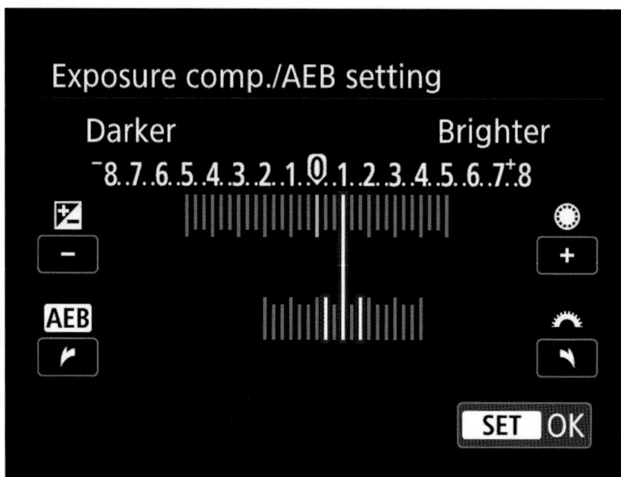

Figure 11.10
Set the range of the bracketed exposures.

base exposure point from the metered (0) value and biasing the bracketing toward underexposure (rotate left) or overexposure (rotate right).

When AEB is activated, the bracketed shots will be exposed in this sequence: metered exposure, decreased exposure, increased exposure. You'll find more information about exposure bracketing in Chapter 4.

ISO Speed Settings

Options: ISO speed, Range for stills, Auto range, Minimum shutter speed

My preference: N/A

Use this entry to select a specific ISO speed using a menu instead of the top-panel ISO button/menus, or to limit the range of ISO settings and shutter speeds that the camera selects automatically. The four subentries include:

- **ISO speed.** This scale allows you to choose from the enabled ISO speeds, plus Auto, using a sliding scale that can be adjusted using the QCD, multi-controller, or the touch screen. Press INFO. when the scale is visible to activate Auto.

- **Range for stills.** You can specify the minimum and maximum ISO sensitivity available, including "expanded" settings such as Low (ISO 50 equivalent) and H1 or H2 (ISO 51200 and 102400 equivalent, respectively). I find myself using this feature frequently to keep me from accidentally switching to a setting I'd rather (or need to) avoid. For example, at concerts I may switch from ISO 1600 to 6400 as the lighting changes, and I set those two values as my minimum or maximum. Outdoors in daylight, I might prefer to lock out ISO values lower than ISO 100 or higher than ISO 800.

- **Auto range.** This is the equivalent "safety net" for Auto ISO operation. You can set the minimum no lower than ISO 100 and the maximum to ISO 32000, and no further. Use this to apply your own "smarts" to auto ISO setting.

- **Minimum shutter speed.** You can choose whether to allow the 5D Mark IV to select the slowest shutter speed used before Auto ISO kicks in. The idea here is that you'll probably want to boost ISO sooner if you're using a long lens with P and Av modes (in which the camera selects the shutter speed). If you specify, for example, a minimum shutter speed of 1/250th second, if P or Av mode needs a slower shutter speed for the proper exposure, it will boost ISO instead, within the range you've specified with Auto Range.

  This setting has two modes. In Auto mode, the camera decides when the shutter speed is too low. You can fine-tune this by choosing Slower or Faster on the scale (–3 to +3) that appears. Or, you can manually select the "trigger" shutter speed, from 1 second to 1/8000th second.

  However, if you've handicapped the 5D Mark IV by selecting an Auto ISO range that doesn't include a sensitivity high enough, the camera will *override this setting* and use a shutter speed lower than the minimum you specify anyway. The camera assumes (rightly or wrongly) that your upper ISO boundary is more important than your lower shutter speed limit. The lesson here is that if you really, really want to enforce a minimum shutter speed when using Auto ISO, make sure your upper limit is high enough. Note that the Minimum Shutter Speed setting is ignored when using flash.

Auto Lighting Optimizer

Options: Disable, Low, Standard (default), High

My preference: Disable

The Auto Lighting Optimizer provides a partial fix for images that are too dark or flat. Such photos typically have low contrast, and the Auto Lighting Optimizer improves them—as you shoot—by increasing both the brightness and contrast as required. The feature can be activated in Program, Aperture-priority, and Shutter-priority modes. You can select from four settings: Standard (the default value, which is always selected when using Scene Intelligent Auto mode, and used for Figure 11.11), plus Low, High, and Disable. Press the INFO. button to add/remove a check mark icon that indicates the Auto Lighting Optimizer is disabled during manual exposure. Since you're likely to be specifying an exposure in Manual mode, you probably don't want the optimizer to interfere with your settings, so disabling the feature is the default.

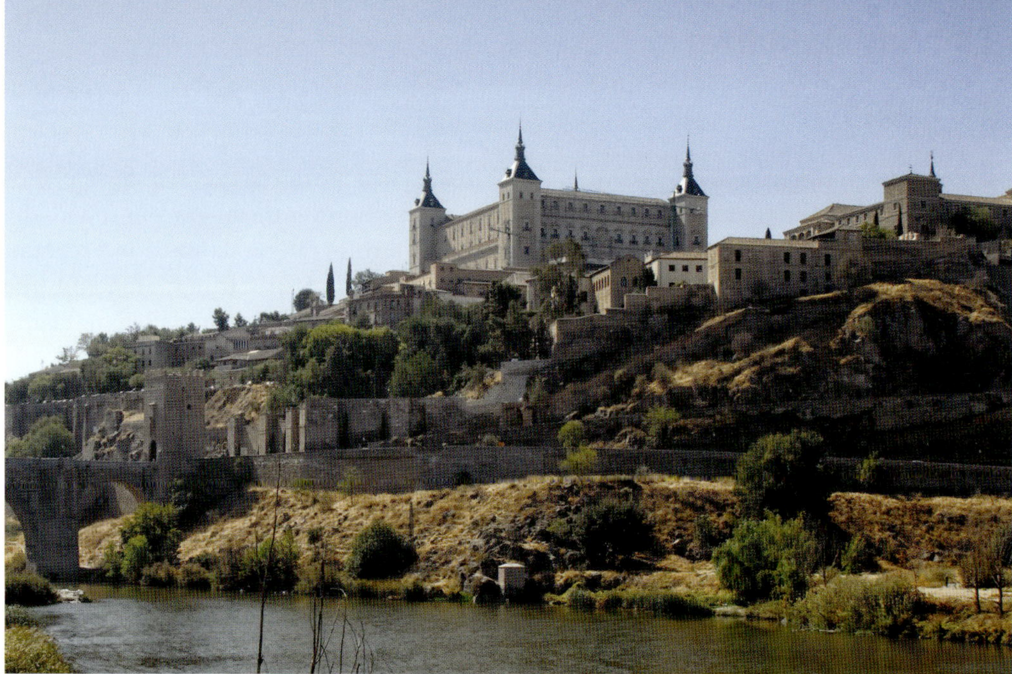

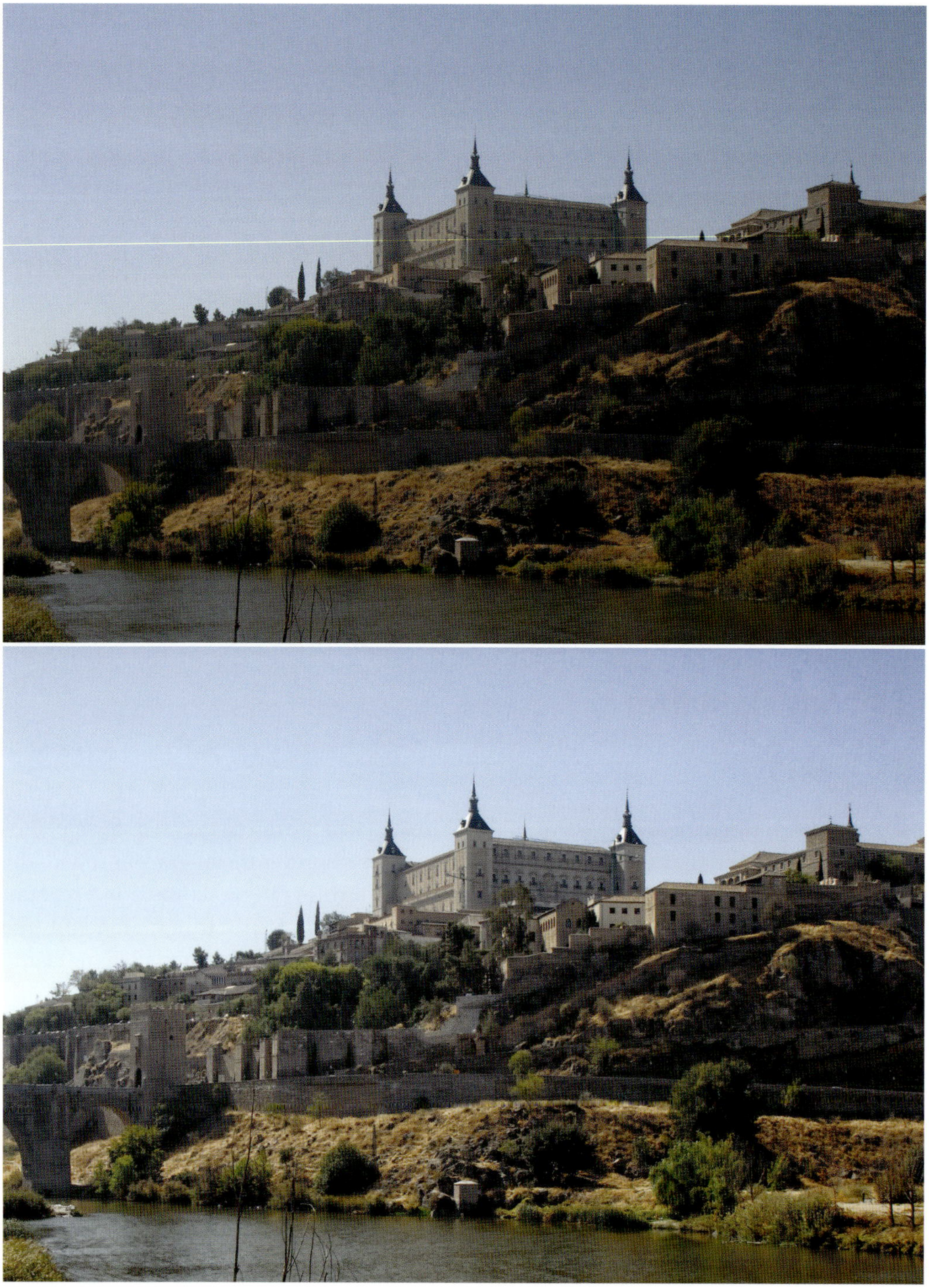

Figure 11.11 Auto Lighting Optimizer can brighten dark, low-contrast images (top), giving them a little extra snap and brightness (bottom).

White Balance

Options: Auto, Daylight, Shade, Cloudy, Tungsten, White fluorescent, Flash, Custom, Color Temperature

My preference: N/A

If automatic white balance or one of the seven preset settings available (Auto, Daylight, Shade, Cloudy, Tungsten, White Fluorescent, or Flash) aren't suitable, you can set a custom white balance using this menu option or a specific color temperature value. The screen shown in Figure 11.12 is identical to the one that pops up when you select White Balance from the Quick Control screen. You can also select White Balance using the Metering Mode/WB button on top of the camera, which produces a slightly different screen that allows you to choose metering mode with the Main Dial, and White Balance with the Quick Control Dial. If you choose the "K" entry, you can select an exact color temperature from 2,500K to 10,000K using the Main Dial.

Of course, unless you own a specialized tool called a color temperature meter, you probably won't know the exact color temperature of your scene. However, knowing the color temperatures of the preset options can help you if you decide to tweak them by choosing a different color temperature setting. The values used by the 5D Mark IV are as follows, with two options available for Auto:

- **Auto (AWB).** 3,000K–7,000K, Press the INFO. button when this is selected to toggle between Ambience Priority (to keep warm color under tungsten light) or White Priority (to produce neutral whites even under tungsten illumination.
- **Daylight.** 5,200K
- **Shade.** 7,000K
- **Cloudy.** 6,000K
- **Tungsten.** 3,200K
- **White fluorescent.** 4,000K

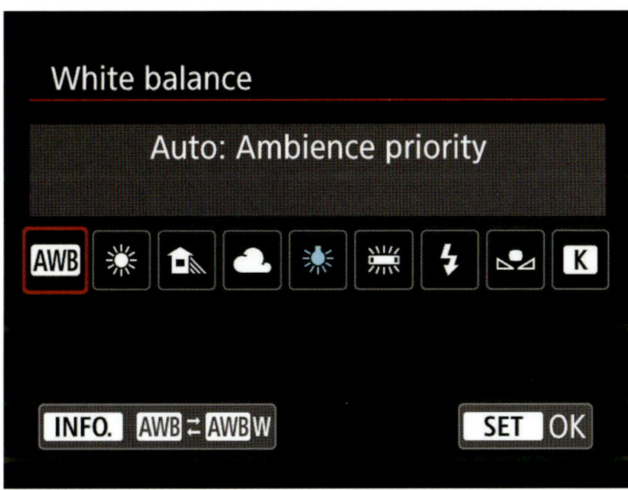

Figure 11.12
White balance presets can be chosen here.

- **Flash.** 6,000K
- **Custom.** 2000K–10000K
- **Color temperature.** 2500K–10000K (Settable in 100K increments)

Choosing the right white balance can have a dramatic effect on the colors of your image, as you can see in Figure 11.13.

The problem with the available presets (Daylight, Shade, etc.) is that you have only six of them, and in any given situation, all of them are likely to be wrong—strictly speaking. The good news is that they are likely to be only a *little bit* wrong. The human eye is very adaptable, so in most cases you'll be perfectly happy with the results you get if you use Auto, or choose a preset that's in the white balance ballpark.

But if you absolutely must have the correct color balance, or are frequently dissatisfied with the color balance the 5D Mark IV produces when using Auto or one of the presets, you can always shoot RAW, and adjust the final color balance in your image editor when converting the .cr2 file. Or, you can use a custom white balance procedure, described next.

If automatic white balance or one of the preset settings aren't suitable, you can set a custom white balance using this menu option. The custom setting you establish will then be applied whenever you select Custom using the White Balance menu entry described earlier.

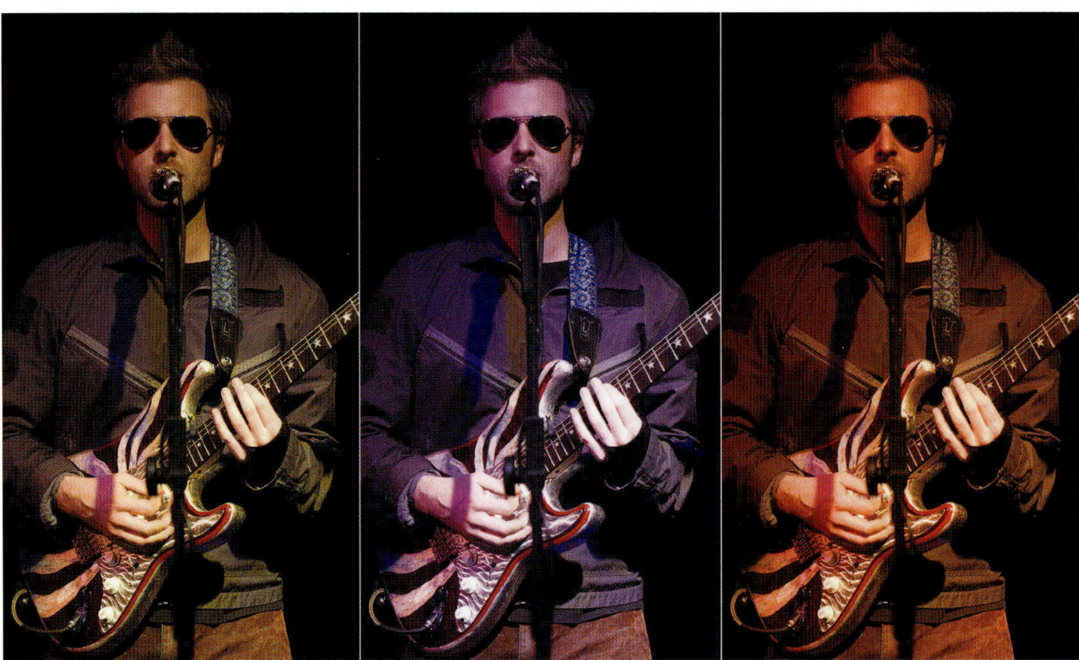

Figure 11.13 Adjusting color temperature can provide different results of the same subject at 3,400K (left), 5,000K (center), and 2,800K (right).

To set the white balance to an appropriate color temperature under the current ambient lighting conditions, focus manually (with the lens set on MF) on a plain white or gray object, such as a card or wall, making sure the object fills the spot metering circle in the center of the viewfinder. Then, take a photo. Next, press the MENU button and select Custom WB from the Shooting 2 menu. Use the Quick Control Dial until the reference image you just took appears and press the SET button to store the white balance of the image as your Custom setting.

Using an ExpoDisc

Many photographers prefer to use a handy gadget called an ExpoDisc, from ExpoImaging, Inc. (www.expoimaging.com), which fits over (or attaches to) the front of your lens and provides a diffuse neutral (or semi-neutral) subject to measure with your camera's custom white balance feature. ExpoDiscs cost $75 to $100 or so, depending on the filter size of your lens, but many just buy the 77mm version and hold it in front of their lens. (There's a strap attached, so you won't lose it.) Others have had mixed success using less-expensive alternatives (such as the lid of a Pringles can). ExpoImaging also makes ExpoCap lens caps with similar diffusing features, and you can leave one of them on your lens at all times (at least, when you're not shooting).

There are two models, the standard ExpoDisc Neutral, and a Portrait model that produces a slightly warmer color balance suitable for portraits. The product produces the best results when you use it to measure the *incident light*; that is, the light falling onto your subject. In other words, instead of aiming your camera at your subject from the shooting position, take the time (if it's possible) to position yourself at the subject position and point your ExpoDisc-equipped lens toward the light source that will illuminate the scene. (However, don't point your camera directly at the sun! Aim at the sky instead.)

I like to use the ExpoDisc in two situations:

- **Outdoors under mixed lighting.** When you're shooting outdoors, you'll often find that your scene is illuminated by direct sunlight as well as by open shade, full shade, or a mixture of these. A custom white balance reading can help you zero in on the correct color balance in a situation that's hard to judge visually.

- **When using studio flash.** It's a nasty secret that many studio flash units change color temperature when you adjust the power slider to scale down the output. Perhaps your 1600ws (watt second) flash puts out too much light to allow you to use a larger f/stop for selective focus. So, you dial it down to 1/4 power. That will likely change the color temperature of the unit slightly, particularly when compared to your 800ws fill light, which you've reduced to *half* power. You can use the ExpoDisc to measure the color temperature of your main light at its new setting, or aim it between two lights to obtain an average reading. The result will probably be close enough to the correct color temperature to satisfy most studio shooters.

Custom White Balance

Options: White balance setting

My preference: N/A

If automatic white balance or one of the preset settings (Daylight, Shade, Cloudy, Tungsten, White Fluorescent, or Flash) aren't suitable, you can set a custom white balance using this menu option. The custom setting you establish will then be applied whenever you select Custom using the White Balance menu.

To set the white balance to an appropriate color temperature under the current ambient lighting conditions, focus manually (with the lens set on MF) on a plain white or gray object, such as a card or wall, making sure the object fills the spot metering circle in the center of the viewfinder. Then, take a photo. Next, press the MENU button and select Custom WB from the Shooting 2 menu. Use the multi-controller until the reference image you just took appears and choose SET to store the white balance of the image as your Custom setting. Only compatible images that can be used to specify a custom white balance will be shown on the screen. Custom white balance images are marked with a custom icon, and cannot be removed (although they can be replaced with a new custom white balance image).

A WHITE BALANCE LIBRARY

Shoot a selection of blank-card images under a variety of lighting conditions on a spare memory card. If you want to "recycle" one of the color temperatures you've stored, insert the card and set the Custom white balance to that of one of the images in your white balance library, as described above.

White Balance Shift/Bracketing

Options: WB bias and WB bracketing

My preference: N/A

White balance shift allows you to dial in a white balance color bias along the blue/yellow-amber dimensions, and/or magenta/green scale. In other words, you can set your color balance so that it is a little bluer or yellower (only), a little more magenta or green (only), or a combination of the two bias dimensions. You can also bracket exposures, taking several consecutive pictures each with a slightly different color balance biased in the directions you specify.

The process is a little easier to visualize if you look at Figure 11.14. The center intersection of lines BA and GM (remember high school geometry!) is the point of zero bias. Move the point at that intersection using the Quick Control Dial to locate it at any point on the graph using the blue/yellow-amber and green/magenta coordinates. The amount of shift will be displayed in the SHIFT box to the right of the graph.

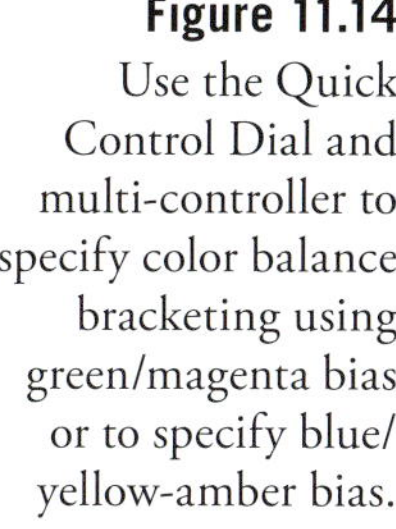

Figure 11.14

Use the Quick Control Dial and multi-controller to specify color balance bracketing using green/magenta bias or to specify blue/yellow-amber bias.

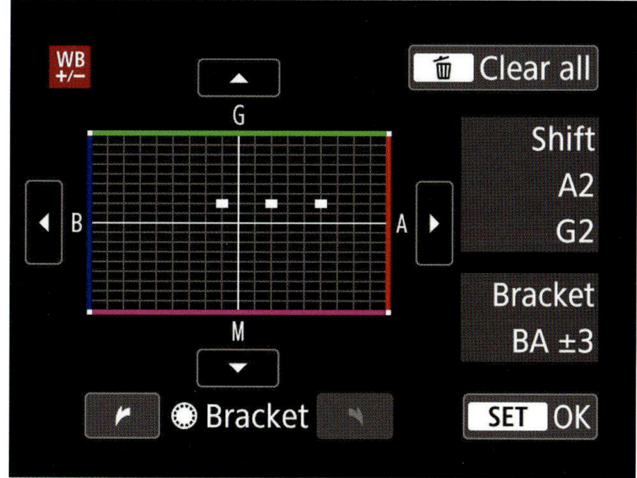

White balance bracketing is like white balance shifting, only the bracketed changes occur along the bias axis you specify. The three squares in Figure 11.14 show that the white balance bracketing will occur in three-stop steps, shifted two increments "up" toward the green bias, and two increments "right" along the blue/yellow-amber axis. The amount of the bracketing is shown in the boxes at the right side of the graph.

This form of bracketing is like exposure bracketing, but with the added dimension of hue. Bias bracketing can be performed in any JPEG-only mode. You can't use any RAW format or RAW+ JPEG format because the RAW files already contain the information needed to fine-tune the white balance and white balance bias.

When you select WB SHIFT/BKT, the adjustment screen appears. First, you press the Quick Control Dial to set the range of the shift in either the green/magenta dimension (move to the left to change the vertical separation of the three dots representing the separate exposures) or in the blue/yellow-amber dimension by pressing to the right. Use the multi-controller to move the bracket set around within the color space, and outside the green/magenta or blue/yellow-amber axes.

In most cases, it's easy to determine if you want your image to be more green, more magenta, more blue, or more yellow-amber, although judging your current shots on the LCD screen can be tricky unless you view the screen in a darkened location so it will be bright and easy to see. Bracketing is covered in Chapter 4.

Color Space

Options: sRGB (default), Adobe RGB

My preference: I use the expanded Adobe RGB color space

When you are using one of the Creative Zone modes, you can select one of two different color spaces (also called *color gamuts*) using this menu entry, shown previously among the other menu choices in Figure 11.9. One color space is named *Adobe RGB* (because it was developed by Adobe Systems in 1998), while the other is called *sRGB* (supposedly because it is the *standard* RGB color space). These two color gamuts define a specific set of colors that can be applied to the images your 5D Mark IV captures.

The Color Space menu choice applies directly to JPEG images shot using P, Tv, Av, and M exposure modes. When you're using Scene Intelligent Auto mode, the 5D Mark IV uses the sRGB color space for all the JPEG images you take. RAW images are a special case. They have the information for *both* sRGB and Adobe RGB, but when you load such photos into your image editor, it will default to sRGB (with Scene Intelligent Auto or Creative Auto shots) or the color space specified here, unless you change that setting while importing the photos. (See the "Best of Both Worlds" sidebar that follows for more information.)

You may be surprised to learn that the 5D Mark IV doesn't automatically capture *all* the colors we see. Unfortunately, that's impossible because of the limitations of the sensor and the filters used to capture the fundamental red, green, and blue colors, as well as that of the elements used to display those colors on your camera and computer monitors. Nor is it possible to *print* every color our eyes detect, because the inks or pigments used don't absorb and reflect colors perfectly. In short, your sensor doesn't capture all the colors that we can see, your monitor can't display all the colors that the sensor captures, and your printer outputs yet another version.

On the other hand, the 5D Mark IV does capture quite a few more colors than we need. The original 14-bit RAW image contains a possible 4.4 *trillion* different hues, which are condensed down to a mere 16.8 million possible colors when converted to a 24-bit (eight bits per channel) image. While 16.8 million colors may seem like a lot, it's a small subset of 4.4 trillion captured, and an even smaller subset of all the possible colors we can see. The set of colors, or gamut, that can be reproduced or captured by a given device (scanner, digital camera, monitor, printer, or some other piece of equipment) is represented as a color space that exists within the larger full range of colors.

That full range is represented by the odd-shaped splotch of color shown in Figure 11.15, as defined by scientists at an international organization called the International Commission on Illumination (usually known as the CIE for its French name *Commission internationale de l'éclairage*) back in 1931. The colors possible with Adobe RGB are represented by the larger, black triangle in the figure, while the sRGB gamut is represented by the smaller white triangle.

Regardless of which triangle—or color space—is used by the 5D Mark IV, you end up with some combination of 16.8 million different colors that can be used in your photograph. (No one image will contain all 16.8 million! If every pixel in a 15-megapixel photo were a different color—which is extremely unlikely—you'd need only 15 million different colors.) But, as you can see from the figure, the colors available will be *different*.

Adobe RGB is what is often called an *expanded* color space, because it can reproduce a range of colors that is spread over a wider range of the visual spectrum. Adobe RGB is useful for commercial and professional printing. You don't need this range of colors if your images will be displayed primarily on your computer screen or output by your personal printer.

Figure 11.15
The outer figure shows all the colors we can see; the two inner outlines show the boundaries of Adobe RGB (black triangle) and sRGB (white triangle).

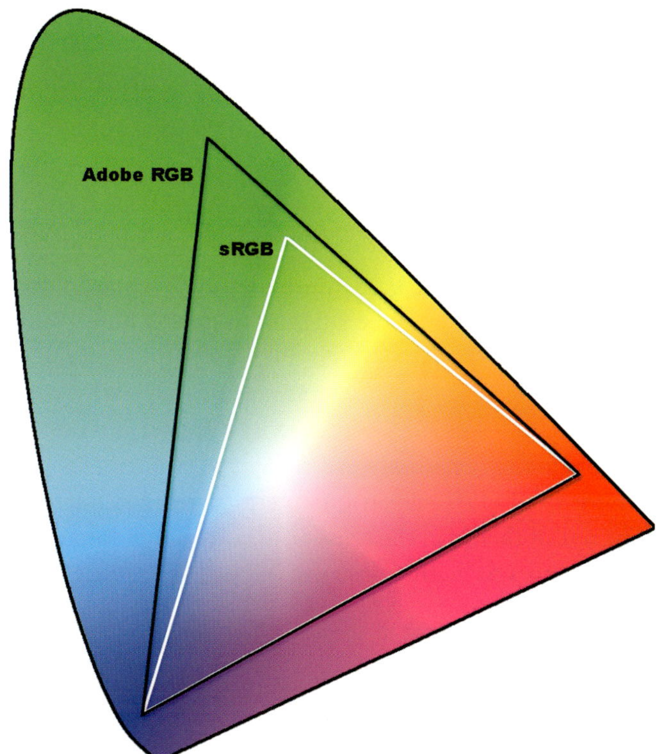

The other color space, sRGB, is recommended for images that will be output locally on the user's own printer, as this color space matches that of the typical inkjet printer fairly closely. While both Adobe RGB and sRGB can reproduce the exact same 16.8 million absolute colors, Adobe RGB spreads those colors over a larger portion of the visible spectrum, as you can see in the figure. Think of a box of crayons (the jumbo 16.8 million crayon variety). Some of the basic crayons from the original sRGB set have been removed and replaced with new hues not contained in the original box. Your "new" box contains colors that can't be reproduced by your computer monitor, but which work just fine with a commercial printing press.

BEST OF BOTH WORLDS

If you choose to set the sRGB color space with this menu entry, you can still easily obtain Adobe RGB versions of your photos if you need them. Just shoot using RAW+JPEG. You'll end up with sRGB JPEGs suitable for output on your own printer, but you can still extract an Adobe RGB version from the RAW file at any time. It's like capturing two different color spaces at once—sRGB and Adobe RGB—and getting the best of both worlds.

Of course, choosing the right color space doesn't solve the problems that result from having each device in the image chain manipulating or producing a slightly different set of colors. To that end, you'll need to investigate the wonderful world of *color management*, which uses hardware and software tools to match or *calibrate* all your devices, as closely as possible, so that what you see more closely resembles what you capture, what you see on your computer display, and what ends up on a printed hardcopy. Entire books have been devoted to color management, and most of what you need to know doesn't directly involve your Canon 5D Mark IV, so I won't detail the nuts and bolts here.

To manage your color, you'll need, at the bare minimum, some sort of calibration system for your computer display, so that your monitor can be adjusted to show a standardized set of colors that is repeatable over time. (What you see on the screen can vary as the monitor ages, or even when the room light changes.) I use a Datacolor (www.datacolor.com) Spyder 4 monitor color correction system for my computer's dual 26-inch wide screen LCD displays. It checks room light levels every five minutes, and reminds me to recalibrate every week or two using a small sensor device that attaches temporarily to the front of the screen and interprets test patches that the software displays during calibration. The rest of the time, the sensor sits in its stand, measuring the room illumination, and adjusting my monitors for higher or lower ambient light levels.

Picture Style

Options: Auto, Standard, Portrait, Landscape, Fine detail, Neutral, Faithful, Monochrome, three User Styles

My preference: Auto

Jump to the Shooting 3 menu, and the entry you'll find at the top of the listings is Picture Style (see Figure 11.16). This feature is one of the most important tools for customizing the way your Canon 5D Mark IV renders its photos. Picture Styles are a type of fine-tuning you can apply to

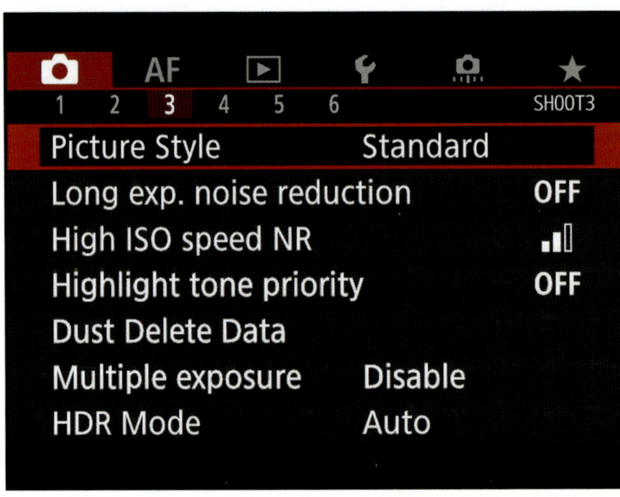

Figure 11.16
Picture Style is the first entry in the Shooting 3 menu.

your photos to change certain characteristics of each image taken using a particular Picture Style setting. The parameters you can specify for full-color images include the amount of sharpness, degree of contrast, the richness of the color, and the hue of skin tones. For black-and-white images, you can tweak the sharpness and contrast, but the two color adjustments (meaningless in a monochrome image) are replaced by controls for filter effects (which I'll explain shortly), and sepia, blue, purple, or green tone overlays.

The Canon 5D Mark IV has preset Picture Styles for Standard, Portrait, Landscape, Fine Detail, Neutral, and Faithful pictures, plus Auto, and three user-definable settings called User Def. 1, User Def. 2, and User Def. 3, which you can define to apply to any sort of shooting situation you want, such as sports, architecture, or baby pictures. There is also a seventh, Monochrome, Picture Style that allows you to adjust filter effects or add color toning to your black-and-white images. See Figure 11.17 for the main Picture Style menu.

Picture Styles are extremely flexible. Canon has set the parameters for Auto and the predefined color Picture Styles and the single monochrome Picture Style to suit the needs of most photographers. But you can adjust any of those "canned" Picture Styles to settings you prefer. Better yet, you can use those three User Definition files to create brand-new styles that are all your own. If you want rich, bright colors to emulate Velvia film or the work of legendary photographer Pete Turner, you can build your own color-soaked style. If you want soft, muted colors and less sharpness to create a romantic look, you can do that, too. Perhaps you'd like a setting with extra contrast for shooting outdoors on hazy or cloudy days.

The current settings for each are arrayed along the top in Figure 11.17 as icons, left to right: S (sharpness strength), F (sharpness fineness), T (sharpness threshold), Contrast (a half white/half black circle), Saturation (a triangle composed of three circles), and Color Tone (a circle divided into thirds). When you scroll down within the Monochrome Picture Style, Filter Effect (overlapping

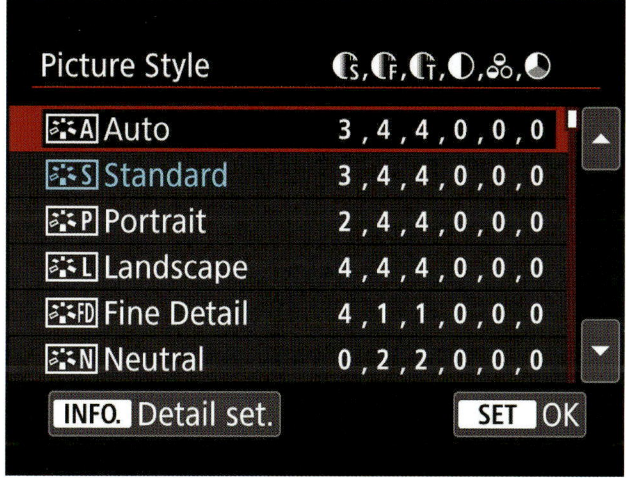

Figure 11.17

Picture Styles are available from this scrolling menu; these six, plus Faithful, Monochrome and three User Def. styles that become visible when you scroll down the list.

circles) and Toning Effect (paintbrush tip) appear. The parameters applied when using Picture Styles are described next.

- **Sharpness.** This parameter determines the apparent contrast between the outlines or edges in an image, which we perceive as image sharpness. When adjusting sharpness, remember that more is not always a good thing. A little softness is necessary (and is introduced by a blurring "anti-alias" filter in front of the sensor) to reduce or eliminate the moiré effects that can result when details in your image form a pattern that is too close to the pattern, or frequency, of the sensor itself. The default levels of sharpening were chosen by Canon to allow most moiré interference to be safely blurred to invisibility, at the cost of a little sharpness. As you boost sharpness (either using a Picture Style or in your image editor), moiré can become a problem, plus, you may end up with those noxious "halos" that appear around the edges of images that have been oversharpened. Use this adjustment with care. You have three individual parameters within this setting that you can adjust individually:

    - **Strength.** Set the intensity of the sharpening on an eight-step scale from 0 (weak outline emphasis) to 7 (strong outline emphasis). Adding too much strength can result in a halo and excess detail around the edges within your image.

    - **Fineness.** This determines which edges will be emphasized, on a scale of 1 (sharpens the finest lines in your image) to 5 (sharpens only larger, coarser lines). Use a lower number if you anticipate your image will have a wealth of fine detail that you want to emphasize, such as a heavily textured subject. A larger number might be better for portraits, so that eyes and hair might be sharpened, but not skin defects. Changes in Fineness and Threshold (which follows) do not apply when shooting movies.

    - **Threshold.** This setting uses contrast between the edges being sharpened and the surrounding areas, to determine the degree of sharpening applied to the outlines. It uses a scale from 1 to 5, with lower numbers allowing sharpening when there is less contrast between the edge and surroundings. There is an increase in noise when a low threshold is set. Higher numbers produce sharpening only when the contrast between edge and adjacent pixels is already high. The highest numbers can produce excessive contrast and a posterlike effect.

- **Contrast.** Use this control, with values from −4 (low contrast) to +4 (higher contrast), to change the number of middle tones between the deepest blacks and brightest whites. Low-contrast settings produce a flatter-looking photo, while high-contrast adjustments may improve the tonal rendition while possibly losing detail in the shadows or highlights.

- **Saturation.** This parameter, adjustable from −4 (low saturation) to +4 (high saturation) controls the richness of the color, making, say, a red tone appears to be deeper and fuller when you increase saturation, and tend more toward lighter, pinkish hues when you decrease saturation of the reds. Boosting the saturation too much can mean that detail may be lost in one or more of the color channels, producing what is called "clipping." You can detect this phenomenon when using the RGB histograms, as described in Chapter 4.

- **Color tone.** This adjustment has the most effect on skin tones, making them either redder (0 to −4) or yellower (0 to +4).

- **Filter effect (Monochrome only).** Filter effects do not add any color to a black-and-white image. Instead, they change the rendition of gray tones as if the picture were taken through a color filter. I'll explain this distinction more completely in the sidebar "Filters vs. Toning" later in this section.

- **Toning effect (Monochrome only).** Using toning effects preserves the monochrome tonal values in your image, but adds a color overlay that gives the photo a sepia, blue, purple, or green cast.

The predefined Picture Styles are as follows:

- **Auto.** Adjusts the color to make outdoor scenes look more vivid, with richer colors.

- **Standard.** This Picture Style applies a set of parameters, including boosted sharpness, that are useful for most picture taking, and which are applied automatically when using Basic Zone modes other than Portrait or Landscape.

- **Portrait.** This style boosts saturation for richer colors when shooting portraits, which is particularly beneficial for women and children, while reducing sharpness slightly to provide more flattering skin texture. The Basic Mode Portrait setting uses this Picture Style. You might prefer the Faithful style for portraits of men when you want a more rugged or masculine look, or when you want to emphasize character lines in the faces of older subjects of either gender.

- **Landscape.** This style increases the saturation of blues and greens, and increases both color saturation and sharpness for more vivid landscape images. The Basic Zone Landscape mode uses this setting.

- **Fine detail.** As you might expect, this setting uses sharpening and contrast to produce an image with optimum detail, at the expense of possibly adding some visual noise.

- **Neutral.** This Picture Style is a less-saturated and lower-contrast version of the Standard style. Use it when you want a more muted look to your images, or when the photos you are taking seem too bright and contrasty (say, at the beach on a sunny day).

- **Faithful.** The goal of this style is to render the colors of your image as accurately as possible, roughly in the same relationships as seen by the eye.

- **Monochrome.** Use this Picture Style to create black-and-white photos in the camera. If you're shooting JPEG only, the colors are gone forever. But if you're shooting JPEG+RAW you can convert the RAW files to color as you import them into your image editor, even if you've shot using the Monochrome Picture Style. Your 5D Mark IV displays the images in black-and-white on the screen during playback, but the colors are there in the RAW file for later retrieval.

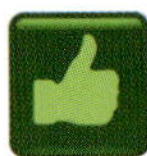

> **Tip**
>
> You can use the Monochrome Picture Style even if you are using one of the RAW formats alone, without a JPEG version. The 5D Mark IV displays your images on the screen in black-and-white, and marks the RAW image as monochrome so it will *default* to that style when you import it into your image editor. However, the color information is still present in the RAW file and can be retrieved, at your option, when importing the image.

Selecting Picture Styles

Canon makes selecting a Picture Style for use very easy, and, to prevent you from accidentally changing an existing style when you don't mean to, divides *selection* and *modification* functions into two separate tasks. There are several different ways to choose from among your existing Picture Styles:

- **Picture Styles menu.** Use this menu entry and scroll down the list shown in Figure 11.17 with the Quick Control Dial or multi-controller until the style you want to use is highlighted. Then press SET.

- **Quick Control screen.** Press the Q button and navigate to the Picture Styles icon at center left of the Quick Control screen with the multi-controller. Press SET, then highlight the Style you want to use and press SET again.

- **Creative Photo button.** The top button in the row of five to the left of the LCD monitor produces a screen allowing you to choose from Picture Style, Multiple Exposure, or HDR. Select Picture Style and press SET and a screen similar to the one shown in Figure 11.18 appears. (This screen is like the one produced by the Quick Control screen.)

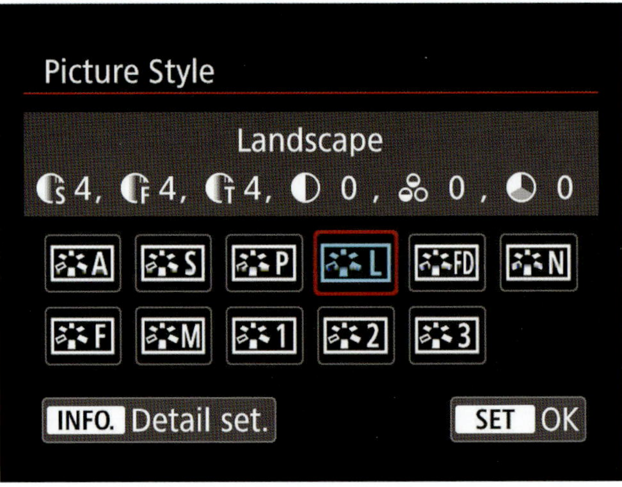

Figure 11.18
Choose Picture Style from the screen produced by the Creative Photo button (a similar screen is summoned from the Quick Control menu).

Defining Picture Styles

Canon makes interpreting current Picture Style settings and applying changes very easy. As you saw in Figures 11.17 and 11.18, the current settings of the visible Picture Style options are shown as numeric values on the menu screen. Some camera vendors use word descriptions, like Sharp, Extra Sharp, or Vivid, More Vivid that are difficult to relate to. You can change one of the existing Picture Styles or define your own whenever the Picture Styles menu is visible. Just press the INFO. button and follow these steps:

1. **Choose a style to modify.** Use the Quick Control Dial to highlight the style you'd like to adjust.

2. **Activate adjustment mode.** Press the INFO. button to choose Detail Set. The screen that appears next will be like the one shown at left in Figure 11.19 for the six color styles or three User Def. styles. The Monochrome screen looks like the one at right in Figure 11.19. In either case, you must scroll down to view all the options.

3. **Choose a parameter to change.** Use the Quick Control Dial to scroll among the parameters, plus Default Set. at the bottom of the screen, which restores the values to the preset numbers.

4. **Activate changes.** Press SET to change the values of a highlighted parameter.

5. **Adjust values.** Use the Quick Control Dial to move the triangle to the value you want to use. Note that the previous value remains on the scale, represented by a gray triangle. This makes it easy to return to the original setting if you want.

6. **Confirm changes.** Press the SET button to lock in that value, then press the MENU button three times to back out of the menu system.

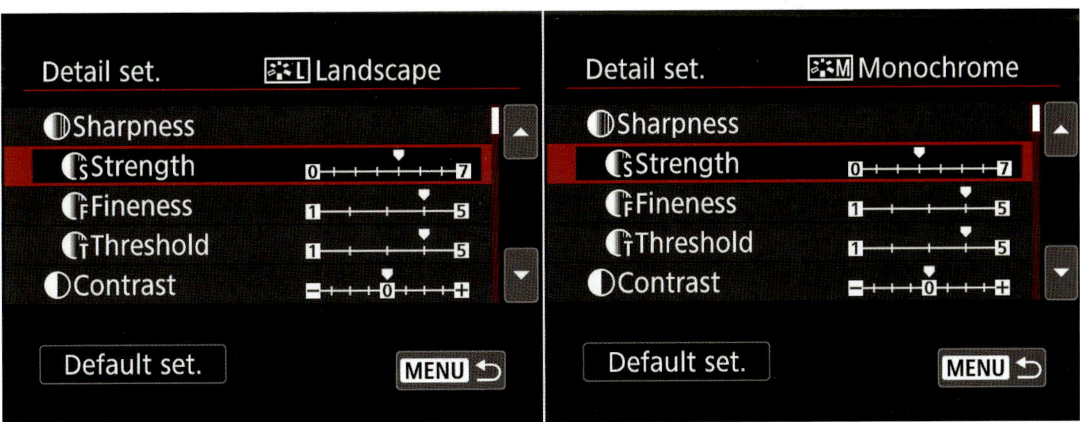

Figure 11.19 Each parameter can be changed separately for color Picture Styles, such as the Landscape style pictured (left), and Monochrome (right).

FILTERS VS. TONING

Although some of the color choices overlap, you'll get very different looks when choosing between Filter Effects and Toning Effects. Filter Effects add no color to the monochrome image. Instead, they reproduce the look of black-and-white film that has been shot through a color filter. That is, Yellow will make the sky darker and the clouds will stand out more, whereas Orange makes the sky even darker and sunsets more full of detail. The Red filter produces the darkest sky of all and darkens green objects, such as leaves. Human skin may appear lighter than normal. The Green filter has the opposite effect on leaves, making them appear lighter in tone. Figure 11.20, left, shows the same scene shot with no filter, then Yellow, Green, and Red filters.

The Sepia, Blue, Purple, and Green Toning Effects, on the other hand, all add a color cast to your monochrome image. Use these when you want an old-time look or a special effect, without bothering to recolor your shots in an image editor. Figure 11.20, right, shows the various Toning Effects available.

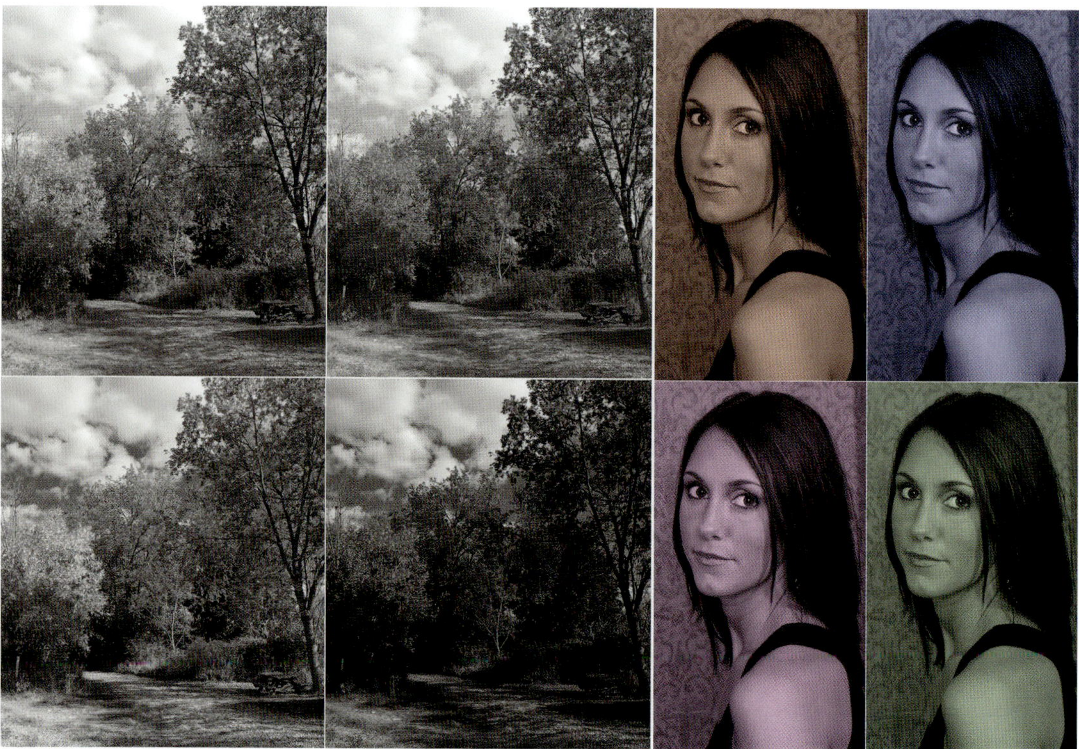

Figure 11.20 Left: Applying color filters: No filter (upper left); Yellow filter (upper right); Green filter (lower left); and Red filter (lower right). Right: Toning: Sepia (top left); Blue (top right); Purple (lower left); and Green (lower right).

Any Picture Style that has been changed from its defaults will be shown in the Picture Style menu with blue highlighting the altered parameter. You don't have to worry about changing a Picture Style and then forgetting that you've modified it. A quick glance at the Picture Style menu will show you which styles and parameters have been changed.

Making changes in the Monochrome Picture Style is slightly different, as the Saturation and Color Tone parameters are replaced with Filter Effect and Toning Effect options. (Keep in mind that once you've taken a JPEG photo using a Monochrome Picture Style, you can't convert the image back to full color.) You can choose from Yellow, Orange, Red, Green filters, or None, and specify Sepia, Blue, Purple, or Green toning, or None. You can still set the Sharpness and Contrast parameters that are available with the other Picture Styles.

Adjusting Styles with the Picture Style Editor

If you'd rather edit Picture Styles in your computer, the Picture Style Editor supplied for your camera in versions for both Windows and Macs allows you to create your own custom Picture Styles, or edit existing styles, including the Standard, Landscape, Faithful, and other predefined settings already present in your 5D Mark IV. You can change sharpness, contrast, color saturation, and color tone—and a lot more—and then save the modifications as a PF2 file that can be uploaded to the camera, or used by Digital Photo Professional to modify a RAW image as it is imported.

To create and load your own Picture Style, just follow these steps:

1. **Load the editor.** Launch the Picture Style Editor (PSE, not to be confused with the *other* PSE, Photoshop Elements).

2. **Access a RAW file.** Load a RAW CR2 image you'd like to use as a reference into PSE. You can drag a file from a folder into the editor's main window, or use the Open command in the File menu.

3. **Choose an existing style to base your new style on.** Select any of the base styles except for Standard. Your new style will begin with all the attributes of the base style you choose, so start with one that already is close to the look you want to achieve ("tweaking" is easier than building a style from the ground up).

4. **Split the screen.** You can compare the appearance of your new style with the base style you are working from. Near the lower-left edge of the display pane are three buttons you can click to split the old/new styles vertically, horizontally, or return to a single image.

5. **Dial in basic changes.** Click the Advanced button in the Tool palette to pop up the Advanced Picture Style Settings dialog box that appears at left in the figure. These are the same parameters you can change in the camera. Click OK when you're finished.

6. **Make advanced changes.** The Tool palette has additional functions for adjusting hue, tonal range, and curves. Use of these tools is beyond the scope of a single chapter, let alone a notation in a list, but if you're familiar with the advanced tools in Photoshop, Photoshop Elements, Digital Photo Pro, or another image editor, you can experiment to your heart's content. Note that these modifications go way beyond what you can do with Picture Styles in the camera itself, so learning how to work with them is worth the effort.

7. **Save your Picture Style.** When you're finished, choose Save Picture Style File from the File menu to store your new style as a PF2 file on your hard disk. Add a caption and copyright information to your style in the boxes provided. If you click Disable Subsequent Editing, your style will be "locked" and protected from further changes, and the modifications you did make will be hidden from view (just in case you dream up your own personal, "secret" style). But you'll be unable to edit that style later. If you think you might want to change your custom Picture Style, save a second copy without marking the Disable Subsequent Editing box.

Uploading a Picture Style to the Camera

Now it's time to upload your new style to your Canon 5D Mark IV into one of your three User Def. slots in the Picture Style array. Just follow these steps:

1. **Link your camera for upload.** Connect your camera to your computer using the USB cable, turn the 5D Mark IV on, launch the EOS Utility, and click the Camera Settings/Remote Shooting choice in the splash screen.

2. **Choose the Shooting menu.** It's marked with an icon of a white camera on a red background, from the menu bar located about midway in the control panel that appears on your computer display.

3. **Select Register User Defined Style.** Click on the box, outlined in red in the figure, to produce the Register Picture Style dialog box.

4. **Choose a User Def. tab.** Click on one of the three tabs, labeled User Def. 1, User Def. 2, or User Def. 3. Each tab will include the name of the current Picture Style active in that tab.

5. **Click the Open File button and choose the Picture Style file to load.** The Picture Styles you've saved (or downloaded from another source) will appear with a PF2 extension. Click on the one you want to use, and then click the Open button in the Open dialog box.

6. **Upload Picture Style to the camera.** The Register Picture Style File dialog box will return. Click OK and the Picture Style will be uploaded to the camera in the User Def. "slot" represented by the tab you've chosen. The name of the Picture Style will appear in the 5D Mark IV's menu in place of User Def. 1 (or User Def. 2/User Def. 3).

Changing a Picture Style's Settings from the EOS Utility

You can modify the settings of a Picture Style that's already loaded into your camera from the EOS Utility when your camera is linked to your computer. Just follow these steps:

1. **Link your camera to the computer.** Connect your camera to your computer using the USB cable, turn the 5D Mark IV on, launch the EOS Utility, and click the Camera Settings/Remote Shooting choice in the splash screen.

2. **Choose the Shooting menu.** It's marked with an icon of a white camera on a red background, from the menu bar located about midway in the control panel that appears on your computer display.

3. **Access the Picture Style.** Click on the Picture Style choice. The currently active Picture Style in the camera will be shown, along with its detail settings.

4. **Choose a Picture Style to modify.** Click the Picture Style box to produce a listing of all the available Picture Styles.

5. **Click Detail Set.** At lower left, Landscape is now highlighted. When you click on Detail Set., a dialog box appears. You can move the sliders to change the settings, as described earlier. You can also click the Default Set. button to return the settings to their original values.

6. **Confirm choice.** Click Return when you've finished making changes, and the Picture Style you've modified will be changed in the camera.

7. **Exit EOS Utility.** Disconnect your camera from your computer, and your modified style is ready to use.

Getting More Picture Styles

I've found that careful Googling can unearth other Picture Styles that helpful fellow EOS owners have made available, and even a few from the helpful Canon company itself. My own search turned up this link: http://web.canon.jp/imaging/picturestyle/file/index.html, where Canon offers a half dozen or more useful PF2 files you can download and install on your own. Remember that Picture Style files are compatible between various Canon EOS camera models (that is, you can use a style created for the Canon 40D with your 5D Mark IV), but you should be working with the latest software versions to work with the latest cameras and Picture Styles. If you installed your software from the CDs that came with your 5D Mark IV, you're safe. If you owned an earlier EOS and haven't re-installed the software since your camera upgrade, you might need to re-install the software. It's available for download from the Canon website.

Try the additional styles Canon offers. They include:

■ **Studio Portrait.** Compared to the Portrait style built into the camera, this one, Canon says, expresses translucent skin in smooth tones, but with less contrast. (Like films in the pre-digital age that were intended for studio portraiture.)

■ **Snapshot Portrait.** This is another "translucent skin" style, but with increased contrast with enhanced contrast indoors or out.

- **Nostalgia.** This style adds an amber tone to your images, while reducing the saturation of blue and green tones.

- **Clear.** This style adds contrast for what Canon says is additional "depth and clarity."

- **Twilight.** Adds a purple tone to the sky just before and after sunset or sunrise.

- **Emerald.** Emphasizes blues and greens.

- **Autumn Hues.** Increases the richness of browns and red tones seen in fall colors.

Long Exposure Noise Reduction

Options: Disable (default), Auto, Enable

My preference: Auto

This entry allows you to enable or disable long exposure noise reduction, or allow the 5D Mark IV to evaluate your scene and decide whether to use this noise-canceling adjustment. Visual noise is that graininess that shows up as multicolored specks in images, and this setting helps you manage it. In some ways, noise is like the excessive grain found in some high-speed photographic films. However, while photographic grain is sometimes used as a special effect, it's rarely desirable in a digital photograph.

The visual noise-producing process is something like listening to a CD in your car, and then rolling down all the windows. You're adding sonic noise to the audio signal, and while increasing the CD player's volume may help a bit, you're still contending with an unfavorable signal-to-noise ratio that probably mutes tones (especially higher treble notes) that you really want to hear.

The same thing happens when the analog signal is amplified: You're increasing the image information in the signal, but boosting the background fuzziness at the same time. Tune in a very faint or distant AM radio station on your car stereo. Then turn up the volume. After a certain point, turning up the volume further no longer helps you hear better. There's a similar point of diminishing returns for digital sensor ISO increases and signal amplification as well.

These processes create several different kinds of noise. Noise can be produced from high ISO settings. As the captured information is amplified to produce higher ISO sensitivities, some random noise in the signal is amplified along with the photon information. Increasing the ISO setting of your camera raises the threshold of sensitivity so that fewer and fewer photons are needed to register as an exposed pixel. Yet, that also increases the chances of one of those phantom photons being counted among the real-life light particles, too.

Fortunately, the 5D Mark IV's sensor and its digital processing chip are optimized to produce the low noise levels, so ratings as high as ISO 800 or ISO 1600 can be used routinely (although there will be some noise, of course), and even ISO 3200 can generate good results.

A second way noise is created is through longer exposures. Extended exposure times allow more photons to reach the sensor, but increase the likelihood that some photosites will react randomly even though not struck by a particle of light. Moreover, as the sensor remains switched on for the longer exposure, it heats, and this heat can be mistakenly recorded as if it were a barrage of photons. This entry can be used to tailor the amount of noise-canceling performed by the digital signal processor.

- **Off/Disable.** Disables long exposure noise reduction. Use this setting when you want the maximum amount of detail present in your photograph, even though higher noise levels will result. This setting also eliminates the extra time needed to take a picture caused by the noise reduction process. If you plan to use only lower ISO settings (thereby reducing the noise caused by ISO amplification), the noise levels produced by longer exposures may be acceptable. For example, you might be shooting a river spilling over rocks at ISO 100 with the camera mounted on a tripod, using a neutral-density filter and long exposure to cause the pounding water to blur slightly. To maximize detail in the non-moving portions of your photos, you can switch off long exposure noise reduction. Because the noise-reduction process used with Auto and On can effectively double the time required to take a picture, Off is a good setting to use when you want to avoid this delay when possible.

- **Auto.** The 5D Mark IV examines your photo taken with an exposure of one second or longer, and if long exposure noise is detected, a second, blank exposure is made and compared to the first image. Noise found in the "dark frame" image is subtracted from your original picture, and only the noise-corrected image is saved to your memory card.

- **On/Enable.** When this setting is activated, the 5D Mark IV applies dark frame subtraction to all exposures longer than one second. You might want to use this option when you're working with high ISO settings (which will already have noise boosted a bit) and want to make sure that any additional noise from long exposures is eliminated, too. Noise reduction will be applied to some exposures that would not have caused it to kick in using the Auto setting.

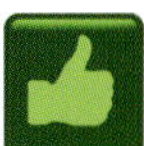

Tip

While the "dark frame" is being exposed, the LCD screen will be blank during Live View mode, and the number of shots you can take in continuous shooting mode will be reduced. White balance bracketing is disabled during this process.

High ISO Speed Noise Reduction

Options: Disable, Low, Standard (default), High, Multi Shot Noise Reduction

My preference: Low, with further noise reduction as required in an image editor

The other type of noise results from using higher ISO settings. This entry allows you to specify just how much or how little of this noise reduction to apply, which can be a valuable option because noise reduction does eliminate detail while blurring the amount of noise. The default is Standard noise reduction, but you can specify Low or High noise reduction, or disable noise reduction entirely. At lower ISO values, noise reduction improves the appearance of shadow areas without affecting highlights; at higher ISO settings, noise reduction is applied to the entire photo. Note that when the High option is selected, the maximum number of continuous shots that can be taken will decrease significantly, because of the additional processing time for the images.

- **Disable.** No additional noise reduction will be applied.
- **Low.** A smaller amount of noise reduction is used. This will increase the grainy appearance, but preserve more fine image detail.
- **Standard.** At lower ISO values, noise reduction is applied primarily to shadow areas; at higher ISO settings, noise reduction affects the entire image.
- **High.** More aggressive noise reduction is used, at the cost of some image detail, adding a "mushy" appearance that may be noticeable and objectionable. Because of the image processing applied by this setting, your continuous shooting maximum burst will decrease significantly.
- **Multi Shot Noise Reduction.** When this option is active, the 5D Mark IV takes four separate shots continuously. It then aligns them (in case there was movement between images) and then merges them, using the dark frame subtraction technique to ignore random pixels caused by noise. The result is a JPEG image that is of better quality than the High setting.

  Multi Shot NR works best if the camera is mounted on a tripod and your subject is not moving. It is not available when Image Quality is set to RAW or RAW+JPEG or Dual Pixel RAW, nor when using flash, live view, shooting multiple or Bulb exposures, or performing autoexposure/white balance bracketing.

Highlight Tone Priority

Options: Disable (default), Enable

My preference: Disable

This setting concentrates the available tones in an image from the middle grays up to the brightest highlights, in effect expanding the dynamic range of the image at the expense of shadow detail. You'd want to activate this option when shooting subjects in which there is lots of important detail in the highlights, and less detail in shadow areas. Highlight tones will be preserved, while shadows will be allowed to go dark more readily (and may exhibit an increase in noise levels). Bright beach or snow scenes, especially those with few shadows (think high noon, when the shadows are smaller) can benefit from using Highlight Tone Priority. Your choices:

- **Disable/OFF.** The 5D Mark IV's normal dynamic range is applied. Note that when Highlight Tone Priority is switched off, the related Auto Lighting Optimizer setting (discussed earlier in this chapter) functions normally.

- **Enable/D+.** Highlight areas are given expanded tonal values, while the tones available for shadow areas are reduced. The ISO 100 sensitivity setting is disabled and only ISO 200 to ISO 32000 (or ISO 200–12800 for movies) are available. You can tell that this restriction is in effect by viewing the D+ icon shown in the viewfinder, on the ISO Selection screen, and in the shooting information display for a particular image. Image noise may slightly increase as the camera manipulates the image. Note that this setting disables the Auto Lighting Optimizer.

Dust Delete Data

Options: Store Delete Data

My preference: N/A

This menu choice lets you "take a picture" of any dust or other particles that may be adhering to your sensor. The 5D Mark IV will then append information about the location of this dust to your photos, so that the Digital Photo Professional software can use this reference information to identify dust in your images and remove it automatically. You should capture a Dust Delete Data photo from time to time as your final line of defense against sensor dust.

To use this feature, select Dust Delete Data, select OK and press the SET button. The camera will first perform a self-cleaning operation by applying ultrasonic vibration to the low-pass filter that resides on top of the sensor. Then, a screen will appear asking you to press the shutter button. Point the 5D Mark IV at a solid-white card with the lens set on manual focus and rotate the focus ring to infinity. When you press the shutter release, the camera takes a photo of the card using Aperture-priority and f/22 (which provides enough depth-of-field [in this case, *depth-of-focus*] to image the dust sharply). The "picture" is not saved to your memory card but, rather, is stored in a special memory area in the camera. Finally, a "Data obtained" screen appears.

The Dust Delete Data information is retained in the camera until you update it by taking a new "picture." The 5D Mark IV adds the information to each image file automatically.

Multiple Exposure

Options: Multiple exposure, Multiple exposure control, Number of exposures, Save source images, Continue multiple exposure, Select image for multi-exposure

My preference: N/A

This option, shown in Figure 11.21, lets you combine two to nine separate images into one photo without the need for an image editor like Photoshop and can be an entertaining way to return to those thrilling days of yesteryear, when complex photos were created in the camera itself. In truth, prior to the digital age, multiple exposures were a cool, groovy, far-out, hep/hip, phat, sick, fabulous way of producing composite images. Today, it's more common to take the lazy way out, snap two or more pictures, and then assemble them in an image editor like Photoshop.

However, if you're willing to spend the time planning a multiple exposure (or are open to some happy accidents), there is a lot to recommend the multiple exposure capability that Canon has bestowed on the 5D Mark IV. For one thing, the camera can combine two or more images using the RAW data from the sensor, producing photos that are blended together more smoothly than is likely for anyone who's not a Photoshop guru. In addition, Canon has eliminated one annoying aspect of the feature found in some cameras: it's not necessary to return to the menu to activate multiple exposure for every set. If you want to take a series of pictures, you can set it once, and forget it. (But don't forget to turn it off when you're done!)

Multiple exposures cannot be captured if white balance bracketing, HDR shooting, or movie-making modes are in use. Before you begin snapping your own multi-exposures, you'll need to set your parameters using the following options discussed below.

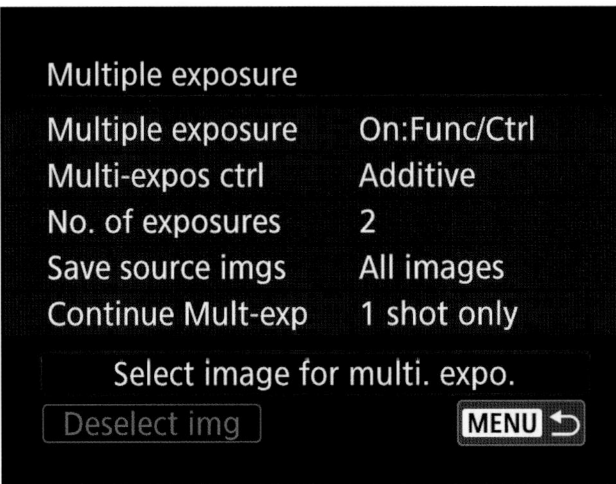

Figure 11.21
Set these parameters to configure your multiple exposures.

Multiple Exposure

The Disable option deactivates the multi-exposure feature, but you can quickly choose either of the two On variations. This is the "master control" that allows you to turn multiple exposure on and off (leaving the other parameters you've set unchanged) and to select from two different multi-exposure modes.

- **Disable.** Deactivates multiple exposure.

- **On: Func/Ctrl.** In the Function and Control Priority mode, the camera snaps off each series, but returns control of the 5D Mark IV to you between each set so you can review your results or make any adjustments in exposure settings or other parameters. I tend to experiment a lot when firing off multiple exposures and prefer this mode for shooting subjects that aren't moving around a lot, and when I want to carefully arrange objects in the frame between shots. Its main disadvantage is that continuous shooting speed is reduced, so it's not the best choice for action.

  Any time during shooting your set when using Function Control Priority, you can press the Playback button to monitor exposure level, overlap alignment, and other factors. If the image doesn't match what you wanted to get, you can press the Trash button and view a set of four options:

  - **Undo last image.** The image you are viewing will be deleted, and the number of remaining shots increases by one.

  - **Save and Exit.** The multiple exposure will be saved, and continued shooting will be aborted. If you've selected All Images for Save Source Images, all the exposures and the merged imaged will be saved. If you've selected Result Only, only the merged image that has already been compiled will be saved. I'll describe the Save Source Images options in more detail shortly.

  - **Exit Without Saving.** Multiple exposure shooting is aborted and no images are saved.

  - **Return to Previous Screen.** Backs up to the last screen viewed.

- **On: ContShtng.** In Continuous Shooting Priority mode, the 5D Mark IV can operate in continuous mode at whatever speed you specify, up to 6 frames per second. I use this when shooting multiple exposures at dance and ballet performances. I can't plan each individual image, anyway, and want to be able to grab separate shots of each movement as they unfold. In this mode, image review, playback, menus, and live view are all disabled while you're shooting. In addition, because of the speed at which images are captured, only the final, combined image is saved on your memory card; the Save Source Imgs option, described below, is disabled. While you can initiate a multiple exposure in this mode while live view is active, the 5D Mark IV flips the mirror back down after the first shot and subsequent images as they are taken can be monitored only through the optical viewfinder.

Multi-Expos Ctrl

This essential parameter can determine how successful your multiple exposure is, by controlling how each individual exposure is merged with the overlapping portions of the other images in the series. Picture an image like the one shown at left in Figure 11.22. The performer, Todd Cooper of the Alan Parsons Live Project, was photographed against a plain, dark background. He happened to be moving, so neither of the two images overlapped with each other, or with any details of the featureless background. But in Figure 11.22, right, the dancer remained in place, so that each subsequent image overlapped the others slightly. The Multi-Exposure Control feature allows you to specify how the images are combined with these choices:

- **Additive.** Each individual shot in the series is, by default, given the full exposure, which is what I used for Figure 11.22, left. Because the background was totally black and the subject was moving and did not overlap, the cumulative exposure effect was to combine two separate images into one image.

   However, you can manually adjust the amount of exposure each shot is given by dialing in exposure compensation, making this mode useful for overlapping images as well. The customary procedure is to specify –1-stop exposure compensation for two shots, –1.5 EV for three-shot multiple exposures, and –2 EV for four-shot multis. Manually calculating the amount of negative exposure compensation allows you to fine-tune the look of overlapping images.

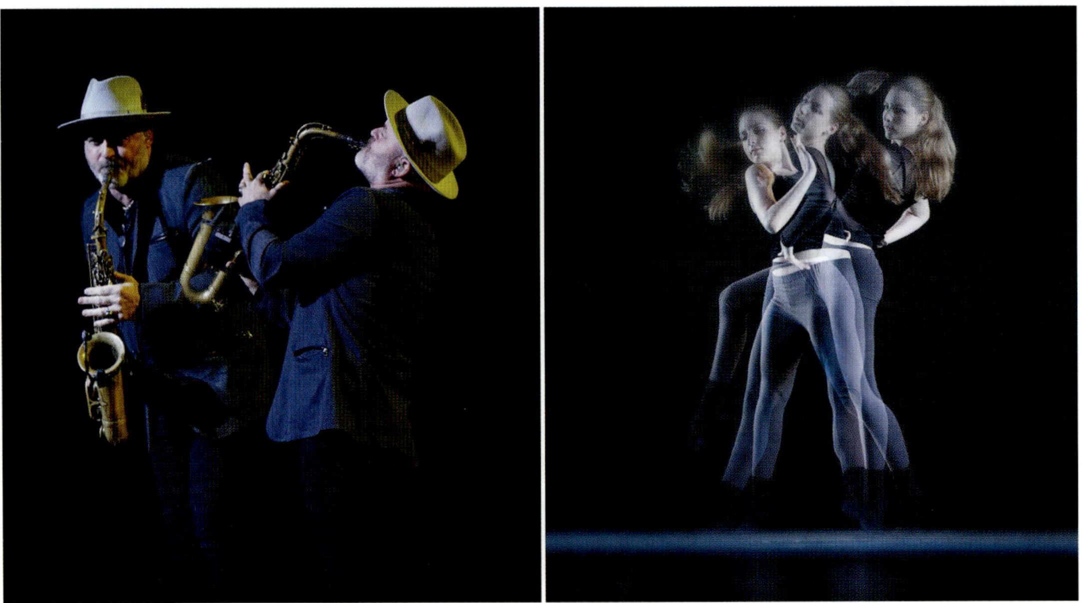

Figure 11.22 Left: Multiple exposure using Additive exposure, and no exposure compensation. Right: Multiple exposure using Average exposure.

- **Average.** Choose this option and the 5D Mark IV will apply appropriate negative exposure compensation for you, based on the number of exposures you're combining into a single image. If your multiple exposures happen to be of the same scene (rather than separate subjects), the camera will attempt to ensure that the background receives the equivalent of a full exposure. I used this option for Figure 11.22, right.

- **Bright.** This mode uses special algorithms to compare the first shot in a series with subsequent images that will be added to that base shot, and then give preference to the brighter parts of the image where pixels overlap. Conceptually, this is like the "lighten" layer merging routines in Photoshop (and other image editors).

- **Dark.** Similar to the Bright option, only preference is given to darker pixels. You may need to use both the Bright and Dark parameters for a while to visualize how they affect your images. I can't really provide hard and fast examples of when to use one or the other; it's a creative process.

No. of Exposures

You can choose from 2 to 9 exposures in each multiple exposure set. Highlight the option, press SET, and spin the QCD to choose the number of exposures. I recommend starting out with three multiple exposures when you begin exploring this tool; you'll quickly discover picture opportunities that call for more or fewer combined shots in a single image.

Save Source Imgs

As you might guess, in producing multiple exposures, the 5D Mark IV takes each shot separately, and then combines them in the camera before saving the combination shot. (In other words, the process is *not* like film multiple exposures, in which the same photosensitive frame collects all the images, adding each subsequent shot to the images that are already there.) Doing it this way keeps the sensor from becoming "overloaded" and losing detail, plus the camera can intelligently combine the images, using exposure compensation and other pixel tricks to produce the final image.

You can elect to save Result Only (just the merged image), or All Images to store each individual image for later use. There are two advantages to the latter approach. You may be able to create a merger of your own manually that is superior to the one generated in the camera. In addition, if one individual shot happens to be a "keeper" on its own, you'll have it available without the distraction of the other merged images. The disadvantage is that saving All Images requires some extra time and memory card space.

Continue Mult-exp

Choose 1 Shot Only or Continuously. Choose the former if you want to take a single multiple exposure series and then return to normal shooting with Multiple Exposure then disabled. Select Continuously if you plan to shoot a batch of different multiple exposures and don't want to return to the menu system to reactivate the feature after each shot.

Select Image for Multi-Exposure

If you like, you can use an image you already took as the base image for a subsequent multi-exposure. The base image can only be a RAW image (not M RAW or S RAW). When RAW images *taken with your camera* (other RAW images on the card cannot be used) are available, this option will be selectable. However, a RAW image that is already a multiple exposure *can* be used as your base image (the mind boggles at the possibilities).

With the option highlighted, press SET and choose the image you want to use. Rotate the QCD to view compatible RAW images and press SET to choose one. Press OK. You can then take the *remaining* exposures in your set. That is, if you've chosen to combine three shots in a multiple exposure, the base image counts as one, so you'll be able to add two more by pressing and holding the shutter release.

Note that images using Highlight Tone Priority or an Aspect Ratio other than 3:2 cannot be used as your base image, and Lens Aberration Correction and Auto Lighting Optimizer will not be applied to your set. If the RAW image specifies the Auto Picture Style, the camera will revert to Standard for the reset of the images.

MULTI NOTES

Some special conditions are required for your 5D Mark IV to shoot multiple exposures. Some features are disabled, and others are locked in at particular values.

- Auto Lighting Optimizer, Highlight Tone Priority, and Peripheral Illumination/Chromatic Aberration Correction are disabled, and the Standard Picture Style will be used if you've chosen the Auto Picture Style setting. Multiple exposures are disabled if your camera is connected to a computer or printer via the USB cable.

- Most settings used for the first shot in a series are locked in for all subsequent images in that series, including image recording quality, ISO sensitivity, Picture Style, high ISO noise reduction, and color space.

- Other functions that cannot be changed while shooting multiple exposures will be dimmed in the camera menu.

HDR Mode

Options: Adjust dynamic range, Effect, Continuous HDR, Auto image align, Save source images
My preference: N/A

I described using the 5D Mark IV's HDR Mode in detail in Chapter 4. To recap, this menu entry has five subentries you can adjust:

- **Adjust dynamic range.** Select Disable HDR, allow the camera to select a dynamic range automatically, or select the range yourself to achieve a particular look. You can choose plus/minus 1, 2, or 3 EV.

- **Effect.** You can add special effects on top of any Picture Style you are using to produce an even more dramatic HDR image. Your choices are as follows:

  - **Natural.** Provides the most useful range of highlight and shadow details.

  - **Art Standard.** Offers a great deal of highlight and shadow detail, but with lower overall contrast and outlines accentuated, making the image look more like a painting. Saturation, bold outline, and brightness are adjusted to the default levels, and tonal range is lower in contrast.

  - **Art Vivid.** Like Art Standard, but saturation is boosted to produce richer colors, and the bold outlines not as strong, producing a poster-like effect.

  - **Art Bold.** Even higher saturation than Art Vivid, with emphasized edge transitions, producing what Canon calls an "oil painting" effect.

  - **Art Embossed.** Reduced saturation, darker tones, and lower contrast give the image a faded, aged look. The edge transitions are brighter or darker to emphasize them.

- **Continuous HDR.** Choose 1 Shot Only if you plan to take just a single HDR exposure and want the feature disabled automatically thereafter, or Every Shot to continue using HDR mode for all subsequent exposures until you turn it off. This is like the multiple exposure option described earlier.

- **Auto image align.** You can choose Enable to have the camera attempt to align all three HDR exposures when shooting hand-held, or select Disable when using a tripod. The success of the automatic alignment will vary, depending on the shutter speed used (higher is better), and the amount of camera movement (less is better!).

- **Save source images.** When the 5D Mark IV has finished creating its HDR image from your three shots, you can choose to save all the images on your memory card (so you can manually combine them later or perform other manipulations using your image editor). Or, you can elect to save your final HDR image only. You might prefer that choice to save card space, reduce the number of images you won't be using anyway, or if shooting a lot of HDR and are confident that the camera's results will suit your needs.

Interval Timer

Options: Disable (default), Enable, Interval, Number of shots

My preference: N/A

This is the first entry on the Shooting 4 menu. (See Figure 11.23.) I explained how to use the Interval Timer in Chapter 6 and will not repeat the discussion here. Press the INFO. button to enter parameters for your timed shoot. Your choices include:

- **Disable/Enable.** Turn the feature on or off.
- **Interval.** Choose the interval between shots up to 99 hours, 59 minutes, and 59 seconds.
- **Number of shots.** Select up to 99 total shots.

Bulb Timer

Options: Disable (default), Enable, Exposure time

My preference: N/A

This feature, available only when the Mode Dial is set to the B (Bulb) position, allows you to specify exposure times up to 99 hours, 59 minutes, and 59 seconds. I described use of this feature in Chapter 6.

Anti-Flicker Shooting

Options: Enable, Disable (default)

My preference: Disable, unless shooting under flickering light source

Novice sports photographers often ask me why shots they take in certain gymnasiums or arenas have inconsistent exposure, wildly varying color, or banding. The answer is that certain types of artificial lighting have a blinking cycle that is imperceptible to the eye, but which the camera can

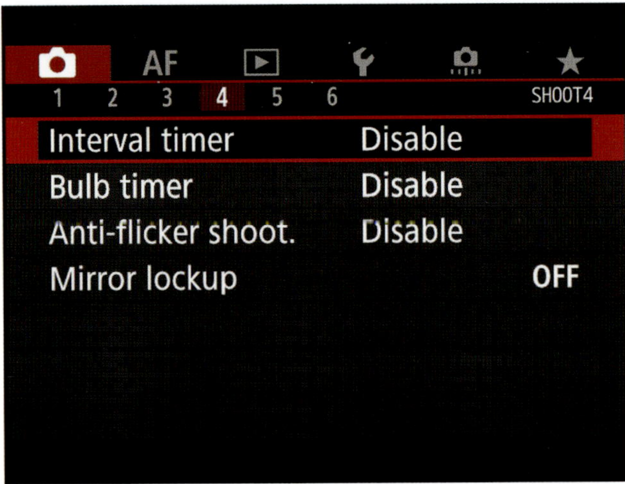

Figure 11.23
The Shooting 4 menu.

capture. This setting, when enabled, detects the frequency (it's optimized for 100 to 120 Hz illumination) of the light source that is blinking, and takes the picture at the moment when the flicker has the least effect on the final image. It cannot be used in live view or movie shooting.

You may experience a slight shutter release time lag as the camera "waits" for the proper instant, and your continuous shooting speed may be reduced, which makes this setting a necessary evil for sports and other activities involving action. Your results may vary when using P or Av modes, because the shutter speed can change between shots as proper exposure requires. You're better off using Tv or M mode, so the shutter speed remains constant.

A handy Flicker! warning will appear in the viewfinder, alerting you that the feature is enabled, as long as you've set Viewfinder Display in the Set-up 2 menu to include that alert. Anti-Flicker is disabled when using Mirror Lockup (explained next), and may not work as well with dark backgrounds, a bright light within the image area, when using wireless flash, and under other shooting conditions. Canon recommends taking test shots to see how effective the feature is under the light source you are working with.

Mirror Lockup

Options: Enable, Disable (default)

My preference: N/A

This option, available only when Anti-Flicker Shooting is disabled, allows you to flip up the 5D Mark IV's mirror prior to exposure. Note that the camera has a second mirror lockup option available under Sensor Cleaning in the Set-up 3 menu. You should be extra careful not to confuse the two. Here is the difference:

- **Mirror lockup.** This option is used while shooting. When enabled from this menu entry, the camera flips the mirror up out of the way when you press the shutter button down all the way. At that point, the viewfinder image will vanish (the mirror is no longer reflecting the image toward the focus screen), and a blinking mirror-up icon appears on the LCD panel. Shooting function settings and menu adjustments are disabled at this point. You must press the shutter release fully a *second* time to take the photo. The net result is that the (minor) vibration caused by the action of the mirror is eliminated, which can be important when shooting with a very long telephoto lens, or taking close-ups.

- **Clean manually.** Select Clean Manually from the Sensor Cleaning entry in the Set-up 3 menu. The mirror will flip up immediately and the shutter will open, exposing the sensor. You can then safely clean your sensor using your favorite method. The shutter won't close and the mirror won't flip down until you power off the camera. The function can't be activated unless your battery or external source has enough power to maintain this configuration.

In general, only advanced dSLRs like the 5D Mark IV offer the Mirror Lockup option in Shooting mode, so you might not even be familiar with its advantages. In recent years, only the cleaning mode mirror flip-up feature has been common. When using Mirror Lockup, keep the following in mind:

- **Avoid excessive lockup times.** Unlike cleaning mode, the shutter remains closed while the mirror is locked up, and, in virtually all cases, a lens will be attached to the camera and focusing light on the sensor plane (or shutter curtains, before exposure). This bright light can damage the shutter, particularly if the camera is accidentally pointed toward the sun. So, a good rule of thumb is to lock up the mirror only just before you want to take the picture (the mirror's vibration will be damped within about one second), and never shoot directly toward the sun. Fortunately, if you lock the mirror up and *don't* take a picture, the mirror will flip back down after 30 seconds automatically.

- **Use a tripod.** Obviously, if you're using mirror lockup to avoid vibration, you're almost certainly working with the camera on a tripod, too. Even with image stabilization, a handheld camera will produce more vibration than any mirror action.

- **Self-timer or remote release recommended.** Even though you've delayed the exposure until mirror vibration has damped, pressing the shutter release (even gently) can introduce a bit of motion to a camera mounted on the sturdiest tripod. The 5D Mark IV's self-timer can be used, but that option doesn't allow you to select the precise moment of exposure. Instead, use a remote release. Perhaps you've framed a shot of some distant wildlife with a super-telephoto. Your first press flips the mirror up to ready the camera for the shot; then, a second or two later your quarry looks toward the camera and you press again to take the picture. With a self-timer, you don't have that flexibility.

- **Self-timer with Bulb exposures.** This combination can be problematic. You'll need to hold the shutter button down during the self-timer countdown when using a Bulb exposure. Releasing the button before the countdown has elapsed eliminates the actual exposure. You'll hear a shutter click, but no picture will be taken. You're better off using a remote release for mirror-up Bulb exposures.

- **No continuous shooting.** Sorry, but you can't lock up the mirror and take a series of shots. Continuous shooting is disabled when Mirror Lockup is active.

Live View Shooting

Options: Enable (default), Disable

My preference: Enable

This menu entry is the first in the Shooting 5 menu (see Figure 11.24). It enables/disables live view shooting and the Live View button. Disabling live view does not affect movie shooting, which is activated by rotating the On/Off/Movie switch to the Movie position and pressing the LV button.

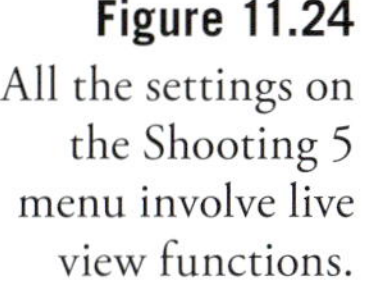

Figure 11.24
All the settings on
the Shooting 5
menu involve live
view functions.

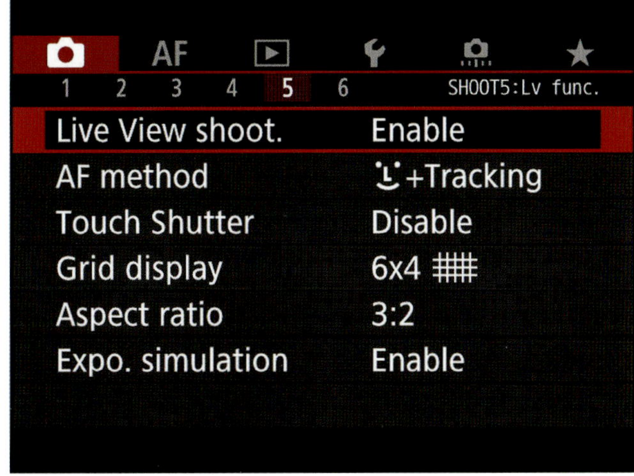

AF Method

Options: Face Detection+Tracking, FlexiZone-Multi, FlexiZone-Single

My preference: FlexiZone-Multi

Here you can select the autofocus mode, Live mode, Face Detection Live mode, and Quick mode, all explained at length in Chapter 5. This menu entry enables and disables the Continuous AF feature, which is the live view equivalent of the AI Servo mode explained in Chapter 5. When activated, the 5D Mark IV will refocus on objects as their distance from the camera changes. The feature is automatically disabled when you choose Quick mode focus.

Touch Shutter

Options: Enable (default), Disable

My preference: N/A

Here you can select the autofocus mode, Live mode, Face Detection Live mode, and Quick mode, all explained at length in Chapter 5. This menu entry enables and disables the Continuous AF feature, which is the live view equivalent of the AI Servo mode explained in Chapter 5. When activated, the 5D Mark IV will refocus on objects as their distance from the camera changes. The feature is automatically disabled when you choose Quick mode focus.

Grid Display

Options: Off, 3 × 3, 6 × 4, 3 × 3+Diagonal

My preference: Off

When enabled, this setting overlays Grid 1 on the screen to help you compose your image and align vertical and horizontal lines, or Grid 2, which consists of four rows of six boxes, which allows finer control over placement of images in your frame. Grid 3 adds diagonal lines. (See Figure 11.25.)

Aspect Ratio

Options: 3:2 (default), 4:3, 16:9, 1:1

My preference: 3:2

Allows you to choose an aspect ratio, or proportions of your image, from 3:2, 4:3, 16:9, or 1:1. JPEG images will be stored using the selected ratio; RAW images will be saved using the default 3:2 proportions, but the desired cropping can be restored in your image-editing software. In Custom Function 2 menu, you can choose either Masked or Outlined for LV Shooting Area Display. The former completely obscures with a black mask the area outside your selected aspect ratio; the latter marks the aspect ratio with lines, but allows you to see the area you are cropping out (this is useful for sports when moving subjects may be entering or leaving the masked area). Note that choosing Off for Custom Function 3 menu's Add Cropping Information entry disables this feature entirely.

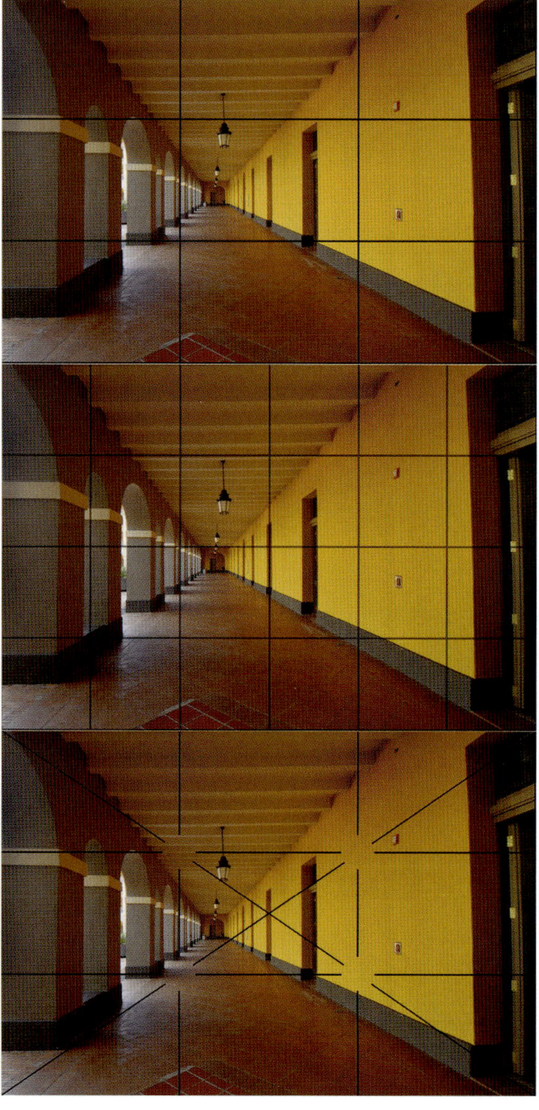

Figure 11.25 Three grids are available to help you align horizontal and vertical subjects.

Selecting proportions other than the 3:2 default results in a cropped image, and the live view display provides a black border on the LCD to show the limits of the image area (see Figure 11.26). At the Large or RAW size setting, you end up with images that measure 6720 × 4480 /30.1MP (3:2 ratio); 5952 × 4480 /26.7MP (4:3 ratio); 6720 × 3776 /25.4MP (16:9 ratio); and 4480 × 4480 /20.1MP (1:1 ratio). At Medium (M), Small 1 (S1), Small 2 (S2), and Small 3 (S3), the images are proportionately smaller.

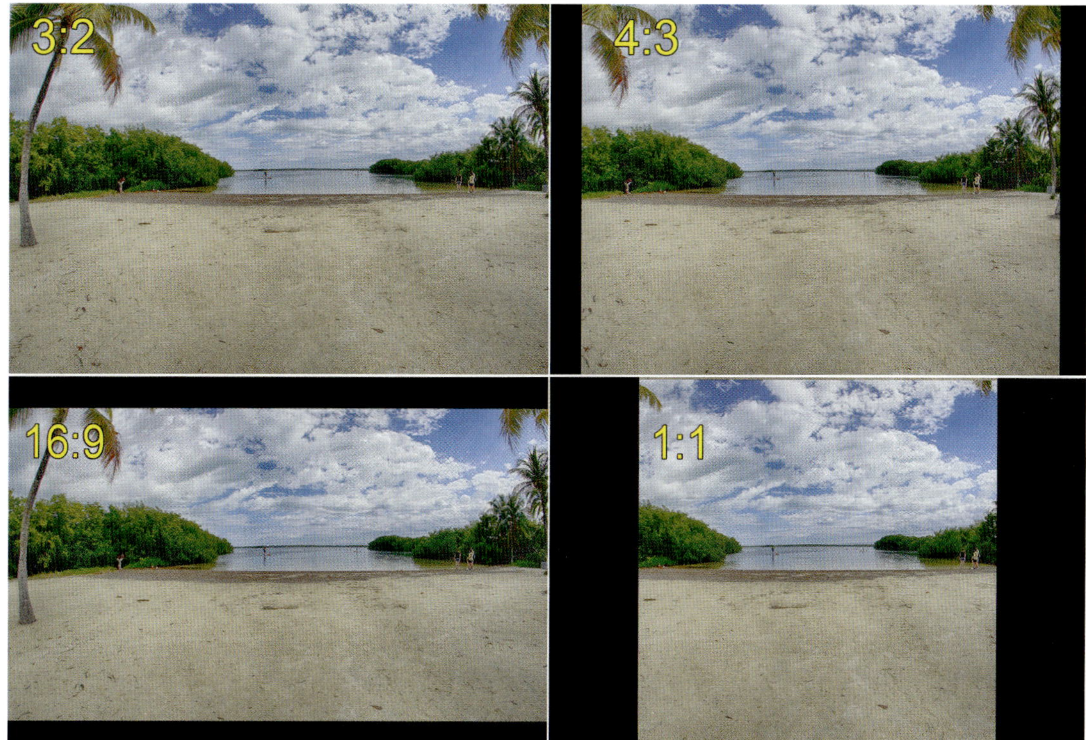

Figure 11.26 You can choose the proportions of your image.

Exposure Simulation

Options: Enable (default), During DOF Preview, Disable

My preference: During DOF Preview

This option allows you to choose whether the live view image mimics the exposure level of the final image, or whether the screen displays a bright image (dependent on the LCD Brightness setting you've specified in the Set-up 2 menu) that may be easier to view under high ambient lighting conditions. Your choices are as follows:

- **Enable.** The live view image on the screen corresponds to the brightness level of the actual image based on the current exposure settings, including any exposure compensation you've specified. Use this option when you want to be able to roughly (but not precisely) monitor the effects of your exposure settings in live view.

- **During DOF Preview.** The live view image is displayed at standard brightness, but will be adjusted to simulate your exposure settings when you press the depth-of-field preview button. This is your best option when you might want to check exposure from time to time during a shooting session. It's the setting I use most often, because I can compose with a big, bright screen, but still stop down to the aperture that will be used and view the effects.

■ **Disable.** The 5D Mark IV ignores any exposure settings and compensation, and shows the live view image at standard brightness. This setting is useful outdoors in full sunlight, because any exposure simulation (dimmed LCD) will be difficult to interpret under high ambient lighting anyway.

Silent LV Shooting

Options: Mode 1 (default), Mode 2, Disable

My preference: Mode 1

This is one of two settings in the Shooting 6 menu (not illustrated). Although it's not possible to completely silence the 5D Mark IV's shutter noise, Canon gives you two options for making the *ker-clunk* a bit less intrusive. Because Live View mode eliminates the noisy mirror-flap action, silent live view shooting *is* fairly quiet. Silent shooting is not available when using an electronic flash, and you'll end up with inconsistent exposures if you use either Mode 1 or Mode 2 with a lens mounted on an extension tube, or if you are working with a Canon tilt-shift (TS-E) lens other than the TS-E17mm f/4L or TSE-E24mm f/3.5L II lenses. Your options are as follows:

■ **Mode 1.** This mode produces a quieter shooting sound level in Live View mode, and enables continuous shooting at up to 7 fps.

■ **Mode 2.** This mode, technically, isn't any quieter, but it separates the *ker* from the *clunk* sounds. Press the shutter release all the way, and the camera emits a small click as the picture is taken, and then camera operation is suspended as long as you hold the shutter button down. If you like, you can wait a moment or two before releasing the button to the halfway position or completely, which produces a second quiet click. It's a tiny bit less intrusive than Mode 1, and with enough ambient sound around you, is the closest you'll get to silent shooting with a digital SLR. Continuous shooting can be specified, but is disabled in this mode. Only a single picture will be exposed. The camera ignores this setting if you're using a remote control, and defaults to Mode 1.

■ **Disable.** Turns off the silent shooting feature, although the resulting noises are roughly the same as Mode 1.

Metering Timer

Options: 4 sec., 8 sec. (default), 16 sec., 30 sec., 1 min., 10 min., 30 min.

My preference: 8 sec. most of the time; I switch to 10 min. when shooting sports

This option allows you to specify how long the EOS 5D Mark IV's metering system will remain active before switching off. Tap the shutter release to start the timer again after it switches off.

12

Customizing with the Autofocus Menus

This chapter contains descriptions of some of the more esoteric options available for the Canon EOS 5D Mark IV's complex autofocus system. Except for the Case options in the AF 1 menu, these are the settings that you'll probably set once and forget for a while, or, at least, until you decide to make a significant change in your camera's autofocus behavior.

As much as I would have liked to present one huge, 100-page chapter on autofocus, it made more sense to describe the basic functions and settings in-depth in Chapter 5, and retain the lesser-used AF menu descriptions here with the camera's other menus. I think the need to jump back and forth will be minimal, although, as with any camera manual, you may need a review of other chapters from time to time as a refresher.

AF 1 Menu

Options: Case 1, Case 2, Case 3, Case 4, Case 5, Case 6

My preference: N/A

This is the menu used to select from among six different factory preset "Cases" with autofocus settings suitable for various types of action scenes. You can also modify those presets to adjust the sensitivity of the camera during tracking of moving objects, its response to acceleration and deceleration, and how quickly it switches between autofocus points as subjects move through the frame.

The icons in the left edge (see Figure 12.1) provide pictogram reminders showing the types of action each Case is designed to cover. Highlight the Case you want to use and press SET to confirm. To change any of the three parameters, press the RATE button and use the QCD, touch screen, or

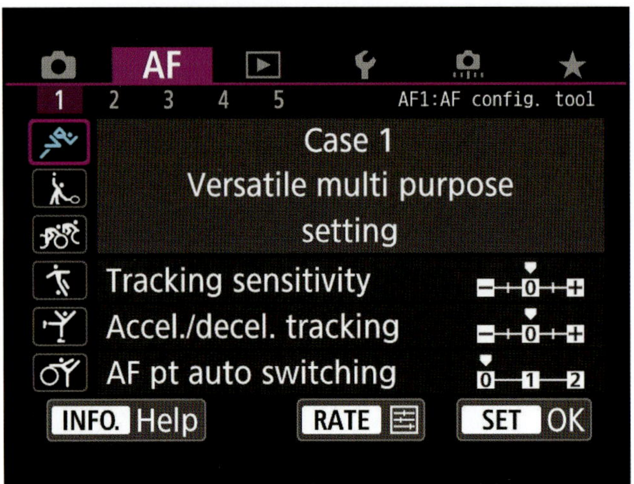

Figure 12.1
The AF 1 menu.

multi-controller joystick to adjust the sliding indicator. The Mark IV provides helpful information about each Case at the press of the INFO. button, and you can read my own detailed recommendations for this menu in Chapter 5. To recap, the parameters you can change include:

- **Tracking sensitivity.** Determines how swiftly the AF system refocuses on a new subject that enters the focus area. Your choices are –2 (Locked On) to +2 (Responsive). Negative numbers allow you to retain focus on the original subject even if it briefly leaves the area covered by the focus points, making tracking easier. Positive numbers switch more quickly to a new subject.

- **Acceleration/deceleration tracking.** Determines how the AF system responds to sudden acceleration, deceleration, or stopping. Your choices are 0 (constant speed) to 2 (sudden changes).

- **AF point auto switching.** Determines how quickly the AF system changes from the current AF point to an adjacent one when the subject moves away from the current point, or an intervening object moves across the frame into the area interpreted by the current point. Your choices are 0 (slower tracking response) to 2 (faster response). This parameter operates in 61 Point Auto Selection, Zone AF, and AF Point Expansion area selection modes.

While you can adjust these parameters for any case, you may find their default values useful:

- **Case 1: Versatile multi-purpose setting.** All-purpose setting that works well with many moving subjects, including motor sports and track, especially with subjects moving toward or away from you.

- **Case 2: Continue to track subject, ignoring possible obstacles.** Excellent for football and other sports where an intervening subject may pass in front of your primary subject. The camera will delay refocusing on the new object long enough to resume following the original subject.

- **Case 3: Instantly focus on subjects suddenly entering AF points.** Ideal when you're photographing a static scene, waiting for a moving subject, such as the winner of a race, a skier, or a bicyclist.

- **Case 4: For subjects that accelerate or decelerate quickly.** I prefer this Case for basketball and soccer, because you can have players racing toward you one instant, and crossing your field of view the next.

- **Case 5: For erratic subjects moving quickly in any direction.** This is my choice for hockey games and anything that involves skates—as well as small children and pets. It's also excellent for that most difficult of subjects: birds in flight.

- **Case 6: For subjects that change speed and move erratically.** This works with 61 Point Auto Selection, Zone AF, and AF Point Expansion area selection modes. (In other words, it doesn't operate with Single-Point Spot AF or Single-Point AF manual selection modes.) An alternative case for basketball, small children, and pets.

See Chapter 5 for step-by-step instructions for adjusting the values of any of the six AF Cases.

AF 2 Menu

This menu has only two options, both of which deal with how the Mark IV autofocuses for the first and second shots in a continuous series when you're working with the AI Servo autofocus mode. The individual options determine whether the camera gives priority to focus (delaying taking a picture until the AF process is complete), or priority to a press of the shutter button (taking the picture when the release is pressed down all the way). Your preference will depend on what type of picture you're taking, as I'll describe next. (See Figure 12.2.)

Figure 12.2
The AF 2 menu.

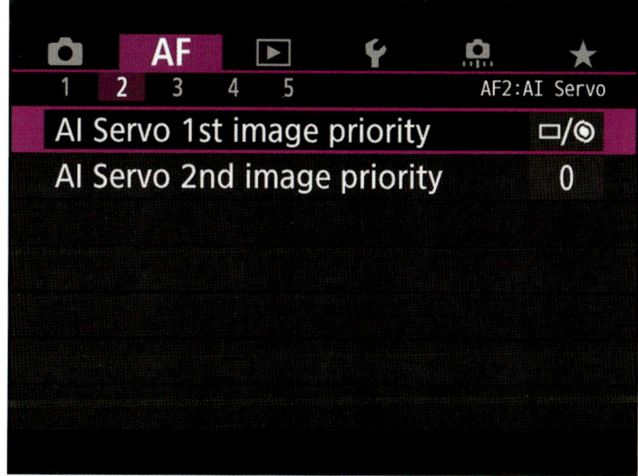

AI Servo 1st Image Priority

Options: Release priority, Equal priority (default), Focus priority

My preference: Release priority for sports, Equal priority for most other subjects

This setting determines the point at which the Mark IV locks in focus when you push the shutter button all the way down when taking a series of photographs. Remember that if you're using a small f/stop with extended depth-of-field, your chances of getting a shot with acceptable depth-of-field are improved at any of these settings. Also, keep in mind that you can further tweak autofocus responsiveness using the AF 1 Case options described in Chapter 5.

Use the Quick Control Dial or multi-controller joystick to move the indicator to any of three positions (see Figure 12.3):

- **Release priority.** The shutter will fire immediately, even if sharp focus has not yet been achieved. Use this setting when getting the shot—any shot—is crucial, and a slightly out-of-focus image would be preferable to none at all. Whether you're a photojournalist or a proud parent snapping Baby's first steps, you'd probably prefer not to miss the shot because the camera is still fine-tuning focus. The 5D Mark IV focuses so quickly that, unless your subject is low in contrast or otherwise problematic, release priority will probably give you a good shot nearly all the time. Remember that if you're using a small f/stop with extended depth-of-field, your chances of getting a shot with acceptable depth-of-field are improved even though you're using release priority.

- **Equal priority.** If focus is important to you, try out this balanced setting that will give the camera a little extra time—but not too much—and improve your chances of getting a precisely focused image without inordinate delay.

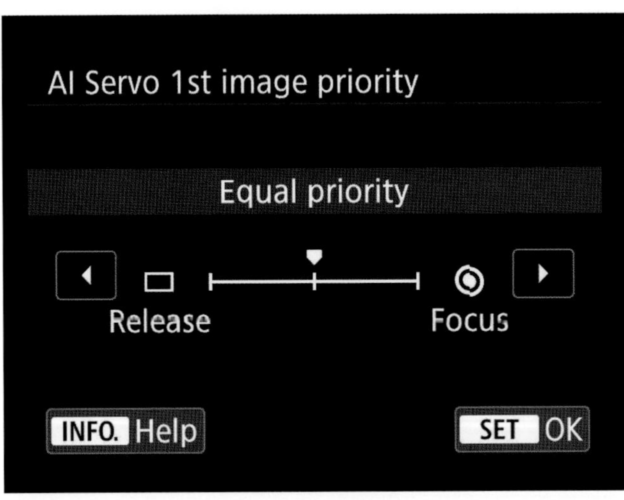

Figure 12.3
Set first image priority.

■ **Focus priority.** Sometimes, accurate focus is all-important, and with a leisurely shooting pace you might not mind waiting an extra fraction of a second while the AF system "hunts" to achieve precise autofocus when faced with the occasional more difficult subject. I tend to use this setting for everything except action shots and birds in flight, because my speedy Mark IV usually doesn't introduce much of a delay as it autofocuses.

AI Servo 2nd Image Priority

Options: Speed priority, Equal priority (default), Focus priority

My preference: Speed priority for sports, Equal priority for most other subjects.

Most of us have an itchy trigger finger, so the first photograph in a series may not capture the decisive moment. When shooting bursts, the Mark IV can continue to fine-tune focus for the second and subsequent images in the series, using the priority you set here. The parameters are similar to those of the previous setting (see Figure 12.4):

■ **Speed priority.** Since this is the second (or ongoing) shot, the shutter has already fired at least once, so this setting tells the camera to keep the same focus setting and continue capturing images. Note that you can select this option regardless of what parameter you've specified for the *first* shot. So, if you've chosen focus priority for the initial image, selecting this setting is a safe bet *if your subject is not moving* quickly enough to require additional focus fine-tuning. But if you selected release priority for the first image, using this setting may mean that the first and all subsequent images may be a little (or a lot) out of focus.

■ **Equal priority.** This balanced setting allows you to express your trust that the Mark IV will provide a reasonable compromise between speed and focus for all images captured after the first.

■ **Focus priority.** Selecting this option can slow down the continuous shooting speed of your camera, but will almost ensure getting a series of shots that are in optimum focus.

Figure 12.4
Set priority for second and subsequent images.

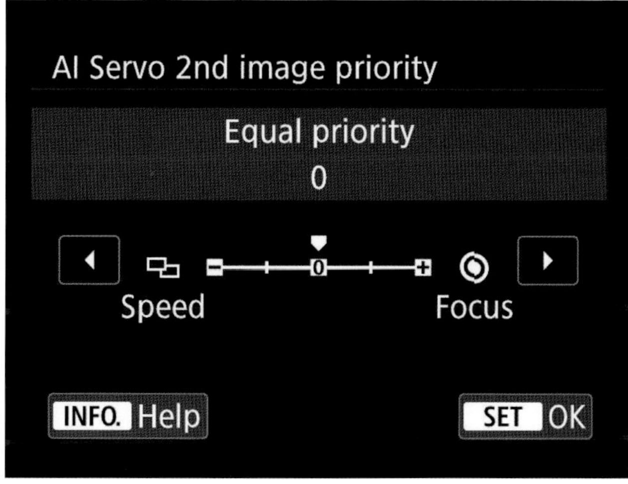

AF 3 Menu

The AF 3 menu (see Figure 12.5) has three entries, all of them easy to understand.

Lens Electronic MF

Options: Enable after One-Shot AF (default), Disable after One-Shot, Disable in AF mode

My preference: Enable after One-Shot AF

A limited number of ten extra-fast Canon prime lenses and one zoom—all of them L lenses with ultrasonic motors—feature super-sensitive electronic focusing rings you can use to fine-tune focus manually after focus has been locked in using One-Shot AF. You might want to disable the use of this ring when using one of the compatible lenses, because even a casual bump against the ring can change focus significantly. The lenses in question are as follows:

EF50mm f/1.0L USM	EF300mm f/2.8L USM	EF600mm f/4L USM
EF85mm f/1.2L USM	EF400 f/2.8L USM	EF1200 f/5.6L USM
EF85mm f/1.2L II USM	EF400mm f/2.8L II USM	EF200mm f/1.8L USM
EF500mm f/4.5L USM	EF28-80mm f/2.8-4L USM	EF40mm f/2.8 STM
EF50mm f/1.8 STM	EF24-105mm f/3.5-5.6 STM	

You have three choices:

- **Enable after One-Shot AF.** When active, you can continue to hold the shutter release halfway, while adjusting focus manually. I use this when shooting portraits with my 85mm f/1.2 lens at a large aperture, allowing me to zero focus in on the near eye of a subject seated on a diagonal angle.

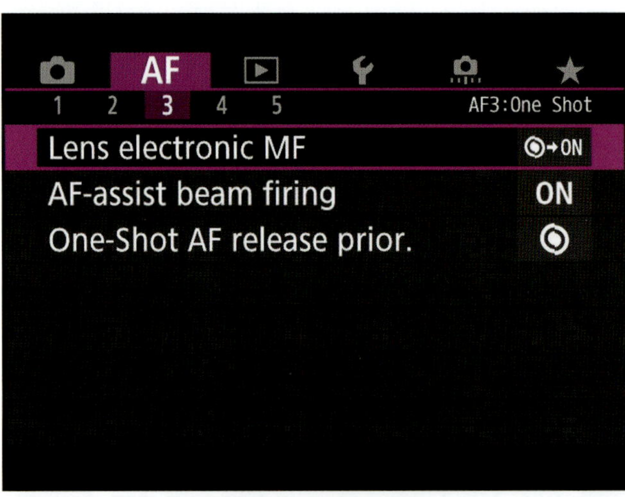

Figure 12.5
The AF 3 menu has just three entries.

- **Disable after One-Shot AF.** Manual focus is disabled. Use this when you are satisfied with the focus set by the camera's autofocus system and don't want to manually tweak it. Remember that if you truly want to use manual focus and bypass the AF system entirely, just slide the AF/MF switch on the lens to the MF position.

- **Disable in AF mode.** Turns off the feature entirely.

AF-Assist Beam Firing

Options: Enable (default), Disable, IR AF assist beam only

My preference: IR AF assist beam only

This setting determines when bursts from an electronic flash are used to emit a pulse of light that helps provide enough contrast for the EOS 5D Mark IV to focus on a subject. You can select Enable to use an attached Canon Speedlite to produce a focus assist beam. Use Disable to turn this feature off if you find it distracting. Keep in mind that if you select Enable and the Speedlite's own AF-Assist Beam Firing is set to Disable, the AF-assist beam will not be emitted (the flash's setting takes precedence).

- **Enable.** The AF-assist light is emitted by the camera's external flash whenever light levels are too low for accurate focusing using the ambient light.

- **Disable.** The AF-assist illumination is disabled. You might want to use this setting when shooting at concerts, weddings, or darkened locations where the light might prove distracting or discourteous.

- **IR AF Assist beam only.** Some Canon flash units, such as the Speedlite 600EX-RT II, have a near-infrared pattern assist beam. Select this option to disable visible light flashes and activate only the less-obtrusive IR beam. Because AF assist is intrusive for the types of subjects I shoot, I prefer to use it only when an IR assist is available from my Speedlite.

One-Shot AF Release Priority

Options: Release priority, Focus priority (default)

My preference: Release priority for sports, Equal priority for most other subjects

This setting can be used to specify whether One-Shot AF uses Focus Priority (the default) or Release Priority. Both modes were described earlier in the AF 2 menu discussion.

AF 4 Menu

The AF 4 menu has seven options, shown in Figure 12.6, all but the first dealing with the selection of AF points and zones.

Lens Drive When AF Impossible

Options: Continue focus search (default); Stop focus search

My preference: Stop focus search

When a scene has little inherent contrast (say, a blank wall or the sky) or if there isn't enough illumination to allow determining contrast accurately (in low light levels, or with lenses having maximum apertures of less than f/5.6), a lens may be unable to achieve autofocus. Very long telephoto lenses suffer from this syndrome because their depth-of-field is so shallow that the correct point of focus may zip past during the AF process before the AF system has a chance to register it.

Use this setting to tell the 5D Mark IV either to keep trying to focus if AF seems to be impossible or to stop seeking focus. Your choices are as follows:

- **Continue Focus Search.** The 5D Mark IV will keep trying to focus, even if the effort causes the lens to become grossly out of focus. Use this default setting if you'd prefer that the lens keep trying. Sometimes you can point the lens at an object with sufficient contrast at approximately the same distance to let the AF system lock on, then reframe your original subject with the hope that accurate focus will now be achieved.

- **Stop Focus Search.** When this option is selected, the camera will stop trying to focus uselessly, allowing you to attempt to manually bring the subject into focus. This setting is best for very long telephoto lenses (around 400mm and up), because they encounter AF difficulties more than most lenses, and are less likely to benefit from extended "hunting."

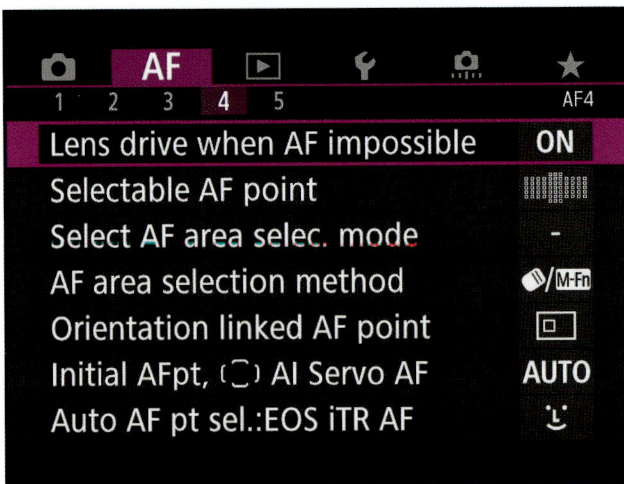

Figure 12.6
The AF 4 menu has seven options.

Selectable AF Point

Options: All points (default), Only cross-type AF points, 15 points, 9 points

My preference: All points

While the Mark IV always uses all 61 AF points (if available with your lens/aperture) when selecting a point automatically, if you're using one of the focus modes that allow specifying the initial focus point or zone, you can select which points will be available. The unavailable points will not be displayed when you press the Point Selection button in the upper-right corner of the back panel. Your options include:

- **All points.** Any of the available 61 focus points can be selected manually. This is my everyday mode. I use the others described next only in specialized situations given in the examples.

- **Only Cross-Type AF points.** Only the (up to) 41 cross-type AF points are shown and available for selection manually. Use this mode when photographing highly detailed subject matter that is likely to confuse the non-cross (linear) focus sensors. I often use this to capture wildlife moving against a complex background.

- **15 points.** Three rows of five columns of sensors in the center of the frame are available for manual selection. I use this a lot for sports like football and track, where I know the action is going to be centered around the middle of the frame.

- **9 points.** Nine points in the center of the viewfinder can be selected. This is my favorite setting for basketball; virtually all the action will be in the center of the frame and involving one or two players, so I won't need to select a focus point from a wider range.

Select AF Area Selection Mode

Options: Manual select: Spot AF, Manual Select: Single Point, Expand AF Area, Expand Area: Surround, Manual Select: Zone AF, Manual Select: Large Zone AF, Auto Selection AF

My preference: All options checked

Here you can choose which of the seven AF area selection modes are available when you use the M-Fn button, AF Area button (on the back of the camera), or Main Dial, depending on the AF Area Selection method (described next), to cycle among them. In effect, you can enable the modes you use most often, and disable those that you rarely or never work with.

When you access this entry, a screen with all seven modes is displayed (see Figure 12.7). Use the Quick Control Dial or multi-controller joystick to highlight a mode you want to activate/deactivate and press SET. A check mark above the icon indicates that the mode will be available. Select OK to confirm your choices. To cycle among the modes you've checked, press the AF Point Selection button on the upper-right corner of the back of the Mark IV and press the M-Fn button, AF Area button, or Main Dial (if selected as your control) until the mode you want to use is selected.

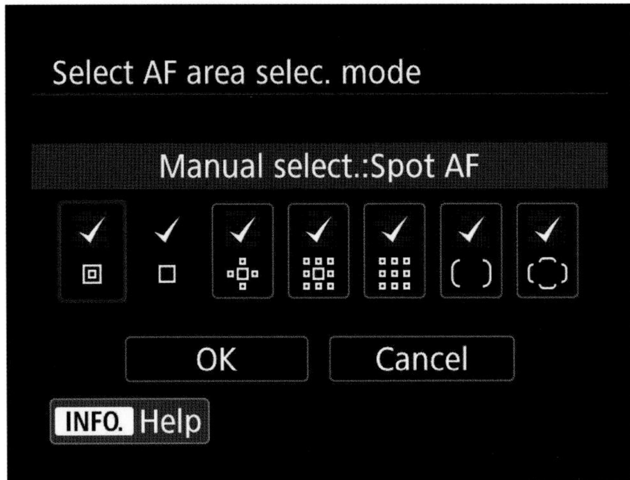

Figure 12.7
Enable or disable any of the seven AF Area Selection modes.

AF Area Selection Method

Options: M-Fn/Area Mode buttons (default), Main Dial

My preference: M-Fn/Area Mode buttons

With this setting, you can customize the controls used to choose an autofocus point manually, perhaps making the selection easier or more intuitive for you, or (as is the default) making this process require the use of two controls so that it can't be done accidentally. Your choices are as follows:

- **M-Fn button/Area Mode button.** To change the AF point that is active, you must press the AF point selection button (to the immediate right of the * button), then press the M-Fn button or Area Mode button (on the back of the camera) multiple times to select the mode you want.

- **Main Dial.** When this option is chosen, you must press the AF point selection button and rotate the Main Dial (or tilt the multi-controller joystick to either side) to select your selection mode.

Orientation Linked AF Point

Options: Same for both vertical and horizontal, Separate AF Points: Area+Point (default), Separate AF points: Point Only

My preference: Separate AF Points: Area+Point

If you have a preference for particular AF area selection modes and a manually selected AF point when composing vertical or horizontal pictures, you can specify that preference using this menu entry, by choosing Select Separate AF Points. Or, you can indicate that you want to use the same mode/point in all orientations (Same for Both Vert/Horiz).

If you'd like to differentiate, there are three different orientations to account for:

- **Same for both vertical and horizontal.** The AF area selection mode *and* the AF point or zone that you select manually are used for both vertical and horizontal images.
- **Separate AF points: Area+Point.** This is my favorite mode. The AF area selection mode *and* AF point or zone that you select manually can be specified for one of three orientations:
  - **Camera held horizontally.** This orientation assumes that the camera is positioned so the viewfinder/shutter release are on top.
  - **Camera held vertically** with the grip/shutter release above the Mode Dial.
  - **Camera held vertically** with the Mode Dial above the grip/shutter release.
- **Separate AF points: Point Only.** The AF area mode remains the same regardless of camera orientation, but you can specify a different AF point in manual point selection modes for each of the three orientations described above. The specified point will remain in force even if you switch from one manual selection mode to another (AF Spot, 1 pt AF, Expand AF Area, or Expand AF Area Surround, as described in Chapter 5).

You might want to use this feature when you want to keep the same initial focus point when photographing certain subjects even if you happen to rotate the camera for certain shots. Perhaps you're shooting candid portraits or fashion, and you'd like the focus point to remain at the "top" of the frame at all times. Just follow these steps:

1. **Choose Select Separate AF Points.** Press SET to confirm.
2. **Select AF Area Selection mode.** Choose any of these modes (Zone AF and 61-Point Automatic are invalid):
   - Single-Point Spot AF (Manual Selection)
   - Single-Point AF (Manual Selection)
   - AF Point Expansion (Manual Selection)
   - AF Point Expansion (Manual Selection/Surrounding Points)
3. **Switch to the orientation you want to define.** You'll need to define all three separately.
4. **Set desired focus point.** Press the Focus Point Select button and then rotate the Main Dial to choose the AF point for that orientation.
5. **Confirm.** Press the Focus Point Select button again and press the LCD Panel Illumination button (the rightmost button on the top panel between the LCD and the Main Dial). A beep will indicate that your setting has been stored.
6. **Define other orientations.** Repeat steps 2–5 for each of the other orientations.

Initial AF Point, Auto Selection, AI Servo AF

Options: Initial Auto Area AF Point Selected, Manual Spot, Manual 1 pt., Expand AF Area, Expand AF Area: Surround., Auto (default)

My preference: Auto

Do you feel that Auto Selection: 61 Pt. AF is *too* automated for you? If you'd like to regain a little control over this automated feature, this is the override for you. You can manually specify the starting point that will be used in AI Servo (continuous autofocus) mode, or mandate that a point you had previously chosen in another AF area selection mode be used when you switch to 61 Pt. AF. If you're confused, this description of your options should clear things up:

- **Initial Auto Area AF pt Selected.** You can use the AF point selection controls to specify any one of the 61 AF points available. When AI Servo AF starts to focus in Auto Selection: 61 pt. AF mode, it will first use the point you have chosen before seeking other points as the 5D Mark IV evaluates your scene. You could use this option when you know that your main subject will *probably* be located in a particular area of the frame (say, a racing car approaching from the left), but still want the camera to refocus as the subject moves. This helps reduce AF confusion from movement elsewhere in the frame that is not your main subject.

- **Manual Spot, Manual 1 pt., Expand AF Area, Expand AF Area: Surround.** If you switch to Auto Selection: 61 pt. AF mode from Manual Select: Spot AF, Manual Selection: 1 pt. AF, Expand AF Area, or Expand Area: Surround, AI Servo will begin operation using the AF point you manually selected in any of those previous modes. This can be a convenient mode to use, because you can define a button to switch from another mode to Auto Selection, using a defined Custom Control under Metering and AF Start. I'll explain the use of Custom Controls in Chapter 13.

- **Auto.** This default value restores the fully automatic operation of the Auto Selection: 61 pt. AF mode. Use this when you trust your 5D Mark IV to make the right selection. For the types of action photography I do, I end up with this setting most of the time. Specifying a start point for auto AF selection can prove distracting when trying to capture moving subjects.

Auto AF Point Selection: EOS iTR AF

Options: EOS iTR AF (Face priority) (default), EOS iTR AF, Disable

My preference: EOS iTR AF; EOS iTR AF (Face priority) when shooting people or events

Your 5D Mark IV includes a feature called EOS iTR, which is capable of using color and facial recognition to identify and track subjects while autofocusing. The feature is processing-intensive, so autofocus takes a bit longer and maximum speed under continuous is limited. It can operate when the AF Area Selection mode is Zone AF, Large Zone AF, or 61 Point Automatic AF.

Your choices are as follows:

- **EOS iTR AF (Face priority).** The autofocus point is based on human faces, color information, and AF phase detection. This mode is most useful when working in AI Servo AF mode (continuous autofocus), because the 5D Mark IV "remembers" the color at the first focus position, and then continues to refocus while tracking your subject using AF points that detect that same color. In One-Shot AF mode, the camera focuses just once, but can identify people more easily. This mode may take longer to achieve focus, and face detection may not occur if the face is small or dimly lit.

- **EOS iTR AF.** The autofocus point is selected using only AF data. Face information or color information is ignored.

- **Disable.** Only the phase detect AF information is used to select a focus point.

AF 5 Menu

You'll find options for selecting AF points here. See Figure 12.8.

AF Point Selection Movement

Options: Stops at AF area edges (default), Continuous

My preference: Stops at AF area edges

This entry simply specifies whether manual focus point selection will stop at the edges of the AF point array, or whether it will wrap around, *Pac-Man* style to continue at the opposite edge (left/right, or top/bottom). The edge stop option is best if you use the points at the edges often and don't want to continue to the opposite side. If you want to move quickly around in the array and aren't worrying about overshooting, then Continuous is the speedier choice.

Figure 12.8
The AF 5 menu has five entries.

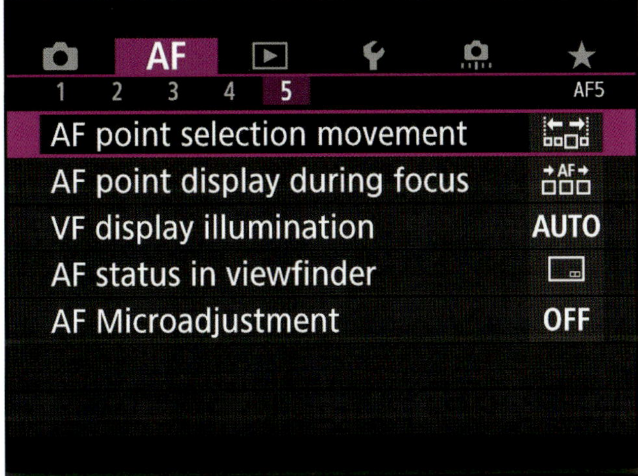

AF Point Display During Focus

Options: Selected (constant) (default), All (constant), Selected (pre-AF focused), Selected AF point (focused), Disable display

My preference: Selected (constant)

Your Mark IV can show you the AF points during shooting, and this entry provides four different options that control the conditions under which the points are displayed. The configuration is largely a matter of personal preference, reflecting when you like to see your focus points or if you find them distracting. The options are as follows:

- **Selected (constant).** The selected AF point(s) (only) are always highlighted. I prefer to see my selected points while I am shooting.

- **All (constant).** All 61 possible AF points are always shown.

- **Selected (pre-AF, Focused).** Focus points are shown when selecting AF point(s); when the camera is ready to shoot, before AF operation; and when focus is achieved (except when using AI Servo AF).

- **Selected AF point (Focused).** Focus points are shown only when selecting AF point(s) or when focus is achieved (except when using AI Servo AF).

- **Disable display.** The selected AF point(s) will *not* be displayed, except if you've chosen Selected (constant).

VF Display Illumination

Options: Auto (default), Enable, Disable

My preference: Auto. I can use the Q button if I need to, as described below.

You can elect to have the AF points and grid in the viewfinder highlighted in red when focus is achieved. Keep in mind that when you press the AF Selection button, the AF points will illuminate regardless of how you have this option set. You can select:

- **Auto.** Points and grid illuminate when focus is achieved under low light only. When selected, you can also specify whether the AF point should also light up in red when you press the Q button while using AI Servo AF. This is especially useful for sports photography and other applications where you want to see the selected focus point. The option does not work if VF Illumination is set to Disable. If the viewfinder electronic level and viewfinder grid are enabled, they will also light up in red.

- **Enable.** Points and grid are illuminated when focus is achieved at all times. The same Q button behavior described above is available.

- **Disable.** Points and grid are never illuminated (except when the AF Selection button is pressed).

AF Status in Viewfinder

Options: Show in field of view (default), Show outside view

My preference: Show outside view

This option lets you place the AF status icon within the field of view, or below the frame underneath the focus indicator. I prefer an uncluttered view, and generally choose the latter.

AF Microadjustment

Options: Disable, All by same amount, Adjust by lens (default)

My preference: Adjust by lens

Caution! Use this control, which allows you to tweak the point of focus of individual lenses, with care. Well-intentioned, but inaccurate adjustments can turn slight focus problems into major ones. I'll cover this drastic correctional step in detail next.

Fine-Tuning the Autofocus of Your Lenses

The Canon EOS 5D Mark IV has a feature called AF Microadjustment, which I hope you never need to use, because it is applied only when you find that a lens is not focusing properly. If the lens happens to focus a bit ahead or a bit behind the actual point of sharp focus, and it does that consistently, you can use the microadjustment feature to "calibrate" the lens's focus.

Why is the focus "off" for some lenses in the first place? There are lots of factors, including the age of the lens (an older lens may focus slightly differently), temperature effects on certain types of glass, humidity, and tolerances built into a lens's design that all add up to a slight misadjustment, even though the components themselves are, strictly speaking, within specs. A very slight variation in your lens's mount can cause focus to vary slightly. With any luck (if you can call it that), a lens that doesn't focus exactly right will at least be consistent. If a lens always focuses a bit behind the subject, the symptom is *back focus*. If it focuses in front of the subject, it's called *front focus*.

You're almost always better off sending such a lens in to Canon to have them make it right. But that's not always possible. Perhaps you need your lens recalibrated right now, or you purchased a used lens that is long out of warranty. If you want to do it yourself, the first thing to do is determine whether your lens has a back-focus or front-focus problem.

For a quick-and-dirty diagnosis (*not* a calibration; you'll use a different target for that), lay down a piece of graph paper on a flat surface, and place an object on the line at the middle, which will represent the point of focus (we hope). Then, shoot the target at an angle using your lens's widest aperture and the autofocus mode you want to test. Mount the camera on a tripod so you can get accurate, repeatable results.

If your camera/lens combination doesn't suffer from front or back focus, the point of sharpest focus will be the center line of the chart, as you can see in Figure 12.9. If you do have a problem, one of

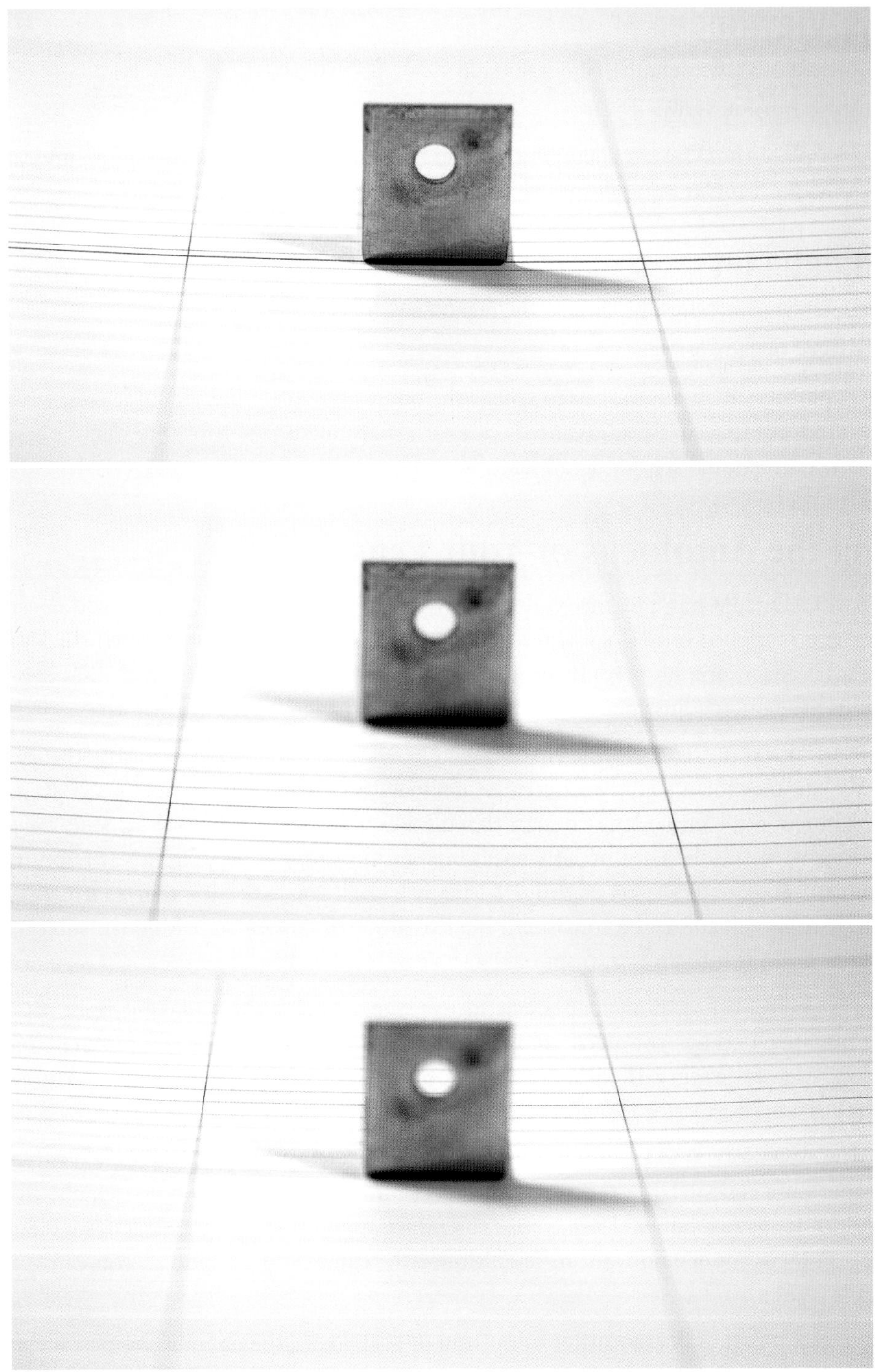

Figure 12.9 Correct focus (top), front focus (middle), and back focus (bottom).

the other lines will be sharply focused instead. Should you discover that your lens consistently front or back focuses, it needs to be recalibrated. Unfortunately, it's only possible to calibrate a lens for a single focusing distance. So, if you use a lens (such as a macro lens) for close focusing, calibrate for that. If you use a lens primarily for middle distances, calibrate for that. Close-to-middle distances are most likely to cause focus problems, anyway, because as you get closer to infinity, small changes in focus are less likely to have an effect.

Lens Tune-Up

Options: Disable (default), Adjust all by same amount, Adjust by lens

My preference: N/A

The key tool you can use to fine-tune your lens is the AF Microadjustment entry. You'll find the process easier to understand if you first run through this quick overview of the menu options:

- **Disable.** Deactivates autofocus micro adjustment.
- **Adjust all by same amount.** The same adjustment is applied to all your lenses. You'd use this if your camera, rather than just a lens or two, requires calibration. (In this case, I particularly recommend sending the camera back to Canon for repair.)
- **Adjust by lens.** You can set an adjustment individually for up to 20 different lenses. If you discover you don't care for the calibrations you make in certain situations (say, it works better for the lens you have mounted at middle distances, but is less successful at correcting close-up focus errors), you can deactivate the feature as you require. Adjustment values range from –20 to +20.

Evaluate Current Focus

The first step is to capture a baseline image that represents how the lens you want to fine-tune autofocuses at a particular distance. You'll often see advice for photographing a test chart with millimeter markings from an angle, and the suggestion that you autofocus on a particular point on the chart. Supposedly, the markings that actually *are* in focus will help you recalibrate your lens. The problem with this approach is that the information you get from photographing a test chart at an angle doesn't tell you what to do to make a precise correction. So, your lens back focuses three millimeters behind the target area on the chart. So what? Does that mean you change the value –3 increments? Or –15 increments? Angled targets are a "shortcut" that don't save you time.

Instead, you'll want to photograph a target that represents what you're trying to achieve: a plane of focus locked in by your lens that represents the actual plane of focus of your subject. For that, you'll need a flat target, mounted precisely perpendicular to the sensor plane of the camera. Then, you can take a photo, see if the plane of focus is correct, and if not, dial in a bit of fine-tuning in the AF Microadjustment menu, and shoot again. Lather, rinse, and repeat until the target is sharply focused.

You can use the focus target shown in Figure 12.10, or you can use a chart of your own, as long as it has contrasty areas that will be easily seen by the autofocus system, and without very small details that are likely to confuse the AF. Download your own copy of my chart from www.dslrguides.com/FocusChart.pdf. (The URL is case sensitive.) Then print out a copy on the largest paper your printer can handle. (I don't recommend just displaying the file on your monitor and focusing on that; it's unlikely you'll have the monitor screen lined up perfectly perpendicular to the camera sensor.) Then, follow these steps:

1. **Position the camera.** Place your camera on a sturdy tripod with a remote release attached, positioned at roughly eye-level at a distance from a wall that represents the distance you want to test for. Keep in mind that autofocus problems can be different at varying distances and lens focal lengths, and that you can enter only *one* correction value for a particular lens. So, choose a distance (close-up or mid range) and zoom setting with your shooting habits in mind.

2. **Set the autofocus mode.** Choose the autofocus mode (One-Shot AF or AI Servo AF) you want to test. (Because AI Auto mode just alternates between the two, you don't need to test that mode.)

3. **Level the camera (in an ideal world).** If the wall happens to be perfectly perpendicular, you can use a bubble level, plumb bob, or other device of your choice to ensure that the camera is level to match. Many tripods and tripod heads have bubble levels built in. Avoid using the center column, if you can. When the camera is properly oriented, lock the legs and tripod head tightly.

4. **Level the camera (in the real world).** If your wall is not perfectly perpendicular, use this old trick. Tape a mirror to the wall, and then adjust the camera on the tripod so that when you look through the viewfinder at the mirror, you see directly into the reflection of the lens. Then, lock the tripod and remove the mirror.

5. **Mount the test chart.** Tape the test chart on the wall so it is centered in your camera's viewfinder.

6. **Photograph the test chart using AF.** Allow the camera to autofocus, and take a test photo, using the remote release to avoid shaking or moving the camera.

7. **Make an adjustment and rephotograph.** Make a fine-tuning adjustment (described next) and photograph the target again.

8. **Evaluate the image.** If you have the camera connected to a monitor or TV with an HDMI cable or through a Wi-Fi connection, so much the better. You can view the image after it's transferred to your computer. Otherwise, *carefully* open the camera card door and slip the memory card out and copy the images to your computer.

9. **Evaluate focus.** Which image is sharpest? That's the setting you need to use for this lens. If your initial range doesn't provide the correction you need, repeat the steps between –20 and +20 until you find the best fine-tuning.

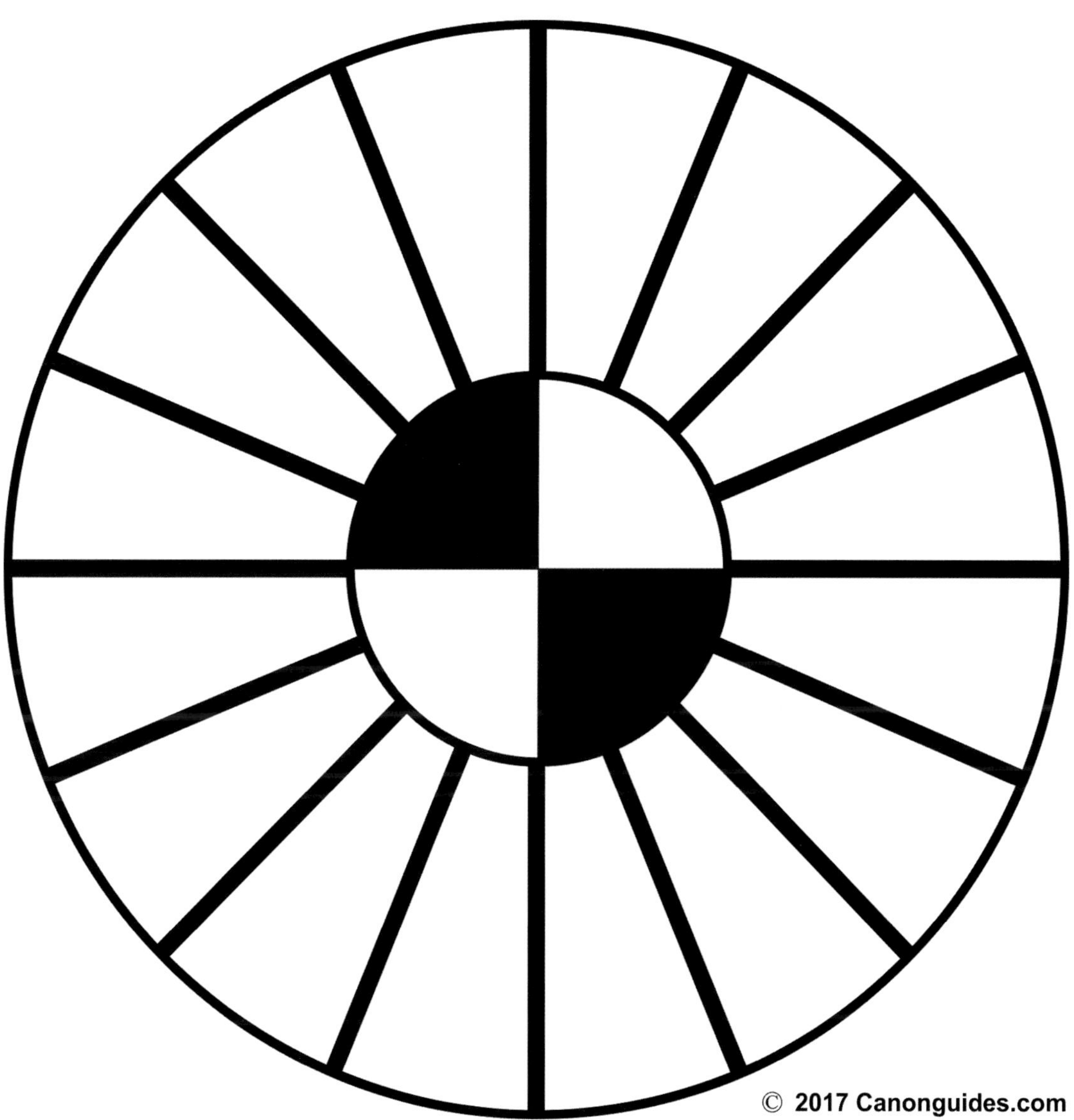

Figure 12.10 Use this focus test chart or create one of your own.

Make Adjustments

Making the adjustments is simple. From the AF 5 menu, select Microadjustment, and choose from Adjust all by same amount, Adjust by lens, or Disable.

- **Adjust all by same amount.** Highlight the entry and press the SET button. Then, press the INFO. button to produce a screen with a scale from –20 to +20. Use the Quick Control Dial to choose a value, and press SET to confirm.

- **Adjust by lens.** Follow these steps:

  1. Highlight Adjust by lens and press the INFO. button. A screen like the one shown in Figure 12.11 will appear. For a prime lens, there will be only a single adjustment scale; for a zoom lens, there will be one scale for W (wide angle) and one for T (telephoto) focal lengths.

  2. Press the INFO. button again. The Review/Edit lens information screen appears. It shows the name of the currently mounted lens and a 10-digit serial number (or 0000000000 if the number cannot be obtained).

  3. If the serial number is obtained, you can select OK to move on to the next step. If you need to edit the serial number, you can use the QCD to highlight any digit, then press SET to edit that digit. Rotate the QCD to increase or decrease the value of the digit. Select OK when finished.

  4. Select the scale and then rotate the QCD to adjust between –20 and +20 (no letters required). Moving the indicator to the right moves the focus point to the rear of the standard point of focus. Adjusting to the left moves the focus point to a position in front of the default focus point.

  5. Press SET to confirm your changes. The 5D Mark IV has enough memory to store values for 40 different lenses or lens+teleextend combinations (handy!). If you want to register more than 40 lenses, select a lens with an adjustment that can be deleted, mount it on the camera, and reset its adjustment to 0. That will free up a slot for a different lens.

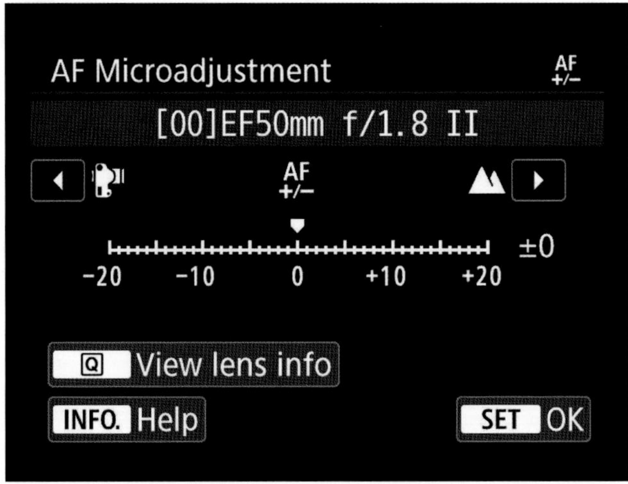

Figure 12.11
Adjustments toward the left move the focus plane closer to the camera; adjustments to the right move it farther away.

13

Customizing with the Playback and Set-up Menus

In the last two chapters, I introduced you to the layout and general functions of the Canon EOS 5D Mark IV's menu system, with specifics on how to customize your camera with the Shooting and Autofocus menus. In this chapter, you'll learn how to work with the Playback and four Setup menus. If you're jumping directly to this chapter and need some guidance in how to navigate the 5D Mark IV's menu system, review the first few pages of Chapter 11. Otherwise, you're welcome to dive right in.

Playback Menu Options

The two blue-coded Playback menus are where you select options related to the display, review, transfer, and printing of the photos you've taken. I won't be showing default values for the Playback menu items, as only three of them have a true default: Image Jump with Main Dial (10 images), Magnification (2X), and Control over HDMI (Disable). The choices you'll find include:

- Protect Images
- Rotate Image
- Erase Images
- Print Order
- Photobook Set-up
- Image Copy
- RAW Image Processing

- Cropping
- Resize
- Rating
- Slide Show
- Image Transfer
- Image Jump with Main Dial

- Highlight Alert
- AF Point Disp.
- Playback Grid
- Histogram Disp.
- Movie Play Count
- Magnification (apx)
- Ctrl over HDMI

Protect Images

Options: Select images, All images in folder, All images on card, Unprotect all images on card
My recommendation: N/A

This is the first of seven entries in the Playback 1 menu (see Figure 13.1). If you want to keep an image from being accidentally erased (either with the Erase button or by using the Erase menu), you can mark that image for protection. There are several ways to protect one or more images.

- **Q button.** This is probably one of the quickest ways to protect a single image. While viewing a photo in playback mode, press the Q button. A Quick Control screen appears with a column of playback function choices in the left column (see Figure 13.2). Protect is at the top, and when highlighted allows you to choose from Disable and Enable to mark an image as protected. A tap or two on the touch screen will do the job, or you can protect the image from this screen using the conventional controls.

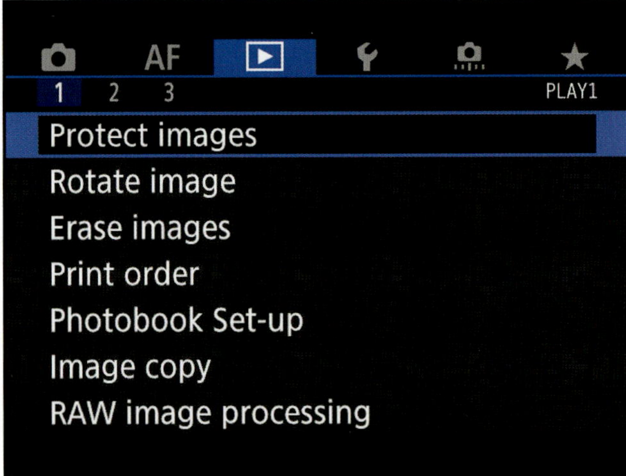

Figure 13.1
The Playback 1 menu.

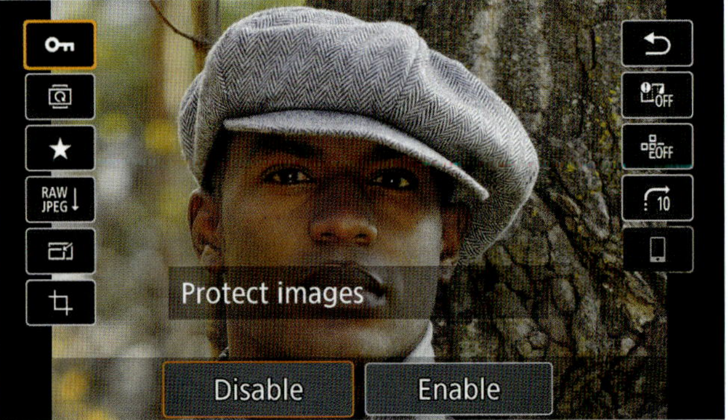

Figure 13.2
Protected images can be locked against accidental erasure (but not preserved from formatting).

■ **Playback menu.** To protect multiple images, you'll probably want to use this menu entry. Choose Protect Images and a screen appears with five options:

- Select Images
- All Images in Folder
- Unprotect All Images in Folder
- All Images on Card
- Unprotect All Images on Card

If you choose Select Images, you can view and select individual images and enable protection by pressing the SET button when they are displayed on the screen. A key icon will appear at the upper edge of the information display while still in the protection screen, and when reviewing that image later. To remove protection, repeat the process. You can scroll among the other images on your memory card using the QCD and protect/unprotect them in the same way. Image protection will not save your images from removal when the card is reformatted.

As always, if you have images stored on both your Compact Flash and SD cards, you can switch the Record/Play function from one card to the other using the Record Func+Card/Folder Sel. entry in the Set-up 1 menu, as described later in this chapter.

■ **RATE Button.** This is the fastest way of all to protect a single image, although you lose the Rate function. You can use the RATE button as a shortcut for protecting images. In the Set-up 3 menu, select Protect as the Rate Btn Function (as described later in this chapter). Then, you can simply press the RATE button during image playback to protect that image.

Rotate Image

Options: Rotate image

My recommendation: N/A

While you can set the EOS 5D Mark IV to automatically rotate images taken in a vertical orientation using the Auto Rotate option in the Set-up 1 menu (as described later in this chapter), you can manually rotate an image during playback using this menu selection. Select Rotate from the Playback 1 menu, use the Quick Control Dial to page through the available images on your memory card until the one you want to rotate appears, then press SET. The image will appear on the screen rotated 90 degrees. Press SET again, and the image will be rotated 270 degrees. (See Figure 13.3.)

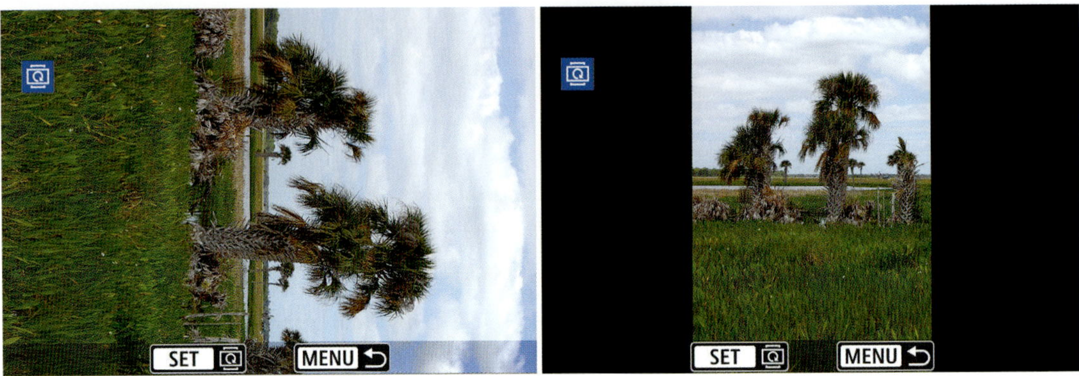

Figure 13.3 A vertically oriented image that isn't rotated appears larger on the LCD (left), but rotation allows viewing the photo without turning the camera (right).

Erase Images

Options: Select and erase images, All images in folder, All images on card

My recommendation: N/A

Choose this menu entry and you'll be given three choices: Select and Erase Images, All Images in Folder, and All images on card. The first option displays the most recent image. Press SET to mark that image for deletion, and then rotate the Quick Control Dial to view other images, using the SET button to mark those you want to delete. When finished marking pictures, press the Trash button, and you'll see a screen that says Erase Selected Images with two options, Cancel and OK. Use the Quick Control Dial to choose OK, then press the SET button to erase the images, or select Cancel and press the SET button to return to the selection screen. Press the MENU button to unmark your selections and return to the menu.

The All Images on Card choice removes all the pictures on the card, except for those you've marked with the Protect command, and does not reformat the memory card. And, as mentioned earlier, if you have images stored on both memory cards, you can switch between them using the Record Func+Card/Folder Sel. entry in the Set-up 1 menu.

Print Order

Options: Number of prints; Select image; Select by folder; All images; Set up: Print type, Date, File number

My recommendation: N/A

The EOS 5D Mark IV supports the DPOF (Digital Print Order Format) that is now almost universally used by digital cameras to specify which images on your memory card should be printed, and the number of prints desired of each image. This information is recorded on the memory card, and can be interpreted by a compatible printer when the camera is linked to the printer using the USB cable, or when the memory card is inserted into a card reader slot on the printer itself. Photo labs are also equipped to read this data and make prints when you supply your memory card to them.

If you don't want to print directly from the camera using PictBridge, you can set some of the same options from the Playback 1 menu's Print Order entry, and designate single or multiple images on your memory card for printing. Once marked for DPOF printing, you can print the selected images, or take your memory card to a digital lab or kiosk, which is equipped to read the print order and make the copies you've specified. (You can't "order" prints of RAW images or movies.)

To create a DPOF print order, just follow these steps:

1. **Access Print Order screen.** In the Playback 1 menu, navigate to Print Order. Press SET.

2. **Access Set up.** The Print Order screen will appear. (See Figure 13.4.) Use the Quick Control Dial to highlight Set Up. Press SET.

3. **Select Print type.** Choose Print Type (Standard, Index/Thumbnails print, or Both), and specify whether Date or File Number imprinting should be turned on or off. (You can turn one or the other on, but not both Date and File Number imprinting.) Press MENU to return to the Print Order screen.

4. **Choose selection method.** Highlight Sel. Image (choose individual images), By Folder (to select/deselect all images in a folder), or All Image (to mark/unmark all the images on your memory card). Press SET.

5. **Select individual images.** With Sel. Image, use the QCD or Main Dial to view the images, and press SET to mark or unmark an image for printing.

Figure 13.4
Select the images to be printed individually, by folder, or all the images on your memory card.

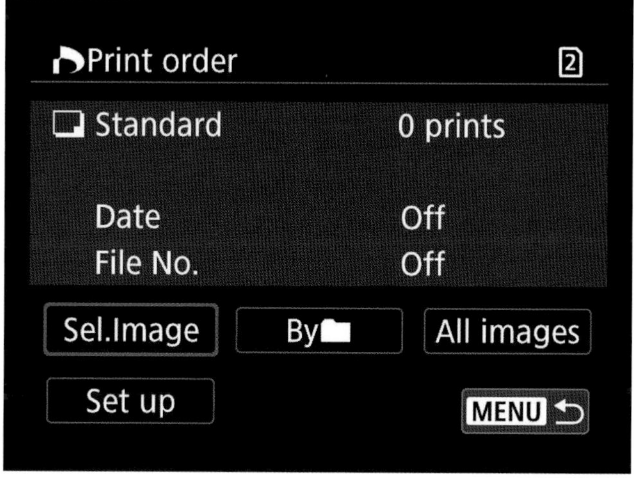

6. **Choose number of prints.** Once an image is selected, rotate the QCD to specify 1 to 99 prints for that image. (For Index prints, you can only specify whether the selected image is included in the index print, not the number of copies.) Press SET to confirm. You can then use the QCD to select additional images. Press MENU when finished selecting to return to the Print Order screen.

7. **Output your hardcopies.** If the camera is linked to a PictBridge-compatible printer, an additional option appears on the Print Order screen—Print. You can select that; optionally, adjust Paper Settings, and start the printing process. Alternately, you can exit the Print Order screen by tapping the shutter release button. Then turn off the camera and printer, remove the memory card, and insert it in the memory card slot of a compatible printer, retailer kiosk, or digital minilab.

Photobook Set-up

Options: Select images, All images in folder, Clear all in folder, All images on card, Clear all on card

My preference: N/A

You can select up to 998 images on your memory card, and then use the EOS Utility to copy them all to a specific folder on your computer. This is a handy way to transfer only specific images to a particular folder, and is especially useful when you're collecting photos to assemble in a photobook. Your choices include:

- **Select images.** You can mark individual images from any folder on your memory card.
- **All images in folder.** Mark all the images in a folder for transfer.
- **Clear all in folder.** Unmark all the images in a folder.
- **All images on card.** Mark all the images on the memory card for transfer to the specific folder.
- **Clear all on card.** Unmark all the images on the card.

Once you marked the images you want to transfer to the specified folder, use the EOS Utility to copy them.

Image Copy

Options: Select image, Select by folder, All images

My recommendation: N/A

Image Copy allows you to make backup or duplicate images of selected photos on your memory card. You can choose individual images, a folder of images, or all images on the default memory card. You can swap the main and secondary cards in the Set-up menu with the Record/Play function in the Record Func+Card/Folder Sel. entry in the Set-up 1 menu, as described later in this chapter. The Image Copy screen will show you the free space available on the target card before the copy function takes place.

Just follow these steps:

1. **Navigate to the Image Copy entry.** Press SET to proceed.

2. **Choose Sel. Image.** Rotate the QCD to highlight Sel. Image and press SET.

3. **Choose folder.** Rotate the QCD to select the folder with the image(s) to be copied, and press SET. A thumbnail of the images to be copied is displayed on the right.

4. **View individual images.** Rotate the QCD to view images. You can press the Magnify button and rotate the Main Dial counterclockwise to switch from a single image to three-image display. (Rotate the Main Dial clockwise to return to the single-image display.)

5. **Mark images.** Press the RATE button to mark an image for copying. A check mark icon will appear at the upper left of the screen.

6. **Choose Target card/folder.** Choose OK when you're ready to select the folder on the target card. You can choose an existing folder or select Create Folder to set up a new folder as the destination.

7. **Begin copying.** Choose OK to copy files. You'll be warned about duplicate file names and offered the choice of skipping the copy, replacing the existing file, or canceling the copy function entirely.

RAW Image Processing

Options: Brightness, White balance, Picture Style, Auto Lighting Optimizer, High ISO Noise Reduction, Image quality, Color space, Lens aberration correction

My recommendation: N/A

You can produce JPEG versions of your full-size RAW images (but not M RAW or S RAW files) right in the camera. The original RAW shot is not modified. When you select this menu entry, only compatible RAW images are offered for your selection. Just follow these steps:

1. **View RAW images.** Rotate the QCD to scroll through compatible images. Press the Magnify button and rotate the Main Dial counterclockwise to view a selection of index images instead.

2. **Select image to process.** Press SET to select an image for processing.

3. **Specify parameters.** A screen appears with a selection of parameters you can adjust. (See Figure 13.5.) Navigate to the parameter you want to manipulate using the joystick-like multi-controller. Your choices include:

   - Brightness
   - White Balance
   - Picture Style
   - Auto Lighting Optimizer
   - High ISO Noise Reduction
   - Image Quality
   - Color Space
   - Lens Aberration Correction

   Press SET to access Peripheral Illumination Correction, Distortion Correction, Digital Lens Optimizer, Chromatic Aberration Correction, or Diffraction Correction.

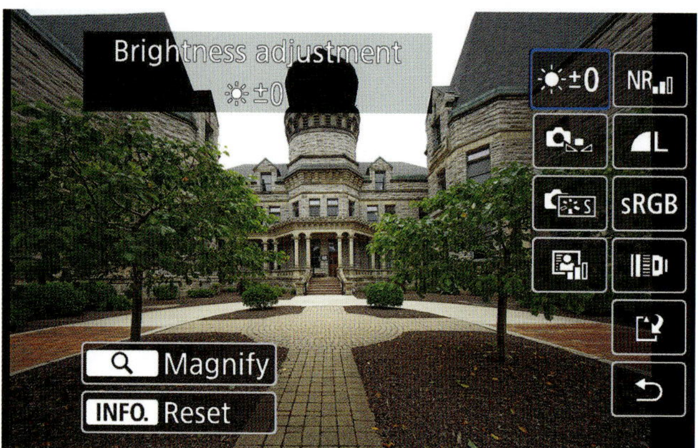

Figure 13.5
Select from eight types of correction using RAW Image Processing.

4. **Make adjustments.** When a parameter is highlighted you can rotate the Main Dial or QCD or press SET to change the settings; press INFO. to reset the settings to the original values of the RAW image; press the Magnify button to zoom in on the image.

5. **Save JPEG.** Navigate to the Save icon at the bottom right of the screen and press SET. Choose OK to save as a new file, or Cancel to abort the process. If the original was shot using live view and an aspect ratio other than 3:2, the image will be displayed in those proportions, and the JPEG will be saved in that aspect ratio.

Cropping

Options: Crop, Aspect ratio

My recommendation: N/A

This entry is the first on the Playback 2 menu. (See Figure 13.6.) If you need to crop an image, you can do it here. You don't have as much control as you would have in an image editor, but if you, say, need to crop an image for emailing or uploading to a social media site, this may do the job. You can crop *only* JPEG images in Large, Medium, S1, or S2 sizes. This function does not work on JPEG S3 images, RAW images, or frames grabbed for 4K movies.

Simply select this menu entry and press SET. A compatible JPEG image appears. Use the QCD to select an image for cropping. Press the Magnify/Reduce button and rotate the Main Dial counter-clockwise to view and select a thumbnail image in index view. Press SET when you've chosen your image. Then, you can apply one of these tools:

- **Enlarge/reduce crop.** Rotate the Main Dial to enlarge and reduce the green cropping frame, seen in Figure 13.7.

- **Position crop frame.** Use the multi-controller joystick to slide the cropping frame around within the image.

■ **Adjust aspect ratio.** Rotate the QCD to cycle the cropping frame's proportions among 3:2, 16:9, 4:3, and 1:1 aspect ratios.

■ **Change crop orientation.** For all aspect ratios except 1:1, you can press the INFO. button to toggle between landscape and portrait orientations.

■ **Check your crop.** Press the Q button and the cropped image will be shown with the area outside the frame removed.

■ **Save cropped image.** Press SET and select OK to save your cropped image as a new file. Your original image is retained unharmed.

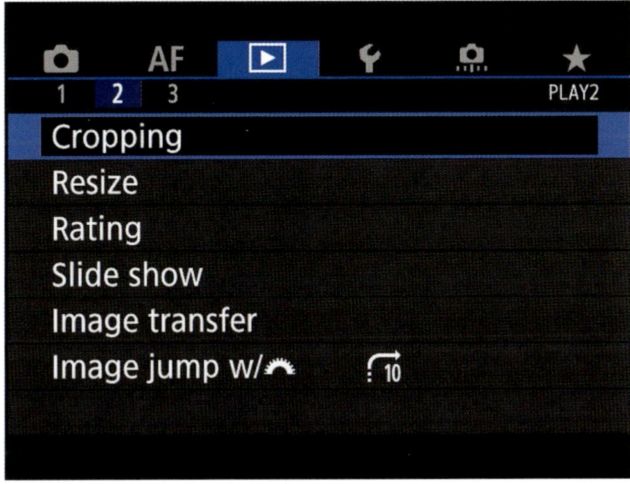

Figure 13.6
Cropping is the first entry in the Playback 2 menu.

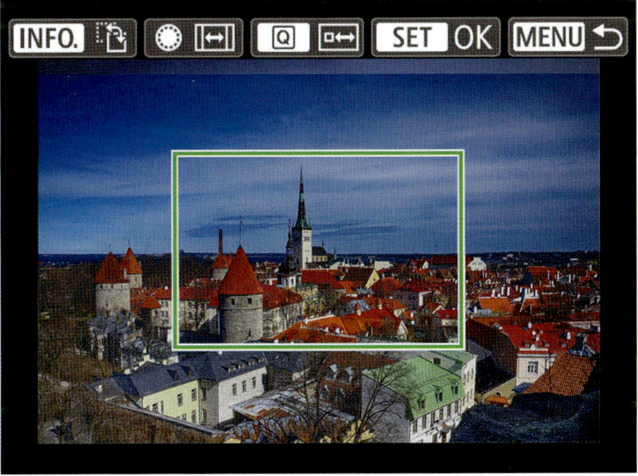

Figure 13.7
The green frame represents the cropped area.

Resize

Options: Medium, Small 1, Small 2, Small 3 image sizes

My recommendation: N/A

If you've already taken an image and would like to create a smaller version (say, to send by e-mail), you can create one from this menu entry. Just follow these steps:

1. **Choose Resize.** Select this menu entry from the Playback 1 menu.

2. **View images to resize**. You can scroll through the available images with the touch screen or directional buttons, or press the Thumbnail/Reduce Image button to view thumbnails and select from those. Only images that can be resized are shown. They include JPEG Large, Medium, Small 1, and Small 2 images. Small 3 and RAW images of any type cannot be resized.

3. **Select an image.** Choose SET to select an image to resize. A pop-up menu will appear on the screen offering the choice of reduced-size images. These include M (Medium: 13MP, 4464 × 2976 pixels); S1 (Small 1: 7.5MP, 3360 × 2240 pixels); S2 (Small 2: 2.5MP, 1920 × 1280 pixels); or S3 (Small 3, .3MP, 720 × 480 pixels). You cannot resize an image to a size that is larger than its current size; that is, you cannot save a JPEG Medium image as JPEG Large.

4. **Resize and save.** Choose SET to save as a new file, and confirm your choice by selecting OK from the screen that pops up, or cancel to exit without saving a new version. The old version of the image is untouched.

Rating

Options: One to five stars

My recommendation: N/A

If you want to apply a quality rating to images or movies you've shot (or use the rating system to represent some other criteria), you can simply press the Rating button during playback multiple times to apply a rating. Or, alternatively, use this entry to give images one, two, three, four, or five stars, or turn the rating system off. The Image Jump function can display only images with a given rating. Suppose you were photographing a track meet with multiple events. You could apply a one-star rating to jumping events, two stars to relays, three stars to throwing events, four stars to hurdles, and five stars to dashes. Then, using the Image Jump feature, you could review only images of one type. As mentioned earlier, you can also redefine the Rating button to apply the Protect attribute to an image in the Set-up 3 menu.

With a little imagination, you can apply the rating system to all sorts of categories. At a wedding, you could classify pictures of the bride, the groom, guests, attendants, and parents of the couple. If you were shooting school portraits, one rating could apply to first grade, another to second grade, and so on. Given a little thought, this feature has many more applications than you might think. Ratings can be used to specify images for a slide show, too, or to select images in Digital Photo Professional.

To use the Ratings menu entry, just follow these steps:

1. Choose the Rating menu item.

2. Use the QCD to select an image or movie. When an image or movie you want to rate is visible, press SET.

3. Now rotate the QCD to apply a one- to five-star rating, or turn a rating off. You can rate up to 999 images.

4. When finished rating, choose MENU to exit.

Slide Show

Options: Select image, Display time, Repeat

My recommendation: N/A

Slide Show is a convenient way to review images one after another, without the need to manually switch between them. To activate, just choose Slide Show from the Playback 2 menu. During playback, you can press the SET button to pause the "slide show" (in case you want to examine an image more closely), or the INFO. button to change the amount of information displayed on the screen with each image. For example, you might want to review a set of images and their histograms to judge the exposure of the group of pictures. To set up your slide show, follow these steps:

1. **Begin setup.** Choose Slide Show from the Playback 2 menu, pressing SET to display the screen shown in Figure 13.8.

2. **Choose image selection method.** Rotate the Quick Command Dial to All Images, and press SET. Then rotate the QCD to choose from All Images, Date, Folder, Movies, Stills, or Rating. Press SET to activate that selection mode. If you selected All Images, Stills, or Movies, skip to Step 4.

Figure 13.8

Set up your slide show using this screen.

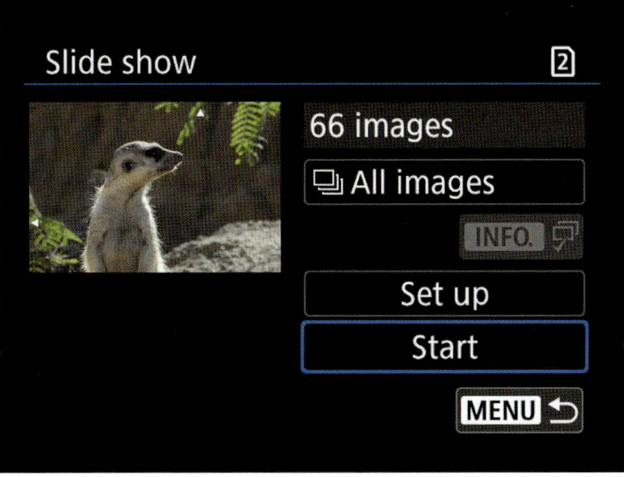

3. **Choose images.** If you've selected Folder, Date, or Rating, press the INFO. button to produce a screen that allows you to select from the available folders, or the available image creation dates or ratings on your memory card. When you've chosen a folder, date, or rating, press SET to confirm your choice.

4. **Choose Play time and Repeat options.** Rotate the Quick Command Dial to highlight Setup and press SET to produce a screen with playing time (1, 2, 3, 5, 10, or 20 seconds per image), and repeating options (Enable or Disable). When you've specified either value, press the MENU button to confirm your choice, and then MENU once more to go back to the main Slide Show screen.

5. **Start the show.** Rotate the QCD to highlight Start and press SET to begin your show. (If you'd rather cancel the show you've just set up, press MENU instead.)

6. **Use show options during display.** Press SET to pause/restart; INFO. to cycle among the four information displays described in the section before this one; MENU to stop the show.

Image Transfer

Options: Image select/transfer, RAW+JPEG transfer, Transfer with caption

My recommendation: N/A

You can specify which images are to be transferred to your personal computer when the 5D Mark IV is linked to the computer with a USB cable. Individual images are "marked" using a review and selection system like the one used to specify print orders. Your options include:

- **Image sel./transfer.** You can choose to select individual images (Sel. Image), a folder (Sel. Folder), or All Images. During transfer, the display shows the total number of images to be transferred, the number of images that failed to transfer properly, and the total transferred. Use the customary image selection screen to move among images with the QCD, pressing the SET button to mark the image for transfer. Once selected, you can rotate the QCD (or tap the arrows at the bottom of the screen) to mark or unmark (using a check mark) the image, and return to the selection screen by pressing MENU. Press the Magnify/Reduce button to zoom in and out of the image.

- **RAW+JPEG transfer.** You can elect to transfer all selected RAW+JPEG images, or, alternatively, tell the camera to transfer either the JPEG images (only) or RAW image (only). For example, if you plan on working with the RAW versions of each shot, you can leave the JPEG files on the memory card, for transfer later, or to discard when you reformat the card.

- **Transfer with caption.** You can create captions in the EOS Utility, register the captions with the camera, and then, using this option (which is available only when images with captions have been captured), transfer the caption information along with the image file.

Image Jump with Main Dial

Options: 1 image, 10 images, 100 images, Date, Folder, Movies only, Stills only, Image rating

My recommendation: N/A

As first described in Chapter 2, you can leap ahead or back during picture review by rotating the Main Dial, using a variety of increments that you can select using this menu entry. The Jump method is shown briefly on the screen as you leap ahead to the next image displayed, as shown in Figure 13.9. Your options are as follows:

- **1 image.** Rotating the Main Dial one click jumps forward or back 1 image.
- **10 images.** Rotating the Main Dial one click jumps forward or back 10 images.
- **100 images.** Rotating the Main Dial one click jumps forward or back 100 images.
- **Date.** Rotating the Main Dial one click jumps forward or back to the first image taken on the next or previous calendar date.
- **Folder.** Rotating the Main Dial one click jumps forward or back to the first image in the next folder available on your memory card (if one exists).
- **Movies Only.** Jumps among movies only using the Main Dial.
- **Stills Only.** Jumps among still photos only using the Main Dial.
- **Image Rating.** When this option is visible, rotate the Main Dial to select the rating you want to use. Then, during picture review, spinning the Main Dial will jump among photos with the rating you selected.

Figure 13.9
The Jump method is shown on the LCD briefly when you leap forward or back using the Main Dial.

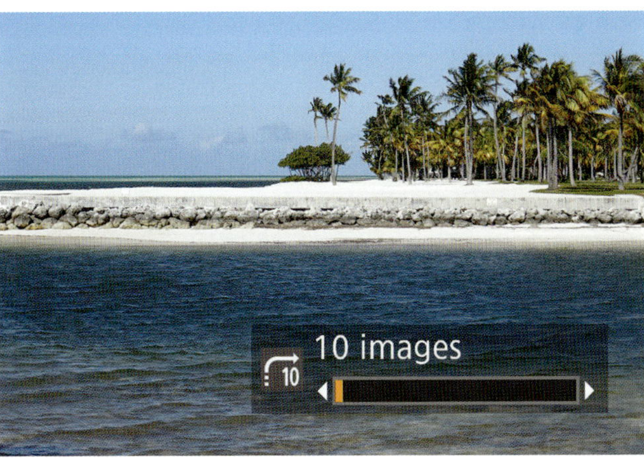

Highlight Alert

Options: Enable, Disable

My recommendation: N/A

Choose Enable, and overexposed highlight areas will blink on the LCD screen during picture review. Set to Disable if you find this alert distracting. Many 5D Mark IV users use the histogram displays during playback as a more precise indicator of over- (and under-) exposure. This is the first entry in the Playback 3 menu. (See Figure 13.10.)

AF Point Disp.

Options: Enable, Disable

My recommendation: N/A

Select Enable, and the exact AF point(s) used to determine focus will be highlighted in red. If automatic AF point selection was used, you may find multiple points highlighted.

Playback Grid

Options: 3 × 3, 6 × 4, 3 × 3+ diagonal lines

My recommendation: N/A

You can superimpose a 3 × 3, 6 × 4, or 3 × 3 plus diagonal lines grid over your image during playback, or disable the grid display entirely. You can review the layout of the grids, which can also be shown during shooting.

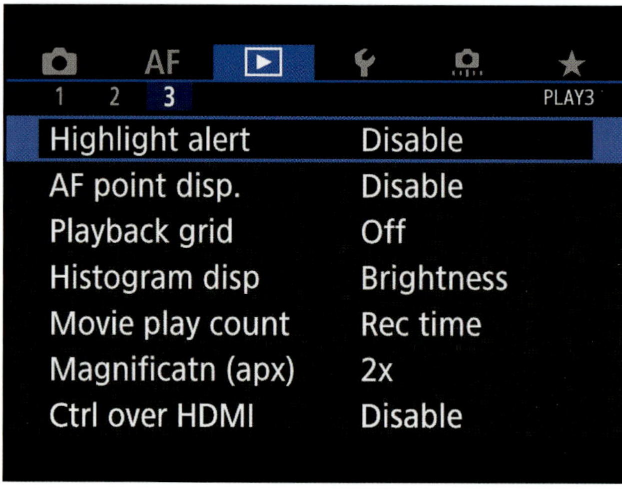

Figure 13.10
The Playback 3 menu.

Histogram Disp.

Options: Brightness, RGB

My recommendation: N/A

Select from Brightness (luminance) or RGB histogram display during playback. I described use of histograms in Chapter 4.

Movie Play Count

Options: Record time, Time code

My recommendation: N/A

Determines whether the movie recording and playback time (Rec Time) is shown on the screen, or whether the Time Code (an absolute positional marker/index) is displayed instead. If you change the Movie Play Count setting in the Shooting 5 (Movie) menu, as described in Chapter 16, or here, the other will be changed automatically. You'll find additional Time Code options in the Shooting 5 (Movie) menu.

Magnification (apx)

Options: 1X, 2X, 4X, 8X, 10X, Actual size, Same as last magnification

My recommendation: Same as last magnification

This setting allows you to specify the initial magnification for magnified view during playback, as well as the starting position on the screen. Choose your starter magnification based on how often you tend to take a close-up look at your images during review. If you're a pixel-peeper, you might want an in-depth 10X view each time you magnify your image. If you're more sedate in your zooming habits, the 1X magnification will start you off with a full-screen view you can zoom in on. I like to use the same magnification I most recently used, because I am likely to examine a series of similar images at the same zoom level during a shooting or review session. Your options are as follows:

- **1X (no magnification).** When you press the Magnify button, the initial view will be the single image display with no magnification. Continue pressing Magnify to zoom in.
- **2X, 4X, 8X, 10X (from the center of the frame).** The initial magnified view will be 2X, 4X, 8X, or 10X (your choice), centered around the middle of the frame.
- **Actual Size (from selected point).** Magnified view starts at 100 percent, centered around the autofocus point used to achieve focus; if manual focus was used, the image will be centered around the middle of the frame.
- **Same as last magnification (from the center point).** The 5D Mark IV uses the same magnification value you last used, centered around the middle of the frame.

Ctrl over HDMI

Options: Enable, Disable

My recommendation: N/A

When enabled, you can control playback operations over the HDMI cable and a television set's remote control when displaying your camera's output on an HDMI CEC–compatible television with a remote control. This option will allow you to access menus, choose a 9-image index, play movies and slide shows, change the amount of information displayed (similarly to the INFO. button), or rotate the image. Set to Disable if you do not have the correct TV hardware, or when testing has shown that your HDMI CEC television does not operate correctly in this mode.

Set-up Menu Options

There are four amber-coded Set-up menus where you adjust how your camera *behaves* during your shooting session, as differentiated from the Shooting menu, which adjusts how the pictures are taken. Your choices include:

- Record Func+Card/Folder Sel.
- File Numbering
- File Name
- Auto Rotate
- Format Card
- Eye-Fi Settings
- Auto Power Off
- LCD Brightness
- LCD Color Tone
- Date/Time/Zone
- Language
- Viewfinder Display
- Touch Control
- Video System
- Battery Information
- Sensor Cleaning
- INFO. Button Display Options
- Custom Quick Control
- INFO. Button Live View Display Options
- RATE Button Function
- HDMI Frame Rate
- GPS Settings
- Communication Settings
- Multi Function Lock
- Custom Shooting Mode (C1-C3)
- Clear All Camera Settings
- Copyright Information
- Certification Logo Display
- Camera Firmware Ver.

Record Funct+Card/Folder Select

Options: Record functions: Standard (default), Auto switch card (overflow), Record separately (both cards), Record to multiple; Record/Play; Folder

My recommendation: Overflow; Record separately for events

This entry, the first in the Set-up 1 menu (see Figure 13.11), determines how the 5D Mark IV specifies the memory card(s)—either the Compact Flash or SD card—and folders where your images are stored. There are three parameters: Record Functions (functions of each slot), which of the two slots is used as the default, and the name of the folder used.

Record Func.

This option is active when you have more than one memory card inserted in the 5D Mark IV. You can select any of four different behaviors:

- **Standard (storage on primary card only).** All images will be recorded only to the memory card specified by the Record/Play setting (described next), either Slot 1 (the CF card) or Slot 2 (the SD card). The file format of the images (any of the RAW, JPEG, or RAW+JPEG options) are set in the Image Quality screen, as detailed in Chapter 11. When that memory card fills up, you must replace it with another card, or switch to the card in the other slot manually. I often use this setting when shooting movies to ensure that my clips are stored on the fastest memory card installed. I can keep a card in the other slot installed for emergencies, but must manually switch to it.

- **Auto switch card (overflow mode).** As with Standard, all images will be recorded only to the memory card specified by the Record/Play setting using the Image Quality specifications you apply, but when that card is full, the camera switches automatically to the other card and creates

Figure 13.11

The Set-up 1 menu.

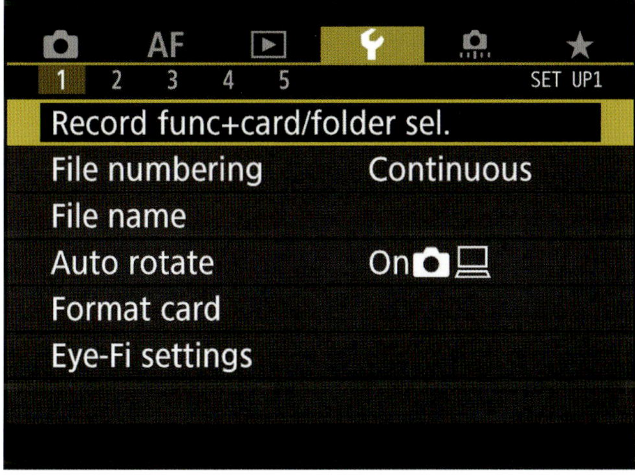

a new folder on that card. I use this setting when I don't want to have to change cards, say, at a wedding or a performance, *and* don't mind having my overflow images diverted to a different, perhaps slower, memory card.

- **Rec. separately (flexible backup).** When this option is active, all images will be stored on *both* cards, but you can specify the image recording quality separately for each memory card in the Image Quality screen. After choosing this option, you'll need to navigate to the Shooting 1 menu and select Image Quality. You'll discover that Slot 1 and Slot 2 are now listed separately. Highlight each one individually and choose one (and only one) of the JPEG or RAW options. (You cannot select RAW+JPEG for a particular slot.)

  This is a very cool feature and is a versatile backup method. For example, you could choose to store a RAW format on a fast Compact Flash card, and your JPEG files (which are smaller) on an SD card. Because JPEG files are more compact, using the slower SD card slot wouldn't bog down your camera as much. You'd still end up with two copies of all your images. If something happened to your CF card (loss, damage, or failure), you'd still have the JPEG copies. Should a mishap befall your SD card instead, you'd not only have the RAW version on the CF card, but could regenerate JPEG copies using an image editor.

  I often use this option for very important shoots, particularly overseas. I carry around plenty of memory cards, so I can keep the backup card, plus copy all the files to my iPad or MacBook Air and have multiple copies. I'd recommend *not* using this setting if you're bracketing, because, even with a modest three-shot bracket, you'd be writing *six* images to your memory cards every time you captured a bracketed set.

- **Rec. to multiple (total backup).** All images are stored on both cards, using the same quality settings you specify in the Image Quality screen. So, if you've selected a RAW+JPEG combination, both images will be written to both memory cards. The process can be fairly slow, so I don't recommend it for fast-moving sports (especially RAW+JPEG; shoot JPEG only for sports) and like the Record Separately option, it's not the best for bracketing. But it does give you total backup of every image you take.

Record/Play or Playback

This option allows you to specify which slot is to be considered the primary for recording or playback, or both (depending on the Record Func. you've selected). Confused? The configurations are simple:

- **For Standard or Auto Switch Card.** In either Standard or Auto Switch Card modes, the camera writes images to only one card, either the default card or the alternate when the default card is full. In that case, the entry reads Record/Play, and you can choose whether all images are written to slot 1 (the CF card) or slot 2 (the SD card). The 5D Mark IV will use that card for both functions, until (if Auto Switch is selected) the card fills and the alternate slot becomes active.

■ **For Rec. Separately or Rec. to Multiple.** In either case, the camera *always* writes to both cards, so you can select *only* which card is to be used for playback. In general, you'll want to select your fastest memory card to be used for playback.

Folder

This option allows you to select which of the folders currently on your memory card should be used to store the images that you capture. You can choose an existing folder from a list, or highlight Create Folder and the camera will create a folder with the folder number incremented. The 5D Mark IV will also create folders for you automatically, and will create a new one when the maximum number of images that can be stored in a specific folder have been deposited. However, you might want to create a new folder on your own. I tend to do that when I am traveling. I can create a new folder each day, making it simple to copy that day's shots to my computer when I return to my hotel room. There's no need to copy the previous files, and since they each have their own folders, the process is simple. You might want to create a new folder for each city you visit, or one for each band or group at the next music festival you attend.

File Numbering

Options: Continuous, Automatic reset, Manual reset

My recommendation: Continuous

The EOS 5D Mark IV will automatically apply a file number to each picture you take, using consecutive numbering for all your photos over a long period, spanning many different memory cards, starting over from scratch when you insert a new card, or when you manually reset the numbers. Numbers are applied from 0001 to 9999, at which time the camera creates a new folder on the card (100, 101, 102, and so forth), so you can have 0001 to 9999 in folder 100, then numbering will start over in folder 101.

The camera keeps track of the last number used in its internal memory. That can lead to a few quirks you should be aware of. For example, if you insert a memory card that had been used with a different camera, the 5D Mark IV may start numbering with the next number after the highest number used by the previous camera. (I once had a brand-new Canon camera start numbering files in the 8,000 range.) I'll explain how this can happen next.

On the surface, the numbering system seems simple enough: In the menu, you can choose Continuous, Automatic reset, or Manual reset. Here is how each works:

■ **Continuous.** If you're using a blank/reformatted memory card, the 5D Mark IV will apply a number that is one greater than the number stored in the camera's internal memory. If the card is not blank and contains images, then the next number will be one greater than the highest number on the card *or* in internal memory. (In other words, if you want to use continuous file numbering consistently, you must always use a card that is blank or freshly formatted.)

Here are some examples.

- You've taken 4,235 shots with the camera, and you insert a blank/reformatted memory card. The next number assigned will be 4,236, based on the value stored in internal memory.
- You've taken 4,235 shots with the camera, and you insert a memory card with a picture numbered 2,728. The next picture will be numbered 4,236.
- You've taken 4,235 shots with the camera, and you insert a memory card with a picture numbered 8,281. The next picture will be numbered 8,282, and that value will be stored in the camera's menu as the "high" shot number (and will be applied when you next insert a blank card).

■ **Automatic reset.** If you're using a blank/reformatted memory card, the next photo taken will be numbered 0001. If you use a card that is not blank, the next number will be one greater than the highest number found on the memory card. Each time you insert a memory card, the next number will either be 0001 or one higher than the highest already on the card.

■ **Manual reset.** The 5D Mark IV creates a new folder numbered one higher than the last folder created, and restarts the file numbers at 0001. Then, the camera uses the numbering scheme that was previously set, either Continuous or Automatic reset, each time you subsequently insert a blank or non-blank memory card.

File Name

Options: Change User Setting 1, Change User Setting 2

My recommendation: N/A

The 5D Mark IV, like other cameras in the Canon product line, automatically applies a file name with a four-digit alphanumeric string, followed by the four-digit image number, such as BB5C0001.jpg or BB5C 0001.cr2 to your image files as they are created. The first four characters are set at the factory and are unique to your camera. However, you can also create two personal User Settings, numbered 1 (with four characters of your choice) and 2 (with three). You can use this menu option to change the names applied to your photos—but only within certain strict limitations. In practice, you can change only four of the eight characters, the *BB5C* (or your camera's counterpart) portion of the file name, using rules and industry conventions, such as those set by the Design Rule for Camera File System (DCF) specification.

DCF limits file names created by conforming digital cameras to a maximum of eight characters, plus a three-character extension (such as .jpg, or .cr2) that represents the format of the file. The eight-plus-three (usually called 8.3) length limitation dates back to an evil and frustrating computer operating system that we older photographers would like to forget (its initials are D.O.S.), but which, unhappily, lives on as the wraith of a file-naming convention.

Of the eight available characters, four are used to represent, in a general sense, the type of camera used to create the image. Canon defaults to your factory-set initial four characters. The remaining four are used for numbers from 0000 to 9999, which is why your 5D Mark IV "rolls over" to *aaaa*0000 again when the 9999 number limitation is reached. When the 5D Mark IV rolls off the factory assembly line, it is configured to provide a choice of three different file-naming schemes:

- **Factory Preset Code.** This is unique to your camera. Every Mark IV has a *different* preset code. When active, your images will be given names like (in my case) *aaaa*0001.jpg when using the sRGB color space. If you switch to Adobe RGB, by industry convention the first character is replaced with an underline, yielding _M4C0001.jpg or _M4C001.cr2 or similar names. You cannot change the factory preset code, but you can switch to one of the alternate naming schemes, as I'll show you next. This is a pretty cool feature, making it easy to tell which of your many Mark IV cameras (it could happen!) was used to take a given image.

- **User Setting 1.** This is one of two user-definable alternative naming schemes. As the camera comes from the factory, it is set to IMG_0001.jpg/cr2/mov (for video) if you're using the sRGB color space, or _IMG0001.jpg (etc.) for Adobe RGB. However, you can specify all *four* initial characters for this setting, and end up with something like 5DM40001.jpg instead, when using sRGB. The underscore still replaces the first characters in the file name when you're using Adobe RGB. So, if you choose *OHIO*, you'll see OHIO0001.jpg for sRGB and _HIO0001.jpg with Adobe RGB.

- **User Setting 2.** This second user-definable setting allows you to specify only the first *three* of the four initial characters. The default is IMG for those characters. The camera uses the fourth position for a code representing the image recording quality. So, if your initial three letters are *ABC*, you might end up with file names like _BCL0001.jpg or ABCL001.jpg. The codes are as follows:

  - **L.** Large Fine JPEG, Large Standard JPEG, or RAW.
  - **M.** Medium Fine JPEG, Medium Standard JPEG, or M RAW.
  - **S.** Small 1 Fine JPEG, Small 1 Standard JPEG, or S RAW.
  - **T.** Small 2 JPEG.
  - **U.** Small 3 JPEG.
  - **_ (underscore).** The file is a movie, and quality setting is not indicated.

Redefining User Settings 1 and 2

To change the two User Settings from their defaults, navigate to the File Name screen, as shown at left in Figure 13.12. Then, follow these steps:

1. **Access menu entry.** Highlight the User Setting you want to modify and press SET. The screen shown at right in Figure 13.12 appears.

2. **Remove old entry.** Press the Trash button at the lower-left corner of the camera repeatedly until the previous entry is removed. A vertical line will be shown at the current cursor position.

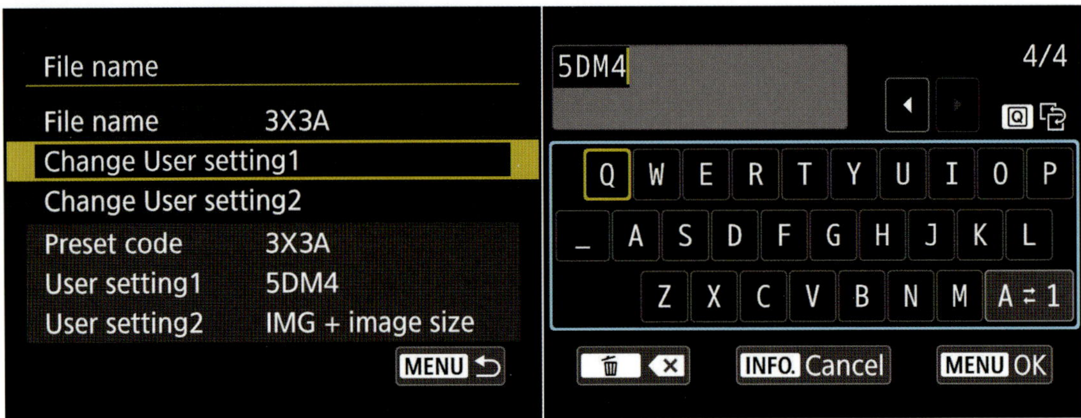

Figure 13.12 Left: Customize and choose your file naming scheme. Right: Enter text here.

3. **Switch to text characters.** The Q button toggles between the text screen at the top and the text characters at the bottom. Press it or tap its icon on the touch screen to jump down to the lower text box.

4. **Select characters.** Use the touch screen or the multi-controller to navigate to the first character you want to choose. Only uppercase letters, an underscore, and numerals are available. You can also navigate with the QCD and Mail Dial, but that is slower. Press the character or press SET to enter the highlighted character.

5. **Choose remaining characters.** The cursor will advance to the next position, and you can repeat Step 4 to enter the remaining characters (a total of four for Setting 1 and three for Setting 2). You can always press the Q button and use the Trash button to remove one or more characters you've entered in error. You cannot use an underscore for any character; that's reserved for the camera's use.

6. **Finish.** Press MENU to confirm your text entry, or INFO. to cancel.

7. **Review.** The updated definitions are shown at the bottom of the screen, as seen at left in Figure 13.12.

Selecting a Naming Scheme

Once you've defined your naming alternatives to your satisfaction, you can switch among them at any time during a shooting session. Just access the File Name screen from the Set-up 1 menu, highlight File Name at the top of the screen, and press SET. You can then choose the factory preset code, User Setting 1, or User Setting 2. Renaming a user setting is so easy that I sometimes do it on the fly during a shoot. If you don't need to differentiate between different cameras or models, you can change the characters to anything else that suits your purposes, including your initials (DDB_ or JFK_, for example) or even customize for a particular shooting session (EUR, GER, FRA, and JAP when taking vacation trips). You can also use the file name flexibility to partially overcome the 9999 numbering limitation. You could, for example, use the template 5D1 to represent the first 10,000 pictures you take with your 5D Mark IV, and then 5D2 for the next 10,000, and 5D3 for the 10,000 after that.

That's assuming you don't rename your image files in your computer. In a way, file naming verges on a moot consideration, because it applies *only* to the images as they exist in your camera. After (or during) transfer to your computer you can change the names to anything you want, completely disregarding the 8.3 limitations (although it's a good idea to retain the default extensions). If you shot an image file named IMG_4832.jpg in your camera, you could change it to Paris_EiffelTower_32.jpg later. Indeed, virtually all photo-transfer programs, including Photoshop Elements Transfer, allow you to specify a template and rename your photos as they are moved or copied to your computer from your camera or memory card.

I usually don't go to that bother (I generally don't use transfer software; I just drag and drop images from my memory card to folders I have set up), but renaming can be useful for those willing to take the time to do it.

Auto Rotate

Options: Camera+Computer, Computer, Off

My recommendation: Camera+Computer

You can turn this feature On or Off. When activated, the EOS 5D Mark IV rotates pictures taken in vertical orientation on the LCD screen so you don't have to turn the camera to view them comfortably. However, this orientation also means that the longest dimension of the image is shown using the shortest dimension of the LCD, so the picture is reduced in size. You have three options. The image can be autorotated when viewing in the camera *and* on your computer screen using your image-editing/viewing software (this choice is represented by a pair of camera/computer screen icons). The image can be marked to autorotate *only* when reviewing your image in your image editor or viewing software (just a computer screen icon is used). This option allows you to have rotation applied when using your computer, while retaining the ability to maximize the image on your LCD in the camera. The third choice is Off. The image will not be rotated when displayed in the camera or with your computer. Note that if you switch Auto Rotate off, any pictures shot while the feature is disabled will not be automatically rotated when you turn Auto Rotate back on; information embedded in the image file when the photo *is taken* is used to determine whether autorotation is applied.

Format Card

Options: Slot 1, Slot 2

My recommendation: N/A

Use this item to erase everything on your memory card and set up a fresh file system ready for use. When you select Format, you'll be given a choice of selecting Slot 1 (CF card) or Slot 2 (SD card). Highlight your preference and press SET. A display pops up showing the capacity of the card, how much of that space is currently in use, and two choices at the bottom of the screen to Cancel or OK (proceed with the format). A blue-yellow bar appears on the screen to show the progress of the formatting step.

Eye-Fi Settings

Options: Enable, Disable, Connection information

My recommendation: Disable

This menu item appears when you have an Eye-Fi card inserted in the camera. You can enable and disable Eye-Fi wireless functions, and view connection information. (See Figure 13.13.) I explained the 5D Mark IV's Eye-Fi options in detail in Chapter 6. The pair of entries allow you to Enable or Disable the card, and view current connection information. Because the Eye-Fi card draws power from the camera even when it's switched off, you might want to Disable the card (or remove it from the camera) when you don't need to use its features.

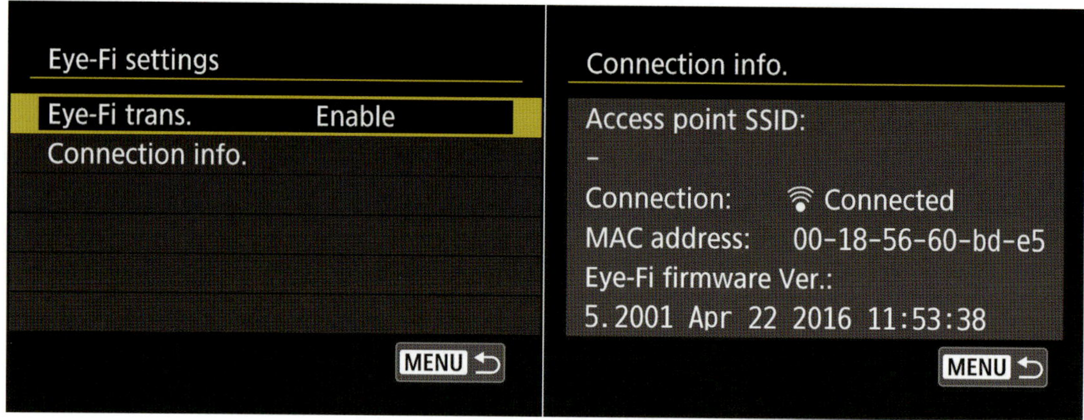

Figure 13.13 Eye-Fi information (left), Connection information (right).

Auto Power Off

Options: 1 (default), 2, 4, 8, 15, 30 minutes, Disable

My recommendation: 2 minutes; 8 minutes when shooting sports

This setting, the first in Set-up 2 menu (see Figure 13.14), allows you to determine how long the EOS 5D Mark IV remains active before shutting itself off. You can select 1, 2, 4, 8, 15, or 30 minutes or Off, which leaves the camera turned on indefinitely. However, even if the camera has shut itself off, if the power switch remains in the ON position, you can bring the camera back to life by tapping the shutter button.

SAVING POWER WITH THE EOS 5D Mark IV

There are three settings and several techniques you can use to help stretch the longevity of your 5D Mark IV's battery. The first setting is the Image Review time option described in Chapter 11 under the Shooting 1 menu. That big 3.2-inch LCD uses a lot of juice, so reducing the amount of time it is used (either for automatic review or for manually playing back your images) can boost the effectiveness of your battery. The second setting, Auto Power Off, turns off most functions (metering and autofocus shut off by themselves about six seconds after you release the shutter button or take a picture) based on the delay you specify. The third setting is the LCD Brightness adjustment described below. If you're willing to shade the LCD with your hand, you can often get away with lower brightness settings outdoors, which will further increase the useful life of your battery. The techniques? Turn off image stabilization if your lens has that feature and you feel you don't need it. When transferring pictures from your 5D Mark IV to your computer, use a card reader instead of the USB cable. Linking your camera to your computer and transferring images using the cable takes longer and uses a lot more power.

Figure 13.14

The Set-up 2 menu has seven options.

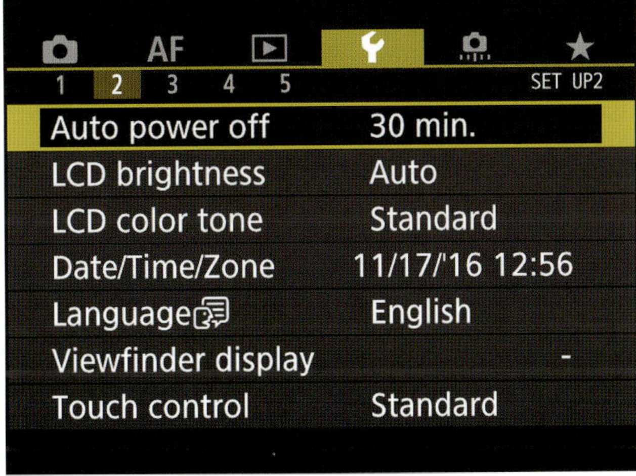

LCD Brightness

Options: Auto (default), Manual

My recommendation: Auto

Choose this menu option, and a thumbnail image with a grayscale strip appears on the LCD, as shown in Figure 13.15. You can select both automatic brightness and manually set brightness.

- **Automatic brightness.** Use the Main Dial to toggle between Auto and Manual brightness settings. You may see the LCD dim when switching to Auto, as the camera adjusts for the light level. If you've chosen this option, you can spin the QCD to change from a default mid-level setting to a lower or brighter setting, and the camera will adjust the brightness from that point automatically.

- **Manual brightness.** If you select Manual, you can use the Quick Control Dial or the multi-controller to adjust the brightness to a comfortable viewing level. Use the gray bars as a guide; you want to be able to see both the lightest and darkest steps at top and bottom, and not lose any of the steps in the middle. Brighter settings use more battery power, but can allow you to view an image on the LCD outdoors in bright sunlight. When you have the brightness, you want, press the SET button to lock it in and return to the menu. I often dial down the brightness to the minimum when shooting at concerts and other events to avoid disturbing the other paying customers.

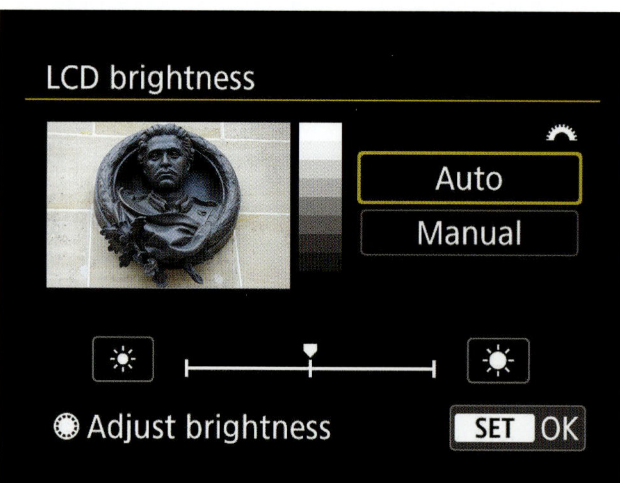

Figure 13.15
Adjust LCD brightness for easier viewing under varying ambient lighting conditions.

LCD Color Tone

Options: 1: Warm tone, 2: Standard (default), 3: Cool tone 1, 4: Cool tone 2

My recommendation: 2: Standard

You can use this setting to adjust the approximate color balance of the LCD monitor to your taste. You'd use it if you consistently find that your images are warmer or cooler than what you view on the LCD, and want to have a (slightly) more accurate preview image. (The LCD will never match your final image precisely, especially when you are shooting RAW, because the 5D Mark IV displays a JPEG version regardless of the format you choose.)

To set the color, activate this entry, and the last image you played back will be displayed on the LCD monitor. You should use the ambient lighting conditions you want to standardize on. Then, highlight 1: Warm tone, 2: Standard, 3: Cool tone 1, or 4: Cool tone 2, and press SET.

Date/Time/Zone

Options: Date, Time, Zone, Daylight Savings

My recommendation: N/A

Use this option to set the date and time, which will be embedded in the image file along with exposure information and other data. As first outlined in Chapter 1, you can set the date and time by following these steps:

1. Access this menu entry from the Set-up 2 menu.

2. Rotate the QCD to move the highlighting down to the Date/Time entry.

3. Press the SET button in the center of the QCD to access the Date/Time setting screen, shown in Figure 13.16.

Figure 13.16
Set the date, time, and time zone here.

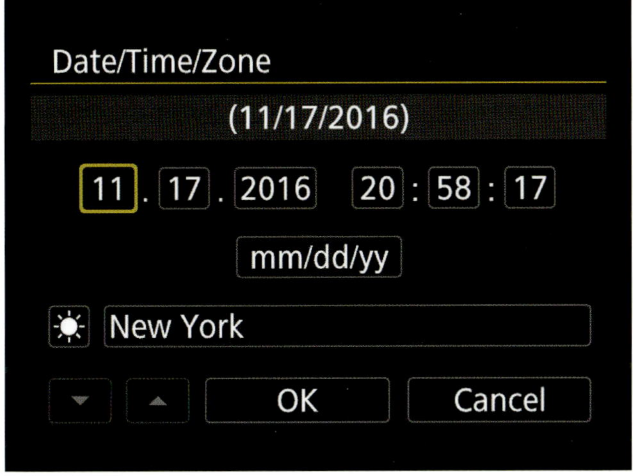

4. Rotate the QCD to select the value you want to change. When the gold box highlights the month, day, year, hour, minute, or second format you want to adjust, press the SET button to activate that value. A pair of up/down pointing triangles appears above the value.

5. Rotate the QCD to adjust the value up or down. Press the SET button to confirm the value you've entered.

6. Repeat steps 4 and 5 for each of the other values you want to change. The date format can be switched from the default mm/dd/yy to yy/mm/dd or dd/mm/yy; you can turn Daylight Savings time on or off, and choose an appropriate time zone.

7. When finished, rotate the QCD to select either OK (if you're satisfied with your changes) or Cancel (if you'd like to return to the Set-up 2 menu without making any changes). Press SET to confirm your choice.

8. When finished setting the date and time, press the MENU button to exit, or just tap the shutter release.

Language

Options: 25 languages

My recommendation: N/A

Choose from 25 languages for menu display, rotating the Quick Control Dial or using the multi-controller joystick until the language you want to select is highlighted. Press the SET button to activate. Your choices include English, German, French, Dutch, Danish, Portuguese, Finnish, Italian, Ukrainian, Norwegian, Swedish, Spanish, Greek, Russian, Polish, Czech, Magyar, Romanian, Turkish, Arabic, Thai, Simplified Chinese, Traditional Chinese, Korean, and Japanese.

If you accidentally set a language you don't read and find yourself with incomprehensible menus, don't panic. Just choose the fifth option from the top of the Set-up 2 menu, and select the idioma, sprache, langue, or kieli of your choice. English is the first selection in the list.

Viewfinder Display

Options: Electronic level, Grid display, Show/Hide in viewfinder

My recommendation: N/A

Thanks to the miracle of modern technology, your optical viewfinder display can be just as crowded with information as the color LCD monitor on the back of your 5D Mark IV. Fortunately, much of this clutter is optional. This menu entry allows you to select which information is shown, and which is hidden.

- **Electronic level.** Hide/Show. The display at the top of the frame (see Figure 13.17, left) shows how much the camera is rotated around the axis passing through the center of the front element of the lens (the horizontal indicators) or tilted up or down (the vertical indicators).

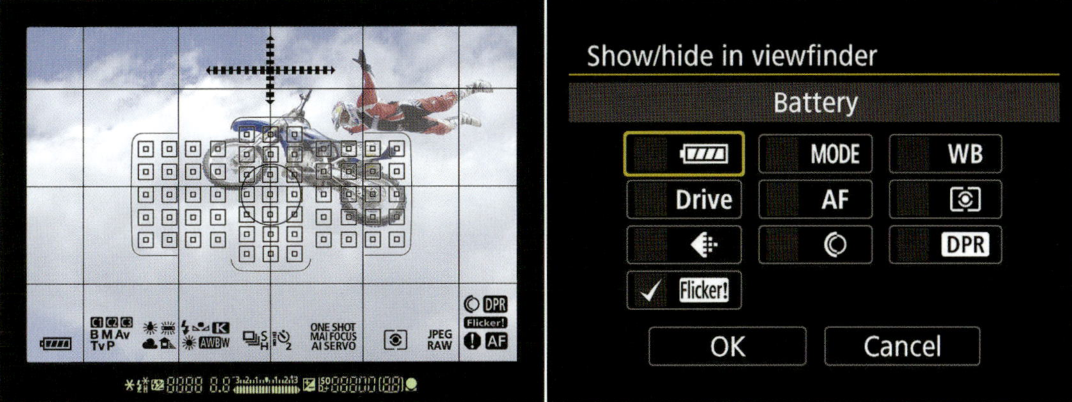

Figure 13.17 The viewfinder screen can become crowded with information (left). Fortunately, you can select which information is shown or hidden (right).

- **Grid display.** Hide/Show. The 24-cell grid on the screen can be used for composition or leveling of horizontal or vertical components in your image, such as the horizon or architectural elements.
- **Show/Hide in viewfinder.** You can select/unselect any or all of 10 different indicators overlaid on the frame area, to custom tailor the amount of information displayed. (See Figure 13.17, right.)

Touch Control

Options: Standard, Sensitive, Disable

My recommendation: Standard

Here you can specify how sensitive the touch screen is to your taps and strokes. You can disable touch control entirely if you never use it, or set the amount of sensitivity that works best for digital control, so to speak.

Video System

Options: For NTSC, For PAL

My recommendation: N/A

This setting, the first on the Set-up 3 screen (see Figure 13.18), controls the output of the 5D Mark IV through the HDMI cable when you're displaying images on an external monitor. You can select either NTSC, used in the United States, Canada, Mexico, many Central, South American, and Caribbean countries, much of Asia, and other countries, or PAL, which is used in the UK, much of Europe, Africa, India, China, and parts of the Middle East.

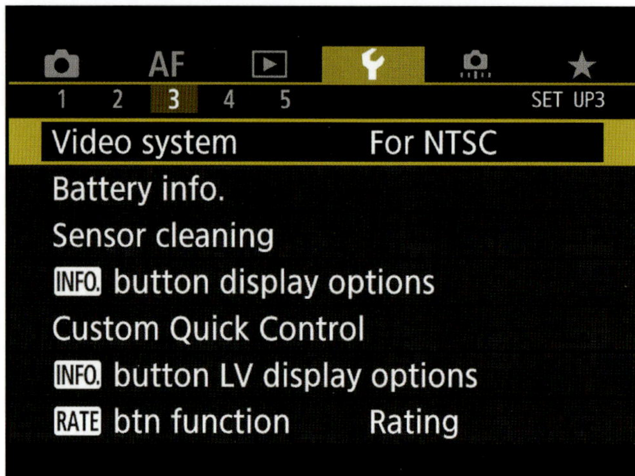

Figure 13.18
The Set-up 3 menu.

VIEWING ON A TELEVISION

Canon makes it quite easy to view your images on a high-definition television (HDTV). Purchase the optional HDMI Cable HTC-100 (or equivalent HDMI Micro C cable) and connect it to the HDMI OUT terminal just above the USB/digital port on the left side of the camera.

Connect the other end to an HDMI input port on your television or monitor (my 42-inch HDTV has three of them; my 26-inch monitor has just two). Then turn on the camera and press the Playback button. The image will appear on the external TV/HDTV/monitor and will not be displayed on the camera's LCD. HDTV systems automatically show your images at the appropriate resolution for that set.

Battery Information

Options: Register, Delete Info.

My recommendation: N/A

This entry is an exceptionally useful feature that allows you to view battery condition information and performance, and track the data among several different batteries. Your EOS 5D Mark IV can keep track of multiple LP-E6 or LP-E6N batteries because each of them is given a unique serial number (which is either printed on or available on a sticker you can affix to the battery). The camera reads this serial number and stores information about each of the batteries that you use and have "registered" separately. I always recommend owning at least two and, preferably three or more batteries. That's especially true if you use the Battery Grip BG-E20, which holds two battery packs itself. I also own the EOS 80D, which uses the same battery, so I'm able to justify four batteries to shuttle between my two cameras.

This feature makes it possible to see exactly how each battery you own is performing, allows you to rotate them to even out the usage, and helps you know when it's time to replace a battery. When you select this menu choice, a Battery info screen like the one shown at left in Figure 13.19 appears, with a wealth of information (if you use two LP-E6/E6N packs in a BG-E20 grip, information about both packs will appear):

- **Battery position.** The second line of the screen includes an icon that shows where the battery currently being evaluated is installed (usually the hand grip if you're not using the BG-E20).

- **Power type.** Next to the position icon is an indicator that shows the model number of the battery installed, or shows that the DC power adapter is being used instead.

- **Remaining capacity.** The Battery check icon appears showing the remaining capacity visually, along with a percentage number that reads out in 1% increments. You can use this as a rough gauge of how much power you have remaining. If you're in the middle of an important shooting session, you might want to switch to a fully charged battery at the 25%–33% level to avoid interruptions at the worst probable time. (If you're using six AA batteries in the BG-E6 grip instead of LP-E6 packs, only this battery capacity notice will appear; the other indicators are not shown.)

- **Shutter count.** Displays how many times the shutter has been actuated with the current charged battery. This info can help you learn just how much certain features cost you in terms of power. For example, if a battery has only 50 percent of its power remaining, but you've taken only a few dozen photos, you know that your power is being sapped by picture review, lots of autofocus, frequent image stabilization because of lower shutter speeds, or (a major culprit) that flip-up flash you've been using. While in most cases knowledge is power, in this instance knowledge can help you *save* power, with a tip-off to use fewer juice-sapping features if the current battery pack must be stretched as far as possible.

- **Recharge performance.** This indicator shows how well your battery pack is accepting and holding a charge. Three green bars mean that the pack's performance is fine; two bars show that recharge performance is degraded a little. A red bar indicates that your pack is on its last legs and should be replaced soon. To lengthen the service time of your batteries, you might want to rotate usage among several different packs, so they all "age" at roughly the same rate.

Registering Your Battery Packs

The EOS 5D Mark IV can "remember" information about up to six LP-E6 battery packs, and provide readouts of their status individually. To register the battery currently in your camera, follow these steps:

1. Access the Battery Info. screen from the Set-up 3 menu.

2. Press the INFO. button, located to the left of the LCD screen.

3. Information about the current battery, including its serial number and the current date, will be shown on a new screen (see Figure 13.19, right).

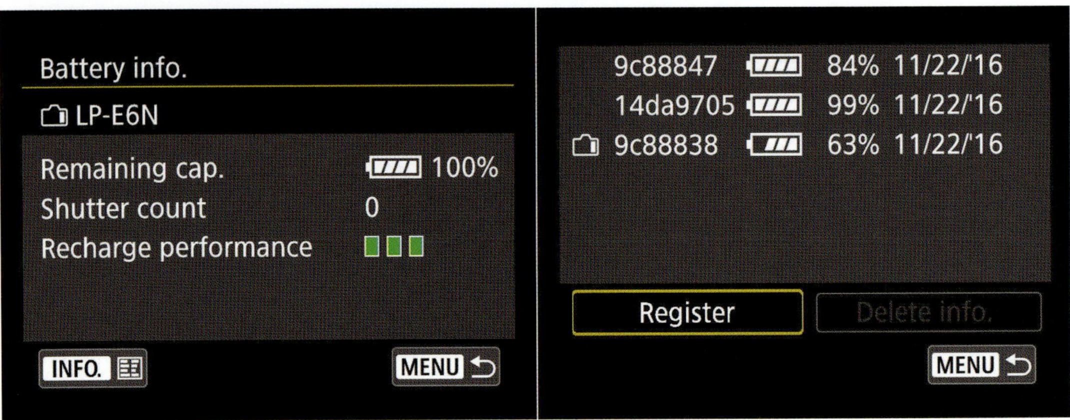

Figure 13.19 View the battery type and position, remaining capacity, number of pictures taken with the current charge, and the performance of your pack (left). Register a new battery (right).

4. Choose Register to log the battery; if the pack has already been registered, you can choose Delete Info. to remove the battery from the list. (You'd want to do this if you already had registered the limit of six batteries and want to add another one.)

5. Press SET to add the battery to the registry.

6. If you're deleting a battery, the 5D Mark IV shows you a Battery Info. delete screen instead. (You can delete a battery pack without having that battery installed in the camera—which could come in handy if you lose one.) Just select the battery (by serial number) and delete.

7. Press MENU to back out of any of the Battery Info. screens.

8. Once a battery has been registered, you can check on its remaining capacity at any time (even if it isn't currently installed in the 5D Mark IV) from the Battery info page. The camera remembers and updates the status of each registered battery whenever it is inserted in the 5D Mark IV. The date the battery was last used is also shown.

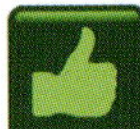

Tip

Use this info with caution, however, as a given battery may have self-discharged slightly during storage and, of course, you may have fully recharged it since the last time it was inserted in the camera. However, this data can be useful in tracking the remaining capacity of several different battery packs during a single shooting session, or over the course of several days when you're not recharging the packs after each session.

Sensor Cleaning

Options: Auto cleaning, Clean now, Clean manually

My recommendation: N/A

One of the Canon EOS 5D Mark IV's most useful features is the automatic sensor cleaning system that reduces or eliminates the need to clean your camera's sensor manually using brushes, swabs, or bulb blowers. Canon has applied anti-static coatings to the sensor and other portions of the camera body interior to counter charge build-ups that attract dust. A separate filter over the sensor vibrates ultrasonically each time the 5D Mark IV is powered on or off, shaking loose any dust, which is captured by a sticky strip beneath the sensor.

Use this menu entry to enable or disable automatic sensor cleaning on power up (select Auto Cleaning to choose) or to activate automatic cleaning during a shooting session (select Clean Now). You can also choose the Clean Manually option to flip up the mirror and clean the sensor yourself with a blower, brush, or swab. If the battery level is too low to safely carry out the cleaning operation, the 5D Mark IV will let you know and refuse to proceed, unless you use the optional AC Adapter Kit ACK-E6N with the DC Coupler DR-E6.

INFO. Button Display Options

Options: Displays camera settings, Electronic level, Quick Control screen, Custom Quick Control screen

My recommendation: N/A

The INFO. button on the back panel of the Canon EOS 5D Mark IV can cycle among up to four different screens on the color LCD monitor, or display a blank screen. The button alternates among Camera Settings, Electronic Level, Quick Control, and Custom Quick Control information displays (see Figure 13.20). If one is shown, press the INFO. button to see the others or to turn off the display entirely. This setting allows you to specify which of the screens are shown. Follow these steps:

1. When you select the menu entry, the INFO. button display options screen appears with four choices. Use the Quick Control Dial or multi-controller to highlight any of the three and press SET to mark or unmark that option.

2. Always mark at least one of the four options. The 5D Mark IV won't allow you to disable all of the display options.

3. When finished, press the SET button to confirm your changes.

4. Press SET to OK or Cancel and exit the screen. (If you exit in any other way, your changes will not be entered.) Once you've left this options screen, you can press MENU or tap the shutter release to return to shooting mode.

5. Thereafter, the 5D Mark IV will cycle among the choices you've activated, plus a blank screen, each time you press the INFO. button.

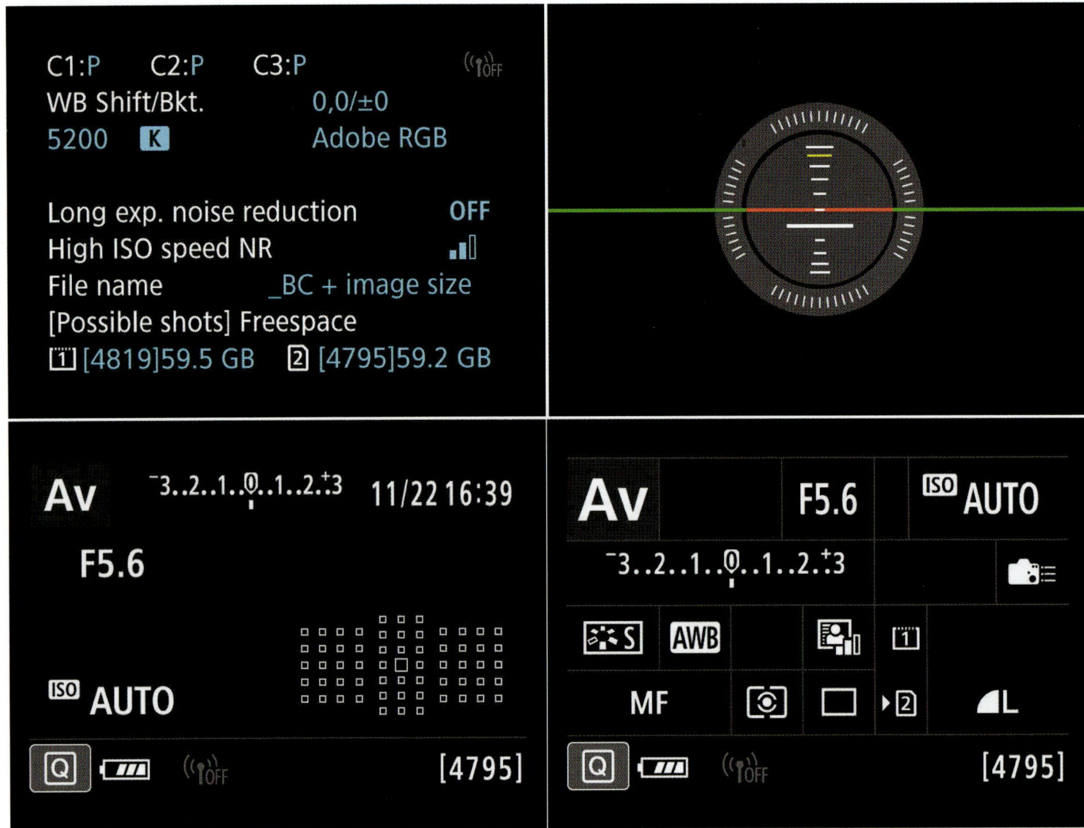

Figure 13.20 The INFO. button cycles among (clockwise from upper left) Camera Settings, Electronic Level, Quick Control, and Custom Quick Control screens.

Custom Quick Control

Options: Edit layout, Revert layout, Clear all items

My recommendation: N/A

This setting allows you to design your own customized Quick Control screen, containing only the items you use most, positioned in the locations most convenient to you, and in a size you select. You can have *two* Quick Control screens at your fingertips: the default screen, and the custom screen, each just a press of the INFO. button away (unless you disable one or the other using the INFO. Button Display Options entry just discussed).

To create your own Custom Quick Control Screen, just follow these steps:

1. **Navigate to the Custom Quick Control entry and press SET.** The screen shown at upper left in Figure 13.21 appears.

2. **Choose Start Editing Layout.** An informational screen appears displaying your available options:

   - **Q.** Add item.
   - **Trash.** Remove item.
   - **SET.** Select and confirm.

3. **To reorder layout.** Highlight the entry you'd like to move, as shown in Figure 13.21, upper right. Then use the QCD to move it down or up and the Main Dial to move the icon horizontally (see Figure 13.21, lower left). Press SET when you're satisfied with the position.

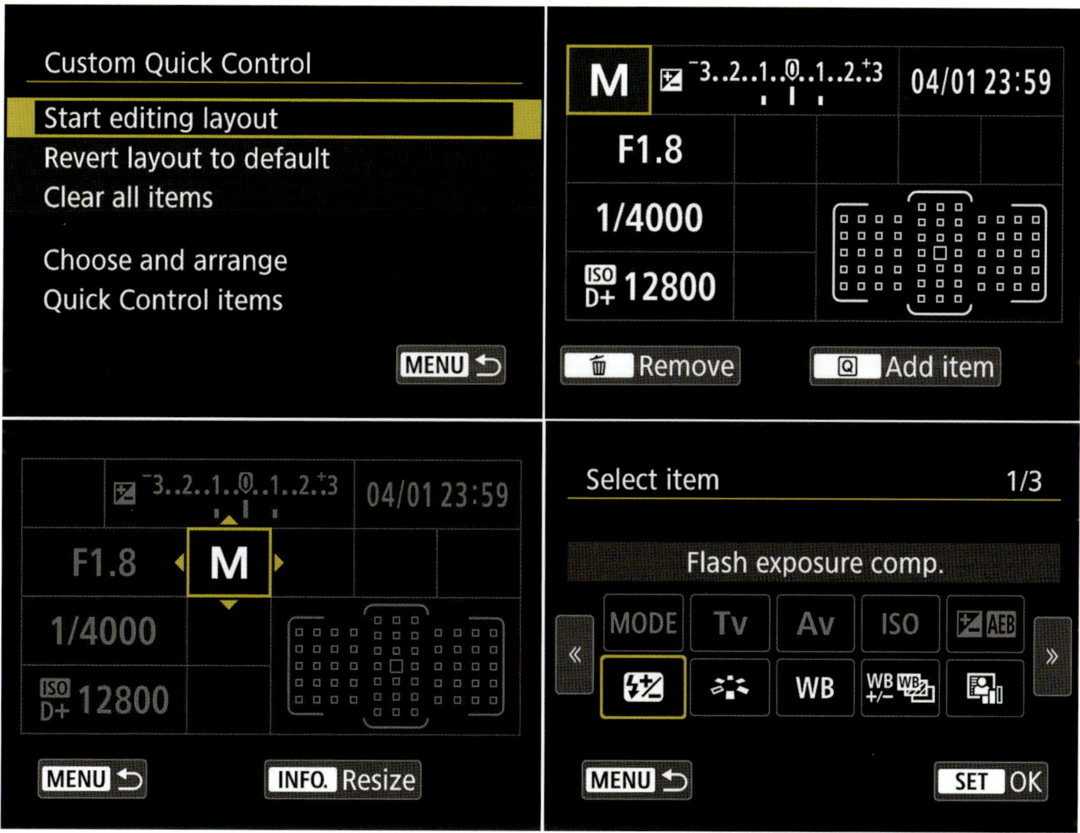

Figure 13.21 To create a Custom Quick Control: Activate editing (upper left); select entry to edit (upper right); move entry (lower left); choose item to add (lower right).

4. **Resize (optional).** Press the INFO. button to resize the highlighted icon. The screen that appears allows you to choose from cell sizes ranging from 1 × 1 to 1 × 3, depending on the sizes available for that icon. Press SET to confirm.

5. **To add an item.** Press the Q button. A screen displaying the available items that can be added to the Custom Quick Control screen is shown, as in Figure 13.21, lower right. Highlight your selection and press SET to confirm.

6. **Return to menu.** When you've returned to the previous menu, you can choose Revert Layout to Default, or Clear All items.

7. **Display Custom Quick Control.** Remember to activate the Custom Quick Control screen in the INFO. Button Display Options entry, as described above. You can disable the default Quick Control display in the same menu entry.

INFO. Button Live View Display Options

Options: Live View INFO. switch setting, Histogram display, Reset

My recommendation: N/A

The 5D Mark IV finally makes it possible to customize and declutter the information displays shown during live view. This setting has three options: Live View INFO. Switch Setting, Histogram Display, and Reset. The last two are easy to understand: you can specify whether the Brightness or RGB histograms are displayed on the live view screen, or you can Reset the live view screens to their factory defaults. The first item shown on the screen (see Figure 13.22) is a bit more complicated. It lets you define which of four information screens is shown, and which icons are available on each.

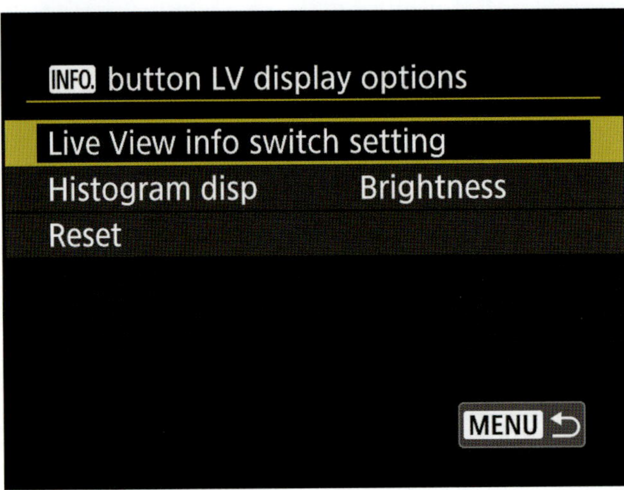

Figure 13.22
INFO. button Live View display options.

Live View INFO. Switch Setting

When you choose this entry, the screen shown in Figure 13.23, left, appears. However, unlike the INFO. Button Display entry above, choosing your display is not a matter of simply checking or unchecking specific elements you want to view. Instead, you mark or unmark any of the four numbers shown in the right-hand column. Each of those numbers represents a different combination of elements:

1. Basic shooting information and on-screen buttons are overlaid on the LCD monitor during live view.

2. Same as #1, but with the addition of detailed shooting information.

3. Same as #2, but with the addition of histogram and electronic level display.

4. Produces a blank screen with none of the elements listed above.

Your options include:

- **Live View INFO. switch setting.** In the column at right in the screen, you'll find numbers 1 through 4. Use the QCD to highlight any of the four and a preview of the information displayed is shown in a thumbnail at left. Press the SET button to check or uncheck one of the four. You cannot hide all of them; at least one must be check marked.

- **Edit screen.** When a screen number is highlighted, press the INFO. button to edit that screen. The Edit screen, like the screen shown at right in Figure 13.23, appears. Highlight the icons you want to show or hide using the QCD, and then press SET to mark or unmark that type of icon. The available icons are as follows:

  - Basic shooting information
  - Detailed Shooting Information
  - On-screen buttons
  - Histogram display
  - Electronic level

The thumbnail image changes to show which of the types of information will be displayed. When finished editing a screen, highlight OK and press SET to exit.

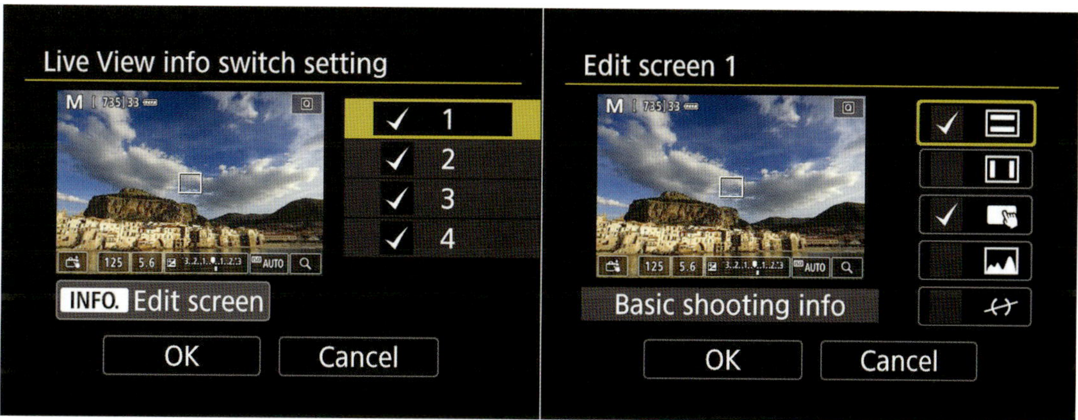

Figure 13.23 Enable or disable an informational screen (left); choose information to appear on each screen (right).

Histogram Display

This entry has two sub-entries. One is Brightness/RGB, which allows you to specify which type of histogram is shown on the LCD monitor during live view, *as long as you've activated display option #3,* described above. The second option is Display Size. You can select Large or Small, depending on how much clutter you can abide on the LCD monitor at one time. Because histograms only appear when the other four screen elements are also displayed, I tend to use Small to produce a slightly less crowded screen.

Reset

Restores the default settings, which are all four Info Switch options, and a large brightness histogram.

RATE Button Function

Options: Rating (default), Protect

My recommendation: N/A

Select whether a press of the RATE button during playback will change the rating of the displayed image, or whether the button will apply the Protect attribute instead. If you elect to retain the Rating function, press the Q button to select which of the one- to five-star ratings can be applied. Highlight a star rating and then press SET to check or uncheck that rating. Highlight the OK or Cancel options at the bottom of the screen to finish.

You might, for example, want to label only the stellar images and turkeys, and so would select only the One-Star and Five-Star ratings, disabling the others. Multiple presses of the RATE button while you are rating images jumps from the starting star rating to the next highest, and then wraps around to the lowest activated rating again. If you never use ratings at all, or apply then from the Playback menu only, you might want to go for the Protect option instead.

HDMI Frame Rate

Options: Auto (default), 59.94i, 59.94p, 23.98p

My recommendation: Auto

This is the first entry on the Set-up 4 menu (see Figure 13.24). Select Auto to allow the camera to choose the appropriate HDMI display protocol when it is connected to a suitable display. Or, you can choose 24 fps progressive scan or 60 fps interlaced or progressive scans. I'll explain more about scan rates in Chapter 16.

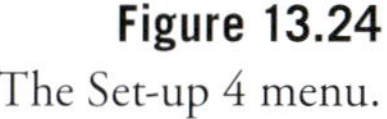

Figure 13.24
The Set-up 4 menu.

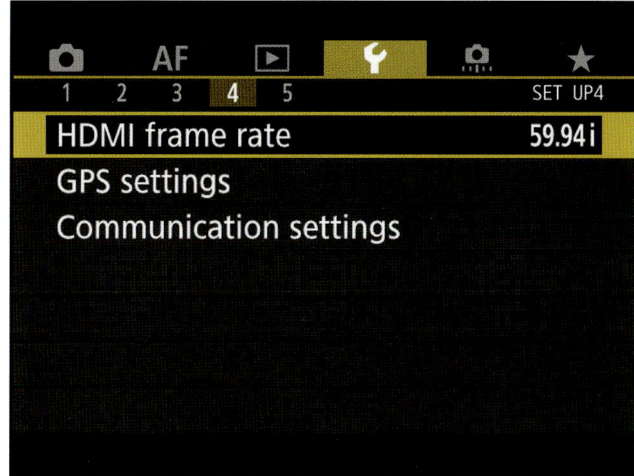

GPS Settings

Options: GPS, Auto time setting, Position update interval, GPS information display, GPS logger
My preference: N/A

Your options for using the built-in GPS device in your 5D Mark IV follow (see Figure 13.25). I discuss GPS use in more detail in Chapter 6. Here are the basics:

- **GPS.** You can choose Disable to switch GPS completely off; Mode 1, in which the GPS remains active even when the camera is off, draining your battery; or Mode 2, which turns GPS off when you physically turn the camera off, saving battery power. However, if the camera powers down after your Auto Power Off setting has elapsed, GPS signals will be received periodically.

  Because the GPS uses a measurable amount of power, you'll want to select the setting best suited for your use of the device. Keep in mind that when GPS is disabled or "asleep" in Mode 2, some time will elapse before the device can acquire satellite signals again and begin functioning normally.

  The GPS data is embedded in your image files as you shoot whenever the GPS entry is set to Enable.

- **Auto Time Setting.** You can choose Auto Update to allow your camera's clock setting to be updated from highly accurate satellite data any time GPS is active; Disable to prevent this from happening, or Set Now to update immediately.

- **Position Update Interval.** Depending on how much you use GPS and how accurate you want the embedded GPS information to be, you can schedule position updates as often as every second to once every 5 minutes. The default value is every 15 seconds.

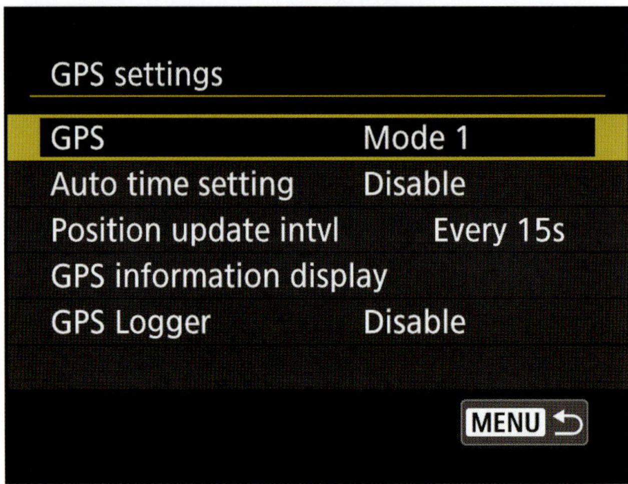

Figure 13.25
GPS settings.

- **GPS Information Display.** This screen shows the camera's current Latitude, Longitude, Elevation, UTC, and strength of Satellite reception. One new feature I'd like to see would be the ability to transmit this information over Wi-Fi so you could quickly locate a lost/stolen camera, like Find My iPhone and comparable phone apps.
- **GPS Logger.** The camera can log your current GPS position, transfer log data to a memory card, or delete log data entirely. The receiver will record your route information internally. Log files can be saved with the Map Utility, and converted to the standard .KMZ file format compatible with Google Earth and other applications.

Communications Settings

Options: Built-in wireless settings, FTP transfer settings

My recommendation: N/A

This entry allows you to specify wireless settings for Wi-Fi/NFC, send images to a smartphone, assign a nickname to your camera, and define File Transfer Protocol settings for uploading files over the Internet. I explained these functions in detail in Chapter 6, and won't repeat those instructions here.

Multi Function Lock

Options: Main Dial, Quick Control Dial, Multi-controller, AF area selection button, Touch control

My recommendation: N/A

This is the first entry on the Set-up 5 menu (see Figure 13.26). Your 5D Mark IV includes a sliding lock switch just beneath the Quick Control Dial. Slide it to the right when you want to prevent the use of the QCD, Main Dial, multi-controller, AF area selection button, or touch controls from accidentally changing a setting. You can select any or all five of the controls to lock, while freeing the others (or none) to act normally. I use this sometimes when I am using manual exposure, especially when I'm fumbling around in a darkened environment, and don't want to unintentionally manipulate my settings. The Multi Function Lock screen has one option for each control; highlight the control and press SET to lock or unlock it. A check mark appears next to the control's name when it's locked, and an L/Lock indicator appears in the viewfinder, top-panel LCD, and shooting settings display (see Figure 13.27). Even if you've locked the QCD, its touchpad functions can still be used during movie shooting even if Silent Control has been activated in the Shooting 5 (Movie) menu.

Figure 13.26
The Set-up 5 menu.

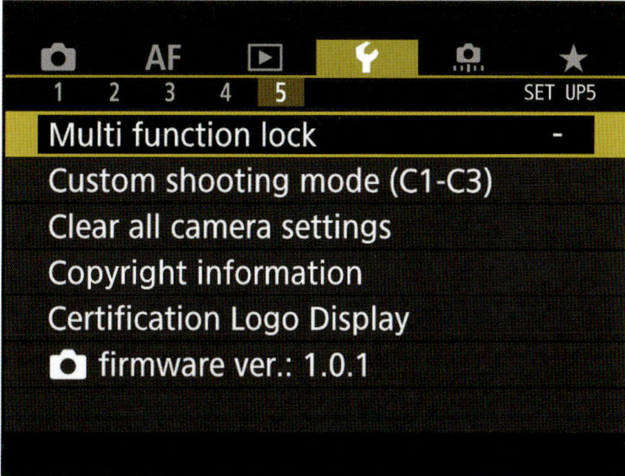

Figure 13.27
Lock any or all of these five.

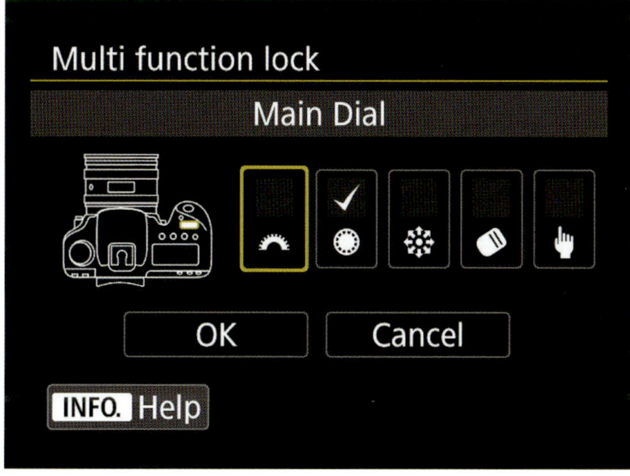

Custom Shooting Mode (C1–C3)

Options: User settings saved in one of three memory slots

My recommendation: N/A

This entry allows you to register your EOS 5D Mark IV's current camera shooting settings and file them away in the C1, C2, or C3 positions on the Mode Dial. Doing this overwrites any settings previously stored at that position. You can also clear the settings for any of the three Mode Dial positions individually, returning them to their factory default values. Table 13.1 shows the settings you can store.

Table 13.1 Stored Camera User Settings	
Mode/Menu	**Settings**
Shooting menu	*Shooting 1:* Image quality; Image review; Beep; Release shutter without card; Lens aberration correction; Flash firing; E-TTL II Flash metering; Flash sync speed in Av mode
	Shooting 2: Exposure compensation/AEB; ISO speed settings; Auto Lighting Optimizer; All white balance settings; Color space
	Shooting 3: Picture Style; Long exposure noise reduction; High ISO speed noise reduction; Highlight tone priority; Multiple exposure; HDR mode
	Shooting 4: Interval timer; Bulb timer; Anti-flicker shooting; Mirror lockup
	Shooting 5 (Live View): Live view shooting; AF mode; Touch shutter; Grid display; Aspect ratio; Exposure simulation
	Shooting 6 (Live View): Silent live view shooting; Metering timer
	Shooting 4 (Movie): Movie servo AF; AF method; Grid display; Movie recording quality; Sound recording; AF speed with Movie Servo AF; Movie Servo AF subject tracking
	Shooting 5 (Movie): Metering timer; Movie recording count; Movie play count; Shutter release function; Time-lapse movie; Remote control

Table 13.1 Stored Camera User Settings (continued)	
Mode/Menu	**Settings**
AF menu	*AF1:* Case 1; Case 2; Case 3; Case 4; Case 5; Case 6
	AF2: AI Servo 1st image priority; AI Servo 2nd Image Priority
	AF3: Lens electronic MF; AF-assist beam firing; One-Shot AF release priority
	AF4: Lens drive when AF impossible; Selectable AF point; Select AF area select. mode; AF area selection method; Orientation linked AF point; Initial AF point with Auto area; Auto AF point selection: EOS iTR AF
	AF5: AF point selection movement; AF point display during focus; VF display illumination; AF status in viewfinder; AF microadjustment (excluding value)
Playback menu	*Playback 2:* Image Jump with Main Dial
	Playback 3: Highlight alert; AF point display; Playback grid; Histogram display; Movie play count; Magnification (approximate)
Set-up menu	*Set-up 1:* File numbering; Auto rotate; Eye-Fi Settings
	Set-up 2: Auto power off; LCD brightness; LCD color tone; Viewfinder display; Touch control
	Set-up 3: Auto cleaning; INFO. button display options; RATE button function
	Set-up 5: Multi-function lock
Custom Functions	*Custom 1:* Exposure level increments; ISO speed setting increments; Bracketing auto cancel; Bracketing sequence; Number of bracketed shots; Safety shift; Same exposure for new aperture
	Custom 2: Set shutter speed range; Set aperture range
	Custom 3: Live view shooting area display; Dial direction during Tv/Av; Custom controls
	Custom 4: Add cropping information; Default erase option; Retract lens on power off; Add IPTC information

This menu choice has only two options: Register (which stores your current settings in your choice of C1, C2, or C3) and Clear settings (which erases the settings in C1, C2, or C3). Note that you must use this menu entry to clear your settings; when using C1, C2, or C3, the Clear Settings option in the Set-up 3 menu is disabled. The Clear all Custom Func. (C.Fn) option in the Custom Functions menu is disabled as well.

Register your favorite settings for use in particular situations. I have stored settings for sports, portraits, and another for landscapes. If you switch to C1, C2, or C3 and forget what settings you've made for that slot, just press the INFO. button to view the current settings. Keep in mind that My Menu settings are not stored individually. You can have only one roster of My Menu entries available for all the Mode Dial's positions.

To perform either of these tasks, just follow these steps:

1. **Make your settings.** Set the EOS 5D Mark IV to an exposure mode other than Scene Intelligent Auto.

2. **Access Camera user settings.** Navigate to the Custom shooting mode option in the Set-up 4 menu, and press SET.

3. **Choose function.** Rotate the Quick Control Dial to choose Register if you want to store your 5D Mark IV's current settings in C1, C2, or C3; or select Clear Settings if you want to erase the settings stored in either location. Press SET to access the settings screen for your choice.

4. **Store/Clear settings.** The individual screens for storing/clearing are virtually identical. Use the QCD to highlight Mode Dial: C1, Mode Dial: C2, or Mode Dial: C3, and press SET to store or clear the settings for that position. (You'll be given a choice to proceed or cancel first.)

5. **Auto update.** Keep in mind that if you change a setting while using one of the custom shooting modes and want to retain the new settings, your stored settings can be automatically updated to reflect the modifications. Select Auto Update Set. and choose Enable to activate this option. If you'd rather retain your custom settings until you manually decide to update, select Disable instead.

6. **Exit.** When you confirm, you'll be returned to the Set-up 4 menu. Press the MENU button or tap the shutter release button to exit the menu system entirely.

Clear All Camera Settings

Options: Clear settings

My recommendation: N/A

This menu choice resets all the settings to their default values. Regardless of how you've set up your EOS 5D Mark IV, it will be adjusted to One-Shot AF mode, Automatic AF point selection, Evaluative metering, JPEG Fine Large image quality, automatic ISO, sRGB color mode, automatic white balance, and Standard Picture Style. Any changes you've made to exposure compensation, flash exposure compensation, and white balance will be canceled, and any bracketing for exposure or white balance nullified. Custom white balances and Dust Delete Data will be erased. Tables showing the factory default settings and my recommendations were provided in Chapter 3.

Remember, Custom Functions and Camera User Settings will *not* be cleared. If you want to cancel those as well, you'll need to use the Custom shooting mode option (described previously) and the Custom Functions clearing option.

Copyright Information

Options: Display copyright information, Enter author's name, Enter copyright details, Delete copyright information

My recommendation: N/A

Here's where you can give yourself credit for the great photos you're shooting with your 5D Mark IV:

- **Display copyright info.** Enable or disable embedding copyright information in your image files. If you're a double-naught secret agent who wants to submit spy photos anonymously, you'll definitely want to disable copyright information.
- **Enter author's name.** You can add your own name (up to 63 characters) to each image file, using a screen like the one shown in Figure 13.12, except with a larger array of alphanumeric characters, using the procedure described earlier in this chapter.
- **Enter copyright details**. You can add more information using the expanded character set. Up to 63 characters can be entered. Note that no copyright symbol is available. While some use a lowercase *c* within parentheses, technically the correct notification would be (Copyright) or (Copr.)
- **Delete copyright information.** This removes all the data you've entered and gives you a clean slate, so to speak.

Certification Logo Display

Options: None

My recommendation: N/A

This is an informational only screen, which allows Canon to add certification data (similar to what is printed on the bottom panel of the camera) via a firmware upgrade, and without the need to manufacture new stickers for the camera bottom.

Camera Firmware Version

Options: Update firmware

My recommendation: N/A

You can see the current firmware release in use in the menu listing. If you want to update to a new firmware version, insert a memory card containing the binary file, and press the SET button to begin the process.

14

The Custom Functions and My Menus

Custom Functions let you tailor the behavior of your camera in a variety of different ways, such as the function carried out when the SET button is pressed. If you don't like the default way the camera carries out a particular task, you may be able to do something about it. You can find the Custom Functions in their own menu, color-coded orange-brown, and visible whenever you are using P, Tv, Av, M, and B exposure modes.

Some Canon EOS cameras (chiefly earlier models and current entry-level cameras) crowded all the Custom Functions on a single screen, with cryptic rows of settings, each with a series of numbers beneath the settings row that represented the current value of that Custom Function. Fortunately, more recent advanced Canon models like the 5D Mark IV have divided all the Custom Functions into five separate screens; all but the last have multiple options. There are 17 C.Fn entries in all, plus Clear All Custom Func.

- Exposure Level Increments
- ISO Speed Setting Increments
- Bracketing Auto Cancel
- Bracketing Sequence
- Number of Bracketed Shots
- Safety Shift
- Same Exposure for New Aperture
- Set Shutter Speed Range
- Set Aperture Range

- Warnings in Viewfinder
- LV Shooting Area Display
- Dial Direction During Tv/Av
- Custom Controls
- Add Cropping Information
- Default Erase Option
- Retract Lens on Power Off
- Add IPTC Information
- Clear All Custom Func. (C.Fn)

Custom Function 1 (C.Fn I): Exposure

This is the Custom Function category you can use to set the increments for exposure and ISO, define bracketing parameters, and other settings. (See Figure 14.1.)

Exposure Level Increments

Options: 1/3 stop (default), 1/2 stop

My preference: 1/3 stop

This setting tells the EOS 5D Mark IV the size of the "jumps" it should use when making exposure adjustments—either one-third or one-half stop. The increment you specify here applies to f/stops, shutter speeds, EV changes, and autoexposure bracketing.

- **1/3 stop.** Choose this setting when you want the finest increments between shutter speeds and/ or f/stops. For example, the 5D Mark IV will use shutter speeds such as 1/60th, 1/80th, 1/100th, and 1/125th second, and f/stops such as f/5.6, f/6.3, f/7.1, and f/8, giving you (and the autoexposure system) maximum control.

- **1/2 stop.** Use this setting when you want larger and more noticeable changes between increments. The 5D Mark IV will apply shutter speeds such as 1/60th, 1/125th, 1/250th, and 1/500th second, and f/stops including f/5.6, f/6.7, f/8, f/9.5, and f/11. These coarser adjustments are useful when you want more dramatic changes between different exposures.

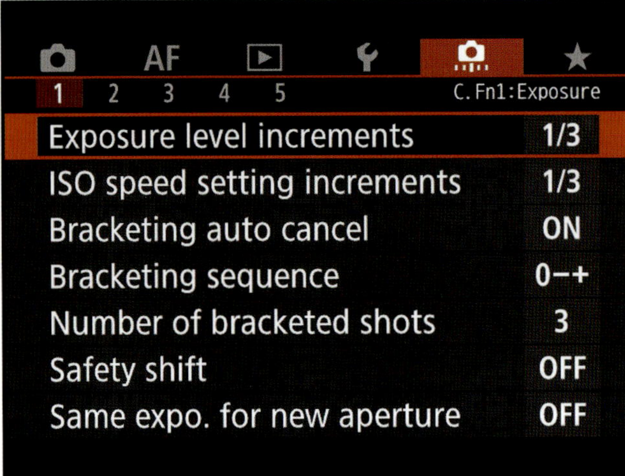

Figure 14.1
The Custom Function 1 menu.

ISO Speed Setting Increments

Options: 1/3 stop (default), 1 stop

My preference: 1/3 stop

This setting determines the size of the "jumps" made when adjusting ISO—either one-third or one full stop. At the one-third stop setting, typical ISO values would be 100, 125, 160, 200, and so forth. Switch to the one-stop setting, and ISO values would be 100, 200, 400, 800, and so forth. The larger increment can help you leap from an ISO setting to one that's twice (or half) as sensitive with one click.

Bracketing Auto Cancel

Options: Enable (default), Disable

My preference: Enable

When Auto Cancel is activated (the default), AEB (Auto Exposure Bracketing) and WB-BKT (White Balance Bracketing) are cancelled when you turn the 5D Mark IV off, change lenses, use the flash, or change memory cards; when Auto Cancel is deactivated, bracketing remains in effect until you manually turn it off or use the flash. When Auto Cancel is switched off, the AEB and WB-BKT settings will be kept even when the power switch is turned to the OFF position. The flash still cancels autoexposure bracketing, but your settings are retained.

I prefer the Enable setting, because I generally shoot a series of bracketed exposures and then turn off the camera when I am finished.

Bracketing Sequence

Options: 0−+ (default), −0+, +0−

My preference: −0+

You can define the sequence in which AEB and WB-BKT series are exposed. For exposure bracketing, you can determine whether the order is metered exposure, decreased exposure, increased exposure; or decreased exposure, metered exposure, increased exposure. Or with white balance bracketing, if your bias preference is set to Blue/Amber in the WB SHIFT/BKT adjustments in the Shooting 2 menu, the white balance sequence when option 0 is selected will be current WB, more blue, more amber. If your bias preference is set to Magenta/Green, then the sequence for option 0 will be current WB, more magenta, more green. Because I shoot so many HDR images to merge in Photoshop, I prefer the −0+ sequence, which starts with less exposure, metered exposure, and plus exposure, as that is the way I bracketed back in the film days.

- **0−+.** Exposure sequence is metered exposure, decreased exposure, increased exposure (0,−,+). White balance sequence is current WB, more blue/more magenta (depending on how your bias is set), more amber/more green (ditto).

- **−0+.** The sequence is decreased exposure, metered exposure, increased exposure (−, 0, +). White balance sequence is more blue/more magenta, current WB, more amber/more green.

- **+0−.** The sequence is increased exposure, metered exposure, decreased exposure. White balance sequence is more amber/more green, current WB, more blue/more magenta.

Number of Bracketed Shots

Options: 2, 3 (default), 5, 7 shots

My preference: 3

Your choices are 2, 3, 5, or 7 shots in a bracket sequence. I find that with an increment of 2/3 or one full stop, three bracketed exposures are enough that one of them will be close to optimum.

Safety Shift

Options: Disable (default), Shutter speed/Aperture, ISO speed

My preference: Disable

Ordinarily, both Aperture-priority and Shutter-priority modes work fine, because you'll select an f/stop or shutter speed that allows the 5D Mark IV to produce a correct exposure using the other type of setting (shutter speed for Av; aperture for Tv). However, when lighting conditions change, it may not be possible to select an appropriate setting with the available exposure options, and the camera will be unable to take a picture at all.

For example, you might be at a concert shooting the performers and, to increase your chances of getting a sharp image, you've selected Tv mode and a shutter speed of 1/250th second. Under bright lights and with an appropriate ISO setting, the 5D Mark IV might select f/5.6, f/4, or even f/2.8. Then, in a dramatic moment, the stage lights are dimmed significantly. An exposure of 1/250th second at f/2 is called for, but your lens has an f/2.8 maximum aperture. If you've used this Custom Function to allow the 5D Mark IV to override your selection, the camera will automatically switch to 1/125th second to allow the picture to be taken at f/2.8.

Safety Shift will make similar adjustments if your scene suddenly becomes too bright; although, in practice, you'll find that the override will be needed most often when using Tv mode. It's easier to "run out of" f/stops, which generally range no smaller than f/22 or f/32, than to deplete the available supply of shutter speeds, which can be as brief as 1/8,000th second. For example, if you're shooting at ISO 400 in Tv mode at 1/1,000th second, an extra-bright beach scene could easily call for an f/stop smaller than f/22, causing overexposure. However, Safety Shift would bump your shutter speed up to 1/2,000th second with no problem.

On the other hand, if you were shooting under the same illumination in Av mode with the preferred aperture set to f/16, the EOS 5D Mark IV could use 1/1,000th, 1/2,000th, 1/4,000th, or 1/8,000th second shutter speeds to retain that f/16 aperture under conditions that are 2X, 4X, 8X, or 16X as bright as normal daylight. No Safety Shift would be needed, even if the ISO were (for some unknown reason) set much higher than the ISO 400 used in this example. These are your options:

- **Disable.** Turn off Safety Shift. Your specified shutter speed or f/stop remains locked in, even if conditions are too bright or too dim for an appropriate exposure. Use this option if you'd prefer to have the shot taken at the shutter speed, aperture, or ISO you've selected under all circumstances, even if it means an improperly exposed photo. You might be able to salvage the photo in your image editor.

- **Shutter speed/Aperture.** Safety Shift is activated for Tv and Av modes. The 5D Mark IV will adjust the preferred shutter speed or f/stop to allow a correct exposure. If you don't mind having your camera countermand your orders, this option can save images that otherwise might be incorrectly exposed. Use when working with a shutter speed or aperture that is *preferable,* but not critical.

- **ISO speed.** This option operates in Program AE (P) mode as well as Tv and Av modes. Think of it as an "emergency" Auto ISO option. You can manually select your preferred ISO setting, and the 5D Mark IV will generally stick with that, but can adjust the ISO setting if required to produce an acceptable exposure. If you've selected a minimum and maximum allowable ISO range in the ISO Speed Settings entry of the Shooting 2 menu (as explained in Chapter 11), this setting will honor those limits *unless* your current manually selected ISO is outside those boundaries.

  For example, if you've chosen a minimum and maximum auto ISO range of ISO 200–800, this setting will stay within that range when adjusting ISO (even though you have Auto ISO off), but if your camera is currently manually set to ISO 100 or a value higher than ISO 800, it will go ahead and use the extra values, too.

Same Exposure for New Aperture

Options: Disable (default), ISO speed, ISO speed/Shutter speed, Shutter speed

My preference: Disable

This entry works in Manual exposure mode to allow you to keep the same exposure when you switch lenses, attach a teleconverter, or use a zoom lens that doesn't have a constant aperture. In all three cases, the reason the manual exposure you've set changes is because your lens (or lens/converter combination) may have a maximum aperture that is different from that when you made your original setting. For example, if you switch from a lens with an f/2.8 maximum aperture to one that opens no wider than f/4, or use, say, a 1.4X tele extender that changes the maximum aperture by one stop, your manually set exposure may be wrong. Similarly, a lens that has a maximum aperture of f/3.5 at its widest setting may have the equivalent of just f/5.6 at its longest telephoto setting. Unless you've set ISO Auto for Manual mode, your exposure can differ from what you intended.

This setting allows you to account for these effects and retain your desired exposure in Manual mode. Note that it does not work with macro lenses that change their effective aperture value as their focus magnification changes. Your choices are as follows:

- **Disable (default).** No automatic compensation is applied. If you switch lenses, use a tele extender, or have a variable aperture lens, you may need to manually adjust your exposure to allow for the "slower" lens speed.

- **ISO speed.** Choose this setting, and the 5D Mark IV will set a higher ISO speed to compensate so your exposure remains the same. The ISO sensitivity will be adjusted within the boundaries you've set for the Range for Stills option in the ISO Speed Settings entry of the Shooting 2 menu, as explained in Chapter 11.

- **ISO speed/Shutter speed (Tv).** In this case, a higher ISO speed will be set first. If the upper boundaries specified in Range for Stills is exceeded, the 5D Mark IV will then change the shutter speed within the range specified for Set Shutter Speed Range on the Custom Functions 2 page (described next).

- **Shutter speed (Tv).** The camera will compensate by using a slower shutter speed to keep the same exposure you set manually. The Set Shutter Speed Range boundaries will be observed, so this setting does not guarantee that your desired exposure will be achieved.

Which should you select? I generally don't use this setting at all, partially because I own very few lenses with variable apertures and, when I change lenses or add a teleconverter, I am (usually) smart enough to know I need to recalculate my manual exposure. You probably do the same. The most common scenario for needing this feature is when you want to use a lens that does have an aperture that changes when you zoom. It's not only cheap lenses that change their aperture: Canon's two EF 100-400mm zooms have an effective aperture of f/4.5 at 100mm, and f/5.6 at 400mm. There are several good lenses, in the 70-300mm range (including one L lens) with f/4-5.6 variable apertures. If you do decide to implement this feature, decide which is most important to you: constant ISO speed or shutter speed. For sports, especially in low-light situations, the ISO speed/Shutter speed (Tv) option is likely to be your best bet.

Custom Function 2 (C.Fn II): Exposure

This is the second Custom Function exposure category, shown in Figure 14.2, that you can use to set both shutter speed and aperture range.

Set Shutter Speed Range

Options: Highest speed: 1/8,000th sec. to 15 sec.; Lowest speed: 30 sec. to 1/4,000th sec.

My preference: N/A

There are times when you want to limit shutter speed range when using Tv or M exposure modes, or the value chosen automatically by the camera in P and Av modes. For example, if you're shooting

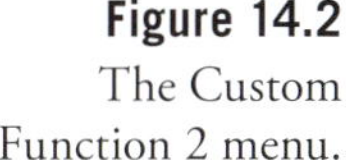

Figure 14.2
The Custom
Function 2 menu.

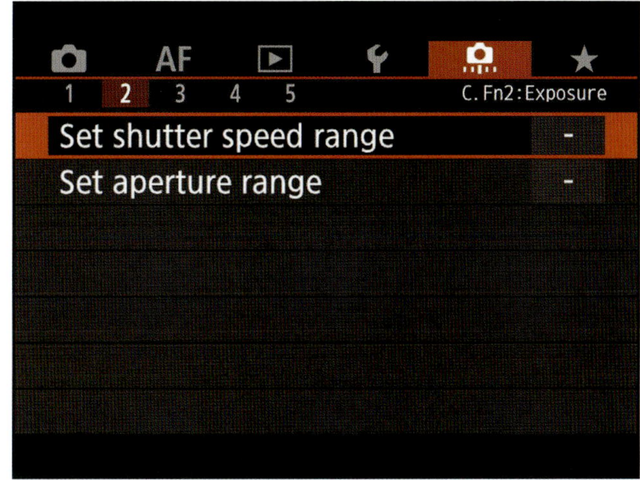

motor sports and want to maintain a bit of blur in the vehicle tires (to avoid that "frozen in time" look), you might want to lock out any shutter speeds higher than 1/500th second. In that case, you might not mind if your aperture changes when the upper limit is reached, or you might let Auto ISO kick in lower sensitivity a notch or two to allow optimum exposure. Going the other way, you might want to avoid shutter speeds lower than, say 1/60th second because you know that's the slowest speed at which a hand-held image is going to be acceptably sharp. This setting lets you specify a "top" shutter speed from 1/8,000th second to 15 seconds, and a "bottom" speed from 30 seconds to 1/4,000th second, depending on your creative needs.

Set Aperture Range

Options: Minimum aperture (smallest lens opening): f/64 to f/1.4; Maximum aperture (largest lens opening): f/1.0 to f/64

My preference: N/A

This entry allows you to specify an aperture range. When using Av, M, and Bulb exposure modes, you can set the aperture manually within the range you specify here. In P and Tv, the aperture will be set automatically within this range when shooting stills. Minimum apertures (the smallest f/stops) can be specified for f/91 to f/1.4, and a maximum aperture of f/1.0 to f/64. These "limits" all depend on the maximum and minimum apertures of your lenses, of course. Use this entry when you want to limit the available f/stops, say, to preserve selective focus or, going the other direction, to maximize depth-of-field (even if it costs you some sharpness because of diffraction). I explained diffraction in Chapter 11.

Custom Function 3 (C.Fn III): Display/Operation

This menu tab offers several options for display and controls, including the important Custom Controls feature. (See Figure 14.3.)

Warnings in Viewfinder

Options: Monochrome Picture Style, WB correction, One-touch image quality, Multi-shot noise reduction, HDR

My preference: N/A

This useful function lets you individually enable or disable five different viewfinder warnings, allowing you to reduce the amount of clutter in your field of view as you frame an image, while retaining the warnings that you really, really want to remain in effect. Mark any or all with a check mark by highlighting the option and pressing SET. Your choices include warnings for the following:

- **Monochrome Picture Style.** If you shoot JPEG most of the time, you might want a tip-off that you've set the camera in black-and-white mode, because color information cannot be added in post-processing. If you generally shoot RAW or RAW+JPEG, you won't care, because the RAW image retains the color information.

- **WB correction.** It's easy to dial in some white balance correction, and easier to forget that you've done so. This warning will let you know—again, very important when shooting JPEG only.

- **One-touch image quality.** Later in this chapter you'll learn how to quickly change image quality using a custom control. You can warn yourself when this capability is available.

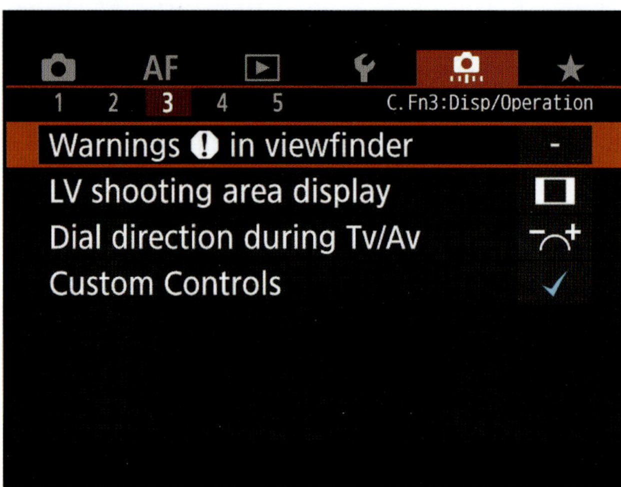

Figure 14.3
The Custom Function 3 menu.

- **Multi-shot noise reduction.** When High-Speed Noise Reduction is set to Multi-Shot Noise Reduction, you'll receive a warning. While the availability of this extreme setting isn't normally a problem, if you feel you're likely to need a tip-off, you can activate this warning.

- **HDR.** Alerts you that HDR is being used.

LV Shooting Area Display

Options: Masked, Outlined

My preference: Outlined for sports; Masked for other subjects

When you're using an aspect ratio other than the default 3:2 in Live View, the 5D Mark IV will always alert you that the full viewable frame is not the active capture area. If you choose Masked, then the extra area will be darkened, which can be very useful in helping you compose your images within the actual proportions of the frame that will be captured. However, you can also choose Outlined, in which case the entire frame can be seen, with lines marking the image area. I like to use this mode when shooting sports in a non-traditional aspect ratio (say, I want the 16:9 wide-screen look in my images), because I can follow moving subjects slightly outside the image area and capture them when framed properly.

Dial Direction During Tv/Av

Options: Normal (–+), Reverse direction(+–)

My preference: Normal

This setting reverses the result when rotating the Quick Control Dial and Main Dial when using Shutter-priority or Aperture-priority (Tv and Av). That is, rotating the Main Dial to the right will decrease the shutter speed rather than increase it; f/stops will become larger rather than smaller. Use this if you find the default rotation scheme in Tv and Av modes are not to your liking. Activating this option also reverses the dial direction in Manual exposure mode. In other shooting modes, only the Main Dial's direction will be reversed.

- **Normal.** The Main Dial and Quick Control Dial change shutter speed and aperture normally.

- **Reverse direction.** The dials adjust shutter speed and aperture in the reverse direction when rotated.

Custom Controls

Options: Redefine 11 buttons

My preference: N/A

If you're eager to totally confuse any poor soul who is not equipped to deal with a custom-configured 5D Mark IV (or, perhaps, even yourself), Canon allows you to redefine the behavior of no less than 11 different controls in interesting, and potentially hilarious ways. Just highlight any of the 11 options (shown in Figure 14.4), press SET to view the functions you can assign, and make your choice. If you see the INFO. icon at bottom left, there are even more decisions to make. You can truly manipulate your camera to work in a way that's fastest and most efficient for you. There are dozens of combinations of control possibilities (some buttons have as many as 12 different options, plus Off), spelled out in a huge matrix+legend description starting on page 496 of your factory manual. The options and explanations would take up half this chapter, so I won't duplicate that information here. Press the Trash button from the Custom Controls screen to return all your settings to the default values shown in Table 14.1.

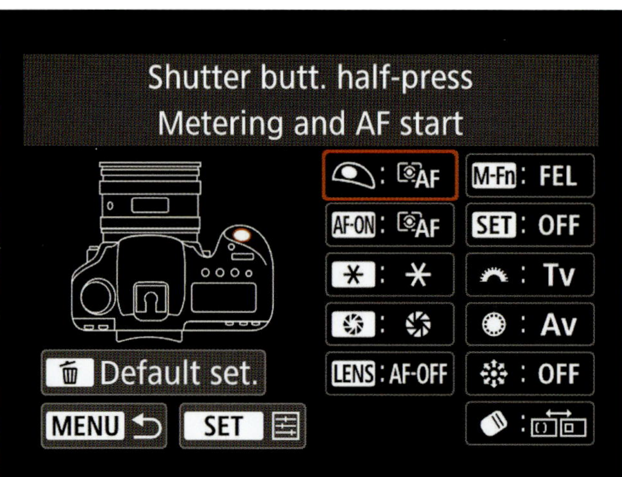

Figure 14.4
Assignable buttons.

Table 14.1 Assignable Controls

Control	Default
Shutter button half-press	Metering and AF start
AF-On button	Metering and AF start
AE Lock button	AE Lock
DOF Preview button	Depth-of-field preview
Lens AF stop button (if available on lens)	AF stop
M-Fn (Multi Function) button	FE lock
SET button	No additional function
Main Dial	Shutter speed setting in Tv and Manual Mode
Quick Control Dial	Aperture setting in Av and Manual Mode
Multi-controller	No additional function
AF area selection button(s)	Direct AF area selection

Custom Function 4 (C.Fn IV): Others

This is the Custom Function "miscellaneous" category that you can use to set the specifications for cropping and erase functions. (See Figure 14.5.)

Add Cropping Information

Options: Off (default), Aspect ratios 6:6, 3:4, 4:5, 6:7, 10:12, 5:7

My preference: Varies depending on print size

If you want to use image crops other than the default 3:2 aspect ratio in live view, but don't want to lock the settings down in stone, this Custom Function, the first on the fourth page of the Custom Function menu, may help you. It allows you to specify one of the optional available crops, such that vertical lines will appear on the live view image to delineate that cropping—but the image you take will be saved in its full-frame form, *without* the actual crop being applied. However, the cropping information *is* embedded in the image file and can be retrieved by compatible software (including Canon's Digital Photo Pro) and used to apply the crop in post-processing.

If you're saying, "Wha?" about now, I can clarify. One of the coolest things about live view is that it mimics the ground glass screen of the medium format (say, 120/220 roll film models) or large format (4 × 5, 5 × 7, or larger-sheet film cameras) that many of us grew up with. That is, as with a medium-format or large-format film camera, the actual film/sensor plane image is there for you to view (although, not necessarily reversed left to right or reversed and inverted as in the good old days).

Figure 14.5

The Custom Function 4 menu.

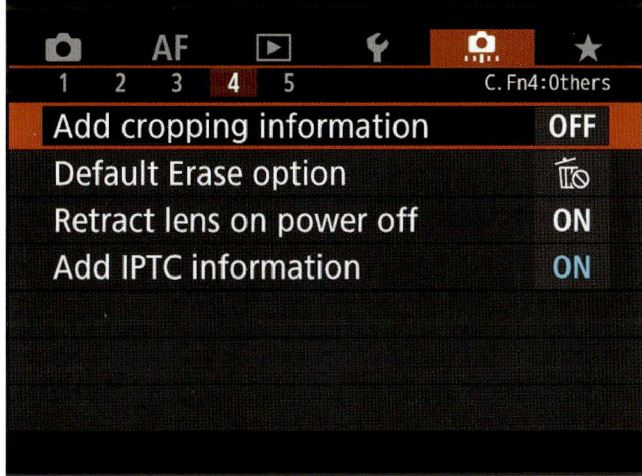

Canon gives you a variety of optional cropping proportions so you can compose and expose your image just as if you were using a camera from those thrilling days of yesteryear—or simply want to use an alternate aspect ratio for creative effect. Your choices include the 6:6 and 6:7 proportions used to create 6cm × 6cm and 6cm × 7cm film images (think Hasselblad or Pentax 67); 4:5 and 5:7 ratios used with 4 × 5–inch, 8 × 10–inch, and 5 × 7–inch sheet film cameras, plus other formats as well. These include 3:4 and 10:12 (the latter perfect for 20 × 24–inch wall prints).

Of course, these days, cameras like the 5D Mark IV have enough resolution that you can easily crop the full-frame image to any proportions you like, but many photographers still enjoy composing within a given aspect ratio.

Default Erase Option

Options: Cancel selected (default), Erase selected

My preference: Erase selected

Specify what happens during image review and playback when you press the Trash button and the Erase Image screen appears. Choose Cancel, and pressing the Trash button a second time backs you out of the screen with no harm done. You'd choose this if you find you accidentally press Trash from time to time. Or, select Erase, and that second press will delete the image, probably forever. It's your choice, but I prefer speed over caution, so I use Erase selected most of the time.

Retract Lens on Power Off

Options: Enable (default), Disable

My preference: Enable

Some lenses that focus using a gear mechanism (such as the EF40mm f/2.8 STM) can retract when the camera is turned off. The retracted lens is smaller and its reduced surface area is better protected against bumps, so I usually leave this setting enabled.

Add IPTC Information

Options: Disable (default), Enable

My preference: Disable

This entry enables you to enable or disable embedding of IPTC (International Press Communications Council) metadata in your JPEG and RAW files. The IPTC standard is the most widely used standard used by news and photo agencies, photojournalists, libraries, and museums. You can load, edit, save, and register specifications using the EOS Utility. Connect your camera to your computer, launch the utility, and navigate to the data entry page shown in Figure 14.6.

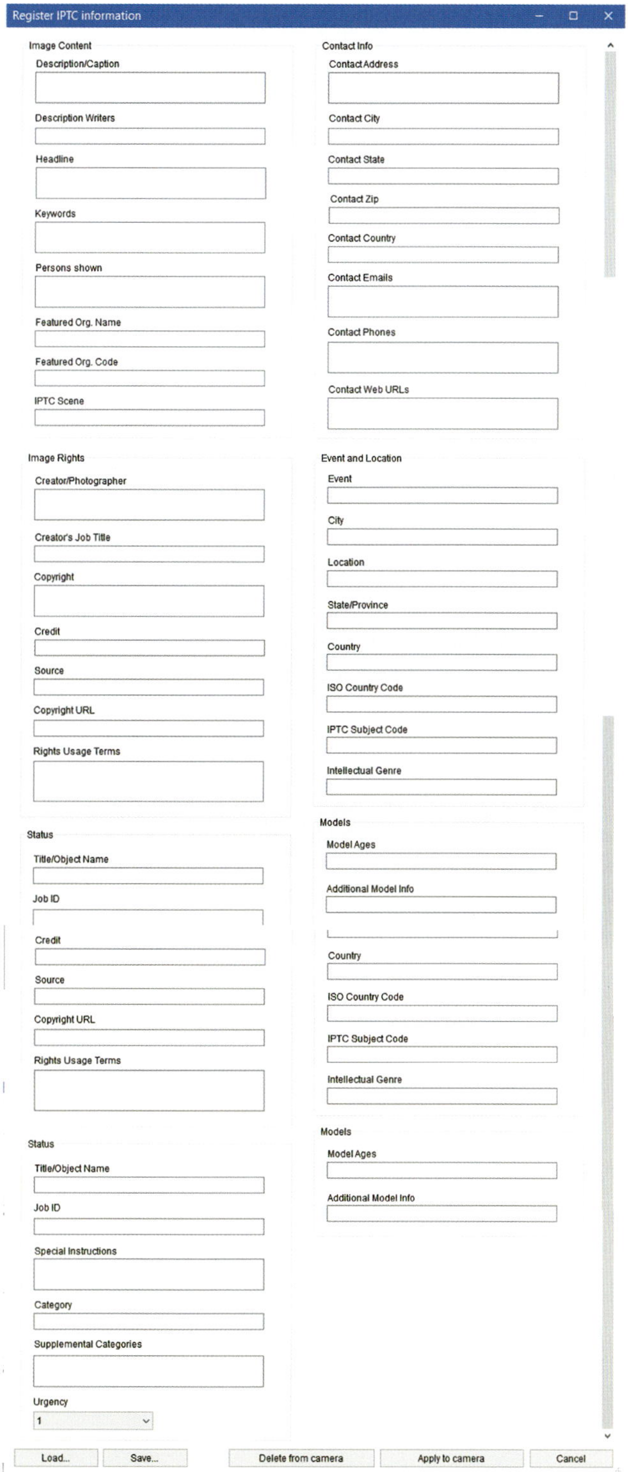

Figure 14.6
IPTC data fields.

Custom Function 5 (C.Fn V): Clear

This is the Custom Function category you can use to clear other functions. (See Figure 14.7.)

Clear All Custom Func. (C.Fn)

Options: Clear

My preference: N/A

Select this entry and choose Cancel (if you chicken out) or OK to return all your Custom Functions to their default values. But don't panic—your matrix of Custom Controls is retained. If you want to zero out those settings, you'll need to access the Custom Controls screen in the Custom Functions 3 menu, and press the Trash button.

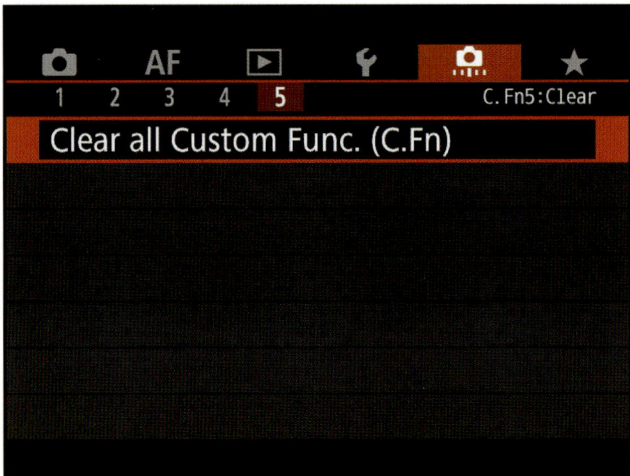

Figure 14.7
The Custom
Function 5 menu.

My Menu

Options: Add My Menu tab, Delete all My Menu tabs, Delete all items, Menu display

My preference: N/A

The Canon EOS 5D Mark IV has a great feature that allows you to define your own menu with multiple tabs, each with just the items listed that you want. Remember that the 5D Mark IV always returns to the last menu and menu entry accessed when you press the MENU button. So, you can set up My Menu to include just the items you want, and jump to those items instantly by pressing the MENU button. Or, you can set your camera so that My Menu appears when the MENU button has been pressed, regardless of what other menu entry you accessed last.

To create your own My Menu, you have to *register* the menu items you want to include. (See Figure 14.8, left.)

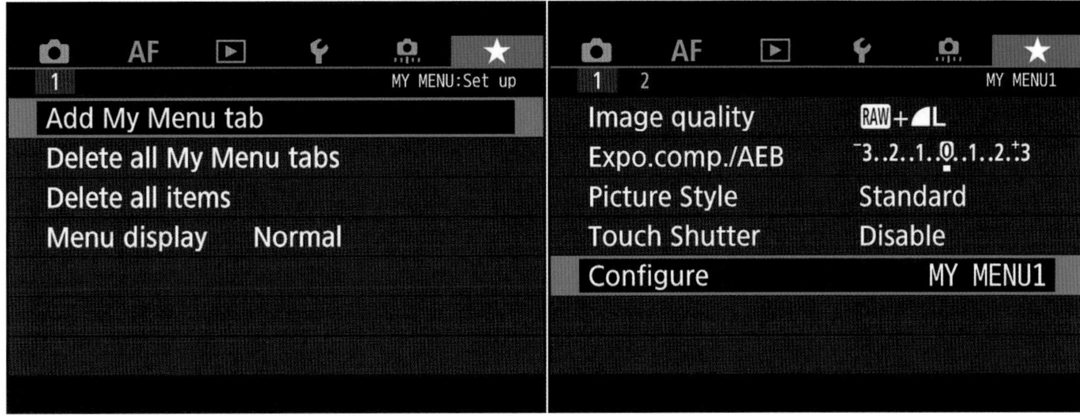

Figure 14.8 Create your My Menu tabs (left) and add entries to them (right).

Just follow these steps:

1. Press the MENU button and use the Main Dial or multi-controller to select the My Menu tab. When you first begin, the personalized menu will be empty except for the My Menu settings shown in the figure.

2. Rotate the Quick Control Dial to select Add My Menu Tab, then press the SET button. Highlight OK in the screen that appears, and press SET once again.

3. The Configure choice will appear. Press SET to view a list of options. Choose Select Items to Register, located at the top of the options screen.

4. Use the Quick Control Dial to scroll down through the continuous list of menu entries to find one you would like to add. Press SET.

5. Confirm your choice by selecting OK in the next screen and pressing SET again.

6. Continue to select more entries for your My Menu tab. You can add up to six for each tab.

7. When you're finished, press the MENU button twice to return to the My Menu screen to see your customized menu, which might look like my example in Figure 14.8, right.

Because you have just added a My Menu tab, My Menu will have two screens. The second screen will contain the options shown in Figure 14.8, right. You can use those entries to:

■ **Add another My Menu tab.** Each time you do, you must use Configure to add at least one entry to the new menu. Your new menus will be assigned names, like MY MENU1, MY MENU2, etc. The original MY MENU: Set up tab will move to the farthest position in the tab lineup. You can have a maximum of five new tabs, plus the sixth Set up tab.

■ **Delete all My Menu tabs.** If you want to start over, you can delete all your tabs.

■ **Delete All items.** This deletes all the registered items on all the tabs you have added. The options in the MY MENU: Set up tab remain. When you delete all items, each will still contain a Configure choice, which allows you to register more entries. The tabs themselves are not removed.

- **Menu display.** This determines which menu screen appears first when the MENU button is pressed. You can choose:
    - **Normal display (default).** Shows the *most recently displayed* menu tab from the Shooting, AF, Playback, Set-up, Custom Settings, and My Menu choices. You'd want this if you prefer to jump back to whichever menu you were working with recently.
    - **Display from My Menu tab.** Shows the My Menu tab only. Use this if you want to bypass the conventional menus and make your menu choices only from your custom My Menu tabs. The other menu tabs are still shown and can be selected.
    - **Display only My Menu tab.** Only the My Menu tabs are available. The others are hidden. Use this only if you do not need to use the conventional menus as you work. You can return to this entry and restore Normal display at any time.

In addition to registering menu items, you can fine-tune each individual tab by selecting Configure. The screen shown in Figure 14.9 appears with these options:

- **Select items to register.** Add new items here.

- **Sort registered items.** Choose this entry to reorder the items in each My Menu tab. Select the menu item and press the SET button. Rotate the Quick Control Dial to move the item up and down within the menu list. When you've placed it where you'd like it, press the MENU button to lock in your selection and return to the previous screen. When finished, press MENU again to exit.

- **Delete selected items, Delete all items on tab, Delete tab.** Use these to remove an individual menu item or all menu items on a tab, or to delete the entire tab itself.

- **Rename tab.** You're not stuck with the MY MENU1, MY MENU2… monikers. This entry allows you to apply a new name for a tab with up to 16 characters. For example, if you created customized Shooting or Autofocus settings, you could name them My Shooting and My Autofocus, respectively.

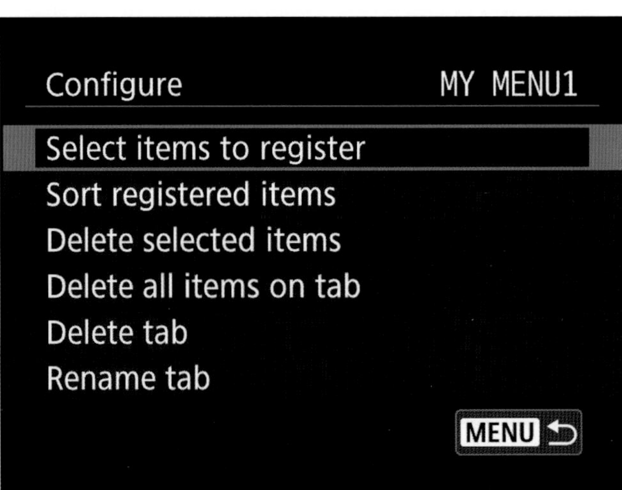

Figure 14.9
You can fine-tune each My Menu tab.

15

Using Live View

Live view has been around long enough that it's becoming old hat for some, but it was really just a precursor to one of the 5D Mark IV's real killer features—full HD video shooting. SNL's Alex Buono shoots the opening montages of *Saturday Night Live* using Canon cameras, so you can see that movie shooting with the 5D Mark IV has a lot of potential. We'll look at movie shooting in Chapter 16, but first it may be useful to learn about live view.

The Canon EOS 5D Mark IV has a gorgeous 3.2-inch LCD that can be viewed under a variety of lighting conditions and from wide-ranging angles, so you don't have to be exactly behind the display to see its live view image clearly while shooting stills or video. It offers a 100 percent view of the sensor's capture area. It's large enough to allow manual focusing—but if you want to use automatic focus the Dual Pixel CMOS AF system provides the best live view autofocus Canon has offered. You still must avoid pointing your 5D Mark IV at bright light sources (especially the sun) when using live view, but the real-time preview can be used for fairly long periods without frying the sensor. (Image quality can degrade, but the camera issues a warning when the sensor starts to overheat.)

You may not have considered just what you can do with live view, but once you've played with it, you'll discover dozens of applications for this capability. Here's a list of considerations:

- **Preview your images on a TV.** Connect your EOS 5D Mark IV to a standard-definition television using the optional HDTV cable, and you can preview your image on a large screen. It's often easier to visualize how a finished photo will look by evaluating a large image that's the same size (or larger) as a print. Portrait photographers, if they wish, can allow clients to watch as a sitting unfolds, and the big screen view will get them thinking about purchasing larger prints for wall display. Instructors can show how they work to a large class.

- **Preview remotely.** Extend the cable between the camera and TV screen, and you can preview your images some distance away from the camera. This technique is not just for covert double-naught spy activities. Perhaps you want to remain some distance from a dangerous activity, or prefer to remain hidden to avoid spooking skittish wildlife. Set up your camera by a stream to capture woodland creatures visiting for a drink while you wait downwind in a camouflaged blind.

- **Shoot from your computer.** Shooting tethered has many useful variations. While you can achieve the remote scenario described above with a long-release cord (or radio control), there's a more flexible approach that allows you to change settings as you shoot. If you are hard-wired to your 5D Mark IV, Canon gives you the EOS Utility software you need to control your camera from your computer, so you can preview images, make a full range of adjustments, and take pictures without physically touching the EOS 5D Mark IV. There are other utilities that allow tethered shooting, including Adobe Lightroom.

- **Shoot from your smart device.** As I explained in Chapter 6, you can easily mount your camera on a tripod and use a live view preview on your smart device to take photos.

- **Continuous shooting.** You can shoot bursts of images using live view, but all shots will use the focus and exposure setting established for the first picture in the series.

- **Shoot from tripod or hand-held.** Of course, holding the camera out at arm's length to preview an image is poor technique, and will introduce a lot of camera shake. If you want to use live view for hand-held images, use an image-stabilized lens and/or a high shutter speed. A tripod is a better choice if you can use one, especially for macro photography.

- **Watch your power.** Live view uses a lot of juice and will deplete your battery rapidly. Canon estimates that you can get 180 to 200 shots per battery when using live view, depending on the temperature. Continuous live viewing/shooting can last about 90 minutes, according to Canon. The optional AC adapter is a useful accessory.

Enabling Live View

You need to take some steps before using live view (or movies). This workflow prevents you from accidentally using live view when you don't mean to, thus potentially losing a shot, and it also helps ensure that you've made all the settings necessary to successfully use the feature efficiently.

Here are the steps to follow:

1. **Choose a shooting mode.** Live view works with any exposure mode available on the Mode Dial, including Scene Intelligent Auto. You can even switch from one mode to another while live view is activated (except that when you change to or from Scene Intelligent Auto while live view is on, it will be deactivated and must be restarted).

2. **Enable live view.** You'll need to activate live view by enabling Live View Shoot from the Shooting 5 menu. (See Figure 15.1, left.) I'll show you more options in the next section. (If the camera is set to Scene Intelligent Auto, which provides a reduced menu set, you'll find the options in the Shooting 3 menu.) Note that disabling live view has no effect on movie shooting.

3. **Choose other live view functions.** Select from the other live view focusing, display, and operational functions using the Shooting 6 menu (Figure 15.1, right), plus additional features available in the Set-up 3 and Custom Settings 3 menus, which I'll describe later in this chapter.

4. **Choose live view or movie shooting.** Rotate the Live View switch, which is concentric with the Start/Stop button to the right of the viewfinder window, to the movie camera or still camera icon.

5. **Begin live viewing.** Press the Start/Stop button to enter live viewing mode. Press again to exit.

6. **Start capture.** Press the shutter release completely to take a picture. After image review, the 5D Mark IV returns to live viewing mode.

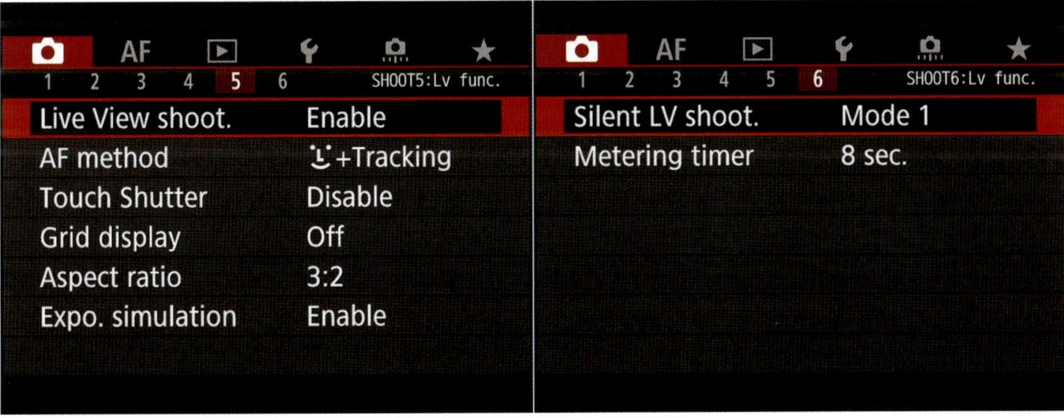

Figure 15.1 The Shooting 5 and 6 menus.

Shooting Menu Options

I described the Shooting 5 and 6 menu options in Chapter 11, but here's a quick recap as a refresher:

- **Live View Shooting.** Enables/disables live view shooting. Disabling live view does not affect movie shooting.

- **AF Method.** Select Face Detection + Tracking mode, FlexiZone Multi mode, and FlexiZone Single mode.

- **Touch Shutter.** Enable or Disable the Touch Shutter feature, which allows you to specify a point of focus, activate AF, and take a picture with a tap on the touch screen.

- **Grid Display.** Overlays Grid 1 on the screen to help you compose your image and align vertical and horizontal lines; Grid 2, which consists of four rows of six boxes; or Grid 3, which adds diagonal lines.

- **Aspect Ratio.** Allows you to choose an aspect ratio, or proportions of your image, from 3:2, 4:3, 16:9, or 1:1. JPEG images will be stored using the selected ratio; RAW images will be saved using the default 3:2 proportions, but the desired cropping can be restored in your image-editing software. During live view, the cropped area is shown either masked or with outlines, using the Custom Function 3 menu, as explained in Chapter 14.

- **Exposure Simulation.** This option determines whether the live view image mimics the exposure level of the final image, or whether a bright image is shown that may be easier to view under high ambient lighting conditions.

    - **Enable.** The live view image corresponds to the brightness level of the actual image using the current exposure/exposure compensation settings.

    - **During DOF Preview.** The live view image is adjusted to simulate your exposure settings only when you press the depth-of-field preview button. This is a handy mode to use if you want the LCD monitor to remain as bright as possible, but retain the ability to preview exposure effects by pressing a button.

    - **Disable.** The live view image is always shown at standard brightness.

- **Silent LV Shooting.** This choice, and Metering Timer, are found on the Shooting 6 menu. Reduce the noise level using either of two modes: Mode 1 produces a quieter shooting sound level in Live View mode, and allows continuous shooting. Mode 2 separates the *ker* from the *clunk* sounds. Press the shutter release all the way, and the camera emits a small click as the picture is taken. When you release the button at least halfway, a discreet second click is heard. Only a single image is captured, even if continuous shooting is enabled. The camera ignores this setting if you're using a remote control, and defaults to Mode 1. Disable turns off silent shooting.

- **Metering Timer.** Specify how long the metering system remains active before switching off. You can select 4, 16, or 30 seconds, plus 1, 10, or 30 minutes. Tap the shutter release to restart the timer.

Activating Live View

Once you've enabled live view in the menu, you can continue taking pictures normally through the 5D Mark IV's viewfinder. When you're ready to activate live view, press the Start/Stop button to the left of the viewfinder. The mirror will flip up, and the sensor image will appear on the LCD. Here are some things you should keep in mind when live view is active:

- **Shooting functions don't interrupt.** You can change settings or review images normally when in Live View mode. Press the WB, DRIVE-AF, or ISO-Flash exposure compensation buttons on the top of the camera, or the Picture Control/Creative Settings button to the left of the LCD, and an overlay appears superimposed on the live view screen. You can use the Quick Control Dial and Main Dial to change those settings. You can also adjust the Auto Lighting Optimizer and change image quality by pressing the Q button on the left side of the camera. If you've chosen AF Quick autofocus mode, you can set the AF point and AF area selection mode, described in Chapter 5.

- **Live view continues.** When you press the shutter release, the 5D Mark IV will take a photo, then display the image you just shot for review, as normal. When picture review is finished, the camera returns to live view. You can take as many consecutive shots using live view as you like, barring sensor overheating. To exit live view entirely, press the Start/Stop button.

- **Metering mode cannot be changed.** Evaluative metering linked to the focus frame is used. You cannot change to Partial, Spot, or Center-weighted metering when live view is active.

- **Fixed continuous exposure.** If you shoot in continuous mode, the exposure determined for the first image will be used for all subsequent images in the series.

- **Watch for overheating.** Leaving live view on for extended periods increases the temperature of the sensor, potentially causing noise or odd colors in your image. If you want to take a long exposure, turn off live view for several minutes before shooting, to allow your sensor to cool. Live view will shut off automatically after a high-temperature icon warns you when things start to heat up.

- **Information display.** During live view, useful information is shown on the screen, such as battery status, Picture Style, and most of the shooting information (shutter speed, f/stop, ISO setting, number of exposures remaining) you'd see through the viewfinder. Press the INFO. button to change the amount of information shown. Figure 15.2 shows the live view screen as it appears when you redirect the 5D Mark IV's output to an external monitor, captured in that mode so the icons could be viewed more easily. When viewed on the LCD monitor, the information is overlaid on the entire frame.

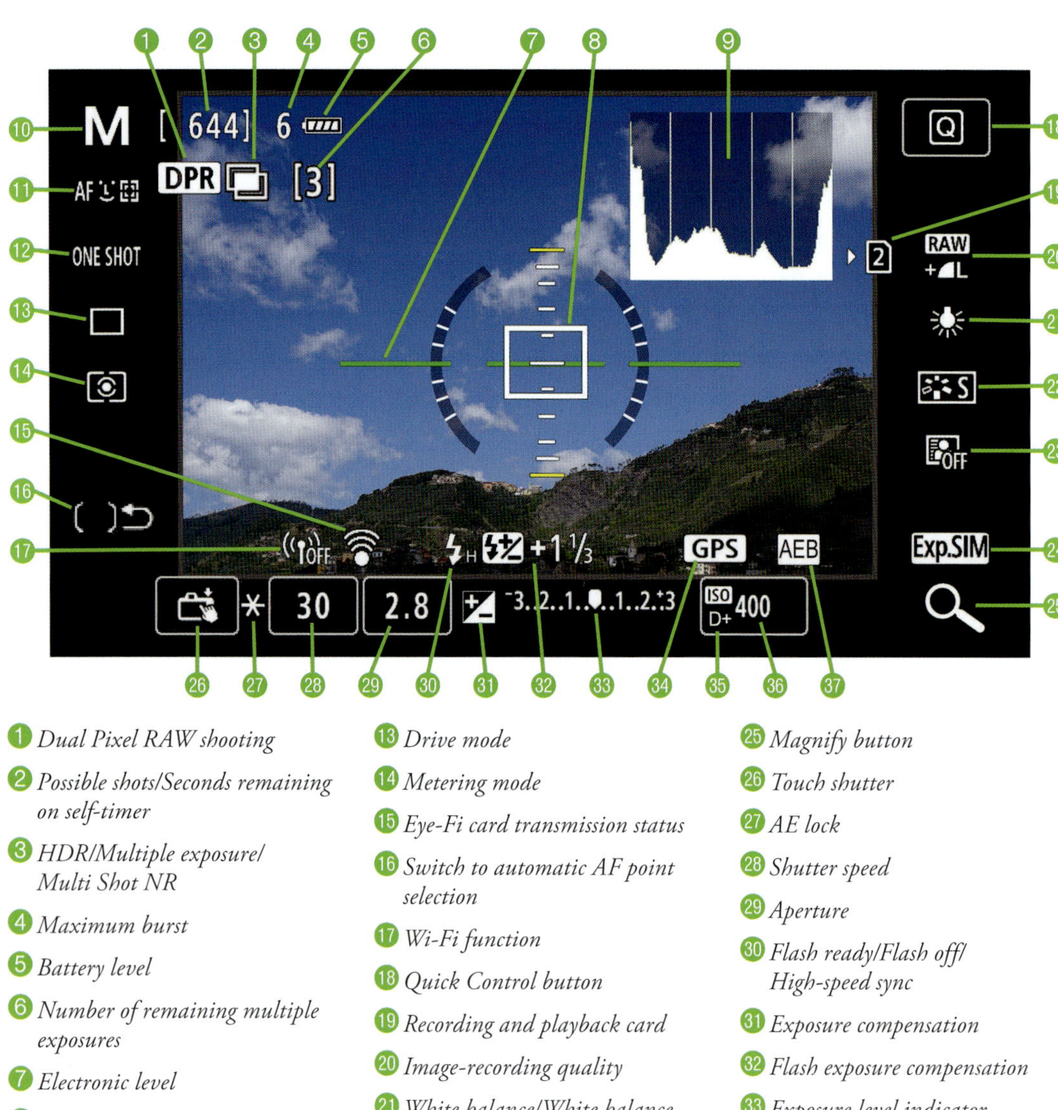

1 Dual Pixel RAW shooting

2 Possible shots/Seconds remaining on self-timer

3 HDR/Multiple exposure/ Multi Shot NR

4 Maximum burst

5 Battery level

6 Number of remaining multiple exposures

7 Electronic level

8 AF point (FlexiZone—Single)

9 Histogram display

10 Shooting mode/Scene icon

11 AF method

12 AF operation

13 Drive mode

14 Metering mode

15 Eye-Fi card transmission status

16 Switch to automatic AF point selection

17 Wi-Fi function

18 Quick Control button

19 Recording and playback card

20 Image-recording quality

21 White balance/White balance correction

22 Picture Style

23 Auto Lighting Optimizer

24 Exposure simulation

25 Magnify button

26 Touch shutter

27 AE lock

28 Shutter speed

29 Aperture

30 Flash ready/Flash off/ High-speed sync

31 Exposure compensation

32 Flash exposure compensation

33 Exposure level indicator

34 GPS acquisition status

35 Highlight tone priority

36 ISO speed

37 AEB/FEB

Figure 15.2 Press the INFO. button to increase or decrease the amount of information shown on the LCD in Live View mode.

Live View Information Screens

You can specify the types and amounts of information shown in the live view information screens using the INFO. Button Lv Display Options entry in the Set-up 3 menu. This screen has two major options, Live View Info Switch Setting and Histogram Display, plus Reset.

In Live View Info Switch Setting there are four available information screens, numbered from 1 to 4, which can individually be enabled or hidden (you cannot choose to hide all of them, however):

- **#1 screen.** Shows basic information, such as shooting mode, shutter speed, aperture, ISO, and exposure settings.
- **#2 screen.** Full information, showing all available active settings.
- **#3 screen.** Same as #2 screen, but with a live histogram and electronic level displayed.
- **#4 screen.** Uncluttered screen showing only the active focus area.

The Histogram Display option allows you to choose either the Brightness or RGB histogram, which were described in Chapter 4. You can also specify whether you want the histogram to appear in large or small size on the LCD monitor. Refer to Chapter 11 for information on customizing the live view information screens. (See Figure 15.3.)

Final Image Simulation

When Exp. Sim. (available with information screens #2 or #3) is displayed in white on the live view screen, it indicates that the LCD screen image brightness is an approximation of the brightness of the image that will be captured. If the Exp. Sim. display is blinking, it shows that the screen image does *not* represent the appearance of the final image because the light level is too dim or too bright. When using flash or bulb exposure, or night scene modes, the Exp. Sim. indicator is dimmed out to show you that the LCD image is not being adjusted to account for the actual exposure.

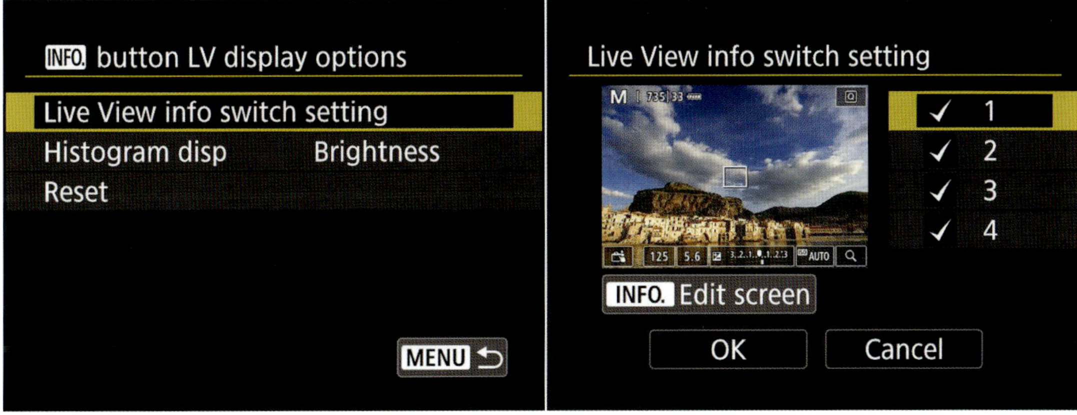

Figure 15.3 You can edit the information appearing on live view screens.

The 5D Mark IV applies any active Picture Style settings to the LCD image, so you can have a rough representation of the image as it will appear when modified. Sharpness, contrast, color saturation, and color tone will all be applied. In addition, the camera applies the following parameters to the live view image shown:

- White balance/white balance correction
- Shoot by ambience/lighting/scene choices
- Metering mode/Exposure
- Auto lighting optimization
- Depth-of-field with DOF button ON
- Auto Lighting Optimizer

- Peripheral illumination correction
- Distortion correction
- Chromatic aberration correction
- Highlight tone priority
- Aspect ratio

Quick Control

Press the Q button or tap the Q icon at the upper right of the touch screen while using P, Tv, Av, M, or B modes in live view, and you can adjust any of the values shown in the left and right columns. These include AF method, AF operation, Drive mode, Metering mode, Image Quality, White balance, Picture Style, and Auto Lighting Optimizer. In Movie mode, you can set AF method, movie recording size, recording level (manual), sound volume (headphones), card selection, white balance, Picture Style, Auto Lighting Optimizer, and HDR movie shooting. Figure 15.4 shows the AF method adjustment screen that appears in still photography live view mode.

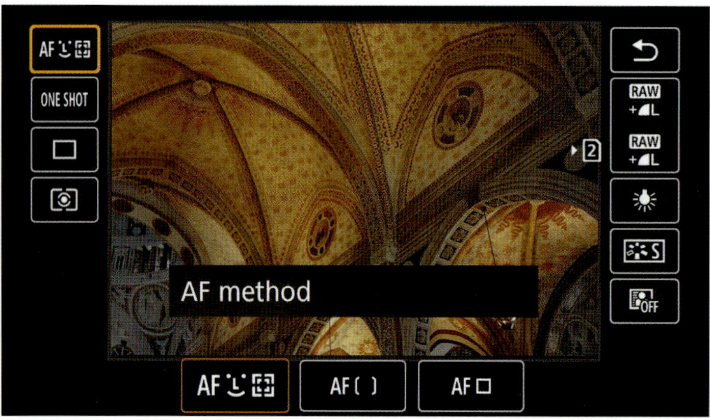

Figure 15.4
Focus mode adjustment Quick Control screen.

Focusing in Live View

Press the shutter button halfway to activate autofocus using the currently set live view autofocus mode. Those modes are Face Detection+Tracking, FlexiZone—Multiple, and FlexiZone—Single. You can also use manual focus. To change the focus mode while using live view, you can access the Quick Control menu with the Q button or by tapping the Q icon on the touch screen, or navigate to the AF Method entry of the Shooting 5 (Live View) menu. I'll describe each of these separately.

AF Operation

Two AF operation modes are available in live view, One-Shot AF and Servo AF. They are comparable to the One-Shot AF and AI Servo AF modes available when using the optical viewfinder (and discussed in Chapter 5), but do not use the 5D Mark IV's AF module located in the floor of the mirror compartment. Instead, live view (and movie shooting) rely on the Dual Pixel phase-detection pixels embedded in the 5D Mark IV's sensor. Press the Drive AF button and choose the AF mode you prefer. Some caveats:

- If you're working with Scene Intelligent Auto, One-Shot AF is enabled automatically and cannot be changed.

- When shooting Continuous High, Servo focus will give priority to shooting speed, which will be limited to about 4.3 frames per second (instead of 7 fps). Select Continuous Low instead, and the camera will attempt to keep your subject in focus, using subject tracking priority.

- When using Servo AF, the beeper will not chirp even when focus is achieved. That mode also disables M RAW and S RAW, and will default to RAW if either is selected. Multi-Shot Noise Reduction is disabled, as well.

AF Methods

Face Detection+Tracking, FlexiZone—Multi, FlexiZone—Single, and Manual focus modes are available. This section will provide descriptions of each of those focus options.

Face Detection+Tracking Mode

This mode also uses phase detection and contrast detection. The 5D Mark IV will search the frame for a human face and attempt to focus on it. Note that when using this mode, a magnified view of your image is not possible. To autofocus using Face Detection+Tracking mode, follow these steps:

1. **Set lens to autofocus.** Make sure the focus switch on the lens is set to AF.

2. **Activate live view.** Press the Start/Stop button. Select Face Detection from the Quick Control menu or the Live View Shooting menu.

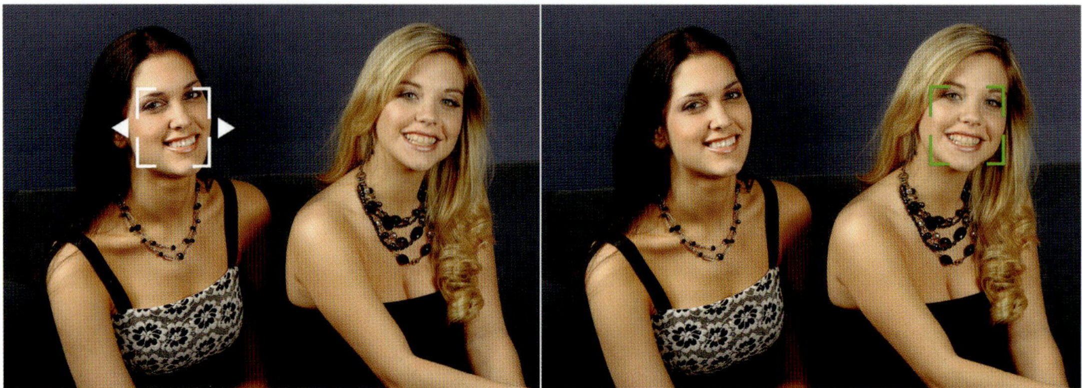

Figure 15.5 If multiple faces are found (left), the bracket can be moved among them. When focus is achieved (right), the bracket turns green.

3. **Face detection.** A frame will appear around a face found in the image. If only one face is detected, the frame will be green; if more than one face is found, the frame will be white and have left/right triangles flanking it. (See Figure 15.5, left.) In that case, use the multi-controller directional controls to move the frame to the face you want to use for focus. You can also tap the touch screen to select a face or other subject. If no face is detected, the 5D Mark IV will switch to FlexiZone—Multi with automatic selection.

   Pressing the SET or Trash buttons activates an AF frame in the center of the screen that you can move to select your subject (human or otherwise), and the 5D Mark IV will continue to track that subject.

4. **Focus.** Press the shutter button halfway to focus the camera on the face within the positioned Face Detection frame. When focus is locked in, the AF frame will turn green and the beeper, if activated, will chime. (See Figure 15.5, right.) If focus cannot be achieved, the AF frame will turn orange.

5. **Press and hold the shutter release to take the picture.** Press the shutter release all the way down to take the picture.

FlexiZone (Multi) Mode

This mode allows focusing over a wide area. In automatic selection mode, the camera selects one of 49 AF points. The 5D Mark IV can automatically select the focus *area* from up to 35 different AF positions in the frame, or any of nine different *zones* you select.

1. **Set lens to autofocus.** Make sure the focus switch on the lens is set to AF.

2. **Activate live view.** Press the Start/Stop button.

3. **Select Automatic or Zone (Manual) Selection.** You can toggle between Automatic and Zone (Manual) Selection by pressing the SET or Trash buttons. When you're using Zone selection, an icon appears in the lower-left area of the screen that you can tap to return to Automatic selection. In Basic Zone modes, Automatic is chosen by default.

- **In Automatic Selection mode,** the 5D Mark IV will choose one of 63 focus areas without input from you. White brackets appear around the area where the focus areas reside, as seen in Figure 15.6, top. That set of brackets cannot be moved. When in Automatic Selection mode, pressing the multi-controller button switches to Zone (Manual) mode.

- **In Zone (Manual) Selection mode,** you can use the multi-controller directional buttons to move a reduced-size frame, seen at bottom of Figure 15.6, around to any of 9 different overlapping areas within the frame.

Figure 15.6
FlexiZone—
Multi AF has both
Automatic (top)
and Zone (Manual)
modes (bottom).

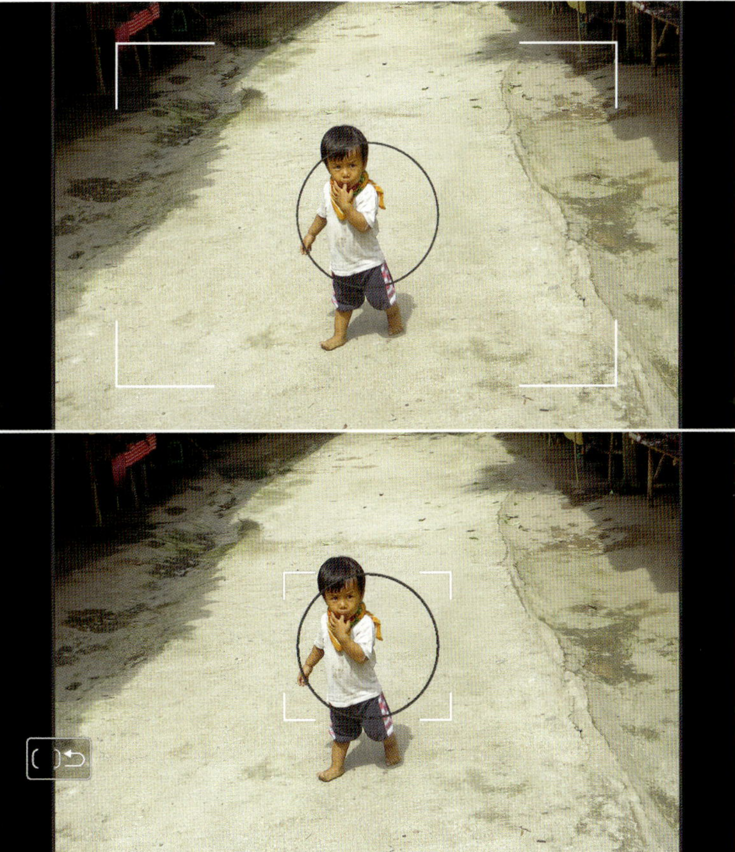

Alternatively, you can tap the touch screen to select a zone. If you have moved the focus area out of the center, pressing the multi-controller button *does not* switch to Automatic mode; instead, either button returns the area selection to the center. If the selection *is in the center already*, pressing the multi-controller button then switches to Automatic mode. This dual behavior of the multi-controller button is confusing at first, but you can get used to it quickly. You can always switch back to Automatic mode by tapping the switch icon at lower left of the touch screen.

4. **Select subject.** Compose the image on the LCD so the selected focus point is on the subject.

5. **Magnify image (optional).** For a closer view when focusing, press the Magnify button to cycle among 1X, 5X, and 10X magnifications.

6. **Press the shutter release button halfway.** When focus is achieved, the AF frame turns green, and you'll hear a beep if the sound has been turned on in the Shooting 1 menu. If the 5D Mark IV is unable to focus, the AF point turns orange instead.

7. **Take picture.** Press the shutter release all the way down to take the picture.

FlexiZone—Single AF Mode

FlexiZone—Single mode allows you to move the AF area around continually from one spot on the sensor to the next, rather than in area/zone "jumps." You can choose any area roughly within the autofocus zone. To autofocus using FlexiZone mode, follow these steps:

1. **Set lens to autofocus.** Make sure the focus switch on the lens is set to AF.

2. **Activate live view.** Press the Start/Stop button.

3. **Choose AF point.** A focus point box will appear (when using Movie Servo AF, the box will be larger). Use the multi-controller directional controls to move the AF point anywhere you like on the screen, except for the edges. Press the multi-controller button to move it back to the center of the screen. You can also tap the touch screen to move the AF point to that location.

4. **Select subject.** Compose the image on the LCD so the selected focus point is on the subject.

5. **Magnify image (optional).** For a closer view when focusing, press the Magnify button (or tap the Magnify icon on the touch screen) to cycle among 1X, 5X, and 10X magnifications.

6. **Press the shutter release button halfway.** When focus is achieved, the AF frame turns green, and you'll hear a beep if the sound has been turned on in the Shooting 1 menu. If the 5D Mark IV is unable to focus, the AF point turns orange instead.

7. **Take picture.** Press the shutter release all the way down to take the picture.

FOCUS ON MAGNIFICATION

- **FlexiZone—Multi mode.** The image is magnified at the center of the frame (Automatic Selection) or center of the zone (Zone Selection).
- **FlexiZone—Single.** The image is magnified at the selected AF point.
- **Move magnified image.** When 5X or 10X magnification is selected, you can move the magnified frame with the multi-controller or by tapping on the triangles on the touch screen.
- **When using Servo AF,** tap the shutter release to exit magnified view.

Manual Mode

Focusing manually on an LCD screen isn't as difficult as you might think, but Canon has made the process even easier by providing a magnified view. Just follow these steps to focus manually.

1. **Set lens to manual focus.** Make sure the focus switch on the lens is set to MF.

2. **Manual Focus appears in the Quick Control menu.** If you press the Q button, you'll see that MF will appear second from the top of the left column, replacing the Focus Method choices when the lens is set to manual focus.

3. **Magnify the frame.** You can press the Magnify/Reduce button to cycle among 1X, 5X, and 10X magnifications. (See Figure 15.7.) When information overlays are visible on the LCD monitor (the INFO. button cycles among the available info screens), you can also tap the magnifying glass icon in the lower-right corner.

Figure 15.7
You can manually focus the center area, which can be zoomed in 5X or 10X.

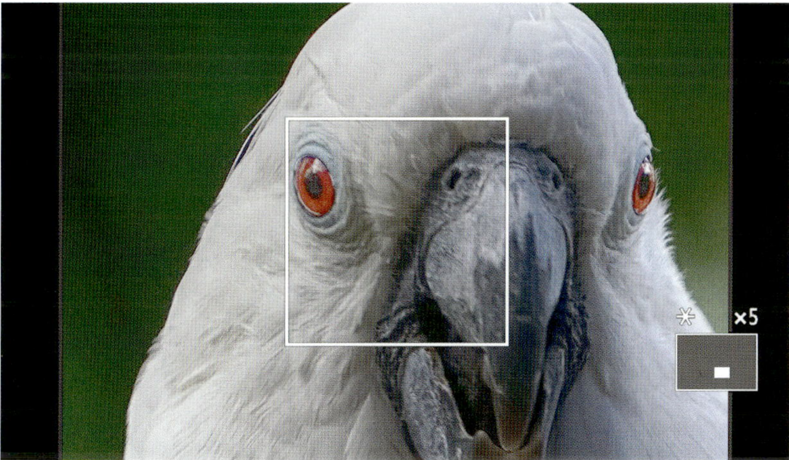

4. **Move magnified area.** While you're zoomed in, use the multi-controller directional controls to move the focus frame that's superimposed on the screen to the location where you want to focus. You can press the multi-controller button to center the focus frame in the middle of the screen. If informational overlays are on the LCD screen, directional arrows will appear at the left/right/top/bottom of the frame. A reference box at lower right shows the relative position of the zoomed area to the full frame.

5. **Focus manually.** The enlarged area is artificially sharpened to make it easier for you to see the contrast changes, and simplify focusing. When zoomed in, press the shutter release halfway and the current shutter speed and aperture are shown in orange. If no information at all appears, press the INFO. button. Use the focus ring on the lens to focus the image. When you're satisfied, use the Magnify/Reduce button to cycle back.

Using the Touch Shutter

In Live View mode, you can activate/deactivate the Touch Shutter feature, which allows you to set focus and take a picture by tapping on your subject on the LCD monitor. It's a convenient way of activating focus and capturing an image with one gesture.

Touch Shutter can be enabled or disabled using the (logically named) Touch Shutter entry in the Shooting 5 (Live View) menu. You can also activate or deactivate the feature by tapping the touch shutter icon at the lower-left corner of the touch screen.

When disabled, you can still tap on the touch screen to specify where you want to focus, but you'll need to press the shutter release to take a picture. When touch shutter is enabled, all you need to do is tap your subject (most often, this will be a person). The 5D Mark IV will focus using Face Detection+Tracking if you've selected that mode, or FlexiZone—Single if you've selected FlexiZone—Multi *or* FlexiZone—Single.

When your subject is focused, the AF point will turn green and a picture will be taken automatically. If the camera was unable to focus, the AF point turns orange. In that case, try tapping again. You can press the SET or Trash buttons to move the focus point to the center of the frame and relocate it manually with the multi-controller directional buttons, if you like, but I find that a screen tap works well. When Touch Shutter is active, Single Shooting is used even if Continuous Shooting has been selected. The Touch Shutter does not work in magnified view.

While Touch Shutter can be used to take bulb/time exposures, I don't recommend it. With the camera set to Bulb, you can tap the screen to start the exposure, and tap it again to stop the exposure. Unless you are very careful, these taps will cause the camera to vibrate, which can spoil your picture even if the camera is mounted on a tripod. Oddly enough, the effects are worst for "shorter" bulb exposures. For exposures longer than 15 seconds, the vibration is likely to subside within the first second or two, and have little effect on your final image.

16

Capturing Video

The Canon EOS 5D Mark IV can shoot full HDTV movies with monaural sound (or stereo sound if you plug in an external microphone) at 4096 × 2160 (4K) resolution, 1920 × 1080 (Full HD) resolution, or video at 1280 × 720 (Standard HD) resolution. In some ways, the camera's Movie mode is closely related to the 5D Mark IV's Live View still mode, and relies on many of the same features for presenting an image, focusing, and other functions, so the information in the previous chapter will serve you well as you branch out into shooting movies with your camera.

To shoot in Movie mode, just rotate the Live View/Movie switch to the Movie position. Press the Start/Stop button to begin/end capture. The screen will look like the one shown in Figure 16.1. That's quite simple, but there are some additional things you need to keep in mind before you start. Before you begin capturing video, you'll want to make certain basic setup adjustments. This section will show you everything you need to know before you begin capturing video in earnest. We'll start with the two Shooting menu movie screens that become visible when the Live View selector switch is rotated left to the Movie camera icon. In that mode, two new menus appear, the Shooting 4 (Movie) and Shooting 5 (Movie) menus.

Shooting 4 (Movie) Menu

Here is an introduction to the options available in the Shooting 4 (Movie) menu (see Figure 16.1). Some of these have counterparts for still shooting and were explained earlier in Chapters 11 and 15. Others are new, and I'll explain them in more detail later in this chapter.

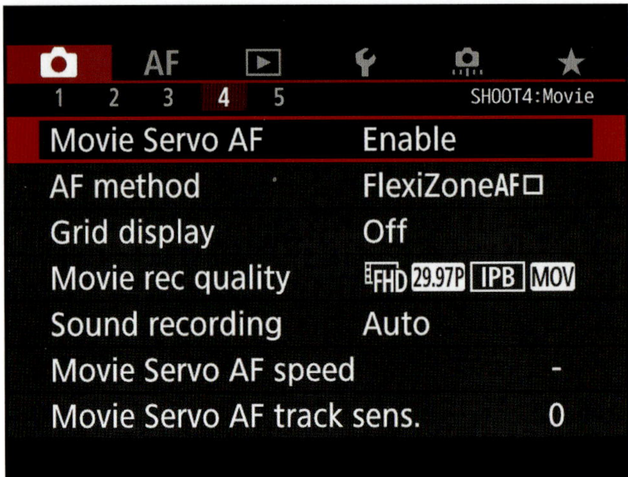

Figure 16.1
The Shooting 4 (Movie) menu.

Movie Servo AF

You can enable or disable this feature, which enables the 5D Mark IV to focus on the subject continuously during movie shooting—even if the shutter button is not held down halfway. It's a battery hog, and the constant refocusing may be undesirable if the noise is picked up by the camera's built-in microphone. To counter that noise, either use an external microphone or temporarily disable movie servo AF using one of the following techniques, which will cease the autofocus operation after you've focused on the plane you want to use:

- **Tap the Servo AF icon.** With the touch screen active, tap the Servo AF icon in the lower-left corner of the screen to stop/start Movie Servo AF.

- **Pause button.** You can define a button to temporarily halt Movie Servo AF, using the Custom Controls entry in the Custom Functions 3 menu. Choose the Pause Movie Servo AF option under the options for the Depth of Preview button. Press the defined button a second time to resume Servo AF.

- **AF Stop button.** You can define several buttons to serve as an AF Stop button, using the AF-Off option found in the AF-ON, AE Lock Button, DOF Preview Button, and Lens AF Stop Button entries of the Custom Controls screen. You must hold down the defined button to stop Servo AF. Release the button to resume.

- **Automatic resume.** If you've paused Movie Servo AF, it will be reactivated automatically if you press the MENU or Playback buttons or change the autofocus method. Note that while Movie Servo AF is paused or disabled, you can use the shutter button or AF-ON button (unless redefined) to start autofocus.

When Movie Servo AF is active, you can define its tracking sensitivity for FlexiZone—Single, as described in a later section.

AF Method

These are the same AF modes available in live view. Select from Face Detection+Tracking, FlexiZone—Multi, or FlexiZone—Single autofocus options. See Chapter 15 for more information on each method.

- **Face Detection+Tracking.** This mode uses phase detection and contrast detection. The 5D Mark IV will search the frame for a human face and attempt to focus on the face. Note that when using this mode, a magnified view of your image is not possible.
- **FlexiZone—Multi.** This mode allows focusing over a wide area. In automatic selection mode, the camera selects one of 63 AF points. The 5D Mark IV can automatically select the focus *area* from up to 35 different AF positions in the frame, or any of nine different *zones* you select.
- **FlexiZone—Single AF.** This mode allows you to move the AF area around continually from one spot on the sensor to the next, rather than in area/zone "jumps."

Grid Display

With this option, you can overlay Grid 1 on the screen to help you compose your image and align vertical and horizontal lines. Alternatively, choose Grid 2, which consists of four rows of six boxes; or Grid 3, which adds diagonal lines. All three variations were shown in Figure 11.25 in Chapter 11.

Movie Recording Quality

The Canon EOS 5D Mark IV has more video recording quality settings than ever before, including 4K video. (See Figure 16.2.) I'll explain the use of these settings in more detail later in this chapter, but, in brief, your choices include the following. **Note:** I'll explain terms like ALL-I, IPB, as well as frame rates in a later section. This description just lists your options. Only NTSC frame rates are

Figure 16.2
Movie Recording
Quality settings.

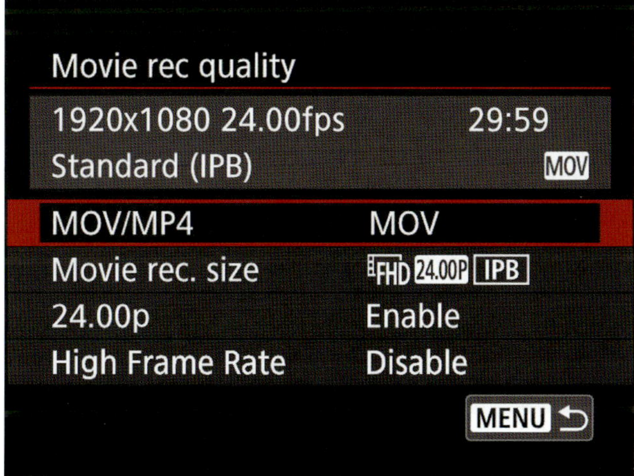

shown; different frame rates are available for use in countries that have standardized on the PAL system, as I'll describe in a later section.

- **MOV/MP4.** You can select the MOV format or MP4 as the "container" for your video files. MOV was developed by Apple for QuickTime and can be used with both Mac and Windows computers, using the MPEG-4 codec (coder/decoder). MP4 is an international standard and more widely supported/used. Your choice may depend on the movie recording size you want to use, as described next. All movies are recorded using progressive scan, described shortly.

- **Movie Recording Size (MOV).** Your choices differ with each recording size you select. When MOV is selected, sizes are as follows (se Figure 16.3, left):

  - **4096 × 2160 resolution (4K)** with 29.97 or 23.98 frame rates and a MJPEG file format. The aspect ratio of the video is 17:9, rather than 16:9 like the other available sizes.

  - **1920 × 1080 (Full HD)** with 59.94/29.97/23.98 frame rates in ALL-I format *or* IPB format, as described later in the chapter.

  - **24.00 fps.** If the 24-fps entry (located just below Movie Recording Size) is Enabled, the only choices available for MOV are 4K MJPG and Full HD ALL-I and IPB.

  - **1280 × 720 (HD)** with 119.9 fps frame rate in ALL-I format. This is available *only* when you have activated High Frame Rate, as I'll describe shortly.

- **Movie Recording Size (MP4).** When MP4 is selected, you can choose only the following, as seen in Figure 16.3, right. You cannot shoot 4K video using MP4.

  - **1920 × 1080 (Full HD)** with 59.94/29.97/23.98 frame rates in IPB format. Note that the selection in the second column of the top row is a "light," more highly compressed version.

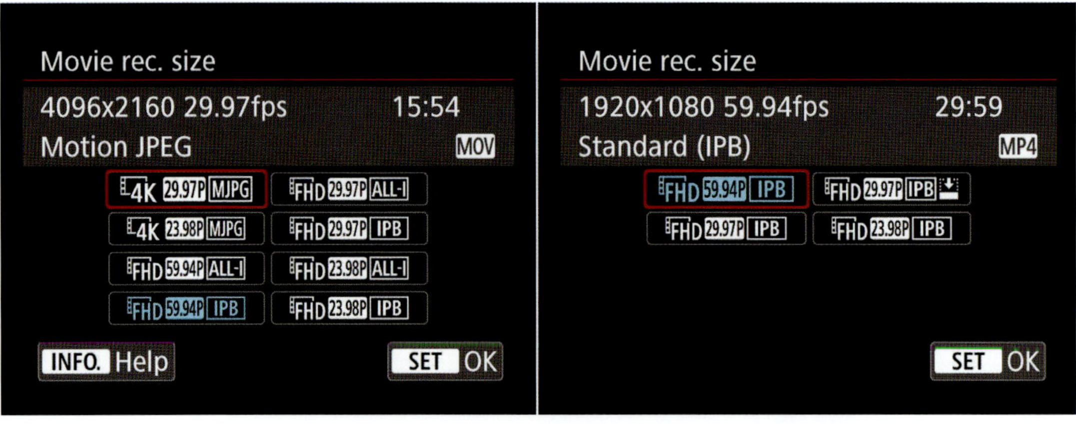

Figure 16.3 Movie Recording Size for MOV (left) and MP4 (right).

- **24.00p.** This choice locks your available movie frame rates at 24 frames per second. With MOV selected, you can choose 4K, Full HD (ALL-I), or Full HD (IPB). When using MP4, only FHD IPB is available.

- **High Frame Rate.** As noted above, the high frame rate choice is available when you are saving as MOV files, and only in standard HD (1280 × 720 pixels) at a fixed 119.9 fps rate (100 fps for PAL video systems, as I'll describe later). You can use this footage for slow-motion playback, as it will be played back at 29.97 (25 for PAL) frames per second, resulting in video at one-quarter actual speed. HFR movies are silent (no sound is available via headphones, either), and limited to 7 minutes and 29 seconds in length for a single clip.

Sound Recording

This setting lets you choose Auto, Manual, or Disable; plus, Enable or Disable the wind filter. (See Figure 16.4.)

- **Auto.** The 5D Mark IV sets the audio level for you.

- **Manual.** Choose from 64 different sound levels. Select Rec Level and rotate the QCD while viewing the decibel meter at the bottom of the screen to choose a level that averages –12 dB for the loudest sounds.

- **Disable.** Shoot silently, and add voice over, narration, music, or other sound later in your movie-editing software. Sound is not output to HDMI, as well.

- **Wind filter/attenuator.** Enable to reduce the effects of wind noise on the microphone. This also reduces low tones in the sound recording. If wind is not a problem, you'll get better quality audio with this option disabled. Even better is to use an external microphone with a wind shield.

Figure 16.4
Sound recording options.

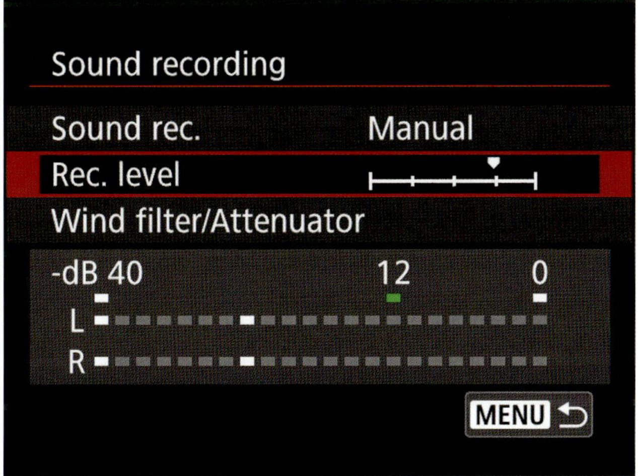

You can use your 5D Mark IV's built-in monaural microphone or plug in a stereo microphone into the 3.5mm jack on the side of the camera. An external microphone is a good idea because the built-in microphone can easily pick up camera operation, such as the autofocus motor in a lens.

Movie Servo AF Speed

This choice is available when Movie Servo AF is set to Enable, and AF Method is set to FlexiZone—Single. If you're using a USM or an STM lens released after 2009, the *slow focus transition* feature, which supplies smoother focus during movie shooting, will be available. Your choices, shown in Figure 16.5, left, are:

- **When Active.** Always On activates the AF adjustment speed setting automatically before and during movie shooting. During Shooting AF speed adjustment is active *only* when you are capturing video.
- **AF Speed.** Highlight this option and press SET. You can then adjust the AF speed using the touch screen, QCD, or multi-controller along a sliding scale from Slow (–7 to 0) to Standard (0) to Fast (+1 to +2).

Movie Servo AF Tracking Sensitivity

Here you can specify how quickly the Movie Servo AF tracking locks onto a moving subject. It's similar to the Tracking Sensitivity you can set for each Case in the Autofocus 1 menu, as described in Chapter 12. As with its still photo counterpart, changing the tracking sensitivity can come in useful when an intervening subject passes through the frame in front of the subject you were capturing. It's also helpful when panning. A sliding scale (shown in Figure 16.5, right) can be adjusted from Locked On (–3 to –1) to Responsive (+1 to +3) or standard at the 0 position. Locked On tells

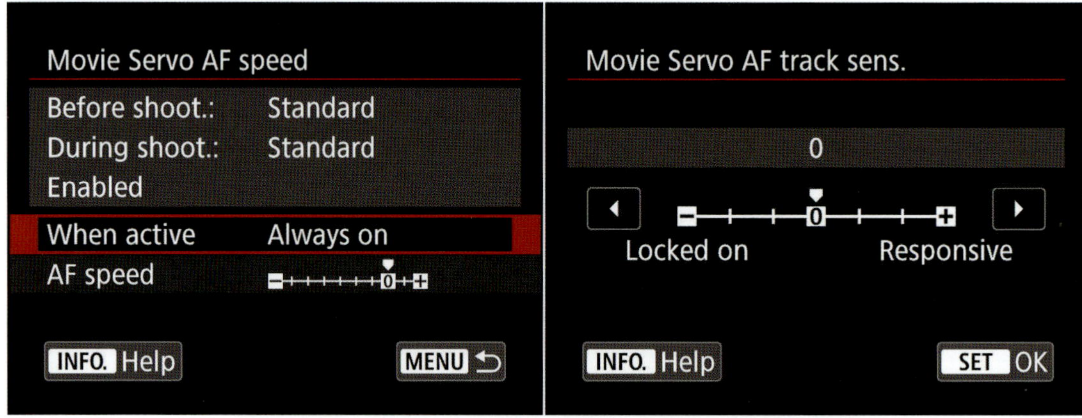

Figure 16.5 Movie Servo AF speed (left), and tracking sensitivity (right).

the camera to stick with the subject currently in focus—like that referee at a football game, or a passerby in an urban scene. Responsive settings tell the camera to switch to track a subject located at the current focus point, even if it's the same subject now moving toward you at a rapid rate, or a different subject that comes into view.

This setting requires the AF method to be set to FlexiZone—Single. At Face Detection+Tracking or FlexiZone—Multi, the 5D Mark IV defaults to the standard (0) setting and does not vary.

Shooting 5 (Movie) Menu

The Shooting 5 (Movie) menu includes the choices shown in Figure 16.6. I'll explain them briefly here, and delve into a little more detail on each later in the chapter.

Metering Timer

Specify how long the metering system remains active before switching off. You can select 4, 16, or 30 seconds, plus 1, 10, or 30 minutes. Tap the shutter release to restart the timer.

Time Code

Advanced video shooters find SMPTE (Society of Motion Picture and Television Engineers)-compatible time codes embedded in the video files to be an invaluable reference during editing. To oversimplify a bit, the time system provides precise *hour:minute:second:frame* markers that allow identifying and synchronizing frames and audio. The time code system includes a provision for "dropping" frames to ensure that the fractional frame rate of captured video (remember that a 24-fps setting actually yields 23.976 frames per second while 30 fps capture gives you 29.97 actual "frames" per second) can be matched up with actual time spans.

Figure 16.6
The Shooting 5 (Movie) menu.

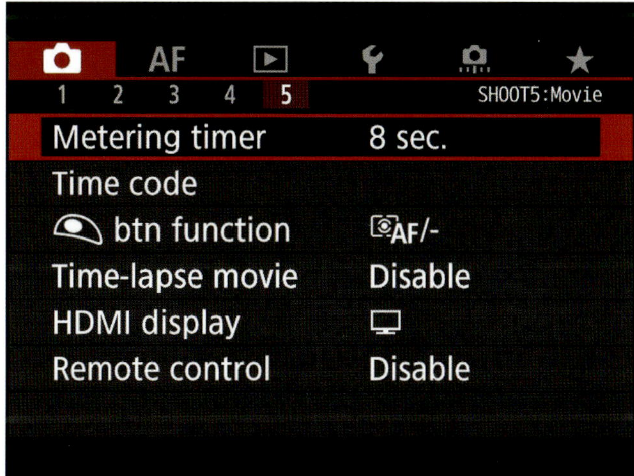

As I noted in the introduction to this book, I won't be covering the most technical aspects of movie shooting in great detail (including time codes, raw HDMI streaming, etc.). If you're at the stage where you're using time codes, you don't need a primer, anyway. However, the Time Code submenu does include the following options:

- **Count up.** Choose Rec Run, in which the time code counts up only when you are actually capturing video, or Free Run (also known as Time of Day), which allows the time code to run up even between shooting clips. The latter is useful when you want to synchronize clips between multiple cameras that are shooting the same event. When using Free Run, even if the cameras record at different times, you'll be able to match the video that was captured at the exact same moment during editing. When Free Run is selected, the time code will always be recorded to the movie file (except for HFR clips).

- **Start Time Setting.** Normally, the 5D Mark IV uses the camera's internal clock to specify the hours:minutes:seconds, with frames set to :00 when you begin shooting. This entry allows you to manually enter any hour:minute:second:frame of your choice, or to Reset the start time to 00:00:00:00.

- **Movie Rec. Count.** Here you can decide whether to display the elapsed time for the current clip on the LCD, or the Time Code while capturing video.

- **Movie Play Count.** This gives you the same choices during playback, allowing you to choose elapsed time or Time Code.

- **HDMI.** You can select Enable to append the time code to the HDMI video output, or Disable to not add it to the output. The Record Command output, when Enabled, allows the camera's Stop/Start action to sync with the external recording device. When Disabled, starting and stopping are controlled by the external recording device.

- **Drop Frame.** As I mentioned, the 30 fps setting yields 29.97 actual frames per second, 60 fps gives you 59.95 frames per second, and HFR provides 119.9 fps, causing a discrepancy between the actual time and the time code that's recorded. Choose enable and the camera will skip some time code numbers in drop-frame mode at intervals to eliminate the discrepancy. When disabled (Non-drop frame), you may notice a difference of several seconds per hour.

Shutter Button Function

This entry gives you four choices for what happens when you half-press the shutter release button, and press it down all the way. (See Figure 16.7.)

Figure 16.7
Shutter button functions.

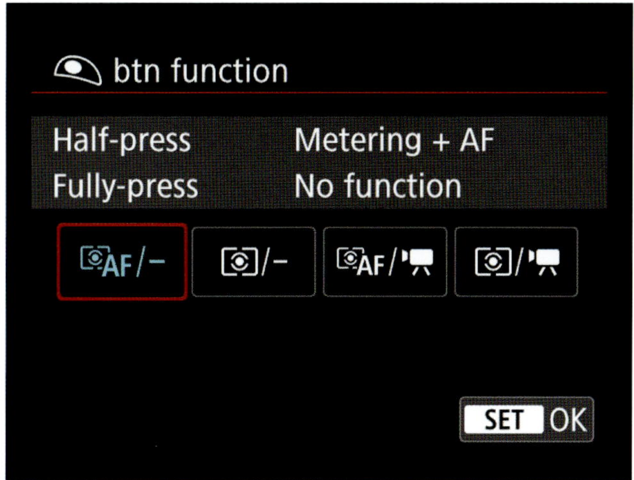

Your choices are as follows:

- **Half-press: Metering+AF; Fully press: No function.** Use if you want a half-press of the shutter button to activate both exposure metering and autofocus (the conventional mode for still photography, too). You'll use the Start/Stop button on the back of the camera to begin/end video capture.

- **Half-press: Metering Only; Fully press: No function.** With this choice, metering and AF initiation are decoupled, much as is done with back-button focus in still mode. When you press the shutter button halfway, metering starts, but, if you're not using Movie Servo AF, focus doesn't start until you press the AF-ON button or other defined AF start button. Use the Start/Stop button on the back of the camera to start/end video capture. You'll retain the ability to take still pictures while capturing video, and don't need to use a remote control to activate capture.

- **Half-press: Metering+AF; Fully press: Start/Stop recording.** This choice is the same as the first in this list, except that video capture can be started and stopped by pressing the shutter release down all the way. In this mode, you can also use any shutter release "alternative" such as the Remote Switch RS-80N3 or Timer Remote Controller TC-80N3. However, because the shutter release is now used to start movie making, you cannot take still photos during capture.

- **Half-press: Metering Only; Fully press: Start/Stop recording.** This choice is the same as the second option on this list, except that video capture can be started and stopped by pressing the shutter release down all the way. In this mode, you can also use any shutter release "alternative," such as the Remote Switch RS-80N3 or Timer Remote Controller TC-80N3. However, because the shutter release is now used to start movie making, you cannot take still photos during capture.

Time-Lapse Movie

The 5D Mark IV's time-lapse movie facility is a still photography mode that shoots images at intervals you specify, and then stitches them together automatically to create a MOV-format movie in Full HD (1920 × 1080) at a playback rate of 30/25 fps. I provided step-by-step instructions for shooting time-lapse clips in Chapter 6, and will not repeat that description here.

HDMI Display

This setting comes into play when you are working with an HDMI external device, such as any of the popular Atomos Shogun line of video recorders/displays. It determines whether the video display is shown on the camera's LCD monitor as well as the external monitor and what information is output to the external device. Note that display of 4K video is not possible under any circumstances. It will be shown in Full HD instead. HDMI output can be used for no more than 30 minutes when not actively capturing video, unless you've Set Auto Power Off to Disable in the Set-up 2 menu. Your three output choices are as follows:

- **External monitor only.** In this case, the output (video and sound) through the HDMI port will be displayed on the external device only, and will include the screen overlay data (if any). You can always press the INFO. button in this mode to cycle through each of the informational screens, and arrive at the plain screen with no overlays. You might want to use this mode if you weren't recording your HDMI output and just wanted to view it on an external monitor with all the information available with a few presses of the INFO. button. Sound is not transferred when Sound Recording is set to Disable.

- **External monitor without info.** You're more likely to use this mode when you're recording your clean video output and absolutely do not want the informational overlays to spoil your footage. Use this if you have no need to view settings information.

- **External monitor plus camera LCD monitor.** This mode displays clean output on the external video monitor/recorder and information with overlays on the camera's LCD. Use this if there is a need for two people to view the capture at one time. The camera operator can see the 5D Mark IV's display with overlay information, while a second person (the director?) can view on an external monitor. It would be useful if the video recording device is located some distance from the camera (even if it's just a few feet).

Remote Control

You can use a remote control to start and stop movie capture, such as the optional Remote Switch RS-80N3 or Timer Remote Controller TC-80N3, which connects to the remote-control terminal on the front of the camera. The infrared Remote Controller RC-6 can also be used if you are facing the front of the camera and are located no more than about 16 feet away. You can enable or disable remote control with this entry.

Compression, Resolution, and Frame Rates

Even intermediate movie shooters can be confused by the number of different choices for compression, resolution, and frame rates. This section will help clarify things for you.

Compression

Compression is easiest to understand, so I'll get it out of the way first. The 5D Mark IV stores files using the standard H.264/MPEG-4 codec ("coder-decoder"). For many of the Movie Size options listed earlier, you can select either ALL-I or IPB compression methods (both Standard and Light).

- **ALL-I (All Intraframe).** This mode, available only when the movie recording format is MOV, is useful for editing and post-processing. In this mode, the camera takes each individual frame that you shoot and attempts to compress it before writing the frame to your memory card. You can think of ALL-I compression as a series of still images, each squeezed down by discarding (hopefully) redundant information. While this compression method is not the most efficient way to reduce file size, because individual frames are stored in their entirety, the resulting files are easier to edit.

- **IPB (Standard).** This is a newer compression method that is considered Standard by Canon. It uses *interframe* compression; that is, only certain "key" frames are saved, with other frames "simulated" or interpolated from information contained in the frames that precede and succeed them. I-frames are the complete or *intraframes* (the only kind used by ALL-I compression); P-frames are "predicted picture" frames, which record *only the pixel changes* from the previous frame (say, a runner traveling across a fixed background); B-frames are "bi-predictive picture" frames, created by using the differences from the preceding *and* following frames. This interpolation produces image quality that is a bit lower and which requires more of your camera's DIGIC+ processing power, but file sizes are smaller.

  Video encoded using IPB must be converted, or transcoded to a format compatible with your video-editing software. The compression scheme can produce more artifacts, particularly in frames with lots of motion throughout the frame. I use this method only when the ability to shoot longer is very important.

- **IPB (Light).** This is available only when the movie recording format is MP4. It is recorded at a bit rate that is lower than IPB (Standard), producing files that are smaller, transfer more quickly, have higher playback compatibility, and provide longer maximum shooting times. If you don't need the maximum resolution possible, this choice can be very useful.

"CLEAN" HDMI OUTPUT

The video is directed through the HDMI port with embedded time code to an external monitor or recorder. As mentioned earlier, you can simultaneously display the video on the color LCD as it is recorded to your memory card. You can choose whether to display the captured image and scene and camera shooting information on the LCD as you shoot. This capability allows professional videographers (or other advanced shooters) more latitude in color correction though the enhanced color space, improved monitoring during the shoot, and more versatile post-production workflow. You can, for example, synchronize the 5D Mark IV's video capture with the start/stop of the external video recorder.

The maximum recording time for a movie clip (other than High Frame Rate movies) is 29 minutes, 59 seconds. Movie shooting will stop automatically, but you can begin shooting a new movie immediately. The EOS Movie Utility can merge multiple MOV files into one longer file. You can also use third-party movie-editing software to edit and combine your clips.

ALL-I files will reach the 4GB limit in about five minutes at 685MB/minute. So, if you really need to capture a continuous shot in *one* file (say, a performance), you might want to use IPB. The 4GB limitation is not as noxious as you might think, and you can continue capture without, in practice, an interruption. Roughly 30 seconds before the 4GB file size is reached, the elapsed shooting time/ time code displayed on the LCD will begin blinking. If you continue past 4GB, a new movie file will be created automatically. This process continues until you've reached the maximum shooting time of 29 minutes, 59 seconds (established because some jurisdictions classify equipment that can capture more than 30 minutes as "camcorders" at higher tax rates). You can patch two or more clips together in editing. Note that the 5D Mark IV will not switch to your second memory card during capture even if Auto Switch Card is activated.

Resolution

Resolution choices are a little less techie:

- **4096 × 2160 (4K).** This ultra-high-definition format is the wave of the future, even if content and display choices are limited at present. As you advance in the video world, you'll probably find yourself shooting 4K a lot, even if you intend to distribute Full HD video. Many editors swear that 4K video converted to Full HD is better than Full HD video captured natively.

- **1920 × 1080 (1080p).** This resolution is so-called "full HD" and is the maximum resolution displayed when using the HDTV format. Many monitors and most HD televisions can display this resolution, and you'll have the best image quality when you use it. Use this resolution for your "professional" productions, especially those you'll be editing and converting to nifty-looking DVDs. However, the top-of-the-line resolution requires the most storage space, approximately 235 to 685 megabytes per minute, as mentioned earlier. This means you can fit a collection of individual clips amounting to no more than about 22 minutes of recording (using ALL-I compression), or 1 hour 4 minutes (using IPB) on a single 16GB memory card.

- **1280 × 720.** "Standard HD" provides less resolution, and can be displayed on any monitor or television that claims HDTV compatibility. If your production will appear only on computer monitors with 1280 × 720 resolution, or on HDTVs that max out at 720p, this resolution will be fine. Don't choose this resolution to stretch your memory cards; it uses a 60/50 fps capture rate that streams an amount of data similar to that of 1080p shooting, so the elapsed time of your clips on a single card will be roughly the same.

Frame Rate

In the 5D Mark IV world, in which all video is shot using *progressive scan* with no *interlaced scan* option, frame rates are easy to choose. (Interlacing is a capture method in which even/odd numbered lines of each frame are captured alternately; with progressive scan, all the lines in a frame are captured consecutively.) Fortunately, one seemingly confusing set of alternatives can be dispensed with quickly: The 50/25 fps and 60/30 fps options can be considered as pairs of *video*-oriented frame rates. The 60/30 fps rates are used only where the NTSC television standard is in place, such as North America, Japan, Korea, Mexico, and a few other places. The 50/25 frame rates are used where the PAL standard reigns, such as Europe, Russia, China, Africa, Australia, and other places. For simplicity, I'll refer just to the 60/30 frame rates in this section; if you're reading this in India, just convert to 50/25.

The third possibility is 24 fps, which is a standard frame rate used for motion pictures. Keep in mind that the rates are *nominal*. A 24-fps setting yields 23.976 frames per second; 30 fps gives you 29.97 actual "frames" per second. The 5D Mark IV's High Frame Rate option captures video at 119.99 fps or, nominally, 120 fps for NTSC and 100 fps for PAL.

The difference lies in the two "worlds" of motion images—film and video. The standard frame rate for motion picture film is 24 fps, while the video rate, at least in the United States, Japan, and those other places using the NTSC standard, is 30 fps. Computer-editing software can handle either type, and convert between them. The choice between 24 fps and 30 fps is determined by what you plan to do with your video.

The short explanation is that shooting at 24 fps gives your movie a "film" look, excellent for showing fine detail. However, if your clip has moving subjects, or you pan the camera, 24 fps can produce a jerky effect called "judder." A 30 or 60 fps rate produces a home-video look that some feel is less desirable, but which is smoother and less jittery when displayed on an electronic monitor. I suggest you try both and use the frame rate that best suits your tastes and video-editing software.

Another consideration that we can't do much about is the difference between a *rolling shutter* and *global shutter*. In progressive scan mode, each line is captured one after another, so that a moving subject may have perceptibly relocated (part of it anyway) during the capture of a frame. The 5D Mark IV's rolling shutter may produce jello-like effects with such motion. A global shutter, like those used in professional videocams, captures the entire frame at once, eliminating that problem. Without benefit of a global shutter in our 5D Mark IV, we at least need to be aware of the possible result when shooting action.

HDR Movies

You can extend the dynamic range of your movies in high-contrast situations by shooting HDR movies. The feature is available with both MOV or MP4 file formats, but the Movie Recording Size under Movie Recording Quality must be set to Full HD 29.9P IPB or Full HD 25.00P IPB. Highlight Tone Priority and Time Lapse Movies must be disabled.

Then, press the Q button to produce the screen shown in Figure 16.8. Scroll down to the HDR Movie entry with the multi-controller and enable it. Then shoot a movie conventionally. Multiple frames are merged to create an HDR movie. You may see excessive noise or some distortion, so you'll want to experiment with this feature to see how useful it is to you.

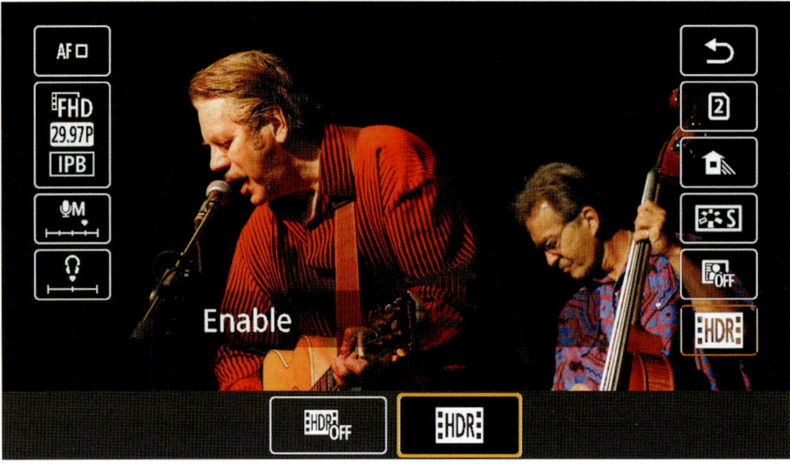

Figure 16.8
Activate HDR Movies in the Quick Control menu.

Exposure Options

You can select fully automatic exposure, elect to specify exposure manually, or choose a shutter speed or aperture setting that you prefer for creative reasons. The 5D Mark II will select an ISO speed for you automatically in all cases, generally sticking to the range ISO 100–12800. (Some oddball exceptions are applied for various combinations of exposure mode and ISO speed settings made in the Shooting 2 menu.) Exposure can be locked with the * button, and cancelled with the AF point selection button located to the right of the * button. Here are your options:

- **Fully automatic exposure.** The 5D Mark IV will automatically select an appropriate exposure for you if the Mode Dial is set to Scene Intelligent Auto, P (program auto exposure), or B (bulb exposure). Note that B will not produce a bulb or time exposure; the camera defaults to P when you use the B position. The idea is to prevent you from losing video capture capabilities if you accidentally select B by mistake. In Scene Intelligent Auto, the 5D Mark IV will analyze your subject and select a Scene type and display it on the upper-left corner of the LCD monitor.

- **Shutter-priority AE.** You can choose Tv on the Mode Dial, exactly as you do when shooting still photographs, and specify a shutter speed, with some limitations. The 5D Mark IV will select an appropriate aperture for you. The available shutter speeds will depend on the frame rate, primarily because you can't (logically) choose a shutter speed that is longer than the length of time needed to expose an individual frame. For example, at 30/25/24 fps, you cannot use a shutter speed longer than 1/30th second. At 60/50 fps, the longest shutter speed available is 1/60th second. In all cases, shutter speeds *shorter* than 1/4000th second (1/8000th) are unavailable.

  Choosing the shutter speed yourself offers two advantages. Even though each frame is captured in about 1/60th–1/30th second, slicing up the time the sensor is exposed to light allows capturing video in a much broader range of lighting conditions. Outdoors in full daylight, 1/30th second would produce an overexposure even with a very small f/stop and an ISO 100 sensitivity setting. In addition, opting for a higher shutter speed allows you to freeze action within each individual frame, reducing or eliminating blur. You might want to use 1/500th second when shooting movies of sports, or stick to 1/30th second when you *want* to include a little motion blur in your video for effect.

- **Aperture-priority AE.** Select Av on the Mode Dial, and you can choose an f/stop that will allow you to maximize or minimize depth-of-field, at your option, for creative effects. There is no limitation on your f/stop selection. However, you should avoid switching to a different aperture while capturing video, as the sudden change can provide a jarring effect.

■ **Manual exposure.** Choose M on the Mode Dial and you can specify ISO speed, shutter speed, and aperture.

- **ISO.** Press the ISO/Flash Exposure Compensation button on top of the camera to view the ISO speed setting screen. Adjust with the Main Dial. Choose Auto and the camera will select an appropriate ISO based on the shutter speed and aperture you have selected. During Manual exposure, the * button locks ISO at its current setting if you have selected Auto.

- **Shutter speed.** Use the Main Dial to select a shutter speed, within the limitations described under Shutter-priority AE earlier.

- **Aperture.** Use the Quick Control Dial to adjust aperture.

    When choosing shutter speed or aperture, you can monitor exposure using the exposure level scale at the bottom of the LCD screen. For an additional check, you can press the INFO. button to view a live histogram.

■ **Scene Intelligent Auto.** The 5D Mark IV will analyze your subject and select a Scene type and display it on the upper-left corner of the LCD monitor.

More on Shutter Speeds

You might think that setting your camera to a faster shutter speed will help give you sharper video frames. But the choice of a shutter speed for movie making is a bit more complicated than that. As you might guess, it's almost always best to leave the shutter speed at 1/30th or 1/60th second, and allow the overall exposure to be adjusted by varying the aperture and/or ISO sensitivity. We don't normally stare at a video frame for longer than 1/30th or 1/24th second, so while the shakiness of the *camera* can be disruptive (and often corrected by your camera's in-lens and in-body image stabilization), if there is a bit of blur in our *subjects* from movement, we tend not to notice. Each frame flashes by in the blink of an eye, so to speak, so a shutter speed of 1/30th or 1/60th second works a lot better in video than it does when shooting stills. Even shots with lots of movement are often sufficiently sharp at 1/60th second.

Higher shutter speeds introduce problems of their own. If you shoot a video frame using a shutter speed of 1/250th second, the actual moment in time that's captured represents only about 12 percent of the 1/30th second of elapsed time in that frame. Yet, when played back, that frame occupies the full 1/30th of a second, with 88 percent of that time filled by stretching the original image to fill it. The result is often a choppy/jumpy image, and one that may appear to be *too* sharp.

The reason for that is more social imprinting than scientific: we've all grown up accustomed to seeing the look of Hollywood productions that, by convention, were shot using a shutter speed that's half the reciprocal of the frame rate (that is, 1/48th second for a 24-fps movie). Professional movie cameras use a rotary shutter (achieving that 1/48th-second exposure by using a 180-degree shutter "angle"), but the effect on our visual expectations is the same. For the most "film-like" appearance, use 24 fps and 1/60th second shutter speed.

Faster shutter speeds do have some specialized uses for motion analysis, especially where individual frames are studied. The rest of the time, 1/30th or 1/60th of a second will suffice. If the reason you needed a higher shutter speed was to obtain the correct exposure, use a slower ISO setting, or a neutral-density filter to cut down on the amount of light passing through the lens. A good rule of thumb is to use 1/60th second or slower when shooting at 24 fps; 1/60th second or slower at 30 fps; and 1/125th second or slower at 60 fps.

Playback and Editing

Select a movie during playback and press SET to commence viewing. As a movie is being played back, a screen of options appears at the bottom of the screen. When the icons are shown, use the QCD, touch screen, or multi-controller to highlight one, and then press the SET button to activate a function. Left to right at the bottom of the figure in the upper-left corner of Figure 16.9, they are as follows:

- **Playback.** Begins playback of the movie or album. To pause playback, press the SET button again. That restores the row of icons so you can choose a function.
- **Slow motion.** Displays the video in slow motion.
- **First frame.** Jumps to the first frame of the video, or the first scene of an album's first video snapshot.

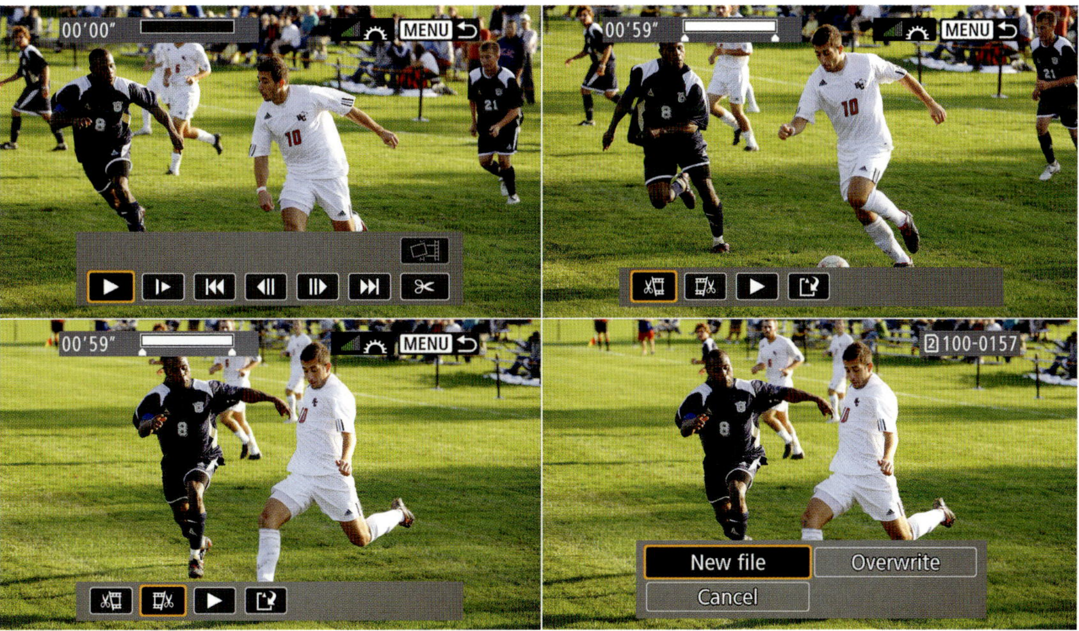

Figure 16.9 Playback and editing options.

- **Previous frame.** Press SET to view previous frame; hold down SET to rewind movie.
- **Next frame.** Press SET to view next frame; hold down SET to fast forward movie.
- **Last frame.** Jumps to last frame of the video, or the last scene of the album's last video snapshot.
- **Edit.** Summons an editing screen.
- **Frame grab.** This icon is located above the Edit scissor icon. It is available only when a 4K movie is being viewed. You can grab the displayed frame and save it as a JPEG image.

Several items are displayed at the top of the playback frame, from left to right:

- **Playback position.** A bar shows the amount of the clip that has been played so far.
- **Playback time.** In minutes and seconds with Movie Play Count: Rec Time enabled.
- **Volume.** Rotate the Main Dial to adjust the volume of the audio.
- **Menu.** Return to single-image display of the movie.

When you select Edit, the screen shown at upper right in Figure 16.9 appears. While reviewing your video, you can trim from the beginning or end of your video clip by selecting the scissors symbol. The icons that appear have the following functions:

- **Cut beginning.** Trims off all video prior to the current point. (Figure 16.9, upper right.)
- **Cut end.** Removes video after the current point. (Figure 16.9, lower left.)
- **Play video.** Play back your video to reach the point where you want to trim the beginning or end.
- **Save.** Saves your video to the memory card. A screen appears offering to save the clip as a New File, or to Overwrite the existing movie with your edited clip. (Figure 16.9, lower right.)
- **Menu.** Exits editing mode.
- **Adjust volume.** Modifies the volume of the sound.

Tips for Shooting Better Video

Producing good-quality video is more complicated than just buying good equipment. There are techniques that make for gripping storytelling and a visual language the average person is very used to, but also unaware of. After all, by comparison we're used to watching the best productions that television, video, and motion pictures can offer. Whether it's fair or not, our efforts are compared to what we're used to seeing produced by experts. While this book can't make you a professional videographer, there is some advice I can give you that will help you improve your results with the camera. There are several different things to consider when planning a video shoot, and when possible, a shooting script and storyboard can help you produce a higher-quality video.

Lens Craft

I covered the use of lenses with the 5D Mark IV in more detail in Chapter 7, but a discussion of lens selection when shooting movies may be useful at this point. In the video world, not all lenses are created equal. The two most important considerations are depth-of-field, or the beneficial lack thereof, and zooming. I'll address each of these separately.

Depth-of-Field and Video

One thing that makes digital still cameras so attractive for professional video shooters—especially now that cameras like the 5D Mark IV support 4K video—is that they have relatively large sensors, which provides improved low-light performance and results in the oddly attractive reduced depth-of-field, compared with many professional video cameras.

But wait! you say. No matter what size sensor is used to capture, say, a full HD video frame, isn't the number of pixels in that video frame exactly the same—1920 × 1080 pixels? That's true—the final resolution of the video image is precisely 1920 × 1080 pixels, whether you're capturing that frame with a point-and-shoot camera, a professional video camera, or a full-frame digital SLR like the Canon 5D Mark IV. But that's only the *final* resolution. The number of pixels used to capture each video frame varies by sensor size.

For example, your 5D Mark IV does *not* use only its central 1920 × 1080 pixels to capture a full HD video frame. If it did that, you'd have to contend with a 3.8X "crop" factor, and the field of view of, say, a 24mm wide angle would be the equivalent of a 90mm telephoto. That doesn't happen! (See Chapter 7 for a longer discussion of the effects of the so-called "crop" factor.) Instead, the 5D Mark IV captures a video frame using the proportions of a 16:9 area of its sensor, producing a negligible crop factor. Your wide-angle and telephoto lenses retain roughly their same fields of view, and you can frame and compose your video through the viewfinder normally, with only the top and bottom of the frame and a little off each side cropped off to account for the wider video aspect ratio. That's why the 5D Mark IV gives you such great video quality, and why your video images retain roughly the same field of view and exact same depth-of-field you get with full-frame still images.

Figure 16.10 shows the approximate capture areas for still photos (the outer green box), Full HD and Standard HD (the white area), and 4K video (the inner red box). You'll note that the Full HD and Standard HD frames are captured from the exact same area of the sensor; the Standard HD frame is reduced in size to 1280 × 720 (and so are High Frame Rate frames) before storing on your memory card. You can also see that a 4K video frame *isn't* captured from the entire 36 × 24mm still frame. A smaller area measuring 4096 × 2160 in a 17:9 aspect ratio is captured instead. That means that any 4K video you shoot will be cropped from the full image, and result in a "magnification" or crop factor of about 1.74X compared to the 3:2 aspect ratio full frame. You'll need to take that into consideration, especially when using wide-angle lenses.

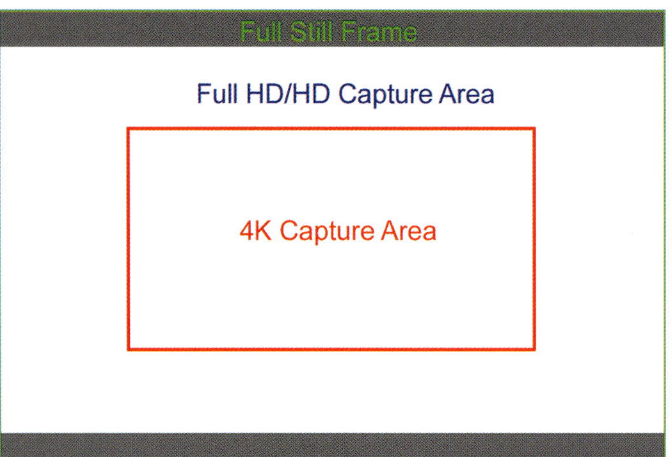

Figure 16.10
Video capture areas.

As I noted in Chapter 7, a larger sensor calls for the use of longer focal lengths to produce the same field of view, so, in effect, a larger sensor has reduced depth-of-field. And *that's* what makes cameras like the 5D Mark IV attractive from a creative standpoint. Less depth-of-field means greater control over the range of what's in focus. Your 5D Mark IV, with its larger sensor, has a distinct advantage over consumer camcorders in this regard, and even does a better job than many professional video cameras. With a really fast lens, such as the Canon 85mm f/1.2 or 50mm f/1.2, some sensational selective focus effects can be achieved.

Zooming and Video

When shooting still photos, a zoom is a zoom is a zoom. The key considerations for a zoom lens used only for still photography are the maximum aperture available at each focal length ("How *fast* is this lens?"), the zoom range ("How far can I zoom in or out?"), and its sharpness at any given f/stop ("Do I lose sharpness when I shoot wide open?").

When shooting video, the priorities may change, and there are two additional parameters to consider. The first two I listed, lens speed and zoom range, have roughly the same importance in both still and video photography. Zoom range gains a bit of importance in videography, because you can always/usually move closer to shoot a still photograph, but when you're zooming during a shot most of us don't have that option (or the funds to buy/rent a dolly to smoothly move the camera during capture). But, oddly enough, overall sharpness may have slightly less importance under certain conditions when shooting video. That's because the image changes in some way many times per second (24/30/60 times per second with the 5D Mark IV in NTSC mode), so any given frame doesn't hang around long enough for our eyes to pick out every single detail. You want a sharp image, of course, but your standards don't need to be quite as high when shooting video.

Here are the remaining considerations:

- **Zoom lens maximum aperture.** The speed of the lens matters in several ways. A zoom with a relatively large maximum aperture lets you shoot in lower light levels, and a big f/stop allows you to minimize depth-of-field for selective focus. Keep in mind that the maximum aperture may change during zooming. A lens that offers an f/3.5 maximum aperture at its widest focal length may provide only f/5.6 worth of light at the telephoto position. If shooting wide open you may want to retain the same maximum aperture regardless of focal length, so depth-of-field (and, along with it, focus) will increase or decrease more predictably from shot to shot, because the *focal length* has changed (that is, going from wide-angle to tele, or the reverse), and not because the *effective aperture* has changed, too.

   In that case, you'll want to use a *constant aperture* lens (sometimes called a *fixed aperture* lens, which can be interpreted two ways). Often, such lenses are Canon L lenses; with less expensive optics with a similar focal length range having a variable maximum aperture. A typical example is the EF 24-105mm f/4L IS USM zoom and EF 28-135 f/3.5-5.6 IS USM. The L lens's maximum aperture is f/4 from 24mm right up to 105mm, while its half-price cousin varies from f/3.5 at 28mm to f/5.6 at the 135mm setting.

- **Zoom range.** Use of zoom during actual capture should not be an every day thing, unless you're shooting a kung-fu movie. However, there are effective uses for a zoom shot, particularly if it's a "long" one from extreme wide angle to extreme close-up (or vice versa). Most of the time, you'll use the zoom range to adjust the perspective of the camera *between* shots, and a longer zoom range can mean less trotting back and forth to adjust the field of view. Zoom range also comes into play when you're working with selective focus (longer focal lengths have less depth-of-field), or want to expand or compress the apparent distance between foreground and background subjects. A longer range gives you more flexibility.

- **Linearity.** Interchangeable lenses may have some drawbacks, as many photographers who have been using the video features of their digital SLRs have discovered. That's because, unless a lens is optimized for video shooting, zooming with a particular lens may not necessarily be linear. Rotating the zoom collar manually at a constant speed doesn't always produce a smooth zoom. There may be "jumps" as the elements of the lens shift around during the zoom. Keep that in mind if you plan to zoom during a shot, and are using a lens that has proved, from experience, to provide a non-linear zoom. (Unfortunately, there's no easy way to tell ahead of time whether you own a lens that is well-suited for zooming during a shot.)

Keep Things Stable and on the Level

Camera shake's enough of a problem with still photography, but it becomes even more of a nuisance when you're shooting video. The image-stabilization feature found in many Canon lenses (and some third-party optics) can help minimize this. Any of them make an excellent choice for video shooting if you're planning on going for the hand-held cinema verité look.

Just realize that while hand-held camera shots—even image stabilized—may be perfect if you're shooting a documentary or video that intentionally mimics traditional home movie making, in other contexts it can be disconcerting or annoying. And even IS can't work miracles. As I'll point out in the next section, it's the camera movement itself that is distracting—not necessarily any blur in our subject matter.

If you want your video to look professional, putting the 5D Mark IV on a tripod will give you smoother, steadier video clips to work with. It will be easier to intercut shots taken from different angles (or even at different times) if everything was shot on a tripod. Cutting from a tripod shot to a hand-held shot, or even from one hand-held shot to another one that has noticeably more (or less) camera movement can call attention to what otherwise might have been a smooth cut or transition.

Remember that telephoto lenses and telephoto zoom focal lengths magnify any camera shake, even with IS, so when you're using a longer focal length, that tripod becomes an even better idea. Tripods are essential if you want to pan from side to side during a shot, dolly in and out, or track from side to side (say, you want to shoot with the camera in your kid's coaster wagon). A tripod and (for panning) a fluid head built especially for smooth video movements can add a lot of production value to your movies.

Shooting Script

A shooting script is nothing more than a coordinated plan that covers both audio and video and provides order and structure for your video when you're in planned, storytelling mode. A detailed script will cover what types of shots you're going after, what dialogue you're going to use, audio effects, transitions, and graphics. A good script needn't constrain you: as the director, you are free to make changes on the spot during actual capture. But, before you change the route to your final destination, it's good to know where you were headed, and how you originally planned to get there.

When putting together your shooting script, plan for lots and lots of different shots, even if you don't think you'll need them. Only amateurish videos consist of a bunch of long, tedious shots. You'll want to vary the pace of your production by cutting among lots of different views, angles, and perspectives, so jot down your ideas for these variations when you put together your script.

If you're shooting a documentary rather than telling a story that's already been completely mapped out, the idea of using a shooting script needs to be applied more flexibly. Documentary filmmakers often have no shooting script at all. They go out, do their interviews, capture video of people, places, and events as they find them, and allow the structure of the story to take shape as they learn more about the subject of their documentary. In such cases, the movie is typically "created" during editing, as bits and pieces are assembled into the finished piece.

Storyboards

A storyboard makes a great adjunct to a detailed shooting script. It is a series of panels providing visuals of what each scene should look like. While the storyboards produced by Hollywood are generally of very high quality, there's nothing that says drawing skills are important for this step. Stick figures work just fine if that's the best you can do. The storyboard helps you visualize locations, placement of actors/actresses, props and furniture, and also helps everyone involved get an idea of what you're trying to show. It also helps show how you want to frame or compose a shot. You can even shoot a series of still photos and transform them into a "storyboard" if you want, such as in Figure 16.11.

Storytelling in Video

Today's audience is used to fast-paced, short-scene storytelling. To produce interesting video for such viewers, it's important to view video storytelling as a kind of shorthand code for the more leisurely efforts print media offers. Audio and video should always be advancing the story. While it's okay to let the camera linger from time to time, it should only be for a compelling reason and only briefly.

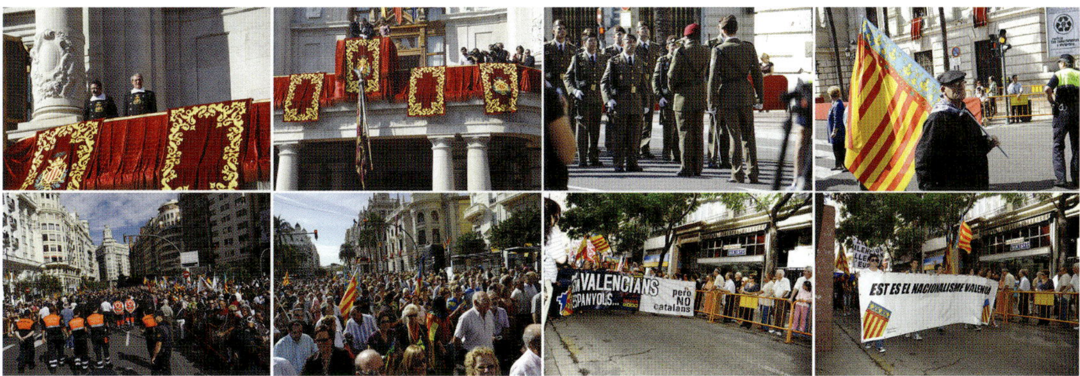

Figure 16.11 A storyboard is a series of simple sketches or photos to help visualize a segment of video.

Above all, look for movement in your scene as you shoot. You're not taking still photographs! Perhaps your ideal still picture of an old castle in Segovia, Spain might be to show the edifice in its modern-day surroundings, but a movie needs to show something *moving,* like the hang glider that soared overhead when I captured the image shown in Figure 16.12. The juxtaposition of old and new added an interesting contrast to the video image (and later narration). If you've seen too many travel videos that looked like they could have been assembled from a series of still photos (a "slide show" so to speak), you'll know that motion is what brings many otherwise static scenes to life.

It only takes a second or two for an establishing shot to impart the necessary information. For example, many of the scenes for a video documenting a model being photographed in a Rock and Roll music setting might be close-ups and talking heads, but an establishing shot showing the studio where the video was captured helps set the scene.

Provide variety too. If you put your shooting script together correctly, you'll be changing camera angles and perspectives often and never leave a static scene on the screen for a long period. (You can record a static scene for a reasonably long period and then edit in other shots that cut away and back to the longer scene with close-ups that show each person talking.)

When editing, keep transitions basic. I can't stress this enough. Watch a television program or movie. The action "jumps" from one scene or person to the next. Fancy transitions that involve exotic "wipes," dissolves, or cross fades take too long for the average viewer and make your video ponderous.

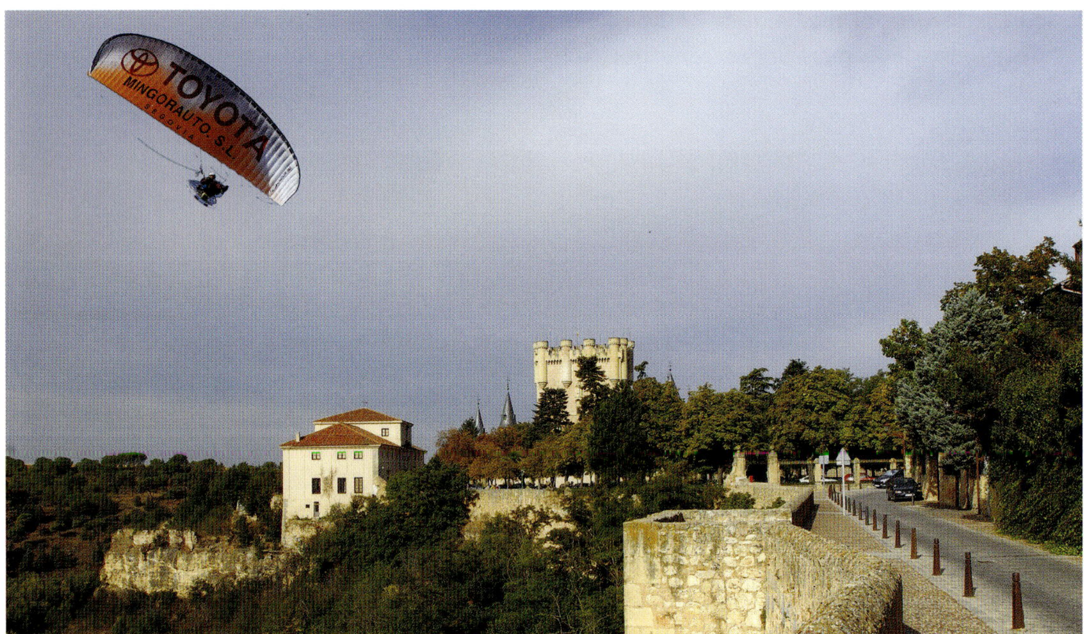

Figure 16.12 Movies need motion to come alive.

Composition

In movie shooting, several factors restrict your composition, and impose requirements you just don't always have in still photography (although other rules of good composition do apply). Here are some of the key differences to keep in mind when composing movie frames:

- **Horizontal compositions only.** Some subjects, such as basketball players and tall buildings, just lend themselves to vertical compositions. But movies are shown in horizontal-format only. So, if you're interviewing a local basketball star, you can end up with a worst-case situation like the one shown in Figure 16.13. If you want to show how tall your subject is, it's often impractical to move back far enough to show him full-length. You really can't capture a vertical composition. Tricks like getting down on the floor and shooting up at your subject can exaggerate the perspective, but aren't a perfect solution.

Figure 16.13
Movie shooting requires you to fit all your subjects into a horizontally oriented frame.

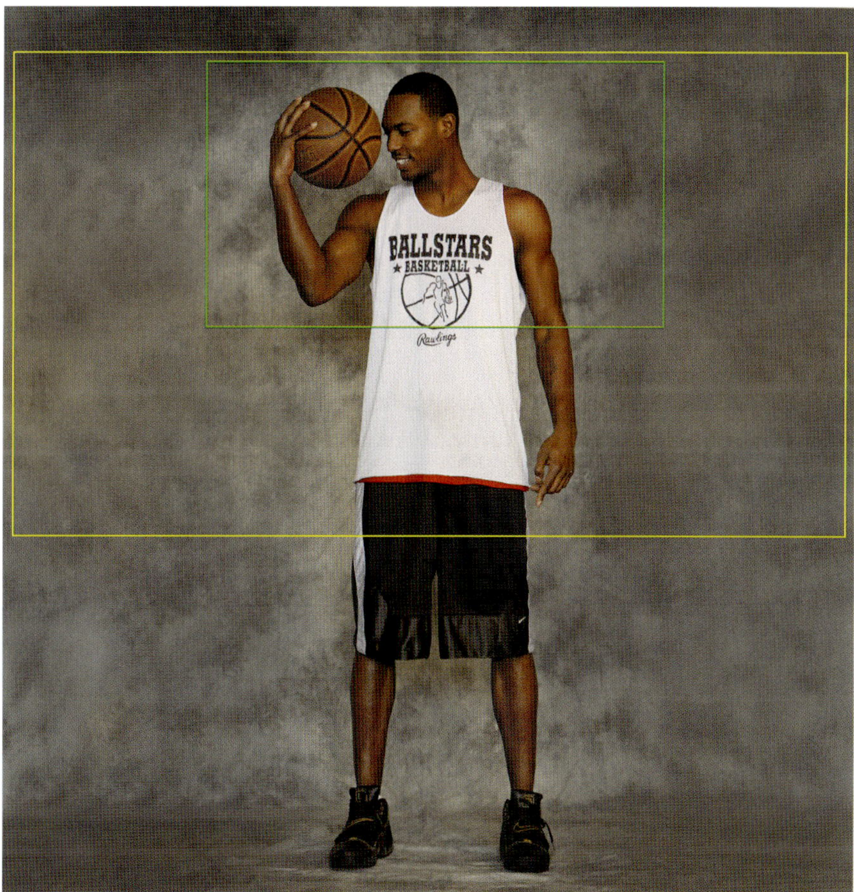

- **Wasted space at the sides.** Moving in to frame the basketball player as outlined by the yellow box in Figure 16.13 means that you're still forced to leave a lot of empty space on either side. (Of course, you can fill that space with other people and/or interesting stuff, but that defeats your intent of concentrating on your main subject.) So, when faced with some types of subjects in a horizontal frame, you can be creative, or move in *really* tight. For example, if I was willing to give up the "height" aspect of my composition, I could have framed the shot as shown by the green box in the figure, and wasted less of the image area at either side.

- **Seamless (or seamed) transitions.** Unless you're telling a story with a photo essay, still pictures often stand alone. But with movies, each of your compositions must relate to the shot that preceded it, and the one that follows. It can be jarring to jump from a long shot to a tight close-up unless the director—you—is very creative. Another common error is the "jump cut" in which successive shots vary only slightly in camera angle, making it appear that the main subject has "jumped" from one place to another. (Although everyone from French New Wave director Jean-Luc Goddard to Guy Ritchie—Madonna's ex—have used jump cuts effectively in their films.) The rule of thumb is to vary the camera angle by at least 30 degrees between shots to make it appear to be seamless. Unless you prefer that your images flaunt convention and appear to be "seamy."

- **The time dimension.** Unlike still photography, with motion pictures there's a lot more emphasis on using a series of images to build on each other to tell a story. Static shots where the camera is mounted on a tripod and everything is shot from the same distance are a recipe for dull videos. Watch a television program sometime and notice how often camera shots change distances and directions. Viewers are used to this variety and have come to expect it. Professional video productions are often done with multiple cameras shooting from different angles and positions. But many professional productions are shot with just one camera and careful planning, and you can do just fine with your 5D Mark IV.

Here's a look at the different types of commonly used compositional tools:

- **Establishing shot.** Much like it sounds, this type of composition, as shown in Figure 16.14, upper left, establishes the scene and tells the viewer where the action is taking place. Let's say you're shooting a video of your offspring's move to college; the establishing shot could be a wide shot of the campus with a sign welcoming you to the school in the foreground. Another example would be for a child's birthday party; the establishing shot could be the front of the house decorated with birthday signs and streamers or a shot of the dining room table decked out with party favors and a candle-covered birthday cake. I wanted to show the studio where the video was shot.

- **Medium shot.** This shot is composed from about waist to head room (some space above the subject's head). It's useful for providing variety from a series of close-ups and makes for a useful first look at a speaker. (See Figure 16.14, upper right.)

- **Close-up.** The close-up, usually described as "from shirt pocket to head room," provides a good composition for someone talking directly to the camera. Although it's common to have your talking head centered in the shot, that's not a requirement. In Figure 16.14, center left, the subject was offset to the right. This would allow other images, especially graphics or titles, to be superimposed in the frame in a "real" (professional) production. But the compositional technique can be used with 5D Mark IV videos, too, even if special effects are not going to be added.

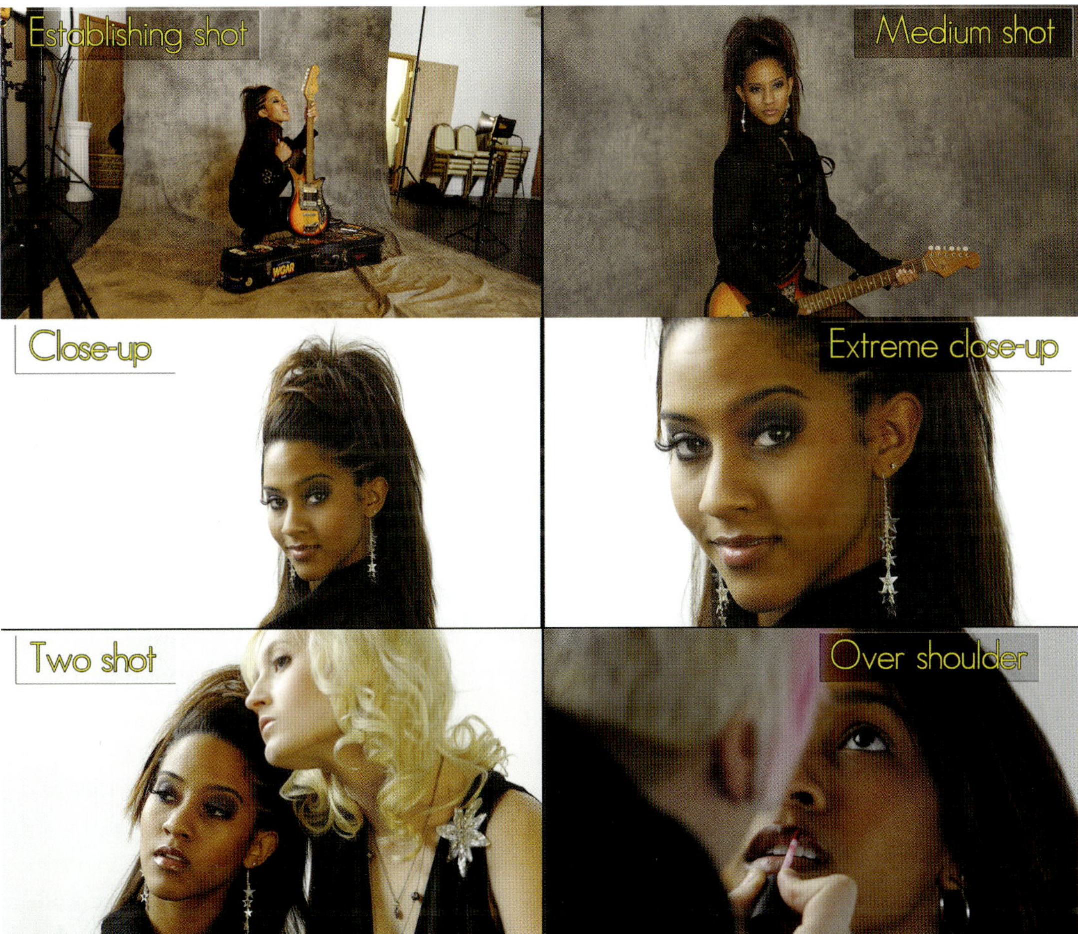

Figure 16.14 Shot choice provides different perspectives on a scene.

- **Extreme close-up.** When I went through broadcast training back in the '70s, this shot was described as the "big talking face" shot and we were actively discouraged from employing it. Styles and tastes change over the years and now the big talking face is much more commonly used (maybe people are better looking these days?) and so this view may be appropriate. Just remember, the 5D Mark IV is capable of shooting in high-definition video and you may be playing the video on a high-def TV; be careful that you use this composition on a face that can stand up to high definition or 4K resolution. (See Figure 16.14, center right.)

- **"Two" shot.** A two shot shows a pair of subjects in one frame. They can be side by side or one in the foreground and one in the background. (See Figure 16.14 lower left.) This does not have to be a head-to-ground composition. Subjects can be standing or seated. A "three shot" is the same principle except that three people are in the frame.

- **Over-the-shoulder shot.** Long a composition of interview programs, the "over-the-shoulder shot" uses the rear of one person's head and shoulder to serve as a frame for the other person. This puts the viewer's perspective as that of the person facing away from the camera. (See Figure 16.14, lower right.)

Lighting for Video

Much like in still photography, how you handle light pretty much can make or break your videography. Lighting for video can be more complicated than lighting for still photography, since both subject and camera movement are often part of the process.

Lighting for video presents several concerns. First off, you want enough illumination to create a useable video. Beyond that, you want to use light to help tell your story or increase drama. Let's take a better look at both.

Illumination

You can significantly improve the quality of your video by increasing the light falling in the scene. This is true indoors or out, by the way. While it may seem like sunlight is more than enough, it depends on how much contrast you're dealing with. If your subject is in shadow (which can help them from squinting) or wearing a ball cap, a video light can help make them look a lot better.

Lighting choices for amateur videographers are a lot better these days than they were a decade or two ago. An inexpensive incandescent video light, which will easily fit in a camera bag, can be found for $15 or $20. You can even get a good-quality LED video light for less than $100. Work lights sold at many home improvement stores can also serve as video lights since you can set the camera's white balance to correct for any color casts. You'll need to mount these lights on a tripod or other support, or, perhaps, to a bracket that fastens to the tripod socket on the bottom of the camera.

Much of the challenge depends upon whether you're just trying to add some fill-light on your subject versus trying to boost the light on an entire scene. A small video light will do just fine for the former. It won't handle the latter. Fortunately, the versatility of the 5D Mark IV comes in quite handy here. Since the camera shoots video in Auto ISO mode, it can compensate for lower lighting levels and still produce a decent image. For best results, though, better lighting is necessary.

Creative Lighting

While ramping up the light intensity will produce better technical quality in your video, it won't necessarily improve the artistic quality of it. Whether we're outdoors or indoors, we're used to seeing light come from above. Videographers need to consider how they position their lights to provide even illumination while up high enough to angle shadows down low and out of sight of the camera.

When considering lighting for video, there are several factors. One is the quality of the light. It can either be hard (direct) light or soft (diffused) light. Hard light is good for showing detail, but can also be very harsh and unforgiving. "Softening" the light, but diffusing it somehow, can reduce the intensity of the light but make for a kinder, gentler light as well.

While mixing light sources isn't always a good idea, one approach is to combine window light with supplemental lighting. Position your subject with the window to one side and bring in either a supplemental light or a reflector to the other side for reasonably even lighting.

Lighting Styles

Some lighting styles are more heavily used than others. Some forms are used for special effects, while others are designed to be invisible. At its most basic, lighting just illuminates the scene, but when used properly it can also create drama. Let's look at some types of lighting styles:

- **Three-point lighting.** This is a basic lighting setup for one person. A main light illuminates the strong side of a person's face, while a fill light lights up the other side. A third light is then positioned above and behind the subject to light the back of the head and shoulders. (See Figure 16.15, top.)

- **Flat lighting.** Use this type of lighting to provide illumination and nothing more. It calls for a variety of lights and diffusers set to raise the light level in a space enough for good video reproduction, but not to create a mood or emphasize a scene or individual. With flat lighting, you're trying to create even lighting levels throughout the video space and minimize any shadows. Generally, the lights are placed up high and angled downward (or possibly pointed straight up to bounce off a white ceiling). (See Figure 16.15, bottom.)

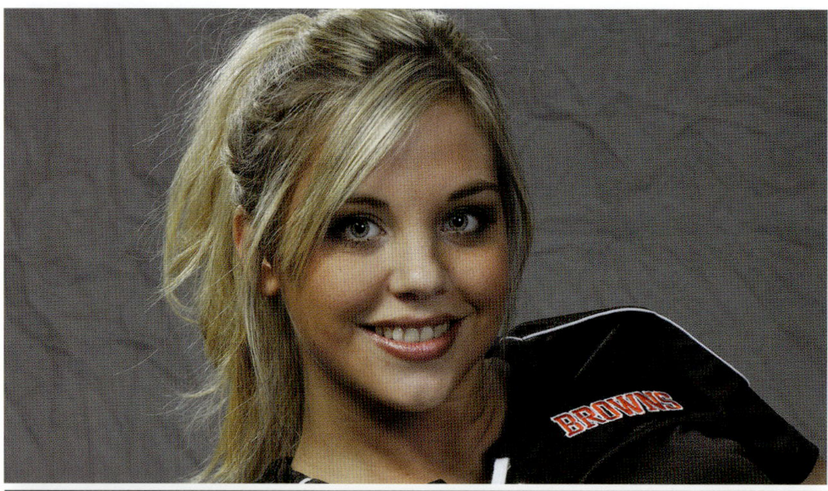

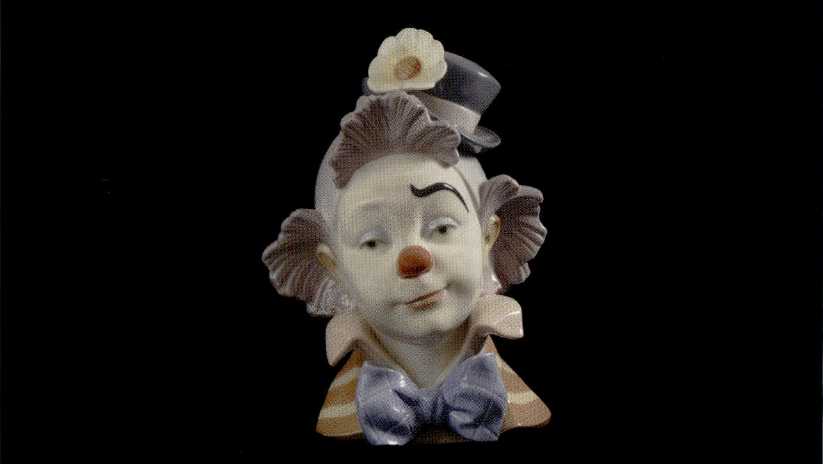

- **"Ghoul lighting."** This is the style of lighting used for old horror movies. The idea is to position the light down low, pointed upward. It's such an unnatural style of lighting that it makes its targets seem weird and "ghoulish."

- **Outdoor lighting.** While shooting outdoors may seem easier because the sun provides more light, it also presents its own problems. As a general rule of thumb, keep the sun behind you when you're shooting video outdoors, except when shooting faces (anything from a medium shot and closer) since the viewer won't want to see a squinting subject. When shooting another human this way, put the sun behind her and use a video light to balance light levels between the foreground and background. If the sun is simply too bright, position the subject in the shade and use the video light for your main illumination. Using reflectors (white board panels or aluminum foil-covered cardboard panels are cheap options) can also help balance light effectively.

Audio

When it comes to making a successful video, audio quality is one of those things that separates the professionals from the amateurs. We're used to watching top-quality productions on television and in the movies, yet the average person has no idea how much effort goes in to producing what seems to be "natural" sound. Much of the sound you hear in such productions is recorded on carefully controlled sound stages and "sweetened" with a variety of sound effects and other recordings of "natural" sound.

Tips for Better Audio

Since recording high-quality audio is such a challenge, it's a good idea to do everything possible to maximize recording quality. Here are some ideas for improving the quality of the audio your camera records:

- **Get the camera and its microphone close to the speaker.** The farther the microphone is from the audio source, the less effective it will be in picking up that sound. While having to position the camera and its built-in microphone closer to the subject affects your lens choices and lens perspective options, it will make the most of your audio source. Of course, if you're using a very wide-angle lens, getting too close to your subject can have unflattering results, so don't take this advice too far. It's important to think carefully about what sounds you want to capture. If you're shooting video of an acoustic combo that's not using a PA system, you'll want the microphone close to them, but not so close that, say, only the lead singer or instrumentalist is picked up, while the players at either side fade off into the background.

- **Use an external microphone.** You'll recall the description of the camera's external microphone port in Chapter 2. As noted, this port accepts a stereo mini-plug from a standard external microphone, allowing you to achieve considerably higher audio quality for your movies than is possible with the camera's built-in microphones (which are disabled when an external mic is plugged in). An external microphone reduces the amount of camera-induced noise that is picked up and recorded on your audio track. (The action of the lens as it focuses can be audible when the built-in microphones are active.)

  The external microphone port can provide plug-in power for microphones that can take their power from this sort of outlet rather than from a battery in the microphone. Canon provides optional compatible microphones such as the Canon BP-512 (around $140); you also may find suitable microphones from companies such as Shure and Audio-Technica. If you are on a quest for superior audio quality, you can even obtain a portable mixer that can plug into this jack. Or, you might be using an Atomos recorder with professional microphone jacks. One good thing about the 5D Mark IV is that so many pro videographers are using it that a wealth of add-on video gear, from monitors to cages and stabilizers are available for it.

- **Hide the microphone.** Combine the first few tips by using an external mic, and getting it as close to your subject as possible. If you're capturing a single person, you can always use a lapel microphone (described in the next section). But if you want a single mic to capture sound from multiple sources, your best bet may be to hide it somewhere in the shot. Put it behind a vase, using duct tape to fasten the microphone, and fix the mic cable out of sight (if you're not using a wireless microphone).

- **Turn off any sound makers you can.** Little things like fans and air handling units aren't obvious to the human ear, but will be picked up by the microphone. Turn off any machinery or devices that you can plus make sure cell phones are set to silent mode. Also, do what you can to minimize sounds such as wind, radio, television, or people talking in the background.

- **Make sure to record some "natural" sound.** If you're shooting video at an event of some kind, make sure you get some background sound that you can add to your audio as desired in postproduction.

- **Consider recording audio separately.** Lip-syncing is probably beyond most of the people you're going to be shooting, but there's nothing that says you can't record narration separately and add it later. It's relatively easy if you learn how to use simple software video-editing programs like iMovie (for the Macintosh) or Windows Movie Maker (for Windows PCs). Any time the speaker is off-camera, you can work with separately recorded narration rather than recording the speaker on-camera. This can produce much cleaner sound.

External Microphones

The single most important thing you can do to improve your audio quality is to use an external microphone. The 5D Mark IV's internal stereo microphones mounted on the front of the camera will do a decent job, but have some significant drawbacks, partially spelled out in the previous section:

- **Camera noise.** There are plenty of noise sources emanating from the camera, including your own breathing and rustling around as the camera shifts in your hand. Manual zooming is bound to affect your sound, and your fingers will fall directly in front of the built-in mics as you change focal lengths. An external microphone isolates the sound recording from camera noise.

- **Distance.** Anytime your 5D Mark IV is located more than 6–8 feet from your subjects or sound source, the audio will suffer. An external unit allows you to place the mic right next to your subject.

- **Improved quality.** Obviously, Canon wasn't able to install a super-expensive, super-high-quality microphone, even on a $3,500 dSLR. Not all owners of the 5D Mark IV would be willing to pay the premium, especially if they didn't plan to shoot much video themselves. An external microphone will almost always be of better quality.

- **Directionality.** The 5D Mark IV's internal microphone generally records only sounds directly in front of it. An external microphone can be either of the directional type or omnidirectional, depending on whether you want to "shotgun" your sound or record more ambient sound.

You can choose from several different types of microphones, each of which has its own advantages and disadvantages. If you're serious about movie making with your 5D Mark IV, you might want to own more than one. Common configurations include:

- **Shotgun microphones.** These can be mounted directly on your 5D Mark IV, although, if the mic uses an accessory shoe mount, you'll need the optional adapter to convert the camera's shoe to a standard hot shoe. I prefer to use a bracket, which further isolates the microphone from any camera noise. One thing to keep in mind is that while the shotgun mic will generally ignore any sound coming from *behind* it, it will pick up any sound it is pointed at, even *behind* your subject. You may be capturing video and audio of someone you're interviewing in a restaurant, and not realize you're picking up the lunchtime conversation of the diners seated in the table behind your subject. Outdoors, you may record your speaker, as well as the traffic on a busy street or freeway in the background.

- **Lapel microphones.** Also called *lavalieres*, these microphones attach to the subject's clothing and pick up their voice with the best quality. You'll need a long enough cord or a wireless mic (described later). These are especially good for video interviews, so whether you're producing a documentary or grilling relatives for a family history, you'll want one of these.

- **Hand-held microphones.** If you're capturing a singer crooning a tune, or want your subject to mimic famed faux newscaster Wally Ballou, a hand-held mic may be your best choice. They serve much the same purpose as a lapel microphone, and they're more intrusive—but that may be the point. A hand-held microphone can make a great prop for your fake newscast! The speaker can talk right into the microphone, point it at another person, or use it to record ambient sound. If your narrator is not going to appear on-camera, one of these can be an inexpensive way to improve sound.

- **Wired and wireless external microphones.** This option is the most expensive, but you get a receiver and a transmitter (both battery-powered, so you'll need to make sure you have enough batteries). The transmitter is connected to the microphone, and the receiver is connected to your 5D Mark IV. In addition to being less klutzy and enabling you to avoid having wires on view in your scene, wireless mics let you record sounds that are physically located some distance from your camera. Of course, you need to keep in mind the range of your device, and be aware of possible signal interference from other electronic components in the vicinity.

WIND NOISE REDUCTION

Always use the wind screen provided with an external microphone to reduce the effect of noise produced by even light breezes blowing over the microphone. Many mics include a low-cut filter to further reduce wind noise. However, these can also affect other sounds. You can disable the low-cut filters for some units by changing a switch on the back from L-cut (low cutoff) to Flat.

17

Troubleshooting and Prevention

One of the nice things about modern electronic cameras like the Canon EOS 5D Mark IV is that they have fewer mechanical moving parts to fail, so they are less likely to "wear out." No film transport mechanism, no wind lever or motor drive, and no complicated mechanical linkages from camera to lens to physically stop down the lens aperture. Instead, tiny, reliable motors are built into each lens (and you lose the use of only that lens should something fail), and one of the few major moving parts in the camera itself is a lightweight mirror that flips up and down with each shot not taken using live view.

Of course, the camera also has a moving shutter that can fail, but the shutter is built rugged enough that you can expect it to last 150,000 shutter cycles or more (according to Canon figures). Unless you're shooting sports in continuous mode day in and day out, the shutter on your 5D Mark IV is likely to last as long as you expect to use the camera.

The only other things on the camera that move are switches, dials, buttons, and the door that slides open to allow you to remove and insert the memory card. Unless you're extraordinarily clumsy or unlucky and manage to bend the internal pins in the card slot, there's not a lot that can go wrong mechanically with your EOS 5D Mark IV.

There are numerous other electrical and electronic connections in the camera (many connected to those mechanical switches and dials), and components like the color LCD and top-panel status LCD that can potentially fail or suffer damage. The camera also relies on its "operating system," or *firmware*, which can be plagued by bugs that cause unexpected behavior. Luckily, electronic components are generally more reliable and trouble-free, especially when compared to their mechanical counterparts from the pre-electronic film camera days. (Film cameras of the last 10 to 20 years have had almost as many electronic features as digital cameras, but, believe it or not, there were whole generations of film cameras that had *no* electronics or batteries.)

Digital cameras have problems unique to their breed, too; the most troublesome being the need to clean the sensor of dust and grime periodically. This chapter will show you how to diagnose problems, fix many common ills, and, importantly, learn how to avoid them, when possible, in the future.

Updating Your Firmware

As I said, the firmware in your EOS 5D Mark IV is the camera's operating system, which handles everything from menu display (including fonts, colors, and the actual entries themselves), what languages are available, and even support for specific devices and features. Upgrading the firmware to a new version makes it possible to add new features while fixing some of the bugs that sneak in.

Official Firmware

Official firmware for your 5D Mark IV is given a version number that you can view by turning the power on, pressing the MENU button, and scrolling to Firmware Ver. x.x.x in the Set-up 5 menu. The first number in the version string represents the major release number, while the second and third represent less significant upgrades and minor tweaks, respectively. Theoretically, a camera should have a firmware version number of 1.0.0 when it is introduced, but vendors have been known to do some minor fixes during testing and unveil a camera with a 1.0.1 firmware designation. It's likely, however, that any camera you buy new will have the latest firmware, or lag only one release behind. Most updating is done for currently owned cameras that need to keep pace with progress. Firmware upgrades are used most frequently to fix bugs in the software, and much less frequently to add or enhance features. Some of the bug fixes can affect only a tiny number of users or applications.

The exact changes made to the firmware are generally spelled out in the firmware release announcement. My recommendation is always to examine the remedies provided and decide if a given firmware patch is important to you. If not, you can usually safely wait a while before going through the bother of upgrading your firmware—at least long enough for the early adopters to report whether the bug fixes have introduced new bugs of their own. Check with the camera forums to see if the firmware caused more problems than it fixed before proceeding. Each new firmware release incorporates the changes from previous releases, so if you skip a minor upgrade you should have no problems.

Upgrading Your Firmware

If you're computer savvy, you might wonder how your EOS 5D Mark IV can overwrite its own operating system—that is, how can the existing firmware be used to load the new version on top of itself? It's a little like lifting yourself by reaching down and pulling up on your bootstraps. Not ironically, that's almost exactly what happens: At your command (when you start the upgrade process), the 5D Mark IV shifts into a special mode in which it is no longer operating from its firmware but, rather, from a small piece of software called a *bootstrap loader*, a separate, protected software program that functions only at startup or when upgrading firmware. The loader's function is to look for firmware to launch or, when directed, to copy new firmware from a memory card or your computer to the internal memory space where the old firmware is located. Once the new firmware has replaced the old, you can turn your camera off and then on again, and the updated operating system will be loaded.

Because the loader software is small in size and limited in function, there are some restrictions on what it can do. For example, the loader software isn't set up to go hunting through your memory card for the firmware file. It looks only in the top or root directory of your card, so that's where you must copy the firmware you download. Once you've determined that a new firmware update is available for your camera and that you want to install it, just follow these steps. (If you chicken out, any Canon service center can install the firmware upgrade for you.)

Note that, from time to time, Canon changes the firmware updating procedure. The Canon website will always provide directions for the latest method. Follow those directions if the steps below are slightly different.

> **WARNING**
>
> Use a fully charged battery or Canon's optional ACK-E6N AC adapter kit to ensure that you'll have enough power to operate the camera for the entire upgrade. Moreover, you should not turn off the camera while your old firmware is being overwritten. Don't open the memory card door or do anything else that might disrupt operation of the 5D Mark IV while the firmware is being installed.

1. Download the firmware from Canon (you'll find it in the Downloads section of the Support portion of Canon's website) and place it on your computer's hard drive. The firmware is contained in a self-extracting file for either Windows or Mac OS. It will have a name such as 5D400113.fir.

2. In your camera, format a memory card. Choose Format from the Set-up menu, and initialize the card (make sure you don't have images you want to keep before you do this!).

3. You can copy the upgrade software to the card either using a card reader or by connecting the camera to your computer with a USB cable and using the EOS Utility application furnished with your camera (and described in the next section).

4. Insert the card in the camera and then turn the camera on. With the 5D Mark IV set to P or any other exposure mode other than Scene Intelligent Auto, press MENU and scroll to Firmware Ver. x.x.x in the Set-up 5 menu and press the SET button. The camera displays a message alerting you that a memory card containing new firmware is required to update. Select OK, and it will check to see if there is a firmware file on the card.

5. If a firmware file is found, you'll see the current firmware version, and an option to update. Choose OK and press the SET button to begin loading the update program.

6. A confirmation screen will appear. Select OK and press SET to continue. As the Firmware Update Program loads, you'll see a progress screen.

7. Next, you'll get the opportunity to confirm that the version you're upgrading to is the one you want. You can press the MENU button to cancel. (Yes, I know there are a lot of confirmation screens; Canon wants to make sure you don't upgrade your firmware by accident, or, possibly, intentionally.)

8. Finally, the very last confirmation screen. Select OK, and press SET, and, I promise, the actual firmware update will really begin.

9. While the firmware updates, you'll be warned not to turn off the power switch or touch any of the 5D Mark IV's buttons.

10. When the update complete screen appears, you can turn off the EOS 5D Mark IV, remove the AC adapter, if used, and reinsert the battery. Then turn the camera on to boot up your camera with the new firmware update.

11. Be sure to reformat the card before returning it to regular use to remove the firmware software.

Using Direct Camera USB Link to Copy the Software

The procedure is slightly different (and a little more automated) if you choose to transfer the firmware software to the camera through a USB linkup. Follow these instructions to get started:

1. Connect the camera (with a freshly charged battery or attached to AC Adapter) to the computer using the USB cable and turn it on.

2. Load the EOS Utility.

3. Click the Camera/Settings/Remote Shooting button.

4. Select the firmware update option. When the Update Firmware window appears at the bottom of the EOS Utility, choose OK.

5. Click Yes in the confirmation screen.

6. Follow the instructions in the dialog boxes that pop up next by pressing the SET button on the camera.

Protecting Your LCD

The 3.2-inch color LCD on the back of your EOS 5D Mark IV almost seems like a target for banging, scratching, and other abuse. Fortunately, it's quite rugged, and a few errant knocks are unlikely to shatter the protective cover over the LCD, and scratches won't easily mar its surface. However, if you want to be on the safe side, there are several protective products you can purchase to keep your LCD safe—and, in some cases, make it a little easier to view. Here's a quick overview of your options.

- **Plastic overlays.** The simplest solution (although not always the cheapest) is to apply a plastic overlay sheet or "skin" cut to fit your LCD. These adhere either by static electricity or through a light adhesive coating that's even less clingy than stick-it notes. You can cut down overlays made for PDAs (although these can be pricey at up to $19.95 for a set of several sheets), or purchase overlays sold specifically for digital cameras. These products will do a good job of shielding your 5D Mark IV's LCD screen from scratches and minor impacts, but will not offer much protection from a good whack.

- **Acrylic/glass shields.** These scratch-resistant panels, laser cut to fit your camera perfectly, are my choice as the best protection solution, and what I use on my own 5D Mark IV. A company called GGS makes some nice glass protectors (see Figure 17.1); they're available for about $12 from eBay, Amazon.com, and other online vendors.

- **Magnifiers.** If you look hard enough, you should be able to find an LCD magnifier that fits over the monitor panel and provides a 2X magnification. These often strap on clumsily, and serve better as a way to get an enlarged view of the LCD than as protection. Hoodman and other suppliers offer these specialized devices.

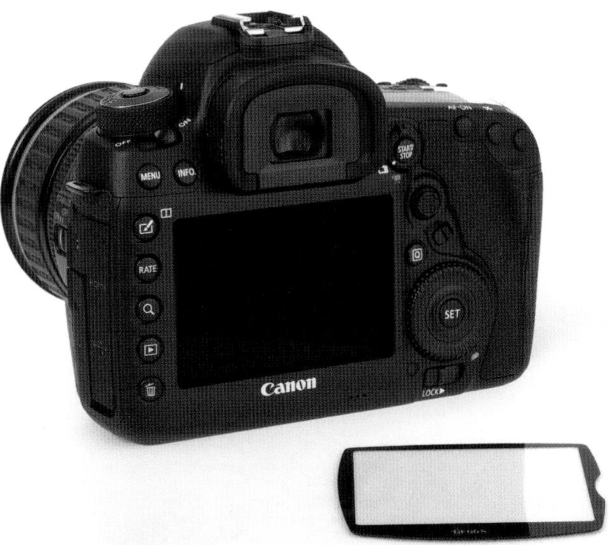

Figure 17.1
A tough glass shield can protect your LCD from scratches.

Troubleshooting Memory Cards

Sometimes good memory cards go bad. Sometimes good photographers can treat their memory cards badly. It's possible that a memory card that works fine in one camera won't be recognized when inserted into another. In the worst case, you can have a card full of important photos and find that the card seems to be corrupted and you can't access any of them. Don't panic! If these scenarios sound horrific to you, there are lots of things you can do to prevent them from happening, and a variety of remedies available if they do occur. You'll want to take some time—before disaster strikes—to consider your options.

All Your Eggs in One Basket?

The debate about whether it's better to use one large memory card or several smaller ones has been going on since even before there were memory cards. I can remember when computer users wondered whether it was smarter to install a pair of 200MB (not *gigabyte*) hard drives in their computer, or if they should go for one of those new-fangled 500MB models. By the same token, a few years ago, the user groups were full of proponents who insisted that you ought to use 128MB memory cards rather than the huge 512MB versions. Today, most of the arguments involve 32GB cards versus 64GB or 128GB cards, and I expect that as prices for 256GB and the still-scarce 512GB memory cards continue to drop, they'll eventually find their way into the debate as well. Size is especially important when you're using a camera like the 5D Mark IV that captures 30-megapixel images.

Why all the fuss? Are 64GB memory cards more likely to fail than 16GB cards? Are you risking all your photos if you trust your images to a larger card? Isn't it better to use several smaller cards, so that if one fails you lose only half as many photos? Or, isn't it wiser to put all your photos onto one larger card, because the more cards you use, the better your odds of misplacing or damaging one and losing at least some pictures?

In the end, the "eggs in one basket" argument boils down to statistics, and how you happen to use your 5D Mark IV. The rationales can go both ways. If you have multiple smaller cards, you do increase your chances of something happening to one of them, so, arguably, you might be boosting the odds of losing some pictures. If all your images are important, the fact that you've lost 100 rather than 200 pictures isn't very comforting.

Also, consider that the eggs/basket scenario assumes that the cards that are lost or damaged are always full. It's actually likely that a 32GB card might suffer a mishap when it's less than half-full (indeed, it's more likely that a large card won't be filled before it's offloaded to a computer), so you really might not lose any more shots with a single 32GB card than with multiple 16GB cards.

If you shoot photojournalist-type pictures, you probably change memory cards when they're less than completely full in order to avoid the need to do so at a crucial moment. (When I shoot sports, my cards rarely reach 80 to 90 percent of capacity before I change them.) Using multiple smaller cards means you must change them that more often, which can be a real pain when you're taking a lot of photos.

There are only two good reasons to justify limiting yourself to smaller memory cards when larger ones can be purchased at the same cost per-gigabyte. One of them is when every single picture is precious to you and the loss of any of them would be a disaster. If you're a wedding photographer, for example, and unlikely to be able to restage the nuptials if a memory card goes bad, you'll probably want to use *both* memory slots in your camera to store each image on both in backup mode. You might even have an assistant ready to copy each card removed from the camera onto a backup hard drive or DVD on-site.

To be even safer, you'd want to alternate cameras or have a second photographer at least partially duplicating your coverage so your shots are distributed over several memory cards simultaneously. (Strictly speaking, the safest route of all is to backup as you shoot to an on-site external drive through Wi-Fi in tethered shooting mode.)

If you deem none of these options sufficient, consider *interleaving* your shots. Say you don't shoot weddings, but you do go on vacation from time to time. Take 50 or so pictures on one card, or whatever number of images might fill about 25 percent of its capacity. Then, replace it with a different card and shoot about 25 percent of that card's available space. Repeat these steps with diligence (you'd have to be determined to go through this inconvenience), and, if you use four or more memory cards, you'll find your pictures from each location scattered among the different memory cards. If you lose or damage one, you'll still have *some* pictures from all the various stops on your trip on the other cards. That's more work than I like to do (I usually tote around a portable hard disk and copy the files to the drive as I go), but it's an option.

What Can Go Wrong?

There are lots of things that can go wrong with your memory card, but the ones that aren't caused by human stupidity are statistically very rare. Yes, a memory card's internal bit bin or controller can suddenly fail due to a manufacturing error or some inexplicable event caused by old age. However, if your card works for the first week or two that you own it, it should work forever. There's not a lot that can wear out.

The typical memory card is rated for a Mean Time Between Failures of 1,000,000 hours of use. That's constant use 24/7 for more than 100 years! Per the manufacturers, they are good for 10,000 insertions in your camera, and should be able to retain their data (and that's without an external power source) for something on the order of 11 years. Of course, with the millions of memory cards in use, there are bound to be a few lemons here or there.

Given the reliability of solid-state memory, compared to magnetic memory, though, it's more likely that your memory problems will stem from something that you do. Memory cards, particularly the SD variety, are small and easy to misplace if you're not careful. For that reason, it's a good idea to keep them in their original cases or a "card safe" offered by Gepe (www.gepecardsafe.com), Pelican, and others. Always placing your memory card in a case can provide protection from the second-most common mishap that befalls memory cards: the common household laundry. If you slip a memory card in a pocket, rather than a case or your camera bag, often enough, sooner or later it's going to end up in the washing machine and probably the clothes dryer, too. There are plenty of reports of relieved digital camera owners who've laundered their memory cards and found they still worked fine, but it's not uncommon for such mistreatment to do some damage.

Memory cards can also be stomped on, accidentally bent, dropped into the ocean, chewed by pets, and otherwise rendered unusable in myriad ways. It's also possible to force a card into your 5D Mark IV's memory card slot incorrectly if you're diligent enough, doing little damage to the card itself, but bending the CF connector pins in the camera, eliminating its ability to read or write to any memory card. Or, if the card is formatted in your computer with a memory card reader, your 5D Mark IV may fail to recognize it. Occasionally, I've found that a memory card used in one camera would fail if used in a different camera (until I reformatted it in Windows, and then again in the camera). Every once in a while, a card goes completely bad and—seemingly—can't be salvaged.

Another way to lose images is to do commonplace things with your memory card at an inopportune time. If you remove the card from the 5D Mark IV while the camera is writing images to the card, you'll lose any photos in the buffer and may damage the file structure of the card, making it difficult or impossible to retrieve the other pictures you've taken. The same thing can happen if you remove the memory card from your computer's card reader while the computer is writing to the card (say, to erase files you've already moved to your computer). You can avoid this by *not* using your computer to erase files on a memory card but, instead, always reformatting the card in your 5D Mark IV before you use it again.

What Can You Do?

Pay attention: If you're having problems, the *first* thing you should do is *stop* using that memory card. Don't take any more pictures. Don't do anything with the card until you've figured out what's wrong. Your second line of defense (your first line is to be sufficiently careful with your cards that you avoid problems in the first place) is to *do no harm* that hasn't already been done. Read the rest of this section and then, if necessary, decide on a course of action (such as using a data recovery service or software described later) before you risk damaging the data on your card further.

Now that you've calmed down, the first thing to check is whether you've actually inserted a card in the camera. If you've set the camera in the Shooting menu so that Shoot w/o Card has been turned on, it's entirely possible (although not particularly plausible) that you've been snapping away with no memory card to store the pictures to, which can lead to massive disappointment later. Of course, the No Card Message appears on the LCD when the camera is powered up, and it is superimposed on the review image after every shot, but maybe you're inattentive, aren't using picture review, or have purchased one of those LCD fold-up hoods mentioned earlier in this chapter. You can avoid all this by turning the Shoot w/o Card feature off and leaving it off.

Things get more exciting when the card itself is put in jeopardy. If you lose a card, there's not a lot you can do other than take a picture of a similar card and print up some Have You Seen This Lost Flash Memory? flyers to post on utility poles all around town.

If all you care about is reusing the card, and have resigned yourself to losing the pictures, try reformatting the card in your camera. You may find that reformatting removes the corrupted data and restores your card to health. Sometimes I've had success reformatting a card in my computer using a memory card reader (this is normally a no-no because your operating system doesn't understand the needs of your 5D Mark IV), and *then* reformatting again in the camera.

If your memory card is not behaving properly, and you *do* want to recover your images, things get a little more complicated. If your pictures are very valuable, either to you or to others (for example, a wedding), you can always turn to professional data recovery firms. Be prepared to pay hundreds of dollars to get your pictures back, but these pros often do an amazing job. You wouldn't want them working on your memory card on behalf of the police if you'd tried to erase some incriminating pictures. There are many firms of this type, and I've never used them myself, so I can't offer a recommendation. Use a Google search to turn up a ton of them. I use a software program called RescuePro, which came free with one of my SanDisk memory cards.

A more reasonable approach is to try special data recovery software you can install on your computer and use to attempt to resurrect your "lost" images yourself. They may not actually be gone completely. Perhaps your card's "table of contents" is jumbled, or only a few pictures are damaged in such a way that your camera and computer can't read some or any of the pictures on the card. Some of the available software was written specifically to reconstruct lost pictures, while other utilities are more general-purpose applications that can be used with any media, including floppy disks and hard disk drives. They have names like OnTrack, Photo Rescue 2, Digital Image Recovery, MediaRecover, Image Recall, and the aptly named Recover My Photos.

DIMINISHING RETURNS

Usually, once you've recovered any images on a memory card, reformatted it, and returned it to service, it will function reliably for the rest of its useful life. However, if you find a card going bad more than once, you'll almost certainly want to stop using it forever. See if you can get it replaced by the manufacturer, if you can, but, in the case of card failures, the third time is never the charm.

Cleaning Your Sensor

There's no avoiding dust. No matter how careful you are, some of it is going to settle on your camera and on the mounts of your lenses, eventually making its way inside your camera to settle in the mirror chamber. As you take photos, the mirror flipping up and down causes the dust to become airborne and eventually make its way past the shutter curtain to come to rest on the anti-aliasing filter atop your sensor. There, dust and particles can show up in every single picture you take at a small enough aperture to bring the foreign matter into sharp focus. No matter how careful you are and how cleanly you work, eventually you will get some of this dust on your camera's sensor. Some say that CMOS sensors, like the one found in the EOS 5D Mark IV, "attract" less dust than CCD sensors found in cameras from other vendors. But even the cleanest-working photographers using Canon cameras are far from immune.

Fortunately, one of the EOS 5D Mark IV's most useful features is the automatic sensor cleaning system that reduces or eliminates the need to clean your camera's sensor manually. Canon has applied anti-static coatings to the sensor and other portions of the camera body interior to counter charge build-ups that attract dust. A separate filter over the sensor vibrates ultrasonically each time the 5D Mark IV is powered on or off, shaking loose any dust.

Although the automatic sensor cleaning feature operates when you power the camera up or turn it off, you can activate it at any time. Choose Sensor Cleaning from the Set-up 3 menu, and select Clean Now. If you'd rather turn the feature on or off, choose Auto Cleaning instead, and then choose either Enable or Disable with the Quick Control Dial. Press SET, then press the MENU button to return to the Set-up 3 menu.

If some dust does collect on your sensor, you can often map it out of your images (making it invisible) using software techniques with the Dust Delete Data feature in the Shooting 3 menu. Operation of this feature is described in Chapter 11. Of course, even with the EOS 5D Mark IV's automatic sensor cleaning/dust-resistance features, you may still be required to manually clean your sensor from time to time. This section explains the phenomenon and provides some tips on minimizing dust and eliminating it when it begins to affect your shots.

Dust the FAQs, Ma'am

Here are some of the most frequently asked questions about sensor dust issues.

Q. I see tiny specks in my viewfinder. Do I have dust on my sensor?

A. If you see sharp, well-defined specks, they are clinging to the underside of your focus screen and not on your sensor. They have absolutely no effect on your photographs, and are merely annoying or distracting.

Q. I can see dust on my mirror. How can I remove it?

A. Like focus-screen dust, any artifacts that have settled on your mirror won't affect your photos. You can often remove dust on the mirror or focus screen with a bulb air blower, which will loosen it and whisk it away. Stubborn dust on the focus screen can sometimes be gently flicked away with a soft brush designed for cleaning lenses. I don't recommend brushing the mirror or touching it in any way. The mirror is a special front-surface-silvered optical device (unlike conventional mirrors, which are silvered on the back side of a piece of glass or plastic) and can be easily scratched. If you can't blow mirror dust off, it's best to just forget about it. You can't see it in the viewfinder, anyway.

Q. I see a bright spot in the same place in all of my photos. Is that sensor dust?

A. You've probably got either a "hot" pixel or one that is permanently "stuck" due to a defect in the sensor. A hot pixel is one that shows up as a bright spot only during long exposures as the sensor warms. A pixel stuck in the "on" position always appears in the image. Both show up as bright red, green, or blue pixels, usually surrounded by a small cluster of other improperly illuminated pixels, caused by the camera's interpolating the hot or stuck pixel into its surroundings, as shown in Figure 17.2. A stuck pixel can also be permanently dark. Either kind is likely to show up when they contrast with plain, evenly colored areas of your image.

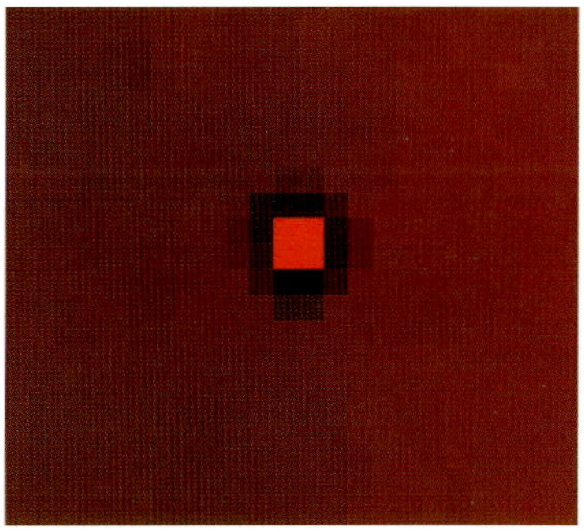

Figure 17.2 A stuck pixel is surrounded by improperly interpolated pixels created by the 5D Mark IV's demosaicing algorithm.

Finding one or two hot or stuck pixels in your sensor is unfortunately fairly common. They can be "removed" by telling the 5D Mark IV to ignore them through a simple process called *pixel mapping*. If the bad pixels become bothersome, Canon can remap your sensor's pixels with a quick trip to a service center.

Bad pixels can also show up on your camera's color LCD panel, but, unless they are abundant, the wisest course is to just ignore them.

Q. I see an irregular out-of-focus blob in the same place in my photos. Is that sensor dust?

A. Yes. Sensor contaminants can take the form of tiny spots, larger blobs, or even curvy lines if they are caused by minuscule fibers that have settled on the sensor. They'll appear out of focus because they aren't on the sensor surface but, rather, a fraction of a millimeter above it on the filter that covers the sensor. The smaller the f/stop used, the more in-focus the dust becomes. At large apertures, it may not be visible at all.

Q. I never see any dust on my sensor. What's all the fuss about?

A. Those who never have dust problems with their EOS 5D Mark IV fall into one of four categories: those for whom the camera's automatic dust removal features are working well; those who seldom change their lenses and have clean working habits that minimize the amount of dust that invades their cameras in the first place; those who simply don't notice the dust (often because they don't shoot many macro photos or other pictures using the small f/stops that makes dust evident in their images); and those who are very, very lucky.

Identifying and Dealing with Dust

Sensor dust is less of a problem than it might be because it shows up only under certain circumstances. Indeed, you might have dust on your sensor right now and not be aware of it. The dust doesn't settle on the sensor itself, but, rather, on a protective filter a very tiny distance above the sensor, subjecting it to the phenomenon of *depth-of-focus*. Depth-of-focus is the distance the focal plane can be moved and still render an object in sharp focus. At f/2.8 to f/5.6 or even smaller, sensor dust, particularly if small, is likely to be outside the range of depth-of-focus and blur into an unnoticeable dot.

However, if you're shooting at f/16 to f/22 or smaller, those dust motes suddenly pop into focus. Forget about trying to spot them by peering directly at your sensor with the shutter open and the lens removed. The period at the end of this sentence, about .33mm in diameter, could block a group of pixels measuring 40 × 40 pixels (160 pixels in all!). Dust spots that are even smaller than that can easily show up in your images if you're shooting large, empty areas that are light colored. Dust motes are most likely to show up in the sky, as in Figure 17.3, or in white backgrounds of your seamless product shots and are less likely to be a problem in images that contain lots of dark areas and detail.

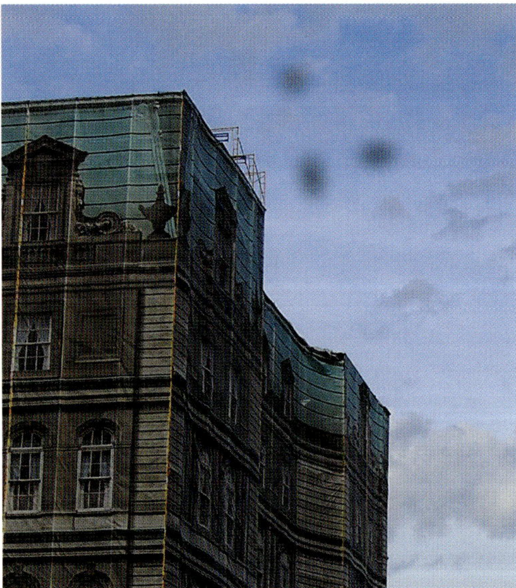

Figure 17.3
Only the dust spots in the sky are apparent in this shot.

To see if you have dust on your sensor, take a few test shots of a plain, blank surface (such as a piece of paper or a cloudless sky) at small f/stops, such as f/22, and a few wide open. Open Photoshop, copy several shots into a single document in separate layers, then flip back and forth between layers to see if any spots you see are present in all layers. You may have to boost contrast and sharpness to make the dust easier to spot.

Avoiding Dust

Of course, the easiest way to protect your sensor from dust is to prevent it from settling on the sensor in the first place. Some Canon lenses come with rubberized seals around the lens mounts that help keep dust from infiltrating, but you'll find that dust will still find a way to get inside. Here are my tips for eliminating the problem before it begins.

- **Clean environment.** Avoid working in dusty areas if you can do so. Hah! Serious photographers will take this suggestion with a grain of salt, because it usually makes sense to go where the pictures are. Only a few of us are so paranoid about sensor dust (considering that it is so easily removed) that we'll avoid moderately grimy locations just to protect something that is, when you get down to it, just a tool. If you find a great picture opportunity at a raging fire, during a sandstorm, or while surrounded by dust clouds, you might hesitate to take the picture, but, with a little caution (don't remove your lens in these situations, and clean the camera afterward!) you can still shoot. However, it still makes sense to store your camera in a clean environment. One place cameras and lenses pick up a lot of dust is inside a camera bag. Clean your bag from time to time, and you can avoid problems.

- **Clean lenses.** There are a few paranoid types that avoid swapping lenses to minimize the chance of dust getting inside their cameras. It makes more sense just to use a blower or brush to dust off the rear lens mount of the replacement lens first, so you won't be introducing dust into your camera simply by attaching a new, dusty lens. Do this before you remove the lens from your camera, and then avoid stirring up dust before making the exchange.

- **Work fast.** Minimize the time your camera is lens-less and exposed to dust. That means having your replacement lens ready and dusted off, and a place to set down the old lens as soon as it is removed, so you can quickly attach the new lens.

- **Let gravity help you.** Face the camera downward when the lens is detached so any dust in the mirror box will tend to fall away from the sensor. Turn your back to any breezes, indoor forced air vents, fans, or other sources of dust to minimize infiltration.

- **Protect the lens you just removed.** Once you've attached the new lens, quickly put the end cap on the one you just removed to reduce the dust that might fall on it.

- **Clean out the vestibule.** From time to time, remove the lens while in a relatively dust-free environment and use a blower bulb like the one shown in Figure 17.4 (*not* compressed air or a vacuum hose) to clean out the mirror box area. A blower bulb is generally safer than a can of compressed air, or a strong positive/negative airflow, which can tend to drive dust further into nooks and crannies.

- **Be prepared.** If you're embarking on an important shooting session, it's a good idea to clean your sensor *now*, rather than come home with hundreds or thousands of images with dust spots caused by flecks that were sitting on your sensor before you even started. Before I left on my recent trip to Spain, I put both cameras I was taking through a rigid cleaning regimen, figuring they could remain dust-free for a measly 10 days. I even left my bulky blower bulb at home. It was a big mistake, but my intentions were good.

- **Clone out existing spots in your image editor.** Photoshop and other editors have a clone tool or healing brush you can use to copy pixels from surrounding areas over the dust spot or dead pixel. This process can be tedious, especially if you have lots of dust spots and/or lots of images to be corrected. The advantage is that this sort of manual fix-it probably will do the least damage to the rest of your photo. Only the cloned pixels will be affected.

- **Use filtration in your image editor.** A semi-smart filter like Photoshop's Dust & Scratches filter can remove dust and other artifacts by selectively blurring areas that the plug-in decides represent dust spots. This method can work well if you have many dust spots, because you won't need to patch them manually. However, any automated method like this has the possibility of blurring areas of your image that you didn't intend to soften.

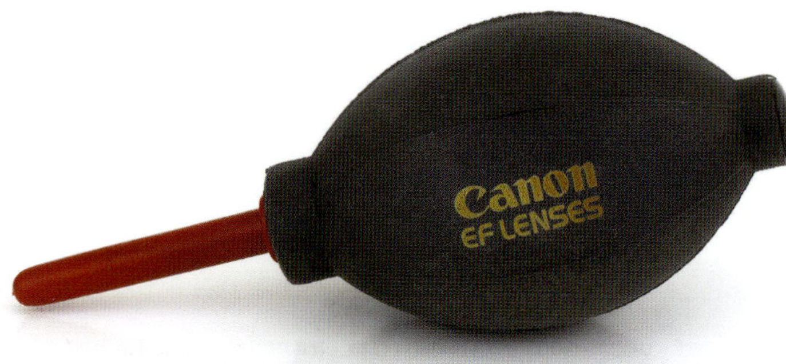

Figure 17.4
Use a robust air bulb for cleaning your sensor.

Sensor Cleaning

Those new to the concept of sensor dust actually hesitate before deciding to clean their camera themselves. Isn't it a better idea to pack up your 5D Mark IV and send it to a Canon service center so their crack technical staff can do the job for you? Or, at the very least, shouldn't you let the friendly folks at your local camera store do it?

Of course, if you choose to let someone else clean your sensor, they will be using methods that are more or less identical to the techniques you would use yourself. None of these techniques are difficult, and the only difference between their cleaning and your cleaning is that they might have done it dozens or hundreds of times. If you're careful, you can do just as good a job.

Of course, vendors like Canon won't tell you this, but it's not because they don't trust you. It's not that difficult for a real goofball to mess up his camera by hurrying or taking a shortcut. Perhaps the person uses the "Bulb" method of holding the shutter open and a finger slips, allowing the shutter curtain to close on top of a sensor cleaning brush. Or, someone tries to clean the sensor using masking tape, and ends up with goo all over its surface. If Canon recommended *any* method that's mildly risky, someone would do it wrong, and then the company would face lawsuits from those who'd contend they did it exactly in the way the vendor suggested, so the ruined camera is not their fault. If you visit Canon's website, you'll find this recommendation: "If the image sensor needs cleaning, we recommend having it cleaned at a Canon service center, as it is a very delicate component."

You can see that vendors like Canon tend to be conservative in their recommendations, and, in doing so, make it seem as if sensor cleaning is more daunting and dangerous than it really is. Some vendors recommend only dust-off cleaning, using reasonably gentle blasts of air, while condemning more serious scrubbing with swabs and cleaning fluids. However, these cleaning kits for the exact types of cleaning they recommended against are for sale in Japan only, where, apparently, your average photographer is more dexterous than those of us in the rest of the world. These kits are like those used by official repair staff to clean your sensor if you decide to send your camera in for a dust-up.

As I noted, sensors can be affected by dust particles that are much smaller than you might be able to spot visually on the surface of your lens. The filters that cover sensors tend to be hard compared to optical glass. Cleaning the 24mm × 36mm sensor in your Canon 5D Mark IV within the tight confines of the mirror box call for a steady hand and careful touch. If your sensor's filter becomes scratched through inept cleaning, you can't simply remove it yourself and replace it with a new one.

There are three basic kinds of cleaning processes that can be used to remove dusty and sticky stuff that settles on your dSLR's sensor. All of these must be performed with the shutter locked open.

- **Air cleaning.** This process involves squirting blasts of air inside your camera with the shutter locked open. This works well for dust that's not clinging stubbornly to your sensor.

- **Brushing.** A soft, very fine brush is passed across the surface of the sensor's filter, dislodging mildly persistent dust particles and sweeping them off the imager.

- **Liquid cleaning.** A soft swab dipped in a cleaning solution such as ethanol is used to wipe the sensor filter, removing more obstinate particles.

Placing the Shutter in the Locked and Fully Upright Position for Landing

Make sure you're using a fully charged battery or the optional AC Adapter Kit ACK-E6N.

1. Remove the lens from the camera and then turn the camera on.

2. Set the EOS 5D Mark IV to any one of the non-fully automatic modes. The shutter cannot be locked open in Auto.

3. You'll find the Clean Manually menu choice in the Set-up 3 menu under Sensor Cleaning. Press the SET button.

4. Select OK and press SET again. The mirror will flip up and the shutter will open (see Figure 17.5).

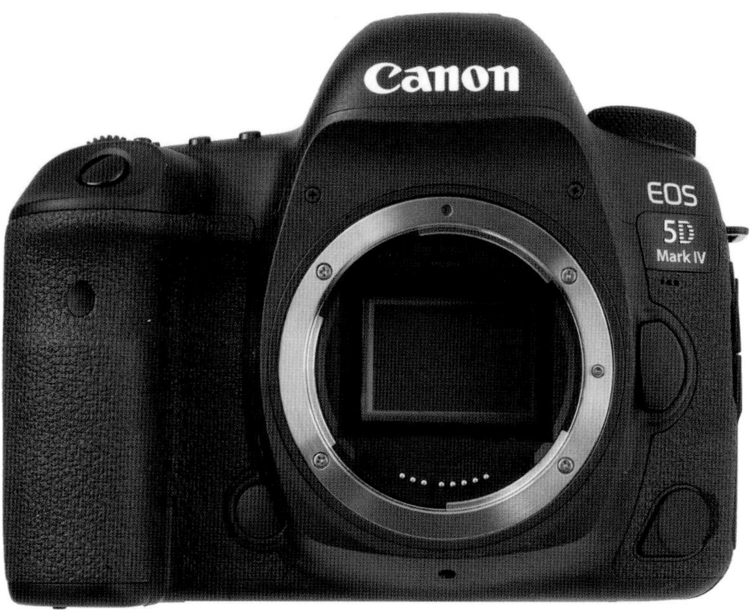

Figure 17.5
With the shutter open and the mirror locked up, you can commence cleaning the exposed sensor.

5. Use one of the methods described below to remove dust and grime from your sensor. Be careful not to accidentally switch the power off or open the memory card or battery compartment doors as you work. If that happens, the shutter may be damaged if it closes onto your cleaning tool.

6. When you're finished, turn the power off, replace your lens, and switch your camera back on.

Air Cleaning

Your first attempts at cleaning your sensor should always involve gentle blasts of air. Many times, you'll be able to dislodge dust spots, which will fall off the sensor and, with luck, out of the mirror box. Attempt one of the other methods only when you've already tried air cleaning and it didn't remove all the dust.

Here are some tips for air cleaning:

- **Use a clean, powerful air bulb.** Your best bet is bulb cleaners designed for the job, like the Giottos Rocket. Smaller bulbs, like those air bulbs with a brush attached sometimes sold for lens cleaning or weak nasal aspirators, may not provide sufficient air or a strong enough blast to do much good.

- **Hold the EOS 5D Mark IV upside down.** Then look up into the mirror box as you squirt your air blasts, increasing the odds that gravity will help pull the expelled dust downward, away from the sensor. You may have to use some imagination in positioning yourself. (See Figure 17.6.)

- **Never use air canisters.** The propellant inside these cans can permanently coat your sensor if you tilt the can while spraying. It's not worth taking a chance.

- **Avoid air compressors.** Super-strong blasts of air are likely to force dust under the sensor filter.

Figure 17.6
Hold the camera upside down when cleaning to allow dust to fall out.

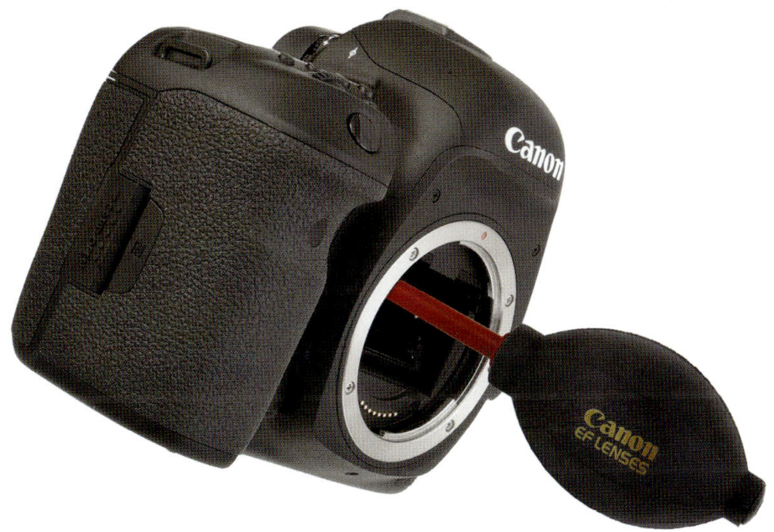

Brush Cleaning

If your dust is a little more stubborn and can't be dislodged by air alone, you may want to try a brush, charged with static electricity that can pick off dust spots by electrical attraction. One good, but expensive, option is the Sensor Brush sold at www.visibledust.com. You need one like the Artic Butterfly shown in Figure 17.7, that can be stroked across the short dimension of your 5D Mark IV's sensor.

Ordinary artist's brushes are much too coarse and stiff and have fibers that are tangled or can come loose and settle on your sensor. A good sensor brush's fibers are resilient and described as "thinner than a human hair." Moreover, the brush has a non-conducting handle that reduces the risk of static sparks.

Brush cleaning is done with a dry brush by gently swiping the surface of the sensor filter with the tip. The dust particles are attracted to the brush particles and cling to them. You should clean the brush with compressed air before and after each use, and store it in an appropriate air-tight container between applications to keep it clean and dust-free. Although these special brushes are expensive, one should last you a long time.

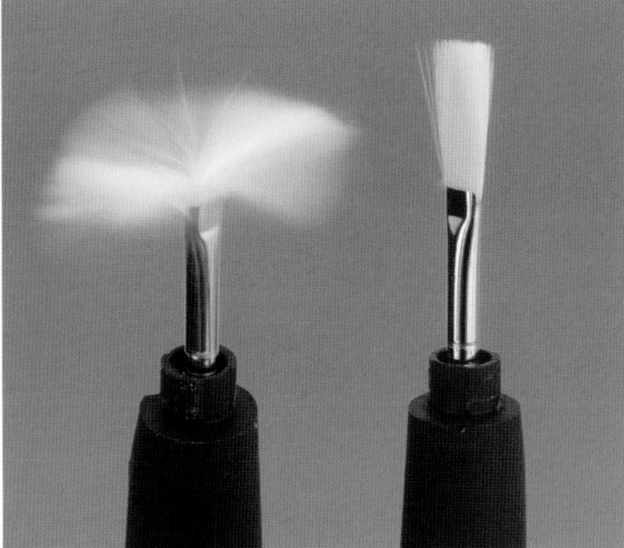

Figure 17.7
The motor in the Arctic Butterfly flutters the brush tips for a few minutes to charge them for picking up dust (left). Then, turn off the power and flick the tip above the surface of the sensor (right).

Liquid Cleaning

Unfortunately, you'll often encounter stubborn dust spots that can't be removed with a blast of air or flick of a brush. These spots may be combined with some grease or a liquid that causes them to stick to the sensor filter's surface. In such cases, liquid cleaning with a swab may be necessary. During my first clumsy attempts to clean my own sensor, I accidentally got my blower bulb tip too close to the sensor, and some sort of deposit from the tip of the bulb ended up on the sensor. I panicked until I discovered that liquid cleaning did a good job of removing whatever it was that took up residence on my sensor.

You can make your own swabs out of pieces of plastic (some use fast-food restaurant knives, with the tip cut at an angle to the proper size) covered with a soft cloth or Pec-Pad, as shown in Figure 17.8. However, if you've got the bucks to spend, you can't go wrong with good-quality commercial sensor cleaning swabs, such as those sold by Photographic Solutions, Inc. (www.photosol.com).

You want a sturdy swab that won't bend or break so you can apply gentle pressure to the swab as you wipe the sensor surface. Use the swab with methanol (as pure as you can get it, particularly medical grade; other ingredients can leave a residue), or the Eclipse solution also sold by Photographic Solutions. Eclipse is quite a bit purer than even medical-grade methanol. A couple drops of solution should be enough, unless you have a spot that's extremely difficult to remove. In that case, you may need to use extra solution on the swab to help "soak" the dirt off.

Once you overcome your nervousness at touching your 5D Mark IV's sensor, the process is easy. You'll wipe continuously with the swab in one direction, then flip it over and wipe in the other direction. You need to completely wipe the entire surface; otherwise, you may end up depositing the dust you collect at the far end of your stroke. Wipe; don't rub.

Figure 17.8
You can make your own sensor swab from a plastic knife that's been truncated.

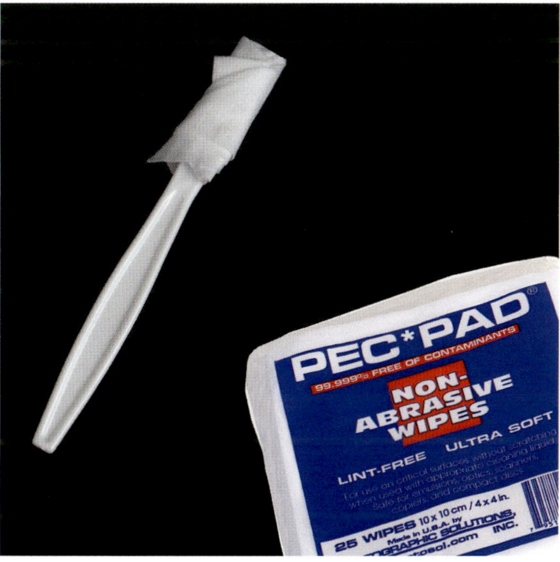

If you want a close-up look at your sensor to make sure the dust has been removed, you can pay $50–$100 for a special sensor "microscope" with an illuminator. (See Figure 17.9.) Or, you can do like I do and work with a plain old Carson MiniBrite PO-55 illuminated 5X magnifier, as seen in Figure 17.10. It has a built-in LED and, held a few inches from the lens mount with the lens removed from your 5D Mark IV, provides a sharp, close-up view of the sensor, with enough contrast to reveal any dust that remains. If you'd like to buy one for less than $10, I provide a link at my website, www.dslrguides.com/carson.

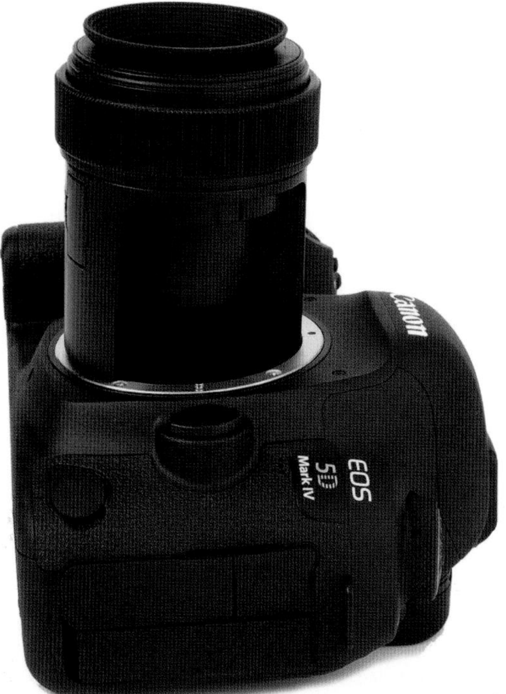

Figure 17.9
This SensorKlear magnifier provides a view of your sensor as you work.

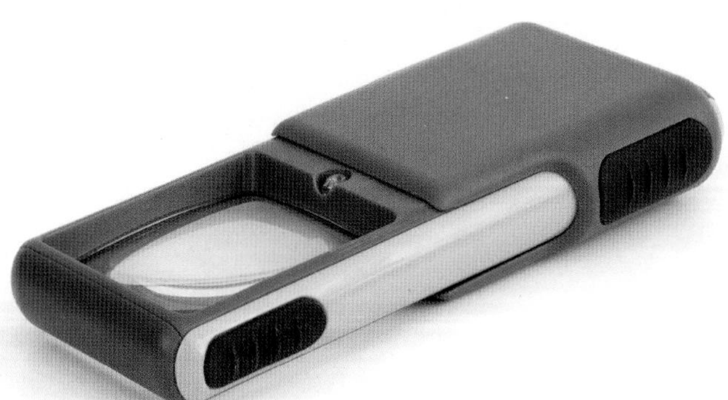

Figure 17.10
An illuminated magnifier like this Carson MiniBrite PO-55 can be used as a 'scope to view your sensor.

Index

HSS (high-speed sync)
information display, 394
using, 45, 207, 222–223
HTC-100 HDMI cable, 4

I

IFC-150U II interface cable, 2
illumination, evenness of, 187–188. *See also*
light, illumination, and exposure
Image Copy options, 332–333
iMage Gateway, uploading to, 166
Image Jump with Main Dial options, 339
Image Quality options, 32, 255–259
Image Recording settings defaults, 55
Image Review option, 259–260
Image stabilizer switch, 43
Image Transfer options, 338
image-recording quality, 394
images. *See also* **flat images; ghost images;**
photos; pictures; two-image display
advancing through, 19
backing up, 332
categorizing, 36
checking, 20
combining, 294
comparing, 20
copying, 332
darkness, 271–272
displaying, 18
duration of display on LCD, 259–260
erasing, 19, 330
final simulation, 395–396
grouping by venue, 36
jumping ahead or back, 19
placing in frames, 304
previewing on TV, 389
protecting, 37, 328–329
rating, 36–37
recovering, 445
resizing on touch screen, 50
reviewing, 18–20
rotating, 329–330
scrolling on touch screen, 50
zooming in on, 19

incandescent/tungsten light, 194
index views, navigating, 20–21
Index/Magnify/Reduce button, 19, 29, 34
INFO. button
description and location, 29
detail screens, 34–35
display options, 359–360
live view display options, 362–364
Live View mode, 34
modes, 34
Movie shooting modes, 34
Playback mode, 34
pressing, 12, 19, 394
turning off, 30
using, 34
information display, changing, 19
infrared sensor, 25–26, 43–44
Initial AF Point options, 318
interface cable IFC-150U II, 2
interframe compression, 413
interlaced scan, 415
interval/time lapse photography, 42, 151–155,
300
IPB (Standard) compression, 413
IPTC (International Press Communications
Council), 384–385
IPTC and GPS information, displaying, 34
ISO. *See also* **High ISO noise reduction**
adjusting, 17
displaying in LCD panel, 42
ISO expansion, enabling, 82
ISO sensitivity in exposure triangle, 62–63
ISO settings, using to adjust exposure, 81–85
ISO speed
information display, 394
readout, 42
setting increments options, 375
settings, 270–271
on Shooting Functions screen, 32
in viewfinder, 45
ISO/Flash exposure compensation, 40–41

J

JPEG compression

> aspect ratio, 304

> Image Quality option, 255–256

> versus RAW, 257–259

> in viewfinder, 45

Jump method, using with images, 339

K

Kelvin scale, 192

Kodak gray card, using, 69

L

landscapes

> recommended settings, 60

> style, 283

> Tv (Shutter-priority) mode, 77

> using Aperture-priority, 74–75

Language options, 354

lapel microphones, using, 435

Large Zone AF

> focus point, 15

> mode, 124, 126

LCD Brightness options, 352

LCD Color Tone options, 353

LCD display versus INFO button, 12–13

LCD illuminator button, 40

LCD monitor

> description and location, 29

> information displayed on, 42, 394

> protecting, 441

> setting color balance, 353

LC-E6/LC-E6E battery charger, 2, 4–5

Lens Aberration Correction option, 260–266

Lens Drive When AF Impossible options, 314

Lens Electronic MF option, 312–313

lens groups and AF points, 116–117

lens hood bayonet mount, 43

lens index indicator, 43

lens mounts

> bayonet, 44

> index mark, 27

> variety, 177

lens release button and locking pin, 25

Lens Tune-Up options, 323–325

lenses. *See also* **Canon lenses; Digital Lens Optimizer option; EF lenses; focus**

> aperture, 173

> buying and expanding, 174–175

> compatibility and limitations, 176–178

> components, 43–44

> cost considerations, 173

> EF-S type, 7

> Extender EF, 184

> fast/close focusing, 173

> fine-tuning autofocus, 321–326

> and f/stops, 65

> image quality, 173

> macro, 184

> Mark II, 172

> mounting, 6–7

> Retract Lens on Power Off options, 384

> size, 173

> telephoto, 184

> TS-E 90 mm/f/2.8, 184

> for video, 421–423

> zoom range, 173

level position. *See* **electronic level**

light, illumination, and exposure, 62–66. *See also* **ambient light sensor; continuous lighting; illumination**

light field photography, 132

light meters, calibration of, 69–70

light stands, using for lighting, 199

light trails, producing, 148–149

lighting

> with desk lamps, 196–197

> DIY (do-it-yourself), 196

> for video, 430–432

lighting accessories

> backgrounds, 200

> light stands, 199

> snoots and barn doors, 200

> soft boxes, 199

> tents, 198

> umbrellas, 197–198

P

P (Program) AE mode, 77–78

P (Program) mode, 12

and electronic flash, 209

menu tabs, 252

pairing smartphones, 161

Partial metering mode, 13–14, 71

PCs. *See* **computers**

PC/X port, 27–28

Pec-Pad, using to clean sensors, 455

perspectives, experimenting with, 144

phase detection, 109–112

phone connections via Wi-Fi, 155

Photobook Set-up options, 332

Photomatrix, 63

photos, transferring to computers, 21–22. *See also* **images; pictures**

Picture Style options

accessing, 30–31

Auto, 283

Autumn Hues, 290

changing settings, 289

Clear, 290

Color tone, 283

Contrast, 282

defining, 285

displaying, 280

Emerald, 290

Faithful, 283

Filter effect, 283

Fine detail, 283

information, 394

Landscape, 283

Monochrome, 283

Neutral, 283

Nostalgia, 290

parameters, 282

Picture Style Editor, 287–288

Portrait, 283

presets, 281

Saturation, 282

selecting, 284

Sharpness, 282

on Shooting Functions screen, 32

Snapshot Portrait, 289

Standard, 283

Studio Portrait, 289

Toning effect, 283

Twilight, 290

uploading styles to camera, 288

pictures. *See also* **images; photos**

snapping without memory cards, 260

taking, 18

pinch gesture, using on touch screen, 50

pincushion distortion, 262

pixels

getting stuck, 447

mapping, 447

playback, options on touch screen, 48

Playback button, description and location, 29, 36

Playback Grid options, 340

Playback image button, 19

Playback menu options

AF Point Disp., 340

Cropping, 334–335

Ctrl over HDMI, 342

Erase Images, 330

Highlight Alert, 340

Histogram Disp., 341

Image Copy, 332–333

Image Jump with Main Dial, 339

Image Transfer, 338

Magnification (apx), 341

Movie Play Count, 341

Photobook Set-up, 332

Playback Grid, 340

Print Order, 330–332

Protect Images, 328–329

Rating, 336–337

RAW Image Processing, 333–334

Resize, 336

Rotate Image, 329–330

Slide Show, 337–338

storing user settings, 369

Playback mode, INFO. button, 34

playback of video, 419–420

S